BRAHMANISM AND HINDUISM

BRAHMANISM AND HINDUISM

OR,

RELIGIOUS THOUGHT AND LIFE

IN INDIA,

AS BASED ON THE VEDA AND OTHER SACRED BOOKS OF THE HINDUS

MONIER MONIER-WILLIAMS, K.C.I.E.

GYAN

Published by

Gyan Publishing House
5, Ansari Road
Daryaganj, New Delhi-110002
Phone: 011-47034999, 9811692060
E-mail: books@gyanbooks.com

Distribution Network
gyanbooks.com
India, USA, Canada, UK, Australia, France

ISBN: 978-81-212-8961-0 (PB)
First Published, 1887

2nd Impression 2023

Printed at: Gyan Press, Delhi.

BRAHMANISM AND HINDUISM
AUTHOR: MONIER MONIER-WILLIAMS

BRĀHMANISM AND HINDŪISM.

PORTRAIT OF MR. GAURĪ-ŚAṄKAR UDAY-ŚAṄKAR, C.S.I.
NOW SVĀMĪ ŚRĪ SAĆĆIDĀNANDA-SARASVATĪ.

Seated, as a Brāhman Sannyāsi, in meditation (described at p. xxi of the Preface).

BRĀHMANISM AND HINDŪISM;

OR,

RELIGIOUS THOUGHT AND LIFE IN INDIA,

AS BASED ON THE VEDA AND OTHER SACRED BOOKS OF THE HINDŪS.

BY

SIR MONIER MONIER-WILLIAMS, K.C.I.E.,

M.A., HON. D.C.L. OXFORD, HON. LL.D. CALCUTTA, HON. PH.D. GÖTTINGEN, V. P. OF THE ROYAL ASIATIC SOCIETY, HON. MEMBER OF THE ASIATIC SOCIETIES OF BENGAL AND BOMBAY, AND OF THE ORIENTAL AND PHILOSOPHICAL SOCIETIES OF AMERICA, BODEN PROFESSOR OF SANSKṚIT, ETC.

FOURTH EDITION,

ENLARGED AND IMPROVED.

NEW YORK:
MACMILLAN AND CO.
1891.

PREFACE.

The present volume, although it professes to be only a new edition of a book which has already met with considerable acceptance[1], contains so many improvements and additions that it may be regarded as almost a new work, and as needing a new Preface.

Its aim has been stated in the first page of the introductory observations, but there is one expression in the second line which requires explanation. The word 'Englishmen' must be understood to include all English-speakers everywhere.

It has been my earnest endeavour in the following pages to give such a clear account of a very obscure and intricate subject as shall not violate scholarly accuracy, and yet be sufficiently readable to attract

[1] The first edition was called 'Religious Thought and Life in India' (denoted by the initials RTL. in the new edition of my Sanskṛit-English Dictionary published by the University of Oxford), that title being given to it because it was intended to be the first volume of a series treating of the religions of India. When, however, my volume on 'Buddhism' appeared—a volume printed in larger type—it was thought better to distinguish the third edition of the present work by the title 'Brāhmanism and Hindūism,' and this title has also been adopted for this new edition.

he is bound to bring his knowledge of Sanskṛit to bear not only on the promotion of philological studies, but also on the elucidation of Indian religious systems with a view to their refutation.

This is no easy task and its difficulty is enhanced by the close intertwining of religion with social and domestic life in every part of India.

It is often asserted that the Hindūs are the most religious people in the world. Those who make this assertion ought, of course, to define what they mean by the word 'religious.' What is really meant, I think, is that among all the races of mankind the Hindūs are the greatest slaves to the bondage of immemorial tradition—not so much in its bearing on religious beliefs, or even on moral conduct, as on social usages, caste practices, and domestic ceremonial observances.

In proof of this it is only necessary to refer to their marriage-customs (see p. 355); but other evidences of this bondage force themselves on the attention of the inquiring traveller at almost every step of his journeyings—in highways and by-ways, on the hills and in the valleys, in towns and in villages, in the dwellings of rich and poor, prince and peasant.

And yet, strange to say, these traditional customs, usages, and ceremonial observances, although they constitute the chief element in a Hindū's religion, are nowhere throughout India regulated or enforced by the delegates or representatives of any supreme Head or central religious authority. No doubt one explanation of this fact may be that an Indian's excessive respect for tradition makes the establishment of any central source of ecclesiastical power, and the exercise of any regularly organized religious government unnecessary.

Reverence for opinions and practices held sacred by his ancestors is ingrained in every fibre of a Hindū's character, and is, so to speak, bred in the very bone of his physical and moral constitution.

Day by day the pious Hindū offers homage to his father, grandfather, and progenitors, including all the seers, holy men, and patriarchs of antiquity.

And even if this were not so, any centralization of religious authority would be almost impossible, because the Indian body politic is divided into a countless number of distinct castes, communities and sects, each of which has its own usages and its own form of self-government, consisting, perhaps, of a kind of council and presiding Head, whose office is to prevent the violation of its own traditions, customs, and rules.

It must be borne in mind, too, that there is one tradition respected by all castes and all sects alike—namely the superiority of the Brāhmans and their right to superintend domestic ceremonies. But see p. 386.

Nevertheless it might certainly be expected that at any rate the Brāhmans to whom obedience is by common consent due, would be subject to some one supreme Head—to some one centralized spiritual government or authority—from which their sacerdotal powers would be derived. But no such central authority exists in India. And the Brāhmans are themselves split up into priests and laymen, besides countless subdivisions each with its own rules carried out by its own separate council and leaders.

Unquestionably this absence of all religious organization among the dense populations of our Indian empire has led to an almost total want of order and unity; yet it is attended with one beneficial result, inasmuch as India, with all its intense religiousness, with all its exaggerated sacerdotalism and ceremonialism, is free from the despotism,—is unfettered by the dictation of any one autocratic pontiff.

At the same time it must be understood that the almost infinite divisions of caste and varieties of caste-observance rest on one unvarying substratum of theological dogma of which the Brāhmans are the keepers and exponents. It may be very true that a Hindū who is bound to conform strictly to the social, domestic, and individual observances prescribed by his own caste, is nevertheless allowed great laxity of opinion in regard to his religious creed. It may also be true that he is permitted to choose for himself his own special or favourite divinity, without accepting all the gods of the Hindū Pantheon. It may even be true that while accepting Hindūism he may be at the same time a believer in Buddhism, in Muhammadanism, in Judaism, in Christianity; or may call himself a Theist, a Deist, a Polytheist, a Theosophist, or even an Agnostic. Still for all that, all the varieties of caste-usage, all the multiplicity of domestic ceremonies, all the diversities of sceptical belief are, so to speak, 'roped together' by one rigid and unyielding line of Brāhmanical pantheistic doctrine.

Any one who glances at the table of contents appended to these prefatory remarks will see at once that a great proportion of the volume before him is employed in expounding the evolution of that doctrine.

I fear, however, that some inquirers may possibly consult its pages, who have little time to pursue step by step the gradual development of Indian religious thought, as I have endeavoured to trace it. These need, as an introduction, a more concise answer to the question, What is a Hindū and what is Hindūism?

For their benefit, therefore, I will here endeavour to condense some of the more important points which are set forth at full length in the succeeding pages.

And first I may point out that the name Hindū is now usually restricted to those who are adherents of the form of religion which the present volume aims at explaining.

It is, indeed, a solemn thought that at least 200 millions of our fellow-subjects are adherents of that religion. And yet it is a remarkable characteristic of Hindūism that it neither requires nor attempts to make converts. Nor is it by any means at present diminishing in numbers. Nor is it at present being driven off the field, as might be expected, by being brought into contact with two such proselyting religions as Christianity and Muhammadanism. On the contrary, it is at present rapidly increasing; for a man becomes a Hindū by merely being born a Hindū; so that every day adds to the adherents of Hindūism through the simple process of the daily increase of births over deaths, which in India is everywhere considerable.

And far more remarkable than this—it will be seen

from what I have written in Chapter iii, that another characteristic of Hindūism is its receptivity and all-comprehensiveness. It claims to be the one religion of humanity, of human nature, of the entire world. It cares not to oppose the progress of any other system. For it has no difficulty in including all other religions within its all-embracing arms and ever-widening fold.

And, in real truth, Hindūism has something to offer which is suited to all minds. Its very strength lies in its infinite adaptability to the infinite diversity of human characters and human tendencies. It has its highly spiritual and abstract side suited to the metaphysical philosopher—its practical and concrete side suited to the man of affairs and the man of the world—its æsthetic and ceremonial side suited to the man of poetic feeling and imagination—its quiescent and contemplative side suited to the man of peace and lover of seclusion. Nay, it holds out the right hand of brotherhood to nature-worshippers, demon-worshippers, animal-worshippers, tree-worshippers, fetish-worshippers. It does not scruple to permit the most grotesque forms of idolatry, and the most degrading varieties of superstition. And it is to this latter fact that yet another remarkable peculiarity of Hindūism is mainly due—namely, that in no other system of the world is the chasm more vast which separates the religion of the higher, cultured, and thoughtful classes from that of the lower, uncultured, and unthinking masses.

The former religion I call Brāhmanism, the latter I call Hindūism; but, as I have shown at length in the present volume, the two are really one, and the higher, purer, and more spiritualistic system has led to the lower, more corrupt, and more materialistic form of doctrine, through the natural and inevitable development of its root-ideas and fundamental dogma.

In brief, Hindūism is founded on that highly subtle theory of pantheistic philosophy which was excogitated by the Brāhmans at the time when they began to think out for themselves the problem of existence several centuries before the Christian era—a theory, which every human intellect most naturally thinks out for itself—a theory, too, which is, in some respects, almost identical with that thought out by Spinoza and the profoundest thinkers of modern Europe.

Indeed, if I may be allowed the anachronism, the Hindūs were Spinozaites more than 2,000 years before the existence of Spinoza; and Darwinians many centuries before Darwin; and Evolutionists many centuries before the doctrine of Evolution had been accepted by the Scientists of our time, and before any word like Evolution existed in any language of the world.

The Hindūs, in fact, have for centuries believed that their one god Brăhmă (neuter)—their one impersonal spiritual Essence or Energy—identified with everything, and constituting everything—is for ever evolving itself out of its own inner substance; like a vast tree[1] with countless branches for ever expanding

[1] The name for the one Self-existent God, Brăhmă, is neuter and derived from the same root as Vṛiksha, 'a tree'—namely, the root *Vṛih* or *Bṛih*, 'to grow.' By referring, however, to p. 95, note 2, of this

itself out of an eternal seed, and then for ever drawing back and being re-absorbed into itself, and disappearing again and again into formlessness and impersonality.

And the first evolution, according to their belief, is the development of a triple personality; first, as God, the personal Creator, called Brăhmā (masculine); secondly, as God the personal Preserver or Maintainer, called Vishṇu (masculine); thirdly, as God the personal Dissolver or Disintegrator (but also the Re-creator and Regenerator after dissolution), called Śiva (masculine). These three masculine deities are sometimes regarded as co-equal and represented by three noble heads rising out of one body. Often their functions are held to be interchangeable, or sometimes one, sometimes the other, may be thought to be the greatest of the three (see pp. 45, 65).

Brāhmanism, then, in its simplest form, consists in a fixed belief that the one eternal impersonal Essence—the sole, really existing Being—expands itself into three principal divine co-equal personalities, which are constantly manifested and ultimately re-absorbed.

Then a further belief was soon developed out of this earlier creed—a belief that each of the three male divinities possesses maternal or feminine attributes as well as masculine. And hence it followed that each personal god became in due course associated with a wife—regarded as half the god's essence (p. 389).

---

volume, it will be seen that the earliest word for the one Spirit of the Universe was Ātman (masc.). Then to distinguish the spirit of man from the Universal Spirit, the latter was afterwards called Paramātman, 'the Supreme Spirit.' Mahātmā—a word now much used by Theosophists—is pure Sanskṛit and means 'having a great spirit,' 'noble-spirited.'

Then, again, the process of divine developments was soon supposed to go on indefinitely. There are, therefore, any number of gods, goddesses, and superhuman beings in a Hindū's pantheon, although his Ishṭa-devatā, or 'Favourite deity,' is generally either Vishṇu or Śiva, or some deity connected with these two personalities. Nay, according to the Hindū pantheistic theory, all great, useful, and good men are personal manifestations of the one impersonal Spirit—and every man's individualized spirit, released from his body by death, must migrate into higher or lower corporeal states, and so pass through innumerable forms of existence, *according to his deeds*, until it is re-absorbed into the one self-existent Spirit of the Universe.

Every man's future, then, depends upon himself. Moreover his passage through these various changes of existence may take place as much in other worlds as in the present; but wherever such changes occur they must remain fixed until another change is caused by dissolution. Hence all the distinct classes of men—such as Brāhmans, soldiers, agriculturists and servants—remain unalterably distinct from each other from birth to death, without any more power of altering their condition than if they were quadrupeds, birds, reptiles or fish (see p. 53).

This may give some idea of the close connexion of the Indian caste system with the Hindū religion, and of the iron sway which it exercises over the people, and of its consequent influence for evil, though in some cases for good also (see Chapter xviii).

It might be thought, perhaps, that the idea of men

and women being, as it were, portions of the divine Essence, would have a good effect in ennobling life. But unhappily the pantheistic philosophy of India leads to many monstrous paradoxes, and one of these is that the divine Essence may become, through the force of an awful law, devilish or demoniacal.

A Hindū, therefore, holds that, as there are any number of good incarnations, so there are any number of evil. And this is not all. It is held that two antagonistic principles are for ever opposing and counteracting each other in the universe around us, and that the vast pantheon is counterbalanced by an equally vast pandemonium. There are, in short, demons without number and of all kinds, just as there are gods without number and of all kinds; demons peopling the atmosphere around us; demons both good and bad, male and female; the good for ever engaged in unceasing conflict with the bad, the bad for ever impeding every good work, for ever causing accidents, diseases, plague, pestilence and ruin (see Chapter ix).

Then, again, there is another noteworthy paradox involved in a Hindū's pantheistic creed. For, although human beings are believed to be portions of Brăhmă the one God, yet that God nevertheless delights in acting as a hard taskmaster towards all these portions of himself, imposing on them intolerable burdens. Hence a pious Hindū who considers himself to be part of the one God, will still feel himself impelled by some law of necessity to propitiate that god by the severest self-imposed religious tasks (pp. 393, 560). It should be noted, too, that the idea of God as an angry avenger is an essential element in later Hindūism. The god of destruction delights in destruction for its own sake (p. 82). But his wife, the goddess Kālī, is the more bloodthirsty of the two. Blood of some kind she will have. Thousands of goats and buffaloes are therefore daily offered upon her altars throughout India (see pp. 189, 431, 575).

Finally there is the paradox of a purely spiritual Essence identifying itself with animals, trees, images and stones.

How, then, can the intelligent and well-educated Hindū—trained by us to think accurately, and instructed by us in the facts, phenomena, and laws of European science—acquiesce in these extravagances? 'There is but one God'—an educated native would probably say, in explanation of the apparent incongruity:—'There is but one God by whatever form He is worshipped in Asia or in Europe. He (the one God) is in His essence impersonal and formless, though He delights in manifesting Himself in infinite developments, in infinite evolutions and personalities; and though He chooses to ignore Himself in the distinct individualities created by Himself. Hence the separate existence of you, and of me, and of the world around us, is a mere illusion. When, through protracted self-discipline, the illusion is made to vanish, we are again absorbed into the one God. Idols are not intended to be worshipped; they are merely useful as helps to devotion. They enable ignorant people to form some idea of God's countless manifestations. They are a necessary assistance to the masses of our illiterate population, whose mental condition is that of children, and who cannot read those written descriptions of God which exist in the Scriptures of all nations, and equally give God human attributes—figure, face, hands, and feet.'

Such would probably be an intelligent Hindū's apology for his national religion. And by this peculiar method of mental engineering is the devious tortuosity of the Hindū pantheistic system made straight, and the vast chasm which separates the creeds of the educated and uneducated classes bridged over. And thus, too, it is that the most highly educated natives acquiesce apathetically in all the strange and monstrous forms of their country's superstitions, and are quite content to remain Hindūs in name and in religion to the end of their lives.

The above summary will, I trust, be useful as an introduction to the study of the evolution of Indian religious thought and life, as I have striven to elucidate it in the present volume. At any rate it may help to make clear how it is that the religion of the Hindūs—rooted in a super-subtle form of spiritual Pantheism—has branched out into numerous ramifications which have gradually extended themselves over the entire area of an immense site, without check or restraint, without order, organization or coherency, by a process of successive growth, decay, recuperation, and accretion carried on for more than three thousand years.

To denote the composite and complex character of this wholly unsystematic system, we have called it 'Brāhmanism and Hindūism,' but we have been careful to make it understood that these names are not accepted by its own adherents (see p. 20).

Its present aspect may be compared to an immense mosaic which, having had no one maker, has been compacted together by a succession of artificers and inlaid with every variety of strange and fanciful image. Or rather perhaps may we liken it to a colossal edifice formed by a congeries of heterogeneous materials, without symmetry or unity of design—a vast, overgrown, irregular structure—which, although often falling into decay in its outlying extremities, still rises from its ruins, still goes through repeated processes of repair, still holds its own with obstinate pertinacity, and still belies the expectations of those who are looking for its downfall.

It will be readily admitted, then, that the duty of finding my way through such a confused congeries of matter has been one requiring much time and labour.

But even more beset with difficulties has been the task of trying to clear the way for others—of trying to assist the investigations of students bent on penetrating the mysteries of Brāhmanical philosophy, and arriving at the inner meaning of forms, symbols, and observances, which even the most pious Hindū is often himself unable to explain, except by saying that they have descended from his forefathers.

I need scarcely say, therefore, that my explanations have been written under a deep sense of the responsibility which these difficulties have laid upon me.

I have felt, indeed, that even the most profound Orientalists who have never come in contact with the

Indian mind, except through the study of books or possibly through making the acquaintance of a few stray Indian travellers in European countries, commit themselves to mischievous and misleading statements, when they venture to dogmatize in regard to the present condition—religious, moral, and intellectual—of the inhabitants of India; while, on the other hand, the ablest men who have passed a great portion of their lives in some one Indian province, without acquiring any scholarlike knowledge of Sanskṛit—the master-key to Hindū religious thought—are liable to imbibe very false notions in regard to the real meaning of the religious practices carried on before their eyes, and to do serious harm if they attempt to propagate their misapprehensions in books, pamphlets, and reviews.

The present volume, therefore, is not merely the outcome of fifty years study of Sanskṛit literature. It is the result of my personal researches in India itself, and is put forth from the vantage-ground of personal contact and personal intercourse with the Hindūs in their own land. I have, during my tenure of the Boden Professorship at Oxford, felt it my duty to visit India three times, and to make three journeys through the length and breadth of the entire peninsula from Cashmere to Cape Comorin, from Bombay to the confines of Tibet.

Possibly those who know my companion volume on Buddhism (the 2nd edition of which was published last year[1]) may be disposed to inquire how it is that the

[1] 'Buddhism in its connexion with Brāhmanism and Hindūism and in its contrast with Christianity (John Murray, Albemarle Street).'

present work has not as many oases in its desert of dry matter. But it must be borne in mind that Buddhism offers an unusual focus of interest in the personal character and biography (however legendary) of its founder; whereas Brāhmanism and Hindūism have no one central personality capable of attracting the attention of general readers. Nevertheless, those who work their way conscientiously and persistently through all that I have here written will not fail, I think, to find their fatigue alleviated by a few refreshing and attractive episodes, if not by any very extensive tracts of interesting and pleasant reading.

Perhaps I may draw especial attention to the later chapters, beginning at Chapter xii. Perhaps, too, I may here state that the chapters on modern Indian Theists were submitted by me to the venerable Debendra-nāth Tāgore himself, when I was staying at Calcutta, and were revised by him in his own handwriting.

It will be seen at once that Chapters xxi and xxii are almost entirely new, and a large number of additions and improvements will be discovered in nearly every page of the entire volume by any one who compares this edition carefully with its predecessor.

Furthermore it will be observed that the Index has been improved and enlarged in a corresponding manner; while at the same time, in almost every case, the figures in the present Index suit the pagination of the previous editions.

In conclusion I may be permitted to repeat what I stated in the Preface to the first edition, that the most cursory perusal of the following pages will show that my sympathy with the natives of our great Dependency and my cordial appreciation of all that is good and true in their own sacred literature (see p. 533) and in their codes of morality, have not led me to gloss over what is false and impure in their systems of belief and objectionable in their social practices.

M. M.-W.

ENFIELD HOUSE, VENTNOR,
October, 1891.

NOTE.

The interesting portrait opposite to the title-page of this volume requires some explanation. The portrait is also to be found in my volume on Buddhism, but is only inserted there to illustrate the connexion between Brāhmanism and Buddhism. It is really an engraving from an excellent photograph of an eminent Brāhman which was taken not long ago at Bombay, and may be regarded as furnishing good evidence of the fact that orthodox Brāhmanism has not yet died out in India. By referring to p. 362 it will be seen that every Brāhman, when he arrives at the fourth stage of life, ought to become a Sannyāsī—that is, to withdraw from all active duties and devote the rest of his days to religious meditation. The person represented was an able prime minister of the native State Bhaunagar, and in consequence of his eminence was created a C. S. I. by our Government. He has recently retired from his high office and become a Sannyāsī. A Rudrāksha rosary is suspended round his neck (see p. 67). In front of his raised seat are various ceremonial implements. Near the right-hand corner of his seat is a Kamaṇḍalu or water-gourd. In front of the seat, on the right of the figure, is an Upa-pātra or subsidiary vessel used with the Kamaṇḍalu. In the middle is the Tāmra-pātra or copper vessel for containing the water used at the performance of ceremonies, and on the left is the Pañća-pātra for the purifying water measured out with the Āćamanī, or spoon used at Āćamana (see p. 402). Near the left-hand corner are the wooden clogs. In his left hand is the Daṇḍa or staff called Sudarśana. It is a mystical weapon employed against evil spirits and consists of a bamboo with six knots. The mystic white roll, which begins above the left hand and ends before the fifth knot, is called the Lakshmī-vastra. The projecting piece of cloth, folded in the form of an axe (Paraśu), represents the weapon of Paraśu-rāma (see pp. 110, 270) with which he subdued the enemies of the Brāhmans.

With reference to p. 460, I am informed by Mr. William Crooke, of the Bengal Civil Service, that in Upper India the village potter (Kumbhār, Kumhār) is 'very low in social rank. He is one of the *begār* or persons bound to contribute their productions to visitors free of charge.'

CONTENTS.

INTRODUCTORY OBSERVATIONS.

PAGE

Three principal stages or phases of the Hindū religion. Definition of Vedism, Brāhmanism, and Hindūism. First seat of the Āryans. Origin of religion among the primitive Āryans. Worship of natural objects 1-6

CHAPTER I.

VEDISM.

Four Vedas. Gods of the Veda. Ideas expressed by the term sacrifice. Use of Soma plant. Animal sacrifice. Remarkable hymns of the Veda. Examples of hymns. Social condition of the people 7-19

CHAPTER II.

BRĀHMANISM.

Four phases. I. Ritualistic Brāhmanism. Development of the idea of sacrifice. II. Philosophical Brāhmanism. Upanishads. Sūtras. Subtle and gross bodies. Sāṅkhya philosophy. Vedānta. Tri-unity of entities. Three corporeal envelopes. Vedānta and Sāṅkhya systems compared. Nyāya philosophy. Metempsychosis. III. Mythological Brāhmanism. Buddhism. Tri-mūrti. Descents of Vishṇu. IV. Nomistic Brāhmanism. Three codes of law . 20-53

CHAPTER III.

HINDŪISM. GENERAL OBSERVATIONS.

Distinction between Brāhmanism and Hindūism. The philosopher Śaṅkara. Inter-relationship and distinction between Śaivism and Vaishṇavism. Six principal sects. Doctrine of incarnation. Śaiva and Vaishṇava marks. Rosaries. Symbols and images 54-72

CHAPTER IV.

ŚAIVISM.

PAGE

Definition of Śaivism. Worship of Rudra-Śiva. Description of Śiva. Śaiva sects. Ceremonies performed at Walkeśvar temple. Ceremonies performed at Bhuvaneśvara temple . . . 73-94

CHAPTER V.

VAISHṆAVISM.

Chief characteristics of Vaishṇavism. Tolerance. Religious credulity. Incarnations of Vishṇu. Vaishṇava sects. Initiation. Sect founded by Rāmānuja. Two antagonistic parties. Privacy in eating. Sect founded by Madhva. Common ground with Christianity. Sect founded by Vallabha. Profligacy of Vallabha Mahārājas. Sect founded by Ćaitanya. Four leaders. Ceremonies at a Vaishṇava temple, Poona 95-145

CHAPTER VI.

VAISHṆAVISM. MINOR SECTS AND REFORMING THEISTIC MOVEMENTS.

Sects founded by Nimbārka; by Rāmānanda; by Svāmi-Nārāyaṇa. Interview between Bishop Heber and Svāmi-Nārāyaṇa. Temples at Wartāl and Ahmedābād. Svāmi-Nārāyaṇa's Directory. Theistic sect founded by Kabīr. Examples of his precepts. Sikh sect founded by Nānak. Features of his teaching. Antagonism between Sikhs and Muhammadans. Govind founder of Sikh nationality. Deification of the Sikh bible. Examples of precepts. Metempsychosis. Govind's shrine at Patnā. Golden temple at Amṛitsar 146-179

CHAPTER VII.

ŚĀKTISM, OR GODDESS-WORSHIP.

Worship of the female principle. Two systems. Mysticism. Mother-goddesses. Devī. Kālī. Initiation. Wine-drinking. Mantras, Bījas, spells. Mystic diagrams. Amulets, gestures. Tantras . 180-208

CHAPTER VIII.

TUTELARY AND VILLAGE DEITIES.

Gaṇeśa and Su-brahmaṇya. Ayenār. Hanumān. Monkey-worship. Duality in unity. Worship of Mothers. Pantheism. Specialities of the Mothers of Gujarāt 209-229

CHAPTER IX.

DEMON-WORSHIP AND SPIRIT-WORSHIP.

PAGE

Seven upper and seven lower worlds. Nature and differences of demons. Corporeal organization. Two grand divisions. Triple classification. Methods of neutralizing influences of demons. Men-demons. Demons in the South and West. Devil-dances. Structures connected with devil-worship. Bishop Caldwell on the Shānārs. Devil-expulsion. Incantations. Evil eye. Charms, amulets. Sorcery 230–256

CHAPTER X.

HERO-WORSHIP AND SAINT-WORSHIP.

No limit to deification of great men. Rāma and Kṛishṇa. Local deifications. Viṭhobā; Tukā-rāma; Khaṇḍo-ba; Jñāneśvara; Dattātreya; Svāmi-Nārāyaṇa. Other examples. Paraśu-rāma, or Rāma with the axe. Five Pāṇḍava princes; Karṇa 257–273

CHAPTER XI.

DEATH, FUNERAL RITES, AND ANCESTOR-WORSHIP.

Universal prevalence of homage to the dead. Object of Hindū funeral rites. Ceremonies in Vedic times, and as prescribed by Āśvalāyana. Other rules for funeral rites. Bone-gathering ceremony. Śrāddha ceremonies. Modern practice of funeral and Śrāddha ceremonies. Character and functions of Yama, god of death. Description of the treatment undergone by a deceased man subject to Yama. Piṇḍas offered to form an intermediate body. Ceremonies to secure immunity from future punishment. Twenty-one different Hells. River Vaitaraṇī. Bone-gathering ceremony at Bombay. Śrāddha ceremonies. Śrāddhas distinguished under twelve heads. Śrāddha for a recently deceased parent. Śrāddhas at Gayā. Piṇḍas or balls of rice and milk 274–312

CHAPTER XII.

WORSHIP OF ANIMALS, TREES, AND INANIMATE OBJECTS.

Motives for worshipping animals. Metempsychosis. Worship of cows and bulls; of serpents; of Nāgas; of Snakes; of Monkeys and various animals. Marriage of animals. Worship of trees and plants; of the Tulasī; of the Pippala; of the Bilva tree. Marriage of trees. Worship of natural objects; of sun, moon, planets, water, mountains, rocks, stones 313–350

CHAPTER XIII.

THE HINDŪ RELIGION IN ANCIENT FAMILY-LIFE.

PAGE

No congregational religion. Domestic religion and usages superintended by Brāhmans. Twelve purificatory rites. Importance of a son. Initiation. The sacred thread. Four stages of a Brāhman's life. Ancient marriage-ceremonial. Ancient fire-worship. Ancient sacrificial rites. Soma-sacrifices 351–369

CHAPTER XIV.

THE HINDŪ RELIGION IN MODERN FAMILY-LIFE.

Name-giving ceremony. Birth-record and Horoscopes. Shaving and tonsure-rite. Betrothal. Initiation. Marriage ceremonies. Wedding of Sir Maṅgaldās Nathoobhāī's sons. Choice of profession. Status of women. Three objects of human life. The model wife 370–389

CHAPTER XV.

RELIGIOUS LIFE OF THE ORTHODOX HINDŪ HOUSEHOLDER.

Description of a modern Hindū house. Some Vedic rites still maintained. A Brāhman's daily duties. Dress. Sacredness of the kitchen. Omens; auspicious and inauspicious sights. Religious inferiority of women. Teeth-cleaning. Application of ashes. Morning Sandhyā service. Midday and Evening service. Brāhma-yajña service. Tarpaṇa service. Pañćāyatana ceremony. Vaiśvadeva ceremony. Bali-haraṇa ceremony. Dining. Prayer before eating 390–425

CHAPTER XVI.

HINDŪ FASTS, FESTIVALS, AND HOLY DAYS.

Hindū powers of fasting. Special fasts. Makara-saṅkrānti. Vasanta-pañćamī. Śiva-rātri. Holī. Rāma-navamī. Nāga-pañćamī. Kṛishṇa-janmāshṭamī. Gaṇeśa-ćaturthī. Durgā-pūjā. Kālī-pūjā. Rāma-līlā. Dīvālī. Illuminations. Kārttika-pūrṇimā . . 426–433

CHAPTER XVII.

TEMPLES, SHRINES, AND SACRED PLACES.

Benares described. Tanjore temple. Madurā temple. Rāmeśvara. Trichinopoly. Jambukeśvara. Kāñjīvaram. Tinnevelly temples. Jagan-nāth in Orissa. Śrī-raṅgam. Temple girls. Courtesans 434–451

CHAPTER XVIII.

CASTE, ESPECIALLY IN RELATION TO OCCUPATIONS.

PAGE

The four restrictions of Caste. Caste and occupations are part of religion. State of trades and industries in India. Village communities. Tillers of soil. Village functionaries. Arts, jewelry, sculpture, painting. Delicacy of Indian hand-work. Tyranny of caste; its advantages and disadvantages 452–474

CHAPTER XIX.

MODERN HINDŪ THEISM. RĀMMOHUN ROY.

Theism no new doctrine in India. Life of Rāmmohun Roy. His death at Bristol 475–490

CHAPTER XX.

MODERN HINDŪ THEISM. RĀMMOHUN ROY'S SUCCESSORS.

Dwārkanāth Tāgore. Debendra-nāth Tāgore. Ādi Brāhma-Samāj. Keshab Chandar Sen. Brāhma-Samāj of India. Sādhāraṇa Brāhma-Samāj. Ārya-Samāj. Dayānanda Sarasvatī . 491–531

CHAPTER XXI.

Examples of the moral precepts of Brāhmanism and Hindūism 532–554

CHAPTER XXII.

SUPPLEMENTARY.

Worship of Brahmā at Pushkara. 'Arrowy-bed' form of self-mortification. Account of the late Mahārāṇī of Nuddea's cremation. Account of the daily Deva-pūjā of the Mahārāja of Dholpur. Account of the customs and religious tenets of the Santāls. Conclusion 555–586

INDEX 587–603

CORRECTIONS.

Page 44, l. 19 from top, strike out the word 'note'.

" 53, l. 9 from bottom, for 'Sannyasī' read 'Sannyāsī'. (In a few other instances the long mark has dropped out.)

" 451. Strike out *Sacred Symbols* from the Heading.

TABLE OF

SYSTEM OF TRANSLITERATION

USED IN THIS VOLUME

WITH

EQUIVALENT SANSKṚIT LETTERS AND PRONUNCIATION.

VOWELS.

A, *a*, for अ, pronounced as in rur*a*l; *Ā*, *ā*, for आ, ा, as in t*a*r, f*a*ther; *I*, *i*, for इ, ि as in f*i*ll; *Ī*, *ī*, for ई, ी, as in pol*i*ce; *U*, *u*, for उ, ु, as in f*u*ll; *Ū*, *ū*, for ऊ, ू, as in r*u*de; *Ṛi*, *ṛi*, for ऋ, ृ, as in mer*ri*ly; *Ṛī*, *ṛī*, for ॠ, ॄ, as in ma*ri*ne; *E*, *e*, for ए, े, as in pr*e*y; *Ai*, *ai*, for ऐ, ै, as in *ai*sle; *O*, *o*, for ओ, ो, as in g*o*; *Au*, *au*, for औ, ौ, as in H*au*s (German); *ṇ* or *ṃ*, for ं, i.e. the Anusvāra, sounded like *n* in French mo*n*, or like any nasal; *ḥ*, for ः, i.e. the Visarga or a distinctly audible aspirate.

CONSONANTS.

K, *k*, for क्, pronounced as in *k*ill, see*k*; *Kh*, *kh*, for ख्, almost as in in*kh*orn; *G*, *g*, for ग्, as in *g*un, do*g*; *Gh*, *gh*, for घ्, almost as in lo*gh*ut; *Ṅ*, *ṅ*, for ङ्, as in si*ng* (si*ṅ*).

Ć, *ć*, for च्, as in dol*ć*e (in music), = English *ch* in *ch*ur*ch*, lur*ch* (lur*ć*); *Ćh*, *ćh*, for छ्, almost as in chur*chh*ill (ćur*ćh*ill); *J*, *j*, for ज्, as in *j*et; *Jh*, *jh*, for झ्, almost as in he*dge-h*og (he*jh*og); *Ñ*, *ñ*, for ञ्, as in si*nge* (si*ñj*).

Ṭ, *ṭ*, for ट्, as in *t*rue (*ṭ*ru); *Ṭh*, *ṭh*, for ठ्, almost as in an*th*ill (an*ṭh*ill); *Ḍ*, *ḍ*, for ड्, as in *d*rum (*ḍ*rum); *Ḍh*, *ḍh*, for ढ्, almost as in re*dh*aired (re*ḍh*aired); *Ṇ*, *ṇ*, for ण्, as in *n*o*n*e (*ṇ*u*ṇ*).

T, *t*, for त्, as in wa*t*er (as pronounced in Ireland); *Th*, *th*, for थ्, almost as in nu*t-h*ook (but more dental); *D*, *d*, for द्, as in *d*ice (more like *th* in *th*is); *Dh*, *dh*, for ध्, almost as in a*dh*ere (more dental); *N*, *n*, for न्, as in *n*ot, i*n*.

P, *p*, for प्, as in *p*ut, si*p*; *Ph*, *ph*, for फ्, almost as in u*ph*ill; *B*, *b*, for ब्, as in *b*ear, ru*b*; *Bh*, *bh*, for भ्, almost as in a*bh*or; *M*, *m*, for म्, as in *m*ap, ja*m*.

Y, *y*, for य्, as in *y*et; *R*, *r*, for र्, as in *r*ed, yea*r*; *L*, *l*, for ल्, as in *l*ie; *V*, *v*, for व्, as in *v*ie (but like *w* after consonants, as in t*w*ice).

Ś, *ś*, for श्, as in *s*ure, se*ss*ion; *Sh*, *sh*, for ष्, as in *sh*un, hu*sh*; *S*, *s*, for स्, as in *s*ir, hi*ss*. *H*, *h*, for ह्, as in *h*it.

Note that the above system differs in one or two trifling points from that used in my 'Practical Grammar of the Sanskṛit Language,' fourth edition, published by the Delegates of the University Press, Oxford, and from that used in my Sanskṛit-English Dictionary, published by the same.

BRĀHMANISM AND HINDŪISM.

Introductory Observations.

THE present work is intended to meet the wants of those educated Englishmen who may be desirous of gaining an insight into the mental, moral, and religious condition of the inhabitants of our Eastern empire, and yet are quite unable to sift for themselves the confused mass of information—accurate and inaccurate—spread out before them by writers on Indian subjects. It will be seen that its aim is to present trustworthy outlines of two important phases of religious thought in India, namely, Brāhmanism and Hindūism, as based on the Veda and the other sacred books of the Hindūs. It is a companion to my volume on Buddhism[1], and these two works will, I hope, be followed by one embodying what I have already written on Zoroastrianism and Muhammadanism. It is my desire to give a clear sketch of the most remarkable features of all these systems, and to note some of the chief points in which they may be contrasted with Christianity.

Having been a student of Indian sacred literature for nearly fifty years, and having thrice travelled over every part of India, from Bombay to Calcutta, from Cashmere to Ceylon, I may possibly hope to make a dry subject fairly attractive without any serious sacrifice of scientific accuracy, while I strive at the same time to hold the scales impartially between antagonistic religious systems and, as far as possible, to do justice to the amount of truth that each may contain.

[1] Published by Mr. Murray (Albemarle Street) in 1890 (2nd edit.).

Brāhmanism and Hindūism may justly claim our earnest consideration, not only for the reason that about two hundred millions of the population of India are adherents of these systems, but because of the intricacy of the doctrines contained in them and the difficulty of making them intelligible to European minds.

With a view to greater perspicuity it is desirable to make use of the word Vedism, as a convenient expression for the earliest stage or phase in the development of Indian religious thought.

I. Vedism, then, was the first form of the religion of the Indian branch of the great Āryan family—the form which was represented in the songs, invocations, and prayers, collectively called Veda, and attributed to the Ṛishis, or supposed inspired leaders of religious thought and life in India. It was the worship of the deified forces or phenomena of Nature, such as Fire, Sun, Wind, and Rain, which were sometimes individualized or thought of as separate divine powers, sometimes gathered under one general conception and personified, though in a very vague way, as one God.

II. Brāhmanism grew out of Vedism. It teaches the identification of all the forces and phenomena of Nature with one spiritual Being—the only real Entity—which, when unmanifested and impersonal, is called Brahmă (neut.); when manifested as a creator, is called Brahmā (masc.); as a disintegrator, Śiva; as a preserver, Vishṇu; and when manifested in the highest order of men, is called Brāhmaṇa ('the Brāhmans'). Brāhmanism is rather a philosophy than a religion. Its fundamental doctrine is spiritual Pantheism. Hence Brahmā is only a creator in the sense of being the first Evolution out of the one Spirit, the evolution out of which all other evolutions have proceeded. He is not a creator in the sense of creating the world out of nothing. The only Creator or, more correctly, Evolver, is the neuter entity called Brahmă, the source of all created things. Hence according to the Śatapatha-brāhmaṇa (XI. 2, 3, 1 etc.) we find it stated:—

'In the beginning Brahmă was this (universe). He created gods. Having created gods, he placed them in these worlds. Having gone to the most excellent worlds he considered: How can I pervade all these worlds? He then pervaded them with form and with name. He who knows these two great manifestations of Brahmă becomes himself a great manifestation.' (Muir's Texts, v. 388.)

III. Hindūism grew out of Brāhmanism. It is Brāhmanism, so to speak, run to seed and spread out into a confused tangle of divine personalities and incarnations. The one system is the rank and luxuriant outcome of the other. Hindūism is chiefly to be distinguished from Brāhmanism in this—that it takes scant account of the primordial, impersonal Essence Brahmă, as well as of its first personal manifestation Brahmā; but honours, in place of both, the two popular personal deities Śiva and Vishṇu (pp. 54, 73). Be it noted, however, that Hindūism includes Brāhmanism. It is indeed a somewhat unsatisfactory term. Unhappily there is no other expression sufficiently comprehensive to embrace that all-receptive, all-absorbent system, which, without any one Founder, was the product of Brāhmanism amplified by contact with its own offspring Buddhism, and with various pre-existing cults. Hindūism is Brāhmanism modified by the creeds and superstitions of Buddhists and Non-Āryan races of all kinds, including Drāviḍians, Kolarians, and perhaps pre-Kolarian aborigines. It has even been modified by ideas imported from the religions of later conquering races, such as Islām and Christianity.

I propose therefore to trace the gradual development of Indian religious thought through these three phases which really run into and overlap each other. In so doing I shall examine it, as in fairness every religion ought to be examined, from the point of view of its best as well as of its worst side.

But I ought to premise that the mass of the Hindūs think

far more about the observance of caste-rules and social customs and the propitiation of local deities and evil demons than about any of the theological creeds excogitated by their religious teachers. Hindūism with the masses is little more than a system of social rules and local superstitions.

It is probable that one of the earliest homes (if not the first seat[1]) of the members of the great Āryan family was in the high land surrounding the sources of the Oxus, to the north of the point connecting the Hindū Kūsh with the Himālayas. The highest part of this region is called the Pamīr plateau, and, like the table-land of Tibet, with which it is connected by a lofty ridge, it well deserves the title of 'the roof of the world' (*bām-i-dunyā*). The hardy inhabitants of these high-lands were a pastoral and agricultural race, and soon found themselves straitened for room within the limits of their mountain tracts. With the increase of population they easily spread themselves westwards towards Balkh, and southwards, through the passes of Afghānistān on the one side and Cashmere on the other, into Northern India.

There they developed high mental capacities and moral feelings. They possessed great powers of appreciating the magnificent phenomena of nature. They were endowed with a deep religious sense—a consciousness of their dependence on the invisible forces which regulated the order of the world. They were fitly called 'noble' (*ārya*), and they spoke a language which was ultimately called 'polished' or 'carefully constructed' (*Saṉskṛita*).

To trace the origin of religion among such a people requires no curious metaphysical hypotheses. We have only to ask ourselves what would be the natural working of their devotional instincts, unguided by direct revelation. Their material

---

[1] According to Dr. Schrader's theory the cradle-land of the primitive Āryans was in the Steppes of Southern Russia. Others place it in Northern Europe. Others dispute both theories, and hold to the old idea of 'somewhere in Central Asia.' I also hold to the old idea.

welfare depended on the influences of sky, air, light, and sun (sometimes fancifully imaged in the mind as emerging out of an antecedent chaotic night); and to these they naturally turned with awe and veneration. Soon all such phenomena were believed to be animated by intelligent wills. At first the relationship between spirit, mind, and matter was imperfectly apprehended. Whatever moved was believed to possess life, and with life was associated power. Hence light, fire, air, and storm were thought of as mysterious forces, whose favour required propitiation. Next they received homage under the general name of Devas, 'luminous ones.' Then, just as men found themselves obliged to submit to some earthly leader, so they naturally assigned supremacy to one celestial being called the 'light-father' (Dyu-pitar, Dyaus, *Ζεὺς πατήρ*, Jupiter). Or, again, a kind of pre-eminence was accorded to the all-investing sky or atmosphere (Varuṇa, *Οὐρανός*), the representative of an eternal celestial Presence watching men's actions, and listening to their words by night as well as by day. Then of course closely connected with light and sky was the actual orb of the Sun called Mitra, often associated with another aspect of the Sun, Aryaman, whose influences fertilized lands, enriched pastures, and fructified crops.

Then other phenomena, connected with Sun and fire (Agni, Latin Ignis), such as the dawn (Ushas, 'Ηώς, Aurora), and Iḍā or Irā (Iris), were by degrees regarded with varying degrees of veneration. They all had names which still exist under different modifications among different branches of the Āryan stock, leading us to infer that they were among the most ancient objects held sacred in the original abode of the Āryan race, before the several members of the family separated.

There is even ground for conjecturing that triads of natural objects, such as Sky, Atmosphere, and Sun, or three forms of the Sun, called Aryaman, Varuṇa, and Mitra, were associated together and worshipped by the primitive Āryans in the earliest times. It is certain that the Āryan race, from the first development of its religious sense on the soil of India, has shown a tendency to attach a sacred significance to the number three, and to group the objects of its adoration in triple combinations.

Not that the nascent religious ideas of a people naturally devout were regulated or circumscribed in ancient times by any definite rules or precise limitations. The objects and forces of nature received homage in different ways—sometimes singly, as if impelled by separate and independent wills; sometimes in groups, as if operating co-ordinately; sometimes collectively, as if animated and pervaded by one dominating Spirit—the maintainer of law and order in the Universe.

As to the form of worship, that, too, was a natural process not yet burdened by tedious ceremonial observances. When men had personified and deified the forces with which they were surrounded, they gave them characters like their own. They attributed to them human tastes, likings, and predilections. They propitiated them by praise and flattery, accompanying their hymns and invocations with such presents and offerings of food and drink as would be deemed acceptable among themselves, and would be needed for the maintenance of their own vigour and vitality.

Perhaps the earliest and commonest offerings were rice and clarified butter. Then the exhilarating juice of the Soma plant, afterwards an essential ingredient in both Āryan and Iranian sacrifices, was used as a libation. But the form of worship, like the creed of the worshipper, was unfettered by precise rule or ritual. Each man satisfied his own religious instincts, according to his own conception of the character of the supernatural being or beings on whose favour his welfare was thought to depend.

CHAPTER I.

Vedism.

So much has been of late years written and spoken about the Veda, that to go minutely into this subject would be, according to a Hindū saying, 'to grind ground corn.'

When the Indian branch of the Āryan family settled down in the land of the seven rivers (*Sapta Sindhu*, cf. Ṛig-veda X. 75, Zend *Hapta Hendu*), now called the Panjāb, about the fifteenth century B.C., their religion was still nature-worship. It was still adoration of the forces everywhere in operation around them for production, destruction, and reproduction. But it was physiolatry developing itself more distinctly into forms of Anthropomorphism, Polytheism, Theism, and Pantheism. The phenomena of nature were thought of as something more than radiant beings, and something more than powerful forces. To the generality of worshippers they were more distinctly concrete personalities, and had more personal attributes. They were addressed as kings, fathers, guardians, friends, benefactors, guests. They were invoked in formal hymns and prayers (mantras), in set metres (ćhandas).

These hymns were composed in an early form of the Sanskṛit language, at different times—perhaps during several centuries, from the fifteenth to the tenth B.C.—by men of light and leading (Ṛishis) among the Indo-Āryan immigrants, who were afterwards held in the highest veneration as patriarchal saints. Eventually the hymns were believed to have been directly revealed to, rather than composed by, these Ṛishis, and were then called divine knowledge (Veda), or the eternal word heard (Śruti), and transmitted by them.

These Mantras or hymns were arranged in three principal collections of continuous texts (Saṃhitās). The first and earliest was called the Hymn-Veda (Ṛig-veda). It was a collection of 1017 hymns, arranged for mere reading or reciting. This was the first bible of the Hindū religion, and the special bible of Vedism. We might imagine it possible to have collected the most ancient hymns and psalms of our own Sacred Scriptures in the same manner.

The second, or Sacrificial Veda (Yajur), belongs to the sacrificial phase of the Vedic system. It was a liturgical arrangement of part of the same collection of hymns, with additions[1] for intoning in a peculiar low tone at sacrificial ceremonies. Be it noted, however, that some of the hymns of the Ṛig-veda (for example, the horse-sacrifice or Aśva-medha hymn, I. 162) presuppose a ritual already definite and systematized.

The third, or Chant-Veda (Sāma), was another liturgical arrangement of some of the same hymns for chanting at particular sacrifices in which the juice of the Soma plant was the principal offering (pp. 12; 368).

A fourth collection—which might suitably be called the Spell-Veda—was added at a later period. It was a collection of hymns—some of them similar to those of the Ṛig-veda, but the greater part original—composed by a particular class of priests called Atharvans[2]. Many of the texts and formularies of this Atharva-veda were ultimately used as charms and spells, and are still so used in various parts of India.

By some of the earliest hymn-composers the gods continued to be regarded as one family—children of the old pre-Vedic heavenly father (Dyo or Dyaus), while Earth (Pṛithivī) was fabled as a divine mother. To other sacred poets the pre-

[1] Certain passages in prose were added, which were especially called *Yajus*.

[2] This was a generic name for a class of priests, descended from a man named Atharvan, who appears to have been the first to institute the worship of fire, before the Indians and Iranians separated. It is certain that particular priests both in India and Persia were called Atharvans.

Vedic deification of the Sky (Varuṇa, Οὐρανός) remained a principal object of adoration. He was still occasionally exalted to the position of a Supreme Being. A well-known hymn in the Atharva-veda (IV. 16) describes him as ruling the world, as penetrating the secrets of all hearts, as detecting the plots of wicked men, as sending down countless messengers who for ever traverse the earth and scan its inmates, as numbering every wink of men's eyes, as wielding the whole universe in the manner of a gamester handling dice.

But the true gods of the Veda constituted a triad of deities. They were the Fire-god (the earth-born Agni), the Rain-god (the air-born Indra), and the Sun-god (the sky-born Sūrya or Savitṛi, pp. 19; 341)—one for each of the three worlds, earth, air, and sky (bhūr, bhuvaḥ, svar). These three were the special objects of worship of the early Indo-Āryans. All their other principal deities were either modifications of, or associated with, one or other of the members of this Vedic triad. For example, the wind (Vāyu) and the storm-gods (Maruts), led by the destroying god (Rudra), were regarded as intimate associates of the Rain-god Indra, and were really only forms and modifications of that god. On the other hand, the ancient Āryan deities, Varuṇa and Mitra, with Vishṇu, were all mere forms of the Sun (Sūrya or Savitṛi, also called Pūshan). Of course the Dawn (Ushas) was also connected with the Sun, and two other deities, the Aśvins—probably personifications of two luminous points in the sky—were fabled as his twin sons, ever young and handsome, travelling in a golden car as precursors of the Dawn.

As to the Fire-god (Agni), he had various attributes significant of his interest in the world of human beings. He was God on the earth and therefore more accessible than other deities. He was manifested by the friction of the two pieces of the sacred fig-tree called Araṇi, and consequently always to be found at hand. He was visibly present in every household. He was man's domestic friend, the father of the sacrifice, the mediator between men and gods, the bearer of hymns and prayers from every family altar upwards towards heaven.

Fire, in fact, may be regarded as the next god to the Rain-god in the estimation of Vedic worshippers; and certainly he takes precedence over every other god in connection with sacrificial rites. Even the Sun-god, who is generally first in all Pagan systems, is held to be a form of heavenly fire. Fire has always been an object of veneration among all nations.

A conjecture may even be hazarded that the three letters A, U, M, which combine to form the sacred syllable Om—afterwards typical of the Brāhmanical triad (pp. 44; 403)—were originally the initial letters of the names of Fire, Wind, and Sun, i.e. Agni, Vāyu or Varuṇa (for Indra), and Mitra. It must not be forgotten, however, that both Indra and Agni were, like Varuṇa, often addressed as if each deity were supreme. Moreover, the god of fire was sometimes held to possess a kind of triple essence in himself, consisting of terrestrial fire, celestial lightning, and solar heat. Sometimes he represented a simple creative energy, which evolved all things out of its own eternal essence.

There are allusions, too, in the Ṛig-veda to thirty-three gods (I. 34. 11; I. 45. 2), or to the three groups consisting of eleven Rudras, eight Vasus, and twelve Ādityas with Heaven and Earth. Their names are given variously, but they are little more than modifications of the three leading personifications.

Only two or three instances occur of Vedic deities who stand alone. One of the most remarkable is Yama, god of departed spirits. It is noteworthy that the spirits of departed ancestors (Pitṛis) who have attained to heavenly bliss, are believed to occupy three different stages of blessedness,—the highest inhabiting the upper sky, the middle the intermediate air, and the lowest the atmospheric region near the earth. Adoration is to be offered them, and they are presided over by Yama, leader of the spirits of the dead, both good and bad.

The earliest legends represent Yama as the first of created

men (his twin-sister being Yamī) and the first of men who died. Hence he is supposed to guide the spirits of other men who die to the world of spirits. Sometimes Death is said to be his messenger; he himself dwelling in celestial light to which the departed are brought, and where they enjoy his society and that of the patriarchs. In the later mythology he is Judge of the dead and punisher of the wicked (p. 289). In the Veda he has no such office,—but he has two terrific dogs, with four eyes, which guard the way to his abode (p. 17).

In brief, enough has been said to show that the early religion of the Indo-Āryans was a development of a still earlier belief in man's subjection to the powers of nature and his need of conciliating them. It was an unsettled system which according to one view assigned all the phenomena of the universe to one Cause; or again, attributed them to several Causes operating independently; or again, supposed the whole visible creation to be a manifestation of one universal all-pervading spirit. It was a belief which, according to the character of the worshipper, was now mere animism, now monotheism, now tritheism, now polytheism, now pantheism. But it was not yet idolatry. Though the forces of nature were thought of as controlled by divine persons, such persons were not yet idolized. There is no evidence from the Vedic hymns that images were actually worshipped, though they appear to have been occasionally employed[1].

The mode of divine worship continued to be determined from a consideration of human likings and dislikings. Every worshipper praised the gods because he liked to be praised himself. He honoured them with offerings because he liked to receive presents himself. He pretended to feed them because he required food himself. This appears to have been the simple origin of the sacrificial system—a system which was afterwards closely interwoven with the whole Hindū religion.

---

[1] For example, in Ṛig-veda II. 33. 9 an image of Rudra is alluded to; and in I. 25. 13, V. 52. 15, visible forms of some kind seem implied.

What, then, were the various ideas expressed by the term sacrifice? In its purest and simplest form it denoted a dedication of some simple gift as an expression of gratitude for blessings received. Soon the act of 'making sacred' became an act of propitiation for purely selfish ends. The favour of celestial beings who were capable of conferring good or inflicting harm on crops, flocks, and herds, was conciliated by offerings and oblations of all kinds, and especially of the products of the soil.

With this idea the gods were invited to join the every-day family meal. Then they were invoked at festive gatherings, and offered a share of the food consumed. Their bodies were believed to be composed of ethereal particles, dependent for nourishment on the invisible elementary essence of the substances presented to them, and to be furnished with senses capable of being gratified by the aroma of butter and grain offered in fire (homa)[1]; and especially by the fumes arising from libations of the exhilarating juice extracted from the Soma plant.

This plant—botanically known as *Sarcostema Viminalis*, or *Asclepias Acida*, a kind of creeper with a succulent leafless stem—which was indigenous in the ancient home of the Āryans, as well as in the soil of India and Persia, supplied an invigorating beverage supposed to confer health and immortality, and held to be the vital sap which vivified the world. Hence its juice became an important ingredient at every sacrifice, and was the subject of constant laudation in numerous Vedic hymns. It was believed to be peculiarly grateful to the Rain-god (Indra), while oblations of butter were specially presented to the god of fire. Eventually the great esteem in which the Soma plant was held led to its being itself personified and deified. The god Soma was once the Bacchus of India. The whole ninth Book of the Ṛig-veda is devoted to his praise.

---

[1] Compare Gen. viii. 21.

And yet this sacred plant has fallen into complete neglect in modern times. When I asked the Brāhmans to procure specimens of the true Soma for me, I was told that the sinful condition of the world had caused the holy plant to cease growing on earth, though it was to be found in heaven [1].

Nor were these the only offerings. In process of time, animal sacrifice was introduced. At great solemnities goats and other animals were killed by hundreds. Portions of the flesh were consumed in the fire, and portions were eaten. Gods, priests, and people feasted together. Of course all offerings were accompanied with hymns of praise. A tedious ceremonial was gradually added. The whole sacrificial service was called Yajña. By diligent performance of Yajña a man gained admittance to Indra's heaven (Svarga, see p. 49).

I close this sketch of Vedism by citing portions of my translations of a few remarkable hymns in the Ṛig-veda, as given by me in 'Indian Wisdom.' One hymn (Maṇḍala X. 129) describes the origin of creation thus :—

In the beginning there was neither nought nor aught;
Then there was neither sky nor atmosphere above.
What then enshrouded all this teeming universe?
In the receptacle of what was it contained?
Was it enveloped in the gulf profound of water?
Then was there neither death nor immortality;
Then was there neither day, nor night, nor light, nor darkness,
Only the Existent One breathed calmly, self-contained.
Nought else but he there was—nought else above, beyond.
Then first came darkness hid in darkness, gloom in gloom;
Next all was water, all a chaos indiscrete,
In which the One lay void, shrouded in nothingness.
Then turning inwards, he by self-developed force
Of inner fervour and intense abstraction, grew.
First in his mind was formed Desire, the primal germ
Productive, which the Wise, profoundly searching, say
Is the first subtle bond, connecting Entity
And Nullity.

---

[1] A creeper, said to be the true Soma, was pointed out to me by the late Dr. Burnell in Southern India, and is still, I believe, used by those orthodox Brāhmans in the Marāṭha country who attempt to maintain the old Vedic worship. A specimen was given by me to the Indian Institute.

In the foregoing hymn we detect the first dim outline of the later philosophical theories, both Sāṅkhyan and Vedāntic.

The idea of the female principle as necessary to the act of creation is also, as may be seen, vaguely implied—an idea which gathered such strength subsequently that every principal deity in the later mythology has his feminine counterpart, who shares the worship paid to the male god, and who sometimes receives the greater homage of the two. That this idea is not fully developed in the Ṛig-veda is proved by the fact that the wives of the chief gods, such as Indrāṇī, Agnāyī, etc., are not associated with their husbands as objects of worship, and even Lakshmī and Sarasvatī, though named, are not adored.

The next example from the 121st hymn of the tenth Maṇḍala is often quoted to furnish an argument for maintaining that the original faith of the Hindūs was monotheistic. The hymn is addressed to Hiraṇya-garbha, a form of the Supreme Being, no doubt originally a personification of the Sun. In the Vedānta philosophy, Hiraṇya-garbha represents the third condition of the Supreme Spirit (see p. 35). In the later system he must be regarded as related to the God Vishṇu. He is thus described:—

> What god shall we adore with sacrifice?
> Him let us praise, the golden child that rose
> In the beginning, who was born the lord—
> The one sole lord of all that is—who made
> The earth, and formed the sky, who giveth life,
> Who giveth strength, whose bidding gods revere,
> Whose hiding-place is immortality,
> Whose shadow, death; who by his might is king
> Of all the breathing, sleeping, waking world.
> Where'er let loose in space, the mighty waters
> Have gone, depositing a fruitful seed,
> And generating fire, there *he* arose
> Who is the breath and life of all the gods,
> Whose mighty glance looks round the vast expanse
> Of watery vapour—source of energy,
> Cause of the sacrifice—the only God
> Above the gods.

The following is a portion of a well-known hymn to the Sky-god (Varuṇa) from the Atharva-veda (IV. 16):—

The mighty Varuṇa, who rules above, looks down
Upon these worlds, his kingdom, as if close at hand.
When men imagine they do aught by stealth, he knows it.
No one can stand, or walk, or softly glide along,
Or hide in dark recess, or lurk in secret cell,
But Varuṇa detects him, and his movements spies.
Two persons may devise some plot, together sitting,
And think themselves alone; but he, the king, is there—
A third—and sees it all. His messengers descend
Countless from his abode, for ever traversing
This world, and scanning with a thousand eyes its inmates.
Whate'er exists within this earth, and all within the sky,
Yea, all that is beyond, king Varuṇa perceives.
The winkings of men's eyes are numbered all by him:
He wields the universe as gamesters handle dice.

Here follow portions of hymns addressed to the Vedic triad. Firstly, the Fire-god (Agni):—

Agni, thou art a sage, a priest, a king,
Protector, father of the sacrifice.
Commissioned by us men, thou dost ascend
A messenger, conveying to the sky
Our hymns and offerings. Though thy origin
Be threefold, now from air, and now from water,
Now from the mystic double Araṇi,
Thou art thyself a mighty god, a lord,
Giver of life and immortality;
One in thy essence, but to mortals three;
Displaying thine eternal triple form,
As fire on earth, as lightning in the air,
As sun in heaven. Thou art the cherished guest
In every household—father, brother, son,
Friend, benefactor, guardian, all in one.
Deliver, mighty lord, thy worshippers,
Purge us from taint of sin, and when we die,
Deal mercifully with us on the pyre,
Burning our bodies with their load of guilt,
But bearing our eternal part on high
To luminous abodes and realms of bliss,
For ever there to dwell with righteous men.

Secondly, the Rain-god (Indra, afterwards lord of Svarga):—

Indra, twin-brother of the god of fire,
When thou wast born, thy mother, Aditi,

Gave thee, her lusty child, the thrilling draught
Of mountain-growing Soma—source of life
And never-dying vigour to thy frame.
Thou art our guardian, advocate, and friend,
A brother, father, mother—all combined.
Most fatherly of fathers, we are thine,
And thou art ours. Oh! let thy pitying soul
Turn to us in compassion when we praise thee,
And slay us not for one sin or for many.
Deliver us to-day, to-morrow, every day.
Vainly the demon [1] dares thy might, in vain
Strives to deprive us of thy watery treasures.
Earth quakes beneath the crashing of thy bolts.
Pierced, shattered lies the foe—his cities crushed,
His armies overthrown, his fortresses
Shivered to fragments; then the pent-up waters,
Released from long imprisonment, descend
In torrents to the earth, and swollen rivers,
Foaming and rolling to their ocean-home,
Proclaim the triumph of the Thunderer.

Thirdly, the Sun-god (Sūrya, Ṛig-veda, I. 50):—

Behold the rays of dawn, like heralds, lead on high
The Sun, that men may see the great all-knowing God.
The stars slink off like thieves, in company with Night,
Before the all-seeing eye, whose beams reveal his presence,
Gleaming like brilliant flames, to nation after nation.
Sūrya, with flaming locks, clear-sighted god of day,
Thy seven ruddy mares bear on thy rushing car.
With these thy self-yoked steeds, seven daughters of thy chariot,
Onward thou dost advance. To thy refulgent orb
Beyond this lower gloom, and upward to the light
Would we ascend, O Sun, thou god among the gods.

The thoughts contained in various hymns addressed to the 'god of departed spirits' (Yama, p. 11) are so remarkable that a few are here given:—

To Yama, mighty king, be gifts and homage paid.
He was the first of men that died, the first to brave
Death's rapid rushing stream, the first to point the road
To heaven, and welcome others to that bright abode.
No power can rob us of the home thus won by thee.

[1] The demon Vṛitra, who is supposed to keep the waters imprisoned in thick clouds.

O king, we come; the born must die, must tread the path
That thou hast trod—the path by which each race of men,
In long succession, and our fathers, too, have passed.
Soul of the dead! depart; fear not to take the road—
The ancient road—by which thy ancestors have gone;
Ascend to meet the god—to meet thy happy fathers,
Who dwell in bliss with him. Fear not to pass the guards—
The four-eyed brindled dogs—that watch for the departed.
Return unto thy home, O soul! Thy sin and shame
Leave thou behind on earth; assume a shining form—
Thy ancient shape—refined and from all taint set free.

I add a few verses from the celebrated Purusha hymn (Ṛig-veda, Maṇḍala X. 90, as freely translated by me in another work). It illustrates the intertwining of polytheism, monotheism, and pantheism. It also foreshadows the idea of sacrifice, as well as the institution of caste[1], which for so many centuries has held India in bondage. The one Spirit is supposed to take a body and then allow himself to be sacrificed.

The embodied spirit has a thousand heads,
A thousand eyes, a thousand feet, around
On every side enveloping the earth,
Yet filling space no larger than a span.
He is himself this very universe;
He is whatever is, has been, and shall be;
He is the lord of immortality.
All creatures are one-fourth of him, three-fourths
Are that which is immortal in the sky.
From him, called Purusha, was born Virāj,
And from Virāj was Purusha produced,
Whom gods and holy men made their oblation.
With Purusha as victim, they performed
A sacrifice. When they divided him,
How did they cut him up? What was his mouth?
What were his arms? and what his thighs and feet?
The Brāhman was his mouth, the kingly soldier
Was made his arms, the husbandman his thighs,
The servile Śūdra issued from his feet.

Further examples and a fuller account of the Veda will be found in my book called 'Indian Wisdom.' The above

[1] This hymn (generally admitted to be a comparatively modern production) is the only hymn in the Ṛig-veda which alludes to the distinctions of caste.

selected examples would, if taken alone, encourage a false estimate of the merits of the Vedic hymns. Although the majority of the Hindūs believe that the four Vedas contain all that is good, great, and divine, and although many of the hymns are to this day in constant daily use and form part of the religious services of every orthodox Brāhman (see pp. 403, 406), yet Vedic compositions will be found, when taken as a whole, to abound more in puerile ideas than in lofty conceptions. At the same time it is clear that they give no support to any of the present objectionable usages and customs for which they were once, through ignorance of their contents, supposed to be an authority. The doctrine of metempsychosis or transmigration of souls, which became an essential characteristic of Brāhmanism and Hindūism in later times, is scarcely hinted at in the religion of the Veda[1]. Nor do the hymns give any sanction to the prohibition of widow-marriages, the general prevalence of child-marriages, the tyrannical sway of caste, the interdiction of foreign travel, and the practice of idolatry.

The social condition of the people, when the hymns were composed, was marked by considerable civilization. They were rich in flocks and herds; they understood the principles of agriculture; they built towns and fortified places; they had some knowledge of arts and of working in metals; they engaged in philosophical speculations; they had political rulers, and a high type of morality; they were separated into classes, though they were not yet divided off by iron barriers of caste; polygamy existed, though monogamy was the rule; they killed animals for sacrifice; they ate animal food, and did not even object to the flesh of cows; among their weaknesses was a fondness for gambling and intoxicating beverages.

---

[1] Maṇḍala I. 164. 32 *bahu-prajaḥ* is explained by *bahu-janma-bhāk*, 'subject to many births;' but it may mean 'having abundant offspring.' There is another text (VIII. 101. 14) beginning Prajā ha tisro atyāyam īyuḥ.

And it is to be observed that, just as the children of Israel found the land of Canaan pre-occupied by Hittites, Perizzites, and Philistines, so the Āryan immigrants, when they advanced into India, found the soil held by previous races, variously called Drāviḍas, Dasyus, Anāryas, Nishādas, etc., and even by more primitive aboriginal tribes, contact and intercourse with whom very soon affected them socially, morally, and religiously.

Monsieur A. Barth[1] comes to the conclusion that the Vedic hymns give evidence of an exalted morality, and draws attention to the fact that they acknowledge no wicked divinities.

Worship of the gods was performed by sacrifice (yajña), invocation (āvāhana), prayer (prārthanā), praise (stuti), and meditation (upāsanā); and the name Brahman (nom. Brahmă), ultimately applied to the one Universal Spirit, was often identified with Prayer.

Finally be it observed that the most sacred and the most universally used of all Vedic prayers is that called Gāyatrī, or, as addressed to the Vivifying Sun-god, Sāvitrī:—

'Let us meditate on that excellent glory of the Divine Vivifying Sun; may he enlighten our understandings[2].' This is still a Brāhman's daily prayer (see below, pp. 403, 406).

Yet the author, or, as a Brāhman would say, the Seer (Ṛishi), of this celebrated prayer was Viśvāmitra—a man originally of the Kshatriya or military caste, once opposed to the Brāhmanical. It should be noted that this Gāyatrī is often personified and worshipped as identified with Sarasvatī and as the mother of the Vedas.

---

[1] His work on the religions of India is excellent, but some of his opinions are new. He sees no 'primitive natural simplicity' in the hymns, and denies that the Vedas represent the general belief of a race.

[2] Tat Savitur vareṇyam bhargo devasya dhīmahi, Dhiyo yo naḥ praćodayāt (Ṛig-veda III. 62. 10). In my opinion the Sandhyā (p. 401) derives its name from the root *dhī* for *dhyai*, 'to meditate,' in this prayer.

CHAPTER II.

Brāhmanism.

THE second phase of Indian religious thought may be suitably called Brāhmanism. The Brāhmans themselves would reject such a title. They call their religion Ārya-dharma, 'the religion of the Āryas' (or Vaidika-dharma, or Ṛishi-sampradāyo dharmaḥ, Patañjali I. 1. 1). They of course regard it as the only true religion, and have no difficulty in including all other religions—such as Muhammadanism and even Christianity—under it.

As Brāhmanism was the outgrowth of Vedism, so it cannot be separated from Vedism. Its development was gradual, just as the development of Hindūism out of it was. Vedism, Brāhmanism, and Hindūism are all closely inter-connected.

It is interesting to trace the crystallization of the rudimentary doctrines of Brāhmanism into definite shape. In Vedic times there was, as we have seen, a feeling after one Supreme Being, if haply He might be found. The hymn-composers gave expression to man's craving for some perception of the Infinite. To satisfy this craving they turned to personifications of the Sky, Sun, Fire, Air, Water, Earth.

What the deepest thinkers, even at that early period, felt with ever-increasing intensity was that a Spirit (Ātman), beyond the cognizance of sense, permeated and breathed through all material things. They bethought them with awe of this same Spirit vivifying their own bodies with the breath of life—of this mysterious Presence enshrined in their own consciences. Then they identified this same Spirit with the divine afflatus thrilling through the imaginations of their own hymn-composers—with the spiritual efficacy of the hymns themselves, with the mystic power inherent in divine knowledge and prayer. This mysterious, all-pervading, vague spiritual Power and Presence, which was wholly unbound by limitations of personality and individuality, became at last a reality. This Breath of Life (Ātman) received a name. They called it Brahman (nominative neuter Brahmă, from the root *bṛih*, 'to expand'), because it expanded itself through all space. It was a pure essence which not only diffused itself everywhere, but constituted everything. Men, gods, and the visible world were merely its manifestations.

Such was the fundamental doctrine of Brāhmanism. Such was Brāhmanism in its earliest origin. Soon, however, it became a more complex system—a system which may be regarded as possessing four sides, or rather four phases running into each other and nowhere separable by sharply defined lines, namely (1) Ritualistic, (2) Philosophical, (3) Mythological or Polytheistic, (4) Nomistic.

Ritualistic Brāhmanism.

This phase of the Brāhmanical system has for its special bible the sacred treatises called Brāhmaṇas, added to the Mantra or Hymn portion of each Veda (for example, the Aitareya, Śatapatha, Tāṇḍya, and Gopatha Brāhmaṇas added to the Ṛig, Yajur, Sāma, and Atharva Vedas respectively). They consist of a series of rambling prose compositions, the oldest of which may have been written seven or eight centuries B.C. Their relationship to the Vedic hymns resembles in some respects that of the book of Leviticus to the Psalms in our own sacred Scriptures. They are an integral portion of the Veda, and are supposed to contain that portion of divine knowledge or revelation particularly adapted to serve as a directory for the Brāhmans in the conduct of the complicated sacrificial ceremonies. For if it was deemed necessary in the early Vedic period to propitiate and maintain the energies of nature by means of invigorating offerings of food, it was clearly still more incumbent on men to make offerings to these same forces when personalized and endowed with forms acknowledged to be perishable. In fact the necessity for sacrificial acts (*karman*) to secure the favour of the gods became ingrained in the whole Brāhmanical system. Not even Jewish literature contains so many words relating to sacrifice as the literature of the Brāhmans. The due presentation of sacrificial offerings formed the very kernel of all religious service. Hymn, praise, and prayer, preaching, teaching, and repetition of the sacred words of scripture were only subsidiary to this act. Every man throughout his whole life rested his whole hopes on continually offering oblations of some kind to the gods, and the burning of his body at death was held to be the last offering of himself in fire (antyā ishṭi or antyeshṭi).

But the idea of the great efficacy of sacrifice was developed gradually. In the Brāhmanical, as in the earlier system, the first aim of sacrifice was to present a simple thank-offering. The second aim was to nourish the gods with the essence of the offered food (as with that of the Soma-juice, p. 369), and so strengthen them for their duty of maintaining the universe. The next idea was that of making these oblations the means of wresting boons from the invigorated and gratified deities, and so accomplishing some specific earthly object, such, for example, as the birth of a son. A still more ambitious idea was that of employing sacrifice as an instrument for the attainment of superhuman powers and even exaltation to heaven (svarga, see p. 49).

All this involved the elaboration of a complicated ritual, and the organization of a regular hierarchy. To institute any sacrificial rite (e.g. the Aśvamedha, or the Jyotishṭoma Soma-sacrifices, Agnishṭoma, Aptoryāma, or that called Vājapeya, 'strengthening drink,' p. 368), and to secure its being conducted with the proper intonation of innumerable hymns and texts from the Veda, and the accurate observance of every detail of an intricate ritual by a full complement of perhaps sixteen different classes of priests, every one of whom received adequate gifts, was the great object of every pious Hindū's highest ambition. Every ceremonial rite, too, had to be performed with *saṅkalpa*, i.e. voluntarily, with earnest resolution and conscious will. The whole course of prayer, praise, ritual, and oblation—sometimes lasting for weeks and even years—though called, as in Vedic times, Yajña, 'sacrifice,' was very inadequately expressed by that term. It was like an intricate piece of mechanism, or a chain of which every link required to be complete and perfect in all its parts. It could then effect anything. It was the great preservative from all evil, the great maintainer of the energies of the Universe, the great source of all benefits. It could procure a whole line of sons and grandsons[1], or secure admission into Indra's heaven (svar, svarga, see p. 49), or even raise the sacrificer to the level of the highest deities. It was believed that the gods themselves had attained their celestial position by performing sacrifices. 'By sacrifices,' says the Taittirīya-brāhmaṇa, 'the gods obtained heaven.'

The most preposterous of all the ideas connected with the sacrificial act was that of making it the instrument of creation. In the Purusha hymn of the Ṛig-veda (X. 90) the gods are represented as cutting up and sacrificing Purusha, the primeval Male, and then forming the whole Universe from his head and limbs (see p. 17). The Tāṇḍya-brāhmaṇa makes the lord of creatures offer himself up as a sacrifice. Even Sacrifice (Yajña) itself was sometimes personified as a god.

Lastly, the shedding of blood was believed by some to expiate sin. The victim consigned to the fire was thought to be an expiation for sins committed by the gods, the fathers, and men. Probably the idea was not so much that of killing an innocent victim for the removal of guilt as of warding off the punishment which an angry Being was likely to inflict.

---

[1] An uninterrupted line of sons, grandsons, and great-grandsons was needed for the due performance of funeral rites, through which alone the bliss of a man after death could be secured (see pp. 274–312).

It is even probable that human sacrifice was once part of the Brāhmanical system. The Aitareya-brāhmaṇa (VII. 13) has the well-known story of Hariśćandra and Śunaḥśepa which points to its prevalence. The same Brāhmaṇa records the substitution of the sacrifice of four kinds of animals—horses, oxen, sheep, and goats—for that of men. Sometimes numbers of animals were tied to sacrificial posts (yūpa), some being killed and some liberated at the end of the ceremony. As to the Horse-sacrifice (Aśva-medha) see p. 329.

One of the most noteworthy ideas to be found in the Brāhmaṇas is that the gods were merely mortal till they conquered Death by sacrifices. Death is thereupon alarmed lest men also should be victorious over him and deprive him of all his rights; but the gods promise that those who perform sacrifices should not become immortal without first offering him their bodies, and that non-sacrificers should present him their bodies in many successive births.

The following is a free translation of a passage of the Śatapatha-brāhmaṇa :—

> The gods lived constantly in dread of Death—
> The mighty Ender—so with toilsome rites
> They worshipped and repeated sacrifices
> Till they became immortal. Then the Ender
> Said to the gods, 'As ye have made yourselves
> Imperishable, so will men endeavour
> To free themselves from me; what portion then
> Shall I possess in man?' The gods replied,
> 'Henceforth no being shall become immortal
> In his own body; this his mortal frame
> Shalt thou still seize; this shall remain thy own,
> This shall become perpetually thy food.
> And even he who through religious acts
> Henceforth attains to immortality
> Shall first present his body, Death, to thee.'

Other passages in the Brāhmaṇas prove that the doctrine of transmigration was beginning to be developed at this period.

It is certainly remarkable that the idea of sacrifice as an atonement for sin seems never to have taken firm hold of the

Hindū mind. Goats were generally sacrificed by Vaidika Brāhmans at their Soma-yāgas, but only in connexion with the central offering of the Soma or liquor of immortality, and mainly with the idea of nourishing the gods who were their friends. Fire was the chief god, not only because he was visibly present, but because he carried up the essence of the oblation to the other gods. In later times the deities were thought to have a malevolent side to their characters, and when sacrifice was needed for the propitiation of an angry deity, it was called Bali. Goats and buffaloes are now immolated in India with the view of appeasing the goddess Kālī, who delights in blood. But in this there is no idea of effacing guilt or making a vicarious offering for sin.

The ordinary Hindū wholly rejects the notion of trusting to anything for salvation but his own self-righteousness; that is, to his own merit (puṇya) acquired through his own pious acts, or through the karma-mārga, 'way of ceremonial acts,' presided over by the Brāhmans.

Philosophical Brāhmanism.

The second or philosophical phase of Brāhmanism cannot be marked off by any decided line from the other phases. Its rudimentary ideas are found in the earlier system, and had their germ in Vedism. It laid stress on the knowledge (jñāna) of the one universally diffused spiritual essence (Brahman) which constitutes everything, and in which all things are merged. This purely spiritual way or way of knowledge (jñāna-mārga) made sacrificial ceremonies useless.

In fact, a reaction from an overdone ritual was inevitable. People became wearied with sacrifices and sacrificers. The minds of thinking men found no rest in the blood of slaughtered victims. It only remained to take refuge in metaphysical investigations. If every man was a part of God, what necessity was there that God should propitiate himself? If a portion of the one self-existent Spirit chose for a time to ignore itself, to invest itself with a body, to fetter itself with actions and their inevitable results, the consequences could only be borne by itself in its passage through numberless births. Nor could there be any final emancipation from a continued succession of corporeal existences, till action ceased and the consciousness of identity with the one universal Spirit returned.

The Upanishads, or hidden spiritual doctrine of the Veda, are the special bible of this phase of Brāhmanism. Many treatises so called were added to the Mantra and Brāhmaṇa portion of the Veda (such as the Īśā, Kaṭha, Ćhāndogya, Muṇḍaka, and Bṛihad-āraṇyaka Upanishads). The aphorisms (sūtras) of the three systems of philosophy with their three so-called branches (that is, the Nyāya with Vaiśeshika; Sāṅkhya with Yoga; Vedānta with Mīmāṉsā) were connected with these writings; but only the Sāṅkhya and Vedānta can be said to be really founded on them.

According to a learned Brāhman who is now a convert to Christianity, the Upanishads are to the Mantras and Brāhmaṇas what our New Testament is to the Old.

They were compositions which expressed the desire of the living personal spirit (jīva or jīvātman) for deliverance from a long series of separate earthly existences and from liability to pass through a variety of bodies—gods, men, animals, plants, stones—and its longing for final reunion with the one self-existent Spirit of the Universe (*Ātman*, afterwards called *Brahman*). And here it may be noted that Philosophical Brāhmanism was not philosophy in the European sense of the word. It was no mere search for truth, for truth's sake. It was rather a form of mystical religious speculation. Nor was it an expression of the soul's desire to be released from the burden of sin. It was rather an inquiry into the best method of its escape from transmigration; the dread of continued metempsychosis being the one haunting thought which colours the whole texture of Indian philosophy. If an Indian metaphysician sets himself to inquire into the nature of spirit and matter, and their relation to each other, his investigations are sure to be conducted with the sole object of liberating the spirit of man from the bondage of repeated earthly existence, and reuniting it with the one Universal Spirit as a river is reunited with the ocean. This is called the way of knowledge (jñāna). This constitutes the right measure (pramā) of all difficulties. This is the summum bonum (niḥśreyasa) of Brāhmanical philosophy.

What, then, are the articles of a Hindū philosopher's creed?

Most Hindū thinkers agree that the one Spirit[1] is eternal, both retrospectively and prospectively. The Spirit of God and the spirit of man must have existed from all eternity and must continue to exist. The two spirits are not really distinct; so says the Vedāntist. The living spirit of man (jīva) —the human Self (Ātman)—is identical with God's Spirit. It is that Spirit limited and personalized by the power of Illusion; and the life of every living spirit is nothing but an infinitesimal arc of the one endless circle of infinite existence.

Again, Hindū philosophers agree that the mind (manas) is distinct from the spirit. Mind is not eternal in the same way. It is an internal organ of the body, standing between the five organs of perception and the five organs of action, connected with both, receiving the impressions conveyed by both, and directing both through the exercise of volition. To the mind appertains the faculties of perception (buddhi), volition (saṅkalpa, vikalpa), self-consciousness and thought, and the spirit cannot possess these, unless joined to mind and invested with a bodily covering or vehicle.

And of actual bodily coverings there are two (though the

---

[1] It is generally better to translate the philosophical terms Ātman, Brahman, and Purusha by 'spirit' rather than by 'soul,' because the expression 'soul' is liable to convey the idea of thinking and feeling, whereas pure Ātman, Brahman, and Purusha neither think, nor feel, nor are conscious. The translation 'Self' is not universally suitable.

Vedānta system reckons three[1]):—first, the subtle body (liṅga or sūkshma-śarīra or ātivāhika[2]), which incloses a portion of the universal spirit in three sheaths (kosha), cognitional, sensorial, and aerial, constituting it a living individual personal spirit (jīvātman), and carrying it through all its corporeal migrations, till, on its reunion with its source, even its subtle body becomes extinct; secondly, the gross body (sthūla-śarīra), which surrounds the subtle vehicle, and is of various forms in the various conditions of existence through animate or inanimate, organic or inorganic life.

And mark that this gross body is of three kinds—divine, earthly, and intermediate—the intermediate being that peculiar frame which the departed spirit receives, after the burning of the earthly gross body and during the interval preceding the assumption of another gross body. This intermediate body (called preta-śarīra, 'the departed man's body,' or, philosophically, Adhishṭhāna-deha) serves, as it were, to clothe the departed spirit during its several residences in the world of departed spirits (pitṛi-loka). It is of the same nature, though inferior to the divine body which belongs to the gods; and it should be noted that this divine intermediate body is really composed of gross (sthūla) particles, though of a more ethereal substance than the earthly body. Without it the departed spirit would have no vehicle but the subtle body, and would be incapable of enjoying bliss or suffering misery in the temporary paradise, or purgatory[3], through which all the departed have to pass before returning to earth (see pp. 292–294).

And be it noted that the union of spirit with a succession of bodily forms is dreaded as the worst form of bondage.

---

[1] In the Vedānta system there are three bodily coverings, the Causal body (Kāraṇa-śarīra) coming first; but this is merely another name for Ajñāna (see p. 35), and can scarcely be regarded as a material substance.

[2] Its minuteness is denoted by its being described as 'of the size of a thumb' (aṅgushṭha-mātra), though some apply this expression to the intermediate body.

[3] The heaven and hell of orthodox Brāhmanism are only temporary.

The spirit, so united, commences acting, and all actions, good or bad, lead to consequences, and these consequences must have their adequate rewards or punishments. It is on this account that the departed spirit must of necessity be removed to temporary heavens or hells. Thence it must migrate into higher, intermediate, and lower earthly forms, according to its various degrees of merit or demerit, till it attains the great end—entire emancipation from the bondage of repeated bodily existence, and reabsorption into the one Spirit of the Universe.

With regard to the external world, it is a fixed dogma of every Hindū philosopher that *Nāvastuno vastu-siddhiḥ* there cannot be the production of something out of nothing (*ex nihilo nihil fit*). Therefore, the external world is eternal, though according to one view, it is evolved out of an eternally existing productive germ united to eternally existing individual spirits; and according to another, it is evolved out of the Illusion which from all eternity overspreads the one eternal Spirit, though having no real existence. These two theories in regard to the creation or evolution of the world—the first in the Sāṅkhya, the second in the Vedānta system—are both of great antiquity.

The first shadowing forth of the mystery of the creation of male and female, and of the living world through their union, is traceable in some of the Vedic hymns. The well-known hymn of the Ṛig-veda (X. 129. 4), already quoted, asserts that first 'in that One Being arose Desire, which was the primal germ of Mind, and which the wise, searching out in their thoughts, discovered to be the subtle bond connecting Non-entity with Entity.'

Again, the Śatapatha-brāhmaṇa (XIV. 4. 2. 4, etc.) and Bṛihad-āraṇyaka Upanishad (I. 3) declare that 'the One Being was not happy, being alone. He wished for a second. He caused his own nature to fall in twain, and thus became husband and wife. He approached her, and thus were human beings produced' (see p. 182).

In this latter passage is the first clear statement of a duality in the divine unity—an idea which took root in the Hindū mind quite as strongly as the doctrine of a Triad (Tri-mūrti) did in the minds of later thinkers—an idea, too, which had been adumbrated in the supposed marriage of Heaven and Earth for the production of gods, men, and all creatures.

The idea was expanded in the mythical cosmogony of Manu, Book I. 5, etc. There it is said that the universe first existed only in darkness as if immersed in sleep. Then the Self-existent (Svayam-bhū) still undeveloped (A-vyakta), having willed to produce various beings from his own substance, first with a mere thought created the waters, and placed on them a productive seed or egg (bīja). Then he himself was born in that egg in the form of Brahmā. Next he caused the egg to divide itself, and out of its two divisions framed the heaven above and the earth beneath. Afterwards, having divided his own substance, he became half male, half female (I. 32), and from that female produced Virāj, from whom was created Manu, the secondary progenitor of all beings. The order of creation of the five elements is, 1. Ether (Ākāśa); 2. Air (Vāyu); 3. Fire (Tejas or Jyotis); 4. Water (Āpaḥ, pl.); 5. Earth (Pṛithivī or Bhūmi); but these were produced from a previous creation of five subtle elements (tan-mātra). The Nyāya-sūtra reverses the order, placing Earth first.

So again in the Sāṅkhya philosophy, there are two eternally existing principles—the Producer and the Spirit. The former is an eternal procreant germ or Creative Force which is called Pra-kṛiti (fem.), because it produces (root kṛi) twenty-three products; these twenty-three, with the Producer, being called the twenty-four Tattvas. It is also called Pradhāna, because it is the fixed material cause of everything except the Spirit—which is the twenty-fifth Tattva. The infinitely subtle elementary germ, Prakṛiti or Pradhāna, though one, is supposed to be made up of a triad of co-eternal primordial substances or essences in equipoise (sāmya). These are called Guṇas, but they are not properly 'qualities,' though certain qualities result from them.

The term Guṇa simply denotes that these constituent essences of Prakṛiti act like cords to bind the spirit with triple bonds. They are, 1. Sattva, 'purity' or 'goodness;' 2. Rajas, 'passion' or 'activity;' and 3. Tamas, 'darkness' or 'apathy;' sometimes regarded as equivalent to happiness, pain, and ignorance, or denoted by white, red, and black respectively.

The Spirit or second eternally existing principle called Purusha (the Male or Self) is not, like Prakṛiti, one; nor does it produce anything. It is multitudinous. Spirits are innumerable, each separate Spirit being co-eternal with Prakṛiti, but doing nothing and creating nothing. When human beings or any other beings are created, the creation is always effected through evolution out of Prakṛiti, which is nevertheless a merely blind and dark force; no creation at all being apparent unless this force brings itself into union with some one eternally existing separate Spirit. Prakṛiti, in short, unites itself with a Spirit or Self and binds it with the triple bond of the three above-named Guṇas [1] in order that this Spirit may reflect the evolved world as a clear river reflects dark trees, while they darken the river, or as a bright crystal vase illumines a flower, while the flower colours the crystal.

The first step in the evolution out of Prakṛiti is the production of Intellect or intelligent perception (Buddhi). Next comes the faculty of Self-consciousness or personality, called the I-maker (Ahaṃ-kāra), and then the five subtle and five gross elements, the latter being the product of the former. Last in the series come the five organs of perception, the five organs of action and the internal organ, mind (Manas), which holds a position between the ten other organs, mediating between them as an instrument of volition between perception and action [2]. These, with the Spirit (Purusha), constitute the twenty-five principles (Tattvas) of the Sāṅkhya system.

---

[1] The Spirit before its association with these Guṇas is called Nirguṇa; and when bound by them, Saguṇa.

[2] In this and in the Nyāya system Buddhi, 'intellect,' is anterior and

The noteworthy point is that self-consciousness, cognition, will, and thought do not belong to the creative force Prakṛiti and its creations, Intellect, the I-maker, and Mind (Buddhi, Ahaṃ-kāra, Manas, which together make up Antaḥkaraṇa) when existing separately, nor to a Spirit (Purusha) when existing separately, but only to the two when united, or to the Antaḥkaraṇa illuminated by a Spirit. In short, two factors —the active, creative but blind force, and the inactive, passive but illuminating spirit—must come together before there can be even any self-consciousness or sense of personality. And yet the creation is not supposed to take place for the sake of the two together, but only that it may be illuminated and observed by each separate individual spirit or soul, which nevertheless is a wholly apathetic, isolated, and indifferent spectator of the act. It is clear from this how easy it became to confuse Purusha with Prakṛiti and to regard either the one or the other or the union of both as the source of the external world[1].

Of course when any being is created the three primordial essences, Purity, Passion, and Darkness, are no longer equally balanced as they are in the creative germ, Prakṛiti. Creation is a result of the disturbance of this equilibrium. One or other quality is then in excess, making a being unselfish and good, selfish and energetic, bestial and ignorant, according as purity, passion, or darkness may happen to preponderate.

I need not point out that this remarkable theory of innu-

---

superior to Manas, 'mind,' which is merely the instrument of thought. It governs the mind, and causes it to decide. Manu's theory is a combination of Sāṅkhya and Vedānta. In Book I. 14, etc. it is said that Brahmā, when born from the egg deposited by the Self-existent, drew out the external world from pure spirit (Ātman). The first product was the principle of thought (Manas = Buddhi or Mahat). Next came Personality (Ahaṃ-kāra), and then the seven subtle elements (Tanmātras). From these seven active principles (called 'the seven Purushas,' I. 19)—viz. Mahat or Buddhi (called *Manas* in I. 14, 74, 75), Ahaṃ-kāra, and the five subtle elements—were evolved in the five gross or material elements (*mahā-bhūta*), the organs of sense, and the whole world of sense.

[1] Professor A. E. Gough in his 'Philosophy of the Upanishads' has thrown great light on the Sāṅkhya and Vedānta systems.

merable personal creations for the sake of individual spirits is not without its counterpart in European systems[1]. In India the idea of a separate spiritual force combining with a primordial material force for the creation of all things was, as we have seen, of great antiquity. And notwithstanding the metaphysical subtleties with which it was connected, the notion of a universe proceeding from a male principle or generator, and a female principle regarded as an energy or capacity (śakti), commended itself to the popular mind as harmonizing with the operations and phenomena everywhere apparent in nature. To this day it is symbolized all over India by temples dedicated to the male and female sex (in the union of the sexual symbols called Liṅga and Yoni). It is clear that in such a system there can be no need for the existence of any supreme Spirit as distinct from the personal spirit, even though such a supreme Being be theoretically admitted (as in the Yoga branch of the Sāṅkhya).

The so-called pantheistic theory of the Vedānta philosophy is even more attractive to the majority of Hindū thinkers. It is true that both the Sāṅkhya and Vedānta together underlie Brāhmanism; but the Vedānta is, so to speak, the latest revelation of the Veda, teaching the non-duality and non-plurality of Spirit—that is, the real existence of only one Spirit called Ātman[2] (nom. Ātmā) or Brahman (nom. Brahmă, see p. 43) instead of many; the separation of human spirits and of all the phenomena of nature from that one Spirit being only effected when it is enveloped in Illusion. In other words, the separate existence of man's spirit and of all natural phenomena is only illusory.

This doctrine is said to rest on another well-known hymn of the Veda (X. 90) called the Purusha-sūkta. There the one embodied Spirit is called Purusha (see p. 17), and is said to be 'everything, whatever is, has been, and shall

[1] The Sāṅkhya has much in common with the Idealism of Berkeley.

[2] One etymology given for Ātman is *an*, 'to breathe.' Compare p. 20.

be.' The same doctrine is briefly formulated in three words (from the Ćhāndogya Upanishad) used as a creed in the present day by Indian Theistic as well as Pantheistic sects—*Ekam eva advitīyam*, 'there is but one Being, without a second.' Nothing really exists but the one impersonal Spirit, called Ātmā or Brahmă (=Purusha). Brahmă is real, the world is an illusion (Brahma satyaṃ Jagan mithyā). From it everything is born, in it everything breathes and is dissolved (tajjalān). That Spirit, *in the illusion which overspreads it*, is to the external world what yarn is to cloth, what milk is to curds, what clay is to a jar; but only in that illusion[1]. As ether contained in various vessels, and as the sun reflected on various mirrors, is one but apparently many, so the spirit is one and many. The potter by the help of clay makes various pots, but the Spirit itself evolves its own various forms. As an actor paints his body with colours and assumes various forms, so the Spirit assumes the bodies caused by its deeds. This self-existent, eternal, impersonal Ātmā or Brahmă is absolutely One (unlike the Sāṅkhyan Spirit or Purusha, which is multitudinous); yet it is made up of a triad of essences—to wit, pure Existence (Sat), pure Thought (Ćit)[2], and pure Bliss (Ānanda), and it may assume three bodily envelopes and three conditions or Guṇas (p. 36).

And here let me observe that more than one Christian writer has compared this tri-unity of Entities with the Trinitarian doctrine of God the Father, who is the Author of all Existence; God the Son, who is the Source of all Wisdom and Knowledge; and God the Holy Spirit, who is the Source of all Joy. But it is a mistake so to compare it; because, with the Vedāntist, Brahmă is only Existence in the negation

---

[1] He is not the *actual* material cause of the world as clay of a jar, but the *illusory* material cause as a rope might be of a snake; see p. 37, l. 14.

[2] Ćit, 'pure thought,' or its equivalent Ćaitanya, is often used alone for Brahmă, the one Self-existent Being. Sat may also be so used. Brahmă is also described in the Upanishads as Truth, Knowledge, Infinity.

of non-existence, only Thought in the negation of non-thought, only Bliss in the negation of non-bliss and in freedom from the miseries incident to life and transmigration.

When this impersonal Spirit—which is without self-consciousness—assumes consciousness of a personal self; that is, when it begins to exist in anything external to itself, and when it begins to think about anything or be joyful about anything besides itself—it does so by the power of Illusion (Māyā) and by investing itself with three corporeal envelopes.

First, the causal body (kāraṇa-śarīra) identified with Ajñāna or Ignorance (Illusion)[1]; secondly, the subtle body (liṅga-śarīra); and thirdly, the gross body (sthūla-śarīra). In this way the impersonal Spirit is converted into a personal God who can be worshipped, and so becomes the Supreme Lord (Īśvara, Parameśvara) and creator of a world of illusion. To be accurate. however, it should be stated that the Vedānta theory makes the assumption of these three bodies involve the assumption of three distinct mystical personalities, each of which is supposed to invest a particular condition of spirit. Thus, with the first or causal body, the impersonal Spirit becomes the Supreme Lord, Parameśvara, supposed to represent and embody the mystical totality of dreamless spirits; with the second or subtle body the impersonal Spirit becomes Hiraṇya-garbha (or Sūtrātman, or Prāṇa), supposed to represent the aggregate of dreaming spirits (connecting them like the Sūtra or thread of a necklace); with the third or gross body it becomes Virāj (or Vaiśvānara, Prajā-pati, Purusha), supposed to represent and embody the aggregate of waking spirits (compare p. 28).

This third condition of spirit or that of being wide awake,

---

[1] The Kāraṇa-śarīra is not only identified with Ignorance (Ajñāna or Avidyā), but also with Illusion (Māyā). It is, therefore, no real body. Both Ignorance and Illusion together cause the separation of the personal supreme Spirit and the personal human Spirit from the one impersonal Spirit. In the same way they are the cause of every existing thing.

though with us considered to be the highest state, is by Hindū philosophers held to be the lowest, because farthest removed from pure impersonalized Spirit. In fact, beyond and underlying all three conditions of spirit is the fourth (turīya) or pure unconditioned, unembodied, impersonal Spirit (Brahmă) itself.

Of course these hyper-subtleties are beyond the scope of ordinary philosophic thought ; but they show how great is the difference between the Pantheism of India and that of Europe. A Vedāntist believes in one impersonal Spirit, who, by association with Illusion, becomes the one Supreme personal God (Parameśvara) of the world (of illusion). And it is this personal God who, when he engages in the creation, preservation, and dissolution of an illusory Universe, is called Sa-guṇa because believed to be associated with the three Guṇas which are held to be substances (dravya) and are the supposed constituents of his causal body, identified, as it is, with Ignorance [1]. These three Guṇas are the same as those which in the Sāṅkhyan system are the constituent essences or ingredients of Prakṛiti, resulting in the three conditions of Activity, Goodness, and Apathy called Rajas, Sattva, Tamas [2]. They are the same as those which in the later doctrine of the Purāṇas separate the one Supreme Being into the three divine personalities of Brahmā (nom. case masc.), Vishṇu, and Rudra-Śiva, each accompanied by his own consort [3].

Dominated by Activity (Rajas), the one Universal Spirit is Brahmā, the Creator ; by Goodness (Sattva), it is Vishṇu, the Preserver ; by Indifference (Tamas), it is Rudra, the Dissolver.

---

[1] In other words, the Kāraṇa-śarīra—consisting of Ignorance, and therefore made up of the three Guṇas—is the illusory corporeal disguise (upādhi), or investing envelope, or triple bond of the impersonal Spirit Brahmă, by which it becomes the personal God Parameśvara.

[2] See top of p. 31. These Guṇas of activity, goodness, and apathy are not properly identical with the so-called qualities, but are rather constituent substances or essences or ingredients, though they may result in such qualities.

[3] In the later mythology the term Śakti, 'active energy' (rather than Māyā, Prakṛiti, and Ajñāna), is used for the female half of the personal God.

Pure Vedāntism, then, is not only a belief in one impersonal Spirit made up of three abstract essences. It is a belief that a kind of threefold triad of essences—to wit, three spiritual essences, three corporeal envelopes, and three dominating conditions or qualities—together constitute one personal God, while constituting at the same time every human personality.

It is by reason, then, of association with Illusion or Ignorance (made up of the three Guṇas or Conditions), that the Supreme Spirit (Paramātman) enshrined in the personal God, and the living spirit (jīvātman) enshrined in the personal man, believe in their own individuality, mistaking it and the world for realities, just as a rope in a dark night might be mistaken for a snake. When the personalized spirit sets itself free from the power of Illusion the consciousness of its own identity and of the identity of the whole universe with the one impersonal Spirit, (Ātman = Paramātman, Brahmă), is re-established. Strange to say, this Illusion or Ignorance is held, like the one eternal Brahmă[1], to have an existence from all eternity, though, owing to the fact that such existence is unreal, and the whole evolved world unreal too, it follows that nothing really existent is left but Brahmă. In other words, all that really exists is identical with Brahmă.

In fact, the more evidently physical and metaphysical speculations are opposed to common sense, the more favour do they find with some Hindū thinkers. Common sense tells an Englishman that he really exists himself, and that everything he sees around him really exists also. He cannot abandon these two primary convictions. Not so the Hindū Vedāntist. Dualism is his bugbear, and common sense, when it maintains any kind of real duality, either the separate independent existence of a man's own Spirit and of God's Spirit or of spirit and matter, is guilty of gross deception.

---

[1] Māyā-ćid-yogo 'nādiḥ, 'the union of Ćit (p. 34) and Māyā is from all eternity.' See Professor Gough's able and instructive articles on the Philosophy of the Upanishads.

And yet, after all, when the Vedāntist theory, as held at present, is closely examined, it turns out to be virtually as dualistic, in regard to spirit and matter, as the Sāṅkhya; the only difference being that the source of the material world (Prakṛiti) in the Sāṅkhya is held to have a real existence (though one of its names is still Māyā) instead of a merely illusory existence[1]. Brahmă and Māyā (Illusion) in the Vedānta, Purusha and Prakṛiti (Māyā) in the Sāṅkhya, must be united in the act of creation. The external world is the product of two principles (which some compare to Knowledge and Ignorance, Light and Darkness). The chief difference between the two systems lies in the unity of Spirit taught by the Vedānta, as distinguished from the plurality of spirits taught by the Sāṅkhya.

Yet the Vedāntist virtually believes in three conditions of being, viz. the real, the practical, and the illusory; for while he affirms that the one Spirit Brahmă alone has a real (pāramārthika) existence, he allows a practical (vyāvahārika) separate existence to human spirits, to the world, and to the personal God or gods, as well as an illusory (prātibhāsika) existence.

Hence every object is to be dealt with practically as if it were really what it appears to be. A god is practically a god; a man, a man; a beast, a beast; so that when a man feeds a horse he does not feed him as a portion of God, but as an animal kept for riding. The Vedānta theory, like the Sāṅkhya, has taken deep root in the Indian mind. A mixture of both is the source of the popular religion and mythology of the Hindūs. Both permeate their literature and give a colour to every thought and feeling of their daily lives.

---

[1] Perhaps the only true monistic theory is that of the Buddhist, who affirms that nothing exists but the self-creative Universe, which, however, he also calls Māyā, 'Illusion.' A Vedāntist is Brahmă-vādī, 'one who affirms that Brahmă "Spirit" is the only reality;' a Buddhist is Śūnya-vādī, 'one who affirms a blank for God;' and a Sāṅkhya is Pradhāna-vādī, 'one who affirms that all material things proceed from Pradhāna (Prakṛiti).'

And hence it is not difficult to understand how a people imbued with the idea that the world is an illusion should have neglected all historical investigations. No such thing as genuine history or biography exists in Sanskṛit literature. Historical researches are to a Hindū simple foolishness.

The third philosophical system, called Nyāya—or the act of going into any subject analytically (opposed to Saṅkhyā or synthetic enumeration)—is not so closely connected with religion and metaphysical speculation as the Sāṅkhya and Vedānta. Yet it offers more interesting parallels to European philosophical and scientific ideas. It is much studied in modern Sanskṛit schools of learning, as an analytical inquiry into all the objects and subjects of human knowledge, including, among others, the process of reasoning and logic.

In regard to the subject of reasoning, the Nyāya proper, as I have shown in 'Indian Wisdom' (p. 72), propounds in its first Sūtra sixteen topics, the first of which is Pramāṇa, that is, the means or instrument by which knowledge or the right measure (pramā or pramiti) of a subject is to be obtained. The means are four, viz. perception by the senses (pratyaksha); inference (anumāna); comparison (upamāna); verbal or trustworthy authority (śabda or āptopadeśa), including revelation [1].

Of these four processes, 'inference' is divided into five members (avayava). 1. The pratijñā, or proposition (stated hypothetically). 2. The hetu, or reason. 3. The udāharaṇa, or example (=major premiss). 4. The upanaya, or application of the reason (=minor premiss). 5. The nigamana, or conclusion, i.e. the proposition re-stated as proved. Thus: 1. The hill has fire; 2. for it smokes; 3. whatever smokes has fire, as a kitchen-hearth; 4. this hill smokes; 5. therefore this hill has fire.

---

[1] The Sāṅkhya rightly includes the third of the four Pramāṇas in the second, and the Vedānta adds two others to the four, viz. negative proof (an-upalabdhi, abhāva) and inference from circumstances (arthāpatti). The Vaiśeshika includes both the third and fourth in the second.

Here we have a clumsy combination of enthymeme and syllogism, which must be regarded not as a syllogism, but rather as a full rhetorical statement of an argument.

The most noticeable peculiarity in the Indian method, stamping it as an original analysis of the laws of thought, is the employment of the terms 'invariable concomitance or pervasion' (vyāpti), 'invariable pervader' (vyāpaka), and 'invariably pervaded' (vyāpya). Fire is the pervader, smoke the pervaded. The argument is thus stated: 'The mountain has invariably fire-pervaded smoke; therefore it has fire.'

The Nyāya, like the Sāṅkhya, believes the individual spirits of men (jīvātman) to be eternal, manifold, eternally separate from each other, distinct from the body, senses, and mind, and infinite. A peculiar tenet of the Nyāya is that spirits are ubiquitous, and *diffused everywhere throughout space*, so that a man's spirit is as much in England as in Calcutta, though it can only apprehend, and feel, and act, where the body happens to be.

Its idea of the mind (manas), which it calls an internal instrument or organ, is that it is a substance (dravya) as eternal as the spirit. Instead, however, of being diffused everywhere like spirit, it is atomic, like earth, water, fire, and air, and can only admit one perception or act of volition at a time. It is simply an eternal insentient substance, like an atom of earth.

In its cosmogony the Nyāya is dualistic in assuming the existence of *eternal atoms*, side by side with *eternal spirits.* Atoms are not like Prakṛiti one, but innumerable.

We know that the true Sāṅkhya (as distinct from the Yoga) recognized no Supreme Spirit. Probably the true Nyāya was in this respect like the Sāṅkhya. In any case neither of these systems admits the absolute unity of one all-pervading Spirit. If they acknowledge a Supreme presiding Spirit at all, it can only be as forming one of innumerable other spirits—though superior to them—and as co-eternal and (in the case of the Nyāya) as co-omnipresent with them.

The foregoing three systems, with their sub-systems, constitute the philosophical phase of Brāhmanism. Clearly one of its aims is to teach men to abstain from action of every kind, good or bad—as much from liking as disliking, as much from loving as hating. The whole external world is an illusion. Actions and feelings are a mistake. They are the fetters of the soul which bind it with bonds of iron to continual bodies.

Transmigration or Metempsychosis is the great bugbear—the terrible nightmare and daymare of Indian philosophers and metaphysicians. All their efforts are directed to the removal of this oppressive scare. 'As the embodied soul,' says the Bhagavad-gītā, 'moves swiftly on through boyhood, youth, and age, so will it pass through other forms hereafter.'

For although the human spirit is really one with the Supreme, yet while it continues in ignorance it may commit sins which it must get rid of by expiatory rites (prāyaśćitta) or by passing through purgatorial hells and successive births. Even virtuous acts involve heaven and re-births.

The question, therefore, is not: What is truth? The one problem is: How is a man to break this iron chain of repeated existences, and to shake off all separate personality? How is he to return to complete union with (sāyujya) pure Spirit? Or, if this object be beyond his reach, how is he to work his way through 8,400,000 successive births to any one of the three inferior conditions of bliss—1. living in the same heaven (sālokya) with the personal God; 2. close proximity to him (sāmīpya); 3. assimilation to his likeness (sārūpya)?

Mythological or Polytheistic Brāhmanism.

The Mythological or Polytheistic phase of Brāhmanism has for its bible the two great legendary heroic poems (Itihāsa) Mahā-bhārata and Rāmāyaṇa, and in later times the Purāṇas. Its development was probably synchronous with that of Buddhism.

Buddhism, like philosophical Brāhmanism, was a disbelief in the efficacy of ritual to secure beatitude, and, like it, taught the uselessness of sacrificial ceremonies and even of austerities for the attainment of true knowledge, which was only to be obtained through self-introspection, abstract meditation, and suppression of all desires. It substituted a blank for God; it denied the existence of a separate spirit, and of everything but body, mind, and sensations—earth, heavens, and hells, which, according to the Buddha, are always, through the force of works, tending to disintegration and re-integration in perpetual cycles. But while Buddhism repudiated priestcraft, it founded a monastic brotherhood and supplied the people with an object of veneration in its founder Gautama—who was styled 'the Enlightened' (Buddha). Its propagation was in a great measure due to the reverence which the Buddha inspired by his own personal character. He was the ideal man—the perfection of humanity. He practised faithfully what he preached effectively. Adherents gathered in crowds around his person, and Gautama himself became the real god of his own popular faith. Everywhere throughout India thousands were drawn towards his teaching. His doctrines of universal charity, liberty, equality, and fraternity were irresistibly attractive. The only hope of competing with the Buddhistic movement lay in inventing human gods and a religious system equally attractive, equally popular, equally suited to the needs and capacities of the mass of the people.

In all probability the Brāhmans commenced popularizing their pantheistic doctrines about the time of the rise of Buddhism in the fifth century B.C. The Buddha died, and, according to his own teaching, became personally annihilated, but the remains of his body were enshrined as relics in various parts of India, and his memory was worshipped as devotedly as his person had once been revered. Of course the religious instincts of the mass of the Hindūs found no real satisfaction in the propitiation of the forces of nature and spirits of the air, or in the cold philosophy of pantheism, or in homage paid to the memory of a teacher held to be nowhere existent. They needed devotion (bhakti) to personal and human gods, and these they were led to find in their own heroes. The Rāmāyaṇa and Mahā-bhārata represent the use made by the Brāhmans of the martial songs of the people, as well as of their local legends, traditions and superstitions. The principal heroes, whose achievements were the subject of epic song and recitation, underwent a process of deification. The great warrior dynasties were made to trace back their origin, through Brāhmanical sages, to the sun-god and the moon-god. Myths and stories confirmatory of the divine origin of every great hero were invented and inserted into the body of the poems. In this manner a kind of anthropomorphic religion, well adapted to the popular mind, was devised. Nor was any amount of anthropomorphism, polytheism, polydemonism, and even fetishism incompatible with pantheistic doctrines. The Brāhmans in their popular teaching were simply carrying out their own doctrine of evolution. The only problem which they set themselves to solve was: how could their theory be made to adapt itself to existing superstitions and be accepted as consistent with all the ideas of a popular mythology?

Nothing, then, was easier for them than to maintain that the one sole, self-existing Supreme Spirit, the only real existing Essence, exercises itself, as if sportively (līlayā), in infinite expansion, in infinite manifestations of itself, in infinite creation, dissolution, and re-creation, through infinite varieties and diversities of operation. The very name 'Brahmă' (derived from the root bṛih, 'to increase'), given to this one eternal Essence, was expressive of this growth, this expansive power, this universal development and diffusion.

Hence all visible forms on earth, said the Brāhmans, are emanations from the one eternal Entity, like drops from an ocean, like sparks from fire. Stones, mountains, rivers, plants, trees, and animals—all these are traceable upwards as progressive steps in the infinite evolution of his being. The highest earthly emanation is man, and the emanation of men is in classes and also traceable upwards according to a graduated scale, the highest class being that of the Brāhmans.

Fitly, too, are the highest human manifestations of the eternal Brahmă called Brāhmans: for they are the appointed mediators between earth and God. None of these emanations can alter their condition in each separate state. But according to their acts, they may pass into temporary heavens or hells, and thence into higher or lower grades of being.

For be it observed that a series of higher forms of existence above that of human beings, such as demigods, supernatural beings, inferior gods, superior gods, is traceable upwards from man to the primeval male god Brahmā—the first personal product of the purely spiritual Brahmă when overspread by Māyā or illusory creative force; this male god Brahmā standing at the head of the so-called creation as the first evolution out of which all other beings and objects are evolved (see note, p. 2) To draw any line of separation between stocks, stones, plants, animals, men, demigods, and gods is, according to the theory of Brāhmanism, impossible. They are all liable to pass into each other[1]. The number of gods is popularly said to be 330 millions, though I have not found this stated in any ancient text (cf. p. 10).

But the act of creation or evolution involves the two other acts of maintenance of being and disintegration. Hence the god Brahmā is associated with two other personal deities, Vishṇu, the Preserver, and Rudra-Śiva, the Dissolver and Reproducer. These three gods, concerned in the threefold operation of integration (or evolution), maintenance, and disintegration (*sṛishṭi-sthiti-laya*), are typified by the three letters composing the mystic syllable Om (AUM),—three letters originally

[1] The whole series of evolutions is sometimes spoken of as Brahmādi-stamba-paryantam, extending from Brahmā to a stump (or tuft of grass).

typical of the earlier Vedic triad (wrongly called a trinity), and, in the mysticism of the Upanishads, of three personalizations of the Universal Spirit (Parameśvara, Hiraṇya-garbha, and Virāj [1]). Like the earlier Vedic gods, the three later deities were not only personifications of the three forces of integration, disintegration, and reintegration. They probably symbolized three principal objects in nature, Earth, Water or Sun, and Fire; or the three worlds, Earth, Air, and Sky; or the three forms of matter, Solid, Liquid, and Gaseous (p. 10). They constitute the well-known *Tri-mūrti*, or triad of forms which characterizes Hindūism, and their bodies, like those of human beings, are composed of gross material particles though of a divine and ethereal character (see p. 28).

These three deities, too, are often, as we have seen, connected with the Guṇas of philosophy. In its highest state the one Spirit is Nirguṇa, 'devoid of all conditions or qualities.' It is only when dominated by either activity or goodness or apathy that the impersonal Spirit becomes either Brahmā, the Evolver, or Vishṇu, the Preserver, or Śiva, the Dissolver (see p. 36).

Properly, according to the true theory of Brāhmanism, no one of these three ought to take precedence over the other two. They are equal, and their functions are sometimes interchangeable, so that each in turn may become the Supreme Lord (Parameśvara), and each may take the place of the other, according to the sentiment expressed by the greatest of Indian poets, Kālidāsa (Kumāra-sambhava, Griffith, VII. 44):—

> In those three Persons the one God was shown—
> Each first in place, each last—not one alone;
> Of Śiva, Vishṇu, Brahmā, each may be
> First, second, third, among the blessed Three.

There is a well-known Tri-mūrti sculptured out of the rock in the caves of Elephanta, at Bombay. Three majestic heads

---

[1] See pp. 14, 35, and Māṇḍūkya Upanishad, which makes the whole monosyllable Om stand for the impersonal Brahmā. According to some A stands for Vishṇu, V for Śiva, and M for Brahmā.

are represented springing out of one body. The triangle (*Trikoṇa*) is also used to symbolize this triune co-equality.

In the later mythology this co-equality was denied, the difference in the characters of the three gods being well illustrated by a story from the Bhāgavata-purāṇa, X. 89 :—

> A dispute once arose among the sages which of the three gods was greatest. They applied to the greatest of all sages—Bhṛigu—to determine the point. He undertook to put all three gods to a severe test. He went first to Brahmā, and omitted all obeisance. The god's anger blazed forth, but he was at length pacified. Next he went to the abode of Śiva, and omitted to return the god's salutation. The irascible god was enraged, his eyes flashed fire, and he raised his Trident weapon to destroy the sage. But the god's wife, Pārvatī, interceded for him. Lastly, Bhṛigu went to the heaven of Vishṇu, whom he found asleep. To try his forbearance, he gave the god a good kick on his breast, which awoke him. Instead of showing anger, Vishṇu asked Bhṛigu's pardon for not having greeted him on his first arrival. Then he declared he was highly honoured by the sage's blow. It had imprinted an indelible mark of good fortune on his breast. He trusted the sage's foot was not hurt, and began to rub it gently. 'This,' said Bhṛigu, 'is the mightiest god; he overpowers his enemies by the most potent of all weapons—gentleness and generosity.'

The three gods differ from, and are superior to, all other divine and human organisms, in that they are not subject to transmigrations. They are beings who have attained the highest condition possible, short of absorption into Brahmă.

And of these three, Vishṇu, the Maintainer and Preserver of all nature, is the most human, as he is also the most humane, in his character, attributes, and sympathies, and therefore devotion (bhakti) to him is, of all forms of Hindu religion, the most popular. He has four arms, symbolical of the power he exerts in the deliverance of his worshippers. Portions of his divine nature have descended into earthly incarnations to deliver the earth in times of danger and emergency. They are still continually descending in good men and living teachers (see p. 103).

Whether, in fact, Vishṇu be connected with light, with heat, with air, or with water, it is evident that his function is that of a divine Pervader, infusing his essence for special purposes into created things, animate and inanimate; for example, into stones, such as the black Śālagrāma; into rivers, such as the Ganges; into trees and plants, such as the Tulasī; into animals, such as a fish, a tortoise, a boar; and lastly, into men (see pp. 103–116).

And here be it noted that the idea of incarnation, like every other idea in religion, morality, and science, when manipulated by the Brāhmans, was by them subtilized and exaggerated. Hence the incarnations of Vishṇu are really descents (avatāra) on earth of portions of the essence of a divine person already possessing a material form (see pp. 63, 103). These descents were undertaken, reasonably enough, for preserving the world when in pressing danger from the malice of evil demons; and they are of four kinds and degrees.

First, the full descent, as in Kṛishṇa, one of the heroes of the Epic poem called Mahā-bhārata.

Secondly (though chronologically anterior), the half-essence descent, consisting of half the god's nature, as in Rāma, hero of the other Epic called Rāmāyaṇa.

Thirdly, the quarter-essence descent, as in Rāma's brother Bharata; fourthly, the eighth-part descent, as in Rāma's two other brothers, Lakshmaṇa and Śatrughna. Other special descents are described at pp. 107–115.

Distinct from these is the constant infusion of portions of the divine essence into ordinary men, animals, and inanimate objects. All men whose lives are remarkable for any peculiar circumstances are held by the Hindūs to be partial incarnations of the divine nature, and worshipped accordingly.

The other two members of the Indian triad, Brahmā and Śiva, have no human incarnations exactly comparable with those of Vishṇu, though Brahmā is, as it were, humanized in his representatives the priests, called Brāhmans.

It is true that certain incarnations of both Brahmā and

Śiva are sometimes mentioned (as, for example, that of Śiva called Vīrabhadra, p. 79), and there are local manifestations of these deities and local descents of Śiva in human form. Moreover, Brahmā and Śiva resemble Vishṇu in having wives. Brahmā's wife is Sarasvatī[1], Vishṇu's is Lakshmī, Śiva's is Pārvatī, and it may be noted that Śiva has two sons, Gaṇeśa, lord of the demon hosts, and Subrahmaṇya (also called Skanda and Kārttikeya), general of the celestial armies, whereas Vishṇu has no sons except in his human incarnations[2].

But it would be a great mistake to suppose that many deities and divine manifestations are generally worshipped. The gods of the Hindū Pantheon to whom temples are reared and prayers offered are not numerous. Forms of Vishṇu, Śiva, and their consorts, with the two sons of Śiva (Gaṇeśa and Subrahmaṇya, p. 211), and Hanumān (p. 220) are the chief temple-deities of India. But there are an infinite number of divine and semi-divine beings, good and evil demons, every one of which is held in veneration or dread, and every one of which, from the highest to the lowest, is, like all the others, subject to the universal law of re-absorption into the one divine universal Essence (Brahmă). Indeed, at the end of vast periods, called days of Brahmā, each lasting for 4,320,000,000 human years, the whole universe is so re-absorbed, and after remaining dormant for equally long periods, is again evolved.

Where, then, lies the motive for self-knowledge and self-discipline, if every man is really God? It is that the One Spirit, as if for diversion, ignores itself, submits to the influence of an illusory creative force, and permits the unity of its nature to be partitioned into an infinite number of individual

---

[1] Dubois (p. 371) relates a legend which makes Brahmā guilty of incest in that he was both the father and husband of Sarasvatī.

[2] Nor were Vishṇu's incarnations prolific, unless we reckon the 108,000 mythical sons of Kṛishṇa (see pp. 113, 114). The great Rāma had twin sons, Kuśa and Lava, born when Sītā had been banished to the hermitage.

personal spirits, which, while they continue in ignorance, are liable to commit error. And no such spirit can recover identity with the Supreme Spirit except by purificatory rites and by raising itself, through the exercise of self-knowledge and self-discipline in many births, to a state of cessation from action (vairāgya). In fact, a condition of entire mental vacuity (ćitta-vṛitti-nirodha) or trance (samādhi) is of all states the most desirable as leading to complete identification with the one universal Spirit. Not that a man need aim at immediate union with that Spirit.

He may simply aspire to re-absorption into the one absolute Spirit; or may simply devote himself to one of the personal gods, Brahmā, Vishṇu, or Śiva, so as to become, by union with them, only one degree removed from re-absorption, and incapable of further transmigrations (p. 41, ll. 11–20). Or he may simply aim at admission to their heavens (p. 70), or to the temporary heaven Svarga (presided over by Indra), the only paradise of orthodox Brāhmanism; or at escaping one of the purgatorial hells (pp. 232, 293).

We may note that Svarga, as an abode of light, is mentioned once in the Ṛig-veda (X, 95, 18); oftener in the Atharva-veda and Brāhmaṇas.

And here lies the motive for religious worship addressed to personal gods and visible forms. For the one universal Spirit is manifested in such forms. Yet it is a cardinal feature of the Brāhmanical system, that the one universal Spirit can never itself be directly worshipped, except by turning the thoughts inwards. No shrine or temple to Brahmă is to be found throughout all India. The one self-existent Brahmă can only become an object of meditation and knowledge. The Spirit is to be known by the spirit; for he is enshrined in every man's heart; and this internal meditation is regarded as the highest religious act. In short, Brahmă is properly only an object of internal knowledge (jñeyam), not an object of external worship (upāsyam).

And here mark the vast difference between the Hindū idea of a triad and the Christian Trinity. Brahmā, Vishṇu, and Śiva are not self-existent. They have only secondary existences, though the One Spirit may be worshipped through these three manifestations, or any one of the three. It is even possible for the members of this triad to worship the One Spirit through the worship of each other, each being in turn regarded as inferior (see p. 45).

Again, it is to be noted that homage may be paid to the one Spirit by and through the worship of the inferior gods, goddesses, departed ancestors, living Brāhmans, heroes, animals, and plants. Even stocks, stones, and images may represent the divine presence, and so become media through which the One Spirit may become an object of adoration. Nay, the very demons may receive worship both from gods and men, if by mortification and meditation they attain nearness to re-absorption into the great Spirit of the Universe.

I once asked a Brāhman, residing at Thānā (Tanna) near Bombay, to give me some explanation of the fact that even Indians of cultivated intellect who assert the unity of God, appear to us Europeans to be worshippers of many gods. His answer was to the following effect:—

'All orthodox Hindūs believe in one universal Spirit, who becomes Supreme Lord over all (Parameśvara). At the same time they believe that this one God has taken various forms, all of which may be worshipped; just as gold is one everywhere, though it may take different forms and names in different places and countries. Every man chooses his favourite god or divine object to which he pays especial homage. Thus Agnihotṛi-Brāhmans regard fire as their favourite form of the deity. They call him Agni-nārāyaṇa. Vedic Brāhmans make a god of the Veda, calling it Veda-nārāyaṇa. Different places have also their favourite presiding deities. Benares is specially watched over by a form of Śiva (called Viśveśvara); Paṇḍharpur, by a form of Kṛishṇa (called Viṭhobā). Here in

Thānā we have temples of Vishṇu, Rāma, Kṛishṇa, Viṭhṭhal, Hanumān, Śiva, Gaṇeśa, and Devī. The oldest and most sacred of all is one of Śiva, in the character of Kaupīneśvara. We may propitiate every one of them with ceremonies and sacrifices, but the Supreme Being present in these gods is the real object of all our offerings and religious services. At the end of each we say: "By this act may the Supreme Lord be gratified!" Hence, though to you we appear Polytheists, we are really Monotheists. Nor are we Pantheists in your sense of the term. Only our deepest thinkers look beyond the personal God to the impersonal Spirit which underlies everything. We educated Brāhmans are practically Theists.'

We might add that the Ṛig-veda asserts that the gods are one Being under different names (I. 164. 46; VIII. 58. 2).

Nomistic Brāhmanism.

The fourth phase of Brāhmanism may be called the Nomistic or Preceptive phase, because it represents that period in Indian religious history when the Brāhmans composed codes of law (smṛiti-śāstra, dharma-śāstra) and laid down precise precepts for the constitution of the Hindū social fabric, for the due co-ordination of its different orders and castes, for the regulation of every-day domestic life and for the enforcement of moral conduct.

Indeed the laxity and liberty allowed by Brāhmanism in regard to all forms of religious belief and philosophical thought, is curiously contrasted with the strictness and rigidity of its rules and ordinances in regard to every act of a man's domestic life, according to his social status or caste.

These rules are contained in three principal codes—(1) the code of Manu; (2) that of Yājñavalkya; (3) that of Parāśara. The first is held to be the most sacred of the three. It was originally a local code, embodying rules and precepts—perhaps by different authors, some of whom may have lived in the fifth century B.C., others in the second century B.C., and others even later. It was at first current among a particular tribe of Brāhmans called Mānavas, who probably occupied part of the North-western region between the rivers Sarasvatī and Dṛishadvatī, but afterwards became generally adopted. The name of the real author of this great work (which as a mere literary production is one of the most remarkable to be found anywhere) is concealed under the title Manu[1]. The code of Yājñavalkya is founded on that of Manu, but introduces many additional rules, some of which are probably as late as the first or second century of our era. It is always associated with its commentary, the Mitāksharā. The code of Parāśara is a still more modern work. It enacts special laws adapted to the fourth or most depraved age of the world (called Kăli). The three codes together constitute a kind of bible of Nomistic Brāhmanism, much in the same way as the Brāhmaṇas of the three Vedas are the exponent of Ritualistic Brāhmanism. The Brāhmaṇas are concerned with public Vedic ritual and sacrifice (śruti-karman), the law-books with domestic ceremonies (smṛiti-karman).

In short, the three chief codes are mirrors of Indian domestic customs, little affected as these have been by the lapse of more than two thousand years. They illustrate very strikingly the close intertwining of politics, morality, and social life with religion and religious ordinances. 'The root of all law,' says Manu, 'is the Veda and the traditions of those who know the Veda.' Accordingly we find that in Manu's code the rules of judicature and of caste are mixed up with the dogmas of religion and philosophy.

Then again, blended with these are high religious and moral precepts—many of them worthy of Christianity (see

---

[1] Manu is supposed to speak as far as I. 60, and after that another sage called Bhṛigu. The entire code is fully analysed and described in my 'Indian Wisdom,' pp. 211-294. The late Dr. A. Burnell's opinion was that the date of the work as we now possess it must be placed in the fourth century of our era. I cannot agree with his views.

Chap. XXI)—while the punishment assigned to every offence is carried beyond the grave into future states of existence, the doctrine of transmigration of souls through celestial and terrestrial bodies from gods to stones being implied throughout. Manu declares that a triple order of metempsychosis through higher, middle, and lower stages of existence results from the force of good, middling, or bad acts, words, and thoughts in every man's present life (Manu XII. 3–40).

The theory of caste and the superiority of the Brāhmans is the hinge on which the whole social fabric turns. The Brāhmans form the central body around which all other classes revolve like satellites. Not only are they invested with divine dignity, but they are bound together by the most stringent rules. Two other castes—viz. Kshatriyas and Vaiśyas—are with them called 'Twice-born,' through the Initiation rite (p. 360) which admitted all three to certain privileges.

The doctrine of Manu was that the deity created distinct classes of men, as he did animals and plants; and that the four chief classes—Brāhmans, soldiers (Kshatriyas), agriculturalists (Vaiśyas), and servants (Śūdras)—were born and must remain as distinct from each other as elephants, lions, oxen, and dogs, wheat, barley, rice, and beans (pp. 452–474).

A Brāhman was to pass through four stages of life; 1. Unmarried religious student (Brahma-ćārin); 2. Married householder (Gṛihastha); 3. Anchorite (Vānaprastha); 4. Abandoner of worldly concerns (Sannyāsin or Sannyāsī, pp. 55, 362). As a householder he could have four wives belonging to any of the three lower castes. Intermarriage could also take place between members of all the four classes, or, again, between the castes resulting from such intercourse. Hence arose an endless number of mixed castes, and castes within castes, each restricted to its own occupation and bound by its own rules.

Examples of moral precepts will be found at Chap. XXI.

CHAPTER III.

Hindūism a Development of Brāhmanism.

General Observations.

We now pass on to the third stage of Hindū religious thought, which has its bible in the Purāṇas. And we may here take note of a fact illustrated by the whole history of the world's religious thought, that a merely spiritual and impersonal religion is quite incapable of taking hold of the masses of mankind. Something more is needed for illiterate unthinking populations earnestly craving for concrete objects of faith and visible objects of devotion.

The chief point, then, which distinguishes Hindūism as a system of creeds from Brāhmanism is that it subordinates the worship of the purely spiritual Brahman (nom. Brahmă) with its first manifestation Brahmā (p. 47), to that of Śiva and Vishṇu, or of their wives, or of some form of these deities; while each sect exalts its own god to the place of the Supreme. Yet we must guard against the idea that theistic Hindūism has superseded pantheistic Brāhmanism; for in India forms of pantheism, theism, and polytheism are ever interwoven with each other. Brahmă has still the spiritual worship of the thoughtful, though he has neither temple nor image; while Brahmā has still two temples in India, and is represented by four-faced images, and is also worshipped under the symbol of Śiva (pp. 44, 79, 83, and Chapter XXII). He has also his own heaven called Brahma-loka (cf. pp. 70, 291).

Moreover it is certain that the worship of personal gods was a part of pantheistic Brāhmanism long before Śiva and Vishṇu became the exclusive favourites of particular sects. Perhaps the best exponent of the Brāhmanical system was the great teacher Śaṅkara (Śaṅkarāćārya), a native of Kerala (Malabar), who lived about the beginning of the eighth century of our era. He was a Sannyāsī (p. 362) and an unmarried Smārta Brāhman[1] under a vow of celibacy, and is often styled Paramahaṉsa-parivrājakāćārya. For it is one of the inconsistencies of the Hindū religion, that it enjoins the duty of marriage upon all, yet honours celibacy as a condition of great sanctity and a means of acquiring extraordinary religious merit and influence. Undoubtedly Śaṅkara was the very incarnation of strict Brāhmanism; and if it be possible to name any one real historical concrete personality as a typical representative of Brāhmanical doctrines, it is undeniable that we must point to Śaṅkara rather than to the legendary Vyāsa, even though the latter be the alleged author of the Vedānta-Sūtra.

Yet so utterly barren is India in both history and biography, that very little is known of the life of perhaps one of the greatest religious leaders she has ever produced.

It is nevertheless a fact that Śaṅkara founded the monastery (maṭha) of Śṛiṅgeri (Śṛiṅga-giri) in Mysore, as well as three others in Northern, Western, and Eastern India[2]; to the Headship over which his chief disciples were appointed by himself; the spiritual powers of the first Head being transmitted through a line of successors, regularly elected.

The most noted successor of Śaṅkara at the Śṛiṅgeri

---

[1] A Sannyāsī may have been once a married man. But there are Sannyāsīs (such as the late Dayānanda) who have become so without going through the previous stages of Gṛihastha and Vānaprastha. Equivalent expressions for Sannyāsin are Parivrājaka, Bhikshu, Daṇḍin, and Maskarin (Pāṇini VI. 1. 154); but the term Bhikshu is now applied in Western India to those clerical Brāhmans (as opposed to lay) who perform religious ceremonies and are not engaged in worldly pursuits.

[2] That in the North is at Badrināth in the Himālayas, that in the West at Dvārikā in Kāthiāwār, that in the East at Jagannāth-purī.

monastery was Sāyaṇa (Mādhava[1]), the well-known author of the Ṛig-veda commentary, who lived in the fourteenth century. Śaṅkara himself, though he managed to write a vast number of treatises on the Vedānta philosophy, led an erratic, restless, controversial life, and died early, probably at Kedārnāth in the Himālayas, at the age of thirty-two.

He is thought by some to have inculcated the preferential worship of the god Śiva[2], of whom some declare him to have been an incarnation. Others maintain that he himself had a preference for Vishṇu, the real fact being that he looked on both these gods as equally manifestations of the one Universal Spirit. For, in truth, all orthodox Brāhmans are in a general way both Śaivas and Vaishṇavas, and any Brāhman may have a preference for the worship of either Śiva or Vishṇu without any necessary exclusive devotion to either, and without identifying either—to the exclusion of the other—with the one Spirit of the Universe, as many Paurāṇika sectarians do. It is well known, in fact, that most Smārta Brāhmans in the present day, who are followers of Śaṅkarāćārya, have a leaning towards the worship of the one personal deity Śiva[3].

On the other hand, very few even of the most ignorant and bigoted Hindūs who are exclusive worshippers of the personal deities Śiva, Vishṇu, or their consorts, and whose highest spiritual aim is to be a dweller in the heaven of one of those

---

[1] The identity of Sāyaṇa and Mādhava is disputed; the preponderance of evidence seems now to be against the late Dr. A. Burnell's view of their identity as expressed in his Vaṉśa-brāhmaṇa.

[2] His sanctity was in such repute that he was held to have worked several miracles, amongst others, transferring his own soul for a time into the dead body of a king Amaru, that he might become the husband of the king's widow for a brief period, and so learn by experience how to argue on amatory subjects with the wife of a Brāhman named Maṇḍana, who was the only person he had never conquered in argument. This is described in a poem called Amaru-śataka, to which a mystical interpretation is given.

[3] Two Smārta Brāhmans accompanied me round the temple of Śiva at Tinnevelly. They both had three horizontal lines (tri-puṇḍra) made with Vibhūti on their foreheads, which proved their preference for Śiva.

gods, are uninfluenced by an undercurrent of pantheistic ideas. Nor would it be easy to find any thoughtful Hindū who, if closely questioned, would repudiate as untenable the doctrine of an omnipresent, impersonal, bodiless and passionless (nirguṇa) spiritual Essence, of which every being in the Universe is a portion. In short, the more closely the theistic phase of Hindūism is examined, the more plainly will it be found to rest on a substratum of pantheistic Brāhmanism. The one system is to a great extent a development of the other, and to draw a line of separation between the two is impossible. Metempsychosis is equally the dread of both.

Nevertheless Hindūism is by no means a simple form of theism, or even polytheism. It presents for our investigation a complex congeries of creeds and doctrines which in its gradual accumulation may be compared to the gathering together of the mighty volume of the Ganges, swollen by a continual influx of tributary rivers and rivulets, spreading itself over an ever-increasing area of country, and finally resolving itself into an intricate Delta of tortuous streams and jungly marshes.

Nor is it difficult to account for this complexity. The Hindū religion is a reflection of the composite character of the Hindūs, who are not one people but many. It is based on the idea of universal receptivity. It has ever aimed at accommodating itself to circumstances, and has carried on the process of adaptation through more than three thousand years. It has first borne with and then, so to speak, swallowed, digested, and assimilated something from all creeds. Or, like a vast hospitable mansion, it has opened its doors to all comers; it has not refused a welcome to applicants of every grade from the highest to the lowest, if only willing to adopt caste-rules; insomuch that many regard Hindūism as a system of social rules rather than of religious creeds.

In this manner it has held out the right hand of brotherhood to the Fetish-worshipping aborigines of India; it has stooped to the demonolatry of various savage tribes; it has not scrupled to encourage the adoration of the fish, the boar[1], the serpent, trees, plants, stones, and devils; it has permitted a descent to the most degrading cults of the Drāviḍian races; while at the same time it has ventured to rise from the most grovelling practices to the loftiest heights of philosophical speculation; it has not hesitated to drink in thoughts from the very fountain of Truth, and owes not a little to Christianity itself. Strangest of all, it has dissipated the formidable organization which for a long period confronted Brāhmanism, and introduced doctrines subversive of Sacerdotalism. It has artfully appropriated Buddhism, and gradually superseded that competing system by drawing its adherents within the pale of its own communion. Without doubt the most remarkable fact in the history of the interaction between Brāhmanism and the mighty movement initiated by one of the greatest of this earth's teachers, was the resolution of Buddhism into Ṡaivism and Vaishṇavism. To say that these two systems in their present form preceded Buddhism is inaccurate. Probably they co-existed with it in some form or other. Undeniably they became amplified and modified by its absorption.

This interchangeableness between Buddhism, Ṡaivism, and Vaishṇavism will be more fully explained hereafter. It will be sufficient at present to note that Gautama Buddha had two distinct characters. In his first and earliest character he was the typical monk (Ṡramaṇa[2]), the great teacher of the power to be gained by meditation and by conquest of the passions. In his second, he was the great friend of the common people who advocated universal brotherhood, universal equality, and universal compassion for all forms of animal

---

[1] A fish and a boar form two of Vishṇu's incarnations. The former is also the emblem of the Pāṇḍya kingdom in the South, and Mīnāćī, the goddess worshipped in the great temple of Madurā, is said to mean fish-ruler, though the Brāhmans have converted it into 'fish-eyed' (Mīnâkshī).

[2] See my work on 'Buddhism,' p. 75 (John Murray, Albemarle Street).

life. In both these characters the personal god Śiva and the incarnated Vishṇu were his counterparts, and ultimately superseded him[1]. Śiva was the Buddha in his monastic character. Vishṇu was the Buddha in his character of a beneficent and unselfish lover and friend of the human race.

And as Śaivism and Vaishṇavism superseded Buddhism, so they became the chief constituents of modern Hindūism. All the shades and subdivisions of Hindū sectarianism may be included under one or other of these two heads.

Nevertheless it is customary to speak of Hindūism as divided into five principal sects: 1. Worshippers of Śiva (Śaivas). 2. Worshippers of Vishṇu (Vaishṇavas). 3. Worshippers of the female personifications of energy, regarded as the wives of the deities (Śāktas, p. 180). 4. Worshippers of Gaṇeśa or Gaṇa-pati—the god of luck and good fortune (Gāṇapatyas, p. 215). 5. Sun-worshippers (Sauras, p. 341). Besides these five, a sixth called Pāśupata (or, by Ānanda-giri, Kāpālika), chiefly found in the South of India, is occasionally added, though this is nothing but a subdivision of the Śaivas. All these six sects are said by South-Indian Pandits to have been founded by Śaṅkarāćārya, who is therefore often called Shaṇ-mata-sthāpaka, 'the establisher of six forms of doctrines.' In reality that great teacher was, as we have seen, utterly opposed to all sectarian ideas. In the Śaṅkara-vijaya of Ānanda-giri (a work written by one of his disciples in the ninth or tenth century) he is described as having traversed India in every direction for the purpose of combating and refuting an immense number of sectarian systems which had taken root in the country. There were at that time, besides the worshippers of Śiva and Vishṇu, votaries of Brahmā, of the Sun, Moon, Kubera, Yama, Varuṇa, Śesha, and others innumerable. Many of these were extirpated through Śaṅkara's instru-

[1] There are clear traces that the great Vaishṇava temple of Jagan-nāth in Orissa was originally dedicated to some Buddhist tooth-relic.

mentality, and many have since disappeared; but, curiously enough, it is alleged that out of pity to the present degenerate age (Kali-yuga), when men are incapable of apprehending the pure unity of the Godhead, Śaṅkara allowed six sects to remain. It was only by degrees that the sectarian character of all but the first two disappeared.

What then is the present idea implied by Hindū sectarianism? It is clear from what has been already stated that every Hindū creed ought to be regarded as unorthodox which exalts favourite personal deities to the position of the one eternal, self-existing Spirit (Ātman or Brahmă), in contravention of the dogma that even the highest divine personalities are finite beings destined ultimately to be absorbed into that one infinite Spirit.

Of course it must be understood that when Śaivism and Vaishṇavism deny this dogma they offend against orthodoxy. But Śaivism and Vaishṇavism constitute, so to speak, the very warp and woof of the later Hindū religion, and it is possible to be a worshipper of Śiva or Vishṇu (as manifestations of Brahmă) without being a sectarian. Hence it seems better to apply the term 'sect' to separate religious communities within the pale of these two chief systems, organized and consolidated by particular teachers with the object of inculcating entire devotion towards, and exclusive dependence on either Śiva or Vishṇu, and securing through the instrumentality of one or other of these gods the welfare and salvation of every individual among his worshippers.

At the same time, it must be carefully noted that Hindū sectarianism is something more than the mere exclusive worship of a personal god. It implies more or less direct opposition to the orthodox philosophy of Brāhmanism, in regard to the identity of man's spirit with God's spirit. Man's spirit is held to have a separate personality, but the doctrine of metempsychosis or transmigration is perhaps insisted on with even greater intensity in Śaivism and Vaishṇavism than in pure Brāhmanism. Nevertheless it must, as we have already seen, be borne in mind that vague pantheistic ideas may always be found lurking at the root of every variety of Hindū sectarian doctrine. Such ideas are naturally inwoven into the very texture of every Hindū mind.

But Hindūism bristles with contradictions, inconsistencies, and surprises; and it is remarkable that the generally prevalent Brāhmanical doctrine of the identification of the living personal Spirit of man with the one universal Spirit of the universe is the peculiar dogma which various sects of both Śaivas and Vaishṇavas—especially the latter—theoretically repudiate, dilute, or qualify. For indeed the spirit of man if it strives to give expression to its feelings of complete and exclusive devotion to a personal deity as to a Creator and Saviour, cannot at the same moment assent to doctrines which destroy its own separate personality.

To mark this complete and exclusive devotion more clearly, and to bind each sect together by some common bond of union, a short form of words called a Mantra (e.g. *Om Rāmāya namaḥ*, reverence to Rāma, see p. 117), expressive of exclusive and absolute trust in the particular god worshipped as representing the Supreme Ruler of the world, is taught by each community and its repetition every day is made a necessary condition of salvation through him.

Moreover, the privilege of imparting this secret (rahasya) Mantra belongs to a regularly constituted order of men (Guru). The communication of it (usually in a whisper) is called initiation (dīkshā), and acquaintance with it is held to be essential to admission within the pale of the society. When any such system has been fully organized it is called a Sampradāya—a word meaning a particular body of traditionary doctrines handed down through a succession of teachers[1].

---

[1] It may also be designated by such terms as Darśana or Mata—that is, particular views or opinions on religion or philosophy. The term

As a matter of fact the Sampradāyas or separate religious denominations of the present day are nearly all mere subdivisions of Vaishṇavism. Not that Śiva has been dethroned by Vishṇu, or has lost any of his importance as one of the two chief deities of modern Hindūism. What is meant is that, although all Hindūs pay homage to Śiva, to his Consort or Śakti, and to his two sons Gaṇeśa and Skanda, few attach themselves to these deities as to personal benefactors—and although many repeat their Mantras, few pray to them *exclusively* as to their personal creators and saviours.

Certainly no one, so far as I have been able to ascertain, turns to these gods, or invokes their intervention and assistance in the hour of death[1] (see p. 297). Similarly all Hindūs adore the Sun in their daily prayers (pp. 342, 406), but very few in the present day ever worship him exclusively or in what may be called a spirit of sectarianism. Several sects of Sun-worshippers are known to have once existed and to have had many adherents, but they have generally died out.

In reality the principle of faith and devotion as displayed towards personal gods could scarcely have taken deep root in India, except in connexion with the worship of a god who descended upon earth as the child of earthly parents for the promotion of man's welfare, and whose nature in his incarnations became quite as human as it was divine.

And here mark that the doctrine of incarnation among the Hindūs is in many important respects different from the Christian idea. The Sanskṛit language, which is the only language of the Hindū religion and the only source of theological terms, has no exact equivalent for incarnation[2].

Darśana, however, is more usually restricted to the six regular philosophical systems.

[1] The names invoked at death are generally those of Rāma and Nārāyaṇa (p. 297). The late Dr. Burnell told me that he once witnessed the execution of thirteen criminals in India who were all Śaivas, and yet all called on the name of Rāma before being hanged.

[2] Unless it be compounds formed with *deha*, *mūrti*, and *sākshāt*.

The common word is Avatāra, which means 'descent.' Furthermore, it must be noted that intervening between the one Self-existent Being and these Avatāras must be placed the forms of personal deities such as Brahmā, Vishṇu, and Śiva—each of whom possesses a body composed, like human bodies, of gross, though divine and ethereal, particles[1]. Strictly, therefore, the so-called incarnations, represented by heroes like Rāma, ought to be regarded as incarnations of incarnations; for they are the descent of portions of the essence of personal divinities, who, already possessing bodies composed of gross, though divine particles, condescend by being born of earthly parents to assume bodies composed of human gross particles. Such descents are attributed, not only to the personal gods Vishṇu, Śiva, and Brahmā, but even to other gods such as Indra, Vāyu, Śesha; Arjuna and the heroes of the Mahā-bhārata being also regarded as incarnated descents of various deities. Yet the only universally acceptable and generally worshipped incarnated descents are those of Vishṇu, as Rāma son of Daśaratha, and as Kṛishṇa son of Vasudeva. When once the feeling of affection for Rāma and Kṛishṇa had rooted itself in the religious sense of the people, it rapidly gathered strength and dominated over every other feeling.

It was thus that the way of devotion (bhakti-mārga) as propounded in the Purāṇas and Tantras[2] superseded the other two ways of salvation—knowledge and works (jñāna-mārga and karma-mārga); though it must be borne in mind that bhakti, 'devotion,' is really a kind of 'meritorious work,' and not equivalent to 'faith' in the Christian sense.

It even triumphed over caste; for an enthusiastic love of

---

[1] See the account of the structure of the bodies of the gods at p. 28.

[2] Doubtless a form of the doctrine of bhakti may be traced back to early times, but for its full development we must look to the Bhagavad-gītā, a comparatively modern episode of the Mahā-bhārata, to the Purāṇas and Tantras, and to a scientific formulation of the doctrine in the Bhakti-sūtra of Śāṇḍilya probably about the twelfth century.

Rāma or Kṛishṇa was theoretically a bond of union among human beings stronger than all social ties, and was incompatible with differences of rank or antagonisms of interest.

In fact the leaders of religious thought in India were all disciples in the school of the great Buddha, to the extent, at least, of imitating his wisdom by advocating social union and fraternity. They saw that their popularity as reformers depended on their attracting adherents from all ranks, high and low. Hence, every great religious leader proclaimed the brotherhood and equality of all who enrolled themselves under his leadership. Buddha was the son of a petty Rājā or landowner, but addressed himself to all ranks. In the same way Vishṇu, in his descent as Kṛishṇa, though of the kingly caste, was the favourite of the common people. But just as Buddhism ultimately fell back into Brāhmanism, so has every movement in the direction of liberty, equality, and fraternity ended by a return, more or less complete, to the original condition of subjection to Brāhmanical authority, ceremonial observances, and caste.

Practically, therefore, we must regard Vaishṇavism as the principal home of Hindū religious sectarianism. All the chief modern sects have resulted more from differences of opinion between various schools of Vaishṇavas, than from antagonism between Śaivism and Vaishṇavism. Nor are Śaivism and Vaishṇavism in their essence antagonistic systems. They represent different lines of religious thought; such lines expressing a contrast rather than an opposition. So far indeed from any necessary opposition between the systems, they are a necessary complement of each other. For the worship of the composite deity Rudra-Śiva is nothing but the expression of the awe felt by human beings in the presence of the two mutually complementary forces of disintegration and reintegration; while the worship of the personal god Vishṇu in his descents upon earth in human form is nothing but the expression of the very natural interest felt by man in his own preservation and in the working of the physical forces which resist dissolution.

Certainly in the present day Śaivas and Vaishṇavas are tolerant of each other's creeds, both appealing to the Purāṇas as their special bible, and each acknowledging the gods of the other as proper objects of worship. This is remarkably illustrated by the fact that in some parts of the country a god called Hari-Hara (Vishṇu-Śiva) is worshipped, who represents the union of the two divine personalities in one. There is a long hymn in praise of this twofold deity in the Hari-vanśa (181st chapter), and images of him may be seen here and there in Southern India. For example, in the great temple at Madurā a fine carving was pointed out to me which proved to be a representation of Śaṅkara-Nārāyaṇa (= Hari-Hara)[1]. One side of the figure represents half the body of Vishṇu with a hand holding a Śaṅkha, while the other represents that of Śiva surmounted by half a head-dress twisted into a matted coil with the lunar crescent conspicuous on it. Then again, wherever in any city a large temple has been erected to Śiva, a similar temple dedicated to Vishṇu is sure to be conspicuous near at hand. Indeed the shrines of the two gods are not unfrequently found in close juxtaposition within the same sacred enclosure. For instance, on the hill of Pārvatī (wife of Śiva) near Poona, and in the enclosure of her temple, I saw a shrine of Vishṇu, another of his vehicle Garuḍa, and images of nearly every deity of the Hindū Pantheon[2].

Nor can any student of the Mahā-bhārata and Purāṇas doubt the interchangeableness of the functions of Śiva and Vishṇu, or fail to perceive that each divine personality has a tendency to blend or merge in the other. In the Liṅga-

[1] In the South of India a legend is current which makes Vishṇu assume the form of a fascinating woman (mohinī) and so connect himself with Śiva. By Śāktas Vishṇu is often held to be female.

[2] So also in the precincts of the temple of Hanumān at Kaira I saw a shrine of Śiva and nearly every other god ordinarily worshipped.

purāṇa (I. 18 ff.) both Brahmā and Vishṇu are said to spring from Śiva. On the other hand, in the Mahā-bhārata (Vana-parvan 499 ff. and Anuśāsana-p. 6806 ff.) Brahmā is described as springing from the navel of Vishṇu when he was lying in placid repose on the serpent of infinity, and enjoying the most perfect serenity of mind [1]; whilst Śiva or Rudra is said to have been produced from Brahmā's (or according to some Vishṇu's) forehead when he happened one day to be roused to anger.

Again, Vishṇu, speaking of himself (Śānti-parvan 13140, etc.), says: 'I am the soul of all the worlds. It was myself whom I formerly worshipped as Rudra. If I were not to worship the boon-bestowing Śiva, no one would worship myself. He who knows him knows me; he who loves him loves me (Yas taṃ vetti sa māṃ vetti yo 'nu taṃ sa hi mām anu).' But the true explanation of the homage paid by each member of the Triad to the other (cf. p. 106) is to be sought for in the pantheistic ideas which underlie Hindūism.

Still it must be admitted that Śaivism and Vaishṇavism are quite distinct systems, and that each sect is inclined to lay an exaggerated stress on its own particular doctrines.

In ancient times these differences not unfrequently led to rancorous antagonism, and sometimes even to violent conflicts. This was especially the case in the South, where Śaivism generally triumphed over and displaced Vaishṇavism [2]. Even in the present day, when universal toleration is the rule, Śaivas and Vaishṇavas like to maintain their distinct characteristics, which they exhibit conspicuously to the eye by a distinctive mark on their foreheads (called tilaka, puṇḍra, and, in the South of India, nāma or gandha).

---

[1] One reason I often had given to me in India for the present merging of Brahmā in Vishṇu was that Brahmā sprang from the body of Vishṇu.

[2] I noticed many traces of the conflict in the South; for example, Vaishṇava sculptures have been left on the Gopuras in the Śaiva temple of Tanjore.

That of the Śaivas consists of three horizontal strokes (tri-puṇḍra) made with the white ashes of burnt substances (vibhūti), to represent, perhaps, the disintegrating forces belonging to their god Śiva[1], and that of the Vaishṇavas is an upright mark (ūrdhva-puṇḍra) made with bright red, yellow, and white colouring substances (the white called Gopī-ćandana[2]), to represent the foot-print of their human and humane god Vishṇu.

Again, it is important to note that both Śaivas and Vaishṇavas differ in the mode of branding their breasts, arms, and other parts of their bodies with other distinctive marks of their sect. Such marks are burnt in with red-hot stamps, sometimes made of gold. In the case of Śaivas they represent the weapons and symbols of Śiva, such as the trident and the liṅga; while the favourite brands of Vishṇu are the discus, the club, and the conch-shell. This practice was severely denounced by Śaṅkara[3], but apparently with little effect.

In regard to rosaries, the rosary (japa-mālā) used by Śaivas is a string of 32 rough berries (or that number doubled) of the Rudrāksha tree (Elæocarpus Ganitrus), while that of the Vaishṇavas is made of the wood of the sacred Tulasī (Tulsī) shrub, and generally consists of 108 beads (see pp. 117, 135 with notes). Such rosaries may be worn as necklaces, though their chief use is to be employed as an aid in the recitation of the names of the deity or of prayers. Occasional varieties in the material and form of the rosaries may be noticed[4]; for example, Śaiva ascetics sometimes carry rosaries formed of the teeth of dead bodies (danta-mālā), or sling serpents round

---

[1] The ashes probably denote that the body must ultimately be reduced to ashes.

[2] This is said to be the soil of a pool near Dvārikā in which the Gopīs drowned themselves on learning of the death of Kṛishṇa.

[3] The Śaṅkara-vijaya shows how Śaṅkara offered the most strenuous opposition to this practice of branding, stigmatizing it as a heretical and ridiculous practice.

[4] See especially my book 'Modern India and the Indians,' p. 108.

their necks for necklaces. On the other hand, Vaishṇava rosaries are occasionally but rarely made of lotus-seeds (kamalāksha).

But the most important difference to be noted between Śaivas and Vaishṇavas is in the use they make of idols, images, and symbols. Śiva, we must remember, is a less human and far more mystical deity than the incarnated Vishṇu. The character in which he is most frequently worshipped is that of an omnipotent God, taking the place of Brahmā the Creator, and granting new life to all created things, but only through death and disintegration. Hence he is not represented by the image of a man, but by a mystic symbol[1]—perhaps the best symbol of delegated creative power—which is not dressed or fed or put to sleep like Vishṇu's idols, but is supposed to be in a condition of perpetual heat and excitement, and requires to be cooled and appeased by constant sprinklings (abhisheka) of cold Ganges water and cooling Bilva leaves applied throughout the day by those who worship him[2] (see pp. 90, 439). Moreover food is not generally offered to Śiva, or, if occasionally so offered, is not afterwards eaten by his votaries (except in certain special localities), for the obvious reason that inauspicious (amaṅgala) ideas are supposed to be connected with his office of causing death[3].

On the other hand, since Vishṇu is god in his more

---

[1] That is, by the liṅga or image of the distinctive organ of the male sex (the phallus), never in the mind of a Śaiva connected with indecent ideas nor with sexual love, though impure practices have certainly been introduced in connexion with the worship of Śiva's wife. In fact, sexual passion is chiefly associated with the worship of Vishṇu, as Kṛishṇa. It is curious that Vaishṇavas dislike the Śaiva liṅga and yet allow the most impure and indecent representations on the walls of their temples.

[2] Another mode of worship is by pradakshiṇā or circumambulation, keeping the right side towards the object worshipped. In many Liṅga shrines a space is left for this kind of homage.

[3] The precept is, 'Leaves, flowers, fruit, and water must not be taken after being offered to Śiva.' But at the great temple of Bhuvaneśvara and a few other places an exception is made.

human and humane aspect, sympathizing with men's trials and condescending to be born of human parents, he is usually represented by the complete image of a well-formed human being—generally that of Kṛishṇa or Rāma—which is every day roused from a supposed nocturnal slumber, dressed, decorated with gold and jewels, bathed, fed with offerings of cooked and uncooked grain, sweetmeats and fruits, undressed and put to sleep again like an ordinary man, while the remains of the food offered (prasāda) are eagerly consumed by the priests and attendants[1] (see p. 145).

And here I may point out that a great distinction is to be made in regard to the comparative sanctity of different kinds of symbols and images. Some are called Svayam-bhū, that is, existing spontaneously, and are of their own nature pervaded by the essence of the deity. These are either not carved at all, or very slightly moulded into shape. They are merely rough stones or rocks supposed to have descended direct from heaven or to have appeared miraculously on the soil. They are the most sacred of all objects of adoration, and when discovered, temples are built over them. The most usual idols of this kind are stones supposed to represent the Liṅga of Śiva, and when shrines are built round them, a Yoni (to represent the female organ) is usually added.

Not less sacred than these rough stones are certain small pebbles found in rivers and polished by the action of the water[2]. Of these the pebbles representing the Liṅga of Śiva, called Bāṇa-liṅga or Vāṇa-liṅga, and apparently of white quartz, are found in the bed of the Narbadā river. The black pebbles representing Vishṇu or Kṛishṇa, called Śāla-grāma (popularly śāl-grām), and generally containing am-

---

[1] This will account for the fact that few villages can afford to keep a temple dedicated to Kṛishṇa. The vestments, ornaments, decorations, and paraphernalia needed are too expensive; whereas all the requisites for the worship of Śiva are a stone liṅga, bilva leaves, and water.

[2] Some of them appear to be artificially rounded and polished.

monites imbedded in the stone, are chiefly found in the river Gaṇḍakī. Both kinds of pebble are employed in the domestic worship of Śiva and Vishṇu known as Pañćāyatana-pūjā (to be described pp. 410–416), and performed by householders in their own houses. Both are held to be of their own nature pervaded by the special presence of the deity and need no consecration. Offerings made to these pebbles—such for instance as Bilva leaves laid on the white stone of Śiva—are believed to confer extraordinary merit.

A second form of idol is wholly artificial. This is carved by masons or sculptors and not held sacred until the Brāhmans have consecrated it by a long ceremony called Prāṇa-pratishṭhā, 'endowing with breath.' When such idols have been placed in shrines they can be looked at by an unbeliever, even though the consecration they have received is supposed to have filled them with the spirit (prāṇa) of the god they represent. Artificial idols and symbols of this kind are manufactured in large numbers in holy cities, not so much for general worship as for votive offerings to be set up with the customary form of dedication (pratishṭhā) in the galleries or vestibules of temples, or under sacred trees, or to be kept as objects of adoration in the private rooms of houses.

Pious persons reckon it a work of religious merit to cause such idols and symbols to be made and dedicated. I have seen thousands so dedicated, and others exposed for sale in the streets. Some Liṅgas are carved out of stone; some are made of glass. Serpents are occasionally carved round these symbols, as well as round the images of Śiva in human form.

An account of the ceremonies performed in worshipping idols will be given subsequently (see pp. 90–94; 144, 145).

Another difference between Śaivism and Vaishṇavism must be noted. Each system has its own heaven. That of Śiva is Kailāsa; that of Vishṇu is Vaikuṇṭha; that of Kṛishṇa is Go-loka (see pp. 118, 291). The first is supposed to be in the Himālaya mountains; while the two latter are believed (like

Svarga, p. 49) to be somewhere on the mythical Mount Meru[1]. To these heavens the faithful worshippers of Śiva, Vishṇu, and Kṛishṇa are respectively transported. There amid eternal snows and inaccessible crags they are thought to be safe from future transmigrations. There, too, they may attain to the highest pinnacle of beatification, not so much by absolute absorption (sāyujya) into the one supreme Spirit according to the Vedānta doctrine (see p. 41)—for such complete union would involve loss of personality—but rather by dwelling in the same abode with their god (sālokya), by nearness to him (sāmīpya), by assimilation to his likeness (sārūpya).

I may mention here that the cultus of the god Śiva in some of his forms, as well as that of some forms of Vishṇu, has been held by more than one authority to be traceable to the practices of pre-Āryan and non-Āryan tribes. But the explanations I have given tend to show that Śiva and Vishṇu are both Brāhmanical gods and have their origin in the Veda, though they have been often made to do duty for local deities outside the true circle of Brāhmanism.

Finally whatever differences exist between the sects of Hindūism, there are two characteristics common to all—viz. a pessimistic view of life and salvation by works.

Self-righteousness lies at the root of Hindūism. Let it be granted that this complex system reckons three ways of deliverance from the misery of life: (1) The way of sacrifices and ceremonial rites, or *karma-mārga*; (2) the way of devotion to personal deities, or *bhakti-mārga*; (3) the way of spiritual knowledge, or *jñāna-mārga*; yet each of these three systems, or all three together, are only followed for the merit (puṇya) to be gained through them, and Hindūism accounts no man righteous except through his own works, acts, and deservings.

---

[1] The temple of Śrī-raṅgam at Trichinopoly is supposed to be a counterpart of Vaikuṇṭha (see p. 448), and the excavated temple at Ellorā is a counterpart of Kailāsa (see p. 447).

It is true that expiatory rites, external purifications, lustral washings, and ceremonial observances performed incessantly by, or through, or with the aid of Brāhmans, or even without their aid, purifies from natal sin (see p. 354), and delivers from constantly contracted impurity and guilt and its consequences, yet, for all that, the dictum of Manu (XII. 3) holds good in Hindūism, and is believed in everywhere throughout India :

> Action of every kind, whether of mind
> Or speech or body, must bear fruit, entailing
> Fresh births through multifarious conditions,
> In highest, mean, and lowest transmigrations.

Doubtless Manu laid stress on the need of internal purity of heart, but this internal purity must be self-accomplished. Then as to the way of devotion to personal duties, sometimes called 'the way of faith,' this again depends on the exercise of a man's own will. Lastly, as to the way of knowledge, this, no doubt, is held to be the highest way, according to the following statement in the Mahā-bhārata (XII. 8810, etc.) :—'By works a creature is bound ; by knowledge he is liberated ; wherefore devotees gifted with perfect insight perform no works. Through works a creature is born after death with a body of (one or other of) sixteen descriptions ; by knowledge he becomes the Eternal, Imperceptible, Undecaying' (Muir's Texts, V. 327). But this knowledge is only obtainable through man's own intuition or through abstract meditation ; for, just as Hindūism knows nothing of purity of heart communicated by an infinitely Pure and Holy Being external to itself, so it knows nothing of any knowledge except that which is Self-evolved.

There is a fourth way which might be included under the first—namely, the way of Tapas, or self-imposed bodily mortification common to all forms of Hindūism, but especially connected with Śaivism (see pp. 83, 87), and with the Yoga philosophy (see my work on 'Buddhism,' p. 226).

We now pass on to a more detailed account of the divisions of Hindūism.

CHAPTER IV.

Śaivism or Worship of Śiva.

Śaivism[1] may be defined to be the setting aside of the triune equality of Brahmā, Śiva, and Vishṇu, and the merging of Brahmā and Vishṇu in the god Śiva. But it is also more than this. It is the exaltation of Śiva (whether as one person or as associated with a consort) to the position of a Supreme Being, exempt from subjection to the law of ultimate absorption into the Universal Spirit. It is his identification with Brahmă as well as with Brahmā; with the one impersonal Spirit as well as with the one personal God; with the Ātman and Māyā of the Vedānta philosophy; with the Purusha and Prakṛiti of the Sāṅkhya system; with the male and female generative energies operating in the Universe.

Yet it ought to be clearly understood that the identification of Śiva with the one impersonal Spirit of the Universe is rarely asserted categorically by Śaiva sectarians; for it must always be borne in mind that the very meaning of Śaivism is exclusive devotion to a *personal* god Śiva, who unlike the impersonal Spirit, possesses a body, and can think, feel, and act. In entering, therefore, on the subject of Śaivism we are passing from pantheistic to theistic ideas.

The Śaiva bible or supposed inspired authority for this elevation of the god Śiva to the highest position in the Hindū system must be sought for among the eighteen Purāṇas. These writings are more generally in favour of the supremacy

[1] Śaiva and Vaishṇava are the Sanskṛit adjective forms of Śiva and Vishṇu; hence may be formed the words 'Śaivism' and 'Vaishṇavism.'

of Vishṇu, but a certain number, such as the Liṅga, Śiva, Kūrma and Skanda Purāṇas, make Śiva supreme [1].

We have already pointed out that the idea of a Tri-mūrti or triple embodiment and triple personification of the phenomena and powers of Nature was adumbrated in the Veda and fully developed in the Mahā-bhārata.

In the Veda special homage is given to three gods who are the representative deities of the three worlds and of the elements they contain. (1) To the god of Fire (Agni), who is the god on the earth. (2) To the god of Rain associated with the gods of Storm (Indra-Rudra), who are the gods in the atmosphere. (3) To the Sun-god (Sūrya), who is the god in the heavens (see p. 9). In mythological Brāhmanism—of which the Mahā-bhārata is the chief exponent—these three Vedic gods pass into Brahmā the creator, Rudra-Śiva [2] the destroyer and recreator, and Vishṇu (p. 75) the preserver. But the act of the Creator was a single act. Once completed, it received scant recognition at the hands of the beings created. And, as a matter of fact, the worship of Brahmā fell into desuetude [3].

On the other hand, the acts of disintegration, reintegration, and maintenance of being were continuous acts of the deepest and most momentous interest to the whole human race. Hence it happened that the homage paid to the deities who presided over these operations increased in intensity and developed into a system of the grossest superstition. For, indeed, three remarkable phenomena could not fail to impress themselves on the most superficial observers of the processes of nature. First, that mysterious and awe-inspiring forces are ever at work for the disintegration of every material object in the universe; secondly, that vivifying forces are

---

[1] The colossal sculpture of the Tri-mūrti in the caves of Elephanta, excavated twelve or thirteen centuries ago, represents Brahmā in the centre, Vishṇu on the right, and Śiva on the left (see p. 45).

[2] I use this compound for convenience. There is really no such word.

[3] My visit to Brahmā's temple near Ājmere is described in Chap. XXII.

ever being exerted for the reintegration of material entities through the disintegration of other entities; thirdly, that every existing material entity is maintained in existence by the agency of sustaining forces which help it to resist the action of the forces of dissolution. In short, it was clear that the three processes of disintegration, reintegration, and maintenance of being are perpetually recurring in an eternal cycle —that each follows on the other and that each is necessary to the other.

Now, it might have been expected that the authors of Hindū mythology would have placed these three distinct processes under the control of three distinct deities. But so close was believed to be the connexion between the work of disintegration and that of reintegration that both were assigned to the presidency of one divine personification, who, in this two-fold character of Destroyer and Re-constructor, may most fitly be designated by the composite name Rudra-Śiva. For it is only as Rudra that he is the Lord of Death and the active agent in dissolution; and it is only as Śiva, 'the auspicious,' that he reconstructs after destruction.

And here at the outset it is important to note that, in his character of both Rudra and Śiva, this god enjoys a cultus which reaches much further back than that of Vishṇu the maintainer and preserver. Of the two deities Śiva is manifestly the more ancient. He was the first to receive special adoration; and although in the present day he has fewer *exclusive* adorers than the god Vishṇu, his worship is even now more generally extended (compare note 1, p. 78).

The name of Vishṇu occurs, it is true, in the Ṛig-veda, but only as a secondary designation of the Sun, that luminary being better known by other more important names—such as Sūrya, Savitṛi, Āditya, Mitra.

On the other hand, Rudra appears quite early in the Veda with a well-recognised and well-marked personality of his own. He is an important deity, whose anger is to be dreaded and whose favour is to be propitiated. Probably the first office or function connected with him was that of directing and controlling the rage of the howling storms [1]. As god of gale and tempest he is father of the destructive storm-winds, who are also called Rudras, and generally identified with the Maruts. And in this character Rudra is closely connected with the Vedic Rain-god (Indra), and with the still more highly esteemed Vedic deity Fire (Agni), which, as a destroying agent, rages and crackles like the roaring tempest. He is also nearly related to Time (Kāla), the all-consumer, and indeed afterwards identified with him [2]. But he has also a more agreeable aspect even in the Veda. He is not merely the awful and inauspicious god whose thousand shafts bring death or disease on men and cattle [3]. He is present in those health-giving winds which chase away noxious vapours. He is addressed as a healer, as a benefactor, as a benevolent and auspicious being; the epithet Śiva being applied to him in the Veda euphemistically as a title rather than as a name.

Again, in the later Vedic period his personality becomes still more intensified, and his name, attributes, and functions infinitely amplified, varied, and extended. For example, in the Vājasaneyi-saṃhitā of the Yajur-veda (XVI. 1, etc.) there is a well-known hymn or litany called the Śatarudriya, addressed to Rudra in his hundred aspects and surrounded by his countless hosts of attendants. In this hymn—a hymn which is of the greatest interest, because constantly used in the present day—he is described as possessing many contradictory, incongruous, grotesque, and wholly ungodlike attributes; for example, he is a killer and destroyer; he is terrible, fierce (ugra), inauspicious; he is a deliverer and saviour; he causes

---

[1] The root *rud* meaning 'to roar' or 'howl' as well as 'to weep.'

[2] In the Kailāsa cave at Ellorā I noticed that Śiva in his character of Kāla was represented as a skeleton.

[3] Death is always connected in the Hindū mind with something inauspicious (amaṅgala) and impure.

happiness, and prevents disease; he has a healing and auspicious body (śivā tanūḥ); he is yellow-haired, brown-coloured, copper-coloured, ruddy, tall, dwarfish; he has braided locks (kapardin), wears the sacred thread, and is clothed in a skin; he is blue-necked and thousand-eyed; he dwells in the mountains, and is the owner of troops (gaṇa-pati) of servants who traverse the earth obeying his orders; he is ruler and controller of a thousand Rudras who are described as fierce and ill-formed (virūpa); he has a hundred bows and a thousand quivers; he is the general of vast armies; he is lord of ghosts, goblins, and spirits; of beasts, horses, and dogs; of trees, shrubs, and plants; he causes the fall of leaves; he is lord of the Soma-juice; he is patron of thieves and robbers[1], and is himself a thief, robber, and deceiver; he presides over carpenters, chariot-makers, blacksmiths, architects, huntsmen; he is present in towns and houses, in rivers and lakes, in woods and roads, in clouds and rain, in sunshine and lightning, in wind and storm, in stones, dust, and earth.

If then this great deity was distinguished even in the Vedic period by so great a variety of attributes, and was held capable of so many functions, it was only to be expected that the plasticity and all-comprehensiveness of his godhead should have increased with the advance of time. It was only natural, too, that the desire to propitiate him should have become more generally diffused. His terrific and ungodlike character was, therefore, kept well in the background, and his epithet 'the blessed or auspicious one (Śiva),' who brought life out of death, who re-created after dissolution, passed into his principal name.

---

[1] In the drama called Mṛiććhakaṭikā some burglars invoke Skanda son of Śiva as their patron deity. At present nearly all the degrading characteristics of the god have been transferred to the form of his consort called Kālī. That goddess is to this day the patron of thieves, robbers, Thugs, murderers, and every kind of infamous rascal (see Chap. XXII).

Hence also Śiva became to his worshippers the great god (Mahā-deva) and lord of the universe (jagat-pitṛi, viśva-nātha), who, although he has numerous forms, is generally worshipped under one mystical shape—a plain upright stone, the sign or symbol (liṅga) of generative and creative power—scattered in millions of shrines over every part of India[1]. And hence, too, it came to pass that, in the end, this so-called great god was often identified with the one universal, all-pervading, self-existent Spirit of Brāhmanical philosophy[2].

Yet it is remarkable that with the increasing tendency to exalt the deity Śiva to the highest pinnacle in the Hindū system, the desire to intensify his more human character and to multiply those inferior attributes which deprive him of all title to be called a god at all, increased also. In the later Indian scriptures he has 1008 names (enumerated in Śiva-purāṇa LXIX, Anuśāsana-parvan XVII, see pp. 105–107 of this volume), besides local appellations and a corporeal existence almost as anthropomorphic as that of Vishṇu.

It is true that the god Śiva never passed through the processes of birth, childhood, manhood, or any of the stages of a recognized human existence in the way that Rāma and Kṛishṇa did[3], yet he has his local incarnations (see p. 266), and, irrespectively of these, a distinct personality of his own, and a biography capable of being written with more precision than that of Vishṇu, by putting together the allusions and descriptions in the Epic poems and Purāṇas.

In the first place, with regard to his supposed residence, we are informed in these writings that his abode is Kailāsa in the Himālaya, which is also that of his countless troops

---

[1] The number of Liṅgas in India is estimated at three krores (=30 millions).

[2] Sāyaṇa, the great commentator on the Ṛig-veda, in the opening prayer to Śiva (as identified with the Supreme) asserts that the Veda was his breath (uććhvasitam).

[3] Only a few local South-Indian legends make him go through human births.

(Gaṇas) of servants[1], as well as of Kubera, god of wealth, who is in a similar manner surrounded by his attendants the Yakshas. This mountain-residence is, as we have already seen, the special heaven of Śiva, just as Vaikuṇṭha is of Vishṇu. Thither his worshippers hope to be ultimately transported, and there he lives with his wife Pārvatī (also called Durgā, Kālī, Umā, Bhavānī, Satī, etc.), with the divine hero Vīrabhadra, who is a manifestation of his own energy, and with his two sons Skanda and Gaṇeśa. The latter two control Śiva's troops, leading some to battle against evil demons, and restraining others who are themselves mischievous imps and would turn the whole world into a scene of confusion unless kept in check[2]. It is probable that in surrounding the god Rudra-Śiva with armies of demons and impish attendants, and making his sons lead and control them, Hindū mythologists merely gave expression to an idea inveterate in the Indian mind, that all disease, destruction, and dissolution are the result of demoniacal agency.

With regard to the bodily form, mode of life, and behaviour attributed to Śiva in his later character of lord of Kailāsa, it is not surprising that these should to some extent be borrowed from the ancient description of him in the Śatarudriya hymn before quoted (p. 76). But many new and supernatural features symbolical of his later functions and actions are added.

In the first place, in regard to his corporeal aspect, he has sometimes five faces (Pañćānana)[3], sometimes one face, with

---

[1] In the temple at Madurā I saw a representation of Śiva borne on one of the Gaṇas. Some of his more personal attendants have special names, such as Nandin (often confounded with his vehicle the bull, see p. 81), Bhṛiṅgin, and Taṇḍu, the last being the original teacher of dancing.

[2] It must be borne in mind that the troops of Śiva are represented as addicted to strong drink as well as to other excesses, and in this respect their master Śiva sets them an example; see pp. 84, 85.

[3] It is probable that the five faces or mouths symbolize the five Vedas (Ṛig, Yajus, Sāma, Taittirīya, and Vājasaneyin), or perhaps the five Pāṭhas (Saṃhitā, Pada, Krama, Jaṭā, and Ghana), or the five Gāyatrīs. The Kulārṇava Tantra says that the five Āmnāyas (the eastern, western,

three eyes, which are thought to denote his insight into past, present, and future time.

The third eye is in his forehead, and a moon's crescent above it marks the measuring of time by months, while a serpent round his neck denotes the endless cycle of recurring years, and a second necklace of skulls with numerous other serpents about his person [1] symbolizes the eternal revolution of ages, and the successive dissolution and regeneration of the races of mankind. His body is generally covered with ashes, and his hair thickly matted together, and gathered above his forehead into a coil, so as to project like a horn. On the top of it he bears the Ganges, the rush of which he intercepted in its descent from Vishṇu's foot, that the earth might not be crushed by the weight of the falling stream. His complexion is sometimes white [2], from the reflection of the snows of Kailāsa, sometimes dark, from his identification with the dark destroyer Time (Kāla). His throat is blue, from the stain of the deadly poison which

southern, northern, and upper) issued from Śiva's five mouths. Or the five elements may be symbolized. So Brahmā's four faces are said to symbolize the source of the four Vedas. So also many images of Buddha in India and Ceylon have five rays of light issuing from the head.

[1] Serpents, as we have seen, are associated with both Śiva and Vishṇu. The latter, as is well known, sleeps on a serpent, and I have often seen Liṅgas in the South with a canopy formed of a five-headed serpent. Images of Kṛishṇa and of Buddha are also so represented. The interchangeableness of Buddhism, Śaivism, and Vaishṇavism is everywhere apparent.

[2] There is a legend that Śiva appeared in the Kali age, for the good of the Brahmāns, as Śveta 'the white one,' and that he had four disciples, to all of whom the epithet Śveta is applied. Possibly the attribution of a white complexion to Śiva may be due to the fact that the Brāhmans of Cashmere, who are almost as fair as Europeans, were the first adherents of Śiva. Then as his cultus passed southwards the god naturally received a complexion more in keeping with that of his worshippers there. Or it may be that white and black, like day and night, symbolized the close connexion and succession of the destroying and regenerative principles. Śiva's wife Pārvatī is also often called Gaurī, the pale-coloured.

would have destroyed the world, had not Śiva in compassion for the human race undertaken to drink it up, on its production at the churning of the ocean. He rides a white bull (called Nandi), images of which are often placed outside his shrines and probably typify generative energy. He is sometimes represented clothed in a deer-skin, sometimes in the skin of a tiger alleged to have been formerly killed by him when created by the magical arts of some Ṛishis who tried to destroy the god, because his beauty had attracted the amorous glances of their wives. Sometimes, again, he appears wearing an elephant's skin which had belonged to a demon of immense power named Gaya, whom he conquered and slew. As Śiva is constantly engaged in battle with mighty demons (such as Pura, Tripura, Andhaka), all of whom he fought and slew, he is armed with special weapons, suited to his warlike needs; for example, he carries a three-pronged trident (triśūla,) which may either denote the three attributes of Creator, Destroyer, and Regenerator, or else all-destroying Past, Present, and Future Time; a bow called Ajagava (and Pināka), a thunderbolt (vajra), an axe, and a nondescript weapon called Khaṭvāṅga, consisting of a kind of staff with transverse pieces surmounted by a skull. He also holds in his hand a noose (pāśa) for binding his enemies, and a kind of rattle or drum, shaped like an hour-glass, called Ḍamaru, which he uses as a musical instrument to keep time while dancing.

It is clear from all this symbolism that the god Śiva, as depicted by his special worshippers, assumes a very bewildering and confusing variety of personalities at different times. His functions, as indicated by his 1008 names (see p. 106), are innumerable and his nature all-comprehensive. Yet an attempt may be made to disentangle the confusion by pointing out that there are really five chief characters of the god which stand out prominently from his general portraiture and are capable of being brought out into definite relief.

I. In the first place, he is, as we have seen, the impersonation of the dissolving and disintegrating powers and processes of nature. These ought really to be regarded as set in action by a beneficent being who performs a necessary operation, but in the later phases of Hindūism the idea of dissolution is invested with terror. Śiva himself is converted into a fierce universal destroyer (Sarva-bhūta-hara), who annihilates at the end of every great age (kalpa) not only men and all created things, but good and evil demons, and even Brahmā, Vishṇu, and all the inferior gods. He is then called Rudra, Mahā-kāla, Hara, Anala (Fire), etc. One legend makes him wear the bones and skulls of the gods as ornaments and garlands.

Another legend describes how at the end of one of the early ages of the universe he burnt up the gods by a flash from his central eye, and afterwards rubbed their ashes upon his body; whence the use of ashes is considered of great importance in his worship. Another legend accounts for the use of Rudrāksha berries in the rosaries of Śiva by describing how he once let fall some tears of rage which became converted into these seeds. Their connexion with Śiva-worship is probably due to their roughness and to their possessing five divisions corresponding to the god's five faces.

It is easy to see how it came to pass that the god in this later character is believed to delight in destruction for its own sake. He is called Śmaśāna-vāsin, 'dweller in burial-places.' Cemeteries and burning-grounds are his favourite haunts; imps and demons (bhūtas and piśāćas) are his ready servants; ferocity and irascibility, on the slightest provocation, constitute his normal condition of mind. For example, on one occasion, when the sage Daksha omitted to invite him and his wife Satī to a great sacrifice at which all the gods were guests, he without the slightest hesitation decapitated the unfortunate sage and replaced his head by that of a ram. So again a sculpture in the caves of Elephanta represents him with eight arms in the act of immolating a child. In this character he is called Bhairava, 'the terrible;' Vīra-bhadra being sometimes identified with him. But in the present day these terrible attributes are generally transferred from the male deity to his wife in the form Durgā or Kālī.

II. In the second place, Śiva is the impersonation of the eternal reproductive power of Nature, perpetually reintegrating after disintegration (whence his names Pitṛi, Mātṛi, Bhūta-bhāvana, Sarva-bhāvakara; see pp. 106, 107). It is especially in this personality that he is worshipped as if he were Brahmā 'the Creator' and called 'the eternally blessed one,' 'the causer of blessings' (Śiva, Sadā-Śiva, Śaṅkara, and Śambhu) —not, however, under the form of a man, but under the often misunderstood symbol of the Liṅga[1] (see p. 68 and note), which is sometimes represented with four faces (see Chap. XXII).

III. In the third place, Śiva is the typical ascetic and self-mortifier (Yogī, Tapasvī), who has attained the highest perfection in abstract meditation and austerity (whence his names Mahā-tapāḥ, Mahā-yogī). In this character he appears quite naked (Dig-ambara), with only one face, like an ordinary human being, with ash-besmeared body and matted hair (whence his name Dhūrjaṭi) sitting in profound meditation under a Banian tree (=Vaṭa or Baṛ tree), and often, like the contemplative Buddha, under a canopy formed by a serpent's head[2]. There he is supposed to remain passionless, motionless, immovable, as the trunk of a tree (sthāṇu), and perhaps rooted to the same spot for millions of years.

Another legend describes how Śiva, when engaged in a course of asceticism, scorched the god of love (Kāma-deva) to ashes by a flash of rage from his central eye, because that

---

[1] The Liṅga (or representation of the male organ) is sometimes denounced as 'an abominable symbol.' Nevertheless it is never by Śaivas connected with the passion of love. This passion belongs to Vaishṇavism rather than to Śaivism. Some think that the worship of the Liṅga was borrowed from pre-Āryan or aboriginal tribes, but see p. 71.

[2] The serpent is often five-headed, which appears to have some connection with Śiva's five faces. Compare note 3, p. 79.

deity attempted to inflame him with passion for his consort Pārvatī.

It is in his character of Yogī that he teaches men by his own example the power to be acquired by mortification of the body, suppression of the passions, and abstract contemplation, as leading to the loftiest spiritual knowledge and ultimately effecting union with himself in Kailāsa.

IV. In the fourth place, the god Śiva is a contemplative philosopher and learned sage, the revealer of Grammar to the greatest of Indian grammarians, Pāṇini[1]. And in this character he is represented as a Brāhman wearing the Brāhmanical thread[2], well-skilled in the Veda, and especially conversant with the Krama arrangement of the text. So much so that a saying is current among the Pandits: 'No one, who is not Rudra, can repeat the Krama' (nārudraḥ Krama-pāṭhakaḥ). Among his names, too, are Mantra-vid, Brahma-vid, Brahma-ćārī, and Paṇḍitaḥ. This, in fact, is one of many proofs that at least one form of Śaivism is as much the peculiar system of Brāhmans, learned men, and the higher classes of the Hindū community, as Vaishṇavism is of men of the world, kings, heroes, and the lower classes[3]. In fact, a verse from the ancient version of Manu is often quoted:—'Śiva is the god of the Brāhmans, Kṛishṇa (Vishṇu) of the Kshatriyas, Brahmā of the Vaiśyas, and Gaṇeśa of Śūdras.'

V. In the fifth place, Śiva is exactly the opposite of an ascetic and philosopher. He is a wild and jovial mountaineer (Kirāta), addicted to hunting and wine-drinking, fond of dancing (Nṛitya-priya, also called Naṭeśvara, 'lord of

---

[1] The first fourteen sūtras of Pāṇini are called the Śiva-sūtras, and the whole grammar is believed to be a revelation from Śiva, whence one of Śiva's names is Vyākaraṇottaraḥ. The miracle is made more remarkable by representing the reputed author Pāṇini as naturally stupid.

[2] I noticed that a carving of Śiva in the caves of Ellorā represents him with the Brāhmanical thread. His son Gaṇeśa also wears this thread.

[3] There is another common saying, Nāvishṇuḥ pṛithivī-patiḥ, 'No one except he resemble Vishṇu ought to be a king.'

dancers'), often dancing with his wife the Tāṇḍava dance, and surrounded by dwarfish, buffoon-like troops (gaṇa) of attendants, who, like their master, are fond of good living and occasionally inebriated by intoxicating liquors. The worshippers of Śiva in this character usually (but not invariably) belong to the sect called Śāktas, who are devoted to the wife of the god, and are given to self-indulgence and sensual gratification. Their religious books are called Tantras, and their tenets will be explained under the head of Śāktism (see p. 180).

A still more remarkable aspect of the god is as a being half-male, half-female (Ardha-nārī)[1]. This seems to be connected with the second of the characters just described. It symbolizes both the duality and unity of the generative act and the production of the universe from the union of two eternal principles (Prakṛiti and Purusha, Māyā and Brăhmăn), according to the Sāṅkhya and Vedānta systems (see p. 183).

Further, it should be noted that, according to some Purāṇas, there are eight principal personal manifestations of Śiva, called Rudra, Bhairava (or Bhīma), Ugra, Īśvara (or Īśāna or Īśa), Mahādeva (or Maheśvara), Paśu-pati, Śarva (Sarva), and Bhava.

Again, he is specially manifested in eight material forms (Tanus)—Fire, Water, Earth, Air, Ether (which are the five elements, typified by his five faces), the Sun, Moon, and the sacrificing Brāhman. By these he upholds the world.

In Southern India Śiva is celebrated as the worker of 64 special miracles. He raised the dead, healed the blind, deaf, lame, etc., and gave similar powers to 63 of his saints. The story of these miracles is given in the Madhurā-sthala-purāṇa, and I saw many representations of them both at Madurā and Tanjore. (For other names of Śiva, see pp. 106, 107.)

---

[1] In the caves of Elephanta I saw a fine carving of Śiva and Pārvatī thus united in one body. The female side forms the left side of the god, and is represented holding a looking-glass. It is noticeable that the wife is always on the left side, except as a bride at the nuptial ceremony.

The great variety of Śiva's characters does not seem to have led to a corresponding variety of Śaiva sects. We find that Śaivism has not, like Vaishṇavism, resolved itself into many separate organized societies under great religious leaders. It would in truth be difficult to name any conspicuous apostle and teacher of pure Śaivism (certainly not Basaba, p. 88), like the celebrated Vaishṇava teachers Rāmānuja, Madhva, Vallabha, and Ćaitanya (pp. 119–145). For we have already seen that the great Śaṅkara, though held by some to have Śaiva proclivities, abstained from inculcating devotion to any one god more than to another.

Unquestionably all Hindūs, even the strictest Vaishṇavas, are ready to pay homage to Śiva in his first and second characters of Dissolver and Regenerator. It is clear, too, that in the days of Śaṅkara several sects of Śaivas existed and became the object of his controversial onslaughts. In the Śaṅkara-vijaya six are named: to wit, 1. the Śaivas, *par excellence*, who had the Liṅga branded on both arms; 2. the Raudras, who had the trident branded on the forehead; 3. the Ugras, who had the Ḍamaru (see p. 81) branded on the two arms; 4. the Bhaṭṭas, who had the Liṅga on the forehead; 5. the Jaṅgamas, who bore the trident on the head and carried a Liṅga made of stone on their persons; 6. the Pāśupatas, who had the latter symbol branded on the forehead, arms, breast, and navel.

These sects are described in the Śaṅkara-vijaya as hostile to the doctrine of Non-duality (Advaita-drohiṇaḥ). Their practice of branding is denounced by Śaṅkara on the ground that various gods are present in the limbs of the human body[1], who are driven away by the burning (tāpana) of the skin.

Of the six sects named only the two last are numerous in the present day, and both these have altered not a few of their tenets and practices. In modern times Śaiva sectarians are

---

[1] May we not compare the Christian idea of the sanctity of the body as the temple of the Holy Ghost?

generally followers of Śiva in his third character of an ascetic. They profess to practise, like their god, severe austerities and bodily mortifications. Numbers of them may be seen at sacred places of pilgrimage, where their appearance as self-mortifying mendicants is often revolting to Europeans.

Those who call themselves Sannyāsīs are the most respectable. Indeed all twice-born men towards the close of their lives ought to abandon their wives and all worldly ties and become Sannyāsīs (p. 53). But the ordinary Sannyāsīs are not of the orthodox type. They are often confounded with other orders of mendicant devotees such as Vairāgīs (held to be Vaishṇavas), Gosāins, and Yogīs (Jogīs); the latter being a general name for all Tapasvīs who seek by their austerities (tapas) to achieve union (yoga) with the deity[1].

Self-mortification (tapas, tapasyā), in fact, and the practice of Yoga is not confined to Śaivism (see p. 72) or even to Hindūism (see my book on Buddhism, p. 226).

The theory is that a Hindū who aims at perfection ought to go through six successive courses of austerity (tapas) for twelve years each, rising by degrees up to the highest order of all—the Parama-haṉsa, who is supposed to be wholly absorbed in meditating on Brahman, and to do nothing else whatever.

Then there is an order of Śaiva ascetics called Daṇḍin, or staff-bearers, ten divisions of whom—called Daśa-nāmī Daṇḍins, said to carry ten different forms of staff—are alleged to have been founded by Śaṅkarāćārya.

There are also the Aghora-panthīs (panthī from Sanskṛit pathin), who propitiate Śiva by their revolting diet, feeding on filth and animal excreta of all kinds. It is asserted that some eat corpses stolen from Muhammadan burial-grounds, and that the head of the Aghorīs near Siddhapur subsists on

---

[1] They are sometimes called Sādhus, and often Fakīrs. The latter name ought to be restricted to Muhammadan mendicants. Bhagat (probably for Bhakta) is sometimes used for Vaishṇava devotees. Mahant is applied to a leader of one of these sects, or to the head of a monastery.

scorpions, lizards, and loathsome insects left to putrefy in a dead man's skull (Āgama-prakāśa, p. 7). Happily the number of these disgusting ascetics is decreasing. I only met one in the whole course of my travels—a revolting creature at Benares.

Then there are the Ūrdhva-bāhus, who extend one or both arms over the head and hold them in that position for years. This kind of devotee, too, is not so common as in former days. During the whole course of my travels I only saw two examples, one at Gayā and the other at Benares. The arm of the former was quite withered, and his fist was so tightly clenched that the nails were growing through the back of his hand. The latter looked like a piece of sculpture, sitting in a niche of the Anna-pūrṇā temple, perfectly motionless and impassive, with naked body smeared all over with white ashes, matted hair, and the forefinger of the upraised hand pointing to the heaven to which in imagination he seemed to be already transporting himself.

There are also the Ākāśa-mukhins, who keep their necks bent back looking up at the sky; the Kāpālikas, who use a dead man's skull for a drinking-cup[1]. (See also Chap. XXII.)

Most of these Śaiva ascetics are disreputable in character and decidedly dirty in their habits. Cleanliness is said to be next to godliness, and Hindūs in their general habits are quite as cleanly as Europeans; yet dirt appears to be regarded as a necessary accompaniment of particular forms of sanctity[2].

We may also note that a sect of Śaivas exists in the South of India—mostly in the Mysore and Kanarese country—who were formed into a religious community about the eleventh or twelfth century by a leader named Basaba (for Sanskṛit Vṛishabha), and are called Liṅgavats (popularly Lingāits), because they wear the Liṅga in a silver or metallic casket

---

[1] This order is said to have been founded by Śaṅkara; compare p. 59.

[2] But only in the case of ascetics. The late Lord Beaconsfield was right when he said that Moses, Muhammad, and Manu all make cleanliness a religious duty.

suspended round their necks with a cord like a necklace. They are usually identified with the Jaṅgamas of Śaṅkara's day, described as utterly unorthodox.

In fact, this sect is opposed to all the orthodox practices and usages of the Hindūs, such as caste-distinctions[1], the authority of the Brāhmans, the inspiration of the Veda, and Brāhmanical sacrifices; and they bury instead of burning their dead. Their tenets are embodied in the Basaba-purāṇa.

With regard to Śaiva philosophical doctrines it should be observed that, like those of the Vaishṇava sects, they deviate more or less from the orthodox Vedānta doctrine of the identity of the Supreme and human Spirit, the amount of deviation depending of course on the intensity of the personality attributed to Śiva.

A particular Śaiva philosophy, which may be called the Śaiva-darśana *par excellence*, was taught in India about the eleventh century. It was handed down in twenty-eight books, called Āgamas, almost all of which are lost. This philosophy is followed by a sect in the South, and is opposed to the non-duality of the Vedānta. It taught a kind of Viśishṭādvaita—like that of the Vaishṇava teacher Rāmānuja (see p. 119)—the distinctive feature of which was that three entities have a separate existence. 1. The Lord (Śiva) called Paśu-pati, 'lord of the soul' (Paśu). 2. The human soul called Paśu, 'an animal.' 3. Matter called Pāśa, 'a fetter.' The soul which belongs to the Lord as to a master, is bound by matter as a beast (paśu) is by a fetter; and of course the great aim of this Śaiva philosophy is to set it free and restore it to its rightful owner. These doctrines have evidently much in common with the theistic Sāṅkhya.

Another Śaiva sect, called Pāśupata, already noticed (pp. 59,

---

[1] The Lingāits of the present day are said to be returning to caste-rules, and only to disregard caste on certain days of the week. I have heard some declare that they belong to a fifth caste (pañćama) which is superior to the four castes of the Brāhmanical system.

86) is connected with the preceding, much as the Madhva is with the Rāmānuja; for instead of affirming the separate existence of three entities they only distinguish between two—Pati and Paśu. The former (Pati) is the Lord (Īśvara), the cause and evolver (kartā) of all things; the latter is the effect (kārya) or that which is evolved out of the cause and wholly dependent on it. The Pāśupatas induce ecstatic union with their lord by singing, dancing, and gesticulations.

I defer to a subsequent chapter a description of the principal Śaiva temples visited by me (see p. 434).

Nevertheless, an account of the ceremonies I saw performed at a Liṅga shrine near Bombay may be introduced here.

It has been already stated that on ordinary occasions the form of worship consists in simply pouring water over the Liṅga and offering Bilva leaves (see p. 68). On great festivals a more complicated ceremonial is observed. In the year 1877 I visited the temple dedicated to Śiva at Walkeśvar, near Bombay, on the morning after the Śiva-rāt (rāt=rātri) or fast kept in honour of the god. The Liṅga shrine there is not large, and the symbol is not too sacred to be exposed to observation. I was permitted, in fact, to stand close to the entrance of the small sanctuary and to note down all I witnessed. In the centre of the shrine was the Liṅga, a plain upright stone, which on the occasion of the Śiva-rāt ceremony was covered with a pile of Bilva (Bīl[1]) leaves. Near it there were several high candlesticks with lights kept continually burning. Behind, in a niche, was the image of Śiva's wife Pārvatī, which on the occasion of my visit was loaded with sacred flowers resembling marigolds. In front, looking into the sanctuary, was the image of a bull made of brass; the bull being Śiva's vehicle, and, like the Liṅga, symbolical of reproductive energy. Above the upright stone was hanging a large vase full of water. It had a perforation in its

[1] The Bilva, corrupted into Bīl, is the Ægle Marmelos, a very astringent plant.

lowest part through which the liquid trickled out, drop by drop, falling at regular intervals on the symbol underneath. When I asked a bystander the meaning of this constant dripping (see p. 68), he replied with much naïveté: 'Holy water from the Ganges is falling on the head of God.' No further explanation appeared to him to be needed. In front of the porch before the door of the sanctuary were three long rows of bells, and above them a line of svastikas or sacred crosses[1] interspersed with trees and figures of elephants, and over all the hood of a cobra snake. Above the door itself was the image of Śiva's son Gaṇeśa.

Outside the shrine, on the morning of my visit, stood a row of male worshippers (three or four women standing near), and in front of them a priest, holding a tray of Bilva leaves, supposed to possess cooling properties grateful to the god Śiva. Some of these the priest placed in the hands of each worshipper, at the same time muttering prayers and texts. Next he dipped his finger in a vase of holy water and touched the two eyes and breasts of each. To me, a spectator, it seemed exactly as if he were making the sign of a cross on their bodies. Then each of the worshippers heaped the leaves received from the priest on the head of the bull. I noticed that some also besprinkled it with saffron (kuṅkuma) powder, which they purchased from a man standing near.

This preliminary ceremony ended, all entered the shrine, and after ringing the bells at the entrance, prostrated themselves before the central symbol, touching the ground with their foreheads. Their next act was to pile more Bilva leaves on the stone symbol. Then taking small lotās of holy water, they poured abundance of the sacred liquid over both leaves and symbol. All the worshippers then seated themselves in a circle round the central stone while the priest

---

[1] The Svastika mark is an auspicious symbol with four arms in the form of a Greek cross, the termination of each arm being bent round in the direction of the sun's course. See note 1, p. 104.

lighted lamps and waved them before it. Every now and then a fresh worshipper entered the shrine, ringing one of the bells at the door before entering. Moreover, in the shrine there was a constant ringing of small portable bells and clapping of hands, as if to draw the attention of the deity worshipped to the prayers muttered by his worshippers, while a number of priests in another part of the sanctuary intoned texts and chanted hymns in chants very like Gregorian.

Outside the shrine, on one side, sat a nearly naked ascetic, with long matted hair coiled round and round into a high peak, his face and body covered with white ashes. On the other side sat a Brāhman with a little wooden table before him, on which was a lotā of holy water, several implements of worship, and a copy of one of the Purāṇas or ancient sacred scriptures. He had three white streaks on his forehead and the same on his shoulders to denote his devotion to Śiva. Hanging over his left shoulder and under his right arm was the sacred cord of three coils of cotton—the mark of his second birth—and his right hand was inserted in a Gomukhī or rosary bag. I asked what he was doing. 'He is counting the beads of his rosary,' said a bystander, 'and each time he tells his beads he repeats one of the 1008 names of the god Śiva over and over again, but this operation must on no account be seen, and so the hand and rosary are concealed in the bag.'

No doubt he was muttering to himself, but in so low a tone that no sound was audible; and his eyes were intently fixed, as if in profound meditation, which neither my presence nor anything passing around appeared to distract for a single instant.

Another devotee was also seated cross-legged outside the entrance to the shrine, whose intoning of one of the Śiva-purāṇas and muttering of prayers (japa) was audible to every one. He had before him a low wooden table, on which was a Rudrāksha rosary (see p. 82), a Liṅga-purāṇa, a little metal saucer of rice, a small lotā of holy water on a three-legged stand, a little spoon, a heap of Bilva leaves, a sacred conch-shell (śaṅkha)—sometimes blown like a horn or used as a Śaiva symbol, though usually appropriated to Vishṇu—three green mangoes, a small bell, a leaf full of dates, and a little bag containing the Vibhūti or white ashes for marking his forehead with the three Śaiva streaks. While I was taking this catalogue he took no notice of my proceedings, but continued muttering his prayers with intense earnestness, as if quite abstracted from the world around him.

Though greatly interested in all I was allowed to witness, I came away sick at heart. No one could be present at such a scene without feeling depressed by the thought that, notwithstanding all our efforts for the extension of education and the diffusion of knowledge, we have as yet done little to loosen the iron grip of idolatry and superstition on the masses of the people. Indeed it would be easy to show that other forms of Śiva-worship are characterized by superstitious observances of a still lower type. Turn we, for example, to the ceremonies performed at the great Śaiva temple of Bhuvaneśvara in Orissa. These are so unique that I may be pardoned for giving some idea of them before concluding this chapter. My authority is Dr. Rājendralāla Mitra, who has described the ceremonial in the second volume of his work on Orissa. Śiva is worshipped at that particular locality under the form of a large uncarved block or slab of granite, about eight feet long, partly buried in the ground, partly apparent above the soil to the height of about eight inches. The block is believed to be a Liṅga of the Svayam-bhū class (see p. 69), and is surrounded by a rim, supposed, of course, to represent the female organ (Yoni). The daily worship consists of no less than twenty-two ceremonial acts.

(1) At the first appearance of dawn bells are rung to rouse the deity from his slumbers; (2) a lamp with many wicks is waved in front of the stone; (3) the god's teeth are cleaned

by pouring water and rubbing a stick about a foot long on the stone; (4) the deity is washed and bathed by emptying several pitchers of water on the stone; (5) the god is dressed by putting clothes on the stone; (6) the first breakfast is offered, consisting of grain, sweetmeats, curd, and cocoanuts; (7) the god has his principal breakfast, when cakes and more substantial viands are served; (8) a kind of little lunch is offered; (9) the god has his regular lunch; (10) the mid-day dinner is served, consisting of curry, rice, pastry, cakes, cream, etc., while a priest waves a many-flamed lamp and burns incense before the stone; (11) strains of noisy discordant music rouse the deity from his afternoon sleep at 4 P.M., the sanctuary having been closed for the preceding four hours; (12) sweetmeats are offered; (13) the afternoon bath is administered; (14) the god is dressed as in the morning; (15) another meal is served; (16) another bath is administered; (17) the full-dress ceremony takes place, when fine costly vestments, yellow flowers, and perfumery are placed on the stone; (18) another offering of food follows; (19) after an hour's interval the regular supper is served; (20) five masks (p. 79) and a Ḍamaru (p. 81) are brought in and oblations made; (21) waving of lights (ārti; Sanskṛit, ārati) is performed before bedtime; (22) a bedstead is brought into the sanctuary and the god composed to sleep.

Of course the offerings are ultimately eaten by the priests and attendants, the superfluity being sold as sacred food.

This Bhuvaneśvara ceremonial seems to be an imitation of the forms of worship offered to the images of Kṛishṇa.

It is satisfactory to find that many enlightened Brāhmans in the present day are not afraid to express their disapproval of idol-offerings. In a Gujarātī work written by a learned Brāhman (Āgama-prakāśa, p. 162) we read: 'When one remembers the greatness of the perfect God who is Existence, Thought, and Bliss (p. 34), how can any idea be formed of offering food and oblations to such a Being?'

CHAPTER V.

Vaishṇavism or Worship of Vishṇu.

THE preceding chapters of this work will, I trust, have made it clear that, in respect of religious belief, the Hindūs of the present day may be broadly divided into three principal classes[1], namely, (1) Smārtas, (2) Śaivas, (3) Vaishṇavas.

The first (p. 55) believe that man's spirit is identical with the one Spirit (Ātmā, Brahmă[2]) which is the essence and substratum of the Universe and only cognizable through internal meditation and self-communion. They regard that Spirit as the highest object of all religious knowledge and aspiration. They are also believers in the Tri-mūrti; that is, in the three personal gods, Brahmā, Śiva, and Vishṇu—with their train of subordinate deities—but only as coequal manifestations of the one eternal impersonal Spirit, and as destined ultimately

---

[1] These, of course, are capable of subdivision.

[2] It is worthy of note that Ātman (which is the earlier word for the one Spirit of the Universe) is masculine, while Brahman, the later word, is neuter. The etymology of Ātman is doubtful. Some derive it from *at*, to move; others from *ah*, connected with *aham*, I; others from *vā*, to blow as the wind; and others (as we have seen) from *an*, to breathe (compare p. 20). No doubt ātman was originally the breath of life—the breath that animates the Universe and man's living soul—the power in which and by which man lives, and moves, and has his being. In the well-known hymn Ṛig-veda I. 115. 1, the Sun (Sūrya)—interpreted by advanced Pandits to mean the Supreme Being—is called the Soul (Ātman) of the Universe (that is, of all that moves and is immovable); and in the Taittirīya Āraṇyaka, VIII. 1, the ethereal element called Ākāśa (supposed to fill and pervade the Universe and to be the vehicle of life) is said to be produced from Ātman. The name Brahman, which is the most usual name for the one Spirit of the Universe in later writings, was at first connected with the spiritual power inherent in the Vedic hymns and prayers. The Veda itself is often called Brahmă, and described as the breath (uććhvasita) of the Supreme.

to be reabsorbed into that Spirit and so disappear[1]. This is the only orthodox form of Brāhmanical religious thought, and those Brāhmans who follow it claim Śaṅkara (see p. 55) as their authoritative guide. It is a form of Pantheism, but differs widely from that of European philosophical systems.

The second great religious class of the Hindūs consists of Śaiva sectarians, who, as we have seen, are believers in the one god Śiva, not only as Dissolver and Regenerator, but as Creator and Preserver, and as the one self-existent Being, identified with the one Universal Spirit, and therefore not liable to lose his personality by reabsorption into that Spirit.

The third class consists of Vaishṇava sectarians, who are believers in the one personal god Vishṇu, not only as Preserver, but as Creator and Dissolver. It should be noted, too, that both Śaivas and Vaishṇavas agree in attributing an essential form and qualities to the Supreme Being. Vishṇu as the Supreme reposes upon his serpent-couch; till affected with the quality of activity he awakes, and, as Brahmā (p. 105), creates the world. See Vishṇu-purāṇa, Chap. II.

Vaishṇavism then is, like Śaivism, a form of Monotheism. It is the setting aside of the triune equality of Brahmā, Śiva, and Vishṇu, in favour of one god Vishṇu (often called Hari), especially as manifested in his two human incarnations Rāma and Kṛishṇa. 'Brahmā and Śiva,' said the great Vaishṇava teacher Madhva, 'decay with their decaying bodies; greater than these is the undecaying Hari.' And here, at the outset, it may be well to point out that Vaishnavism, notwithstanding the gross polytheistic superstitions and hideous idolatry to which it gives rise, is the only Hindū system worthy of being called a religion. At all events it must be admitted that it has more common ground with Christianity than any other form of non-Christian faith. Vedism was little more than reveren-

---

[1] Brahmā, Śiva, and Vishṇu are manifested by the simple *will* of the Supreme, whereas in the creation of living human beings (jīva) the influence of karma, 'act,' is an important element.

tial awe of the forces of Nature and a desire to propitiate them. Brāhmanism was simply an Indian variety of pantheism. Buddhism was a product and a reform of Brāhmanism, and gained many followers by opening its arms to all castes and by offering deliverance from the slavery of passion and from the miseries of life and the burden of ritualism and priestcraft; but, in its denials of the existence of both a Supreme and human spirit, was no religion at all; and in its negations never commended itself generally to the Indian mind. Śaivism, though, like Vaishṇavism, it recognized the eternal personality of one Supreme Being, was too severe and cold a system to exert exclusive influence over the great majority. Vaishṇavism alone possessed the elements of a genuine religion.

Who can doubt that a God of such a character was needed —a God who could satisfy the yearnings of the heart for a religion of faith, love and prayer rather than of knowledge and works? Such a God was believed to be represented by Vishṇu, who evinced his sympathy with mundane suffering, by frequent descents on earth, for the delivery of men from the threefold miseries of life, viz. (1) from the diseases incident to body and mind, such as those resulting from lust, anger, avarice, etc.; (2) from the miseries inflicted by material environment, —by beasts, snakes, wicked men, etc.; (3) from those inflicted by unseen demoniacal agency. Indian philosophy, however, claimed the power of getting rid of all these three miseries (see Sāṅkhya-kārikā, 1).

Hence teachers arose (among whom was Śāṇḍilya the author of the Bhakti-sūtra) who insisted on the doctrine of salvation by love and devotion (Bhakti)—a doctrine dimly adumbrated in portions of the Veda, and fully propounded in the Bhagavad-gītā and Bhāgavata-purāṇa (see p. 63).

Intense devotion, then, to a personal god Vishṇu, and belief in his power to elevate his worshippers to eternal bliss in his own heaven (Vaikuṇṭha, see p. 118), is the chief characteristic of Vaishṇavism; for Vaishṇavism, like Śaivism, dissents from the vague impersonal Pantheism of Brāhmanical philosophy, whose one God is the substratum of everything and himself nothing. Nor can we wonder that devotion to Vishṇu in his two human incarnations, Rāma and Kṛishṇa, became the most popular religion of India. These two heroes were of the kingly or Kshatriya caste, and greatly beloved as popular leaders. It is usual to assert that the Brāhmans are the highest objects of worship and honour among the Hindūs. This is not the case among the countless adherents of the Vaishṇava religion. The mass of the people of India exalt the divine right of kings and the divine right of the government of the day above all other forms of power, and worship every great and heroic leader as an incarnation of the deity.

Yet, with all its popularity, Vaishṇavism is not an example of a house at peace within itself. It has split up into various subdivisions, which display no little of the odium theologicum in their opposition to each other. Possibly antagonism of some kind is a necessary condition of religious vitality. At any rate in India all religious systems inevitably break up into sects, and seem to gather strength and vigour from the process.

It is not uncommon, indeed, to hear it asserted that Hindūism is rapidly falling to pieces, and destined soon to collapse altogether. One reason given for the doom supposed to be impending over its future is, that it is not a proselyting religion. And the truth certainly is that no stranger can be admitted as a convert to Hindūism either by making any particular confession of faith, or by going through any prescribed forms. The only acknowledged mode of admission is by birth. To become a Hindū one must be born a Hindū. Yet Hindūism is continually growing within itself. In its tenacity of life and power of expansion it may be compared to the sacred banian-tree, whose thousand ramifications, often issuing from apparently lifeless stems, find their way into walls, undermine old buildings, or themselves send down roots which become fixed in the soil, and form fresh centres of growth and vitality.

And it cannot be doubted that one great conservative element of Hindūism is the many-sidedness of Vaishṇavism. For Vaishṇavism is, like Buddhism, the most tolerant of religious systems. It is always ready to accommodate itself to other creeds, and delights in appropriating to itself the religious ideas of all the nations of the world. It admits of every form of internal development. It has no organized hierarchy under one supreme head, but it may have any number of separate associations formed by separate teachers, who are ever springing up and extending their religious authority over ever-increasing masses of the population. It has no formal confession of faith, but it has an elastic creed capable of adaptation to all varieties of opinion and practice. It has no one bible—no one collection of writings in one compact volume, with lines of teaching converging towards one great central truth; yet, while making use of the Veda it has a series of sacred books of its own (such as the Purāṇas, the Bhagavad-gītā, etc.), each of which professes to be a revelation from the Supreme Being, and claims to constitute an authority for the establishment of almost any kind of doctrine. It can, like Brāhmanism, be pantheistic, monotheistic, dualistic, polytheistic. It can, like Śaivism, enjoin asceticism, self-mortification, and austerity. It can, like Śāktism, give the reins to self-indulgence, licentiousness, and carnality. It can, like Buddhism, preach liberty, equality, fraternity; or inculcate universal benevolence, and avoidance of injury to others. It can proclaim Buddha or any other teacher or remarkable man to be an incarnation of Vishṇu. It can even set its face against idolatry[1], and can look with sympathizing condescension on Christianity itself, or hold it to be a develop-

[1] There can be no doubt that the anti-idolatrous sect founded by Kabīr (see p. 158) grew out of Vaishṇavism.

ment of its own theory of religion suited to Europeans. It is owing to this all-comprehensiveness of the Vaishṇava system that any new doctrine, or any new view of old doctrines, may be promulgated with an almost certain prospect of success. And indeed the theological laxity of the inhabitants of India increases in proportion to the tenacity of their adherence to caste customs and traditions. Broken up as they are into a multitude of separate peoples, comparatively few individuals have any desire for national union or intellectual progress, and these few owe their ideas to the education we have imparted. Few wish to leave the path trodden by their forefathers, or deviate from the old indurated ruts. The masses can neither read nor write. They care nothing for science. History, biography, and political economy are to them a terra incognita. Their whole desire is to be left undisturbed in their social customs, family traditions, and caste usages—constituting as these do their chief religion.

It seems, indeed, as if religion of this kind is the only force which has power to rouse the masses from their normal condition of torpor. The stern necessity of conforming to domestic usages is ever present to a Hindū's mind, colouring all his ideas, running through every fibre of his being, and constituting the Alpha and Omega of his earthly career. If this be religion, he is born religious, and dies religious. He is religious in his eating and drinking, in his sleeping and waking, in his dressing and undressing, in his rising up and sitting down, in his daily work and daily amusement. Nay, religious ceremonies anticipate his birth, prolong his marriage-rite into a triple act lasting for years (p. 379), and follow him after death. Yet any social innovation he utterly repudiates. It is only in religious doctrine that he evinces credulity and receptivity. Let any earnest preacher of any new creed appear in any assemblage of ordinary Hindūs—let him announce that he has come as a messenger from heaven, and he may generally reckon on being believed. And if to his other qualifications he adds a character for self-denial and asceticism, he cannot fail to attract disciples; for nowhere in the world are family ties so binding as in India, and yet nowhere is such homage paid to their abandonment. The influence of any new religious teacher (āćārya) who is known to live a life of abstinence, bodily mortification, and suppression of the passions, is sure to become unbounded, either for good or evil.

Probably, during the leader's lifetime, he is able to restrain the enthusiasm of his converts within reasonable limits. It is only when he dies that they are apt to push his opinions to extremes never intended by himself. Eventually they develop his teaching into an overgrown unhealthy system, the internal rottenness of which disgusts all sensible men, even among its own adherents. Then some new teacher arises to re-establish purity of doctrine. He is, of course, in his turn a man of earnestness and energy, with a strong will, and great powers of persuasion. He collects around him with equal facility a number of followers, and those in their turn carry his teaching to preposterous lengths.

Hence the condition of Vaishṇavism, which depends far more than Śaivism on personal leadership and influence, is one of perpetual decay and revival, collapse and recovery. Its fluctuations resemble those of a vast ocean heaving this way and that in continual flux and reflux.

It is doubtless true that all human systems are liable to similar alternations. But in India every tendency of humanity seems intensified and exaggerated. No country in the world is so conservative in its traditions, yet no country has undergone so many religious changes and vicissitudes. To follow out in detail the whole drama of Vaishṇavism would require volumes. Even the first act presents us with a succession of shifting scenes.

In all likelihood the primary idea of a god Vishṇu (a name derived from root vish, 'to pervade'), permeating and infusing his essence into material objects, was originally connected with the personification of the infinite heavenly space. We know that in the Ṛig-veda Vishṇu is a form of the ever-moving solar orb, and in a well-known hymn (I. 22, 16, 17), still commonly used by the Brāhmans, he is described as striding through the seven worlds [1] in three steps, and enveloping the universe with the dust of his beams. A later work, the Aitareya-brāhmaṇa of the Ṛig-veda, opens with the following remarkable statement: 'Fire (Agni) has the lowest place among the gods, Vishṇu the highest; between them stand all the other deities.' (Haug's edition, 1.)

Elsewhere the god Vishṇu is connected with water. In Manu's Law-book (I. 10) the Universal Spirit is called Nārāyaṇa, as moving on the waters; in harmony with which idea Vishṇu is often represented in sculptures, images, and pictures as Nārāyaṇa in human form, reposing on the thousand-headed serpent and floating on the ocean.

In the later mythology of Brāhmanism, when the doctrine of the triad of personal gods (Tri-mūrti) had been fully developed and Vishṇu had taken his place as the second person of that triad, he has a less distinctly marked human personality —*antecedent to his incarnated descents*—than the god Śiva.

To write a biographical account of the god Vishṇu's life in his own heavenly abode, like the life of his rival Śiva (p. 78), would be difficult. The truth is that the development of his personality, which is really greater than that of any other god in the Hindū pantheon, must be looked for on earth in his descents (avatāra) as Rāma and Kṛishṇa.

Nevertheless, it must be borne in mind that the god Vishṇu really possesses a corporeal character of his own quite irrespective of and anterior to his incarnated descents. He is described

[1] There are seven lower regions, viz. Atala, Vitala, Sutala, Rasātala, Talātala, Mahātala, and Pātāla; above which are the seven Lokas or worlds, called Bhūr (the earth), Bhuvar, Svar, Mahaḥ, Janaḥ, Tapaḥ, and Brahma or Satya. Sometimes the first three of these, the earth (Bhū), atmosphere (Bhuvar), and heavens (Svar), are supposed to comprehend all the worlds (see p. 403). For the hells see pp. 232–233.

as living in his heaven Vaikuṇṭha—a locality more inaccessible and less easy to identify with any definite spot on earth than Śiva's abode Kailāsa (p. 79). He has a wife Lakshmī or Śrī, the goddess of fortune and beauty, who is fabled to have sprung, with other precious things, from the froth of the ocean when churned by the gods and demons (see p. 108). And as Vishṇu in his non-Avatāra condition lives a life which has fewer features in common with humanity than that of Śiva, so is his wife Lakshmī less human than Śiva's wife Pārvatī. In fact the more human side of both Vishṇu and Lakshmī is reserved for their descents in human form —Vishṇu as Rāma and Kṛishṇa, Lakshmī as Sītā and Rukmiṇī. Nevertheless some details of Vishṇu's separate personality, as distinct from his Avatāras, may be gathered from the Purāṇas. For example, we are told that he has a peculiar auspicious mark (Śrī-vatsa) on his breast[1]. He has four arms, and holds a symbol in each of his four hands; namely, a wheel or circular weapon (ćakra) called Sudarśana, a conch-shell[2] (śaṅkha) called Pāñćajanya, a club (gadā) called Kaumodakī, and a lotus-flower (padma). Of these the circular symbol may possibly have been borrowed from Buddhism. If so, it was originally significant of the wheel

---

[1] Described as a peculiar twist or curl of the hair. In one form of Kṛishṇa (as Viṭho-bā in the Marāṭha country) his breast has a foot-mark, believed to be the indelible impress of the blow from the sage Bhṛigu's foot (see the story at p. 45).

[2] One account describes the sacred conch-shell as thrown up by the sea when churned by the gods and demons (see p. 108). Another account makes Vishṇu's shell consist of the bones of the demon Pañćajana. According to the Vishṇu-purāṇa (V. 21), 'this demon lived in the form of a conch-shell under the ocean. Kṛishṇa (Vishṇu) plunged into the waters, killed him, took the shell which constituted his bones, and ever afterwards used it for a horn. When sounded it fills the demon-hosts with dismay, animates the gods, and annihilates unrighteousness.' Vishṇu is believed to take such delight in this shell, that a small shell of the same species is used in pouring holy water over his idols and symbols in the performance of his worship. It is also frequently branded on the arms of his worshippers.

of the Buddhistic law, or of the cycles of existence peculiar to that system. Or, bearing in mind Vishṇu's connection with the Sun, we may regard it as emblematical (like the Svastika[1]) of the Sun's circular course in the heavens. In the later mythology, however, it represents a missile weapon hurled by Vishṇu, like a quoit, at the demons who are ever plotting evil against gods and men, and with whom he is always at war[2]. Similarly the conch-shell is blown by him like a trumpet in his battles; its miraculous sound filling his enemies with terror and helping him to secure victory. The club is also used in Vishṇu's conflicts with his demon-foes. Moreover he is armed with a wonderful bow called Śārṅga and a sword Nandaka. He has a jewel on his wrist named Syamantaka, and another on his breast called Kaustubha. When he moves through space to the aid of his worshippers he is borne on the mythical bird Garuḍa[3], closely related to the Sun and compared to an eagle, but represented as semi-human in form and character, with a bird-like face. Possibly this Garuḍa may be a personification of the sky

---

[1] The Svastika mark may be a kind of curtailed form of this wheel, consisting of four spokes crossing each other at right angles and a portion of the circumference which is left to denote the direction in which it must turn to symbolize the Sun's course in the heavens. This conjecture, which I formed long ago, is confirmed by the late Mr. Edw. Thomas's article in the Numismatic Chronicle.

[2] The names of some of the chief demons thus destroyed by Vishṇu (or Kṛishṇa identified with Vishṇu) are Madhu, Kaṉsa, Bāṇa, Bali, Mura, etc.

[3] In some parts of India (especially in the South) Garuḍa is an object of worship. I frequently came across images of him in Vaishṇava temples. He is the son of Kaśyapa and Vinatā, and hence Aruṇa the Dawn, regarded as charioteer of the Sun, is his younger brother. Most of the Hindū deities are described as associated with or attended by their own favourite animals, which they sometimes use as vehicles (vāhana). Brahmā is attended by a goose or swan (haṉsa); Śiva by a bull (see p. 81); Kārttikeya or Skanda by a peacock; Indra by an elephant; Yama by a buffalo (mahisha); Kāma, 'god of love,' by a parrot; Gaṇeśa by a rat; Agni by a ram; Varuṇa by a fish; Durgā by a tiger. Serpents are associated with both Śiva and Vishṇu.

or ethereal element which supports Vishṇu—identified with the Sun—one of whose names is 'Air-borne' (Vāyu-vāhana). It is noteworthy that Garuḍa, like the Kṛishṇa form of Vishṇu, is the destroyer of serpents which typify destruction and evil (compare p. 113). Yet serpents have also their contrary character, and even divine attributes; for at the dissolution of the Universe and between the intervals of creation, Vishṇu, as the Supreme Being, floating on the waters (p. 102), reclines in profound repose on the thousand-headed serpent Śesha—typical of infinity—while his wife Lakshmī chafes his feet, and out of his navel grows the lotus which supports Brahmā, the active agent in reproducing the world. Finally, Vishṇu has the river Ganges issuing from one of his feet, whence it flows through the sky before it falls on Śiva's head (p. 80).

And here it may be noted that the devotional enthusiasm of Vishṇu's worshippers has endowed him with a thousand names and epithets[1]. This is exactly eight less than the Śaivas have lavished on Śiva, and, considering the rivalry between the followers of the two deities, must be regarded as a modest allowance. The repetition of any or all of these names (nāma-saṅkīrtana), either with or without the help of a rosary, constitutes an important part of daily worship, and is productive of vast stores of religious merit. They are all enumerated with those of Śiva in the Anuśāsana-parva of the Mahā-bhārata (1144–1266, 6950–7056)[2].

---

[1] Of course the greater number of the names are simply epithets. The Muhammadans reckon ninety-nine names and epithets of God, and make the repetition (zikr) of them a work of enormous religious merit. In the same way the Jews attach great efficacy to the repetition of the Divine epithets. Christianity reckons, I believe, about ninety epithets of Christ, but no Christian thinks of repeating them as a meritorious exercise. Aristotle, it is said, enumerates more than a hundred names and epithets applicable to Zeus; but the Greeks and Romans do not appear to have believed in any religious advantage attending the mere mechanical recital of such names.

[2] I notice several repetitions of the same name in the catalogue; for instance, Āditya, Sthāṇu, Srashṭṛi.

In comparing the two catalogues it is interesting to observe how many names are common to both deities. Vishṇu, especially, has a large number of names which he shares with the rival god, and is even called Śiva 'the Auspicious;' while Śiva is called Vishṇu, 'the Pervader,' each in fact usurping the functions of the other. Moreover, to both deities is allotted an ample assortment of the usual titles expressive of almighty power—such as 'all-creating,' 'all-seeing,' 'all-knowing,' 'infinite,' 'self-existent,' 'all-pervading'—mixed up with many which are unworthy of beings claiming divine homage. Vishṇu has certainly fewer objectionable epithets than Śiva.

Many names of both gods are simply taken from those of the Sun, Fire, and Wind; and many are expressive of lofty divine attributes—once believed to be the peculiar property of Christian theology. For example, Vishṇu is called 'the holy Being' (Pavitram, also applied to Śiva), 'the True' (Satyaḥ), 'the Pure Spirit' (or 'having a pure spirit,' Pūtātmā), 'the Way' (Mārgaḥ), 'the Truth' (Tattvam), 'the Life' (Prāṇaḥ), 'the Physician' (Vaidyaḥ), 'the World's Medicine' (Aushadhaṃ or Bheshajaṃ Jagataḥ), 'the Father' (Pitā), and even 'the Holy of the Holy' (Pavitram Pavitrāṇām)[1]—an epithet which it is difficult to reconcile with some of the actions of his Kṛishṇa manifestation.

On the other hand, Śiva is called by the following names in addition to those already mentioned at pp. 81–85:—'the Mother' (Mātā, as well as Pitā, 'the Father'), 'Extinction' (Nirvāṇam), 'the Year-causer' (Saṃvatsara-karaḥ), 'the great Illusionist' (Mahāmāyaḥ), 'the Night-walker' (Niśā-ćaraḥ),

[1] Other remarkable names and epithets of Vishṇu are the following:—'the Bridge' (Setuḥ), 'the Guide' (Netā), 'the All' (Sarvaḥ), 'the Refuge' (Śaraṇam), 'the Friend' (Suhṛid), 'the Affectionate' (Vatsalaḥ), 'the Benefactor' (Priya-kṛit), 'the Witness' (Sākshī), 'the Patient' (Sahishṇuḥ), 'the Peace-giver' (Śānti-daḥ), 'the Authority' (Pramāṇam), 'the Mysterious one' (Guhyaḥ), 'the Undying-bodied one' (Amṛita-vapuḥ), 'the Holy' (Brahmaṇyaḥ), 'the Winkless' (Animishaḥ), 'the Desired one' (Ishṭaḥ), 'the Who?' (Kaḥ), 'the What' (Kim).

'the Submarine Fire' (called Baḍavā-mukhaḥ, 'Mare-faced'), 'the White One' (Śuklaḥ), 'the Enraged' (Mahākrodhaḥ), 'the Root' (Mūlam), 'the Ill-formed' (Virūpaḥ), 'the Mule' (Haya-gardabhiḥ, mixture of the qualities of horse and ass?).

Again, some of Vishṇu's designations as Kṛishṇa, such as Pārtha-sārathi, 'Charioteer of Arjuna' (under which title he is worshipped at Madras), and Veṅkaṭeśa, 'Lord of the hill Veṅkaṭa,' are, like those of Śiva, merely local epithets; and some (as for example Viṭho-bā, worshipped at Paṇḍharpur) are the result of his identification with particular local heroes.

I need scarcely repeat that the chief distinguishing characteristic of the god Vishṇu is his condescending to infuse his essence into animals and men with the object of delivering his worshippers from certain special dangers or of otherwise benefiting mankind. The peculiar nature of these descents (Avatāra), and the vast difference between the Hindū and Christian idea of incarnation, have been already described (p. 63). Vishṇu, in fact, is believed to exist in an eternal body antecedent to his earthly incarnations. In some of the Purāṇas Vishṇu's ten incarnations are multiplied to twenty-two, twenty-four, and twenty-eight. The ten best known are :—

1. 'The Fish' (Matsya). Vishṇu is believed to have infused a portion of his essence into a fish—or rather perhaps to have taken the form of a fish—to save Manu [1], the primeval man and progenitor of the human race, from the universal deluge. This Manu, like Noah, conciliated the Deity's favour by his piety in an age of depravity. Hence he was warned of the approaching deluge, and was commanded to build a ship and go on board with the seven Ṛishis, or patriarchs, and the seeds of all existing things. Manu did so. The flood came, and Vishṇu took the form of a vast fish with a horn on its head, to which the ship's cable was fastened. The ship was thus

[1] That is, the Manu of the present period—not to be confounded with Brahmā's grandson, the supposed author of the well-known Law-book. The name Manu is from the root man, 'to think.'

supernaturally drawn along and secured to a high crag till the flood had passed.

2. 'The Tortoise' (Kūrma). Vishṇu infused a portion of his essence into the body of an immense tortoise to aid in producing or recovering certain valuable articles, some of which had been lost in the deluge. For this purpose he stationed himself at the bottom of the sea of milk—one of the seven concentric circular seas surrounding the seven concentric circular continents of the earth—that his back might serve as a pivot for the mountain Mandara, around which the gods and demons twisted the great serpent Vāsuki. They then stood opposite to each other, and using the snake as a rope and the mountain as a churning-rod, churned the milky ocean violently, till, one by one, fourteen inestimably valuable and typical objects emerged[1]. 1. The nectar conferring immortality (Amṛita). 2. The physician of the gods and holder of the nectar (Dhanvantari). 3. The goddess of good fortune and beauty, wife of Vishṇu (Lakshmī or Śrī). 4. The goddess of wine (Surā)[2]. 5. The moon (Ćandra). 6. The nymph Rambhā, celebrated as a kind of prototype of lovely women. 7. A fabulous high-eared horse (Uććaiḥ-śravas), the supposed prototype of the equine race. 8. The miraculous jewel Kaustubha, afterwards appropriated by Kṛishṇa. 9. A celestial tree (Pārijāta) yielding all desired objects. 10. The cow of plenty (Kāma-dhenu or Surabhi), granting all boons. 11. A mythical elephant (Airāvata)—afterwards appropriated, as a vehicle, by the god

[1] When I asked an Indian Pandit how it was possible to believe in what to us appears an extravagant fable, I was told that it was simply allegorical, and only intended to typify the truth that nothing valuable can be produced without extraordinary exertion.

[2] This is one proof out of many that the drinking of wine and spirits was once not only common in India, but also sanctioned by religion. In Vedic times wine appears to have been preserved in leathern bottles, see Ṛig-veda I. 191. 10 (Rājendralāla Mitra's Essays, VII). Unhappily the sect of Śāktas (see pp. 192, 193) may claim scriptural authority for their orgies, and appeal to the example of their gods Śiva and Bala-rāma.

Indra—prototype of the elephantine race. 12. A sacred conch-shell (Śaṅkha), afterwards the property of Vishṇu (or Kṛishṇa), and supposed, when blown as a horn, to insure victory over his enemies (see note, p. 103). 13. A miraculous unerring bow (Dhanus)[1]. 14. A deadly poison (Visha).

3. 'The Boar' (Varāha). Vishṇu infused a portion of his essence into the body of a huge boar—symbolical of strength —to deliver the world from the power of the demon Hiraṇyāksha, who had seized the earth and carried it down into the depths of the ocean. The divine boar dived down into the abyss, and after a contest of a thousand years, slew the monster and brought back the earth to the surface. Another variety of this legend (given in the Vana-parva of the Mahābhārata) represents the earth as submerged by a deluge—pressed down by an ever-increasing and superabundant population—till the boar descended into the waters, upheaved it on one of his tusks, rescued it from its watery grave, and made it fit to be reinhabited.

4. 'The Man-lion' (Nara-siṇha). Vishṇu assumed the shape of a creature, half man, half lion, to deliver the world from the tyrant Hiraṇya-kaśipu, who had obtained a boon from Brahmā that he should not be slain by either god or man or animal. Hence he became powerful enough to usurp the dominion of the three worlds. He even appropriated the sacrifices intended for the gods and necessary for their support. When his pious son Prahlāda praised Vishṇu, the tyrant tried to destroy the boy; but Vishṇu appeared suddenly out of the centre of a pillar in a shape neither god, nor man, nor animal, and tore Hiraṇya-kaśipu to pieces.

These first four incarnations are said to have taken place in the first and best (satya) of the four ages of the world.

---

[1] Two such bows are mentioned in Hindū mythology, one the property of Śiva and the other of Vishṇu. It was by bending Śiva's bow—which no other merely human suitor was able to do—that Rāma won Janaka's daughter Sītā (see Rāmāyaṇa I. 57).

5. 'The Dwarf' (Vāmana). In the second (Tretā) age of the world[1], Vishṇu infused a portion of his essence into the body of a dwarf to wrest from the tyrant-demon Bali (the analogue of Rāvaṇa and Kaṇsa, the two opponents of the Rāma and Kṛishṇa incarnations respectively) the dominion of the three worlds. The apparently contemptible little dwarf presented himself one day before the Tyrant, and solicited as much land as he could step in three paces. No sooner was his request granted than his form expanded, and he strode in two steps over heaven and earth, but out of compassion left the lower world in the demon's possession.

6. 'Rāma with the axe' (Paraśu-rāma). Vishṇu infused a portion of his essence into the axe-armed Rāma, son of the Brāhman Jamadagni and descendant of Bhṛigu, in the second age, to prevent the military caste (see p. 270) from tyrannizing over the Brāhmanical. Paraśu-rāma is said to have cleared the earth twenty-one times of the whole Kshatriyȧ race.

Vishṇu's essence seems to have deserted this hero before his death, as implied in the account of the great Rāma's victory over Paraśu-rāma, given in Rāmāyaṇa I. 75, 76.

7. In the seventh descent Vishṇu infused half of his essence into the great Rāma, commonly called Rāma-ćandra, 'the moon-like Rāma[2].' This celebrated hero was believed to have been manifested at the close of the second or Tretā age to destroy the tyrant-demon Rāvaṇa who reigned in Ceylon. India was never under one monarch, and in ancient times its kings were simply petty princes and chieftains, who ruled over districts of more or less extended area, and Oudh (Ayodhyā) was probably one of the more powerful principalities. As a historical fact Rāma was no doubt one of the four sons of a king of Oudh, named Daśa-ratha, of the so-called Solar race, and

---

[1] This would be the third age reckoning backwards, and is therefore called Tretā.

[2] In paintings he is represented with a peculiar greenish complexion. The word ćandra is often added to names to express beauty.

therefore a Kshatriya. The real date of Rāma's birth, in the absence of all trustworthy historical records, can only be a matter of the most uncertain conjecture. He is celebrated throughout India as the model son, brother, and husband, who was banished by his father to the southern forests. There his pattern wife Sītā was carried off by Rāvaṇa, the tyrant-king of Ceylon, and recovered by Rāma after making a bridge of rocks to the island. He was aided by Hanumān—a powerful chief of one of the aboriginal tribes, poetically compared to monkeys. This story forms the subject of one of the two great Indian Epics—the Rāmāyaṇa—and no story in the world has obtained a wider circulation and celebrity. Every man, woman, and child in India is familiar with Rāma's exploits for the recovery of his wife, insomuch that a common phrase for an ignorant person is 'one who does not know that Sītā was Rāma's wife.' From Kaśmīr to Cape Comorin the name of Rāma is on every one's lips. All sects revere it, and show their reverence by employing it on all occasions. For example, when friends meet it is common for them to salute each other by uttering Rāma's name twice. Then no name is more commonly given to children, and no name is more commonly invoked at funerals and in the hour of death. It is a link of union for all classes, castes, and creeds. And yet it is highly probable that, during his lifetime, Rāma received little more than the usual homage offered to every great, good, and brave man. His apotheosis did not take place till after his death, when he was converted into one of the most popular incarnations of Vishṇu; his servant Hanumān also receiving divine honours.

8. The eighth descent was as Kṛishṇa, 'the dark hero-god'; the most popular of all the later deities of India. This descent of Vishṇu at the end of the Dvāpara or third age of the world, as the eighth son of Vasu-deva and Devakī, of the Lunar race of Kshatriyas (called Yādavas), was for the destruction of the tyrant Kaṇsa, the representative of the principle of evil—the analogue of Rāvaṇa in the previous incarnation.

According to some, Kṛishṇa ought not to be reckoned as one of the ten Avatāras or descents of portions of Vishṇu's essence; for he was nothing short of Vishṇu's whole essence.

Those who hold this doctrine substitute Bala-rāma, 'the strong Rāma,' an elder son of Vasudeva and Devakī, and therefore elder brother of Kṛishṇa, as the eighth incarnation of Vishṇu. This Bala-rāma is more usually regarded as an incarnation of the great serpent Śesha. He is sometimes called the Indian Hercules, but without any very good reason. No special prodigies of strength are recorded of him, though he wields a formidable weapon in the shape of a plough-share, as well as a pestle-shaped club (musala). He is chiefly remarkable for his love of strong drink, in which, with his wife Revatī, he frequently indulges to the verge of inebriation (p. 108, note 2; p. 270). When he died a serpent came out of his mouth and entered the ocean (Mahā-bhārata XVI. 117).

The details of the later life of Kṛishṇa are interwoven with the later portions of the Mahā-bhārata, but do not belong to the plot, and might be omitted without impairing its unity. He is certainly not the hero of the great epic. He merely appears as a powerful chief[1] who takes the side of the real heroes—the Pāṇḍavas—and his claims to divine rank are often disputed during the progress of the story. Even since his apotheosis Kṛishṇa has always been peculiarly the god of the lower classes; for, although of the kingly caste, he was brought up among cowherds, cowherdesses, and the families of peasants. His juvenile biography is given with much minuteness of detail in the Bhāgavata-purāṇa, from which we learn that Vasudeva of the Lunar race of princes —who probably occupied the part of India now called

[1] Kṛishṇa was no doubt a powerful chief of the Yādava tribe, who were probably Rājputs occupying a district of Central India south of Muttra (Mathurā) and east of the Jumnā. The real date of his birth, though kept as a holy day and holiday throughout a great part of India, cannot be fixed with any more certainty than that of Rāma; but in all probability he lived in more recent times than Rāma.

Rājputāna[1]—had two wives, Rohiṇī and Devakī. The latter had eight sons, of whom the eighth was Kṛishṇa. It was predicted that one of them would kill Kaṇsa, chief of Mathurā (Muttra), and cousin (not brother) of Devakī. Kaṇsa therefore imprisoned Vasudeva and his wife, and slew their first six children. Bala-rāma, the seventh, was abstracted from Devakī's womb, transferred to that of Rohiṇī, and so saved. The eighth was Kṛishṇa, born with a black skin, and the mark Śrī-vatsa on his breast[2]. His father Vasudeva escaped from Mathurā with the child, and, favoured by the gods, found a certain herdsman named Nanda, whose wife had lately had a child. To his care he consigned the infant Kṛishṇa. Nanda settled first in Gokula or Vraja, and afterwards in Vṛindāvana, where Kṛishṇa and Bala-rāma grew up together, roaming in the woods, and joining in the sports of the herdsman's sons and daughters. While still a boy, Kṛishṇa gave proof of his divine origin by working a few startling miracles. Thus he destroyed the serpent Kāliya—probably a type of evil and malignity—by trampling and dancing on his head. He lifted up the mountain-range Govardhana on his finger to shelter the herdsmen's wives from the wrath of Indra. Yet in spite of these evidences of his supramundane powers, Kṛishṇa was addicted to very mundane practices. He constantly sported with the Gopīs or wives and daughters of the cowherds; on one occasion stealing their clothes when they were bathing and making them come to him naked. Eight were his favourites, especially Rādhā. In time Kṛishṇa migrated to Gujarāt, built Dvārikā on the coast, and thither transported the inhabitants of Mathurā after killing

---

[1] The two most powerful lines of Indian princes, those of Oudh and Rājputāna, were careful to trace back their pedigree to superhuman origins, the former claiming the Sun-god and some of the latter the Moon-god as their primeval progenitors. Udaipur and others claim the Sun.

[2] Compare note 1, p. 103. The day of his birth is called Janmāshṭamī. It is kept on the eighth day of the dark half of the month Bhādra in some places, and of Srāvaṇa in others.

Kaṇsa. He is fabled to have had countless wives and 108,000 sons, and one called Pradyumna by Rukmiṇī. It is said that while Kṛishṇa was lying on the ground in meditation, a hunter, named Jarā, mistook him for game and killed him by piercing the sole of his foot (Mahā-bhārata XVI. 126).

9. Buddha. The adoption of Buddha as one of the ten incarnations of Vishṇu appears to have been the result of a wise compromise with Buddhism; the Brāhmans asserting that Vishṇu, in his compassion for animals, descended as the sceptical Buddha that he might bring discredit on Vedic sacrifices (see Gīta-govinda I. 13); or, according to another theory, that wicked men might bring destruction on themselves by accepting Buddhism and denying the supremacy of the gods. The fact was that the Brāhmans appropriated Buddha much as some of them are willing to appropriate Christ, and make Him out to be an incarnation of Vishṇu.

10. Kalki or Kalkin. The descent of Vishṇu in this character has not yet taken place. Nor is he to appear till the close of the fourth or Kali age, when the world has become wholly depraved. He is then to be revealed in the sky, seated on a white horse, with a drawn sword blazing like a comet, for the final destruction of the wicked, for the redemption of the good, for the renovation of all creation and restoration of the age of purity (Satya-yuga). From the fact of the horse playing an important rôle in this incarnation, it is sometimes called Aśvāvatāra. Some of the degraded classes of India comfort themselves in their present depressed condition by expecting Kalki to appear as their future deliverer, and as the restorer of their social position. Indeed it is a remarkable fact that a belief in a coming Redeemer seems to exist in all religions, not excepting Buddhism and Muhammadanism [1].

Looking more closely at these ten special incarnations,

[1] In Buddhism there is the future Buddha; in Islām the Mahdī. The succession of Buddhas may be compared to that of Vishṇu's descents.

we may observe that the god Vishṇu, in conformity with his character of a Maintainer of life, discharges his functions in his first three descents by pervading the bodies of animals. It is remarkable, too, that these three zoomorphic incarnations all have reference to the tradition of a general deluge. In his fourth descent Vishṇu takes the form of a being half animal, half man. Possibly this combination may be intended as a kind of intermediate link, to connect the deity with higher forms. From half a man, the transition is to a complete man, but the divine essence on passing into human forms commences with a dwarf—the smallest type of humanity. Thence it advances to mighty heroes, sent into the world to deliver mankind from the oppression of tyrants—represented as evil demons—whose power increases with the increase of corruption and depravity during the four ages. The eighth is the highest and so to speak culminating incarnation; for in this Kṛishṇa is believed to be, not a part of Vishṇu's essence, but a complete manifestation of Vishṇu himself. The ninth may be passed over as a mere device on the part of the Brāhmans to account for the existence of Buddhism. The tenth and final incarnation, which remains to be revealed, will surpass all the others in importance. In it evil and wickedness are to be entirely rooted out, and the age of purity restored. Possibly this progressive series of what to us appear exceedingly absurd metamorphoses may be connected with the idea of continuous development; and just as the souls of men, regarded as emanations from the Deity, pass into stones, plants, and animals, or rise to the bodies of higher beings, so portions of the essence of Vishṇu pass through progressive stages of embodied existence for the maintenance of the order of the universe.

As we have already seen, Vishṇu's essence divided itself into male and female, but he had no children in his Non-avatāra condition, as Śiva had, unless Kāma-deva, god of love, said to have been his mind-born son (afterwards incarnate in

Pradyumna, p. 114), be so regarded. When the male essence descended as Rāma, the female was born as Rāma's faithful wife Sītā; and when the male descended as Kṛishṇa, the female became Krishṇa's favourite, Rādhā.

We now proceed to give a description of the more important Vaishṇava sects,—beginning with those founded by Rāmānuja, Madhva, Vallabha, and Ćaitanya; and first we may direct attention to some points in which they all agree.

In the first place, it must be understood that all the sects agree in maintaining, at least theoretically, that devotion to Vishṇu supersedes all distinctions of caste (compare p. 64). As a matter of fact, however, it is not to be supposed that a Vaishṇava Brāhman ever really gives up his claim to superiority over the inferior classes.

Next, it must be borne in mind that all the Vaishṇava sects are more or less opposed to the non-duality (advaita) doctrine of Śaṅkarāćārya (see p. 55) which makes the spirit of man identical with the one Spirit of the Universe (Ātmā, Brahmă).

Further, we may note that the bible of all worshippers of Vishṇu in his most popular manifestation—that of the hero Kṛishṇa, with his favourite wife Rādhā—consists of two chief books, the Bhāgavata-purāṇa and the Bhagavad-gītā portion of the Mahā-bhārata; and that those who pay exclusive adoration to the other popular manifestation—the hero Rāma—also acknowledge two special bibles in Vālmīki's Rāmāyaṇa, and in the Rāmāyaṇa of Tulsī-dās (Tulasī-dās). Undoubtedly these four books ought to find a place among the 'Sacred Books' of our Indian Empire.

Then it must not be forgotten that all agree in the worship of existing religious teachers who are supposed to be embodiments, not only of divine wisdom, but of the very essence of divinity. In the foremost rank must always come the original founder of each particular sect, whose title is Āćārya. He is regarded as little inferior to Kṛishṇa himself, and may even be identified with him. As to the living teacher of the day, if not elevated to equal rank, he is a greater reality. He receives homage as a visible and tangible mediator between earth and heaven. He is to the mass of Vaishṇavas even more than a mediator between themselves and God. He is the living embodiment of the entire essence of the deity (sarva-deva-mayaḥ). Nay, he is still more. He is the present God whose anger is to be deprecated and favour conciliated, because they make themselves instantly felt.

Next, all the Vaishṇava sects agree, as we have seen (p. 61), in requiring a special ceremony of initiation (dīkshā) into their communion, accompanied by the repetition of a formula of words, significant of reverence for either Kṛishṇa or Rāma, such as, 'homage to the divine son of Vasudeva' (Om namo Bhagavate Vāsudevāya), 'homage to the adorable Rāma' (Śrī Rāmāya namaḥ), or the eight-syllabled formula, 'adorable Kṛishṇa is my refuge' (Śrī Kṛishṇaḥ Śaraṇam mama).

Children are admitted to the religion of Vishṇu at the age of six or seven years or, by some sects, earlier. A rosary or necklace (kaṇṭhī) of one hundred and eight beads [1], usually made of tulsī wood (pp. 67, 333), is passed round their necks by the priest (Guru), and they are taught the use of one of the foregoing formulas, which is repeated by the Guru, very much as the sacred words 'In nomine Patris,' etc. are repeated by the priest at the Christian rite of baptism.

Then, at the age of twelve or thirteen, another rite is performed, corresponding to our confirmation. With the Vallabha sect it is called the 'Dedication rite' (Samarpaṇa); that is, the consecration of body, soul, and substance (tan, man, dhan) to Kṛishṇa; the formula taught being to the following effect:—'I here dedicate to the holy Kṛishṇa my bodily organs, my life, my inmost soul, and its faculties, with my wife, my house, my children, with all the wealth

---

[1] According to Dr. Rājendralāla Mitra this is merely to aid the possessor in repeating any one of Vishṇu's names 800 times, the eight additional beads marking each hundred recitation.

I may acquire here or hereafter, and my own self. O Kṛishṇa, I am thy servant.' These ceremonies may, in the case of all but Brāhmans, take the place of the initiatory rite of orthodox Brāhmanism, performed by investiture with the sacred thread (to be described at p. 360).

Another general characteristic of all the Vaishṇava sects is tenderness towards animal life. In this respect Vaishṇavism contrasts favourably with Śaivism. No life must be taken by a worshipper of Vishṇu, not even that of a minute insect, and not even for sacrifice to a deity (as, for example, to Kālī), and least of all must one's own life be taken. It is usual for missionaries to speak with horror of the self-immolation alleged to take place under the Car of Jagan-nāth (Kṛishṇa). But if deaths occur, they must be accidental, as self-destruction is wholly opposed both to the letter and spirit of the Vaishṇava religion.

Then, of course, the several sects agree in enjoining the use of the perpendicular coloured marks on the forehead, called Ūrdhva-puṇḍra (described at p. 67). They are supposed to denote the impress of either one or both the feet of Vishṇu, and to possess great efficacy in shielding from evil influences and delivering from sin. In addition to these frontal marks, most of the sects brand the breast and arms with the circular symbol and conch-shell of Vishṇu.

Finally, all the sects believe that every faithful and virtuous worshipper of Vishṇu is transported to his heaven, called Vaikuṇṭha, or to that of Kṛishṇa, called Go-loka (instead of to the temporary Svarga of orthodox Brāhmanism, p. 49), and that when once admitted there, he is saved from the misery of further transmigration. There, according to the merit of his works, he may enjoy any of the three conditions of bliss, Sālokya, Sāmīpya, or Sārūpya (p. 41; compare p. 234). Whether a Vaishṇava may be supposed capable of achieving the highest condition of beatification—conscious absorption into the divine essence (Sāyujya)—depends of course on the philosophical views of the sect to which he belongs (see p. 95). One point requires to be well understood in comparing the Vaishṇava religion with Christianity—namely, that God, with Hindū Theists, can only be propitiated by works. He may be called merciful, but He only shows mercy to those who deserve it by their actions, and if He accepts faith it is only because this also is a meritorious act. Every man's hope of heaven, and of salvation from the misery of successive births, depends on the amount of merit he has accumulated during life. We must also bear in mind that although Vishṇu is supposed to be a Creator as well as a Saviour, yet he is not so in the Christian sense of the word; for all the sects believe in some material cause (upādana)—some eternal substance out of which the Universe is evolved.

Let us now advert to the principal Vaishṇava sects.

Sect founded by Rāmānuja.

The Vaishṇava form of the Viśishṭādvaita philosophy[1] was taught by Rāmānuja, or as he is called Rāmānujāćārya, who was born about A.D. 1017 at Śrī Parambattūr, a town about twenty-six miles west of Madras. He is believed to have been an incarnation of Śesha or Ananta (pp. 105, 323) and is known to have taught at Kāñći-puram (Kāñjīvaram, p. 446), to have travelled twice through India, and to have finally settled at Śrī-raṅgam, near Trichinopoly. He is said to have lived for one hundred and twenty years and died in 1137. He is buried in the great temple of Śrīraṅga-nāth (see p. 447). The distinctive point of his teaching, according to the Sarva-darśana-saṅgraha (Cowell and Gough), was his assertion of the existence of a triad of principles (padārtha-tritayam),—namely, 1. the Supreme Spirit (Para-brahman or Īśvara);

[1] There is also a Śaiva form; see above, p. 89, and see 'a catechism of the Viśishṭādvaita' printed and published in 1887 by N. Bhāshyāćārya, Pandit of the Adyar Library, Madras, who is my authority for some statements here.

2. the separate spirits (Ćit) of men; and 3. non-spirit (A-ćit). Vishṇu is the Supreme Being; individual beings are separate spirits; the visible world (dṛiśyam) is non-spirit. All three have an eternal existence and are inseparable, yet Ćit and A-ćit are different from Īśvara and dependent on Īśvara.

This doctrine was clearly antagonistic to that of the great Brāhmanical revivalist Śaṅkara, who lived three or four centuries before (see p. 55). According to Śaṅkara, as we have seen, the separate existence of the spirit of man, as distinct from the one Universal Spirit, was only illusory. Illusion (Māyā), too—existing from all eternity—was the only material or substantial cause (upādāna-kāraṇa) of the external world, though this eternally creative Illusion was powerless to create the world except in union with the one Spirit. Rāmānuja, on the other hand, contended that the spirits of men are truly, essentially, and eternally different from the one Spirit, though dependent on it. With regard to the external world his views appear to have been less dualistic than those of the Sāṅkhya, and even than those of the Vedānta, for in these systems we have either Prakṛiti or Māyā, as the material cause (upādāna) out of which the Universe was created; whereas Rāmānuja held that God is himself both the creator (Kartā) of the world and the substantial cause or material out of which it is formed. He appears, too, to have asserted that the world and God stand towards each other in the relation of body and spirit, and that body and spirit are virtually one. It will be found, in fact, that the doctrine 'ex nihilo nihil fit' in some form or other holds good in every religious system which India has produced independently of Christian influences.

In support of the doctrine that the spirits of men are really and eternally distinct from the one Universal Spirit he appealed to a passage in the Muṇḍaka Upanishad, which rests on a well-known text of the Ṛig-veda (I. 164. 20): 'Two birds—the Supreme and Individual Spirits—like closely associated friends, occupy (cling to) the same tree (abide in the same body). One of them (the Individual Spirit) enjoys the sweet fruit of the fig (or consequences of acts), the other, without eating, looks on as a witness.'

As Rāmānuja admitted the dependence of the human spirit on the divine, so he urged the duty of striving after complete, though conscious, union with the Supreme—identified with Vishṇu:—'Cut is the knot of man's heart, solved are all his doubts, ended are all his works, when he has beheld the Supreme Being[1].'

A good account of Rāmānuja's opinions is given by the late Dr. K. M. Banerjea ('Dialogues on Hindū Philosophy'). His account is founded on Rāmānuja's own commentaries on the Vedānta-sūtras (called Śārīraka-bhāshya, Vedānta-dīpa, Vedānta-sāra, Vedārtha-saṅgraha), and his commentary on the Bhagavad-gītā, etc.

We may suppose Rāmānuja himself to be speaking as follows:—

'All the Śāstras tell us of two principles—knowledge and ignorance, virtue and vice, truth and falsehood. Thus we see pairs everywhere, and God and the human spirit are also so. How can they be one? I am sometimes happy, sometimes miserable. He, the Spirit, is always happy. Such is the discrimination. How then can two distinct substances be identical? He is an eternal Light, pure, without anything to obscure it—the one superintendent of the world. But the human spirit is not so. Thus a thunder-bolt falls on the tree of non-distinction. How canst thou, O slow of thought, say:—I am He, who has established this immense sphere of the universe in its fulness? Consider thine own capacities with a candid mind. By the mercy of the Most

---

[1] This is given in the Sarva-darśana-saṅgraha as one of Rāmānuja's precepts. Compare a similar precept at the end of the Kaṭhopanishad. I once heard an excellent sermon on this text delivered by Professor Bhāṇḍārkar in the house of prayer of the Prārthanā-Samāj in Bombay.

High a little understanding has been committed to thee. It is not for thee, therefore, O perverse one, to say, I am God. All the qualities of sovereignty and activity are eternally God's. He is therefore a Being endowed with qualities, but not under the influence of illusion (māyā). You cannot, if you believe Him to be all truth, allow the possibility of His projecting a deceptive spectacle. Nor can you, if you believe Him to be all knowledge and all power, assent to the theory of His creating anything under the influence of Avidyā, or Ignorance.'

Yet, notwithstanding the manifestly dualistic teaching of Rāmānuja in regard to the Supreme and human spirit, he is usually credited with a modified acquiescence in the non-duality doctrine of Śaṅkara. According to some, in fact, he merely propounded a new view of the Vedānta non-duality (a-dvaita) doctrine; that is, the non-duality of the one Spirit qualified by its connexion with Ćit and A-ćit, and therefore called 'qualified non-duality' (viśishṭādvaita). In the Sarva-darśana-saṅgraha it is stated that Rāmānuja's teaching, regarded from different points of view, was open to the charge of admitting the three ideas of unity, duality, and plurality. Unity, it alleges, was admitted by him in saying that all living beings and visible forms constitute the body of the one Supreme Spirit. Duality was admitted in saying that the Spirit of God and of man are distinct. Plurality was admitted in saying that the Spirit of God, the spirits of men which are multitudinous, and the visible world are distinct. (Cowell and Gough's translation, pp. 73, 75.) The first of these admissions is said to amount to qualified unity, and is therefore styled Viśishṭādvaita.

Rāmānuja also held that at great periodical dissolutions of the Universe human spirits and the world are re-absorbed into God, but without losing their separate identity and consciousness. In the Tattva-muktāvali (see Dr. Banerjea's 9th Dialogue) we find Rāmānuja represented as saying, 'Many flavours of trees there are in honey, and they are separable from it. How otherwise could it remove the three-fold disorders (p. 97)? Spirits, in like manner, are absorbed in the Lord at the dissolution of all things, but are not unified with Him, for they are again separated at the creation. As there is a difference between rivers and the sea, between sweet and salt waters, so is there a difference between God and human spirits, because of their characteristic distinctions. Rivers, when joined with the sea, are not altogether unified with it, though they appear inseparable. There is a real difference between salt and sweet waters. Even milk, when mixed with milk, and water with water, do not obtain unification, merely because they are supposed to be unified[1].'

With regard to the various manifestations of the Supreme Being and the duty of worshipping Him, Rāmānuja held that God is present on earth in five ways: 1. in forms and images (mūrti); 2. in partial divine embodiments (as Rāma); 3. in full divine embodiments (as Kṛishṇa); 4. in the subtle (sūkshma) all-pervading spirit; 5. in the internal spirit controlling the human soul (antaryāmin). The worshipper may be incapable of rising at once to any high act of adoration; in which case he must begin by adoring Vishṇu as manifested in the first of these five ways—that is to say, in images and idols. He may afterwards ascend by regular steps through the other four modes of worship till he reaches the fifth. If he ever succeeds in attaining to this highest stage and so becomes capable of worshipping the internal Spirit enshrined in his own heart, then Vishṇu identified with that Spirit raises him to his own heaven Vaikuṇṭha, whence there is no return to human existence, and where he enjoys the exquisite bliss of conscious assimilation to the God whom he has adored on earth, and even

---

[1] The twenty-ninth Sūtra of Śāṇḍilya (translated by Prof. E. B. Cowell) mentions a sage Kāśyapa who appears to have held doctrines coinciding to a certain extent with those of Rāmānuja.

of conscious absorption into that God[1]. Possibly this theory of conscious absorption may constitute another reason for attributing the doctrine called 'qualified non-duality' (viśishṭādvaita) to Rāmānuja. Nevertheless the impression left on the mind by the account of his system in the Sarva-darśana-saṅgraha is that Rāmānuja was even more opposed to the doctrine of unity in regard to the divine and human spirits than his brother sectarian Madhva. This impression is borne out by the fact that his system is treated of before that of Madhva, and so placed lower down in that ascending scale which is supposed to culminate in the orthodox Advaita. Probably the real reason for its being so placed is that he asserts three principles—the Spirit of God, the spirit of man, and the visible world—as his first axiom; whereas Madhva only asserts two (see p. 131).

Rāmānuja had numerous disciples, and among them seventy-four special teachers called Āćārya-purushas appointed by himself. These were all married men, and the children of some of them succeeded to the Āćāryaship. One of the most celebrated of his followers was Vyāsāćārya, who wrote a commentary on Rāmānuja's works. Of course many of these followers modified his teaching in the usual manner, introducing doctrines and practices which the founder of the sect had not enjoined and would not have sanctioned. Then, in the 13th century or about six hundred years ago, another of his followers—a learned Brāhman of Kāñjīvaram, named Vedāntāćārya—put himself forward as a reformer, giving out that he was commissioned by the god Vishṇu himself to purify the faith; that is, to sweep away incrustations, and restore the doctrines of the original founder. These doctrines, he affirmed, had been more carefully preserved by the Northern Brāhmans than by the Southern. Hence arose irreconcilable differences of opinion, which resulted in two

[1] See Sarva-darśana-saṅgraha (Prof. A. E. Gough's translation of the Rāmānuja system), p. 79.

great antagonistic parties of Rāmānujas—one called the northern school, Vada-galai (for Vada-kalai, Sanskṛit kalā), the other the southern school, Ten-galai (for Ten-kalai[1]). They are far more opposed to each other than both parties are to Śaivas. The northern school accept the Sanskṛit Veda. The southern (Ten-galai) have compiled a Veda of their own, called 'the four thousand verses' (Nālāyira), written in Tamil, and held to be older than the Sanskṛit Veda, but really based on its Upanishad portion. According to Pandit N. Bhāshyāćārya this work is called Divya-prabandha. In all their worship they repeat selections from these Tamil verses.

An important difference of doctrine, caused by different views of the nature of the human spirit's dependence on Vishṇu, separates the two parties. The view taken by the Vada-galais corresponds, in a manner, to the Arminian doctrine of 'free-will.' The human spirit, say they, lays hold of the Supreme Being by its own will, act, and effort, just as the young monkey clings to its mother. This is called the monkey-theory (markaṭa-nyāya). The view of the Ten-galais is a counterpart of that of the Calvinists. It is technically styled 'the cat-hold theory' (mārjāra-nyāya). The human spirit, they argue, remains passive and helpless until acted on by the Supreme Spirit, just as the kitten remains passive and helpless until seized and transported, nolens volens, from place to place by the mother-cat.

Again, the Ten-galais maintain that the Śakti, or wife of Vishṇu, is a created and finite being, though divine, and that she acts as a mediator or minister (purusha-kāra), not as an equal channel of salvation; whereas the Vada-galais regard her as, like her consort, infinite, and uncreated, and equally to be worshipped as a channel or means (upāya) by

[1] The Sātāni branch of the Rāmānujas is not a separate school. It consists of a body of Śūdras who are opposed to Brāhmanical usages. It represents, in fact, the low-caste or out-caste converts to Vaishṇavism. It is among the Rāmānuja Vaishṇavas what the Liṅgāit sect is among Śaivas (see p. 88).

which salvation may be attained. I heard it remarked by a learned Ten-galai Brāhman that no educated men believe Vishṇu to be really married. 'What most Ten-galais hold,' he said, 'is that Lakshmī is an ideal personification of the deity's more feminine attributes, such as those of mercy, love, and compassion; while some philosophers contend that the Hindū gods are only represented with wives to typify the mystical union of the two eternal principles—spirit and matter—for the production of the Universe. The central red mark, therefore, is, in the one case, the mere expression of trust in God's mercy; in the other, of belief in the great mystery of creation and re-creation.'

No Arminians and Calvinists have ever fought more rancorously over their attempts to solve insoluble difficulties than have Vada-galais and Ten-galais over their struggles to secure the ascendency of their own theological opinions. The fight has ended in a drawn battle. The two opposite parties, exhausted with their profitless logomachy and useless strivings after an impossible unity of opinion, have agreed to differ in abstruse points of doctrine.

Their disputes are now chiefly confined to externals of the most trivial kind. It is the old story repeated. The Sibboleths are intolerant of the Shibboleths. The Vada-galais contend that their frontal mark (puṇḍra, pp. 66, 118, 400) ought to represent the impress of the right foot of Vishṇu (the supposed source of the Ganges), while the Ten-galais maintain that equal reverence is due to both the god's feet. It is certainly convenient from a social point of view that a man's religious idiosyncrasies should be stamped upon his forehead. Accordingly, the two religious parties are most particular about their frontal emblems, the Vada-galais making a simple white line between the eyes (curved like the letter U) to represent the sole of one foot, and adding a central red mark—emblematical of Lakshmī; while the Ten-galais employ a more complicated device symbolical of both feet, which are supposed to rest on a lotus throne, denoted by a white line drawn half down the nose. The complete Ten-galai symbol has the appearance of a trident, the two outer prongs (painted with white earth) standing for Vishṇu's two feet, the middle (painted red or yellow) for his consort, Lakshmī, and the handle (or white line down the nose) representing the lotus throne. The worst quarrels between the two divisions of the sect arise from disputes as to which mark is to be impressed on the images worshipped in the Vaishṇava temples, to which all Rāmānujas resort indifferently. Tedious and expensive law-suits are often the result.

Both sects, however, agree in stamping or branding the same emblems of Vishṇu—the discus, the conch-shell, the club, and the lotus—but more generally the former two only, on their breasts, shoulders, and arms (p. 118).

Another point which distinguishes the Ten-galais is that they prohibit their widows from shaving their heads. Every married woman in India rejoices in long, fine hair, which she is careful to preserve intact. In the case of men, regular shaving is not only a universal custom, it is a religious duty. But for women to be deprived of any portion of their hair is a shame. A shorn female head is throughout India the chief mark of widowhood. The general rule is that every widow should submit her growing locks periodically to the family barber, though child-widows among the Marāṭhas are exempt. I believe also that in Northern India widows are not obliged to shave. It is certain that the Ten-galai widows are exempted from all obligation to dishonour their heads in this manner[1] (compare 1 Cor. xi. 5).

Again, a peculiarity common to both Rāmānuja sects is the strict privacy with which they eat and even prepare their

---

[1] The Ten-galais quote a verse of Vṛiddha-Manu, which declares that if any woman, whether unmarried or widowed, shave her head, she will be condemned to dwell in the hell called Raurava for one thousand times ten million ages.

meals. No Indians like to be looked at while eating. They are firm believers in the evil influence of the human eye (dṛishṭi-dosha).

Cooking is an affair of equal secrecy. We Europeans cannot understand the extent to which culinary operations may be associated with religion. The kitchen in every Indian household is a kind of sanctuary or holy ground—almost as hallowed as the room dedicated to the family gods. No unprivileged person must dare to intrude within this sacred enclosure. The mere glance of a man of inferior caste makes the greatest delicacies uneatable, and if such a glance happens to fall on the family supplies during the cooking operations, when the ceremonial purity of the water used[1] is a matter of almost life and death to every member of the household, the whole repast has to be thrown away as if poisoned. The family is for that day dinnerless. Food thus contaminated would, if eaten, communicate a taint to the souls as well as bodies of the eaters—a taint which could only be removed by long and painful expiation. In travelling over every part of India, and diligently striving to note the habits of the natives in every circumstance of their daily life, I never once saw a single Hindū, except of the lowest caste, either preparing or eating cooked food of any kind. The Rāmānujas carry these ideas to an extravagant extreme. They carefully lock the doors of their kitchens and protect their culinary and prandial operations from the gaze of even high-caste Brāhmans of tribes and sects different from their own.

Each of the present chiefs (āćāryas) of the two Rāmānuja sects lays claim to be the true descendant of the founder himself in regular, unbroken succession. The Vada-

---

[1] Caste-rules are an essential part of the Hindū religion. It is the fashion for enlightened men who still keep up caste to excuse themselves on the plea that many of the rules originated in social convenience, or the need of sanitary precautions. Nothing is so necessary for the preservation of health in India as attention to the purity of water.

galai successor (named Ahobala) lives at a monastery (Maṭha) in the Kurnool district. The Ten-galai successor (named Vānamāmala) lives in the Tinnevelly district. Though they preside over monasteries, they are both married; whereas the successors of the orthodox Brāhman Śaṅkara (who live at Śṛiṅgeri in Mysore) are celibates. The two Rāmānuja Āćāryas, however, are strict Ayengār Brāhmans, and will probably in their old age become Sannyāsīs, according to the teaching of the ancient lawgiver Manu, who ordained that the discharge of household duties is incompatible with the attainment of greater nearness to the Supreme Being, and that therefore every twice-born man as he advances in life is bound to give up all family ties (p. 362, Manu VI. 1).

Each Āćārya makes a periodical visitation of his diocese, and holds a kind of confirmation in every large town. That is to say, every child or young person who has been initiated is brought before him to be branded or stamped as a true follower of Vishṇu. Boys may be branded at the age of seven or upwards; girls only after their marriage. A sacred fire is kindled, two golden instruments are heated, and the symbols of the wheel-shaped discus and conch-shell of Vishṇu are impressed on the breast, arms, or other parts of the body. I was informed by an intelligent Brāhman at Madurā that the Āćārya, or chief of the sect from the Ahobala Maṭha, visits that town once every eight or ten years, when as many young persons as possible take the opportunity of being branded. Even those who have been invested with the Brāhmanical thread require the addition of the Vaishṇava brand. The Āćārya is put to no expense. He is the guest of some well-to-do Brāhman in the town, and reaps a rich harvest of fees.

We pass on to the second great Vaishṇava sect—that founded by Madhva—whose adherents are called Mādhvas. They are chiefly found in Southern India.

Sect founded by Madhva.

The next most important of the Vaishṇava sects is that of the Mādhvas. They were founded by a Kanarese Brāhman named Madhva—otherwise called Ānanda-tīrtha—said to have been born about the year 1200 of our era, at a sacred place called Udipi, in South Kanara (sixty miles north of Mangalore), and to have been educated in a convent at Anantešvar. His doctrine is commonly called Duality (Dvaita), and is well known for the intensity of its opposition to the Non-duality (Advaita) doctrine of the great Vedāntist Šaṅkarāćārya. The school he founded is sometimes called Pūrṇa-prajña—a name also applied to its founder.

In fact the teaching of Madhva is by some thought to owe no little of its distinctive character to the influence of Christianity, which had made itself felt in the South of India before the thirteenth century. No evidence whatever is forthcoming on this subject. Nor has his system really much common ground with Christianity. Nor would it be easy to give a thoroughly exhaustive account of his doctrines[1]. Still their general drift may be correctly gathered from the Sarva-daršana-saṅgraha, though the points in which he differs from Rāmānuja are rather obscurely stated in that work.

Of course Madhva, like Rāmānuja, taught that there was only one God, whose principal name was Vishṇu (or Hari), and who was the one eternal Supreme Being, all other gods being subject to the law of universal periodical dissolution.

'Brahmā, Šiva, and the greatest of the gods decay with the decay of their bodies; greater than these is the undecaying Hari.' (Professor Gough's translation.)

Perhaps the chief distinctive feature of Madhva's teaching was that his first axiom asserted categorically that there

[1] I repeatedly questioned some of Madhva's more intelligent followers whom I met in the South of India as to the exact distinction between his views and those of Rāmānuja, but no one was able to give me any very satisfactory reply.

are two separate eternal principles (instead of three, as asserted by Rāmānuja, p. 119), and that these two are related as independent and dependent, as master and servant, as king and subject. The one is the independent principle, God (identified with Vishṇu), the other is the dependent principle consisting of the human spirit, or rather spirits; for these are innumerable as in the Nyāya and Sāṅkhya.

It was Madhva's unqualified denial of the unity of the Supreme and human spirits which made him the opponent of the followers of Śaṅkara.

The Vedāntists maintained, as we have seen, that the difference between one thing and another and between one spirit and another was wholly illusory and unreal. Madhva affirmed that a real and inextinguishable duality was to be proved both by perception and by inference [1].

'The Supreme Lord,' said Madhva, 'differs from the individual spirit because the Lord is the object of its obedience. A subject who obeys a king differs from that king. In their eager desire to be one with the Supreme Being, the followers of Śaṅkara lay claim to the glory of his excellence. This is a mere mirage. A man with his tongue cut off might as well attempt to enjoy a large plantain.'

Again, according to Madhva the Vedic text, 'This is Self—That art thou,' points to similarity, not identity.

'Like a bird and the string; like the juices of various trees; like rivers and the sea; like fresh and salt water; like a robber and the robbed; like a man and his energy; so are the human spirit and the Lord diverse and for ever different.'

Nor have these two principles a qualified unity comparable to the union of spirit and body, as affirmed by Rāmānuja. They are absolutely distinct. With regard to the visible world, he taught that its elements existed eternally in the Supreme Being, and were only created by Him in the sense of being shaped, ordered, and arranged by His power and will.

[1] See pp. 88, 90 of Cowell and Gough's 'Sarva-darśana-saṅgraha.'

Practically he seems to have asserted three principles quite as plainly as Rāmānuja did; for his doctrine was that, when once the world had emanated from the Supreme essence, it remained a distinct entity to all eternity. 'There is a difference,' he affirmed, 'between human souls and God, and a difference between insentient matter (jaḍa) and God.' Probably, like Bishop Berkeley, he saw the difficulty of proving the existence of matter externally to the mind, and therefore contented himself with asserting two distinct principles, the Supreme and the human spirit. In short, his dogma was that as the visible world emanated from God it was not distinguishable, as an original principle, from God, and was not even as distinct as the human spirit and body, though, when once produced, it was as distinct from its Producer as an effect from its cause [1].

According to Madhva the Supreme Being is to be honoured in three ways—by naming, by worship, and by branding.

The act of naming (nāma-karaṇa) is performed by giving a child one of the thousand names of Vishṇu—such as Keśava—as a memorial of his dedication to the service of the god.

The act of worship is threefold:—(1) with the voice—by veracity, right conversation, kind words, and repetition of the Veda; (2) with the body—by giving alms to the poor, by defending and protecting them; (3) with the heart—by mercy, love, and faith. This is a mere repetition of the old triple division of duties, according to thought, word, and deed.

With regard to the rite of branding (called aṅkana), the Mādhva sect, like the Rāmānujas and other Vaishṇavas, lay great stress on marking the body indelibly with the circular discus and shell of Vishṇu. They firmly believe that it is the duty of Vaishṇavas to carry throughout life a memorial of their god on their persons, and that such a lasting outward and visible sign of his presence helps them to obtain salvation through him.

[1] This was very much the doctrine of the Kabbalists, who equally held that nothing could be produced from nothing. It resembles also the theory of the Stoics.

'On his right arm let the Brāhman wear the discus, on his left the conch-shell!'

When I was at Tanjore I found that one of the successors of Madhva had recently arrived on his branding-visitation. He was engaged throughout the entire day in stamping his disciples and receiving fees from all according to their means.

Texts are recited at the time of branding, and in Sāyaṇa-Mādhava's time the following prayer was said:—'O Discus (Sudarśana), brightly blazing, effulgent as ten million suns, show unto me, blind with ignorance, the everlasting way of Vishṇu. Thou, O Conch-shell, aforetime sprangest from the sea, held in the hand of Vishṇu, adored by all the gods, to thee be adoration.' (Sarva-darśana-saṅgraha, Cowell and Gough, p. 92.)

I learnt, too, that no less than eight Āćāryas, established in eight different monasteries (Maṭhs) with temples attached, claim to be successors of Madhva. There are also two principal religious parties among the Mādhvas, who, no doubt, quarrel over their Shibboleths like the two divisions of Rāmānujas. At Udipi itself (p. 130), there are eight Maṭhs, and the place is much frequented by pilgrims from Mysore.

The frontal mark of all the Mādhvas is the same, consisting of two thin vertical lines meeting below in a curve, like that of the Vada-galai Rāmānujas. But a central black line is generally made with charcoal taken from incense burnt before the idols of Vishṇu.

So much for the doctrines of two sects which have some common ground with Christianity and are therefore worthy of especial attention. Perhaps Madhva's system is the more interesting in its relation to European thought, but his Theism, like that of Rāmānuja and of every other Hindū Theistic system, differed widely in many important points from the Theism of Christianity, especially in making God the substantial as well as efficient cause of the visible world.

Sect founded by Vallabha.

The third great Vaishṇava sect is that founded by Vallabha, or, as he is called by his followers, Vallabhāćārya (Mahā-prabhu), said to have been born in the forest of Ćampāraṇya about A.D. 1479. He was believed to have been an embodiment of a portion of Kṛishṇa's essence, and various stories are fabled about him. For instance, his intelligence is alleged to have been so great that when he began learning at seven years of age, he mastered the four Vedas, the six systems of Philosophy, and the eighteen Purāṇas in four months.

After precocity so prodigious he was able at the age of twelve to formulate a new view of the Vaishṇava creed, but one which was to a great extent derived from a previous teacher named Vishṇu-svāmī. Soon he commenced travelling to propagate his doctrines. When he reached the court of Kṛishṇa-deva, King of Vijaya-nagar, he was invited to engage in a disputation with a number of Smārta Brāhmans. In this he succeeded so well that he was elected chief Āćārya of the Vaishṇavas. He then travelled for nine years through different parts of India, and finally settled in Benares, where he is said to have composed seventeen works, among which was a commentary on the Bhāgavata-purāṇa. This last, especially its tenth book—descriptive of the early life of Kṛishṇa—is the authoritative source of the doctrines of the sect. Vallabhāćārya's view of the Vaishṇava creed has been called Pushṭi-mārga, the way of eating, drinking, and enjoying oneself. But in real fact he simply dissented from the doctrine that asceticism was a mode of commending man to God. He maintained that worship of the Deity ought not to be accompanied with fasting and self-mortification, because every individual soul was a portion of the Supreme Soul, and every man ought therefore to reverence, and even foster, his own body which contained it.

He held, in short, that individual human spirits were like

sparks from the Supreme Spirit, and, though separate, identical in essence with it. His doctrine is called pure non-duality (Śuddhādvaita), to distinguish it from the qualified non-duality (Viśishṭādvaita) of Rāmānuja; but, when closely examined, it seems to be a nominal distinction without much real difference. He is known to have died at Benares; but, according to his disciples, was transported to heaven while performing his ablutions in the Ganges.

His followers are numerous in Bombay, Gujarāt, and Central India, particularly among the merchants and traders called Baniyas and Bhāṭiyas. He left behind him eighty-four principal disciples, who disseminated his doctrines in various directions. But the real successor to his Gādī (gaddī) or chair was his second son, Viṭṭhal-nāth, sometimes called Gosāinjī from his having settled at Gokul, Kṛishṇa's abode near Muttra. This Viṭṭhal-nāth had seven sons, each of whom established a Gādī in different districts, especially in Bombay, Kutch, Kāṭhiāwār, and Mālwa. The influence of Vallabhāćārya's successors became so great that they received the title Mahārāja, 'great king,' the name Gosāin (for Go-svāmin—lord of cows—an epithet of Kṛishṇa) being sometimes added.

As was naturally to be expected, his followers exaggerated his teaching, especially in regard to his non-ascetical view of religion. They have been called 'the Epicureans of India.' Their spiritual leaders, the Mahārājas, dress in the costliest raiment, feed on the daintiest viands, and abandon themselves to every form of sensuality and luxury.

The children of the Vallabhāćāryans are admitted to membership at the age of three or four years, or, in some parts of India, later. A rosary, or necklace (kaṇṭhī) of one hundred and eight beads[1], made of tulsī wood, is passed round their necks by the Mahārāja, and they are taught the use of the

[1] These help in the recitation of the chief names of Kṛishṇa as the Supreme Being (see p. 105), or of similar epithets applied to the successors of Vallabha; but see note to p. 117.

eight-syllabled prayer, 'The adorable Kṛishṇa is my soul's refuge' (Śrī-Kṛishṇaḥ śaraṇam mama).

The god worshipped is the Kṛishṇa form of Vishṇu, as he appeared in his boyhood, when, as a mere child, he gave himself up to childish mirth, and condescended to sport with the Gopīs or cowherdesses of Mathurā (Muttra).

I was once present at a kind of revivalist camp-meeting near Allahābād, where a celebrated Hindū preacher addressed a large assembly of people and magnified this condescension as a proof of Kṛishṇa's superiority to all other gods.

Then, again, images used in the temples of the sect represent Kṛishṇa in the boyish period of his life (in the form called Bāla-Kṛishṇa), supposed to extend to his twelfth year. According to the higher Vaishṇava creed, Kṛishṇa's love for the Gopīs—themselves the wives of the cowherds—and the love of the Gopīs for Kṛishṇa are to be explained allegorically, and symbolize the longing of the human soul for union with the Supreme (Brahma-sambandha). When I have asked strict Vaishṇavas for an explanation of Kṛishṇa's alleged adulteries, I have always been told that his attachment to the Gopīs was purely spiritual, and that, in fact, he was only a child at the time of his association with them.

Yet it is certain that the followers of Vallabha interpreted that attachment in a gross and material sense. Hence their devotion to Kṛishṇa has degenerated into the most corrupt practices, and their whole system has become rotten to the core. It is even said that the male members of the sect sometimes seek to win the favour of their god by wearing long hair and assimilating themselves to females; and even their spiritual chiefs, the Mahārājas, the successors of Vallabhāćārya, sometimes simulate the appearance of women (that is, of Gopīs) when they lead the worship of their followers.

But the real blot, or rather foul stain, which defaces and defiles the system, remains to be described. These Mahārājas have come to be regarded as representatives of Kṛishṇa upon earth, or even as actual incarnations or impersonations of the god. So that in the temples where the Mahārājas do homage to the idols, men and women do homage to the Mahārājas, prostrating themselves at their feet, offering them incense, fruits and flowers, and waving lights before them, as the Mahārājas themselves do before the images of the gods. One mode of worshipping the boyish Kṛishṇa is by swinging his images in swings. Hence, in every district presided over by a Mahārāja, the women are accustomed to worship not Kṛishṇa but the Mahārāja by swinging him in pendent seats. The Pān-supārī ejected from his mouth, the leavings of his food, and the very dust on which he has walked, are eagerly devoured by his devotees, while they also drink the water rinsed from his garments, and that used in the washing of his feet, which they call Ćaraṇāmṛita, 'feet nectar.' Others, again, worship his wooden shoes, or prostrate themselves before his seat (gādī) and his painted portraits. Nay, infinitely worse than all this: it is believed that the best mode of propitiating the god Kṛishṇa in heaven is by ministering to the sensual appetites of his successors and vicars upon earth. Body, soul, and property (in popular language tan, man, dhan) are to be wholly made over to them in a peculiar rite called Self-devotion (samarpaṇa, see p. 117), and women are taught to believe that highest bliss will be secured to themselves and their families by the caresses of Kṛishṇa's representatives.

The profligacy of the Mahārājas was exposed in the celebrated trial of the Mahārāja libel case, which came before the Supreme Court of Bombay on the 26th of January, 1862. The evidence given, and the judgment of the judges, have acted as some check on the licentious practices of the sect, but it is still held to represent the worst and most corrupt phase of the Vaishṇava religion.

The reformation of the Vallabhāćārya system effected by Svāmi-Nārāyaṇa will be afterwards described (see p. 148).

Sect founded by Ćaitanya.

The fourth principal sect of Vaishṇavas is found in Bengal. They are the followers of a celebrated teacher named Ćaitanya, and their precepts and practices have a close community with those of the Vallabhāćāryans already described. The biography of Ćaitanya, as given by native writers, is, as usual, chiefly legendary. Only scattered elements of truth are discoverable amidst a confused farrago of facts, fiction, and romance. What respect, indeed, for chronological or historical accuracy can be expected in a people who are firmly convinced that their own existence and that of every one else is an illusion?

I believe it is pretty certain that Ćaitanya was born at Nadīya (=Navadvīpa) in Bengal in the year 1485 of our era, two years after Luther in Europe. His father was an orthodox Brāhman named Jagan-nāth Miśra. His mother was the daughter of Nīlāmbar Ćakravartī. Since Ćaitanya is held to have been an incarnation of Kṛishṇa, various prodigies are described as having marked his first appearance in the world. He was thirteen months in the womb. Then soon after his birth, at the end of an eclipse, a number of holy men (among whom was his future disciple Advaita) arrived at the house of his parents to do homage to the new-born child, and to present him with offerings of rice, fruits, gold and silver. In his childhood he resembled the young Kṛishṇa in condescending to boyish sports (līlā). Yet his intellect was so acute that he rapidly acquired a complete knowledge of Sanskṛit grammar and literature. His favourite subject of study was the Vaishṇava bible, consisting of the Bhāgavata-purāṇa, and Bhagavad-gītā.

Yet Ćaitanya, notwithstanding his devotion to religious study, did not shrink from what every Hindū believes to be a sacred obligation—the duty of marrying a wife, and becoming a householder (gṛihastha). He even married again when his first wife died from a snake-bite. At the age of twenty-five (A. D. 1509) he resolved to abandon all worldly connexions, and gave himself up to a religious life. Accordingly, like Vallabhāćārya and at about the same period, he commenced a series of pilgrimages. His travels occupied six years, and he is known to have visited some of the most celebrated shrines of India, especially those of Benares, Gayā, Mathurā, Śrīraṅgam, and ultimately the temple of Jagan-nāth at Purī in Orissa.

Having thus prepared himself for his mission, he addressed himself to the real work of preaching and propagating his own view of the Vaishṇava creed. It is noteworthy that just about the time that Luther was agitating the minds of men in Europe, Ćaitanya was stirring the hearts of the people of Bengal. After making many converts he seems to have appointed his two most eminent followers, Advaita and Nityānanda, to preside over his disciples in that part of India. He himself settled for twelve years at Kaṭak in Orissa. There he lived for the rest of his life in close proximity to the great temple of Jagan-nāth, and contributed to the reputation of the shrine by his presence at the annual festivals.

His success as a preacher was remarkable. Even his enemies were attracted by the persuasiveness of his manner and the magnetic power of his eloquence. The lower classes flocked to him by thousands. Nor was their admiration of him surprising. The first principle he inculcated was that all the faithful worshippers of Kṛishṇa (=Vishṇu) were to be treated as equals. Caste was to be subordinated to faith in Kṛishṇa[1]. 'The mercy of God,' said Ćaitanya, 'regards neither tribe nor family.'

[1] This was his theory, but among his numerous followers of the present day the doctrine of equality does not overcome caste-feeling and caste-observances except during religious services. The food presented to the idol of Jagan-nāth is distributed to all castes alike, and eaten by all indiscriminately at the annual festival.

By thus proclaiming social equality he secured popularity. In this respect he wisely imitated the method of Buddhists and Śāktas. The doctrine of the latter, who abounded everywhere in Bengal, was that magical powers might be acquired by the worship of the female principle or generative energy (śakti) in nature, personified as Śiva's wife. They believed that the male principle, personified as the male god Śiva, the great Reproducer, was helpless in the work of Reproduction without the energizing action of the female principle. Hence the union of the sexes was thought by some to be typical of a great cosmical mystery. This will be more fully explained in the chapter on Śāktism (p. 180).

Ćaitanya professed to oppose these Śākta doctrines, both as tending to licentious practices, and as ignoring the supremacy of the god Vishṇu over Śiva. Yet his system, like that of Vallabha, had a tendency in the same direction. He taught that the devotion of the human soul to Vishṇu was to be symbolized under the figure of human love. '"Thou art dear to my heart, thou art part of my soul," said a young man to his loved one; "I love thee, but why, I know not." So ought the worshipper to love Kṛishṇa, and worship him for his sake only. Let him offer all to God, and expect no remuneration. He who asks for a return acts like a trader.' Such are the words of a modern exponent of this Vaishṇava system.

I have already pointed out that the idea of devotion (bhakti) as a means of salvation, which was formally taught by the authors of the Bhagavad-gītā, Bhāgavata-purāṇa and Śāṇḍilya-sūtra, was scarcely known in early times. The leading doctrine of the Vedic hymns and Brāhmaṇas is that works (karma), especially as represented by the performance of sacrifices (yajña), constitute the shortest pathway to beatitude, while the Upanishads insist mainly on abstract meditation and divine knowledge (jñāna) as the true method. Ćaitanya affirmed that intense devotion—displayed by complete union of the spirit with Kṛishṇa—was the only real salvation. Devotion, in fact, superseded all other duties. 'Whatever is accomplished by works, by penance, by divine knowledge, by suppression of the passions, by abstract meditation, by charity, by virtue, by other excellences,—all this is effected by devotion to me. Paradise, Heaven, beatitude, union with the Supreme Spirit,—every wish of the heart is obtainable by devotion to me.' Such are Kṛishṇa's own words, according to the belief of Ćaitanya and other Vaishṇava teachers. (Bhāgavata-purāṇa XI.)

But the devotional feelings of Kṛishṇa's votaries are supposed to be susceptible of five phases, or rather, perhaps, to be exhibited in five different ways, which are thus enumerated:—1. Calm contemplation of the godhead (śānti); 2. Active servitude (dāsya); 3. A feeling of personal friendship (sakhya); 4. A feeling of filial attachment like that of a child for its parent (vātsalya); 5. A feeling of tender affection like that of a girl for her lover (mādhurya).

The last of these is held to be the highest feeling. Indeed, Ćaitanya taught that the great aim of every worshipper of Kṛishṇa ought to be to lose all individuality and self-consciousness in ecstatic union with his god; and it is on this account that he is believed to have held the dualistic non-duality doctrine (dvaitādvaita of Nimbāditya, see p. 147). To bring about a condition of intense religious fervour various practices were enjoined—for example, incessant repetition of the deity's name (nāma-kīrtana), singing (saṅkīrtana), music, dancing, or movements of the body allied to dancing, such as were also practised by certain Śaiva devotees[1]. Ćaitanya was himself

[1] These correspond to the Zikr and religious dancing of the Muhammadan dervishes. For even cold Islām has its devotees who aim at religious ecstasy, resorting to expedients very similar to those of the Ćaitanyas. I have been twice present at the weekly services of the Cairo dervishes. One sect repeat the name of God with violent ejaculations and contortions of the body, while another fraternity whirl themselves round till they swoon away in the intensity of their fervour.

in the constant habit of swooning away in paroxysms of ecstatic emotion, which at last affected his reason. His biographers assert that in one of these fits he was translated directly to Vishṇu's heaven (Vaikuṇṭha). According to some accounts he ended his life by walking into the sea near Purī in Orissa, fancying he saw a beatific vision of Kṛishṇa sporting on the waves with his favourite Gopīs. Certain it is that he disappeared mysteriously about A.D. 1527, at the age of forty-two.

Then happened what has constantly taken place in the religious history of India. Men of high aspirations, who have laboured for the revival or reformation of religion, and received homage as inspired teachers from crowds of disciples during life, have been worshipped as actual deities at death. The only question in the minds of Ćaitanya's devoted followers was as to whether he was a full manifestation of the Supreme Being (Kṛishṇa) or only a descent of a portion (aṇśa) of his essence. The difficulty seems to have been settled by deciding that Ćaitanya was none other than very Kṛishṇa incarnate, and that his two principal disciples, Advaita and Nityānanda, were manifestations of portions of the same deity. These three leaders of the sect are therefore called the three great lords (Prabhus). They constitute the sacred triad of this phase of Vaishṇavism.

But a fourth leader, named Hari-dās, who during his lifetime was a companion of Ćaitanya, is worshipped as a separate divinity in Bengal. Indeed, all the living successors and the present leaders of the sect, called Gosāins (=Gosvāmins), are venerated as little less than deities by the Vaishṇavas of this school. For the worship of living religious leaders and teachers (usually called by the general name Guru) is a marked feature of this, as of all forms of Vaishṇavism. The Guru with Vaishṇavas is indeed more than a teacher, and even more than a mediator between God and men. He is the present god—the visible living incarnation of the deity. His anger and favour make themselves instantly felt. He is on that account even more feared and honoured than the very god of whom he is the representative and embodiment.

Another feature of the system is the extraordinary value attached to the repetition of Kṛishṇa's names, especially of his name Hari. The mere mechanical process of constantly repeating this name Hari—though the mind be vacant or fixed on some other object—secures admission to Vishṇu's heaven. Religious ceremonies are comparatively useless. This idea, however, prevails among all Vaishṇavas. Hari-dās is said to have retired to a secluded place for the purpose of repeating the word Hari 300,000 times daily.

Even a blasphemous repetition of Kṛishṇa's name may secure beatitude. In the Marāṭha country there is a form of devotion called Virodha-bhakti, which consists in a man's pretending to oppose the deity with the sole object of achieving the bliss of being killed by him, and so transported to the god's heaven. So it is said that Śiśu-pāla was saved by constantly thinking of Kṛishṇa through enmity; and the cowherdesses by thinking of him through lust (kāmāt).

It is related of a certain wicked godless man that he had a son named Nārāyaṇa (one of the principal names of Vishṇu). On his death-bed, and just before breathing his last, the father called out his son's name without the most remote intention of invoking the god. The effect was that Yama's messengers, who stood ready to convey the reprobate's soul to a place of punishment, were obliged to make way for the emissaries of Vishṇu, who carried the spirit off in triumph to the god's paradise.

The repetition of particular Vedic texts is by some regarded as equally efficacious. A story is told of a certain converted Hindū who took occasion to recount his experiences before becoming a Christian. It appears that he had been troubled with a constant longing for a vision of Vishṇu, and in his distress consulted a Brāhman, who informed him that to obtain the desired vision he would have to repeat a particular text (Mantra) 800,000 times. This he accomplished by dint of hard work night and day in three months, and, on complaining to his friend the Brāhman that no result followed, was told that he must have made some slight verbal mistake in the repetition of some one text, and that any such slip necessitated his going through the whole process again.

Many treatises held in high repute have been written by the disciples of Ćaitanya in support of his tenets (e.g. the Ćaitanya-ćaritāmṛita by Kṛishṇa-dās in 1590).

The ceremonial acts practised in worshipping the image of Kṛishṇa (described at pp. 90–94) have many points of resemblance to those of Śiva, but I had few opportunities of witnessing them.

I visited the temple of Dākor in Gujarāt, where there is a noted idol of Kṛishṇa (or Raṇ-chor, see p. 152) brought from Dvārikā (p. 113). I was made to take off my shoes before ascending the steps of the temple, but was not permitted to see the image closely or to note the process of worshipping it.

On one occasion, however, I was allowed to look through an accidental crevice into the shrine of a Vaishṇava temple at Poona while the early morning service (pūjā) was performed. The idol of the god Kṛishṇa first underwent a process of being roused from its supposed nocturnal slumbers by the attendant priest, who invoked the deity by name. Then a respectful offering of water in a boat-shaped vessel was made to it. Next the whole idol was bathed and holy water poured over it from a small perforated metal lotā. Then the attendant priest standing near applied sandal-paste (ćandana) with his finger to the idol's forehead and limbs, and, taking a brush, painted the face with a bright colouring substance, probably saffron. Next, the idol was dressed and decorated with costly clothes and ornaments. Then the priest burnt camphor and incense and waved lights before the image, at the same time ringing a small bell (ghaṇṭā). Then flowers (pushpa) and the leaves of the sacred tulsī plant were offered, followed by an oblation of food (naivedya), consisting of cooked rice with sugar. Next water was taken out of a small metal vessel with a spoon and was presented for sipping (āćamana). The god was of course supposed to consume the food or feast on its aroma, receiving at the end of the meal an offering of betel for the supposed cleansing of the mouth after eating, and a spoonful more water for a second sipping. Finally the priest prostrated himself before the idol, and terminated the whole ceremony by putting the god to sleep for the day.

While he was going through these ceremonial acts, he appeared to be muttering texts, and I observed that during the whole service a Brāhman was seated on the ground not far off, who intoned portions of the tenth book of the Bhāgavata-purāṇa, descriptive of the life of Kṛishṇa, from a copy of the work placed before him. At the same time a band over the entrance to the temple played a loud accompaniment with tom-toms, fifes, and drums.

In the evening the process of waking, undressing, redressing the image, and putting it to sleep was repeated, but without bathing. Flowers and food were again offered, texts intoned, and musical services performed.

The cooked food offered to the idol is ultimately eaten by the priests. In large temples it is also distributed to the worshippers, who receive it eagerly as divine nutriment, called *prasāda* (p. 69), and at some places (for example at a particular temple in Benares) considerable portions are sold at high prices to outside applicants.

The water in which the idol is washed is called tīrtha (or sometimes ćaraṇāmṛita), and is drunk as holy water.

Sometimes the mode of worship by Pradakshiṇa (or Pradakshiṇā)—that is, circumambulation, with the right side kept towards the object (following the course of the sun)—is performed. The same sort of circumambulation—but often on the knees—is performed round the holy house at Loretto in Italy.

CHAPTER VI.

Minor Vaishṇava Sects. Reforming Theistic Movements.

WE cannot quit the subject of Vaishṇavism without giving some account of its more important minor sects, as well as of certain reforming theistic movements which may be said to have grown out of it. We may begin with the

Sect founded by Nimbārka or Nimbāditya.

This is perhaps one of the oldest of the known minor sects. Its founder Nimbārka or Nimbāditya, whose followers are sometimes called Nīmānandīs, sometimes Nīmāvats, is held to have been identical with the astronomer Bhāskarāćārya, who flourished about the twelfth century. The poet Jaya-deva, who is also supposed to have lived in the twelfth century, may have been his disciple. If so, it is certain that the disciple did more than his master to promote the doctrine of devotion to Kṛishṇa. In Jaya-deva's mystical poem, called the Gīta-govinda (compared by some to our Song of Solomon), are described the loves of Kṛishṇa and the Gopīs (wives and daughters of the Cowherds), and especially of Kṛishṇa and Rādhā, as typical of the longing of the human spirit or soul for union with the divine.

Others again believe Nimbārka to have been an actual incarnation of the Sun-god, and maintain that he derived his name of 'Nimb-tree-Sun' from having one day stopped the course of the sun's disk, dislodged it from the heavens, and confined it for a brief season in a Nimb (Nīm) tree. This remarkable miracle was worked to enable Nimbārka to offer food just before sunset to a holy guest whose religious vows prevented his eating after dark.

Nimbārka propounded a philosophical theory which, like that of Rāmānuja, amounted to a compromise between dualism and non-dualism, and was called dualistic non-dualism (Dvait-ādvaita). He held that every man's spirit was capable of being absorbed into God's Spirit, and that such an end was to be aimed at. His followers, who are not very numerous, are devoted to the worship of the goddess Rādhā in conjunction with Kṛishṇa.

Sect founded by Rāmānanda.

Rāmānanda is said to have been born in the thirteenth century. The sect founded by him in the fourteenth century has many adherents in Gangetic India, especially around Agra. They are often called Rāmānandis or Rāmavats, and are sometimes confounded with the Rāmānujas, the fact being that Rāmānanda was probably one of Rāmānuja's disciples. The Rāmānanda Vaishṇavas, however, have distinctive doctrines of their own. They worship Vishṇu under the form of Rāma (the hero of the Rāmāyaṇa) either singly or conjointly with his wife Sītā, and they are not, like the Rāmānujas, hyper-scrupulous about the privacy of their meals. Their favourite book is the Bhakta-mālā of Nābhājī—a work interesting for its biographies of certain Vaishṇavas and adherents of the sect, among whom are included two well-known poets, Sūr-dās and Tulasī-dās (commonly Tulsī-dās). The former was blind. He wrote a great many stanzas in praise of Vishṇu, and is regarded as a kind of patron of blind men, especially if they roam about as wandering musicians.

Tulsī-dās, whose verses are to this day household words in every town and rural district where the Hindī language is spoken, ranks as a poet of higher order. He was born near Ćitra-kūṭa about A.D. 1544, and settled at Benares, where he became an enthusiastic worshipper of Rāma and Sītā. His Hindī poem, the Rāmāyaṇa, or history of Rāma, is no mere translation of Vālmīki's great work. It has all the freshness of an independent and original composition. He died about 1624.

But Rāmānanda is chiefly noted for his twelve immediate disciples, the most celebrated of whom were Kabīr, Pīpā, and Ravi-dās. Of these again by far the most remarkable was Kabīr. He was an enthusiastic reformer, who founded a distinct theistic sect to be described hereafter (see p. 158).

Let us first conclude our description of strictly Vaishṇava sectarianism by giving some account of the comparatively modern Vaishṇava sect founded by Svāmi-Nārāyaṇa. This sect is worthy of notice, both because it affords a good example of the best aspect of modern Vaishṇavism, and because the efforts of its founder to deliver the system of Vallabhāćārya from the corrupting influences of the profligate Mahārājas (see pp. 136, 137) is worthy of all praise.

Sect founded by Svāmi-Nārāyaṇa.

Svāmi-Nārāyaṇa, whose proper name was Sahajānanda, was a high-caste Brāhman. He was born at Chapāī, a village one hundred and twenty miles to the north-west of Lucknow, about the year 1780. He was a Vaishṇava, but disgusted with the manner of life of the so-called followers of Vallabhāćārya, whose precepts and practice were utterly at variance, and especially with the licentious habits of the Bombay Mahārājas (see p. 137), he determined to denounce their irregularities and expose their vices. He himself was a celibate, virtuous, self-controlled, austere, ascetical, yet withal large-hearted and philanthropic, and with a great aptitude for learning. He left his home about the year 1800, and took up his abode at a village within the jurisdiction of the Junagaṛh Nawāb. There he placed himself under the protection of the chief Guru, named Rāmānanda-Svāmī. When that holy man removed to Ahmedābād, in 1804, Sahajānanda followed him.

In a large and populous city a man of evident ability and professed sanctity could not fail to attract attention. Soon Sahajānanda collected about his own person a little band of disciples, which rapidly multiplied into an army of devoted adherents. Some attribute his influence to a power of mesmerizing his followers, but he probably owed his success to a remarkable fascination of manner combined with consistency of moral character, and other qualities which singled him out for a leader. His disciples increased so rapidly that the Brāhmans and magnates of Ahmedābād began to be jealous of his popularity. He was obliged to fly, and sought refuge at Jetalpur, twelve miles south of Ahmedābād. There he invited all the Brāhmans of the neighbourhood to the performance of a great sacrifice. The native officials no sooner heard of the proposed assemblage than, fearing a collision between his followers and other religious parties, they had him arrested on some frivolous pretext and thrown into prison. Such an act of tyranny defeated its own object. It excited universal sympathy, and increased his influence. He was soon released. Hymns were composed in which his merits were extolled. Verses were written descriptive of his sufferings. Curses were launched against the heads of his persecutors.

Jetalpur then became the focus of a great religious gathering. Thousands flocked to the town and enrolled themselves as the followers of Sahajānanda, who took the name of Svāmi-Nārāyaṇa.

Bishop Heber, in his Indian Journal, gives the following interesting account of an interview with him at this period of his career:—

About eleven o'clock I had the expected visit from Svāmi-Nārāyaṇa. The holy man was a middle-sized, thin, plain-looking person, about my own age, with a mild and diffident expression of countenance, but nothing about him indicative of any extraordinary talent. He came in somewhat different style from all I had expected, having with him nearly two hundred horsemen. When I considered that I had myself an escort of more than fifty horse I could not help smiling, though my sensations were in some degree painful and humiliating at the idea of two religious teachers meeting at the head of little armies, and filling the city which was the scene of their interview with the rattling of quivers, the clash of shields, and the tramp of the war-horse. Had our troops been opposed to each other, mine, though less numerous, would have been doubtless far more effective, from the superiority of arms and discipline. But in moral grandeur what a difference there was between his troops and mine! Mine neither knew me nor cared for me, though they escorted me faithfully. The guards of Svāmi-Nārāyaṇa were his own disciples and enthusiastic admirers, men who had voluntarily repaired to hear his lessons, who now took a pride in doing him honour, and who would cheerfully fight to the last drop of blood rather than suffer a fringe of his garment to be handled roughly. In my own parish of Hodnet there were once, perhaps, a few honest countrymen who felt something like this for me, but how long a time must elapse before a Christian minister in India can hope to be thus loved and honoured.—Chap. xxv.

It soon became clear to Sahajānanda that the success of his future operations would depend on the consolidation of his party. He therefore retired with his followers to the secluded village of Wartāl, where he erected a temple to Nārāyaṇa (otherwise Kṛishṇa, or Vishṇu, as the Supreme Being) associated with the goddess Lakshmī. It was from this central locality that his crusade against the licentious habits of the Vallabhāćāryans was principally carried on. His watchword seems to have been 'devotion to Kṛishṇa (as the Supreme Being) with observance of duty and purity of life.'

He was in the habit of making periodical tours in Gujarāt, like a bishop visiting his diocese. It was in one of these that Svāmi-Nārāyaṇa was struck down by fever at Gadaḍā in Kāṭhiāwār, where he died.

His disciples now number more than 200,000 persons. They are broadly divided into two classes—Sādhus, 'holy men,' and Gṛihasthas, 'householders.' These correspond to clergy and laity; the former, who are all celibates, being supported by the latter. Those Sādhus who are Brāhmans are called Brahma-ćārīs (cf. p. 362 of this volume). Of these there are about 300 at Wartāl, the whole body of Sādhus, or holy men, numbering about 1,000. A still lower order is called Pāla. Of these there are about 500.

The two principal temples of the sect are at Wartāl (for Sanskṛit Vṛittālaya or better Vratālaya, 'abode of religious observances') about four miles to the west of the Baroda railway, and at Ahmedābād. The former is the most important and best endowed, but both are presided over by Mahārājas, neither of whom is willing to yield the precedence to the other. Jealousies are already springing up between them. Probably, in process of time, a schism will take place, and perhaps two antagonistic parties be formed, as in the other Vaishṇava sects.

In company with the Collector of Kaira I visited the Wartāl temple on the day of the Pūrṇimā, or full moon of the month Kārttik—the most popular festival of the whole year. The Mahārāja greeted us at the Borehavi station of the Baroda railway with a choice of conveyances—an elephant, a bullock-carriage, a palanquin and four saddle-horses, with a mounted guard. I chose the palanquin and found myself moving comfortably forward, while my companion's vehicle oscillated violently in response to the inequalities of the road. The Svāmi-Nārāyaṇa sect are a wealthy community, but clearly object to spend their money on improving their access to their chief temple. One reason for this may be that a shrine's inaccessibility enhances the merit of pilgrimage.

We were met at the entrance to the court of the temple (mandira) by the Mahārāja himself, attended by his minister—an old Brahmaćārī, or unmarried Brāhman. The temple dedicated to Lakshmī-Nārāyaṇa, erected about sixty years ago, is a handsome structure. It has the usual lofty cupolas, and stands in the centre of a courtyard, formed by the residences of the Mahārāja and his attendants, the great hall of assembly, and other buildings.

We were conducted by the Mahārāja through a crowd of at least ten thousand persons who thronged the quadrangle and all the approaches to the temple. They were waiting to be admitted to the ceremony of the day—the one object that had drawn so many people to the spot—the privilege of Darśana; that is, of seeing and adoring the idol. It was a moment of intense excitement. Let a man but bow down before the jewelled image on this anniversary of its manifestation to the multitude, and the blessing of the god attends him for the whole year. The vast concourse swayed to and fro like the waves of a troubled sea, each man vociferating to his neighbours in a manner quite appalling. I could not help thinking of our apparent helplessness in the surging crowd, and asking myself how two solitary Europeans would be likely to fare, if, from some accidental circumstance, the religious fanaticism of a myriad of excited Hindūs were to break loose and vent itself upon us.

But the ten thousand people were docile as children. At a signal from the Mahārāja they made a lane for us to pass, and we entered the temple by a handsome flight of steps. The interior is surrounded by idol shrines. On the occasion of the present festival the principal images were almost concealed from view by rich vestments and jewelry.

The two principal shrines have three figures. One of them has an idol of Kṛishṇa in his character of Raṇ-chor, 'deliverer from evil[1],'—a form of Kṛishṇa specially worshipped at Dvārikā and throughout Gujarāt (see p. 144),—on the left of the spectator. An image of Nārāyaṇa (Vishṇu as the Supreme Being) is in the middle; and Lakshmī, consort of Vishṇu, is on the

[1] So the name was interpreted to me, but it properly means 'fight-quitter,' and rather refers to Kṛishṇa's declining to take part in the great war of the Mahā-bhārata, between the sons of Pāṇḍu and Dhṛita-rāshṭra.

right. A gong to be struck in the performance of worship (pūjā) hangs suspended before the shrine. The other principal sanctuary has Kṛishṇa in the middle, his favourite Rādhā on the right, and Svāmi-Nārāyaṇa, the founder of the sect, on the left. The latter is here worshipped, like other great religious leaders, as an incarnation of a portion of Vishṇu—that is, he is held to be one of the numerous Narāvatāras or descents of parts of the god's essence in the bodies of men. In an adjacent shrine are his bed and clothes, the print of his foot, and his wooden slippers.

We were next conducted to the Sabhā-maṇḍapa, or great hall of assembly, on one side of the quadrangle. Here about three thousand of the chief members of the sect, including a number of the Sādhus or clergy, were waiting to receive us. Chairs were placed for us in the centre of the hall, and before us, seated on the ground, with their legs folded under them in the usual Indian attitude, were two rows of about thirty of the oldest Sādhus, three or four of whom had been actually contemporaries of Svāmi-Nārāyaṇa. These old men were delighted when we questioned them as to their personal knowledge of their founder. The only inconvenience was that they all wanted to talk together. I felt indisposed to check their garrulity, but the Mahārāja had no such scruples and invited us to another hall in the story above, where a select number of their best Pandits and officials were assembled to greet us. The regular Darbār or formal reception took place in this room. Here we were garlanded with flowers, besprinkled with rosewater, and presented with fruits, sweetmeats, and pān-supārī, in the usual manner. I found the Pandits well versed in Sanskṛit. One or two astonished me by the fluency with which they spoke it, and by their readiness in answering the difficult questions with which I tested their knowledge.

The Mahārāja's last act was to conduct us to an adjacent building, used as a lodging-house or asylum (dharma-śālā) for the clergy. On the present anniversary at least six hundred of these good men were collected in long spacious galleries called Āśramas (places of retreat). They were all dressed alike in plain salmon-coloured clothes, each man being located in a small separated space not more than seven feet long, by three or four broad. Above his head, neatly arranged in racks, were his spare clothes, water-jar, &c. When we were introduced to the six hundred Sādhus they were all standing upright, motionless, and silent. At night they lie down on the hard ground in the same narrow space. These holy men are all celibates. They have abandoned all worldly ties, that they may go forth unencumbered to disseminate the doctrines of their founder. They itinerate in pairs, to cheer, support, and keep watch on each other. They travel on foot, undergoing many privations and hardships, and taking with them nothing but a staff, the clothes on their back, their daily food, their water-jar, and their book of instructions. They may be seen here and there in the ordinary coarse salmon-coloured dress of ascetics, striving to win disciples by personal example and persuasion rather than by controversy. Surely other proselyting societies might gain some useful hints by a study of their method.

What I saw of their whole system convinced me that the Svāmi-Nārāyaṇas are an energetic body of men and their sect an advancing one. Notwithstanding the asceticism of their clergy, the leading members of the community have a keen eye to worldly wealth and the acquisition of land, and are perhaps not over-scrupulous in carrying out their plans of aggrandisement. Without doubt the tendency of their doctrines is towards purity of life, which is supposed to be effected by suppression of the passions (udāsa), and complete devotion to the Supreme Being in his names of Nārāyaṇa, Vishṇu, and Kṛishṇa. In an honest desire to purify the Vaishṇava faith the sect has done and is doing much good; but there can be no question that its doctrines, like its gods, its idols, and its sectarian marks, are part and parcel of genuine Hindūism. At any rate the system lacks the true vivifying regenerating force which can alone maintain it in vigour, and, like other Indian reformations and religious revivals, is, I fear, destined in the end to be drawn back into the all-absorbing vortex of corrupt Hindūism.

After my discussion with the Pandits I was presented with their Śikshā-patrī, or manual of instructions, written in Sanskṛit (with a long commentary), and constituting the religious directory of the sect. It was compiled by their founder, with the aid of a learned Brāhman named Dīna-nāth, and is a collection of two hundred and twelve precepts—some original, some extracted from Manu and other sacred Śāstras, and many of them containing high moral sentiments worthy of Christianity itself. Every educated member of the sect appeared to know the whole collection by heart[1].

Some of the verses were recited to me by the Pandits in the original Sanskṛit, and as they fairly represent the purer side of Vaishṇavism (which has been much corrupted by recent teachers), as well as its confused ideas on all religious and philosophical subjects, I here append a translation of a few selected specimens. The figures at the end of each precept refer to the number of the verses in the Śikshā-patrī.

No disciples of mine must ever intentionally kill any living thing whatever, not even a flea or the most minute insect (11).

The killing of any animal for the purpose of sacrifice to the gods is forbidden by me. Abstaining from injury is the highest of all duties (12).

Suicide at a sacred place of pilgrimage, from religious motives or from passion, is prohibited (14).

No flesh meat must ever be eaten, no spirituous or vinous liquor must ever be drunk, not even as medicine (15).

All theft is prohibited, even under pretence of contributing to religious objects (17).

No male or female followers of mine must ever commit adultery (18).

No false accusation must be laid against any one from motives of self-interest (20).

---

[1] The text has been edited by me with a complete translation, and is published in the Journal of the Royal Asiatic Society for October 1882.

Profane language against the gods, sacred places, Brāhmans, holy men and women, and the Vedas, must never be used (21).

A truth which causes serious injury to one's self or others ought not to be told. Wicked men, ungrateful people, and persons in love are to be avoided. A bribe must never be accepted (26).

A trust must never be betrayed. Confidence must never be violated. Praise of one's self with one's own lips is prohibited (37).

Holy men should patiently bear abusive language, or even beating, from evil-minded persons, and wish good to them (201).

They should not play at any games of chance, nor act as informers or spies; they should never show love of self, or undue partiality for their relations (202).

Wives should honour their husbands as if they were gods, and never offend them with improper language, though they be diseased, indigent, or imbecile (159).

Widows should serve the god Kṛishṇa, regarding him as their only husband (163).

They should only eat one meal a day, and should sleep on the ground (168).

Every day let a man awake before sunrise, and, after calling on the name of Kṛishṇa, proceed to perform the rites of bodily purification (49).

Having seated himself in some place apart, let him cleanse his teeth, and then, having bathed with pure water, put on two well-washed garments, one an under garment, and the other an upper (50).

My male followers should then make the vertical mark (emblematical of the footprint of Vishṇu or Kṛishṇa) with the round spot inside it (symbolical of Lakshmī) on their foreheads. Their wives should only make the circular mark with red powder of saffron (52).

Those who are initiated into the proper worship of Kṛishṇa should always wear on their necks two rosaries made of Tulsī wood, one for Kṛishṇa and the other for Rādhā (4).

After engaging in mental worship, let them reverently bow down before the pictures of Rādhā and Kṛishṇa[1], and repeat the eight-syllabled prayer to Kṛishṇa (*Śrī-Kṛishṇaḥ śaraṇam mama*, 'Adorable Kṛishṇa is my soul's refuge') as many times as possible. Then let them apply themselves to secular affairs (54).

Devotion to Kṛishṇa unattended by the performance of duties must on no account be practised (39).

The duties of one's own class and order must never be abandoned, nor the duties of others meddled with (24).

Nowhere, except in Jagan-nāth-purī, must cooked food or water be accepted from a person of low caste, though it be the remains of an offering to Kṛishṇa (19).

---

[1] It is a characteristic of the Svāmi-Nārāyaṇa sect that pictures, instead of images, are used in some of their temples.

Duty (dharma) is that good practice which is enjoined both by the Veda (Śruti) and by the law (Smṛiti) founded on the Veda. Devotion (bhakti) is intense love for Kṛishṇa accompanied with a due sense of his glory (103).

An act promising good reward, but involving departure from proper duties, must never be committed (73).

If by the great men of former days anything unbecoming has been done, their faults must not be imitated, but only their good deeds (74).

If knowingly or unintentionally any sin, great or small, be committed, the proper penance must be performed according to ability (92).

Every day all my followers should go to the Temple of God, and there repeat the names of Kṛishṇa (63).

The story of his life should be listened to with the greatest reverence, and hymns in his praise should be sung on festive days (64).

All males and females who go to Kṛishṇa's temple should keep separate and not touch each other (40).

Vishṇu, Śiva, Gaṇa-pati (or Gaṇeśa), Pārvatī, and the Sun; these five deities should be honoured with worship (84).

Nārāyaṇa and Śiva should be equally regarded as part of one and the same Supreme Spirit, since both have been declared in the Vedas to be forms of Brahmă (47).

On no account let it be supposed that difference in forms (or names) makes any difference in the identity of the deity (112).

That which abides within the living human spirit in the character of its internal regulator (*antaryāmitayā*) should be regarded as the self-existent Supreme Being who assigns a recompense to every act (107).

That Being, known by various names—such as the glorious Kṛishṇa, Param Brahma, Bhagavān, Purushottama—the cause of all manifestations, is to be adored by us as our one chosen deity (108).

Having perceived, by abstract meditation, that the spirit is distinct from its three bodies (viz. the gross, subtle, and causal bodies) and that it is a portion of the one Spirit of the Universe (Brahmă), every man ought to worship Kṛishṇa by means of that soul at all times (116).

Towards him alone ought all worship to be directed by every human being on the earth in every possible manner. Nothing else except devotion (bhakti) to him can procure salvation (113).

The philosophical doctrine approved by me is the Viśishṭādvaita (of Rāmānuja, see p. 122), and the desired heavenly abode is Goloka. There to worship Kṛishṇa and be united with him as the Supreme Soul is to be considered salvation (121).

The twice-born should perform at the proper seasons, and according to their means, the twelve purificatory rites[1] (saṉskāra), the (six) daily

[1] Of these only six are now generally performed, viz.:—(1) the birth-ceremony, or touching the tongue of a new-born infant with clarified butter, etc.; (2) the name-giving ceremony on the tenth day; (3) tonsure; (4) induction into the privileges of the twice-born, by investiture

duties[1], and the Śrāddha offerings to the spirits of departed ancestors (91).

The eleventh day of the waxing and waning moon should be observed as fasts, also the birthday of Kṛishṇa; also the night of Śiva (*Śiva-rātri*) with rejoicings during the day (79).

A pilgrimage to the Tīrthas, or holy places, of which Dvārikā (Kṛishṇa's city in Gujarāt) is the chief, should be performed according to rule. Almsgiving and kind acts towards the poor should always be performed by all (83).

A tithe of one's income should be assigned to Kṛishṇa; the poor should give a twentieth part (147).

Those males and females of my followers who will act according to these directions shall certainly obtain the four great objects of all human desires—religious merit, wealth, pleasure, and beatitude (206).

We now pass on to the reformed theistic sects founded by Kabīr and Nānak.

Theistic Sect founded by Kabīr.

There can be no doubt that the teaching of Kabīr exercised a most important influence throughout Upper India in the fifteenth and sixteenth centuries. That it formed the basis of the Sikh movement in the Panjāb is clear from the fact that Kabīr's sayings are constantly quoted by the Guru Nānak and his successors, the authors of the sacred writings which constitute the bible (Grantha) of the Sikh religion.

Kabīr was a weaver, and in all probability a Musalmān by birth. He is believed to have lived partly at Benares and partly at Magar, near Gorakhpur, in the reign of Sikandar Shāh Lodi, between 1488 and 1512. According to a legend he was miraculously conceived by the virgin widow of a Brāhman. His name Kabīr—an Arabic word meaning 'Great'—gives support to the now generally accepted opinion

with the sacred thread; (5) solemn return home from the house of a preceptor after completing the prescribed course of study; (6) marriage. They are described at p. 353.

[1] The six daily duties (called Nitya-karma) according to Parāśara are:—(1) bathing; (2) morning and evening prayer (sandhyā); (3) offerings to fire (homa); (4) repetition of the Veda; (5) worship of ancestors; (6) worship of the gods.

that he was originally a Musalmān. But he never had any sympathy with Muhammadan intolerance and exclusiveness. It is certain that in the end he became a pupil of Rāmānanda (see p. 147), and for a time a true Hindū, and, what is important to bear in mind, a true Vaishṇava, who, like other Vaishṇava leaders, had much of the democratic, tolerant, and liberal spirit of Buddhism. No wonder, then, that he laboured to free the Vaishṇava creed from the useless and senseless incrustations with which it had become overlaid. But he did more than other Vaishṇava reformers. He denounced all idol-worship and taught Vaishṇavism as a form of strict monotheism. True religion, according to Kabīr, meant really nothing but devotion to one God, who is called by the name Vishṇu, or by synonyms of Vishṇu such as Rāma and Hari, or even by the names current among Muhammadans. For Kabīr, in his tolerance, had no objection to regard Muhammadans as worshipping the same God under a different name. In this way he was the first to attempt a partial bridging of the gulf between Hindūism and Islām. Nor did he reject all the pantheistic ideas of Brāhmanism.

We have already noted how in India all phases of religious belief are constantly meeting and partially fusing into each other. Polytheism is continually sliding into Monotheism, Monotheism into Pantheism, and this back to Polytheism. Vaishṇavism and Śaivism in their universal receptivity are open to impressions from Islām; Islām, notwithstanding its exclusiveness, is adulterated with Vaishṇavism and Śaivism. Hence it happens that Vaishṇavism and Śaivism, however decidedly they may insist on the separate personality of the Godhead, are perpetually slipping back, like a broad wheel, into old pantheistic and polytheistic ruts. And Islām, however uncompromising its views of the Unity of the Deity, has its school of Sūfī philosophers, who hold opinions almost identical with those of the Vedānta Pantheists. It is no wonder, therefore, that Kabīr—while asserting the Unity of God, the

Creator of the world, who is admitted to have attributes and qualities and to assume any shape at will—also maintained that God and man are parts of one essence, and that 'both are in the same manner everything that lives and moves and has its being.'

Kabīr's adherents—still very numerous in Northern India—are generally called Kabīr-panthīs. His doctrines and precepts are embodied in the Sukh-nidhān and other Hindī works, as well as in the Sikh Grantha. His successors have added precepts of their own, many of which are attributed to Kabīr. His alleged sayings are innumerable.

I here subjoin a few specimens [1]:—

Hear my word; go not astray.

My word is from the first. Meditate on it every moment.

Without hearing the word, all is utter darkness. Without finding the gateway of the word, man will ever go astray.

There are many words. Take the pith of them.

Lay in provender sufficient for the road while time yet serves. Evening comes on, the day is flown and nothing will be provided.

With the five elements is the abode of a great mystery. When the body is decomposed has any one found it? The word of the teacher is the guide.

That a drop falls into the ocean all can perceive; but that the drop and the ocean are one, few can comprehend.

The dwelling of Kabīr is on the peak of a mountain, and a narrow path leads to it.

No act of devotion can equal truth; no crime is so heinous as falsehood; in the heart where truth abides, there is my abode.

Put a check upon the tongue; speak not much. Associate with the wise. Investigate the words of the teacher.

When the master is blind, what is to become of the scholar? When the blind leads the blind both will fall into the well.

It is evident from these examples that the key-note of Kabīr's teaching was the duty of obeying spiritual teachers. He maintained, in fact, that every man was bound to search for a true and trustworthy spiritual pastor (Guru), and, having found one, to make him his master—to submit mind, conscience, and even body to his will and guidance. Yet he

[1] Selected from H. H. Wilson's 'Hindū Religious Sects.'

never claimed infallibility for his own utterances. He constantly warned his own disciples to investigate for themselves the truth of every word he uttered.

And this leads us to the religious system founded in the Panjāb by Kabīr's most celebrated follower Nānak, about the time of the Emperor Bābar.

The Sikh Theistic Sect, founded by Nānak.

It is well known that certain sects of Christians call themselves 'brethren,' to denote their relationship to each other and to their Head as members of a religious society typified by a family. Much in the same way the sect founded by Nānak styled themselves Sikhs or 'disciples' to express their close dependence on their teachers or Gurus. For if the 'diapason' of Kabīr's doctrine, and, indeed, of all Vaishṇava teaching, was, 'Hear the word of the Guru, the word of the Guru is the guide,' much more did Nānak insist on a similar submission. Literally interpreted, the Sanskṛit terms Guru (derived from the Sanskṛit root gṛī, 'to utter words'), and Ṡishya—corrupted into Sikh—meaning in Sanskṛit 'one who is to be instructed,' are merely correlatives like teacher and taught. Hence, the system might as suitably be called Guruism as Sikhism.

Great light has been thrown on its religious aspect by the labours of the late Professor Trumpp, of Munich. He was commissioned by our Government to translate what is called the Ādi-Granth, or first Sikh bible, and his work appeared in 1877 with valuable introductory essays. It is chiefly by studying this book that we are able to form an accurate idea of one of the most interesting and important religious and political movements in the history of India. With some difficulty I myself procured a copy of the Ādi-Granth at Amṛitsar.

In the light, therefore, of Professor Trumpp's investigations, and my own inquiries at Lahore, I proceed to give a brief account of Nānak and the characteristic features of Nānak's teaching.

It appears to be a well-ascertained fact that this great teacher was born, not in Lahore itself, but in a neighbouring village, called Talvandī, on the river Rāvī, not far from Lahore, in the year 1469, a few years before Ćaitanya in Bengal and Martin Luther in Europe. Of course the various biographies of Nānak—called Janam-sākhīs, and written in the Panjābi dialect — are filled with myths and stories of miraculous events, invented to justify the semi-deification of the founder of the sect soon after his death. That all the Hindū gods appeared in the sky and announced the birth of a great saint (Bhagat) to save the world, is not quite capable of proof. Nor can we quite accept as a fact another statement of his chroniclers, that one day angels seized him while bathing, and carried him bodily into the presence of the Deity, who presented him with a cup of nectar and charged him to proclaim the one God, under the name of Hari, upon earth. But we need not disbelieve the statement that at an early age he became a diligent student of Vaishṇava religious books, and that in his youth he imitated the example of other incipient reformers, wandering to various shrines in search of some clue to the labyrinth of Hindūism. It is even affirmed that his travels included the performance of a hajj to Mecca, and that on being reproved by the Kāzī for lying down with his feet towards the Ka'bah, he replied: 'Put my feet in that direction where the house of God is not.'

Nānak, however, laid no claim to be the originator of a new religion. His teaching was mainly founded on that of his predecessors, especially on that of Kabīr, whom he constantly quoted. He was simply a Guru, or teacher, and his followers were simply Sikhs or disciples. But he was also a reformer who aimed, as other reformers had done before him, at delivering Hindūism, and especially the Vaishṇavism of Northern India, from its incubus of caste, superstition, and idolatry.

Yet it does not appear that Nānak directly attacked caste or denounced it in violent language. He simply welcomed persons of all ranks as his followers, and taught that the Supreme Being was no 'respecter of persons.'

The plain fact was that Nānak found himself in a part of India where Muhammadans formed the majority of the population. Though himself originally a Hindū, he became partially Islāmized, to the extent at least of denouncing idolatry. His idea was to bring about a union between Hindūs and Muhammadans on the common ground of a belief in one God. Yet the creed of Nānak was really more pantheistic than monotheistic. God, he said, is Supreme Lord over all (Parameśvara). He may be called Brahmă, or by other names, such as Govinda, etc., but his especial name is Hari (=Vishṇu). This Supreme Being does not create the Universe out of nothing, but evolves it out of himself. It is a kind of expansion of his own essence which takes place for his own amusement (khelā)—such expansion being made up of the three Guṇas—Sattva, Rajas, and Tamas—in perfect equilibrium (see p. 31). It is Illusion or Māyā which disturbs this equilibrium and causes the apparent separation between God, the world, and the human soul. All this is pure Brāhmanism. We find also that, except in denouncing idolatry, Nānak differed very little from a pure Vaishṇava, for he taught that in the present age (Kali-yuga) the repetition of the name of Hari is the only means of salvation from the misery of successive births—notwithstanding the merit to be gained by works and ceremonies—and that the knowledge of this name is only to be acquired through a properly ordained teacher (Guru). It is curious, too, that a religious movement which commenced in an effort to draw the adherents of Sikhism and Muhammadanism together, should have ended in exciting the bitterest animosity between them.

Nānak's death is known to have occurred on the 10th of October, 1538. One of his sons expected to succeed him, but to the surprise of those who were present at his death, he passed over his own son and nominated, as second Guru, his disciple Lahanā, whose name had been changed to Aṅgada because of his devotion. He had, so to speak, given up his person (aṅga) to the service of his master. This appears to have been his chief merit. He was quite illiterate, though tradition makes him the inventor of the peculiar alphabet called Guru-mukhī (a modification of the Deva-nāgarī) in which the Sikh bible was written. Aṅgada nominated Amar-dāṣ to succeed him as third Guru. Seven others were appointed to the succession in a similar manner. These make up the ten chief Gurus of the Sikh religion. They were, 4. Rām-dās; 5. Arjun; 6. Har-Govind; 7. Har-Rāi; 8. Har-Kisan (for Har-Kṛishṇa); 9. Teg-Bahādur; and 10. Govind-Siṇh.

Professor Trumpp has given an interesting account of each, though he does not vouch for the truth of the native biographies from which his details are taken. One thing is certain, that notwithstanding the agreement of Sikhs and Muhammadans in regard to the great doctrine of the Unity of the Godhead, a violent political antagonism soon sprang up between them. The truth was, that when the Sikhs began to combine together for the promotion of their worldly as well as spiritual interests, they rapidly developed military tastes and abilities. This was the signal for an entire change of attitude between Sikhs and Muhammadans. So long as the former were a mere religious sect they were left unmolested; but when they began to band themselves together for purposes of political aggrandizement, they encountered opposition and persecution. The Muhammadan Government naturally took alarm. It could not permit the growth of an *imperium in imperio*. Internecine struggles followed. Both parties treated each other as deadly enemies; but the hardy and energetic Sikhs, though occasionally vanquished and dispersed, were not to be driven off the field. Nor is it surprising that they gradually developed a taste for rapine and spoliation. The decaying Mogul Empire was quite unable to hold its own against their aggressiveness. Ultimately, they combined into powerful associations (misals) under independent marauding chiefs, seized large tracts of land, and took possession of the whole Panjāb.

The first to inspire the Sikhs with a desire for political union was the fourth Guru, Rām-dās. He was himself a quiet unassuming man, but he understood the value of money and the advantage of organization. His affable manners attracted crowds of adherents, who daily flocked to his house and voluntarily presented him with offerings. With the contributions thus received he was able to purchase the tank called Amṛita-sar (Sanskṛit, Amṛita-saras, 'lake of nectar'), and build the well-known lake-temple at the place now known as Amṛitsar (Umritsur), which afterwards became a rallying-point and centre of union for the whole Sikh community.

Rām-dās conveyed his precepts to his followers in the form of verses. Many of his stanzas, together with the sayings of the previous Gurus, and especially of the first Guru, Nānak, were for the first time collected by his son, the fifth Guru, Arjun, who was appointed by his father to the Guruship just before his death in 1581. From that time forward the succession was made hereditary, and the remaining five Gurus were regarded as rulers rather than as teachers.

With regard to the fifth Guru, Arjun, it may be observed that he was a worthy successor of his father. He perceived that to keep his Sikhs or disciples together, it would be necessary to give them a written standard of authority, and some sort of machinery of government. It is to him, therefore, that the Sikhs owe the compilation of their first bible—called the Granth, or book (Sanskṛit, Grantha)—and to him is due the establishment of an organized system of collecting a regular tax from all adherents of the sect in different localities. Moreover, under him the sacred tank and temple founded by Rām-dās became the nucleus of the sacred town Amṛitsar, which is still the metropolis of the Sikh religion. He was the first Sikh Pope who aimed at temporal as well as spiritual power. It is not surprising, then, that his death is said to have been brought about by the Emperor Jahāngīr.

The lives of the sixth, seventh, and eighth Gurus may be passed over as unimportant. The ninth Guru, Teg-Bahādur, attracted the attention of the Emperor Aurangzīb. This fanatical monarch, who was bent on forcing the whole world to embrace Islām, did not long leave the Sikhs undisturbed. He imprisoned Teg-Bahādur, and tortured him so cruelly that the Guru, despairing of life, induced a fellow-prisoner to put an end to his sufferings. But Aurangzīb's tyranny was quite powerless to suppress the Sikh movement. It was rather the chief factor in Sikh progress. The murder of the ninth Guru was the great turning-point in the history of the sect. Thenceforward the Sikhs became a nation of fighting men.

Teg-Bahādur's son, Govind-Siṇh, succeeded as tenth Guru. Burning to avenge his father's death, he formed the ambitious design of establishing an independent dominion on the ruins of the Muhammadan Empire. He was a man of extraordinary energy and strength of will, but, born and brought up at Patnā, was deeply imbued with Hindū superstitious feelings. The better to prepare himself for what he felt was too gigantic a task to be accomplished without supernatural assistance, he went through a course of severe religious austerity. He even so far abjured the principles of his predecessors as to propitiate the goddess Durgā. Nay, it is even affirmed that, instigated by the Brāhmans to offer one of his own sons as a sacrifice, and unable to obtain the mother's consent, he allowed one of his disciples to be beheaded as a substitute at the altar of the bloody goddess. The story is noteworthy as pointing to the probable prevalence of human sacrifice at that time in Upper India.

In fact, it was the tenth Guru, Govind, who converted the

Sikhs into a nation of fighting men. His character was a curious compound of pugnacity, courage, superstition, and fanaticism. If Nānak, the first Guru, was the founder of the Sikh religion, Govind, the tenth Guru, was the founder of the Sikh nationality. Many reformers had attempted to abolish caste as a part of religion, but Govind regarded its evils from a purely political standpoint. He perceived that great national weakness resulted from the disunion caused by caste. He therefore proclaimed social equality in the Sikh community.

Nor was this all. They were to add the name Siṉh ('lion') to their other names. They were to be distinguished by long hair, they were always to carry a sword—in token of engaging in perpetual warfare with the Musalmāns—to refrain from smoking tobacco, and to wear short trowsers, instead of the ordinary Dhotī. They were to be called Khālsā, or the peculiar property of the Guru, and were to be admitted to discipleship by a kind of baptismal rite called Pāhul—that is to say, sugar was dissolved in water, consecrated by the repetition of certain texts taken from the Granth, and stirred with a two-edged sword. Then part of this decoction—euphemistically styled nectar—was administered to each new disciple, and the rest sprinkled on the head, mouth, eyes, and other parts of his body, while he was made to take an oath not to mix with certain excommunicated persons, not to worship idols, not to bow to any one, except a Sikh Guru, and never to turn his back on a foe.

He was enjoined to repeat the Granth during meals and at other times (both the Jap-jī of Nānak and that of Govind). The Vedas, Śāstras, Purāṇas, and the Kurān were not to be credited; no Hindū ceremonies were to be observed, no Śrāddhas performed, no mark was to be applied to the forehead (see p. 66), no sacred cord was to be worn, no rosary to be used, no tobacco to be allowed, no animal to be eaten, unless killed by a Sikh, and no beef was to be touched. Especial care was to be taken in preparing the Karāh-Prasād. This corresponded to the Hindū Prasāda (see p. 145), and the eating of it in common is compared by Professor Trumpp to the Christian Communion. It was made of flour, sugar, and ghī. When prepared it was distributed to the people who sat round it, praying.

Moreover the Sikh was never to wear a cap, nor to shave his head or beard; nor to take off his turban while eating.

Govind even composed a second bible (Granth), which was added as a supplement to the first, and called the book of the tenth Guru. The precepts of Nānak and his successors, which had been compiled by Arjun, were too full of passages suggestive of meekness and pacific feelings. In his own supplement Govind adhered to the religious teaching of the Ādi-Granth, but he introduced precepts the direct object of which was to rouse the martial ardour of his followers; he substituted war for peace as a religious duty,—reversing the order followed in the Christian Bible, which advances from the sanction of war in the Old Testament to the inculcation of universal peace in the New. Thenceforward they were to imitate the Muhammadans—they were to spread their religion, not by persuasion, but by the sword. Nay, they were to live by the sword, and even to worship the sword.

Govind was himself more of a military than a religious leader. He was not only a brave soldier, but a daring and resolute commander, and his fighting propensities were intensified by his innate superstition and fanaticism.

It need not, therefore, be matter of astonishment that the greater part of Govind's own life was passed in strife and warfare. But he was no match for the Emperor Aurangzīb, who was his equal in fanatical intolerance, and greatly his superior in ability and military resources. Forced to withdraw from a hopeless contest, he retired to Central India and built himself a residence in Mālwā (called Damdamā), which is still a point of resort for the Sikh community. On Aurangzīb's death, Govind gained the goodwill of his successor, Bahādur Shāh, and even accepted a military command in the Dekhan. There a Paṭhān, who owed him a grudge, attempted his assassination and wounded him so severely that he died at the town of Nadēṛ, near the Godāvarī (A.D. 1708).

Perhaps the most remarkable feature of the later Sikh system was the quasi-deification of the sacred book, or Granth. Govind refused to appoint a successor to the Guru-ship, but he well knew that to maintain the Sikh religion as a distinctive creed some visible representative and standard of authority was needed. He therefore constituted the Granth a kind of permanent religious Guru, endowing it with personality, and even with the title Sāhib (Lord). 'After me,' he said, 'you shall everywhere mind the book of the Granth-Sāhib as your Guru; whatever you shall ask it will show you.'

It may be worth while, therefore, to inquire a little more closely into the nature of the book thus exalted to the position of an infallible guide, and made to do duty as a kind of visible vicegerent of God upon earth.

It consists, as we have seen, of two parts, the Ādi-Granth or first book, which is the portion most generally revered, and the book of the tenth Guru, Govind, which finds greater favour with the more fanatical section of the community. We can only here glance at the form and contents of the Ādi-Granth. The translator (Professor Trumpp) considers it to be 'an extremely incoherent and wearisome book, the few thoughts and ideas it contains being repeated in endless variations.' Nor will this estimate of its merits be matter of wonder when it is found that the Ādi-Granth is, in fact, a jumbling together of metrical precepts and apophthegms supposed to have been composed by at least thirty-five different authors, among whom were six of the ten chief Gurus (Nānak, Aṅgada, Amar-dās, Rām-dās, Arjun, and Teg-Bahādur), fourteen Bhagats or saints (Rāmānand, Kabīr, Pīpā, Ravi-dās, Dhannā, Nāmdev, Sūr-dās, etc.), and fifteen Bhāṭs or professional panegyrists, whose names are not worth recording. These latter were employed to write eulogies on the Gurus, and their panegyrics, introduced into the Granth, are curious as specimens of abject adulation, though absolutely worthless in themselves. It is noticeable that one verse by Govind-Siṉh has been appended to the Ādi-Granth, and is regarded as an integral portion of the volume.

The language in which the whole work is written is not so much the old Panjābī dialect as the old Hindī. This ancient dialect was probably used by the Sikh Gurus, though natives of the Panjāb, that they might be better able to commend their utterances to the whole Hindū community. It may be conveniently called Hindū-ī to distinguish it from the modern Hindī[1]. The graphic system used by the writers was a modification of the Deva-nāgarī alphabet, called Guru-mukhī, the peculiarity of which is that it preserves the forms of some Sanskṛit letters, but changes their phonetic power.

Perhaps it is as unjust to disparage the Granth as to exalt its merits unduly. To say that it contains many noble thoughts is as true as to say that it abounds in much silly twaddle and inane repetition. Nor can it be fairly accused of absence of arrangement. The verses, though unconnected, are arranged in six divisions:—(1) we have the Japu (commonly called Jap-jī), which consists of introductory verses by Nānak; (2) then follows the So-daru; (3) the So-purkhu; (4) the Sohilā, three short sections, consisting chiefly of verses adapted for evening devotion; lastly come (5) the Rāgs, verses sung in particular Rāgs or musical keys, thirty-one in number, which constitute the great body of the Granth, especially the first four, called Sirī Rāg, Rāg Mājh, Rāg Gaurī, and Rāg Āsā; and (6) the Bhog, consisting of verses by Nānak, Arjun, and the earlier Gurus, besides others

---

[1] I believe I was one of the first to recommend its being so distinguished, in the Preface to the first edition of my Sanskṛit-English Dictionary, published by the University of Oxford in 1872.

by Kabīr, whose sayings are also scattered everywhere through every section of the Granth.

I select a few examples from the book, slightly abridged, and altered from Professor Trumpp's version :—

At the beginning is the True One.

Know, that there are two ways (that of Hindūs and that of Musalmāns), but only one Lord.

By thyself all the creation is produced ; by thyself, having created, the whole is caused to disappear.

Thou, O Hari, alone art inside and outside ; thou knowest the secrets (of the heart).

Mutter the name of Hari, Hari, O my heart, by which comfort is brought about ; by which all sins and vices disappear ; by which poverty and pain cease.

Thou art I, I am thou, of what kind is the difference ? Like gold and the bracelet, like water and a wave.

By the perfect Guru the name of Hari is made firm in me. Hari is my beloved, my king. If some one bring and unite (him with me), my life is revived.

Thou art my father, my mother, my cousin, my brother, my protector in all places. Then what fear and grief can there be to me ? By thy mercy I have known thee. Thou art my support, my trust. Without thee there is none other ; all is thy play and thy arena, O Lord !

The Lord is my dear friend. He is sweeter to me than mother and father, sister, brother, and all friends ; like thee there is none other, O Lord !

Be united with the Lord of the Universe. After a long time this (human) body was obtained. In some births thou wast made a rock and mountain. In some births thou wast produced as a pot-herb. In the eighty-four lakhs (of forms of existence) thou wast caused to wander about.

No hot wind touches those who are protected by the true Guru. The Guru is the true creator.

Protected by the Guru he is admitted to the true house and palace (of Hari). Death cannot eat him.

I am continually a sacrifice to my own Guru.

I am become a sacrifice to my own Lord. From the Veda, from the book (the Kurān), from the whole world he is conspicuous. The King of Nānak is openly seen.

Having forgotten all things meditate on the One ! Drop false conceit, offer up (thy) mind and body !

The following are examples of Kabīr's sayings quoted in the Granth :—

Kabīr says : I am the worst of all, every one is good except me.

Death, of which the world is afraid, is joy to my mind.

The gate of salvation is narrow, not wider than the tenth part of a mustard-seed.

If I make the seven oceans ink, if I make the trees my pen, if I make the earth my paper, the glory of God (Hari) cannot be written.

Hope should be placed on God (Rām), hope in others is useless.

What thou art doing to-morrow do now; what thou art doing now do at once. Afterwards nothing will be done when death descends on thy head.

It will be sufficiently evident from these passages that Sikhism was a great religious reform, and yet in its essence very little better than either Vaishṇavism or Brāhmanism. The Granth declares the Oneness of the Deity, but when we sound the depths of its inner doctrines we find that this unity is based on a substratum of pantheistic ideas. There is but One God, but He manifests Himself everywhere and is everything. From various passages of the Granth it is clear that the Vaishṇava names Hari, Kṛishṇa, Rāma, and Govinda are accepted by the Sikhs as names of the Supreme. They are even willing to regard the different divine personalities represented by these names as manifestations of the one Supreme Being. The point on which they pride themselves is the prohibition of image-worship. Yet they make an idol of their own sacred book, worshipping it as truly as the Hindūs do their idols, dressing it, decorating it, fanning it, putting it to bed at night, and treating it much in the same manner as the idols of Kṛishṇa are treated.

We have seen that one great distinguishing feature of their system is that war is made an essential part of religion. To indicate their belief in this doctrine they worship the military weapons of the Gurus. In some respects they conform to the customs of the Hindūs. They even surpass the ordinary Hindū in some of his most inveterate superstitions; as, for example, in ascribing divine sanctity to the cow. The killing of a cow is, with Sikhs, the most heinous of crimes[1], meriting

[1] At one time in the Panjāb it was infinitely more criminal to kill a cow than to kill a daughter.

nothing less than capital punishment—not, however, from any injunction to that effect in the Granth, but from simple opposition to the Musalmāns, who, whenever they conquered any district peopled by Hindūs, invariably slaughtered cows, both to ratify their victories and to show their contempt for Hindū superstitions.

Then again they accept in all its fulness the Hindū doctrine of metempsychosis, believing that there are eighty-four lakhs (or eight million four hundred thousand) of forms of existence through which all souls or spirits—represented as flames emanating from the fountain of life—are liable to pass before returning to their source. These forms of life are supposed to consist of 2,300,000 quadrupeds; 900,000 aquatic animals; 1,000,000 feathered animals; 1,100,000 creeping animals; 1,700,000 immovable creatures (such as trees and stones); 1,400,000 forms of human beings. Deliverance from all individual existence (Nirvāṇa) is the summum bonum.

But, after all, the chief distinctive feature of Sikhism is that, accepting the Vaishṇava doctrine of complete submission to the Guru or ordained religious teacher, the Sikh Guru is made, so to speak, to out-Guru all other Gurus. His word is to be law in every single matter, human and divine. First, he baptizes the novice with a decoction of sugar and water, which he has previously consecrated and stirred with a two-edged dagger. Then he imparts the name of Hari to his disciple in a particular sacred text, which loses all its efficacy unless orally communicated. He tells him to mutter it perpetually, enjoins him to fix his mind on Hari's excellences, and never to rest until he has merged his own existence in that of Hari. In return for the instruction thus imparted, the disciple, even in the earliest period of Sikhism, had to render a certain amount of personal and even menial service to his Guru. Then as Sikhism advanced and the Guru gained temporal as well as spiritual authority, he became to his disciples exactly what Muhammad became to his followers in Arabia—not only teacher and spiritual pastor, but master, military leader, and king. Finally, when he had ceased to act as a military leader, he was regarded as an all-powerful mediator between God and man, and even as an actual god to whom prayers were to be addressed as to the Supreme Being Himself.

Before concluding this sketch of one of the most interesting religious movements that has ever taken place in India, I ought to state that I visited the tombs of Ranjit Siṉh and Guru Arjun at Lahore, the birth-place of Govind at Patnā, and the sacred metropolis or Jerusalem of Sikhism at Amṛitsar.

I noticed that the mausoleum which contains the ashes of Ranjit Siṉh at Lahore had idols of the Hindū gods Gaṇeśa and Brahmā over the entrance. Inside, resting on a small elevated platform, was the sacred Granth, and all around were eleven small tombs, mere mounds of earth, under which are preserved the ashes of Ranjit's eleven wives, who became Satīs at his death.

It may be worth while here to mention that it is against the practice of the Hindūs to preserve the remains of their deceased relatives in tombs. The body is burnt, and, however illustrious the man may have been, the ashes are scattered on sacred rivers. The Sikh leaders were, like the Muhammadans, ambitious of perpetuating their own memories after death. They continued the Hindū practice of burning their dead, but, like the Muslims, spent larger sums in erecting magnificent tombs for the reception of their own ashes than in building palaces for their own ease and self-indulgence during life.

The temple dedicated to the tenth Guru Govind, at Patnā, was rebuilt by Ranjit Siṉh about forty years ago. I found it, after some trouble, in a side street, hidden from view and approached by a gateway, over which were the images of the first nine Gurus, with Nānak in the centre. The shrine is open to the air on one side. Its guardian had a high-peaked turban encircled by steel rings (ćakra), used as weapons. He was evidently an Akālī—or 'worshipper of the timeless God'—a term applied to certain Sikh zealots who believe themselves justified in putting every opponent of their religion to the sword. As I entered the court of the temple, accompanied by a Musalmān friend, this Akālī displayed great excitement, and I began to fear an outburst of fanaticism which might have been dangerous to us both. Happily my companion knew the man we had to deal with, and, under a process of judicious handling, the fiery zealot cooled down, and even allowed us to inspect the interior of the tenth Guru's shrine.

On one side, in a small recess—supposed to be the actual room in which Govind was born more than two centuries before—were some of his garments and weapons, and what was once his bed, with other relics, all in a state of decay. On the other side was a kind of low altar, on which were lying under a canopy a beautifully embroidered copy of the Ādi-Granth and of the Granth of Govind. In the centre, on a raised platform, were numerous sacred swords, which appeared to be as much objects of worship as the sacred books.

As to the golden temple at Amṛitsar, called Hari-mandira, 'the temple of Hari,' or sometimes Durbār Sāhib, it may be said to rank next to the Tāj at Agra as one of the most striking sights of India. To form an idea of the unique spectacle presented by this sacred locality, one must picture to one's self a large square sheet of water, bordered by a marble pavement, in the centre of a picturesque Indian town. Around the margin of this artificial lake are clustered many fine mansions, most of them once the property of Sikh chiefs who assembled here every year, and spent vast sums on the endowment of the central shrine. One of the houses is occupied by Sirdār Maṅgal Siṇh Rāmgharia, a well-known and much esteemed member of the Sikh community. It has two lofty towers, from one of which I enjoyed a grand panoramic view of the lake and its vicinity—one of those rare sights seen at intervals during life, which fix themselves indelibly on the memory. In the centre of the water rises the beautiful temple with its gilded dome and cupolas, approached by a marble causeway. It is quite unlike any other place of worship to be seen throughout India, and in structure and appearance may be regarded as a kind of compromise between a Hindū temple and a Muhammadan mosque, reminding one of the attempted compromise between Hindūism and Islām, which was once a favourite idea with both Kabīr and Nānak.

In point of mere size the shrine is not imposing, but its proportions strike one as nearly perfect. All the lower part is of marble, inlaid, like the Tāj, with precious stones, and here and there overlaid with gold and silver. The principal entrance facing the causeway looks towards the north. The interior is even more gorgeous than the exterior. On the ground-floor is a well-proportioned vaulted hall—its richly gilded ceiling ornamented with an infinite number of small mirrors, and its walls decorated with inlaid work of various designs, flowers, birds, and elephants. Four short passages, entered by carved silver doors, one on each of its four sides, lead to this vaulted chamber, giving it a shape not unlike that of a Greek cross. All around on the outside is a narrow corridor. In the interior, opposite the principal entrance, sits the presiding Guru—his legs folded under him on the bare ground—with the open Granth before him. He is attended by other officials of the temple, who assist him in chanting the sacred texts. The Brāhmans maintain that God may infuse his essence into images, but they never make an idol of the written Veda, which, according to their theory, is divine knowledge communicated orally to inspired sages, and by them orally transmitted—not written down. Sikhism, on the contrary, denies that God associates himself with images, but believes that he is manifested in a written book (Granth).

Hence, although the temple is free from images, and is dedicated to the one God under his name Hari (applied also to Kṛishṇa or Vishṇu), a visible representation of the invisible God is believed to be present in the sacred book. The Granth is, in fact, the real divinity of the shrine, and is treated as if it had a veritable personal existence. Every morning it is dressed out in costly brocade, and reverently placed on a low throne under a jewelled canopy, said to have been constructed by Rañjit Siṇh at a cost of 50,000 rupees. All day long chowries are waved over the sacred volume, and every evening it is transported to the second temple on the edge of the lake opposite the causeway, where it is made to repose for the night in a golden bed within a consecrated chamber, railed off and protected from all profane intrusion by bolts and bars. Of this I was myself a witness.

On the occasion of my first visit to the Golden Temple two or three rows of temple officials and others were seated in a circle round the vaulted chamber, to the number of about a hundred, listening to the Granth which was being chanted by the presiding Guru and his assistants in a loud tone, with an accompaniment of musical instruments. The space in the centre was left vacant for offerings, and was strewn with flowers, grain, and small coin. A constant line of worshippers, male and female, entered one after the other, cast down their offerings, bowed their heads to the ground before the Granth and before the presiding Guru, and reverently circumambulated the corridor of the temple. I noticed that one poor old woman threw in two small coins, and then, bending low, touched the marble floor with her forehead.

On leaving the temple I talked for a time with an intelligent Sikh who had received an English education. Pointing to an idol of Kṛishṇa which had been set up on the margin of the lake, I asked whether the Sikhs were returning to the worship of Vaishṇava images. 'Yes,' he said, 'we are gradually lapsing back into our old habits. Our first Guru abolished caste and forbad the worship of idols. Our tenth Guru was a thorough Hindū at heart, and by his own example encouraged the return to Hindū practices; so that of the Sikhs now found in the Panjāb a large number adopt caste, wear the Brāhmanical thread, keep Hindū festivals, observe Hindū ceremonies (such as the Śrāddha), and even present offerings to idols in Hindū temples.'

In short, a careful observation of the present condition of Sikhism must lead to the conclusion that the Sikh reforming movement, like others which preceded it, is gradually being drawn back into the all-absorbing current of ordinary Vaishṇavism. Yet the possession of a distinct rule of faith and standard of doctrine in the Granth must have a prophylactic effect. It must keep the crumbling elements of Sikhism together for a time. Nor need the process of reabsorption involve the obliteration of all distinctive marks. For just as the strength of Hindūism is Vaishṇavism, so the strength of Vaishṇavism is its tolerance of an almost infinite diversity within its own pale. Probably, in the end, the Granth itself will be accepted by the whole body of Vaishṇavas as a recognized portion of their sacred literature.

The census of ten years ago made the number of Sikhs in India amount to 1,853,426, of whom only 806,928 were females.

In regard to the sect called Kūkas see p. 268.

But Sikhism was not the only offshoot of the school founded by the great reformer Kabīr. He is said to have had twelve disciples, like his predecessor Rāmānanda; and each disciple is supposed to have taken a distinct line (panthāḥ) of his own, and to have originated a distinct school of religious thought.

Two of these may be singled out for special notice—the Dādū-panthīs and the Satnāmīs.

The Dādū-panthīs, as their name implies, were founded by Dādū, a cotton-cleaner of Ahmedabad, who flourished about

A.D. 1600. They are really Vaishṇava Theists like the Sikhs; that is, worshippers of the one God under some of the names of Vishṇu, according to the doctrine of Kabīr, on whose precepts the religious works of the sect are all founded.

In the same way the Satnāmīs are only Vaishṇava Theists, who call the one God by a peculiar name of their own (Satnām), and base their doctrines like the Sikhs on Kabīr's school of theology.

According to Professor H. H. Wilson, the founder of the Satnāmīs was Jag-jīvan-dās (for Jagaj-jīvana-dās), a native of Oudh, whose samādh or tomb is at Katwa, between Lucknow and Ajūdhyā. He is said to have flourished about A.D. 1750, and to have written certain tracts in Hindī, called Jñāna-prakāśa, Mahā-pralaya, and Prathama-grantha. When I was last in India I heard of a branch of the Satnāmīs at Chatīsgarh, in the Central Provinces. They are the followers of a low-caste Chamār named Ghāsī-dās and his son Bālak-dās, who flourished about the beginning of this century. I was able to obtain some account of their tenets and practices from the missionaries of the Church Missionary Society at Madras. They are also described in one or two numbers of the Madras Missionary Record for 1872.

Like other varieties of Hindū Unitarians, all of whom mix up pantheistic ideas with monotheistic doctrines, they submit implicitly to their Gurus, regarding them as vicegerents of God upon earth, and occasionally as actual incarnations of the Deity.

The following are a few of their precepts and rules:—

God pervades the universe. He is present in every single thing. The title Lord (Sāhib) should be added to every object in which God is present. God is the spring and source of everything good and evil. Idols must not be worshipped. The ordained religious teacher (Guru) is holy. Even the water in which his feet are washed is holy, and should be drunk by his disciples. Distinctions of caste are not to be observed. Fasts need not be kept. Feed the poor. Wound no one's feelings. When the dead are burned let no one cry or weep; let them only exclaim, 'The Lord gave, and the Lord has taken away!'

CHAPTER VII.

Śāktism, or Goddess-worship.

Śāktism in the simplest acceptation of the term is the worship of force (Sanskṛit *Śakti*) personified as a goddess and subordinately in all women. Doubtless there may be some educated Hindūs whose worship of this goddess amounts to little more than reverence for a personification of the energy of Nature; but a true Śākta adores her with a view to the acquisition of supernatural faculties through her help, or to the destruction of enemies through her co-operation.

Of course it is alleged by all Śaiva and Vaishṇava sectarians that the gods Śiva and Vishṇu, as identified with the Supreme Being, are themselves the source and spring as well as the controllers of all the forces, energies and phenomena of nature. Yet we must bear in mind that it is a rooted idea with all Hindū theologians, of whatever denomination, that the highest condition of the Self-existent Being is a condition of complete quiescence and inactivity, as well as of complete oneness, solitariness, and impersonality.

In fact Brāhmanism holds that the One Universal Self-existent Spirit is Existence, Thought, and Joy—or, in other words—is Life without anything to live for, Thought without anything to think about, Joy without anything to be joyful about. But the moment this one Self-existent pure Spirit begins to be conscious (in our sense) of existence and to exercise thought and feel joy—it assumes personality and material organization. It becomes, in fact, a personal God; and when this personal God wills to put forth energy for the creation or evolution of a world out of himself his nature becomes duplex. Evidently the absolute unity and strictly masculine character of that nature might have been preserved in his personal development, but the idea of a kind of duality in unity very soon suggested itself to the Hindū mind. He was held to possess a double nature, partly male and partly female, the female constituting his left side.

Then, again, this duality might have been evenly balanced, or the preponderance of active energies might have been assigned to the male side. The Hindūs, however, in dividing the divine nature into two halves, had no idea of any due co-ordination of working power between man and woman. The male side of the god was believed to relegate his more onerous executive functions to the female. Hence the female side of the personal god is often more propitiated than the male, and the worshipper is inclined to turn with greater devotion to the goddess than to the god when he supplicates any powerful intervention on his own behalf in circumstances of unusual exigency or peril.

The Kumārī-tantra says: 'The whole world is embodied in the woman. One should be a woman one's self. Women are gods. Women are vitality.'

This I believe to be the true theory of Śāktism in its simplest and most general aspect. It is a theory which is certainly more closely connected with Śaivism than with any other system. Like Śaivism, too, it traces back its origin to philosophical Brāhmanism, and through Brāhmanism to the earliest conceptions foreshadowed in the Veda.

Perhaps the first dawn of the idea of duality in unity is to be found in the well-known 129th hymn of the 10th Maṇḍala of the Ṛig-veda already quoted (p. 13). In that hymn we find it stated that in the beginning when the universe was about to be developed there arose in the One Being Desire which produced Mind and all existing things (p. 29).

But the idea of a universe proceeding from a female principle brought into union with a male is more fully developed in other Vedic texts.

Probably Heaven (Dyaus) and Earth (Pṛithivī) are the most ancient of all Vedic gods, and from their fancied union, as husband and wife, the other deities and the whole Universe were at first supposed to spring. They are often described as parents (janitrī, Ṛig-veda X. 110. 9; pitarā, III. 3. 11; mātarā, I. 155. 3). Or Heaven alone is called father (pitā) and Earth mother (mātā). On the other hand, elsewhere in the Veda the female deity Aditi—probably a personification of the sky or of universal nature—seems to stand alone, taking the place of both Heaven and Earth as parent of the deities, her counterpart being Diti the mother of the demons. Another important goddess in the Ṛig-veda is the Dawn[1] (Ushas, 'Ηώς), the Sky's daughter, who is of course closely connected with the Sun-god; but is not described as married to him, though followed by him, as a mistress is pursued by her lover.

And here it may be noted as remarkable that the wives of two chief Vedic gods, Indra and Agni (Indrāṇī and Agnāyī), are not associated with their husbands or exalted to equal rank as objects of worship. Nor is the popular goddess Lakshmī, afterwards wife of Vishṇu, mentioned at all in the Ṛig-veda[2]. Nor is Sarasvatī held to be the consort of Brahmā. She is rather a river-goddess, though often invoked in other characters, and once associated with a river-god Sarasvat (VII. 96. 4, 6). It is only when we come to the Brāhmaṇas and Upanishads that we find the duality of the divine nature clearly enunciated. For example, in the Śatapatha-Brāhmaṇa (XIV. 4. 2. 4, etc.), before noticed, and Bṛihad-āraṇyaka Upanishad (3) we read to the following

[1] Sometimes spoken of as plural.

[2] Dr. Muir shows this (Sanskṛit Texts, V. 337), and points out that Lakshmī is once used for good-fortune in Ṛig-veda X. 71. 2, and that in Atharva-veda VII. 115. 1 a plurality of Lakshmīs is spoken of. Five are often mentioned. At Madurā I noticed carvings of seven or eight different Lakshmīs who preside over different kinds of good-luck. They are often found over the doors of houses.

effect: 'The One Being did not enjoy happiness when alone. He was desirous of a second. He divided himself into two. Hence were husband and wife produced. Therefore was this (second) only a half of himself, as the half of a split pea is.' It is then related how all beings were produced by the union of the divine male and divine female. Śaṅkara, in his comment on the Upanishad, observes, in relation to the above passage: 'Because this male half is void as wanting the female half, therefore after taking a wife it is completed by the female half, as a split pea is by being joined with its other half' (see Roër's translation).

If we pass on to Manu, we find that the Self-existent is described as dividing his own substance and becoming half male and half female (I. 5, etc.; see p. 30).

Turning next to the Sāṅkhya philosophical system, we know that it teaches the separate existence of eternal Spirit called 'the Self' or 'Male' on the one side and of an eternal productive force or prolific germ (Prakṛiti fem., or Māyā) on the other. The union of the two was believed to be indispensable before any creation could result.

The Vedānta system is virtually very similar (see p. 37).

Of course ordinary thinkers gave a concrete reality to all such metaphysical speculations. The Spirit—which was called 'the Self' (Ātman) in one system and 'the Male' (Purusha) in the other—became in the popular creed a separate male god, while the productive prolific force became a separate female god. The union of the two was expressed in the later mythology by the Ardha-nārī or androgynous form of Śiva—in which the right side of the god is represented as male, and the left side as female (see p. 85)—or by the united male and female symbols (Liṅga and Yoni) set up in innumerable shrines throughout every part of India. (Compare the union of Hermes and Aphrodite.)

The same doctrine is often repeated in the Purāṇas; but even in those writings it is to be noted that although they often countenance and even promote Śākta views by making the active power of the goddess a subject of special laudation, and by according greater honour to the female deity (as for example in placing the goddess first in such compounds as Lakshmī-Nārāyaṇau, Sītā-Rāmau, Rādhā-Kṛishṇau[1]), yet no exclusive or extravagant worship of the goddess is inculcated.

It was reserved for the latest sacred writings called Tantras (see p. 205) to personify Energy or Force as a female deity, and to teach an undue adoration of the wives of Śiva and Vishṇu to the neglect of their male counterparts.

Practically, as we shall see, the Śāktism of the present day is a mere offshoot of Śaivism. It inculcates an exclusive adoration of Śiva's wife as the source of every kind of supernatural faculty and mystic craft. This, in fact, is the central doctrine and leading idea of all Tāntrik writings. For the Tantras, believed as they are to be a direct revelation from Śiva to his wife Pārvatī (p. 205), are the bible of Śāktism, just as the Purāṇas are the bible of ordinary Śaivism and Vaishṇavism. That they are regarded by some as of equal authority with the Purāṇas, and even as a kind of secondary revelation, is evident from a passage in Kullūka's commentary on Manu II. 1. There he asserts that divine truth is of two kinds—'that revealed in the Vedas and that found in the Tantras.' It is even alleged that Śaṅkarāćārya was a Śākta.

Unhappily a vast proportion of the inhabitants of India, especially in Bengal, are guided in their daily life and practices by Tāntrik teaching, and are in bondage to the doctrines inculcated in these writings.

It is noteworthy, too, that the system is closely connected with the mysticism of the Yoga philosophy and with the corrupt forms of Buddhism prevalent in Tibet (see my volume

---

[1] According to a Vārttika on Pāṇini II. 2, 34 (Kāśikā Vṛitti) the more honourable should stand first in a compound, as in Mātā-pitarau, Śraddhā-medhe, Brāhmaṇa-Kshatriya-Viṭ-Śūdrāḥ.

on Buddhism, p. 223). Its demoralizing effect on the life and conduct of the Hindūs cannot be doubted.

And indeed it can scarcely be doubted that Śāktism is Hindūism arrived at its worst and most corrupt stage of development. To follow out the whole process of evolution would not be easy. Suffice it to say that just as Hindūism resolved itself into two great systems—Śaivism and Vaishṇavism—so the adherents of those two systems respectively separated into two great classes. The first are now called 'followers of the right-hand path' (Dakshiṇa-mārgīs). These make the Purāṇas their real Veda (Nigama), and are devoted to either Śiva or Vishṇu in their double nature as male and female. But they do not display undue preference for the female or left-hand side of the deity; nor are they addicted to mystic or secret rites. The second class are called 'followers of the left-hand path' (Vāma-mārgīs). These make the Tantras their peculiar Veda (Āgama), tracing back their doctrines to the Kaula Upanishad, which is held to be the original authority for their opinions; whence their system is called Kaula, as well as Śākta, and they themselves Kaulikas.

And it is these left-hand worshippers who, I repeat, devote themselves to the exclusive worship of the female side of Śiva and Vishṇu[1]; that is, to the goddess Durgā or Kālī (=Ambā, Devī) rather than to Śiva; to Rādhā rather than to Kṛishṇa; to Sītā rather than to Rāma; but above all to Ambā or Devī, the mother-goddess, sometimes confounded with Śiva's consort, but rather, in her more comprehensive character, the great Power (Śakti) of Nature, the one Mother of the Universe (Jagan-mātā, Jagad-ambā)—the mighty mysterious Force, whose function is to direct and control two quite distinct operations; namely, first, the working of the natural appetites and passions, whether for the support of the body

[1] The wives of the deities are generally placed on their left. The only exception is in representations of the marriage ceremony. On that occasion the bride takes her station on the right of the bridegroom.

by eating and drinking, or for the propagation of living organisms through sexual cohabitation; secondly, the acquisition of supernatural faculties (siddhi), whether for a man's own individual exaltation or for the annihilation of his opponents.

And here it is necessary to observe that the Śākta form of Hindūism is equipped with a vast mythological Personnel of its own—an immense array of female personalities, constituting a distinct division of the Hindū Pantheon.

Yet the whole array, spreading out as it does into countless ramifications, has its root in the wife of Śiva. By common consent she is held to be the source or first point of departure of the entire female mythological system. She also stands at its head; and it is remarkable that in every one of the male god Śiva's characteristics, his consort is not only his counterpart, but a representation of all his attributes intensified. We have already pointed out (pp. 76–78) how it came to pass that the male god gradually gathered under his own personality the attributes and functions of all other divinities, and thus became to his own special worshippers the great god (Mahā-devaḥ) of Hindūism [1]. Similarly and in a much greater degree did his female counterpart become the one great goddess (Mahā-devī) of the Śākta hierarchy; representing in her own person all other female manifestations of Brahmā, Vishṇu, and Śiva, and absorbing all their functions. For this reason even the wives of Brahmā and Vishṇu were said to be her daughters. As to the contradictory qualities attributed to her, these are no source of difficulty to a Hindū mind. She is simply in all respects a duplicate of her husband, painted in deeper or more vivid colours.

And just as Śiva (p. 80) is at one time white (Śveta, śukla) both in complexion and character, at another black (Kāla); so his female nature also became one half white (whence her name Gaurī) and the other half black (whence her name Kālī).

[1] At Pokhar and on the road to Amber in Rājputāna I passed two temples where the Liṅga of Śiva has four faces and is worshipped as Brahmā.

Then, again, each of these opposite characters became variously modified and endlessly multiplied. The white or mild nature ramified into the Śaktis called Umā, Gaurī, Lakshmī, Sarasvatī, etc.; the black or fierce nature into those called Kālī, Durgā, Ćaṇḍī, Ćāmuṇḍā, etc. And just as Śiva has 1008 names or epithets, so his wife possesses a feminine duplicate of nearly every one of his designations. At least one thousand distinct appellations are assigned to her, some expressive of her benignant, some of her ferocious character. Notably it is declared in the Tantras that if any one repeats eight of her names containing the letter *m*, kings will become his servants, all men will love him, and all his difficulties come to a happy termination.

In short, all the other Śaktis came to be included by the Śāktas under the Śakti or female energy of Śiva, which eventually developed into innumerable separate personifications.

These personifications, following the analogy of some of Vishṇu's incarnations, are sometimes grouped according to a supposed difference of participation in the divine energy, such for example as the full energy (pūrṇā śakti), the partial (aṉśa-rūpiṇī), the still more partial (kalā-rūpiṇī), and the partial of the partial (kalāṉśa-rūpiṇī), this last including mortal women in various degrees, from Brāhman women downwards, who are all worshipped as forms of the divine mother manifesting herself upon earth; for it must not be forgotten that in the Śākta creed every female is a present divinity.

The more usual classification, however, begins with the Mahā-vidyās. These are held to be ten in number, that number being probably selected to match the ten chief incarnations of Vishṇu. They are called Mahā-vidyās as sources of the goddess's highest knowledge; that is to say, of the knowledge which confers preternatural powers. They have all different attributes, and are thus designated:—1. Kālī (sometimes called Śyāmā), black in colour, fierce and irascible in character. 2. Tārā, a more benign manifestation, worshipped especially in Kaśmīr. 3. Shoḍaśī, a beautiful girl of sixteen (also called Tripurā, worshipped in Malabar). 4. Bhuvaneśvarī. 5. Bhairavī. 6. Ćhinna-mastakā, a naked goddess holding in one hand a blood-stained scimitar and in the other her own severed head, which drinks the warm blood gushing from her headless trunk. 7. Dhūmāvatī. 8. Vagalā or Bagalā or Bagalā-mukhī. 9. Mātaṅgī, 'a woman of the Bhaṅgī caste.' 10. Kamalātmikā or Kamalā. Of these the first two are especially Mahā-vidyās, the next five Vidyās, and the last three Siddha-vidyās.

The next class of personifications or manifestations of the goddess are the Mātṛis or Mātṛikās (or Mahā-mātṛis), the great mothers of the Universe. These are more important than the Mahā-vidyās in their connexion with the prevalence of Mother-worship, a form of religion which, among the peasantry of India, often takes the place of every other creed. This will be more fully explained in the chapter on tutelary deities (p. 209).

The Mātṛis or Mothers are—1. Vaishṇavī. 2. Brāhmī or Brahmāṇī, often represented with four faces or heads like the god Brahmā. 3. Kārttikeyī, sometimes called Māyūrī. 4. Indrāṇī. 5. Yāmī. 6. Vārāhī, connected with the boar incarnation of Vishṇu. 7. Devī or Īśānī, represented with a trident in one hand as wife of Śiva. 8. Lakshmī[1]. Each of these divine Mothers is represented with a child in her lap.

Closely related to the Mothers is a class of female personifications called the eight Nāyikās or mistresses. These, of course, are not necessarily mothers. In fact no other idea is connected with them than that of illegitimate sexual love. They are called Balinī, Kāmeśvarī, Vimalā, Aruṇā, Medinī, Jayinī, Sarveśvarī, and Kauleśī.

Another class of manifestations is that of the Yoginīs.

[1] Some lists give nine Mātṛikās (viz. 1. Nārasiṇhi; 2. Ćāmuṇḍā; 3. Vārāhī; 4. Vāruṇī; 5. Lakshmī; 6. Kālī; 7. Kāpālī; 8. Kurukulyā; 9. Indrāṇī), some sixteen, and some fifty-two, among whom are enumerated Nārāyaṇī, Kaumārī, Aparājitā, Durgā, Maheśvarī, etc.

These are sometimes represented as eight fairies or sorceresses created by and attendant on Durgā, sometimes as mere forms of that goddess, sixty or sixty-five in number, and capable of being multiplied to the number of ten millions.

Other classes not worth enumerating are the Ḍākiṇīs and Śākinīs. These are simply female fiends or ogresses of most repulsive habits, and are not so much manifestations of the goddess as impish servants always attendant on her.

But it is in the form Kālī—the form under which the goddess is worshipped at Calcutta—that she is most terrible.

The following is a free translation of two passages in the Tantras descriptive of Kālī's appearance[1] :—

'One should adore with liquors and oblations that Kālī who has a terrible gaping mouth and uncombed hair; who has four hands and a garland formed of the heads of the demons whom she has slain and whose blood she has drunk; who holds a sword in her lotus-like hand; who is fearless and awards blessings; who is as black as the large clouds and has the whole sky for her clothes; who has a string of skulls round her neck and a throat besmeared with blood; who wears ear-rings (consisting of two dead bodies); who carrries two dead bodies in her hands; who has terrible teeth and a smiling face; whose form is awful and who dwells in burning-grounds (for consuming corpses); who stands on the breast of her husband Mahā-deva[2].'

'A Kaulika (i. e. a Śākta) should worship Kālī, who lives amongst dead bodies; who is terrible and has fearful jaws; who has uncombed hair and a glowing tongue; who constantly drinks blood; who stands over her husband Mahā-kāla[2] and

[1] All my extracts from the Tantras are taken from the Hon. Rao Bahādur Gopāl Hari Deshmukh's work called Āgama-prakāśa, where the original Sanskṛit of all the passages quoted in this chapter will be found.

[2] The images of Kālī at Calcutta represent her trampling on her husband. The explanation of this is that she had a contest with the thousand-headed Rāvaṇa (whose story is told in the Adbhuta-Rāmāyaṇa) for ten years, and, having conquered him, became so elated and danced so

wears a garland of skulls on her blood-besmeared throat; who has prominent breasts; who is waited on by all the Siddhas as well as by the Siddhīs.'

It is this goddess who thirsts for blood, and especially for human blood; and if the blood of animals is not offered to her, she takes that of men. In one of the Tantras kings are directed to appease her by blood and even by human sacrifice (nara-bali). The blood of a tiger is said to satisfy her for 100 years, and that of a man for 1000 years.

It might have been expected that a creed like this, which admits of an infinite multiplication of female deities and makes every woman an object of worship, would be likely to degenerate into various forms of licentiousness on the one hand and of witchcraft on the other. But if such consequences might have been anticipated, the actual fact has been worse than the most gloomy pessimist could possibly have foretold. In Śāktism we are confronted with the worst results of the worst superstitious ideas that have ever disgraced and degraded the human race. It is by offering to women the so-called homage of sensual love and carnal passion [1], and by yielding free course to all the grosser appetites, wholly regardless of social rules and restrictions, that the worshippers of the female power (Śakti) in Nature seek to gratify the goddess representing that power, and through her aid to acquire supernatural faculties, and even ultimately to obtain union with the Supreme Being. Incredible as it may appear, these so-called worshippers actually affect to pride themselves on their debasing doctrines, while they maintain that their creed is the grandest

---

energetically that the Universe would have collapsed under her movements had not Śiva mercifully interposed his body. When the goddess found that she was treading on her husband's sacred person, she suddenly ceased dancing, and, as is not unusual with Hindū women when struck with horror or shame, protruded her red tongue in a manner not altogether consonant with European ideas of womanly dignity.

[1] The Tantras make no secret of the fact that the virile *retas* itself is regarded as the offering most pleasing to the goddess.

of all religions, because to indulge the grosser appetites and passions, with the mind fixed on union with the Supreme Being, is believed to be the highest of all pious achievements. Indeed, according to the distorted ideas and perverted phraseology of the sect, all who are uninitiated into this system are styled 'beasts' (paśu[1]), the initiated being called Siddha, 'the perfect ones.'

The rite of initiation (Dīkshā) must be performed by a proper Guru or teacher, who does little more than impart a knowledge (upadeśa) of certain mystic texts and syllables to the candidate, but the rite ought never to take place unless moon, planets, and stars are favourable. If a pupil can be initiated during the occurrence of a solar eclipse wonderful advantages may be expected to accrue to both teacher and taught.

Of course, the principal rites, or rather orgies, of Śākta worshippers take place in secret and with closed doors. This secrecy is strictly in accordance with Tāntrik precept. Thus, we read:—

'One should not practise the Kaula system in the presence of the uninitiated (Paśus or beasts), any more than one should recite the Veda in the presence of a Śūdra.

'One should guard the Kaula system from the Paśus just as one guards money and grain and clothes from thieves.

'One should conceal the Kaula system like the water in the cocoa-nut; one should be a Kaula internally, a Śaiva externally, and a Vaishṇava when talking at public meetings.

'The Vedas, the Śāstras, and the Purāṇas are clearly like a common woman (open to all), but this mystical Śaiva science is like a high-born woman (kept secluded).'

Hence no one who has been initiated into the practices of the sect can be persuaded to speak of them to the uninitiated. Probably the spread of education and the influence exercised by Christian men and women throughout India are gradually operating to abolish all the grosser forms of Śāktism, as they

---

[1] Another name for an uninitiated person is Kaṇṭaka, 'a thorn.'

have already helped to do away with Satī, female infanticide, human sacrifices, and other monstrous evils. Still it is well known that even in the present day, on particular occasions, the adherents of the sect go through the whole ceremonial in all its revolting entirety. When such occasions occur, a circle is formed composed of men and women seated side by side without respect of caste or relationship[1]. Males and females are held for the particular occasion to be forms of Śiva and his wife respectively, in conformity with the doctrine propounded in one of the Tantras, where Śiva addressing his wife says: 'All men have my form and all women thy form; any one who recognizes any distinction of caste in the mystic circle (Ćakra) has a foolish soul.'

The actual performance of the ceremonial then follows. It consists of five separate actions:—1. The drinking of wine and liquors of various kinds (madya); 2. the eating of meat (māṉsa); 3. the eating of fish (matsya); 4. the eating of parched or fried grain (mudrā); 5. sexual union (maithuna)[2].

With regard to the first four of these acts the Tantras prescribe twelve sorts of liquors, three sorts of wine, and three sorts of meat. Pulastya, one of the ancient sages who are the supposed authors of certain law-books, also enumerates twelve kinds of liquors as follow:—1. liquor extracted from the bread-fruit (panasa), called Jack-liquor; 2. from grapes (drākshā); 3. from date-palm (kharjūrī); 4. from common palm (tālī), or toddy; 5. from cocoa-nut (nārikela); 6. from

---

[1] The verse cited as the authority for the temporary suppression of caste at these meetings is as follows:—Prāpte hi Bhairave ćakre sarve varṇā dvijātayaḥ Nivṛitte Bhairave ćakre sarve varṇāḥ pṛithak pṛithak. 'On entering the circle of Bhairava, all castes are on an equality with the best of the twice-born; on leaving it, they are again separated into castes.'

[2] The five acts are called the five Ma-kāras, because the letter M begins each Sanskṛit word. 'The assemblage of five things beginning with the letter M,' says one of the Tantras, 'satisfies the gods.'

The term Mudrā, which here means 'fried grain,' is also used to denote mystical intertwinings of the fingers.

sugar-cane (ikshu); 7. from the Mādhvīka plant; 8. long-pepper liquor (saira); 9. soap-berry liquor (arishṭa); 10. liquor from the Bassia Latifolia (mādhūka); 11. a kind of rum or liquor prepared from molasses, etc. (called Gauḍī, or sometimes Maireya); 12. arrack, or liquor prepared from rice or other grain (surā, or vāruṇī, or paishṭī).

Besides the above twelve kinds of spirituous drink others are frequently mentioned; for example, Ṭāṅka, made from wood-apple; Kolī, made from the jujube; and Kādambarī; the last being the favourite beverage of Bala-rāma.

The meat may be that of birds, beasts, or fish. The parched grain is eaten, like dry biscuit, as a relish with the wine and spirituous liquors. The drinking of each kind of drink is supposed to be attended with its own peculiar merit and advantage. Thus one liquor gives salvation, another learning, another power, another wealth, another destroys enemies, another cures diseases, another removes sin, another purifies the soul.

The Mātṛikā-bheda Tantra (quoted by Dr. Rājendralāla Mitra) makes Śiva address his own wife thus:—'O sweet-speaking goddess, the salvation of Brāhmans depends on drinking wine. I impart to you a great truth, O mountain-born, when I say that the Brāhman who devotes himself to drinking and its accompaniments, forthwith becomes a Śiva. Even as water mixes with water, and metal blends with metal; even as the confined space in a pitcher merges into the great body of surrounding space on the destruction of the confining vessel, and air mingles with air, so does a Brāhman melt into Brahmā, the universal Soul.

'There is not the least doubt about this. Likeness to the divinity and other forms of beatitude are designed for Kshatriyas and others; but true knowledge can never be acquired without drinking spirituous liquor; therefore should Brāhmans always drink. No one becomes a Brāhman by repeating the Gāyatrī, the mother of the Vedas; he is called a Brāhman only when he has knowledge of Brahma. The ambrosia of the gods is their Brahma, and on earth it is arrack (or liquor distilled from rice); and because one attains through it the condition of a god (suratva), therefore is that liquor called surā.'

It is not surprising, therefore, that in Bengal some respectable mothers of families, who believe the above passage to be a direct revelation from Śiva and who would not dream of drinking spirits for their own gratification, never say their prayers without touching their tongues with a pointed instrument dipped in arrack, and never offer flowers to their god without sprinkling them with a few drops of that liquor.

In short, the drinking of spirituous liquor is as much an essential part of the Śākta ceremonial as the drinking of Soma juice was of the Vedic sacrifices, and the drinking of arrack (surā) was of the Sautrāmaṇi and Vājapeya and other sacrificial rites. Indeed these ancient rites are appealed to in the Tantras as a justification for the Śākta practice.

Nor can there be any doubt that at one time the drinking of wine and spirituous liquors was prevalent all over India[1].

---

[1] This is well shown by Rājendralāla Mitra in one of his Essays on the Indo-Āryans. The reason given for the cessation of the custom of wine-drinking among the Hindūs is that wine and spirituous liquors were on two particular occasions cursed by the gods Śukra and Kṛishṇa. The cause of Śukra's curse is related in the First Book of the Mahābhārata (ch. 76). It appears that Kaća, son of Vṛihaspati, had become a pupil of Śukra Āćārya with a view to learn from him the charm (mantra) for restoring dead men to life, which none else knew. The Asuras came to know of this, and, dreading lest the pupil should obtain, and afterwards impart, the great secret to the Devas, assassinated him, and mixed his ashes with the wine drunk by his tutor, thus transferring him to the bowels of Śukra Āćārya. It happened, however, that during his pupilage Kaća had won the affection of Deva-yānī, the youthful and charming daughter of Śukra Āćārya, and that lady insisted upon her father's restoring the youth to her, threatening to commit suicide if the request was not granted. Śukra, unable to deny any favour to his daughter, repeated the charm, and forthwith, to his surprise, found the youth speaking from his own stomach. The difficulty was now to bring the youth out, for this could not be accomplished without ripping open his tutor's abdomen. Śukra

Some of the gods were supposed to set the example—notably Śiva[1] with his wife Durgā, and Balarāma elder brother of Kṛishṇa with his wife Revatī—and we find that one of the products of the ocean when churned by the gods and demons was Surā, or spirit distilled from rice, and that one of the seven seas encircling the earth was believed to be composed entirely of that liquor[2]. Drunkenness in fact became such an evil that to remedy it a kind of temperance movement appears to have been eventually organized, leading to a complete reaction to the other extreme of total abstinence. Hence we find that in Manu's time the penalty for drinking spirits was to commit suicide by drinking them when in a boiling state (XI. 91).

In the same way the eating of meat was once universal in India; cows were sacrificed[3] and the flesh eaten, especially at Śrāddhas, where the aroma of beef was thought to be an excellent aliment for the spirits of the dead. Manu allows all sorts of animal food to be eaten, provided that small portions are first offered to the gods and to the spirits of

---

Āćārya thereupon taught the youth the great charm, and then allowed himself to be ripped open, and Kaća, in grateful acknowledgment for his own restoration to life, immediately repeated the Mantra and resuscitated his tutor. But Śukra Āćārya, seeing that it was spirituous liquor which had made him swallow the ashes of his pupil, and that pupil a Brāhman, prohibited for ever afterwards the use of any kind of strong drink by Brāhmans. 'From this day forward,' said he, 'the Brāhman, who, through infatuation, drinks arrack (surā) shall lose all his religious merit. The wretch shall be considered guilty of the sin of killing Brāhmans, and be condemned in this as well as in a future world.'

With regard to the curse pronounced by Kṛishṇa on all spirituous liquor, the reason assigned for it is that his kinsmen the Yādavas had brought great trouble on themselves by their potations.

[1] It is said that even in the present day it is not uncommon for the adherents of the Śākta sect to sprinkle spirituous liquor instead of water on the liṅga of Śiva.

[2] See Vishṇu-purāṇa.

[3] The Taittirīya-brāhmaṇa mentions various ceremonies at which cattle had to be sacrificed. All this is well shown by Dr. Rājendralāla Mitra.

departed ancestors (V. 32); and Vālmīki, when he entertained Vasishṭha at his hermitage (as described in the Uttara-Rāma-ćaritra), regaled him with the 'fatted calf.' The Śāktas, therefore, have good ground for asserting that, in drinking wine and eating meat, they are merely reverting to the practice of their ancestors. Yet it is curious that they think it necessary to go through the form of neutralizing the curse of the great Śukra Āćārya (see note, p. 194) before beginning their potations. This they do by repeating three particular Mantras and certain magical formulæ, after drawing a triangle on the ground with the finger dipped in spirituous liquor.

The fifth act of the Śākta ceremonial—the union of the actual man and woman—is held to be the most important of all. In the minds of some it is supposed to symbolize a great cosmical mystery—the production of the universe through the union of Purusha and Prakṛiti (see pp. 30, 31)—a mystery constantly kept before the mind by the worship of the two stone symbols Liṅga and Yoni.

'The only salvation,' says a Tantra, 'is that which results from spirituous liquors, meat, and cohabitation with women.'

The holy circle (śrī-ćakra) or meeting of the members of the sect on solemn occasions (represented by a mystical diagram) is said to be 'the door to the highest form of salvation—complete union with the Supreme Being (sāyujya-mukti, p. 41).'

These circles are of different kinds according to the difference in the rank, character, and occupation of the women (śaktis) present at them. Thus there is the Vīra-ćakra; then the Mahā-ćakra, the Deva-ćakra, the Rāja-ćakra, etc.

It is to be observed, however, that all the five acts we have described do not necessarily take place at every meeting.

Moreover, besides the five so-called ceremonial acts performed by Śāktas at their secret meetings, there are six other methods of propitiating the goddess with a view to acquire superhuman powers (siddhi)—namely, by the use of Mantras, Bījas (or Vījas), Yantras, Kavaćas, Nyāsas, Mudrās.

The subject of the employment of Mantras or sacred texts, their use, misuse, and prostitution to the worst purposes, is one of the greatest interest and importance in its bearing on the past and present religious condition of the Hindūs.

A Mantra, as most persons know, is properly a divinely inspired Vedic text, but with the Śāktas, and indeed with the great mass of the Hindūs in the present day, it loses this character and becomes a mere spell or charm. Even though the text be taken from the Ṛig, Yajur or Atharva-veda (p. 8), and be generally employed as a prayer or invocation with a definite meaning and application attached to the words, it becomes with the Śāktas a mere collection of magical letters and sounds, which, if properly uttered and repeated according to prescribed formularies, possesses in itself a mystical power capable of causing every conceivable good to one's self or evil to one's enemies.

The Bījas, again, are mystical letters or syllables invented for the sake of brevity to denote the root (mūla) or essential part of such Mantras, or the name of the deity to whom it may be addressed, or some part of the body over which that deity presides. For example:—*Am* is said to denote Śiva, *U* Vishṇu, *Hṛim* the sun, *Lam* the earth, *Ṇam* the mind, *Dham* both the goddess Bhuvaneśvarī and the tongue, *Nam* both the goddess Anna-pūrṇā and the nose, *Pam* the ear, etc.

Perhaps the following abridgment of a passage from a little work by Pratāpa-ćandra Ghosha, descriptive of the worship of Durgā (Durgā-pūjā) in Bengal, and giving directions for the performance of a preparatory rite called Bhūta-śuddhi, 'removal of evil demons,' will give the best idea of the uses to which the Bījas are applied:—

Holding a scented flower, anointed with sandal, on the left temple, repeat *Om* to the Gurus, *Om* to Gaṇeśa, *Om* to Durgā. Then with *Om phaṭ* rub the palms with flowers, and clasp the hands thrice over the head, and by snapping the fingers towards ten different directions, secure immunity from the evil spirits. Next utter the Mantra *Ram*, sprinkle water all around, and imagine this water as a wall of fire. Let the priest identify himself with the living spirit (jīvātman) abiding in man's breast, in the form of the tapering flame of a lamp, and conduct it by means of the Sushumṇā nerve through the six spheres within the body upwards to the Divine Spirit. Then meditate on the twenty-four essences in nature; viz. the Producer, Intellect, Egoism, the five subtle and five gross elements, the five external organs of sense, the five organs of action, with mind. Conceive in the left nostril the Mantra *Yam*, declared to be the Bīja or root of wind; repeat it sixteen times while drawing air by the same nostril; then close the nose and hold the breath, and repeat the Mantra sixty-four times.

Then meditate on the Mātṛikā, and say, 'Help me, goddess of speech:' *Am* to the forehead, *Ām* to the mouth, *Im* to the right eye, *Īm* to the left eye, *Um* to the right ear, *Ūm* to the left ear, *Im* to the right cheek, *Īm* to the left cheek, *Ṛim* to the right nostril, *Ṝim* to the left nostril, *Ḷrim* to the right cheek, *Ḷrīm* to the left cheek, *Em* to the upper lip, *Aim* to the lower lip, *Om* to the upper teeth, *Aum* to the lower teeth, *Tam*, *Tham*, *Dam*, *Dham*, and *Nam* to the several parts of the left leg, *Pam* to the right side, *Pham* to the left, *Bam* to the back, *Mam* to the stomach, *Yam* to the heart, *Ram* to the right shoulder, *Lam* to the neck-bone, *Vam* to the left shoulder, *Śam* from the heart to the right leg, *Ham* from the heart to the left leg, *Ksham* from the heart to the mouth.

To us it may seem extraordinary that intelligent persons can give credence to such absurdities, or lend themselves to the practice of superstitions so senseless; but we must bear in mind that with many Hindū thinkers the notion of the eternity of sound—as propounded in Patañjali's Mahābhāshya (I. 1. 1) and in the Pūrva-mīmāṉsā of Jaimini—is by no means an irrational doctrine. According to the well-known Mīmāṉsā aphorisms (I. 1. 18–23), sound is held to have existed from the beginning. Hence the letters of the alphabet, being the ultimate instruments by which sounds are uttered and thoughts expressed, are considered to possess supernatural qualities and attributes and to contain within themselves an occult magical efficacy.

Let a man only acquaint himself with the proper pronunciation and application both of the Mantras and of their Bījas or radical letters, and he may thereby propitiate the Śaktis so as to acquire through them superhuman power (siddhi)—nay, he becomes, through their aid, competent to accomplish every conceivable object.

At the same time it is to be observed that for any ordinary man to make himself conversant with the Mantras is no easy task; if at least we are to believe a statement in the Tantras that the primary Mantras are seventy millions [1] in number, while the secondary are innumerable.

This, no doubt, is an absurd exaggeration; but it must be borne in mind that only a certain number are regarded as efficacious, and that in the present day there are Brāhmans called Mantra-śāstrīs who make a knowledge of these Mantras their peculiar business, learning them by heart with the sole object of using them as spells and charms. Only a few, however, are believed to have acquired perfect mastery over the most powerful Mantras, which must be pronounced according to certain mystic forms and with absolute accuracy, or their efficacy is destroyed. Indeed, this kind of craft, though supposed to endow the possessor of it with very enviable omnipotence, is not unattended with unpleasant risks and drawbacks; for if in the repetition of a Mantra the slightest mistake is made, either by omission of a syllable or defective pronunciation, the calamity which it was intended to bring down on an enemy will inevitably recoil on the head of the repeater. Then, again, there are various methods of obstructing or neutralizing the effect of Mantras used by Mantra-śāstrīs for the destruction or humiliation of others. The difficulty, of course, is to find out the exact Mantra which is being employed for one's injury; but, having done so, every such Mantra is rendered powerless by uttering it with one's face bending over a vessel full of milk and then swallowing the milk, or by writing it on the leaf of a banian tree and throwing the leaf into a river [2].

It must be noted, too, that Mantras are not always repeated without a knowledge of their meaning, though the meaning is

---

[1] The same number is given in the Śaiva-darśana of Mādhava's Sarva-darśana-saṅgraha.

[2] Full directions are given in the Tantra-sāra.

of little importance compared with the magical force of the letter and sound. Their efficacy also is greatly increased if they are employed on lucky days or at particular times and seasons. One Tantra teaches that Mantras should be repeated in the month Ćaitra to give valour; in Vaiśākha to obtain jewels; in Māgha for intelligence; on Sundays for wealth; on Mondays for tranquillity; on Tuesdays for long life, and so on. The intercalary month ought always to be avoided [1]. A few translations of common Mantras [2] are here given:—

'Cause stupefaction (stambhana) of the enemy, paralyze his mouth and tongue; confuse his senses, arrest his speech.'

'Om—reverence to the Lord—svāhā. Let everything be auspicious; let everything opposed to me perish; let everything be favourable.'

'Let Brahmāṇī, Māheśvarī, Kaumārī, Indrāṇī, Ćāmuṇḍā, Vārahī, and Vaishṇavī protect my head, mouth, neck, hands, heart, waist and feet, together with my whole body; protect me, O great goddess, Bhadra-Kālī.' This Mantra is worn as a kavaća or amulet; see p. 204.

'I invoke Bhavānī, accompanied by her husband, attended by her subordinates, by her retinue, by her power (sa-śaktikā), by her vehicle, by her weapons, and by all defensive things.'

'Salutation to the god of love (Kāma-deva) with his five arrows:—the arrow that puts to flight (drāvaṇa-bāṇa); the arrow that enchants (sammohana); the arrow that fascinates (vaśīkaraṇa); the love-kindling arrow (sandīpana); the love-inflaming arrow (santāpana).'

The Gāyatrī or holiest text of the Ṛig-veda (see p. 19) is of course the most potent of all Mantras. It is not surprising, therefore, that many Mantras employed by the Śāktas are composed after the model of that text. The following are translations of Gāyatrī Mantras:—

---

[1] The Tantra-sāra gives full directions on this subject.

[2] The original Sanskṛit text of these, as of all the extracts from the Tantras, will be found in Gopāl Hari Deshmukh's Āgama-prakāśa.

'We meditate on that being who has ashes for weapons; we think of that being who possesses sharp teeth; let our fever (jvara) incite him.' This is called the fever-gāyatrī.

'We meditate on the goddess of nectar; we think of the goddess of love (Kāmeśvarī); let our affection incite him.' This is called the nectar-gāyatrī.

'We meditate on the lord of water (Jaleśvara); we think of the fish-net; let the fish (mīna) incite him.' This is called the fish-gāyatrī.

'We meditate on that being who has a snare for snaring animals; we think of the act of cutting off the victim's head (Śiraś-ćheda); let our offering (bali) incite him.' This is called the bali-gāyatrī.

No magician, wizard, sorcerer or witch whose feats are recorded in history, biography, or fable, has ever pretended to be able to accomplish by incantation and enchantment half of what the Mantra-śāstrī claims to have power to effect by help of his Mantras. For example, he can prognosticate futurity, work the most startling prodigies, infuse breath into dead bodies, kill or humiliate enemies, afflict any one anywhere with disease or madness, inspire any one with love, charm weapons and give them unerring efficacy[1], enchant armour and make it impenetrable, turn milk into wine, plants into meat, or invert all such processes at will. He is even superior to the gods, and can make gods, goddesses, imps and demons carry out his most trifling behests. Hence it is not surprising that the following remarkable saying is everywhere current throughout India:—

'The whole universe is subject to the gods; the gods are

---

[1] Warlike weapons when thus charmed were supposed to possess supernatural powers, and to assume a kind of divine personality like the genii of the Arabian Nights. Certain spells had to be learnt for their restraint as well as for their use. When once let loose, he only who knew the secret Mantra for recalling them could bring them back.

subject to the Mantras; the Mantras to the Brāhmans; therefore the Brāhmans are our gods[1].'

Often these Mantra-śāstrīs are mere fortune-tellers.

I may mention as an illustration that a Śākta Brāhman of this type came to see me one day at Patnā. He asked to look at my hand, and, after examining it for a minute, prophesied that my stay in India would be happy and prosperous, except that on that day fortnight I should meet with a great disappointment. I smiled at the absurdity of his attempting to forecast my future biography, but it is certain that I only met with one unexpected and most mortifying contretemps from the day of my departure from England to the day of my return, and that happened on the very day predicted. It must at least be acknowledged that the coincidence was remarkable.

I may also give an outline of a story told to me by a Marāṭha Pandit, which well illustrates the sort of use these Mantra-śāstrīs are supposed to make of their magical powers. A certain Śākta Brāhman, named Bhāskarāćārya, well-versed in the Mantras, expected to be asked to a dinner-party given by a wealthy friend, but received no invitation. This so irritated the Brāhman that he determined to revenge himself on the householder who had ventured so imprudently to slight him. Having waited till the moment when the assembled guests, with appetites stimulated by the fragrance of an array of choice dishes, were about to feast on the delicacies prepared for their consumption, he quietly in his own house selected a particular Mantra, and by simply repeating it turned all the viands into foul and fetid excrementitious matter. The story goes on to relate how the householder, suspecting the cause of this disastrous metamorphose, sent a messenger in hot haste to implore the immediate presence of the offended Brāhman,

[1] The Sanskṛit version of this saying is given incorrectly by Dubois (p. 77). I have heard it variously rendered. Perhaps the following is the most usual :—Devādhīnaṃ Jagatsarvam Mantrādhīnāś-ća Devatāḥ Mantrāś-ća Brāhmaṇādhīnā Brāhmaṇā mama Devatāḥ.

who thereupon becoming mollified, obligingly consented to repeat another Mantra which reconverted all the filth into the most delicious ambrosial food.

We now pass on to the Yantras. These are mystical diagrams drawn on metallic tablets, often of copper—generally combinations of triangular figures like the inverted triangles of the Freemasons—supposed to possess occult powers.

Each of the goddesses worshipped by the Śāktas has a Yantra assigned to her, which is sometimes placed in the centre of a lotus-diagram, the Bīja belonging to the goddess being also inscribed a certain number of times on each petal.

The Śrī-ćakra or holy circle is delineated in a diagram of this kind and then worshipped. It is supposed to represent the orb of the earth, nine triangles being drawn within the circle to denote the nine continents. In the centre is the drawing of a mouth, which is believed to typify the female energy (Śakti) presiding over the circle. According to some authorities, even the orthodox Śaṅkarāćārya must have been a Śakti-worshipper; for he is known to have placed a representation of the Śrī-ćakra in each of the four monasteries founded by him.

These Yantras or mystic diagrams are thought to be quite as effective in their operation as the Mantras, and of course a combination of both is held to be absolutely irresistible. An enemy may be killed or removed to some other place, or a whole army destroyed, or salvation and supreme felicity in a future state obtained by drawing a six-sided or eight-sided diagram and writing a particular Mantra underneath. If this be done with the blood of an animal[1] killed sacrificially in a place where corpses are burned (Śmaśāna), no power in earth or heaven can resist the terrific potency of the charm. Triangular, pentangular, and nine-triangled Yantras are equally efficacious.

---

[1] It may give an idea of the depths of superstition and degradation to which Śāktism can lead if we note here that the Retas (semen) of either male or female is believed to be still more efficacious.

Let us pass to a brief explanation of the Kavaćas. I need not tell Sanskṛit scholars that the word kavaća properly means a kind of cuirass, breast-plate, or similar armour worn as a defence in battle. With the Śāktas a kavaća is an amulet or talisman worn as a preservative against evil influences, or to bring about the attainment of some desired object. It may consist of a stone, piece of paper, metal, leaf or other material on which Mantras, Yantras, mystical words and formulæ of various kinds are inscribed. It is then worn on the neck, breast, arms, or loins, especially in times of pestilence and sickness. Women often wear kavaćas with the object of propitiating the goddess, and so inducing a condition of body favourable to the production of male offspring.

The term kavaća is also applied to whole hymns when they are used as charms.

As to the Nyāsas, these consist in mentally assigning various parts of the body to the protection of tutelary presiding deities, with imposition of the hand or fingers, and repetition of texts, mystical words, and syllables.

The Mudrās, on the other hand, are intertwinings of the fingers supposed to possess an occult meaning and to have extraordinary efficacy. Their use as well as that of the Nyāsas will be more fully explained in treating of the morning and evening religious services called Sandhyā.

It may be noted here that four days, or rather nights, are kept as principal festivals by the left-hand worshippers:—namely, (1) the night of the Kṛishṇa-janmāshṭamī (see note 2, p. 113), called the Kāla-rātri; (2) the Moha-rātri, or Kālī-ćaturdaśī, kept on the fourteenth day of the second half of Āśvina; (3) the Śiva-rātri or Mahā-rātri, kept on the fourteenth of the dark half of Māgha; (4) the Dāruṇī Rātriḥ, kept on the day before the Holī festival, which is on the fifteenth day of the first half of Phālguna. But besides these four festivals, nine nights in each of the months Āśvina, Ćaitra, Pausha, and Āshāḍha are also observed as holy nights. It is declared that ceremonies performed on any of these nights must of necessity confer superhuman power (siddhi).

Before concluding this part of our subject, it may be well to note a few more particulars in regard to the works we have so often quoted as the chief authority for the doctrines and practices of the Śāktas.

The Tantras, I repeat, are the bible of Śāktism. Like the Purāṇas, they are sometimes called a fifth Veda. Very commonly, too, the name Āgama, 'that which has come down' (also applied to the Brāhmaṇa portion of the Veda), is given to them in contradistinction to Nigama, which is a general name for the Vedas, Dharma-śāstras, Purāṇas, and other Smṛiti works. Sometimes the authorship of the Tantras is attributed to Dattātreya, who is worshipped as an incarnation of Brahmā, Vishṇu, and Śiva (p. 267), but the general opinion is that they were revealed by Śiva alone. None of them have as yet been printed or translated in Europe. They are said to be sixty-four in number, without counting a large collection of works of a Tāntrik character and Śākta tendency. As a general rule they are written in the form of a dialogue between the god Śiva and his wife; and every Tantra ought, like a Purāṇa, to treat of five subjects—the creation, the destruction of the world, the worship of the gods, the attainment of superhuman power, and the four modes of union with the Supreme Spirit (given at p. 41), to which is sometimes added a fifth, Sārshṭi, 'attaining to the same rank as that of the Deity.' In some of the Tantras it is stated that five Āmnāyas or sacred systems of teaching have been handed down from primeval times, one having issued from each of Śiva's five mouths. As a matter of fact very few conform to any systematic arrangement. Those I have examined seem to be mere hand-books for the practices I have attempted to describe, which to Europeans appear so monstrous that the possibility of any persons believing in their efficacy seems in itself almost incredible.

Whole Tantras teach nothing but various methods of making use of spells for acquiring magical power.

Some give collections of charms for making people enamoured, for destroying enemies and rivals, for producing or preventing diseases, for curing blindness, for injuring crops. Others simply describe the most effectual modes of worshipping the Śaktis, Mahā-vidyās, Mātṛis, Yoginīs, Vaṭukās, or by whatever name the innumerable manifestations of Śiva and his wife may be called. Others confine themselves to an explanation of the Yantras, Bījas, and Mudrās (intertwining of the fingers) belonging to each manifestation, the places suited for the worship of each, the names of trees and plants sacred to each, or permeated by each, and the days of the year allotted to each. Some few touch on nearly every conceivable topic of human knowledge, and contain here and there really interesting matter.

Even alchemy comes in for a share of attention; but the Śākta idea of this pretended science (Rasāyana, Raseśvara-vidyā) is that its only use is to enable the devotee to transmute the decaying particles of his body into an incorruptible substance by means of elixirs compounded of mercury and mica, supposed to consist of the essences of Śiva and his wife Gaurī respectively. After long persistence in the practice of swallowing these elixirs the candidate for beatitude becomes immortal, and not merely united with Śiva but identified with him. This kind of transformation is called Jīvan-mukti, 'salvation during life [1].'

So little is known about the composition of the Tantras that it is not possible to decide at present as to which are the most ancient, and still less as to the date to be assigned to

[1] One of the systems described by Mādhava in his Sarva-darśana-saṅgraha is called the Raseśvara-darśana, or the system which teaches the use of mercury or quicksilver as a means of strengthening the body and giving it divine stability capable of resisting death and preventing further transmigration. Mercury is said to be named Pāra-da because it gives *pāra*, or the farther shore of Metempsychosis.

any of them. They are all said to be founded on the Kaulopanishad. It may, however, be taken for granted that the extant treaties are, like the extant Purāṇas, based on older works; and if the oldest known Purāṇa is not older than the sixth or seventh century, an earlier date can scarcely be attributed to the oldest known Tantra. Perhaps the Rudra-yāmala is one of the most deservedly esteemed and most encyclopedic in its teaching[1]. Others are the Ṡakti-saṅgama, Viṡva-sāra, Mahā-nirvāṇa, Vīra, Kulārṇava (a text-book of the Kaulas), Ṡyāmā-rahasya, Ṡāradā-tilaka, Uḍḍīṡa, Kāmākhyā, Vishṇu-yāmala.

Full as the above works are of doubtful symbolism, they are not all necessarily full of impure allusions, though the teaching contained in the best of them unquestionably tends towards licentiousness. When they are better known, their connection with a distorted view of the Sāṅkhya philosophy, and with some of the corrupt forms of Buddhism, will probably be made clearer. Doubtless they have greatly influenced the later Buddhist literature of Nepāl, and would probably throw much light on the magical hymns and spells of the Atharva-veda.

There are also works called Vaishṇava Tantras, such as the Gautamīya and the Sanat-kumāra, but even in these Ṡiva is the narrator and his wife the supposed listener. Moreover their teaching, which makes Rādhā, the wife of Kṛishṇa, take the place of Durgā as the chief object of adoration, has the same tendency as that of the other Tantras, and equally leads to licentiousness.

Happily the worst abominations of Ṡāktism are gradually dying out in British India; and its true character is impressing itself on the convictions of the more highly educated Hindūs.

---

[1] It is said to consist of 100,000 verses. A section of it, called Jāti-mālā, treating of caste, has been printed at Calcutta.

Nor can the power of the Mantra-śāstrīs stand against the moral and intellectual revolution which is slowly but surely upheaving the whole fabric of superstition. That power is already much weakened, and the field for its exercise among a people, steeped for centuries in debasing and degrading religious and social ideas, is daily becoming narrower. Still in most of the native States, where all the grosser forms of Hindūism are still rampant, the whole system is as firmly established as ever. Even those in high positions, who have no faith in it themselves, find themselves unable to offend the prejudices of their subordinates by venturing to engage in any work or perform the most ordinary act without the sanction of crafty and ignorant Brāhmans claiming divine authority and professing to work miracles through their knowledge and application of the Mantras.

Well may the enlightened Brāhman before quoted (see p. 189) give expression to his indignation thus:—

'All sensible people ought to say to the Mantra-śāstrīs, We have suffered much misery through your deceit, we have been taxed very heavily by you, and you have involved us in the results of all your wickedness. It is true your ancestors had some knowledge of different sciences and imparted some of that knowledge to us. In return for these benefits we have fed you and supported you and promoted your interests. When you found your power established over us you abandoned the duty of seeking after knowledge, and worked only mischief. Your teaching is now a mere reflection of your ignorance, wickedness, folly, and hypocrisy. You harass and injure us in a thousand ways. If our knowledge increases, you try to prevent it, thinking that, if inquiry is encouraged, your customers will decrease. We begin to see through your artifices. Begone, every one of you, and don't attempt to deceive us any more.'

CHAPTER VIII.

Tutelary and Village Deities.

It may be said that all deities ought to be called tutelary, and no doubt the idea of protecting from harm is essential to the later idea of a god. But among rude, uncultivated races the first conception of a god is never that of a beneficent saviour. Primitive man, just emerging from the depths of a merely animal existence, finds himself face to face with mighty mysterious natural forces. He sees, feels, and dreads their operation. He personifies and deifies them, and gives them names expressive of the awe with which their power has impressed him, or of his desire to propitiate them. It is a question whether any of the primary names for God in any country are significant of his attributes as a Guardian, Saviour, and Deliverer. In India tutelary functions were no doubt ultimately associated with both Ṡiva and Vishṇu, but in the case of Vishṇu they were delegated, as we have seen, to his incarnations or descents on earth, and in the case of Ṡiva to his sons Gaṇeṡa and Skanda and to his consort the great goddess Devī, regarded as the mother of the world and worshipped under a great variety of different names in different localities. In the South of India another tutelary god named Ayenār, the reputed son of Vishṇu and Ṡiva (see p. 218), is very popular among the peasantry.

Whether the worship of these village deities (grāma-devatā) is a mere offshoot or ramification of the religion of Ṡiva and Vishṇu is very doubtful. It is much more probable that the village gods represent far earlier and more primitive objects of worship. Possibly they may even be developments of local fetishes once held in veneration by uncivilized aboriginal tribes and afterwards grafted into the Hindū system by the Brāhmans, whose wise policy it has ever been to appropriate and utilize all existing cults, customs, and superstitions. It is certain that even in the present day scarcely a village, and indeed scarcely a household in India, is without its tutelary divinity, usually represented by some rudely carved image or symbol, located in homely shrines or over doorways, or, it may be, denoted by simple patches of red paint on rocks or under sacred trees or in cross-ways, and always taking the place of the superior gods in the religion of the lower orders.

The question however arises:—In what sense are these homely village deities tutelary? From whom or what are they believed to protect?

A Christian, when he prays for deliverance from evil, means not only deliverance from a personal evil spirit, but from the evil of sin and from the general evil existing in the world around him.

An ordinary Hindū peasant's religion consists mainly in seeking deliverance from the evil inflicted by demons. The religiously-minded are no doubt sincere in their desire to be freed from inborn sin and its effects through ceremonial washings and purificatory rites (saṇskāras), but the majority are much more eager to escape the calamities which may overtake them through demoniacal, planetary, and atmospheric influences. In truth I am convinced that those Europeans who have lived in closest contact with the Hindū mind will bear me out in my assertion that the great majority of the inhabitants of India are, from the cradle to the burning-ground, victims of a form of disease which is best expressed by the term demonophobia. They are haunted and oppressed by a perpetual dread of demons. They are firmly convinced that evil spirits of all kinds, from malignant fiends to merely mischievous imps and elves, are ever on the watch to harm, harass and torment them, to cause plague, sickness, famine and disaster, to impede, injure and mar every good work.

Hence a tutelary god among the Hindūs is simply one that delivers from the calamities, actual and potential, believed to be due to demons.

Worship of Gaṇeśa (Gaṇa-pati) and Su-brahmaṇya.

At the head of tutelary village deities I place the two sons of Śiva:—1. Gaṇeśa (p. 59)—also called Gaṇa-pati (commonly Gaṇ-pati, and in Southern India Puliyār, 'the son'); 2. Skanda —often called Kārttikeya, and still more commonly Su-brahmaṇya. But in so placing these two gods I must explain that my investigations in India have led me to take a view of their character and functions somewhat different from that hitherto propounded by European writers on Hindū Mythology. It is usual for such writers to describe Gaṇeśa as the god of learning and patron of letters[1]; whereas the whole province of speech, language, and literature is really placed under the presidency of the goddess Sarasvatī[2]. The only possible ground I have been able to discover for connecting Gaṇeśa with the patronage of learning is the circumstance that every Indian book opens with the formula Śrī Gaṇeśāya namaḥ.

But the real explanation of this is that the writing of a book is among Hindūs a very serious and solemn undertaking, peculiarly liable to obstruction from spiteful and jealous spirits of evil, and the favour of Gaṇeśa is invoked to counteract their malignity. It seldom occurs to an ordinary Hindū writer to suppose that the failure of his literary efforts is likely to be due to his own incapacity. In

[1] I find that even M. Barth, in his recent excellent work on the religions of India, falls into this mistake.

[2] Thus we find the first verse of the Mahābhārata addresses homage to Sarasvatī, not to Gaṇeśa.

this, as in all other enterprises, want of success is attributed not to want of skill, energy, or persistency, but to negligence in taking proper precautions against demoniacal jealousy and obstruction.

So far indeed is Gaṇeśa from being the god of learning, he is peculiarly the god of the lower orders and uneducated classes. Hence in a verse said to be extracted from the old version of Manu he is called the god of the Śūdras[1].

Again, it is usual to describe Skanda as the god of war, as if he were a kind of Hindū Mars, whereas his martial qualities are only displayed in leading the armies of the gods against the countless host of their enemies the evil demons.

With a view then to a fuller explanation of the history and character of two gods so generally honoured and propitiated throughout India, I must begin by pointing out that the cultus of both Gaṇeśa and Su-brahmaṇya is a mere offshoot of Śaivism. The very name Gaṇeśa (Gaṇa-īśa) or Gaṇa-pati, meaning 'lord of hosts,' belonged originally to Śiva (see p. 77), for Śiva is, as we have seen, surrounded by countless troops or hosts (gaṇa) of servants and officers, who are constantly in readiness to traverse earth and air for the execution of his orders.

And just as Śiva is ever engaged in two opposite duties—on the one hand, as Rudra and Kāla, directing and controlling dissolution and death, on the other hand, as Śiva and Śambhu, presiding over re-integration and new life—so by a figment of mythology, those of his emissaries who are charged with carrying out the former operation are converted into evil demons, imps, and devils, while those who are agents in the latter are held to be good angels, ministering spirits, and beneficent genii.

And hence it is that two entirely opposite classes of demoniacal beings are believed to be continually roaming about

---

[1] The verse is—Viprāṇāṃ daivataṃ Śambhuḥ Kshatriyāṇāṃ tu Mādhavaḥ Vaiśyānāṃ tu bhaved Brahmā Śūdrāṇāṃ Gaṇa-nāyakaḥ.

earth, air and sky—the one ill-disposed towards all forms of life, human and divine, the other well-disposed; the one destroyers, the other protectors; the one instruments of calamity and disaster, the other agents of good-fortune and prosperity.

It is to be observed, too, that differences of rank, character, and function are supposed to separate both good and bad spirits[1] into various subdivisions. For example, the highest order of evil demons, who may be called arch-fiends, disdain any lower aim than the humiliation and subjugation of the gods; and, to effect this, they will sometimes undergo long courses of austerity and self-mortification, in the hope of making themselves omnipotent. The next in order vent their rancour and hostility upon human beings. Of these, again, some destroy life, some inflict diseases, some disturb religious rites. Another class are mere demons of mischief and obstruction who delight in hindering good works or frightening women and children, like the ghosts, hobgoblins, elves, and bogies of nursery tale and fable.

Similar differences are supposed to divide good demons into various orders and degrees of rank and power.

It is over these countless hosts of good and evil demons that the god Śiva exercises sovereignty. They are all primarily subject to his authority; but the actual command over them is delegated to his two sons, Gaṇeśa and Skanda.

As for Skanda, although the younger and less generally worshipped, he holds the more ambitious office. He is called the god of war, because he is commander-in-chief or generalissimo (Senā-pati) of the good demon armies. These he leads against the hosts of their enemies the evil demons; notably against those rebellious and arrogant arch-fiends who seek to overcome and enslave the gods. He is often called Kārttikeya, from his foster-mothers, the six Kṛittikās

[1] The use of the term 'spirit' for demon is not intended to imply that demons are incorporeal spiritual beings.

or Pleiades, and then has six heads[1] and twelve arms. These are to enable him to hold weapons of different kinds, like a person armed with the many-chambered revolver of modern times.

But he is not seldom represented in other characters. For example, in some places he appears as simply a beautiful youth (Kumāra) riding on a peacock, divested of all martial attributes. Again, in the South of India, where his cultus prevails most extensively, he is not worshipped as presiding over war, but under the name Su-brahmaṇya, 'very pious or sacred.' He is sometimes held to be unmarried, but I found that his temples are either frequented by those who seek through his intervention to be delivered from evil spirits, or else by women who hope by propitiating him to obtain handsome sons. He is himself married, and has two wives popularly called Devayānī and Vallī-amman. These, like their husband, are believed to grant children, to prevent the attacks and thwart the malice of devils, and when evil spirits have actually taken possession of any one, to be capable of casting them out. At Tanjore and other places in the South of India I found the temples of Skanda in his character of Su-brahmaṇya side by side with those of his brother Gaṇeśa, and in some districts Su-brahmaṇya is the more popular. He has a celebrated temple on the Pulney hills.

As to Gaṇeśa, it is certain that he has no pretensions whatever to be regarded as a martial deity. On the contrary, he is essentially a homely village-god. Fighting and activity of any kind are repugnant to his nature, which, however, appears to be somewhat contradictory and full of curious enigmas. His form resembles that of a bloated, well-fed Brāhman seated at his ease with legs folded under him on a lotus-throne, the very beau-ideal of satiated appetite and indolent self-complacency, but with the head of an

---

[1] The six heads were to enable him to be nursed by his six nurses.

elephant to denote shrewdness or wisdom, and with four arms, holding an elephant-hook, a noose, a mace[1], and a cake, one in each of his hands. Not unfrequently he is represented riding on a rat, and is always associated with images of that animal, probably as emblematical of sagacity. In Southern India I occasionally found his idols in company with those of Nāgas or snakes. Sometimes he has a garland round his neck, sometimes the sacred Brāhmanical cord. Unlike Su-brahmaṇya or Skanda, he is not generally represented as married; though according to some he has two wives called Ṛiddhi and Siddhi[2], 'Prosperity' and 'Success.'

Contrasting Gaṇeśa then with Su-brahmaṇya, we must always bear in mind that Gaṇeśa is not the commander and leader, but rather the king and lord of the demon-host, ruling over both good and bad alike, and controlling those malignant spirits who are ever plotting evil and causing hindrances and difficulties. But he controls them, not as Skanda does, by the exercise of bravery and physical energy, but by artifice and stratagem, very much after the manner of some indolent, wily Brāhman who, skilled in the Mantras, sits comfortably at home and by the simple repetition of a few texts, spells and cabalistic words, compels good and evil spirits to obey his behests.

Nor is it out of harmony with this theory of the true character of the god that the Gaṇeśa of modern mythology is thought by some Pandits to be a development of the Vedic Brahmaṇas-pati or Bṛihaspati, 'lord of prayer'—once the personification of religion and devotion—who by the simple force of his supplications protects the pious from the machinations of the impious. It is certain that the

---

[1] Instead of a mace he has sometimes a lotus, and sometimes a fragment of one of his own tusks which he once broke off in a fit of uncontrollable passion.

[2] Others make his two wives Buddhi and Siddhi, 'Intelligence' and 'Success.'

modern popular Gaṇeśa has no place in the Veda, the epithet Gaṇānāṃ Gaṇa-patiḥ, which occurs in Ṛig-veda II. 23. 1, having reference to Brahmaṇas-pati as lord of the Gaṇas or troops of divinities[1].

What the Gaṇeśa or Gaṇa-pati of the present day really represents is a complex personification of sagacity, shrewdness, patience, and self-reliance—of all those qualities, in short, which overcome hindrances and difficulties, whether in performing religious acts, writing books, building houses, making journeys, or undertaking anything. He is before all things the typical embodiment of success in life; with its usual accompaniments of good-living, plenteousness, prosperity, and peace. This is the true secret of his popularity. This is why his images and shrines smeared with red paint are seen everywhere throughout India. In all ceremonies, *except funeral rites*, and in all undertakings Gaṇeśa is first invoked.

It should be noted, however, that although his principal office is to remove impediments, especially from religious rites, he may also cause hindrances; and this in fact is implied in his names Vighneśa and Vighna-rāja, 'lord of obstacles.' So also, although he is essentially a god who presides over domestic happiness and rural prosperity, driving away evil demons from houses, fields, crops, and herds, he may also, if not propitiated, allow malicious imps to haunt houses, infest roads, mar harvests, and cause a murrain among cattle.

When I was nearly dashed to pieces by restive horses, one of which broke away from my carriage and was precipitated over a precipice on the Ghāṭ between Poona and Mahābaleśvar, I was told by a wise-looking native who witnessed the accident that the road in that district was infested by demons who often caused accidents, and that if I had taken care to propitiate Gaṇeśa before starting I should have escaped all molestation and all risk of being upset.

[1] The same expression Gaṇānāṃ Gaṇa-patiḥ occurs also in the Vājasaneyi-Saṃhitā of the Yajur-veda, XXIII. 19.

Altogether, the god Gaṇeśa represents a being who is a curious mixture of divine and demoniacal, benevolent and malevolent, intellectual and animal propensities, all of which are typified by the somewhat grotesque and bizarre assemblage of symbols noticeable in his image.

Notably, too, his worship is combined with that of every other god. For all sects unite in claiming him as their own. It is on this account that his shrines and images are generally found in association with those of other deities, and are usually to be seen in the approaches or vestibules of large temples. Often, however, they stand alone, and are then to be found outside villages, under trees, or in cross-ways, or indeed in any kind of locality, but always smeared with red paint in token of good-luck and auspiciousness. Solitary temples of large size dedicated to Gaṇeśa are rare. The largest I saw anywhere in India was at Wā-i, between Poona and Mahābaleśvar. It contained a colossal image of the god, and in this temple I noticed a singularly simple and easy method of doing him honour. A man entered with a small vessel of holy water from the neighbouring river. He repeated no prayers, but with a diminutive spoon poured a little of the water two or three times on the lower extremities of the huge image and then retired. Another large Gaṇeśa temple which I visited is on the summit of the rock of Trichinopoly, Gaṇeśa being there called Ujjhī Puliyār[1].

In point of fact Gaṇeśa has in the present day few exclusive adorers; that is to say, there are few sectarians who trust to him alone for salvation, though all propitiate him for success. In former times the Gaṇeśa or Gāṇapatya sect, as it was called (see p. 59), was divided into six sub-sects who worshipped six different forms of the god, named respectively (according to the Śaṅkara-vijaya) Mahā-Gaṇapati, Haridrā-

[1] There is also a shrine to Su-brahmaṇya on this celebrated rock, and I noticed as a peculiarity that the image of a peacock was represented looking into Gaṇeśa's shrine, not into that of his brother.

Gaṇapati, Uććhishṭa-Gaṇapati (also called Heramba), Navanīta-Gaṇapati, Svarṇa-Gaṇapati, and Santāna-Gaṇapati[1].

Worship of Ayenār.

Closely allied to the worship of Gaṇeśa and Skanda (Subrahmaṇya), and generally to Śaivism, is the worship of Ayenār; a village-god very popular in the extreme South of India, but little known in other parts. One distinction, however, may be noticed between the worship of Ayenār and that of Śiva's two sons. He is never asked for any positive good. He only protects from harm, and his worship consists solely in propitiation. His name Ayenār is said to be a corruption of Hari-hara (=Vishṇu and Śiva, see p. 65), and he is believed to be the son of both these deities; that is, he is the product of the marriage of Śiva and Vishṇu when the latter took the form of a beautiful woman. He is popularly called Ayenār-appan[2], and sometimes has another name, Śāstā, 'the ruler or governor.'

Like Gaṇeśa and Skanda, the popular deity Ayenār is a lord and leader of the demon-host, and his province is to guard the fields, crops, and herds of the peasantry, and drive away their enemies the devils and fiends, who are ever on the watch to inflict disease, blight, and other calamities. Accordingly, outside every village in Southern India, and generally among a group of trees to the west of the village, may be seen the shrines of Ayenār, surrounded with rude clay or

---

[1] Ḍhunḍhi-rāja, said to mean 'king of Śiva's hosts,' is another popular form of Gaṇeśa at Benares. I noticed numerous worshippers at his shrine, as well as at that of another shrine of the same god in his character of Sākshin or witness. In this latter character he is usually called Sākshi-Vināyaka (vulgarly Sākhi-Vināyaka). Every pilgrim who has been the round of the shrines in the Pañćakośī of Benares must finish up by a visit to Gaṇeśa, 'the witness,' who then bears testimony to the completeness of the difficult task he has accomplished.

[2] Appan is the Tamil for 'father,' as Amman is for 'mother.'

terra-cotta figures of horses and other animals—often of life-size—on which he is supposed to ride when keeping guard. His image is that of a human form painted a reddish colour and very roughly carved, sometimes in a sitting posture, sometimes on horseback. When properly represented, he ought to have a crown on his head, the Śaiva mark on his forehead, a sceptre in his hand, and ornaments on his person. Often images of Gaṇeśa are placed near him. He has two wives (known by the names Pūraṇī and Pudkalā), who generally sit on each side of him, and take an active part in driving away demons, especially at night, when like their husband they ride about the fields on horses. It is on this account that no villager in Southern India likes to be out in the fields at night, and on no account will any one pass near the shrines of Ayenār and his wives after dark. If any venturesome person happens to cross their path when they are careering about the fields, he is liable to be taken for an evil spirit and slain.

After recovery from sickness, or to commemorate any piece of good-fortune, the villagers place fresh clay horses round the shrine of Ayenār, as thank-offerings or in fulfilment of vows. He is also at such times propitiated by offerings of the blood of swine, goats, sheep, cocks and other animals, or by cooked food and libations of strong liquor.

If cholera or pestilence of any kind breaks out, the villagers redouble their offerings to the priests of the shrine, who are generally very poor and of the lowest caste, and are very glad to receive any money or consume any eatables that may be offered to the god.

I examined with great interest many shrines of Ayenār in Southern India, and particularly one at Permagudy, on my way from Madurā to Rāmeśvaram. It was situated close to a grove of small trees not far from the village. Under a rough stone canopy was a rudely carved stone male idol. The wives of the god were not represented, but about twenty-five toy-like terra-cotta horses, some as large as life, were ranged on each side of the shrine. Several of these fictile animals had grotesque images upon them representing riders, and some of them were so badly formed that it was difficult to say whether they were intended for lions or horses. In the front of the shrine was a rude stone altar for sacrifices and oblations, but I saw no signs of any recent offerings, nor was a single worshipper of the god to be seen anywhere. I noticed indeed that all the shrines of Ayenār had a deserted appearance, the fact being that he is never worshipped in our sense of the word. He is only propitiated in emergencies. Every year after harvest-time a festival is kept in his honour, when numerous animals are sacrificed, and images of the god are decorated with ornaments and drawn about through the village streets on the rude clay horses which I have described.

Worship of Hanumān.

In connexion with the subject of local tutelary deities it ought to be mentioned that a very common village-god in the Dekhan, Central and Upper India, is Hanumān (nom. case of Hanumat, a name meaning 'possessing large jaws'). This god derives his popularity from the part he took in assisting Rāma to recover his wife Sītā after she had been carried away to Ceylon by the demon Rāvaṇa. He is one of the chiefs of a host of semi-divine monkey-like beings who, according to the Rāmāyaṇa (I. 16), were created to become Rāma-ćandra's allies. In point of fact, there can be little doubt that Hanumān was originally a mere poetical deification of some well-known leader of the wild aboriginal tribes, whose appearance resembled that of apes, and who really rendered effective assistance to Rāma in his battles with Rāvaṇa. There were several of these powerful aboriginal chiefs, who, from their accomplishing apparently supernatural feats of strength, were held to be the progeny of various gods. Thus the Simian king Sugrīva was said to be a son of the Sun, and another chief named Bali was a son of Indra.

Hanumān, on the other hand, was believed to be a son of the wind (Pavana or Māruta). He could assume any form at will, wield rocks, remove mountains, dart through the air, seize clouds, and rival Vishṇu's divine bird Garuḍa in swiftness of flight. His devotion to Rāma's service was so great that he is worshipped over a great part of India as the type and model of a faithful devoted servant. Many believe that, when propitiated, he can confer supernatural muscular strength and bodily power. His images, which, to denote the reverence in which they are held, are always smeared with vermilion (sindūra) and oil, are generally rudely formed. I noticed, however, that they were most common in the Dekhan, where they are generally found outside villages. Not that there is any lack of them in large towns. In the centre of Poona, I came across a shrine containing a shapeless idol, which was said to be an image of Hanumān several hundred years old. It was set up under a Banian tree. A man was in the act of painting it with bright red paint as I passed, and another man was prostrating himself at full length on the ground before it.

Again, I visited a large temple dedicated to Hanumān outside the town of Kaira. It is said to be well endowed. Offerings of oil are constantly presented to Hanumān, and eighty Maunds of oil had recently been offered to this idol. Within the enclosure of his temple were shrines to Rāma and Kṛishṇa, both of which occupied subordinate positions. Of course the worship of Hanumān is usually connected with that of Vishṇu, but here in this enclosure was also a Liṅga shrine[1], and another of the goddess of small-pox, and all around was a cloister which served as a Dharma-śālā, or lodging for travellers.

---

[1] According to some legends, Hanumān was a son of Śiva.

The veneration in which apes and monkeys of every kind are held throughout India cannot fail to strike a stranger as remarkable. This is doubtless connected with the homage paid to Hanumān. It is not, however, identified with that homage; for although monkeys are believed to be his near relations, they were probably independent objects of worship from the earliest times[1]. Yet these animals are very ungod-like in their habits, and not one whit superior to the most mischievous monkeys in any other part of the world. Often a troop will make its appearance in an Indian village, tear off the roof of a native house, or do even worse damage out of sheer wantonness. Yet no householder would ever dream of reprisals. The sacred character of the monkey shields him from all harm.

Mother-worship.

Undoubtedly the most popular tutelary deities of India are the divine Mātṛis or Mothers. The propitiation of Ayenār and his wives is confined to the South, but mother-worship is extended everywhere throughout India. In the first place, every living mother is venerated as a kind of deity by her children. Then every village has its own special guardian mother, called Mātā or Ambā. Generally there is also a male deity, who protects like the female from all adverse and demoniacal influences. But the mother is the favourite object of adoration; and no wonder; for, as we have seen in the preceding chapter, activity, power, and force (śakti) are supposed to be her peculiar attributes. Perhaps however the real reason for her attracting more homage than the god is that she is held to have a thoroughly feminine nature. She is more easily propitiated by prayer, flattery, and offerings; more

[1] It seems not unlikely that the Vṛishākapi of Ṛig-veda X. 86 may point to a very early veneration of apes, arising, perhaps, from their mysterious resemblance to men.

ready to defend from evil; more irritable, uncertain, and wayward in her temper and moods; more dangerously spiteful, and prone to inflict diseases, if offended by neglect.

In point of fact, the worship of the divine Mothers (Mātṛis) is, as already pointed out, a branch of Śaivism, and particularly of that form of Śaivism called Śāktism (p. 181).

Indeed, one of the most remarkable features of the multiform and many-sided Hindū religion is the efficacy supposed to belong to this form of worship. Probably the idea of Mother-worship had its origin in the patriarchal constitution of ancient Āryan society. Among the early Āryans the paternal and maternal tie, and, indeed, the whole family bond, was intensely strong. If the father was regarded with awe as the primary source of life, the mother was an object of devotion to the children of the family as the more evident author of their existence. And again, if the father was venerated as the food-supplier and protector (pitā), the mother was beloved as the meter out (mātā) of daily nourishment—the arranger of the household, measuring and ordering its affairs as the moon (also called mātā) measured the time. To the Āryan family the father and mother were present gods.

Can we wonder that, with the growth of devotional ideas and the increasing sense of a higher superintending providence, the earliest religious creed was constructed on what may be called paternal and maternal lines? At first the sky (Dyaus, Zeus), bending over all, was personified as a Heavenly Father (Dyaus-pitar, Jupiter), and the Earth as the Mother of all creatures. Then, in place of the Earth, Infinite Space (A-diti) was thought of as an eternal Mother. Then Prakṛiti was the germinal productive principle—the eternal Mother, capable of evolving all created things out of herself, but never so creating unless united with the eternal spiritual principle called the eternal Male (Purusha).

To the prevalence of such ideas must, I think, be attributed the fact that everywhere throughout India are scattered shrines which on inspection are found to contain no images or idols shaped like human beings, but simply stone symbols of a double form, intended to typify the blending of the male and female principles in creation. The casual tourist, whose notions of propriety are cast in a European mould, is shocked by what he considers an evidence of the utter degradation of Indian thought. He turns away in disgust, and denounces the Hindū religion as simple abomination.

My own researches into Indian religious thought have led me to view in these symbols a proof of the hold which the ancient dualistic philosophy has on the Hindū mind. It is common to say that Brāhmanism is Pantheism, and no doubt it is, broadly speaking, true that Brāhmanism is *a kind of Pantheism;* but to apply the term Pantheism, without any qualification, to the ordinary religion of the Hindūs[1] is altogether misleading. A small minority of orthodox Brāhmans are strict Pantheists according to the Vedantic doctrine (see p. 36), but a large majority of the Hindūs are believers in one personal God—that is to say, in either Śiva or Vishṇu or their manifestations—and are therefore Theists. Yet it is true that their Theism is no stern belief in the unity of God. It constantly tends to pantheistic or polytheistic superstitions, and especially to the mystical theory of a duality in unity before explained (see p. 181). Such a theory rests, as we have seen, on the philosophical doctrine of two distinct eternally existing essences—Spirit regarded as a male principle, and Matter or the germ of the external world regarded as a female. Without the union of the two no creation takes place. To any one imbued with these dualistic conceptions the Liṅga and the Yoni are suggestive of no improper ideas. They are either types of the two mysterious creative forces—the efficient and material causes of the universe—or symbols of one divine power delegating procreative energy to male and female organisms. They are mystical representatives, and perhaps the best

[1] As I have heard it applied by Missionaries and others.

possible impersonal representatives, of the abstract expressions 'paternity' and 'maternity.'

Of course, such ideas are too mystical for the masses of the people. Yet the ordinary Hindū finds no difficulty in accepting the theory of a universe proceeding from a divine father and mother. Hence, as we have already seen, some images of Śiva (called Ardha-nārīśa) represent him as female on one side of his body and male on the other, to indicate that he combines in his own person maternal as well as paternal qualities and attributes, and that all the mothers of India are simply manifestations of portions of his essence. I need not repeat here that the god's energy is supposed to be located more especially in the female half of his nature, and that the divine mothers are variously classified according to various degrees of participation in that energy, the highest being identified with different forms of his supposed consort, the lowest including human mothers downwards, who are all worshipped as incarnations of the one divine productive capacity of nature. Compare p. 183.

There are about one hundred and forty distinct Mothers in Gujarāt, besides numerous varieties of some of the more popular forms. In all likelihood every one of these, though declared by the Brāhmans to be separate forms of Śiva's consort Kālī, is really the representative of some local deity (Grāma-devatā), worshipped by the inhabitants from time immemorial. Some are represented by rudely carved images, others by simple symbols, and others are remarkable for preferring empty shrines and the absence of all visible representation.

The first genuine country village I visited on reaching Bombay in 1875 was in Gujarāt. It had as usual two shrines, one to Śiva and his son Gaṇeśa, the other to the local Mātā or Mother, believed to be a manifestation of Śiva's wife and called Khoḍiyār, or 'Mischief.' The attitude of mind and usual disposition of this Mother towards the villagers appears to be anything but maternal. Her shrine when I visited it was of a very rough and ready character, little better than a mere mud shed, open to all the winds of heaven and accessible to all comers—even to unbelievers like myself, quite as much as to her faithful votaries. Her image too was by no means attractive in its contour and accompaniments. It was carved in the rudest manner, and might have done duty for an African fetish. I noticed that in some villages the Mother is represented by a simple unworked stone, but always recumbent, never erect, and occasionally a wall or some markings on it are believed to symbolize the presence of the goddess. It is a mistake to suppose that every Hindū temple has an anthropomorphic idol. I passed a shrine near Allahābād dedicated to a local Mother euphemistically called Alopī or 'Non-destroyer,' who here takes the place of the goddess worshipped in the South under the name of Mārī-amman, the 'Destroying Mother,' or goddess of small-pox (see p. 228). There was no image in Alopī's shrine, only a flat stone slab, on which, in consequence of a late outbreak of small-pox, an immense number of offerings of flowers, cocoa-nuts, and grain were being laid by a succession of worshippers, both Hindū and Muhammadan.

On the other hand, when I visited the village over which Khoḍiyār presides, I found no offerings near her image; or if any had been placed there before my arrival they had disappeared. Most probably the few that had been offered had been already appropriated by the village priest, who was nowhere to be seen. The name Khoḍiyār, 'Mischief,' is very significant of this particular Mother's character, for although her function is to shield from harm, she is more inclined to turn mischievous and cause harm, and will certainly do so if her temper is ruffled by any remissness in the daily process of coaxing and conciliating her.

Hence it is no matter of surprise that an outbreak of sickness in the village was attributed entirely to a little temporary slackness in supplying her with her daily nutriment. Extraordinary offerings, therefore—some of them accompanied by the killing of animals and pouring out of blood—had to be made till the disease had abated. When no sickness remained it was believed that the Mother's anger was appeased, no further trouble was taken, and everything returned to the old routine.

Had any native of the district, who happened to have been educated at the Bombay Presidency College, suggested a little attention to sanitary rules as a more effective remedy against cholera or small-pox, he would have been laughed to scorn by his fellow-villagers.

Each of the remaining 139 Mothers of Gujarāt has some speciality. One, named Bećarājī, has numerous imageless shrines. The shrine most frequented is at a place seventy-five miles north of Ahmedābād. Sometimes she is represented by a coloured square figure, divided into six compartments.

Another, named Uṇṭāi, causes and prevents whooping-cough; another, named Berāī, prevents cholera; another, called Marakī (popularly Markī), causes cholera; another, Haḍakāī, controls mad-dogs and prevents hydrophobia; another, Āśāpūrā, represented by two idols, satisfies the hopes of wives by giving children. Others are Kālkā and Hingrāj.

Not a few are worshipped either as causing or protecting from demoniacal possession as a form of bodily disease. The offering of goats' blood to some of these Mothers is supposed to be very effectual; the animals are not always killed.

A story is told of a Hindū doctor who cured a whole village of an outbreak of virulent influenza, attributed to the malignant influences of an angry goddess, by simply assembling the inhabitants, muttering some cabalistic texts, and solemnly letting loose a pair of scape-goats into a neighbouring wood as an offering to the offended deity.

The small-pox goddess is a form of divine mother universally adored under different names through every part of India.

In the upper provinces she is called Śītalā Devī, or simply Devī. In the South her name is Mārī-amman, 'Mother of Death.' This goddess may either avert small-pox—of which there are three different kinds—cause small-pox, or be herself small-pox. In some parts of the country persons who die of small-pox are not burnt, lest the goddess herself should be burnt too. She also presides over cholera and other diseases causing death. Her shrines are generally found outside villages, under trees, or in groves, and are often associated with the shrines of Gaṇeśa.

Some of the most important local Mothers in the South are deifications of celebrated women who were great benefactresses and came to be regarded after death as manifestations or forms of Śiva's wife. Such are Mīnāćī (for Mīnākshī, worshipped at Madurā), Kāmāćī, Viśālāćī, and others.

In the South of India the Mothers are called Ammans.

Notably a Mother named Ella-amman presides over boundaries, and is supposed to have great power over serpents and to be particularly fond of fish.

Another, called Pīdārī, is said to be 'a queen among the devils,' because all who hang or poison themselves, or die any violent death, are turned into malignant demons who would destroy the whole human race if not kept in check by Pīdārī.

Other Mothers dreaded for their fierce nature are themselves simply demons; for example, Ćāmuṇḍā, Marudāyī, and Kāterī. The last is an evil spirit inhabiting the air, and is thought to be too aerial in character to be represented by an image.

All these Mothers are believed to delight in blood and to drink it. Hence the blood of swine, goats, and cocks, besides all kinds of cooked grain, are offered to them. One Mother called Kulumāndī-amman is said to have a special fancy for black kids, and can only be appeased and prevented from causing sickness and death if the blood of at least three or four thousand such kids is presented to her every year.

Sometimes she is personated by a man who is carried on the shoulders of two other men and sucks up some of the blood of the slaughtered animals.

When a woman dies unpurified within fifteen days after childbirth she becomes a demon called Ćuḍel (Churel). She is then always on the watch to attack other young mothers.

On the other hand, the power of at least one well-disposed Mother in Gujarāt is exerted in a remarkable way for the benefit of women after childbirth. Among a very low-caste set of basket-makers (called Pomlā) it is the usual practice of a wife to go about her work immediately after delivery, as if nothing had happened. The presiding Mātā of the tribe is supposed to transfer her weakness to her husband, who takes to his bed and has to be supported with good nourishing food.

The goddess Shashṭhī (Chaṭhī) protects infants, and is therefore worshipped on the sixth day after delivery. She is represented by a simple stone set up under some tree.

The eight Mothers worshipped by the Tāntrikas of Bengal are each represented with a child in her lap, and it is remarkable that Umā, wife of Śiva, when worshipped as a type of beauty and motherly excellence, is always regarded as a virgin [1].

All the Mothers are believed to have control over magical powers, and especially over the secret operations of nature and all those mysterious occult agencies which are intensified by darkness and invisibility. These powers and preternatural faculties they can impart to their worshippers, if properly propitiated. This is a proof of the intimate connexion subsisting between Mother-worship and the doctrines of Śāktism as described in the preceding chapter.

---

[1] So in particular churches at Munich and elsewhere the shrines of the black Virgin are frequented by vast numbers of pilgrims, who hang up votive offerings, often consisting of waxen arms and legs, around her altar, in the firm belief that they owe the restoration of broken limbs and the recovery from various diseases to her intervention.

CHAPTER IX.

Demon-worship and Spirit-worship.

THIS subject has already been to some extent anticipated in the previous chapter. There I have endeavoured to point out that the universal prevalence of the worship of tutelary deities among the great mass of the population in India is the result of a perpetual dread of evil demons—a dread which haunts Hindūs of all ranks and stations, from the highest to the lowest, with the exception of those fortunate persons whom a European education has delivered from the dominion of superstitious ideas.

My object in the present chapter will be to show that the very demons and evil spirits are as much objects of worship as the gods who defend men from their malice; just as the tutelary deities themselves may under aggravating circumstances turn into angry demons who require to be propitiated (see p. 245).

In fact, a belief in every kind of demoniacal influence has always been from the earliest times an essential ingredient in Hindū religious thought. The idea probably had its origin in the supposed peopling of the air by spiritual beings—the personifications or companions of storm and tempest. Certainly no one who has ever been brought into close contact with the Hindūs in their own country can doubt the fact that the worship of at least ninety per cent. of the people of India in the present day is a worship of fear. Not that the existence of good deities presided over by one Supreme Being is doubted; but that these deities are believed to be too absolutely good to need propitiation; just as in ancient histories of the Slāv races, we are told that they believed in a white and a black god, but paid adoration to the last alone, having, as they supposed, nothing to apprehend from the beneficence of the first or white divinity.

The simple truth is that evil of all kinds, difficulties, dangers, and disasters, famines, diseases, pestilences, and death, are thought by an ordinary Hindū to proceed from demons, or, more properly speaking, from devils, and from devils alone. These malignant beings are held, as we have seen, to possess varying degrees of rank, power, and malevolence. Some aim at destroying the entire world, and threaten the sovereignty of the gods themselves. Some delight in killing men, women, and children, out of a mere thirst for human blood. Some take a mere mischievous pleasure in tormenting, or revel in the infliction of sickness, injury, and misfortune. All make it their business to mar or impede the progress of good works and useful undertakings.

And the remarkable thing is, that the power wielded by certain arch-demons over men, and even gods, is supposed to have been acquired by the practice of religious austerities. It is said of the demon Rāvaṇa, that after undergoing severe austerities in a forest for ten thousand years, standing in the midst of five fires with his feet in the air, he obtained from the god Brahmā powers greater than those possessed by the gods themselves.

We must, however, at the outset guard against the idea that in Hindū mythology the expressions devil and demon—any more than the Greek διάβολος and δαίμων—are convertible terms; or that these two words at all adequately express the immense variety of spiritual beings supposed to hold communication with man or liable to be brought into relationship with him.

It is well known that Indian literature makes constant mention of numerous regions above and below the earth which serve as the abode of such beings. Thus we learn from the Epic poems and Purāṇas that there are seven upper and seven lower worlds[1] (see p. 102, note), and beneath the latter are twenty-one hells. They are enumerated in Manu IV. 88–90, and others are added in Vishṇu-purāṇa II. 6[2].

The hells are for the infliction of various degrees of suffering on sinful men. Yet they are not places of eternal punishment. They are merely temporary purgatories. One is a place of terrific darkness; another consists of heated caldrons (tapta-kumbha); another of red-hot iron (tapta-loha); another contains pits of red-hot charcoal; another of blood; another is a dense forest whose leaves are sharp swords; another is a hell of pincers (Sandaṇśa); another is a sea of fetid mud; another is a plain paved with iron spikes[3]. In

[1] All fourteen worlds are believed to rest on the thousand heads of the great serpent Śesha; or the earth which is the lowest of the seven upper worlds is supposed to be supported at the quarters and intermediate quarters of the sky by eight male and eight female mythical elephants. Then, again, the earth is thought to be composed of seven great circular islands (most of which are known by the name of some tree or plant, such as Jambu, Kuśa, Plaksha, Śālmali), surrounded by seven circular seas, all of which are described in Mahā-bhārata VI. 236, etc., and in the Vishṇu-purāṇa II. 2, etc. See also my 'Indian Wisdom,' p. 419.

[2] This Purāṇa and the Bhāgavata make twenty-eight hells.

[3] In a recent number of a Chicago paper I find the following curiously parallel ideas quoted from a Roman Catholic book for children, by the Rev. J. Furniss: 'The fourth dungeon is the boiling kettle. Listen; there is a sound like that of a kettle boiling. The blood is boiling in the scalded brains of that boy; the brain is boiling and bubbling in his head; the marrow is boiling in his bones. The fifth dungeon is the red-hot oven, in which is a little child. Hear how it screams to come out; see how it turns and twists itself about in the fire; it beats its head against the roof of the oven; it stamps its feet upon the floor of the oven.' The idea of terrific torture lasting to all eternity seems a wholly Western conception. The same Chicago paper goes on to quote from another author: 'The world will probably be converted into a great lake or liquid globe of fire, in which the wicked shall be overwhelmed, which shall always be in tempest, in which they shall be tossed to and fro, having no rest day nor night .... their heads, their eyes, their tongues, their hands, their feet, their loins and their vitals shall for ever be full of a glowing, melting fire, fierce enough to melt the very rocks and elements.' So, again, a celebrated preacher is reported to have said in a sermon: 'When thou diest thy soul will be tormented alone; that will be hell for it; but at the Day of Judgment thy body will join thy soul and thou

the same way the Svarga or heaven of Brāhmanism is merely a temporary paradise (pp. 49; 71).

On the other hand, the seven worlds immediately below the earth are not places of punishment at all. According to the Vishṇu-purāṇa (II. 5) they are regions adorned with beautiful palaces, groves and streams, where the sun diffuses light, not heat, and the moon shines for illumination, not for cold; where the air is resonant with the song of birds, and where are all kinds of delicious food and beverages.

All seven lower regions (which are not to be confounded with the hells), and especially the one called Pātāla, are inhabited by demoniacal creatures—such as the Daityas and Dānavas (p. 238), of a nature not necessarily wicked, and in some respects superior to that of men. According to one legend, the Demon Bali reigns in these regions[1] (see p. 110), but, if this be accepted, he is not to be confounded with Yama (p. 290). Notably they are peopled by a race half men, half serpents, called Nāgas. These serpent-demons (see pp. 321–323), who are described as having jewels in their heads, are fabled to have sprung from Kadrū wife of Kaśyapa, and some of the females among them (nāga-kanyās) are even said to have married human heroes[2]. They are ruled over by three chief serpents called Śesha, Vāsuki, and Takshaka, who also exercise control over the ordinary snakes which infest the earth.

Again, the seven upper worlds, including the world which is

---

wilt have twin hells; thy body sweating drops of blood, and thy soul suffused with agony. In fierce fire, exactly like that we have on earth, thy body will be, asbestos-like, for ever unconsumed; all thy veins roads for the feet of pain to travel on; every nerve a string on which the devil shall for ever play his diabolical tune of hell's unutterable lament.'

[1] At the Calcutta Exhibition of 1883–1884, I was greatly amused by coming across an image of the Demon Bali, which had been labelled by a native clerk 'King of the Netherlands.'

[2] In this way Ulūpī became the wife of Arjuna, and, curiously enough, a tribe of Rājputs, now existing, claims descent from the Nāgas.

the peculiar abode of man, are inhabited by countless hosts of superhuman and semi-divine creatures of all kinds. Apparently some of the highest worlds are set apart for the exclusive occupation of those beatified creatures who have attained a state of absolute perfection; for example, the Siddhas and others. But the regions just above the earth—especially the region corresponding to the atmosphere, called Bhuvar—are tenanted by numerous demonized spirits of dead men and superhuman beings, who, like the inhabitants of the lower worlds, may fitly be designated by the general name 'demons[1].' They have been already alluded to in chapter VIII (p. 209). Like men, they are generally gifted with free-will, and may have good or evil proclivities, and even the best of them may fall away from religion and virtue. They may be pious or impious, benevolent or malevolent, merciful or cruel. They may be obedient to the gods as their servants or followers, or may be opposed to them as enemies. Similarly they may be the friends or foes of man. Some of these beings are constantly traversing the earth and the world immediately above the earth. They are innumerable and constitute a vast Pandemonium, for ever balancing, as it were, the equally vast Pantheon of 330 million gods. Moreover, this Pandemonium is constantly replenished, as we shall see, with new inhabitants from the world of human beings.

And here again we must guard against the notion that the demons, whether good or bad, of Hindū mythology are in their nature and organization wholly spiritual and immaterial. Though they are sometimes called by English writers on Hindū mythology 'spirits,' and though they are certainly endowed with frames of a finer and more ethereal structure than the bodies of men, and not necessarily visible to men, yet these frames have for their essential elements gross (sthūla) material particles. In point of fact, according

[1] The Sanskṛit term Bhūta, though often restricted to evil demons and devils, may be used generally in the same way. Compare p. 242.

to Hindū ideas, the corporeal organization of the generality of demons stands midway between that of men and gods. For it is must be borne in mind that, in accordance with the theory before explained, even the gods have forms, composed of material atoms requiring the support of daily food (see pp. 22, 28, Bhagavad-gītā III. 11), that they are capable of undergoing austerities (see Manu XI. 243, 244), that they are liable to passions and affections like men and animals, and that all, not excepting the one Supreme Personal God, are subject to the inexorable law of disintegration and ultimate absorption into the one universal and sole eternal Essence. In short, gods, demons, and men are so closely connected and inter-related that it is difficult to draw any line of demarcation between them. All three are subject to distinctions of sex; all three have bodies made up of gross elementary (sthūla) particles—these bodies being ethereal in the case of gods, less ethereal in the case of demons, and earthly in the case of men.

It is noticeable, too, that all men living on the earth are said to fall under two categories, those who have divine (daiva) natures, and those who have demoniacal (āsura), and that instances are recorded of demons allying themselves with mortal women. These ideas are quite in keeping with the theory of transmigration (pp. 26–29).

Moreover, it is to be observed that, as it is common to find the bodies of even secondary deities possessed of an extra number of hands and arms, the same is true of the demons. Again, as all the gods have the power of assuming any shape they like and of moving through the air in all directions, so also have the generality of demons. In epic poetry the bodies of the gods are described as very similar to those of men. They differ only in the power of walking above the surface of the ground, in being shadowless, in being free from perspiration, in having eyes that never wink, and flowery ornaments that never wither (Nala V. 24). Whether these latter attributes belong also to all demon-frames is not so clear. Some classes of demons have shapes peculiarly their own which they cannot alter. In general they are dwarfish and shorter than men [1], but the majority enjoy the faculty of assuming any shape suited to their needs, and even that of human beings.

It would be difficult in fact to enumerate all the varieties of these beings, separable as they are, both good and bad, into numberless classes according to differences of rank, powers, and functions.

Nevertheless, it is important to note that they all fall under two grand divisions. The first division embraces all demons created by God at the creation of the world, or brought into existence by the act of superior deities at other times.

The second comprehends all demons whose creation or existence is due to men, that is to say, to the spirits of men who have once lived upon the earth.

To begin with the first of these grand divisions, although it is said to comprise seven principal classes of beings corresponding to the seven worlds—seven demon-kings, with frames in stature equal to a palm-tree, being mentioned in the Śaṅkara-vijaya (chap. LI)—yet it would be easy to show by extracts from both the earlier and later sacred literature that no clearly definite classification or arrangement of demoniacal creatures in any regular series or gradation is possible.

Probably the earliest Sanskṛit expression for a 'demon' is Asura; and we know that although this word is used in the later literature as a general term for evil demons of malignant disposition, it was originally restricted to beings of a god-like nature, and even applied to the gods themselves.

Thus in the Ṛig-veda the word Asura is used as the epithet of Indra, the Maruts, Rudra, and other deities, and is espe-

---

[1] I noticed that all Śiva's troops of demons are represented as dwarfish in the sculptures of the caves of Elephanta.

cially an attribute of the ancient deity Varuṇa, who is first an impersonation of the vault of heaven, and then identified with the Supreme Being.

Furthermore, in the Taittirīya-Saṃhitā (VI. 4. 10. 1) it is said that there was an original equality in goodness and power between the gods and Asuras[1].

In the Taittirīya-Brāhmaṇa, Prajā-pati, or 'the Lord of Creation,' creates the Asuras with his breath (asu). In the Śatapatha-Brāhmaṇa the seventh Manu (or Manu of the present period) is made to produce gods, Asuras, and men. In other passages of the Brāhmaṇas they are said to have their own priests and sacrificial rites.

On the other hand, in the Veda various orders of evil beings are spoken of under the name of Dasyus, Rākshasas, Yātudhānas, Kimīdins, and are described as without religious rites, godless, haters of prayer (brahma-dvish), eaters of flesh (kravyād), monstrous in form, and possessors of magical powers[2].

Then, again, in Manu's law-book (I. 37) we find it stated that the ten Prajā-patis or secondary creators, after creating the gods and great sages, afterwards created various orders of beings, such as the Yakshas, Rākshasas, Piśāćas, Gandharvas, Apsarasas (pl. of Apsaras), Asuras, Nāgas, etc. It is not affirmed that any of these beings were aboriginally evil-minded, though they were certainly capable of becoming so. In the Rāmāyaṇa constant mention is made of beings hostile to gods and men called Rākshasas. They are the haters and disturbers of religious rites, they change their shapes at will, harass holy men and devotees, and utter frightful sounds in the ears of the faithful.

Most Rākshasas are men-eaters, and one, called Virādha, is described as resembling a mountain-peak, with long legs, a crooked nose, hideous eyes, pendant belly, and an open

---

[1] Muir's Sanskṛit Texts, v. 230. [2] Ibid. ii. 418.

mouth like that of death. At the head of them is the Demon Rāvaṇa, who is an impersonation of selfish ambition. It does not appear, however, that in other respects he was innately wicked. On the contrary, it was only by severe religious austerities carried on for ten thousand years that he acquired unbounded power over gods and men. Others, too, of these same Rākshasas are described as virtuous and pious, and among them especially Vibhīshaṇa, who is the brother of Rāvaṇa, and exactly his opposite in character and conduct. In the Mahā-bhārata, again, Kaṉsa, Kali, and numerous other demons are, like Rāvaṇa in the Rāmāyaṇa, impersonations of evil. Kaṉsa is the implacable enemy of Kṛishṇa, and Kali is for ever instilling evil thoughts into men's hearts in an age of universal degeneration.

We may note, too, that in epic poetry frequent mention is made of another class of beings who are more especially hostile to the gods, and for ever engaged in warfare with them. They are called Daityas, as the supposed children of the goddess Diti by Kaśyapa (the gods being children of Aditi). Others, too, are often alluded to under the name of Dānavas, as daughters of Danu. Both of these classes of beings are said in the Vishṇu-purāṇa to occupy some of the seven regions below the earth of which Pātāla is one (II. 5), and appear to belong to a higher order of creation than the Rākshasas, whose nature is of a type inclined to baser forms of wickedness, and whose malignity is more particularly directed against men.

Then there are troops (gaṇas) of beings called Pramathas, who constitute the armies of the god Śiva. There are also the Yakshas, who wait on Kubera (Kuvera), and the Gandharvas (Atharva-veda XI. 5. 2) or heavenly choristers, and their wives the Apsarasas, who attend on Indra. To these may be added the Kinnaras (with human figure and equine head), the Kimpurushas, the Vidyā-dharas, Pannagas, &c.

Most of these creatures are good and benign in character;

but all were created free agents, and are therefore liable to fall away, and, after committing acts of sin or disobedience, may become malignant beings animated with a spirit of bitter hostility towards gods and men.

It is in consonance with the theory of a continual conflict between the powers of good and the powers of evil that we find the chief gods of the Hindū Pantheon constantly represented in the act of crushing their demon foes. Thus Kṛishṇa is seen bruising the head of the great demon serpent Kāliya, while Śiva tramples on the arch-fiend Tripura, and holds venomous serpents in his hands in token of his supremacy over all malignant influences.

Hence, too, a great number of the 1,000 names of both Vishṇu and Śiva will be found to be simple epithets—like Murāri 'enemy of Mura,' Purāri 'enemy of Pura'—significant of their victory over certain typical demon antagonists. Furthermore, the symbols held in the hands of both deities, the discus and club of Vishṇu, and the trident and bow of Śiva, are merely weapons of supposed irresistible efficacy in their conflicts with the spirits of evil.

We pass on now to the second great division of the demon world—that which is said to owe its creation to man. This is by far the more important of the two great divisions in its bearing on the subject of the present chapter, for it is chiefly to those demons whose existence is derived from the departed spirits of human beings that adoration and propitiation are commonly offered.

And, indeed, it is a noteworthy point in the religious creed of all ordinary Hindūs that the majority of malignant devils are believed to have been originally human beings.

If any man is killed by a tiger or the bite of a snake, or has died a sudden violent death of any kind, away from his relations and out of reach of proper funeral ceremonies, he forthwith becomes an unquiet spirit, roaming about with malevolent proclivities. In one place I found people worshipping the ghost of a milkman who was killed by a tiger and became a devil. In another place the ghost of a potter became a devil and a terror to the neighbourhood. The priests of these demons were milkmen and potters respectively.

And a curious notion prevails in some parts of India that, the better the man, the more mischievous will his ghost turn out to be, if his body has not received proper cremation, or if from any accident the succeeding funeral rites have not been carefully performed or partially omitted.

Again, a still more remarkable doctrine is rife in India, especially in the South. There it is a fixed article of belief. that when a man notorious for any particular vices dies, the man himself may become extinct, but his evil nature never dies; nay, every one of his vices may then assume personality and live after him as a demon.

And this applies equally to women, so that the resulting demons may be of either sex, and the female is not unfrequently more spiteful and malignant than the male. It also applies to persons of all castes, high or low, so that the demons created may be of all ranks, and may have either refined or low tastes.

It is thus that legion after legion of foul fiends and unclean spirits, bearing names corresponding to such expressions as deceit-devils, lying-devils, gambling-devils, pride-devils, cruelty-devils, lust-devils, gluttony-devils, strife-devils, drunkenness-devils, are supposed to have originated.

The same applies to a man who has been guilty of great crimes or sins. His crimes and sins live after him in the shape of malignant demons.

Hence have arisen any number of murder-devils, theft-devils, perjury-devils, adultery-devils, blasphemy-devils, who are always on the look-out for weak-minded victims, and ever instigating them to the commission of similar crimes.

Nay, a man may sometimes become a demon without dying; for example, we read in the Mahā-bhārata and Vishṇu-purāṇa that Nahusha son of Āyus was changed into a serpent-demon, in consequence of a curse pronounced on him by the sage Agastya for his excessive pride in having gained by penance the rank of Indra and then insulted some of the Ṛishis (Mahā-bh. V. 343; Vishṇu-purāṇa, p. 413; Manu VII. 41).

Furthermore, all the diseases that either human or bestial flesh is heir to are personified and converted into demons—such as the demons of small-pox, of cholera, and of various forms of typhus and jungle fever, and of cattle-disease. And this idea of personifying and demonizing diseases is extended to unseasonable calamities and disasters, such as hail-storms, drought and blight, which all do duty in the devil army.

Indeed, I found that some villages in India possess a professional exorciser or charmer, called Gārpagārī (probably for Gār-apakārī, gār in Marāṭhī meaning 'hail'), whose peculiar business is to repeat incantations for warding off the hail-storm-demon from the growing crops.

It is important, however, to bear in mind that there is in Hindūism a per-contra side to the vastness of the demon-host. For if it is an awful thought that year after year, and even day by day, men and women are themselves through their sinful habits causing fresh accessions to the demon-armies, it is, on the other hand, a comforting reflection that the ranks of good demons and benevolent spirits are continually recruited by the deaths of righteous men, saints and sages, who are ranged with the gods on the opposite side of the battle-field, and are ever contending with their fiendish antagonists.

It is, then, these lower forms of evil demons—once the occupants of human bodies—that are most dreaded by the generality of Hindūs, and therefore most worshipped. Such demons fitly take rank with devils.

According to some authorities they may be grouped under the three classes of Bhūta, Preta, and Piśāća, each class having a distinct origin.

A Bhūta, they say, is a spirit emanating from a man

who has died a violent death either by accident, suicide, or capital punishment, and has not had proper funeral ceremonies performed afterwards.

A Preta is the spirit of a deformed or crippled person, or of one defective in some limb or organ, or of a child that dies prematurely, owing to the omission of ceremonies during the formation of the embryo. It is not necessarily wicked or malicious or evil-disposed towards living men.

A Piśāća is a demon created by a man's vices. It is the ghost of a liar, drunkard, adulterer, or criminal of any kind, or of one who has died insane.

In real truth, however, this kind of triple classification is nowhere universally accepted, and is never consistently maintained. My own inquiries led me to the conclusion that the terms Bhūta and Preta are as a general rule applied to all demons and ghosts indifferently, and the term Piśāća to malicious and mischievous imps and fiends. Such demons and malicious beings haunt cemeteries or take up their abode in trees, and are addicted to roaming about between the hours of 12 and 3 in the morning. They may take either hideous or beautiful shapes, and even the form of men. They require, as we have seen, the support of food; and what satiates their appetites more than any other kind of nutriment is the blood of living animals. But according to popular belief they may also feed on corpses, ordure and carrion, and may even occupy and vivify dead bodies. Nay, they may enter living bodies through the open mouth, if it happen to be opened imprudently wide. Thus, if a man in an unguarded moment yawns or gapes without holding his hand or snapping his fingers before his face, they may promptly dart in and take up their abode in his interior, feeding on the refuse of the food as it passes through the intestines.

When malignant demons thus take possession of the bodies of living men, they may cause diseases and unpleasant affections of all kinds, or they may agitate the limbs of the person possessed, and impel him to frantic movements, in which all devils take particular delight.

Occasionally they may take the shape or character of a dog, cat, serpent, or other animal. It is fully believed that if a person happens to be possessed by a dog-demon he will take to barking like a dog.

With regard to so-called demon-worship, it must be noted that there is no real worship. Nor has any demon—not even one of the highest class—any imposing temple-like structure erected to him. Often a mere heap of earth piled up in pyramidal shape near some tree, or a similar erection formed with bricks and painted with streaks of white, constitutes the only shrine, while another heap in front with a flat surface does duty for the altar. Sometimes the whole is covered with a wooden roof supported on rough columns. There is rarely any idol; though sometimes, if the demon's origin be traceable to the ghost of some high personage, whose elevation of rank or office made him during lifetime formidable to his followers, he may be represented by a rude image of some of the terrible forms of Śiva. No real prayers are said at such shrines, though incantations may be recited. The propitiation consists in offerings of food, as mentioned in the preceding chapter (p. 221), and in various ceremonies which differ in different localities.

A spirit of one of these classes highly reverenced and very commonly propitiated by villagers in some parts of India is one popularly called Bhūmyā, or the 'earth-spirit.' He is supposed to be the spirit of the founder of the village. If a village is deserted by its inhabitants, no new colony of people will dare to settle there without going through a careful process of propitiating the earth-spirit, who never, under any circumstances, quits his old haunts.

Another class consists of the spirits of young men who have died without becoming fathers. These wander about in a restless miserable manner, like people burdened with an enormous debt which they are quite unable to discharge. They are euphemistically called Pitās, 'fathers,'—that is, by the name to which they are least entitled,—and are propitiated by offerings presented at small shrines of a very simple construction erected near rivers or pools of water. Often these shrines are formed by merely setting up two bricks with a little interval between them covered by another brick.

And here it should be noted that although nearly every village has its own special demon, whose cultus may not only have existed from time immemorial, but may have an origin antecedent to the introduction of Hindūism, yet it is always possible to connect every form and variety of such worship with that of the god Śiva, his consort Durgā (or Devī) and his two sons Gaṇeśa and Su-brahmaṇya (see p. 212).

It is important, too, to bear in mind that as the South of India is the region in which Śaivism is particularly prevalent, so also it is among the inhabitants of the South that devil-worship is most systematically practised. No one who has travelled in that region can doubt that demonophobia is a disease with which the whole Southern population is almost hopelessly and incurably afflicted. Possibly one reason of this may be that when the Drāviḍians invaded India they found the South inhabited by wild aboriginal savages, whose whole aspect and demeanour appeared to them to resemble those of devils. Again, the Āryans as they advanced towards the South found it occupied by hostile Drāviḍian races, as well as by apparently aboriginal tribes, and their excited imaginations converted these powerful enemies into super-natural giants, and the most formidable of them into veritable demons (Rākshasas).

In due time Āryans, Drāviḍians, and aborigines blended amicably together, but the dread of demon-foes remained, and this dread still prevails not only in the South, but over every part of India. In fact, so deep-seated and ineradicable is the fear of evil spirits in the minds of the lower orders, that in many villages of India the doors of the houses are never allowed to face the South, lest the entrance of some dreaded demon should be facilitated. Perhaps, however, the true devil-region is the extreme Southern peninsula, near the Island of Ceylon. The nearer indeed we approach that island, the more do we find the people (like the Shānārs of Tinnevelly) steeped in demonolatry and saturated with every form of superstitious fear of evil spirits, ghosts, and goblins.

Every village has its own peculiar devil or devils, to the attacks of which it is constantly in imagination exposed. Happily every village has also, as we have already pointed out, its own tutelary deities. Curiously, too, many good spirits are believed to be equestrian in their tastes. Possibly the villagers suppose that by turning them into a kind of cavalry regiment they give them an advantage over their impish opponents, who prowl about on foot, and sneak into the village domain at unguarded corners.

Certain it is that to propitiate these tutelary divinities the villagers set up horses of baked clay in their fields—often as large as life, and generally ten or twenty in a row or in a semicircle round a shrine—and present them as offerings to the good divinity of the shrine, in token of gratitude for deliverances.

They are especially presented—though not without other oblations—to the male guardian God Ayenār (see p. 219), who is believed to be a daring horseman capable of clearing hedges and ditches and riding down the most active demon-antagonist.

As to the female tutelary deities called Mothers (see p. 223), we have already seen that if not propitiated by constant offerings, and especially with blood, they will themselves assume the personality of the very demon dreaded by the villagers, and inflict the very plague from which they usually protect them.

The most terrible of all demons are thought to be those

created by Europeans. Of course the propitiating process must vary according to the character of the man whose demonized spirit is to be coaxed into good-humour. His tastes and idiosyncrasies during life must be carefully inquired into and judiciously indulged. The story is told of a certain choleric Englishman who was a terror to the inhabitants of a district in the South of India, and whose ghost after his death had to be constantly appeased by offerings of good cooked meat, brandy, soda-water, and cigars placed daily on his tomb. The same was done to secure the continued good-will of a philanthropic sportsman, who when he was alive delivered a large tract of country from the ravages of tigers.

And here we may note other methods of neutralizing the evil influences of demons prevalent in Southern India. Male and female devils are supposed to delight in dancing, particularly when accompanied with wild cries, violent gesticulations, ringing of bells, and noisy discordant music. Hence it happens that, when pestilence is rife in any district, professional wizard-like exorcisers, or persons selected for the purpose, paint their faces, put on hideous masks, dress up in fantastic garments, arm themselves with strange weapons, and commence dancing. Their object is to personate particular demons, or to induce demoniacal spirits to leave the persons of those possessed by them and to occupy the persons of the dancers, who shriek, fling themselves about, and work themselves up into a phrenzy of excitement, amid beating of tom-toms, blowing of horns, and ringing of bells. When the dancers are thoroughly exhausted by their gesticulations they sink down in a kind of trance, and are then believed to be actually possessed by the spirit of the demon and are turned for a time into demon-mediums, gifted with clairvoyance and a power of delivering prophetic utterances. The spectators ask them questions about missing relatives or future events, and their deliverances are supposed to be oracular. This is akin to Shamanism.

I witnessed such a dance on a dark night in a garden near Colombo in Ceylon. The dancers represented the demons of various forms of typhus fever, carried flaring torches, wore hideous masks, and had jingling bells on their legs. Their wild cries and horrible antics will remain indelibly impressed on my recollection. (See my 'Buddhism,' p. 217.)

When I was at Tanjor the late learned Dr. Burnell, then judge of that district, gave me some interesting information in regard to the demon-festivals which recur periodically in the district of Mangalor, where he held office for some time.

One of the most popular of these festivals, called Illeććhida Nema, is celebrated every fifteen or twenty years. At another called Kallyāta, a wild dance is performed every sixtieth year before a particular rock or stone, which is supposed to tremble and shake periodically.

Sometimes the performance takes place in a large shed in the middle of which burns a common lamp under a canopy. Around are images of the Bhūtas. At the distance of about a foot in front of the lamp is placed a common wooden tripod-stand, two or three feet high, on which is constructed a square frame of cocoa-nut leaves. Inside this frame rice and turmeric are piled up in the form of a pyramid into which a three-branched iron lamp is inserted. Around are arranged offerings consisting of fruits and living victims, such as fowls and goats. The latter are adorned with garlands, and both fowls and goats are afterwards decapitated, the warm blood being either poured out on the ground or on the altar, or else drunk by the officiating priest. The idea is that the demon thirsts for blood, and becomes irritated if his cravings are not satisfied. The sole object of sacrificing animals is to assuage his thirst and appease his anger.

All this is preliminary to the principal performance, which takes place in an open space in front of the slaughtered victims. The priest, or some other devotee who has undergone a long preparatory fasting, comes forward to personate a particular demon. He is dressed up in a fantastic costume, often covered with grotesque dangling ornaments and jingling bells. Sometimes he wears a hideous mask; sometimes his faced is daubed with paint of different colours. In one hand he holds a sword, trident, or other implement, and perhaps a bell in the other. He then commences dancing or pacing up and down in an excited manner, amid beating of tom-toms, blowing of horns, and all kinds of noisy music, while an attendant sings songs, or recites rude poems descriptive of the deeds of the demons. Meanwhile spirituous liquor is distributed, the performer becomes violently excited, and the demon takes complete possession of him. Finally he succumbs in an hysterical fit, and gives out oracular responses to any inquiries addressed to him. Most of the bystanders consult him as to their several wants and destinies, or the welfare of absent relatives, but are not allowed to do so without first presenting offerings.

Of course, variations occur in different districts.

According to Mr. Walhouse, in his paper read before the Anthropological Institute, the structures and observances connected with devil-worship on the Western coast of India are both domestic and public. In villages, and very generally in towns, there is in every house a wooden cot or cradle, placed on the ground or suspended by ropes or chains, and dedicated to the Bhūta of the spot. On these are deposited a bell, a knife or sword, and a pot filled with water, all which are collectively called the Bhāṇḍāra of the Bhūta, and kept either in a part of the house itself, or in a small separate building. The object seems to be to propitiate the spirit that haunts the spot by making a sort of abode for it.

On the last day of every lunar month flowers are laid on the cot, and perfume burnt before it; and once a year, towards the end of April, a ceremony called Tambila is performed. A fire is lit on the spot where the cot and paraphernalia stand, then fried rice, mixed with coarse sugar and grated cocoa-nut kernel, is heaped on two plantain leaves, which are placed on the cot, together with some young cocoa-nuts, pierced ready to drink from. A ball is then formed of boiled rice, coloured yellow with turmeric, and laid on a piece of plantain-leaf on a small stool, which is placed before the cot, with a lighted torch upon it. A fowl is held above the rice-ball and torch, its throat cut, and the blood allowed to drop upon the ball; some perfume is burnt, and the ceremony ends. Should a member of the family be stricken with any unusual attack, a fowl is turned three times round before the patient's face, its neck then twisted, and the blood let fall upon him; the meaning being to offer life for life—the fowl in lieu of the man. The family priest is then consulted, who recommends alms to be given to himself to satisfy the hostile stars, with a promise to perform a special ceremony to the Bhūta.

Mr. Walhouse informs us that these demons have shrines called Bhūta-sthāns, sometimes of considerable size, but far more commonly small plain structures, four or five yards deep by two or three wide, with a door at one end, covered by a portico supported on two pillars with a thatched roof, and windowless. Inside the Bhūta-sthān a number of brass images roughly made in human shape, or resembling animals such as pigs, tigers, fowls, etc., are usually found. The Bhūtas themselves are commonly represented by mere rough stones. These rustic fanes are thickly scattered over the face of the country—under a green-tree, on hill-sides, down in hollows, in jungles, on plains, by roadsides, in villages, amid rice-fields, but always on a small plot of waste ground.

Once a year a festival called Kolla is held. The festival always takes place at night, and about nine o'clock all the villagers assemble in their best attire. Then the Pūjāri, or priest, takes the Bhūta sword and bell in his hands, and whirls round and round, imitating the supposed gestures of the demon. A Dhēr (Dheḍa), or man of the lowest caste—at other times regarded with contempt, but now advanced to the foremost post—comes forward naked, except round the loins, his head and body being grotesquely and frightfully besmeared with white, yellow, and red paint. Meanwhile a dozen or more tom-toms are beaten with a continually increasing din, and the Dhēr (Dheḍa) presently breaks into a maniac dance, capering, bounding, and spinning vehemently. At length he stops; he is full of the demon, and stands fixed and rigid, with staring eyes. Presently he speaks, or rather the demon speaks through him, in loud, hoarse, commanding tones, wholly unlike his own, or indeed any natural voice. Various disputes and litigated matters, especially when evidence and ordinary means of adjustment fail, are then brought forward and submitted to the decision of the Bhūta, and his award, pronounced through the Dhēr, is generally, though not always, submitted to. After this the demon desires to have food, and the Dhēr eats fried rice and drinks the milk of young cocoa-nuts; or, if the demon he represents be one of low degree, he eats animal food and drinks arrack.

Among the demons most feared in Kanara are Kalkatti, Kallurti, and Pañjūrli.

The story of the former two is as follows:—Kalkatti and Kallurti were respectively the son and daughter of one Kalkuḍa, a sculptor, who must have lived in the fifteenth century of our era. Kalkatti was a mason, and one day found fault with his father's work, which so distressed him that he forthwith killed himself. The son then followed his father's trade, and succeeded so well that he made the celebrated Jain statue at Kārakal. After completing this masterpiece he wanted to go elsewhere, but the king of the country forbad him, and to prevent his producing any similar statue cut off his left hand and right leg. Notwithstanding this mutilation he went to Yenūr and made a still larger statue there. His sister Kallurti determined to join him at Yenūr. There they lived together for some time, and then both committed suicide. It was thus that they became formidable demons, who revenged themselves on the king of Kārakal by burning down his palace and town and annoying people throughout the country in various ways. Their story is a long one, and the books which recount it give directions for appeasing their anger.

The story of Pañjūrli is also a long one. He is a terrible pig-faced demon, created, it is said, through a curse of Śiva pronounced on some young pigs which had laid waste his garden, and were thereupon collectively transformed into a single mischievous demon.

In South Kanara, according to Mr. Walhouse, there is a noted temple, which is believed to be the residence of seven most dreaded demons. Certain devil-stones are sold there in which the powers of the Bhūtas are held to be inherent. These are taken home and used by the purchasers against their enemies.

I add an extract from Bishop Caldwell's account of the Religion of the Shānārs, a tribe in the South of India, whose occupation consists in cultivating and climbing the palmyra tree for the sake of its juice. They have been largely converted to Christianity, and chiefly through the Bishop's devoted labours among them.

In his description of their devil-worship, he says:—'Every malady, however trivial, is supposed by the more superstitious to be inflicted by a devil, and a sacrifice is necessary for its removal; but the unusual severity or continuance of any disease, or the appearance of symptoms which are not recorded in the physician's Śāstra, are proofs of possession of which no Shānār can entertain any doubt. The medical science of so rude a people not being very extensive, cases of unquestionable possession are of frequent occurrence. When a woman is heard to weep and laugh alternately, without any adequate cause, or shriek and look wild when no snake or wild beast can be perceived, what Shānār can suppose anything but a devil to be the cause of the mischief?

The native doctor, himself a Shānār, is sent for to give his advice. He brings his library with him (he cannot read, but it is all in his memory), his complete science of medicine in one hundred stanzas, as revealed by the sage Agastya to his disciple Pulastya; but in vain he recites his prescriptions, in vain he coins hard words. As no description of hysterical complaints is contained in his authorities, what can he do but decide that a devil has taken possession of the woman, and recommend that a sacrifice be offered to him forthwith, with a cloth and a white fowl to the doctor?

'Sometimes the friends are not desirous of expelling the evil spirit all at once, but send for music, get up a devil-dance, and call upon the demon to prophesy.

'If they desire to expel the devil, there is no lack of moving ceremonies and powerful incantations, each of which has been tried and found successful innumerable times. If the devil should prove an obstinate one and refuse to leave, charm they never so wisely, his retreat may generally be hastened by the vigorous application of a slipper or a broom to the shoulders of the possessed person, the operator taking care at the same time to use the most scurrilous language he can think of. After a time the demoniac loses his downcast, sullen look. He begins to get angry and writhe about under the slippering, and at length cries, "I go, I go." Then they ask him his name, and why he came there. He tells them he is such and such a devil, whom they have neglected, and he wants an offering; or he calls himself by the name of some deceased relative, who, as they now learn for the first time, has become a demon. As soon as the demon consents to leave, the beating ceases; and not unfrequently immediate preparations are made for a sacrifice, as a compensation to his feelings for the ignominy of the exorcism. The possessed person now awakes as from a sleep, and appears to have no knowledge of anything that has happened.'

I must not omit to note one or two other facts connected with a belief in demoniacal influences and their counteraction.

Demons or evil spirits in India are supposed to be often the cause of what in Europe is called 'an evil eye,' that is, a mysterious power of fascinating, bewitching, or inflicting some injury on others by a fixed look, gaze, or glance. Indeed, a look of admiration from friend or foe is believed to be fraught with great danger and possibly serious calamity to any individual who is the object of it.

Europeans who are often unaware of the universal prevalence of this superstition are occasionally the innocent cause of great distress to the parents of Indian children by looking at them approvingly and uttering some exclamation of praise.

A story was told me with the utmost gravity—as if its truth was beyond all dispute—of a person who was born a twin, but whose twin brother was a spirit who constantly attended him and gifted him with various preternatural faculties, and amongst others the power of an evil eye. It was declared to be a fact, that whatever this person looked at with admiration instantly faded away and perished. Old women who are believed to have this power are particularly dreaded and shunned as dangerous witches.

Another story was told me of a man who fell in love with his neighbour's wife. By calling in demoniacal aid he was able to fix his gaze on her, and after successfully bewitching her to cause her death. Then he managed to get possession of a hair or two from her head. These he handed over to a well-known sorcerer at Lahore, who, once possessed of a portion of her person, had no difficulty in bringing her to life again by his incantations, and in return for a good sum of money delivered her to her lover, who married her.

Some sorcerers, if called upon to get rid of an enemy, mould a human effigy in wax, pronouncing over it a few mysterious cabalistic words. The waxen figure is then placed before a fire, and, as it melts, brings down deadly calamities on the head of the person to be destroyed. Or, if a human bone from a cemetery can be procured, and certain Mantras recited over it, very fatal results will ensue (compare p. 201).

Many charms are used against the misfortunes which may at any time be brought about by malicious spirits, or by evil influences connected with the human eye. In some parts of India a tiger's claw or tooth is worn on the neck and held to be very efficacious. In other places an image of the liṅga[1] is worn, or some bright ornament—such as a string of white cowries—which is supposed to arrest evil glances, or divert them from the person wearing such a necklace. A small iron ring is also commonly carried about as an amulet. It is particularly effective if inlaid with pearls. Frequently a lime is carried in the turban, and great faith is reposed in its prophylactic properties. Or again, any ornament with a figure of Hanumān (p. 220) engraved on it makes an admirable charm which few demons can withstand.

In some districts—especially in the South—I have often remarked white pots, with black marks or grotesque objects covered with streaks of white paint, placed here and there in the fields, and intended to catch the eye so as to avert envious glances or the malignant influences of demons from the growing crops. In remote villages, too, was occasionally to be observed an apparatus for curing cattle-disease, when caused (as universally believed in India) by the machinations of evil demons. At the entrance to the village were two upright posts with a cord stretched between them, on which were hung rude models of ploughs, etc., and in the centre dangled a large pot-cover. On inquiry I found that charms resembling physicians' prescriptions in rather unreadable hieroglyphics were written on this cover, and all the afflicted cattle driven under them. The power of such

[1] In Southern Italy an ornament with a finger pointing downwards is to this day used as a charm against the evil eye.

charms is supposed to depend a good deal on the reputation of the sorcerers employed to write them, and every village does not possess such men. They are sometimes sent for from great distances, and, in my opinion, a long period must elapse before any filtering down of education from the upper classes will avail to undermine the faith of the simple villagers in the efficacy of a pot-cover inscribed with the charms of the more noted sorcerers[1].

---

[1] The following abridgment of an article on Indian 'Haunted Bungalows,' taken from the 'Graphic' newspaper (June 9, 1883), will be interesting in connexion with the subject of the chapter here concluded :—

'The notion of Indian houses being haunted is, on first thought, rather ridiculous. Nevertheless, there is scarcely a station in Hindostan which has not its haunted bungalow. The spirits appear to the appalled beholders by sunlight as well as by night, and are apparently indifferent to the time of day. A curious and very well authenticated instance of this disregard of the hour is that of an *afternoon* ghost, which punctually appears at sunset in a certain house at Madras.

'But there are evil and beneficent spirits in India. There is a well-known haunted house in one of the stations of the North of India, where the "house-ghost," if we may so call him, evinces malicious and malignant idiosyncracies. It is this wretched spirit's mundane amusement to try and upset the charpoy, or bed, on which the bewildered tenant seeks repose; and so persistent are his efforts in this direction, that they have been compared to shocks of earthquake, and to the explosions of subterraneous mines. People laugh, but no one particularly cares to sleep twice in that haunted bungalow.

'Another species of malignant spirit which becomes most intimately associated with an Indian house is a disease. There are houses in Indian towns and stations of which the citizens say it is as much as any man's life is worth to enter them. C., who was superior to superstition, went into a house of this character, just to show the absurdity of believing "in such rot," and speedily lost his wife and three children. It cannot be denied that the mortality in some Indian bungalows of an unlucky reputation is unaccountable.

'It is a relief to turn from the vagaries of evil spirits to the beneficence of the good.

'In England one seldom hears of a good ghost, or of a ghost who puts himself out of his way to oblige any one; but, in India, ghosts of this cheerful temperament are quite common. Sometimes they assume the appearance of Europeans; sometimes that of natives. These ghosts have done the living no end of good. The warnings and other information they have imparted have been endless.'

I also add a statement of one part of the creed of American Spiritualists in the present day (written by the Rev. C. Ware, and quoted in the 'Religio-Philosophical Journal'), as offering many curious analogies to ideas current in India for centuries before 'Spiritualism' was ever heard of in either Europe or America :—

'It is a fact that myriads of disembodied human beings are living in a world that is merely the duplicate or counterpart of the earth, a realm as closely connected with the earth's atmosphere as the atmosphere is with the earth itself; all above it and below it being links of one endless chain. This is what we mean by earth-bound spirits; they are so earthly, their nature is so unrefined, so material in its tendencies, that they cannot rise above their surroundings. They cannot rise to those spheres of light, and love, and blessedness; because the external surroundings of a spirit always correspond with its inward condition; they must remain in that first sphere, which is only a step higher than the earth, until they become spiritually developed.

'Religious professors talk about going on the wings of faith to the home beyond the skies, but, unfortunately for them, everything in the infinite universe is determined by immutable laws, laws which cannot be set aside, laws which are self-operating; and by these laws is the relative position of every individual spirit determined. You will pass into the spirit-world with your spiritual body, but your position there will be determined by the degree of refinement which characterizes that same spiritual body. The tippler, the smoker, the glutton and the sensualist, are, whether they recognize it or not, constantly defiling themselves with the elements which will keep them down to earth. It is such habits and tendencies that make spirits "earth-bound." If these habits are not conquered and overcome here, they will have to be there, before the spirit can rise to association with the pure and the holy.

'This immense realm, then, which is earth's counterpart, surrounds this earth, and its myriads of inhabitants constantly exert an influence upon this world; and this is a solemn thought, when you remember that here dwell millions of ignorant, debased, degraded souls, where they remain exerting their baneful influence, until they are enlightened, purified and reformed.

'More particularly we mean by earth-bound spirits, not only those who, through ignorance, sensual habits, and material tendencies are kept down by their own specific gravity, but also those who are fettered to the earth by wrong-doing, crime and injustice committed. Thousands of such are here wandering, full of remorse; they have to repent, to do their best to repair the wrong and to make atonement, before they can rise.'

CHAPTER X.

Hero-worship and Saint-worship.

THE worship of great men, saints and sages, who have been remarkable for the possession of unusual powers or striking qualities of any kind, is a phase of religious development which perhaps more than any other is the natural outcome of man's primitive devotional instincts. In India a tendency to this kind of worship has always prevailed from the earliest period. Nascent in Vedic times, it speedily grew with the growth of a belief in the doctrine of divine incarnation and embodiment. For although it is true that Indian philosophers disparage the body and invent elaborate schemes for getting rid of all corporeal encumbrances, yet it is equally true that nowhere in the world has the conception of God's union with man, and of His ennobling the bodily frame, not only of men but of animals and plants, by taking it upon Himself, struck root so deeply in the popular mind as in India.

We know indeed that, according to the pantheistic creed of Brāhmanism, God and the Universe are One. His presence pervades inanimate as well as animate objects, and every human being is a manifestation of His energy; but He is believed to be specially manifested in all great, good, and holy men. All such men are held to be entitled to worship at the hands of their less-favoured fellow-men, in virtue of their being embodiments in a higher degree of portions of His essence. The homage they receive may not always amount to actual worship during life, but after their decease their claim to a position in the celestial hierarchy is pretty sure to be fully recognized; and if their lives have been marked by any extraordinary or miraculous occurrences, they soon become objects of general adoration. It is not merely that a niche is allotted to them among the countless gods of the Hindū Pantheon (popularly 330,000,000, see p. 44). A shrine is set up and dedicated to their deified spirits upon earth, and generally in the locality where they were best known. There they are supposed to be objectively present—not indeed visibly to men, and not always represented by visible images or symbols—but as ethereal beings possessed of ethereal frames which need the aroma or essence of food for their support (see p. 12). The idea seems to be that the localizing of a deified or canonized spirit involves the duty of its maintenance. Hence oblations are daily offered, and if by a happy accident some miraculous event, such as the unexpected recovery of a sick man, occurs in the neighbourhood, the celebrity of the new god rapidly rises, till he takes rank as a first-class divinity, and his sanctuary becomes a focus to which tens of thousands of enthusiastic devotees annually converge.

There seems indeed to be no limit to this kind of deification, and it is often a mere device for making some locality popular.

Volumes might be written in describing instances that have occurred and are constantly occurring in all parts of the country. And it is remarkable that the rank or importance to which a canonized or deified human being may attain in the world of spirits does not always depend, as a matter of course, on the estimation in which he was held, or even on the measure of divinity attributed to him while on the earth. Any man of the lowest rank, whose influence during life was perhaps quite insignificant, may be elevated to the highest pinnacle of honour when severed from terrestrial ties, if his relatives can show that his career was marked by any extraordinary act of self-sacrifice or heroism, or so-called miracle. Nevertheless, it is important to note that the idea of divinity seems to be specially associated with five classes of living persons—kings, warriors, Brāhmans, saints, and sages—and that these enjoy a kind of a-priori claim to subsequent apotheosis.

And first in regard to kings—every king is regarded as little short of a present god. In Manu's law-book a king is said to be created by drawing eternal particles from the essence of the eight guardian deities (VII. 4). Again, he says, 'A king, even though a mere child, must not be treated with contempt, as if he were a mortal; he is a great divinity in human shape' (VII. 8).

In proof of the hold which these ideas still have on the people, it is stated in a recent number of a native newspaper, that there is now a sect of persons in Orissa who worship the Queen of England as their chief divinity.

The transition from the worship of kings to that of military heroes and conquerors is of course easy. Great warriors have always in India commanded a large share of popular homage, though their full apotheosis has generally been deferred until after death, and until their human origin has become obscured in the mists of tradition. The most noteworthy instances of such deification have been Rāma and Kṛishṇa, both of whom, notwithstanding their human parentage and human career, were ultimately[1], as we have seen (pp. 110–114), exalted by their worshippers to the first rank among Vishṇu's incarnations.

And, to this day, all living persons remarkable for great personal valour and strength, or for supposed miraculous powers, run the risk—like Paul and Barnabas at Lystra—of being converted into gods. Even any unusual deformity or strange eccentricity may be an evidence of divinity.

[1] In the Mahā-bhārata the divinity of Kṛishṇa is occasionally disputed, as by Śiśu-pāla and others.

The story has often been told of a number of Hindūs in the Panjāb who formed themselves into a sect of Nikkal Sen worshippers. The explanation of this was, that General Nicholson was a soldier of such unexampled bravery and heroism, that neither argument nor force could prevent his native admirers from worshipping him. 'This man,' they said, 'is the great power of God.' He endeavoured by punishing them to put a stop to the absurdity, but this only filled them with greater awe, and made them persist in their pūjā with more obstinate determination.

Nor is the object of such adoration always really worthy of honour, or even decently respectable. It is well known that a certain tribe in India worship a notorious robber, whose deeds merit nothing but general execration. Perhaps, however, a sufficient explanation of this circumstance may be found in the fact that the tribe in question is itself addicted to occasional plundering on its own account.

It was on a similar principle that the Thugs (Ṭhags) worshipped Kālī as goddess of destruction, and strangled their victims in her honour (see chap. XXII).

Another robber, who was hung at Trichinopoly, became so popular, as a demon, that children were constantly named after him.

Turning next to Brāhmans, we find it affirmed by Manu that a 'Brāhman is a mighty god, a supreme divinity, whether he be learned or unlearned, and even if employed in inferior occupations' (IX. 317, 319). 'From his birth alone a Brāhman is regarded as a divinity even by the gods' (XI. 84).

With regard to a Brāhman who is also a Guru or teacher, his person is still more sacred, and he is everywhere the object of divine honours (see p. 117). 'The teacher (Guru) is God, and the teacher is a refuge (gati). If Śiva be angry the teacher becomes a protector, but there is no other refuge if the teacher be offended. Any one who worships another god or goddess when his preceptor is at hand incurs terrible perdition. The preceptor alone is the divine power, whether he be learned or unlearned. His ways may be good or bad, but he is the only safe guide' (Tantra-sāra, p. 1).

In illustration of this I may mention, that I was admitted as a great favour to a sort of religious camp-meeting which took place at one of the most sacred places in all India—the confluence of the Ganges and the Jumnā. There I found that a celebrated preacher was addressing a congregation of about one hundred persons, who hung upon his lips in rapt attention. The subject of the sermon, which was delivered with great eloquence, was the condescension of Kṛishṇa in becoming first a child and then a man for the benefit of the human race. No sooner was the sermon over than certain persons in the audience took lighted lamps, and standing up before the preacher, waved them before him in homage as before the chief deity of the place [1].

Perhaps the most readily conceded of all claims to apotheosis is that of the saint or holy sage who has become a Sannyāsī — that is to say, has renounced all family ties, and lives a life of asceticism, self-denial, and austerity. When such a man dies in India, his body is not burnt but buried, because in fact he is not supposed to die at all. He is believed to lie in a kind of trance, called Samādhi; sanctity exhales from his body, and his tomb—popularly called a Samādh—often becomes a noted place of pilgrimage. resorted to by myriads from all parts of India.

Very similar is the adoration paid to the faithful wife, commonly called Suttee (=Sanskṛit *Satī*), who in former days burnt herself on her husband's funeral pile. Monuments are erected over her ashes, and within the shrine is

---

[1] I witnessed a similar proceeding in a Roman Catholic Cathedral not long ago. During the mass, and after waving the censer full of incense before the altar, one of the officiating attendants waved it before the chief-priests who were present, in token, I presume, of homage.

often a representation of her foot-prints, which are worshipped with the greatest veneration.

Of course jealousies and rivalries occasionally spring up between the adherents and admirers of various departed saints or heroes, especially if much expense has been incurred in erecting shrines and monuments in the hope of attracting pilgrims to particular localities. Nor is there any dominant ecclesiastical authority in India capable of arbitrating between competing claims or fixing the relative rank of fresh accessions to the celestial sphere.

It seems that such things are managed better in China. In that country, according to Sir A. Lyall, 'The Emperor —himself a sacred and semi-divine personage—seems to have gradually acquired something like a monopoly of deification, which he uses as a constitutional prerogative, like the right of creating peers.' In fact, 'The government not only bestows on deceased persons its marks of posthumous approbation and rank in the State Heaven; it also decorates them with titles.' The Peking Gazette of May, 1878, contains a decree conferring a great title upon the dragon spirit of Han Tan Hien, in whose temple is the well in which the iron tablet is deposited. 'This spirit has from time to time manifested itself in answer to prayer, and has been repeatedly invested with titles of honour. In consequence of this year's drought prayers were again offered up, and the provinces (mentioned) have been visited with sufficient rain. Our gratitude is indeed profound, and we ordain that the Dragon Spirit shall be invested with the additional title of the Dragon Spirit of the Sacred Well.' Another spirit had already obtained the title of 'Moisture-diffusing, beneficial-aid-affording, universal-support-vouchsafing-Prince,' and received additional titles in a Gazette of 1877[1].

It might have been conjectured that in India a crafty

---

[1] 'Asiatic Studies,' by Sir Alfred Lyall (John Murray), pp. 138, 139.

priesthood would have taken care to lay its hands on a prerogative so valuable and far-reaching in its effects as that thus exercised by the Chinese government. But we do not find that the Brāhmans have ever claimed the exclusive privilege of converting men into gods, or even of conferring honorary degrees and titles of distinction on departed spirits. The origin of the popularity of many celebrated shrines is lost in remote antiquity, and without doubt it has often been due to a happy hit on the part of the relatives of some well-known character, who have erected a tomb over his ashes or a monument to his memory on simple speculation, and then sent agents everywhere to advertise its virtues or spread reports of great miracles worked in the neighbourhood.

Such shrines may often bring in a large revenue to their proprietors, and may even be more frequented than those of Vishṇu's two most celebrated incarnations, Kṛishṇa and Rāma; but it must be borne in mind that in almost every case where a local hero or remarkable person of any kind has attained to deification, he ends by being worshipped as a form of either Vishṇu or Śiva.

To give a few instances of local deifications which fell under my own observation in India:—It is well known that at Paṇḍharpur in the Deccan (on the Bhīmā, about 112 miles south-east of Poona) and in the surrounding districts the favourite god is Viṭho-bā (also called Viṭhṭhal). Very little is known of his origin, but he is said to have been a Brāhman named Puṇḍarīka (sometimes corrupted into Puṇḍalīka), who gained a great reputation for filial piety, and so pleased Vishṇu that the god, in recognition of his merits, infused into him a large portion of his own essence. Viṭho-bā is now everywhere regarded as a form of Kṛishṇa. Idols of him are common, and have this peculiarity, that he is represented standing on a brick (vīṭ for īṭ) with his arms akimbo, the hands resting on the hips. A legend has been framed to account for this position. Probably it was a favourite attitude of the man before his deification[1]. Some of his images have the impression of a kick given by the sage Bhṛigu's foot clearly marked on the breast (see p. 45).

Paṇḍharpur is one of the most sacred places in the Marāṭha country, and vast numbers of pilgrims flock to the shrine of Viṭho-bā twice a year—once in the month Āshāḍha, and once again in Kārttika. The place was probably at one time a stronghold of the Buddhists. Indeed it was stated to me, as one reason for the great popularity of Viṭho-bā, that his principal idol took the place of an image of the Buddha, and so became acceptable to all castes. Others believe it to have been a Jaina idol. There is no doubt that caste is still to a great extent ignored by the worshippers of Viṭho-bā at times of pilgrimage. It is remarkable, too, that worshippers make him no offerings, nor ask the god for special benefits. He is supposed to love all mankind, and require nothing but love in return; so people simply praise him, and sometimes even embrace his image. The idol, which is said to be svayambhū (p. 69), is dressed every day in jewelled dresses, and hymns are sung before it. It is supposed to change its appearance and look like a child in the morning, a man at noon, and an old man in the evening. Doubtless Viṭho-bā owes much of his celebrity to the songs of the Marāṭha national poet Tukā-rāma. A common devotional service among the pilgrims is a Kīrtana or 'song of praise' extracted from his poems. Hundreds of men and women sit in a circle on the ground, while behind the sitters are many standing. The principal singers form a kind of inner semicircle. The leader thereupon gives out a verse, such as the following: 'All earthly things are vanity; therefore draw thy heart away and elevate it to Viṭho-bā.' These

[1] One of Tukā's Abhaṅgas begins, 'Beautiful is that object, upright on the brick, resting his hands on his loins.' I cannot agree in thinking it possible that the name Viṭho-bā may be derived from *vīṭ* 'a brick,' and *ubhā* 'upright.'

words are caught up by the other performers, and then chanted enthusiastically by all with a vigorous accompaniment of lutes (vīṇās), cymbals, and drums. Sometimes a discourse on the vanity of human life follows the singing.

Even a woman may be the preacher. When Dr. Murray Mitchell visited Paṇḍharpur a widow named Sālu-bāī addressed a large audience, commencing her discourse by uttering the names Rāma, Kṛishṇa, Hari, which were caught up by her hearers in a prolonged shout (Indian Antiquary, June 1882).

A ceremony is also performed which consists in breaking a large black clay-vessel fastened on a tree. The contents, consisting of curdled milk and grain, fall on the ground and are eagerly snatched up by the struggling crowd.

The celebrated national poet of the Marāṭhas, Tukā-rāma, was a Śūdra of the trading caste who lived in the days of Śivā-jī, about 250 years ago, at Dehū near Poona, and wrote about 5,000 hymns. Though he devoted his genius to the extolling of Viṭhō-bā as a form of God, he is himself also an object of adoration, and is believed to have worked many miracles—amongst others ascending in bodily shape to heaven in Vishṇu's car. Dehū is now a much-frequented place of pilgrimage, especially at an annual festival when the poet's ascension is commemorated. People of all castes who worship at this place and at Paṇḍharpur are called Vārkarī. The following is a specimen of the religious sentiments in Tukā-rāma's songs translated by Sir A. Grant:—

> Sing the song with earnestness, making pure the heart;
> If you would attain God, then this is an easy way:—
> Make your heart lowly, touch the feet of Saints,
> Of others do not hear the good or bad qualities.
> Tukā says: Be it much or little, do good to others[1].

---

[1] A musician performed before me on the Sitār at Poona, and sang a song from Tukā-rāma, which may be thus translated: 'O God, grant this boon that I may never forget Thee, and that I may sing Thy praise with zest. This is all the wealth I ask. I desire not extinction, nor riches. I want not emancipation from existence. I pray that I may live to praise Thee, and enjoy the company of the good.'

Another deification, Khaṇḍo-bā (also called Khaṇḍe-Rao), was a personage who lived in the neighbourhood of the hill Jejūrī (=Sanskṛit *Jayādri*), thirty miles from Poona. He is probably a deification of some powerful Rājā or aboriginal chieftain who made himself useful to the Brāhmans. He is now regarded as an incarnation of Śiva in his form Mallāri. The legend is that the god Śiva descended in this form to destroy a powerful demon named Mallāsura, who lived on the hill and was a terror to the neighbourhood. Pārvatī descended at the same time to become Khaṇḍo-bā's wife. His worship is very popular among the Kolis and people of low caste in the Marāṭha country. I was informed that he is the family god of Holkar, who is of the shepherd caste. Sheep are sacrificed at the principal temple on the Jejūrī hill, where there is an image of the Liṅga; and a bad custom prevails of dedicating young girls to the god's service. They are called Muralīs (or Murlīs), and although nominally wives of the god, are simply prostitutes. Khaṇḍo-bā is sometimes represented with his wife on horseback attended by a dog[1].

As to another local deification called Jñāneśvara (pronounced in Marāṭhī Dñyāneśvara and popularly Dñyāno-bā), he was a learned Brāhman, living at a place called Alandi, twelve miles from Poona, who wrote a commentary in verse on the Bhagavad-gītā called Jñāneśvarī. Towards the end of his life he became a Sannyāsī, and on dying, or appearing to die, his body was, as usual, not burnt, but buried, and a tomb (Samādh) erected over it. The belief, of course, is that he merely lies in a trance, and that he occasionally shows himself alive to his worshippers. He is held to have been an incarnation of Vishṇu, and is said to have given evidence of his divinity while he lived as a Brāhman on the earth by one or two notable miracles. For example, he one day caused a buffalo to speak and recite a hymn from the

---

[1] A sect existed in Śaṅkara's time who worshipped Mallāri as 'lord of dogs' (see Śaṅkara-vijaya, chap. 29). So Rudra is lord of dogs (see p. 77).

Veda. On another occasion, he commanded a wall on which he was sitting to transport him for a mile into the presence of a holy person who wished to see him. The wall obeyed, and remains to this day at some distance from the town, but the old mouldering erection seemed likely to disappear under the plundering hands of relic-seekers, and the piety of the inhabitants has therefore recently cased it with stone. It is still, however, greatly venerated, and a hole has been made in the stone-casing to enable pilgrims to express their faith by touching the original structure. Indeed, in the belief of the generality of Hindūs, such miracles are of common occurrence all over India. No one is troubled by any misgivings as to their improbability, or supposes for a moment that a saint of any pretensions could be incapable of working them.

Again, I found that in certain localities in the Marāṭha country a holy Brāhman, named Dattātreya (vulgarly Dattātre), who lived about the tenth century of our era, is worshipped as an incarnation of all three gods, Brahmā, Vishṇu, and Śiva, or, according to some, especially of Vishṇu[1]. He was greatly revered for his wisdom and self-mortification, and before his death became a Sannyāsī. His shrines are scattered here and there in the districts around Poona. I visited a remarkable one at Wāi—a sacred town on the Kṛishṇā (Kistna) near Sattārā—where the image of Dattātreya has three heads, to represent the Hindū triad. Two or three worshippers of the male sex appeared to be engaged in earnest devotion before this idol.

Another deification is that of Vyaṅkaṭeśa (Veṅkaṭeśa) or Tri-pati (for Sanskṛit *Śrī-pati*), a name given to Vishṇu or Kṛishṇa when he became incarnate in a man popularly called Bālā-jī. Little is known about this man, except that he was a person remarkable for many extraordinary

[1] There is a strange legend connected with Dattātreya current in some parts of India. Brahmā, Vishṇu, and Śiva are said to have visited the wife of a holy man and tried to seduce her, but without success.

qualities, and that he lived in the neighbourhood of a hill called Śeshādri in the Madras presidency. It is certain that a celebrated temple dedicated to him has been erected at that place—usually called the Hill of Tri-pati or Vyaṅkaṭa (Veṅkaṭa)—and that pilgrimages are made to it from every part of the country. It is especially resorted to for religious shaving.

Of more recent deifications and canonizations a few examples may be given. I have already described how the followers of a Brāhman named Sahajānanda or Svāmi-Nārāyaṇa, who flourished about the beginning of the present century, regard him as a portion of Vishṇu (see p. 153).

The same may be said of the followers of the cotton-bleacher Dādū, who lived in less recent times (see p. 178).

Then Mīrā-bāī, a princess who lived in the time of Akbar, and married the Rāṇā of Udayapur (Udaipur), is worshipped by a sect, who believe that she disappeared one day into her tutelary idol—an image of Kṛishṇa—which opened to receive her and protect her from persecution. She is the authoress of some religious odes.

Again, Rām-singh, the son of a carpenter, was a man who founded a small sect of Sikhs called Kūkas, which had to be repressed not long since with an iron hand, because in their fanaticism they took to murdering the butchers who killed oxen for food. His followers scarcely worshipped him as a god, yet they fully believed in his power of working miracles. (Compare the last paragraph at p. 172 of this volume.)

Another founder of a sect—Rām-dās—was the Guru of Śivā-jī. His followers, who are numerous in the Marāṭha country, adore him in connexion with the worship of the great Rāma, and therefore also worship Hanumān. His tomb or Samādh is at Parāli, near Sattāra.

I may add, that in a village of Gujarāt called Sārsā there lives (or did live in 1878) a man named Kubera. This man is of the Koli caste. He has been a teacher of religion for more than thirty-five years, and gives himself out to be a portion of the god Kṛishṇa. He has gathered around him at least 20,000 disciples, and formed them into a religious society who call themselves Hari-jana. They are also called Kuber-bhaktas. They worship or worshipped Kubera their founder, as a living incarnation, in his own dwelling, but they have temples or meeting-houses in many villages, and send missionaries to all parts of Gujarāt. Like the Svāmi-Nārāyaṇa sect, they are divided into Sādhus and Gṛihasthas, or Clergy and Laity (see p. 150). At one of their temples (Mandirs) in the town of Nariād, two of their clergy minister daily. Several members of the sect attend and listen to expositions of their sacred books, but worship no idols.

Another considerable temple which I saw at Nariād is dedicated to a holy man named Santa-Rām (probably = Śānta-rāma, or perhaps Santosha-rāma). His body is buried in the precincts of the temple, and I observed that the courtyard around was kept scrupulously clean. He has no very large number of disciples, but they appeared to be very devoted in their homage.

I heard of another man in Gujarāt, named Hari-Kṛishṇa, who not very long ago proclaimed himself to be a manifestation of the Supreme Being, and attracted a few disciples; but he is now dead, and the sect has also, I believe, died out.

Again, when I was at Kaira I visited a small shrine, dedicated to a Sādhu or holy man whose name I understood to be Pariṇāma. There was no image, but only the empty seat which he had once occupied as a religious teacher, with some of the vestments which he wore at the time of his decease. Yet the place was regarded as so sacred that I was not allowed to enter without taking off my shoes.

I believe the followers of this man are gradually decreasing, and will ultimately disappear. In fact, it ought to be noted that the most astounding exploits of great heroes and the most startling miracles of eminent saints are liable to be eclipsed by still greater wonders, wrought by still greater heroes and saints, who are always appearing on the scene and engrossing the attention of an ignorant and superstitious multitude.

In no other way can we account for the little honour now paid to such an eminent hero as Bala-rāma, 'the strong Rāma,' who was an elder brother of Kṛishṇa and brought up with him (see p. 112)[1].

Again, as to the well-known Paraśu-rāma, or Rāma with the axe—he was a Brāhman who achieved so great a reputation in conflicts with the Kshatriyas that his admirers converted him into one of Vishṇu's ten principal incarnations (see p. 110). Yet he is little worshipped except in some parts of the western coast of India. The story of his clearing the earth twenty-one times of the Kshatriya race and of his ultimate defeat by his rival the great Rāma-ćandra, who was the Kshatriya incarnation of Vishṇu and also one of the god's ten principal descents, proves that the axe-Rāma was at one time a man of pre-eminent valour and renown (see p. 110, and Mahā-bhārata Vana-p. 11071; Śānti-p. 1707; Bhāgavata-purāṇa, book IX). Tradition ascribes the colonizing of the Koṅkan—called Paraśu-rāma-kshetra—and the creation of the whole country of Malabar (Kerala) to Paraśu-rāma.

He must have been a very extraordinary personage, for he is believed to have compelled the ocean to retire for the formation of the Malabar coast, and to have caused vast fissures in the Western Ghāṭs and other mountains by blows of his axe[2]. At the same time he is said to have reared great stone cairns on the Travancore mountains, and to have scattered small spangle-like gold coins everywhere on the soil.

---

[1] Both Bala-rāma and Kṛishṇa refused to take any part as warriors in the great war between the Pāṇḍava and Kaurava princes.

[2] Unusual formations in hills and other curious physical phenomena are often attributed to Paraśu-rāma, and sometimes to Bhīma.

It is certain that earthen vessels containing coins are often dug up on the hills. No wonder that he has many followers in Malabar and the Koṅkan[1], but I met with no actual worshippers in other places who adore him as a god.

Similarly the five Pāṇḍava princes, Yudhi-shṭhira, Bhīma, Arjuna, Nakula, and Sahadeva, who are all great heroes of the Mahā-bhārata, receive little actual worship at the present day, though Kṛishṇa, another great hero of the same poem, is universally adored. The five brothers were the reputed children of Pāṇḍu and his wife Kuntī (or Pṛithā), but are believed to have really derived their origin from the gods Yama (= Dharma-rāja), Vāyu, Indra, and the two Aśvins respectively. These deities infused portions of their essences into Kuntī's children, and great prodigies occurred at their birth. When grown up they had one wife in common, called Draupadī. Draupadī (in Southern India Draupadī-Amman) has several shrines, but her five husbands receive little adoration. This story proves the prevalence of polyandry[2].

Nevertheless, any marvel or prodigy, any rock of fantastic shape, or any wonderful work the performance of which appears to be beyond human power, is often ascribed to the Pāṇḍavas. I visited some remarkable Buddhistic caves

---

[1] A tribe of Brāhmans in the Koṅkan called Ćit-pāvans is said to have been created by Paraśu-rāma thus:—After his contest with the Kshatriyas he took up his abode in the mountains of that part of India. There he had a quarrel with some Brāhmans who resided with him in the same region. Then to spite them he went to the sea-shore, and finding fourteen funeral piles (ćitās=ćaityas) with the remains of a number of persons who had been burnt, resuscitated them and converted them into Brāhmans.

[2] Certain hill-tribes in the Himālaya mountains are still given to polyandry. It is practised also among the Todas and the Nayars in Malabar, and among certain tribes in New Zealand, the Pacific islands, the Aleutian islands, Africa, Australia, as well as among the Kalmucks, Iroquois, and in Bhotān and other barren regions where a large population is not easily supported. The ancient Britons, according to Cæsar, were addicted to the same practice. See De Bello Gallico, v. 14. Compare Lubbock's 'Origin of Civilization,' p. 139.

excavated at a considerable height from the ground in the hills near Nāsik. The people of the country fully believe them to have been the work of the Pāṇḍavas, and call them Pāṇḍu-leṇe. It is therefore surprising that so few shrines dedicated to these heroes are found in any part of India.

In one of the galleries of the temple at Tinnevelly I observed well-carved images of all the five brothers; Arjuna being especially conspicuous with his bow Gāṇḍīva, and Bhīma with his club. It is worthy of note, too, that five rough stones smeared with red paint may occasionally be seen set up in fields. These are probably intended to represent the five Pāṇḍava princes who are supposed to guard the crops. Such stones abound in various parts of India, but are not always five in number, sometimes as many as twenty being ranged together in a kind of circle.

Again, I saw images to the honour of the Pāṇḍavas at Madurā, and at Buddha-gayā, but no worshippers were near them[1]. Yet the characters of these heroes are quite as much venerated now as they ever were in ancient times, and their virtues, as narrated in the Mahā-bhārata, are to this day proverbial throughout India. Arjuna, who is the most renowned, is a pattern of bravery and generosity; Yudhi-shṭhira of justice, passionless self-command, and cold heroism; Nakula and Sahadeva of wisdom, temperance, and beauty; while Bhīma is a type of brute courage and physical strength.

Representations of Bhīma's gigantic form are not uncommon, but are rather curiosities to excite wonder, than objects to attract worship. I saw a huge image of him on one of the Ghāṭs at Benares, and another near the Agra fort, and another in a corridor of the Liṅga temple at Tinnevelly. This last is about 20 feet high and holds a huge club. It is painted bright red and made for moving about in processions.

Bhīma's great strength is illustrated by a curious story.

[1] In the Marāṭha country a single rudely-carved figure, especially if mounted, is called a Vīr (*vīra*, hero), or sometimes a Dev (*deva*, god).

Soon after his birth his mother, who was carrying him in her arms up a mountain, accidentally let him fall over a precipice, and on descending in great agony of mind, expecting to find her baby dashed to pieces on the rock beneath, she found to her amazement and delight that the boy was unhurt, and the rock shivered to atoms by contact with his body.

Karṇa, too, another of the Mahā-bhārata heroes (also son of Kuntī by the Sun-god), is greatly revered, and often cited in proverbial expressions, as a model of liberality, chivalrous honour, and self-sacrificing generosity. I saw one or two images of him in Southern India, but met with no shrines dedicated to his worship.

Clearly the hero-worship of India is subject to constant changes and fluctuations. Worshippers are capricious; great warriors, great saints, and great sages have their day and find themselves gradually pushed into the background, while their places are taken by rival warriors, saints, and sages who claim to be still greater[1].

---

[1] That man-worship is not confined to India may be proved by numerous examples drawn from all countries. In Africa the King of Loango is honoured as a god. His person is so sacred that no one is allowed to see him eat. In Peru a particular Inca was adored as a god during his lifetime. In New Zealand the warrior chief, Hongi, was called a god by his followers. At the Society Islands, King Tamatoa was worshipped, and in the Marquesas there are several men named *atua* believed to possess the power of gods. At Tahiti the king and queen were once held so sacred that the sounds forming their names could not be used for ordinary words. See 'Origin of Civilization,' by Sir J. Lubbock, p. 355.

CHAPTER XI.

Death, Funeral Rites, and Ancestor-worship.

In the two preceding chapters we have had occasion to state incidentally the Hindū doctrine in regard to the spirits of the dead. We have seen that they are supposed to pass into one or other of two very different conditions. They may be degraded to the state of evil demons or elevated to the position of divinities[1]. In the former case they are rather feared and propitiated than worshipped; in the latter they are rather reverenced and worshipped than propitiated. In the present chapter I have to point out how far this varying condition of deceased persons depends on the performance of funeral and ancestral rites by living relatives and descendants.

Of all forms of religious devotion homage to dead relations is the most widely extended[2]. It forms a part of nearly all religions, and is an element in the creed of nearly every race[3]. Perhaps the one exception is Protestant Christianity. The Roman Catholic Church, as is well known, teaches that supplications and prayers may avail to improve the condition of departed spirits in purgatory. Not only, therefore does it

---

[1] In the same way among the Romans some souls of the dead were good, pure, and bright, and therefore called Manes; while others, called Larvæ and Lemures, wandered about as unquiet ghosts, and were often regarded as evil spirits. Compare also the Roman ideas respecting the Penates. With regard to the ideas prevalent among the Greeks, the following passages bear on the existence of the ψυχή after death as an εἴδωλον in Hades: Il. xxiii. 72, 104; Od. xi. 213, 476; xx. 355; xxiv. 14.

[2] I refer any one who doubts this fact to Mr. E. B. Tylor's 'Primitive Culture,' vol. ii. chap. xviii.

[3] The Bishop of Madagascar stated not long ago, that when he had to descend a dangerous stream in that island, the boatmen made offerings to the spirits of their ancestors before attempting to shoot the rapids.

permit special masses to be offered for the souls of deceased relations, it introduces a prayer for the dead into the regular daily mass [1].

According to the Protestant creed, on the other hand, the condition of the dead is irrevocably fixed. To think of ameliorating it by human intercession is nothing short of heresy. Nor is it customary to perpetuate by any kind of act, periodically repeated, the memory of one's nearest and dearest relatives. It is no doubt true that tombs are occasionally visited, and, in the case of royal personages, memorial services performed; and an eminent Bishop [2] once gave it as his opinion that the Church of England does not condemn special services for the spirits of the dead [3]; provided, I presume, that their condition is not supposed to be thereby altered.

It is also true that every respectable man who has had a respectable father or mother will be careful to reverence their memory [4], but I question whether the same man ever feels it his duty to bestow a single reverential thought on either of

---

[1] Our prayer for the Church militant has, I believe, taken the place of this. In some Roman Catholic countries it is customary to exhume skeletons at intervals of several years, and to place their skulls in a small chapel adjoining the parish church. This chapel is in German Switzerland called the Schädel-haus, 'Skull-house,' and is used as an oratory where people pray for their dead relations and friends.

[2] According to the late Bishop of Peterborough, the belief was once general in the early Church that the souls of the faithful, though free from all suffering, were capable, while awaiting their final consummation and bliss, of a progress in holiness and happiness; and that prayers for such progress might lawfully be made in their behalf. Accordingly, prayers for 'the rest and refreshment of the departed' abound in the early liturgies of the Church. See the Bishop's letter to the Rev. J. Mason's parishioners who complained of Mr. Mason's having given notice that he intended celebrating the Holy Communion for the repose of Dr. Pusey's soul.

[3] All Souls' day is observed as a festival (on Nov. 2) in the Church of Rome. It is said that in countries where superstition is rife feasting takes place, and the souls of the dead are supposed to join in the festivities and consume the essence of the food before it is eaten.

[4] The feeling seems to find expression in putting periodical advertisements 'in loving memory' in the obituary of modern newspapers.

his departed grandfathers and grandmothers, and whether the world would feel quite sure of the sanity of any one who was in the habit of offering periodical homage to his two great-grandfathers and great-grandmothers.

This utter neglect of one's ancestors, which seems to spring not so much from any want of sympathy with the departed as from a disbelief in any interconnexion between this world and the world of spirits, is perhaps with good reason regarded as a defect in our religious character and practice.

In Eastern countries, especially India, China, and Japan, the opposite extreme prevails. We know that in India, every religious duty is magnified and intensified. There, to speak of mere reverence for the dead is a very inadequate expression. The constant periodical performance of commemorative obsequies is regarded in the light of a positive and peremptory obligation. It is the simple discharge of a solemn debt due to one's forefathers—a debt consisting not only in reverential worship, but in the performance of acts necessary to their support, happiness, and progress onward in the spirit-world. A man's deceased relatives, for at least three generations, are among his cherished divinities, and must be honoured by *daily offerings* (see p. 410), or a Nemesis of some kind is certain to overtake his living family.

Nothing, in fact, seemed to me more noteworthy in comparing Hindūism with other religions, than the elaborate nature of its funeral rites and the extraordinary importance attached to marriage, with a view to providing sons for the due performance of these rites and of the subsequent ceremonial worship called Śrāddha.

And here at the outset it may be well to point out that the main object of a Hindū funeral is very different from that of European obsequial rites.

It is nothing less than the investiture of the departed spirit with a kind of intermediate body—a peculiar frame interposed, as it were parenthetically, between the terrestrial gross body which has just been destroyed by fire, and the new terrestrial body which it is compelled ultimately to assume. The creation of such an intervenient frame—composed of gross elements, though less gross than those of earth—becomes necessary, because the individualized spirit of man, after cremation of the terrestrial body, has nothing left to withhold it from re-absorption into the universal soul, except its incombustible subtle body, which, as composed of the subtle elements, is not only proof against the fire of the funeral pile, but is incapable of any sensations in the temporary heaven or temporary hell (p. 49), through one or other of which every separate human spirit is forced to pass before returning to earth and becoming reinvested with a terrestrial gross body.

Were it not for this intermediate frame—believed to be created by the offerings made during the funeral ceremonies—the spirit would remain with its subtle body in the condition of an impure and unquiet ghost (preta) wandering about on the earth or in the air among demons and evil spirits, and condemned itself to become an evil spirit[1]. Its reception of the intervenient body converts it from a Preta or ghost into a Pitṛi or ancestor; but this does not satisfy all its needs. The new body it has received, though not so gross as that of earth, must be developed and supported. It must, if possible, be rescued from the fire of purgatory. It must be assisted onwards in its course from lower to higher worlds and back again to earth. And these results can only be accomplished by the ceremonies called Śrāddha — ceremonies which may in some

[1] It is curious that the Hindū notion of the restless state of the soul until the Śrāddha is performed agrees with the ancient classical superstition that the ghosts of the dead wandered about as long as their bodies remained unburied, and were not suffered to mingle with those of the other dead. See Od. xi. 54; Il. xxiii. 72; and cf. Æn. vi. 325; Lucan, i, ii; Eur. Hec. 30.

respects be compared to the Roman Catholic masses for the dead. The first Śrāddha—to be described (at p. 303, etc.) —is performed very soon after the funeral rites, and is always a costly affair.

In England, the religious services at a funeral occupy about half an hour, and the entire ceremony, with all its attendant circumstances, is performed in the present day at little cost.

In India, the funeral ceremonies of the older members of a family[1] occupy ten days, and with the succeeding Śrāddha rites—carried on with the help of Brāhmans and including the feasting of numberless guests and the distribution of presents—may involve an enormous expenditure. I found that the cost to even the poorest respectable person was forty rupees, and that any one well-to-do in the world would incur the everlasting obloquy of his family and friends and be almost excommunicated from society if he spent less than six thousand or seven thousand rupees on the funeral of a father and in the carrying out of all the other necessary ceremonies consequent on his death. It is well known that the expenditure incurred on such occasions by rich Bengal Rājās and Zamīndārs of high family has often impoverished them for the remainder of their lives. Instances are on record of a single funeral and Śrāddha costing a sum equivalent to £120,000, the greater part of that amount being squandered on worthless Brāhmans, indolent Pandits, hypocritical devotees, and vagabond religious mendicants.

In truth, the expenditure of time, money, and energy needed to satisfy public opinion before a man is held to have discharged the debt due to a deceased father, and before he is relieved from the long course of fasting and mourning he is expected to undergo, constitutes an evil which has gradually grown till it has become a veritable curse to the country, and one of the principal bars to any

[1] The funeral rites of children are much simpler and shorter.

advance in its social condition (compare p. 532). Nor is there any warrant for the system in the more ancient books held sacred in India as authoritative guides.

Let us try to ascertain the ancient practice by a reference to the Veda and Sūtras.

The ceremonies in Vedic times must have been very simple. We gather from the 18th hymn of the 10th Maṇḍala of the Ṛig-veda that the dead body was, in all probability, not burnt but buried. It was deposited near a grave dug ready for its reception, while the widow lay down or seated herself by its side, and the relatives—female as well as male—ranged themselves in a circle all around. Their first concern seems to have been to propitiate Death, supposed to be personally present and to be naturally eager to take the opportunity of laying his hands on any other member of the family, who might be brought, by the necessity of attending the funeral, within easy and tempting reach of his clutches. Hence the person appointed to perform the ceremony addressed Death, calling upon him to keep clear of the path of the living, and deprecating any attack on the survivors, who were assembled to perform pious rites for their dead relative, but had no idea of yielding themselves up into his power, or renouncing the expectation of a long life themselves. The leader of the funeral next placed a boundary of stones between the dead body and the living relations, to mark off the limits of Death's authority. Then followed a prayer that none of those present might be removed to another world before attaining to the full period of a life lasting for a hundred years. This prayer was no doubt accompanied with oblations in fire, after which the widow's married female relatives were directed by the performer of the ceremony to prepare for the return home. They were to lead the way without weeping or any signs of grief, and without taking off their jewelry[1].

[1] The words of the hymn are, *Anaśravo 'namīvāḥ su-ratnā ā rohantu*

Then the widow herself was told to leave the corpse of her dead husband in the inner circle assigned to Death, and join her surviving relations outside the boundary line. She was addressed in words to the following effect: 'Rise up, O woman (udīrshva nāri), come back to the world of the living; thou art lying by a dead man; come back. Thou hast sufficiently fulfilled the duty of a wife to the husband who formerly wooed thee and took thee by the hand' (Ṛig-veda X. 18. 8). Next, the performer of the ceremony took a bow, previously placed in the hand of the deceased, and gave it to his relatives in token that the manly courage he had displayed during life was not to perish with him, but to remain with his family. Addressing the dead man he said: 'I take the bow out of thy hand for our own protection, for our glory, and for our strength; remain thou here, we will remain here as heroes, so that in all battles we may conquer our foes' (X. 18. 9). The body was then tenderly committed to its 'house of clay' (mṛin-mayaṃ gṛihaṃ, Ṛig-veda VII. 89. 1), with the words: 'Return to thy mother Earth, may she be kind to thee and lie lightly on thee, and not oppress thee;' and with other similar words, which may be thus freely translated:—

> Open thy arms, O earth, receive the dead
> With gentle pressure and with loving welcome.
> Enshroud him tenderly, e'en as a mother
> Folds her soft vestment round the child she loves.
>
> (X. 18. 11.)

Finally, a mound or column (sthūṇā) of earth was reared over the grave, and the Pitṛis or deified ancestors and the god Yama were entreated to preserve it.

---

janayo yonim agre, 'without tears, without sorrow, bedecked with jewels, let the wives go to the house first.' It is said that the Brāhmans fraudulently substituted *agneḥ*, 'of fire,' for *agre*, 'first,' and that this verse was then quoted as the Vedic authority for the burning of widows; whereas neither the Veda nor Manu directed or even hinted at the concremation of the living wife with her dead husband.

It is remarkable that in some passages of the hymns (X. 58. 7; 16. 3) there are dim hints of a belief in the possible migration of the spirits of the deceased into plants, trees, and streams. Compare pp. 18; 24.

It is to be noted, however, that no very distinct account of the condition of the virtuous dead is to be found in the oldest hymns of the Ṛig-veda, although a future life is fully recognized, and although the Pitṛis or departed ancestors are addressed with the utmost reverence (VI. 52. 4; VII. 35. 12; X. 14. 7, 8, etc.). Nor do we find any clear mention of hells or places of torment for the wicked, although we read of dark and deep abysses into which bad men are thrown along with the evil demons[1].

Passing from Vedic times to the period when the Āśvalāyana and other collections of domestic rules (Gṛihya-sūtras) were composed, probably about five or six centuries before Christ, we find that funeral rites, though still conducted with much simplicity, were beginning to be more elaborate and more in unison with present custom. If the practice of cremation was doubtful in Vedic times it was now invariable, except in the case of infants and of great saints. As far as can be gathered from a study of the rules laid down, the ceremonial must have been much as follows:—

When a man died, his immediate family, headed by the eldest son or other near relative, formed a procession to a properly prepared place in the Śmaśāna or 'burning ground,' carrying the sacred fires and sacrificial implements. The younger walked first, the elder behind—the men separated from the women[2]—bearing the corpse, the hair and nails of which had been clipped, and leading the sacrificial animal,

---

[1] 'Indrā and Soma plunge the wicked in inextricable darkness, so that not one of them may again issue from it.' See Ṛig-veda VII. 104. 3, and compare IV. 5. 5; IX. 73. 8.

[2] In the present day the only part women take in funeral ceremonies is that of weeping and wailing and uttering loud cries of grief at home.

either a cow[1] or a black she-goat. The remaining relatives followed with their garments hanging down and their hair dishevelled—the elder in front, the younger behind. When they reached the funeral ground, the son or brother or other near relative appointed to perform the ceremony, taking a branch of the Śamī-tree, sprinkled holy water on the spot excavated and prepared for the pile, repeating Ṛig-veda X. 14. 9: 'Depart (ye evil spirits), slink away from here; the Fathers (his departed ancestors) have made for him this place of rest.'

Then the sacred fires were deposited around the margin of the excavated place, and a heap of fire-wood was piled up inside the sacrificial ground (antar-vedi). Next, a layer of Kuśa grass was spread over the pile along with the black skin of the goat. Then the clipped hair and the dead body were placed upon it, with the feet towards one of the fires and the head towards the other. Next, the widow was made to lie down on the funeral pile north of the body, along with the bow of her deceased husband, but was not allowed to remain there long. Soon the leader of the funeral called upon her to rise, repeating Ṛig-veda X. 18. 8, already quoted (see p. 280).

Next, he took back the bow, repeating Ṛig-veda X. 18. 9 (quoted at p. 280).

Then he placed the various sacrificial implements and portions of the sacrificial animal in the two hands and on different parts of the body of the corpse. This being done, he kindled the three sacred fires. While the body was burning, portions of hymns of the Ṛig-veda (such as

---

[1] The sacrifice of a cow (called Anustaraṇī) at ancient funeral ceremonies proves, according to Dr. Rājendra-lāla Mitra, that in early times there was no law against the eating of flesh, and even of beef. A cow was killed, that the dead might have a supply of the essence of beef for their journey; and when the spirits of the departed had feasted on the aroma of the immolated animal, the actual flesh was left for the living.

X. 14. 7, 8, 10, 11; 16. 1–4; 17. 3–6; 18. 11; 154. 1–5) were repeated.

The following are free translations of some of the verses:—

> Soul of the dead! depart; take thou the path—
> The ancient path—by which our ancestors
> Have gone before thee; thou shalt look upon
> The two kings, mighty Varuṇa and Yama,
> Delighting in oblations; thou shalt meet
> The Fathers and receive the recompense
> Of all thy stored-up offerings above.
> Leave thou thy sin and imperfection here;
> Return unto thy home once more; assume
> A glorious form. By an auspicious path
> Hasten to pass the four-eyed brindled dogs—
> The two road-guarding sons of Saramā;
> Advance to meet the Fathers who, with hearts
> Kindly disposed towards thee, dwell in bliss
> With Yama; and do thou, O mighty god,
> Intrust him to thy guards[1] to bring him to thee,
> And grant him health and happiness eternal.
> (X. 14. 7–11.)

When a dead body was thus burnt the spirit—invested with its incombustible subtle frame—was supposed to rise along with the smoke to heaven.

Then the performer of the ceremony repeated the verse (Ṛig-veda X. 18. 3):—

> We living men, survivors, now return
> And leave the dead; may our oblations please
> The gods and bring us blessings! now we go
> To dance and jest and hope for longer life.

After this they proceeded homewards, the younger walking in front, the elder behind. But before re-entering the house they purified themselves by chewing leaves of the Nimba-tree[2], and by touching fire, grains of barley, oil, and water. During one night they cooked no food, and for three nights ate nothing containing salt.

After the tenth day the bones and ashes of the deceased

---

[1] These are the two four-eyed watch-dogs mentioned at p. 289.

[2] This, however, is not mentioned in the Āśvalāyana Sūtras.

were gathered together and placed in a plain undecorated funeral vase. This particular act, which in modern times is generally performed on the fourth day, was called Asthi-sañćaya, 'bone-collection.' A hole was excavated and the vessel placed in it, while Ṛig-veda X. 18. 10 was repeated: 'Return to thy mother Earth, the Widely-extended, the Broad, the Auspicious; may she be to thee like a young maiden, soft as wool (ūrṇa-mradā)! may she protect thee from the embrace of the goddess of corruption!'

Then earth was scattered over the excavation, with repetition of the twelfth verse of the same hymn. Lastly, a cover was placed over the vase and the hole was filled up with earth, while the thirteenth verse was repeated: 'I raise up the earth around thee for a support, placing this cover on thee without causing injury. May the Fathers guard this funeral monument for thee! May Yama establish a habitation for thee there!'

The principal rite being thus brought to a close, the relations returned home, and after performing an ablution offered the first Śrāddha to the deceased person.

I may mention here that, being one day on the Bombay burning-ground, I was a spectator of a 'bone-gathering' ceremony (see p. 302), which had many features in common with the ancient rite. A Brāhman and five women were seated in a semicircle round the ashes and bones of a young married girl of low caste, whose body had recently been burnt. Before them was an earthenware vase, and around it were flowers, fruits, and betel-leaves. The Brāhman had a metal vase shaped something like a tumbler in his hand containing consecrated or holy water. With a small round spoon or ladle he took out a small portion of the water and poured it into the hands of the woman, at the same time muttering texts and prayers. Then he poured water into the vase, and on the top of the water placed the fruit, flowers, and leaves. Next, he collected the half-calcined bones, and having put them carefully and reverentially into the vase, he made a hole in the ground a few yards off and buried it. I was told that the vase would be left there for ten days, when a Śrāddha would be performed in the same place.

Turning next to the law-books (see p. 51), which follow on the Sūtras and are based on them, we find, as might be expected, that the practice they inculcated differed little from that enjoined in the Sūtras. Funeral rites are called 'the last sacrifice' (antyeshṭi), that is to say, the sacrifice of the body in fire. They are regarded as inauspicious (amaṅgala), because impurity is thought to result from contact with a dead body and from connexion with the departed spirit, which, though released by the burning of the body, is still regarded as impure until the Śrāddha ceremonies are performed. Manu even declares that some implication of impurity attaches to the sound of the Sāma-veda because it is chanted at funeral services.

The Śrāddha, on the other hand, is held to be auspicious (maṅgala), because it is performed for the benefit of a deceased person after he has received an intermediate body and become a Pitṛi or beatified father. It is true that both funeral and Śrāddha ceremonies consist in the offering of balls (piṇḍa) of rice or flour and libations of water, with texts and prayers; but in the funeral rites the ball of rice is for the nourishment of the ghost and for the formation of a body as its vehicle, whereas in the Śrāddha the Piṇḍa is said to represent the body so formed, and is offered as an act of homage. Nevertheless it is plainly declared in Manu (III. 237) and elsewhere that the embodied Pitṛis require the periodical offering of these Piṇḍas and water for their continual nourishment and refreshment.

A large number of relatives are supposed to partake in the benefits of the Śrāddha. They are as follow:—(1) Father, father's father, father's grandfather; (2) Mother, mother's father, mother's grandfather; (3) Stepmother, if any; (4) Father's mother, his grandmother, and his great-grandmother; (5) Father's brothers; (6) Mother's brothers; (7) Father's sisters; (8) Mother's sisters; (9) Sisters and brothers; (10) Fathers-in-law. We know, in fact, that the Hindū family (gotra) is held to be a corporate society, bound together by a right of participation in the Śrāddha offerings. This right furnishes the principal evidence of kinship, on which the title to share in the patrimony is founded, no power of making wills being recognized in Manu or any other authoritative code of Hindū jurisprudence. All who unite in presenting to their deceased ancestors the balls (piṇḍa) of rice or flour and libations of water (udaka), are called Sapiṇḍas[1] and Samānodakas to each other, and a kind of intercommunion and interdependence is thus continually maintained between the dead and living members of a family —between past, present, and future generations. Practically, however, the closeness of the interconnexion extends only to three generations on each side. In this way a kind of family chain, consisting of seven links, is formed. The householder represents the central link, and is himself linked to father, grandfather, and great-grandfather on one side, and to son, grandson, and great-grandson on the other (Manu V. 60). The first three are supposed to be dependent on the living paterfamilias for their happiness and support, through the constant offering of the ball-like cakes and water; and he himself, the moment he dies, becomes similarly dependent on the three succeeding generations.

The connexion which is kept up by the common offering of water lasts longer, and ends only when the family names are no longer known (V. 60). Manu's law-book, however, which stands at the head of all the others and is the earliest in date, makes no positive statement as to the precise dis-

---

[1] According to the Mitāksharā school, Piṇḍa may also signify body, and some interpret *sapiṇḍa* to mean persons united by bodily relationship. The other school is that of the Dāya-bhāga, which prevails in Bengal.

tinction between the funeral or Śrāddha ceremonies. Nor does it discriminate clearly between the subtle, the terrestrial, and the intermediate bodies. It merely affirms that a Śrāddha means an oblation of grain, water, or other substances offered with faith (śraddhā), and that the performance of Śrāddhas by a son is necessary to deliver a father from the hell called Put (IX. 138); whence a son is called Put-tra, 'rescuer from Put[1].' This, of course, sufficiently explains the desire of every Hindū for the birth of a son rather than a daughter.

The law-book of Yājñavalkya is later in date. The precepts it lays down (Book III) prove that in the early centuries of our era funerals were conducted in a simple manner. Still, much of the practice was in harmony with modern usage, as well as with that of the Gṛihya-sūtras (p. 281).

For example, a child under two years of age was not burnt but buried, and no offering of water was made to it. (See also Manu V. 68.) The corpse of any other deceased person, except that of a great saint or ascetic, was accompanied by a procession of relations to the burning-place, and there burnt with common fire (laukikāgninā), while a hymn to Yama was repeated. Next, the relatives poured out a single libation of water to the deceased, uttering his name and family. Then, instead of shedding tears or giving way to grief, the relatives, after performing their ablutions, seated themselves on a spot covered with soft grass, while the elder repeated to the younger some verses from the ancient Itihāsas, such as the following (freely translated):—

> Does it not argue folly to expect
> Stability in man, who is as transient
> As a mere bubble and fragile as a stalk?

---

[1] It is wholly inconsistent with the true theory of Hindūism that the Śrāddha should deliver a man from the consequence of his own deeds. Manu says, 'Iniquity once practised, like a seed, fails not to yield its fruit to him that wrought it' (IV. 173); but Hindūism bristles with such inconsistencies.

Why should we utter wailings if a frame,
Composed of five material elements,
Is decomposed by force of its own acts,
And once again resolved into its parts?
The earth, the ocean, and the gods themselves
Must perish, how should not the world
Of mortals, light as froth, obey the law
Of universal death and perish too?

After hearing verses of this kind they set out homewards, the younger ones leading the way. On reaching the house they made a solemn pause outside the door. Then they all chewed leaves of the Nimba-tree (popularly, Nīm), rinsed their mouths with water, touched fire, water, cow-dung, and white mustard-seed, and placed their feet on a stone; then they slowly re-entered the house. Impurity caused by the ceremonies connected with touching the corpse (śāvam āśaućam) lasted for either three nights or ten nights. In later times the season of mourning and impurity lasted longer (see p. 306, note 3).

Turn we now to the more modern practice.

Perhaps the best authority for the present creed of the Hindūs in regard to the future state of the soul, and the best guide to the right performance of funeral and Śrāddha ceremonies, is the Garuḍa-purāṇa. This is a comparatively modern work—probably not older than the seventh or eighth century, and possibly still more modern. It is written, like other Purāṇas, in the form of a dialogue; and is the more interesting, as portions of it are recited at funerals and Śrāddhas in the present day. The dialogue is between Vishṇu and Garuḍa—the divine bird represented as always attendant on the god and serving as his vehicle (see p. 104). Questioned by Garuḍa, Vishṇu reveals the secrets of the future world and the nature of the punishment in store for the wicked. He also prescribes the proper ceremonies. As a matter of fact, however, the forms now observed do not always agree with the directions in the Garuḍa-purāṇa, or in any other guide. They vary according to different localities and different castes.

To describe all the variations within the limit of a single chapter would be impossible. I can only advert to some principal usages in the case of the death of persons of higher caste. And to make the Hindū theory of a future state clearer — complicated as it is by numerous contradictory statements and inconsistencies—it will be necessary to trace the development of the prevalent ideas concerning the character and functions of the god of death, Yama.

Probably the name Yama in the Veda is to be connected with an obsolete verb *yam*, meaning 'to double' (Lat. gemino). At any rate, the Vedic meaning of the word seems to have been 'twin,' and Yama himself, with his twin sister Yamī, were held to be the first pair of mortals born into the world, being both children of Vivasvat the Sun (see p. 11 of this volume, and compare Ṛig-veda X. 10). As he was supposed to be the first of men who died, it was only natural that the earliest myths should invest him with the office of conducting the spirits of other men who die to the spirit-world—a world which, according to some later authorities, is to be regarded as divided into three regions, the upper sky, middle air, and the atmosphere just above the earth; the ancient patriarchs occupying the highest region, and the more recently deceased, the lowest.

The next of the ancient ideas concerning Yama was that he reigned as a kind of president of the dead (Pitṛi-pati) in the upper sky. There the spirits of the just, invested with celestial lustre, wafted by gentle breezes or borne in heavenly cars, continually arrived, and became themselves gods to be worshipped under the title of Pitṛis. There they enjoyed the society not only of Yama, but of the god Varuṇa, also supposed to dwell there. The road to this abode was guarded by two four-eyed watch-dogs, called Śyāma, 'dark,' and Śabala (or sometimes Karbura), 'spotted' (see Ṛig-veda X. 14. 10–12, and pp. 283, 422). Death, and sometimes Agni (fire), were regarded as Yama's messengers charged with the duty of conducting the spirits of the dead heavenward, while Yama himself was not so much the god as the friend of departed spirits. He was looked up to with veneration, but not by any means with terror, as if he were the god of punishment. (Compare p. 16 of this volume.)

Turning now to the period of the Epic poems and Purāṇas, we find Yama developed into a much more terrific being. He is now the Judge and punisher of the dead, who sits in judgment upon them, and, so to speak, holds the keys of heaven and hell. Hence he is called 'the Restrainer or Punisher' (Yama, from yam, to restrain), or 'the King of Justice' (Dharma-rāja), or simply 'Justice' (Dharma), or 'the Rod-bearer' (Daṇḍa-dhara), or 'Noose-bearer' (Pāśin). Sometimes he is represented as acting in these characters on behalf of Rudra-Śiva, who is the real god of the dead. Many descriptions of his appearance may be found in the Epic poems and Purāṇas. There he is usually depicted as grim and awe-imposing in aspect, green in colour, clothed in red, riding on a buffalo, and holding a club in one hand and a noose in the other. He is also one of the eight guardians of the quarters of the sky, his own quarter being the South, in which direction in some region of the lower world and somewhere on the confines of the places of torment, which are called the 'terrific provinces' of his kingdom (Vishṇu-purāṇa II. 6), are his city and palace called Yama-pura and Yama-sadana. Between the earth and this abode flows the terrible river Vaitaraṇī[1], which all departed spirits must cross. In the later Purāṇas—and especially in the Garuḍa—Yama is generally regarded as a stern and terrible god of punishment only. He is a kind of Hindū Pluto or Minos, and nothing more. But there is this inconsistency in his position, that although he is appointed to punish every man according to his works, he has, in the creed of many Hindūs,

[1] Baitaraṇī (or Vaitaraṇī) is the name of a river in Orissa 45 miles N.E. of Kuttack. On its bank is a shrine called 'Yama's abode.'

no power over those worshippers of Śiva, Vishṇu, Kṛishṇa, and Brahmā, who have lived virtuous lives, and who when they die are transported to the heavens Kailāsa, Vaikuṇṭha, Go-loka and Brahmā-loka respectively [1]. Nor has he power over those whose death-beds are protected by the due performance of the requisite ceremonies and by the payment of sufficient fees to the Brāhmans who superintend such ceremonies. Compare p. 118.

In attempting, therefore, to give some idea of the present creed of the Hindūs in regard to death and a future state, it will be necessary to begin by describing the career and history of a deceased mortal who, from his evil deeds during life or from some defect in the proper ceremonies at his decease, becomes subject to Yama's penalties.

We are told in the Garuḍa-purāṇa that when such a man dies his spirit takes a downward course through the intestines and emerges in the same manner as the excreta; whereas—as we shall see in the sequel—the spirit of a good man finds its way through the tenth aperture of the body, which is a suture at the top of the skull, called the Brahmarandhram, 'Brahma's crevice.'

No sooner has death occurred and cremation of the terrestrial body taken place, than Yama's two messengers (Yama-dūtau), who are waiting near at hand, make themselves visible to the released spirit, which retains its subtle body composed of the subtle elements, and is said to be of the size of a thumb (aṅgushṭha-mātra). Their aspect is terrific; for they have glaring eyes, hair standing erect, gnashing teeth, crow-black skin, and claw-like nails, and they hold in their hands the awful rod and noose of Yama. Then, as if their appearance in this form were not sufficiently alarming, they proceed to terrify their victim by terrible visions of the torments (yātanā) in store for him.

[1] 'The servants and ministers of Yama and his tortures are unavailing against one who places his reliance in Vishṇu.' Vishṇu-purāṇa III. 7.

In a story told in the Vana-parva of the Mahā-bhārata (16,754), Yama himself appears before a dying man. He is clothed in blood-red garments with a glittering crown upon his head, and, like Varuṇa, holds a noose in his hand, with which he binds the spirit and its subtle frame after drawing it from the sick man's body.

The usual theory, however, is that his two messengers perform this office. They then convey the bound spirit along the road to Yama's abode. There being led before Yama's judgment-seat it is confronted with his Registrar or Recorder named Ćitra-gupta[1]. This officer stands by Yama's side with an open book before him. It is his business to note down all the good and evil deeds of every human being committed during his life, with the resulting merit (puṇya) and demerit (pāpa), and to produce a debtor and creditor account made up and balanced on the day of his death, when that being is brought before Yama[2]. According to the balance on the side of merit or demerit is judgment pronounced.

Truly the prospect of so terrible an ordeal to a man conscious of his sins might appear absolutely unbearable, were it not for his belief in the doctrine that the ceremonies performed on his behalf by his relations after his death, have power, if properly carried out, to turn the scale and perhaps place a considerable balance to his credit.

As however a disembodied spirit can neither enjoy heaven nor suffer the pains of hell until reinvested with a physical frame, composed—as already pointed out—of gross though ethereal particles, it is instantly after its sentence hurried back to the place of cremation; where it acquires a frame of the necessary sensibility by feeding on the oblations of rice

[1] It is remarkable that the enterprising and intelligent Writer caste (Kāyastha) of Bengal claim to be descended from a Brāhman, named Ćitra-gupta; and secretaries are sometimes called by that name.

[2] Compare Rev. xx. 12, 'And the dead were judged out of those things which were written in the books, according to their works.'

and libations of water offered for ten consecutive days after the burning of the terrestrial body[1].

On the first day the ball (Piṇḍa) of rice offered by the eldest son, or other near relative, nourishes the spirit of the deceased in such a way as to furnish it with a head; on the second day the offered Piṇḍa gives a neck and shoulders; on the third, a heart; on the fourth, a back; on the fifth, a navel; on the sixth, a groin, and the parts usually concealed; on the seventh, thighs; on the eighth and ninth, knees and feet. On the tenth day the intermediate body is sufficiently formed to produce the sensation of hunger and thirst. Other Piṇḍas are therefore put before it, and on the eleventh and twelfth day[2] the embodied spirit feeds voraciously on the offerings thus supplied, and so gains strength for its journey to its future abode (Garuḍa-purāṇa I. 51, etc.). Then on the thirteenth day after death it is conducted either to heaven or to one of the hells. If to the latter, it has need of the most nourishing food to enable it to bear up against the terrible ordeal which awaits it.

The road by which Yama's two officers force a wicked man to descend to one or other of the twenty-one hells (p. 232) is described in the first two chapters of the Garuḍa-purāṇa. The length of the way is said to be 86,000 leagues (yojanas). The condemned soul, invested with its sensitive body and made to travel at the rate of 200 leagues a day, finds no shady trees, no resting-place, no food, no water. At one time it is scorched by a burning heat, equal to that of twelve meridian suns, at another it is pierced by icy cold winds; now its tender frame is rent by thorns; now it is attacked by lions, tigers, savage dogs, venomous serpents, and scorpions. In one place it has

---

[1] This frame is sometimes called 'the upward-going body' (ūrdhva-deha), whence the obsequial ceremonies that produce it are sometimes called Aurdhva-dehikam. Another name for this body is Adhishṭhāna-deha (see p. 28).

[2] In some parts of India these are also the days on which the relations who are performing the funeral rites have their festive dinners.

to traverse a dense forest whose leaves are swords; in another it falls into deep pits; in another it is precipitated from precipices; in another it has to walk on the edge of razors; in another on iron spikes; here it stumbles about helplessly in profound darkness; there it struggles through loathsome mud swarming with leeches; here it toils through burning sand; there its progress is arrested by heaps of red-hot charcoal and stifling smoke. Compelled to pass through every obstacle, however formidable, it next encounters a succession of terrific showers not of rain, but of live coals, stones, blood, boiling water and filth. Then it has to descend into appalling fissures, or ascend to sickening heights, or lose itself in vast caves, or wade through lakes seething with fetid ordure. Then midway it has to pass the awful river Vaitaraṇī, one hundred leagues in breadth, of unfathomable depth; flowing with irresistible impetuosity, filled with blood, matter, hair, and bones; infested with huge sharks, crocodiles, and sea-monsters; darkened by clouds of hideous vultures and obscene birds of prey. Thousands of condemned spirits stand trembling on the banks, horrified by the prospect before them. Consumed by a raging thirst, they drink the blood which flows at their feet, then tumbling headlong into the torrent they are overwhelmed by the rushing waves. Finally, they are hurried down to the lowest depths of hell, and yet not destroyed. Pursued by Yama's officers they are dragged away and made to undergo inconceivable tortures, the detail of which is given with the utmost minuteness in the succeeding chapters of the Garuḍa-purāṇa.

A description so monstrous would be scarcely worth reproducing in any form, did it not profess to represent an important article of the creed of a vast majority of our fellow-subjects in regard to a future state. It might indeed be thought that a belief in such horrors and in the possibility of undergoing a fate so awful would be calculated to produce a salutary deterrent effect on wicked persons, did we not find that, however intense is a Hindū's belief in the reality of hell's most excruciating torments, as described in the Garuḍa and other Purāṇas, he is equally ready to accept the doctrine laid down in the same works, that by performing certain religious rites and giving gifts to the Brāhmans all the terrific penalties of sin may be avoided and the god of hell disappointed of his victims (compare p. 291, first line).

What, then, is the nature of the various modern ceremonies which secure this immunity from future punishment and make the course of the departed spirit—however guilty—peaceful and pleasant? We can only give an outline of some of those most usually practised in the present day among religious families of the higher classes.

In the first place, when a man becomes seriously ill, it is common for his relatives to assume rather prematurely that his case is hopeless. They therefore make preparations for performing the last offices of religion, in anticipation of his decease, in a manner which to us Europeans would appear not unlikely to hasten on the crisis. Perhaps his only chance of warding off the approach of death may depend on perfect repose of body and mind. Yet how can his kinsmen allow him to run the risk of falling into the hands of the god of punishment, when by a little exertion they may secure for him the protection of the sacred river which flows perhaps not more than ten miles from his abode? Hence, his eldest son and other near relatives lose no time in placing him on a litter and conveying him to the banks of the nearest holy stream. If such a river as the Ganges or Narmadā or Godāvarī or Kṛishṇā (Kistna) happen to be within reach, the relatives of the dying man are the more eager to bring him into close proximity to the sacred waters. At Calcutta this is often done two or three days before death supervenes. According to Mr. S. C. Bose, 'Persons entrusted with the care and nursing of a dying man at the burning-ghāṭ [on the Ganges] soon get tired of their charge, and rather than administer to his comfort, are known to resort to artificial means, whereby death is accelerated. They unscrupulously pour the unwholesome, muddy water of the river down his already choked throat, and in some cases suffocate him to death[1].'

Of course the Ganges is of all rivers held to be the most divine and the most potent in its efficacy. If simply looked upon during the death-agony, the messengers of Yama, who are eager to seize and bind the soul, are powerless to harm it.

But neither the Ganges nor any other sacred stream is always to be reached. In such cases various other preventive measures calculated to keep the officers of Yama at bay or force them to retire, may be resorted to, according to the practice believed to be most efficacious in different localities.

For example, in many families it is thought enough to scatter Sesamum seed and Kuśa grass around the sick man's couch or to encircle it with a kind of cordon of cow-dung; or a Śālagrāma stone (see p. 69) is brought and placed on a stand close to the dying man's side, while at the same time a Tulasī plant is deposited near him. Or again, a sprig of that sacred plant is wound round his head; or its leaves are placed in his mouth[2]; or a piece of gold[3] is inserted between the teeth; or a little mud from a sacred stream may be brought from a distance and plastered on his forehead; or Ganges water may be poured down his throat.

Then again a cow duly decorated is brought close to the moribund man's bed, and he is made to grasp its tail, under

---

[1] 'The Hindoos as they are,' p. 252.

[2] According to the Garuḍa-purāṇa (IX. 7, 8), 'The house in which there is a single sprig of the Tulasī is like a holy place of pilgrimage. Yama's messengers cannot enter it. Yama cannot look upon the man who dies with the Tulasī in contact with his body, even though he may have committed hundreds of crimes.' In verse 11 the same efficacy is ascribed to Kuśa grass, which is said to be pervaded by Brahmā, Vishṇu, and Śiva.

[3] To secure the presence of gold in the mouth at death, a healthy man will sometimes have it inserted in his teeth.

the notion that by the sacred animal's assistance he will be safely transported over the terrible river of death, Vaitaraṇī (see also p. 290). This, however, is a precautionary measure which will be quite ineffectual unless the cow is afterwards handed over as a gift to the Brāhmans.

Others again who believe that the passage of the Hindū Styx is compulsory on all, and that it cannot be accomplished without direct Brāhmanical aid, take care to send for two or three priests for the performance of the Vaitaraṇī-rite. This ceremony, which is very usual in Bengal, consists mainly in paying money to the Brāhmans, who in return mutter a few texts and prayers, supposed to be efficacious in helping the deceased man across the dreaded river.

Of course Mantras or texts from the Vedas are repeated, and hymns to Vishṇu and Śiva are occasionally recited. Then at the last moment the dying man is made if possible to repeat the Tāraka-mantra or 'saving-text,' according to the sect to which he belongs. In most cases it consists in uttering one of the names of Vishṇu, such as Rāma, or Nārāyaṇa (p. 62), or Hari, or the eight-syllabled Mantra, 'Blessed Kṛishṇa is my refuge.' One common formula or cry uttered by the attendants is 'Hari bol'!

When the moment of death arrives the spirit is supposed to escape, invested only with its liṅga-śarīra (see p. 28), through the top of the head or through one of the upper or lower apertures of the body[1], according to the character for good or evil it achieved during life (see p. 291).

The corpse has now to be transported to a place where its cremation may be accomplished in due form and according to prescribed rules, but not until certain other rites have been performed. And first the eldest son or his nearest representative carefully shaves the body[2]. This he does without

---

[1] The seven upper apertures are the mouth, the eyes, the nostrils, and ears.

[2] This is according to the directions in the Garuḍa-purāṇa. At Benares the shaving process generally takes place at the burning-ghāṭ.

removing the hair from under the arms and without clipping the nails. Next he bathes it with water from a sacred stream and decorates it with sandal-wood and garlands; or in place of decoration he may plaster it with mud from the Ganges. Then it is covered with new vestments and placed on the litter; a rice-ball (Piṇḍa) being offered to the guardian deities of the soil, who protect the road to the burning-ground from the attacks of evil spirits. At the same time the name and family of the deceased man are pronounced by his son, while his son's wife and the other women of the household reverently circumambulate the corpse and utter lamentations. The body is now ready to be borne to the place of cremation, which ought, if possible, to be near a river[1]. And here a great difficulty has sometimes to be overcome in finding proper persons to carry the dead body. If the deceased happens to be a Brāhman, four men of his own caste—and, if possible, chosen from his own relations—ought to perform this office, walking behind the son, who leads the funeral procession, holding in his hand an earthen vessel containing fire. Or, according to the Garuḍa-purāṇa (X. 12), the son himself should help to carry the corpse on his shoulder, the other relatives with bare heads following in the rear.

It may be noted here that the rule which prevents Brāhmans from touching the bodies of persons of inferior caste is often a cause of great trouble and difficulty.

Not long ago a very respectable man of the Kāyastha caste died in Khandesh at a place where no male members of his own caste lived. The body had to be burnt immediately, but no one of superior caste could be induced to touch it, and had any one of a lower caste done so, the family would have suffered irretrievable degradation. The difficulty was only

[1] If a place near a river is to be found anywhere within ten or fifteen miles of the dead man's residence the corpse is generally carried there, unless, as we have seen, this is done before the breath leaves the body.

surmounted by the payment of an exorbitant sum to some Brāhmans who at length consented to bear the body to the burning-ground.

This explains the unwillingness of the Hindūs to leave their own country and caste.

The burning of the corpse is the next act in the drama.

A proper spot for the erection of the funeral pile must be chosen. It must be well purified by the sprinkling of holy water. A kind of altar is then made with earth, and the Homa ceremony is performed by casting grain into the sacred fire with repetition of certain Mantras. Then the pile ought, strictly, to be constructed with Tulasī and Palāśa and sandal-wood. Five Piṇḍas or balls of rice are placed on the body, which is made to face the north, and its orifices filled with ghee. The eldest son or his representative applies the fire to the wood, reciting Ṛig-veda X. 17. 3 :—'May the guardian deity Pūshan convey thee hence on thy distant road; may he deliver thee to the Fathers etc.'

Not long ago (and even under our rule till the Act of 1829, p. 481), if the dead man had a faithful wife (satī) she often gave proof of her devotion by allowing her living body to be burnt with her husband's corpse; and the Garuḍa-purāṇa eulogizes the devoted woman who thereby secures bliss for herself and her husband. Sometimes a widowed mother burnt herself with the body of an only son.

When the body is half-burnt the skull ought to be cracked with a blow from a piece of sacred wood. The idea is that the soul may not have been able to escape through the aperture at the top of the head, and that the cracking of the skull may open a crevice and facilitate its exit.

In the case of the death of a holy man whose body is buried and not burnt, the necessary blow is given with a cocoa-nut (śri-phala) or with a sacred conch-shell (śaṅkha).

A story was told me with great seriousness of a sorcerer at Lahore who made it the business of his life to make a collection of the skulls of dead men, which had not been properly cracked in this manner at death and so retained the spirits of the deceased inside. The peasantry in the neighbourhood fully believed that he was able to make use of these spirits for magical purposes, and force them to obey him.

During the process of cremation an oblation of clarified butter ought to be offered in the fire and a Mantra repeated, entreating the god of fire to convey the deceased man to heaven. When the body has been consumed, all present at the funeral bathe or purify themselves with ablutions. Sesamum and water are then offered, while the name and family of the deceased are again repeated.

Finally, a few leaves of the Nimba-tree (Nīm) are chewed by all and the funeral procession returns home, the women walking first and the men behind. Meanwhile the pyre and the products of combustion are left undisturbed to a future day.

The Garuḍa-purāṇa directs that if a man dies in a remote place, or is killed by robbers in a forest and his body is not found, his son should make an effigy of the deceased with Kuśa grass and then burn it on a pile with similar rites.

The Brāhmans who repeat Mantras and officiate at funeral ceremonies are not held in high repute. On the fourth day after cremation the relatives return to the burying-ground, and assembling at the pyre perform the 'bone-gathering' (asthi-sańćaya) ceremony. Three circumambulations are made around the ashes and a Mantra from the Yajur-veda (beginning Yamāya tvā, XXXVIII. 9) is repeated. The calcined bones are then placed in a kind of urn or earthen vessel; a cavity is dug in the ground and the vessel deposited in it. Next a Piṇḍa is offered over the ashes for the removal of the suffering supposed to have been caused by the act of cremation. Then after a few days the vessel is removed from the cavity in order that the ashes and bones may be carried away and thrown into some sacred river—if possible the Ganges. 'Whatever sins,' says the Garuḍa-purāṇa (X. 84), 'a man may have committed during life, if his bones are cast into the Ganges he must certainly go to heaven.'

In illustration of this a story is related in the same Purāṇa of a certain hunter, notorious for his crimes, who was killed by a tiger in an inaccessible corner of a forest. There his body lay for many years and his disembodied spirit became a troublesome devil (compare p. 239), till fortunately the bleached skeleton was spied by a crow, who picking up bone after bone dropped it into the Ganges. Whereupon the demon was suddenly converted into a saint, and transported in a celestial chariot to the mansions of the blessed. This story is narrated with all seriousness by the author of the Purāṇa as if he were recording an historical fact.

In connexion with the same subject I may repeat an anecdote told me by a late member of the Indian Civil Service—once a Magistrate and Collector in North-western India. He was once on a tour of inspection through his district when he overtook a poor old woman trudging along the road with evident difficulty. He inquired in a kindly voice where she was going. 'To the Ganges with my husband,' was the prompt reply. Involuntarily the Magistrate looked back, expecting to see some old man following her, when she calmly opened a handkerchief which she had been carrying slung over her shoulder, and showed him all that remained of her defunct lord and master in the shape of a few half-calcined bones, an old tooth or two, and a little dust and ashes. These she was transporting to the river with the pious object of scattering them on the sacred waters.

I may also put on record how greatly struck I was with the peaceful aspect of a spot of ground called the Asthi-vilaya-tīrtham, 'sacred place for the dissolution of bones,' at Nāsik—the Benares of Western India. There surrounded by trees, temples, and lovely scenery is a consecrated pool, formed by the waters of the Godāvarī, which are here partially diverted from their course and made to flow into a receptacle lined with stone in a secluded bend of the river. This is the cemetery or 'sleeping-place' of myriads of human beings whose ashes are brought at particular holy seasons and scattered on the tranquil waters.

I was also much impressed by another 'bone-gathering' ceremony which I witnessed on the burning-ground at Bombay (see p. 284). On the morning of one of my visits to that place twenty-four men were gathered round the ashes of a man whose body had been burnt two or three days before. The ceremony commenced by one of their number examining the ashes, and carefully separating any portions of the bones that had not been calcined by the flames on the previous day. These he collected in his hands and carried outside the burning-ground, with the intention, I was told, of throwing them into the sea near at hand. This being done, the whole party gathered round the ashes of the pyre in a semicircle, and one of the twenty-four men sprinkled them with water. Then some cow-dung was carefully spread in the centre of the ashes so as to form a flat circular cake of rather more than a foot in diameter, around which a stream of cow's urine was poured from a metal vessel. Next, one of the men brought a plantain-leaf, and laid it on the circle of cow-dung so as to form a kind of dish or plate. Around the edge of the leaf were placed five round balls (Piṇḍas), probably of rice-flour, rather smaller than cricket-balls, mixed with some brown substance. Sprigs of the Tulsī plant and fresh leaves of the betel, with a few flowers, were inserted in each ball, and a coloured cotton cord loosely suspended between them. Next, one of the relations covered the five Piṇḍas with the red powder called gulāl. Then five flat wheaten cakes were placed on the plantain-leaf inside the circle of the five Piṇḍas, and boiled rice was piled up on the cakes, surmounted by a small piece of ghī mixed with brown sugar.

The ceremony being so far completed, the son or next nearest relative took an empty earthenware vase, filled it with water, and held it on his right shoulder. Starting from the north side he commenced circumambulating the five Piṇḍas and the five wheaten cakes, keeping his left shoulder towards them, while one of the relatives with a sharp stone made a hole in the jar, whence the water spouted out in a stream as he walked round. On completing the first circuit and coming back to the north, a second incision was made with the same stone, whence a second stream poured out simultaneously with the first. At the end of the fifth round, when five streams of water had been made to spout out from five holes round the five Piṇḍas, the earthenware vase was dashed to the ground on the north side, and the remaining water spilt over the ashes. Next, one of the relatives took a small metal vessel containing milk, and, with a betel-leaf for a ladle, sprinkled some drops over the rice piled on the wheaten cakes. After which, taking some water from a small loṭā—or rather making another relative pour it into his hand —he first sprinkled it in a circle round the Piṇḍas, and then over the cakes. Finally, bending down and raising his hands to his head, he performed a sort of pūjā to the Piṇḍas, which were supposed to represent the deceased man and four other relations. This was repeated by all twenty-four men in turn. After the completion of the ceremony, the balls and cakes were left to be eaten by animals. The men who performed it probably belonged to a low caste or to some aboriginal tribe.

An account of the late Mahārāṇī of Nuddea's cremation and of the subsequent ceremonies is given further on (Chap. XXII) and is well worthy of attention.

Of course the Śrāddha ceremonies proper (as already shown at pp. 278–285) have many points in common with the antecedent funeral obsequies (antyeshṭi), especially in the nature of the oblations offered and texts repeated, but the balls of rice, etc. (Piṇḍas) are said to represent the deified bodies of the Pitṛis.

According to the Nirṇaya-sindhu a Śrāddha is a gift given

to the Pitṛis, offered with faith (Srăddhā) and with some auspicious exclamation (such as *svadhā*[1]), and followed by gifts to the Brāhmans (compare p. 287).

A Śrāddha, then, is a reverential offering to deceased ancestors. But Śrāddhas are not only acts of homage, they are believed to minister to the welfare of those deceased relatives who through the previous funeral rites have obtained ethereal bodies (divya-deha). Until the Śrāddha is performed the spirit is a Preta, after its performance (pp. 307–312) the spirit takes its place among the Pitṛis or divine Fathers in their blissful abodes called Pitṛi-loka. And the Śrāddhas do this, not so much by supplying them with nutriment in the balls of rice, cakes of meal, and daily water offered[2], as by accumulating merit (puṇya) for them and so accelerating their progress through the heavens to future births and final union with the Supreme. And this accumulation of merit is mainly accomplished by feasting and feeing the Brāhmans, who are held for the time to represent the Pitṛis.

But a Śrāddha is also performed on one's own account. Propitiation and gratification of the Manes are acts fraught with reflex benefits to any one who performs them properly, and may become a means of storing up merit or procuring some advantage for himself and his family. Probably this is the main idea in the minds of those who go through some of the ceremonies so earnestly.

Nor is a Śrāddha by any means necessarily connected with funerals. It may be performed every day, and especially on various occasions of rejoicing. According to the Vishṇu-purāṇa (III. 13): 'A householder should worship the Pitṛis at

---

[1] Requiring the dative case of the object to which the oblation is offered. Other similar exclamations are svāhā, śraushaṭ, vaushaṭ. Svadhā is also a name for the oblation or for its personification.

[2] Yet it is true, as before seen, that Manu and others make the Pitṛis actually feed on the essence of the offerings. In the same way it is said that in Europe in ancient times asphodels were planted near groves to supply the Manes of the dead with nourishment.

the marriage of a son or daughter, on entering a new dwelling, on naming a child, on performing tonsure, on seeing the face of a son.'

It is on this account that the Nirṇaya-sindhu distinguishes Śrāddhas under twelve heads, as follows :—

1. Nitya, 'daily,' 'constant,' consisting of offerings of water to ancestors generally at the daily Tarpaṇa ceremony forming part of the Sandhyā (p. 410). This cannot be performed vicariously, but only by every man in his own person.

2. Naimittika, 'special,' performed on special occasions as at funerals, and having reference to one person (ekoddishṭam) recently deceased. An odd number of Brāhmans (for instance, one, three, five, etc.) are to be feasted at the close of the rite. In contradistinction to Nitya, Naimittika ceremonies admit of being performed through a deputy or representative.

3. Kāmya, 'voluntary,' performed for the accomplishment of some desired object; as, for instance, the obtaining of a son.

4. Vṛiddhi-Śrāddha, 'for the increase of prosperity.'

5. Sapiṇḍana, 'for the benefit of all kinsmen who are Sapiṇḍas,' that is, connected by the offering of the Piṇḍa. This may be performed by women.

6. Pārvaṇa, 'performed at the conjunction of sun and moon,' that is, at new moon and at other periods of the moon's changes.

7. Goshṭhī-Śrāddha, 'performed at any large assembly or family gathering.'

8. Śuddhy-artha, 'for the sake of purification,' and consisting mainly in the feeding of a certain number of Brāhmans, as representatives of the Pitṛis.

9. Karmāṅga, 'performed at certain Saṇskāra rites.'

10. Daivika, 'on behalf of the gods,' especially the Viśve devāḥ, or 'deities collectively.'

11. Yātrārtha, 'for success' on undertaking a journey.

12. Pushṭy-artha, 'for health and well-being of body.'

Other forms of Śrāddha were described to me while I was in India; for example, the one called Hiraṇya-Śrāddha, 'gold Śrāddha,' is said to be performed by giving money to a Brāhman, when no Brāhman can be found who wishes to be fed with cooked food.

Again, Darbha-Śrāddha is where, in the absence of Brāhmans as representatives of the Pitṛis, an effigy of a Brāhman is made with Kuśa grass and worship offered to it.

Of all these Śrāddhas, that performed for a parent recently deceased (and therefore falling under the class Naimittika and called Ekoddishṭa, 'directed towards one person') is the most interesting, as it is the only one accompanied with elaborate ceremonial, costly gifts, and festivities. It must not be deferred too long after the termination of the funeral proper, and must in all cases take place before the end of the first month after death. It ought to be performed by a son and repeated in a simple form every succeeding month for a year[1], and again at every anniversary.

In Bengal, according to Mr. S. C. Bose[2], a son from the hour of his father's death to the conclusion of the funeral ceremony is religiously forbidden to shave, wear shoes, shirts, or any garment other than the piece of white cloth, his food being confined to a single meal consisting of rice, pulse, milk, ghee, sugar, and a few fruits. A Brāhman must continue this course of fasting for ten days[3], a Kshatriya longer. (See the Mahārāja of Nuddea's description, Chap. XXII.)

Then fifteen or sixteen days after the demise of his father the son makes preparation for the approaching Śrāddha. About the twentieth day he walks barefoot to the house of each of his relations to announce that the Śrāddha is to take

---

[1] So in Ireland a mass for the dead is celebrated one month after death.

[2] See 'The Hindoos as they are,' pp. 254–257.

[3] According to the Vishṇu-purāṇa, the time of mourning and impurity is, for a Brāhman, ten days; for a Kshatriya, twelve; for a Vaiśya, fourteen; for a Śūdra, a whole month or thirty-one days. The higher the caste the less the inconvenience imposed.

place on the thirty-first day after death. On the thirtieth day, the son and other near relatives shave, cut their nails, and put on new clothes, giving the old to the barber. Invitations are sent round to the Brāhmans and Pandits requesting their presence at the feast. On the thirty-first day, early in the morning, the son, accompanied by the officiating priest, goes to the river-side, bathes, and performs certain preliminary rites. A quantity of silver and brass utensils, besides shawls. cloth, and hard silver in cash are required for the ceremony and to serve as gifts for the Brāhmans, Pandits, and other guests. From eight in the morning to two in the afternoon the house is crammed to suffocation. The guests arrive early, and are asked to take their seats according to their caste. About ten o'clock the son begins the rite; the officiating priest reciting the formularies (which ought to include Pitṛi-sūktas from the Sāma-veda), and the son repeating them. Meanwhile female singers of questionable character entertain the guests with their songs, while garlands and sandal-paste are distributed.

About one in the afternoon the ceremony is brought to a close by the Brāhmans and Pandits receiving their customary gifts. The first in the list gets, in ordinary cases, about five rupees in cash, and one brass vessel valued at four or five rupees; the second, third, and others in proportion. The Guru or religious teacher and the Purohita or officiating priest carry off the lion's share.

On the following day, according to Mr. Bose, an entertainment is given to the Brāhmans, and until this is done no Hindū can be released from the restrictions of mourning, nor regain his former purity. About twelve, the guests begin to assemble, and when the number reaches two or three hundred, seats of Kuśa grass in long rows are arranged for them, and each man receives a plantain leaf on which are placed fruits and sweetmeats, such as 'ghee-fried loochees' and other delicacies, besides various kinds of confectionery in earthen plates. Every Brāhman before leaving the house is presented with a money gift (dakshiṇā) of one or two annas.

The next day, a similar entertainment with similar gifts is given to Kāyasthas and members of inferior classes.

And here it may be noted that time and place are important factors in the due performance of Śrāddhas. As to time, the month Bhādra—from the middle of August to the middle of September—and especially the Pitṛi-paksha (Pitṛi fortnight) in that month or in the beginning of Āśvina, are believed to be the most auspicious seasons for Śrāddhas.

As to locality, the banks of sacred streams or pools, and places consecrated by the footsteps of Vishṇu, are sought for as the most favourable spots. Śrāddhas are also performed in cow-houses. No place can surpass in suitability the neighbourhood of some of the holy tanks at Benares, except it be the temple built over the footstep of Vishṇu at Gayā, which is more frequented than any other spot in India for the performance of particular Śrāddhas.

At Benares on the Ghāṭ near the pool of Maṇi-karṇikā, on the day I visited it, a man was performing a Śrāddha (perhaps the Kāmya, p. 305) for his mother. The officiating Brāhman began by forming a slightly elevated piece of ground with some sand. This was supposed to constitute a small altar (vedi). It was of an oblong form, but not more than ten inches long by four or five broad. Across this raised sand he laid three stalks of Kuśa grass. Then taking a number of little earthenware platters or saucers, he arranged them round the sand, putting tila or sesamum seed in one, rice in another, honey in a third, areca or betel-nut in a fourth, ćandana or sandal in a fifth. Next, he took flour of wheat or barley and kneaded it into one large Piṇḍa, rather smaller than a cricket-ball, which he carefully deposited in the centre of the sand-altar, scattering over it jasmine flowers, khaskhas grass, and wool, and placing on one side of it a betel-leaf with areca-nut and a single copper coin. Then having poured water from a loṭā into his hand, he sprinkled it over all the offerings, arranged in the manner described. Other similar operations followed:—thus, for instance, an earthenware platter, containing a lighted wick, was placed near the offerings; ten other platters were filled with water, which was all poured over the Piṇḍa; another small platter with a lighted wick was added to the first; then some milk was placed in another platter and poured over the Piṇḍa, which was once more sprinkled with water. Finally, the Brāhman joined his hands together and did homage to the Piṇḍa. The ritual lasted about fifteen minutes, and while it was proceeding, the man for whose mother it was performed repeated prayers under the direction of the officiating Brāhman, quite regardless of my presence and of much loud talking going on around him. The ceremony ended by the 'feeding of a Brāhman,' who was made to sit on the ground near the oblations, and fed with flat cakes, ghee, sweetmeats, vegetables, and curds placed in a plate of palāśa-leaves.

The Brāhmans who assist at Śrāddhas are not considered particularly respectable.

With regard to Gayā, which I visited in 1876, I may mention that the city is most picturesquely situated on the river Phalgu, about sixty miles south-west of Patnā, near some short ranges of hills rising abruptly out of the plain. The Vishṇu-pada temple, where the principal Śrāddhas are performed, is built of black stone, with a lofty dome and golden pinnacle. It contains the alleged footprint of Vishṇu in a large silver basin, under a silver canopy, inside an octagonal shrine. Piṇḍas and various kinds of offerings are placed by the pilgrims inside the basin round the footprint, and near it are open colonnades for the performance of the Śrāddhas.

Let no one suppose that the process of performing Śrāddhas at Gayā is either simple or rapid. To secure the complete efficacy of such rites, a whole round of them must be performed at about a hundred distinct places in and around Gayā, as well as at the most holy spot of all—the Vishṇu-pada temple—the time occupied in the process being at least eight days, and sometimes protracted to fifteen, while the sums spent in fees to the officiating priests (who at Gayā are called Gayāwāls, abbreviated into Gaywāls = Gayā-pālas, regarded as an inferior order of Brāhmans) are often enormous.

The efficacy of Śrāddhas performed at Gayā is this, that wherever in their progress onwards departed relatives may have arrived, the Śrāddhas take them without further impediment or delay to Vishṇu's heaven (Vaikuṇṭha, p. 70).

One or two examples witnessed by me will suffice. A party consisting of six men and one Gaywāl entered one of the colonnades of the temple and seated themselves on their heels in a line, with the officiating priest at their head. Twelve Piṇḍas or balls of rice and milk, not much larger than the large marbles used by boys (called 'alleys'), were formed and placed with sprigs of the sacred Tulasī plant in small earthenware platters. Then on the top of the Piṇḍas were scattered Kuśa grass and flowers. I was told that the Piṇḍas in the present case were typical of the bodies of the twelve ancestors for whom the Śrāddha was celebrated. The men had Kuśa grass twisted round their fingers, to purify their hands for the due performance of the rite. Next, water was poured into the palms, part of which they sprinked on the ground, and part on the Piṇḍas. One or two of the men then took threads off their clothes and laid them on the Piṇḍas. This act is alleged to be emblematical of presenting the bodies of their departed ancestors with garments.

Meanwhile texts and prayers were repeated, under the direction of the Gaywāl, and the hands were sometimes extended over the Piṇḍas as if to invoke blessings. The whole rite was concluded by the men putting their heads to the ground before the officiating Brāhman and touching his feet.

The number of Piṇḍas varies with the number of ancestors

for whom the Śrāddhas are celebrated, and the size of the balls and the materials of which they are composed differ according to the caste and the country of those who perform the rite. I saw one party in the act of forming fourteen or fifteen Piṇḍas with meal, which were of a much larger size than large marbles. This party was said to have come from the Dekhan. Sometimes the Piṇḍas were placed on betel-leaves with pieces of money, which were afterwards appropriated by the priests; and sometimes the water used was taken out of little pots by dipping stalks of Kuśa grass into the fluid and sprinkling it over the balls. At the end of all the ceremonies a prayer was said for pardon lest any minute part of the ceremonial had been unintentionally omitted. Then finally all the earthen platters employed were carried to a particular stone in the precincts of the temple and dashed to pieces there. No platter is allowed to be used a second time. The Piṇḍas are left to be eaten by birds and other animals, or reverently deposited in the river.

It is remarkable that some of the most enlightened men of India are unable to resist the impulse which takes every Hindū on a pilgrimage once in his life, if possible, to both Benares and Gayā, though they are perfectly aware that from the moment of their arrival within ten miles of these sacred localities they are certain to become the prey of a well-organized army of rapacious priests. Mr. Deshmukh gave me a brief account of his visit to Gayā in 1876[1]. He went there, like others of his fellow-countrymen, with the object of performing some of the Śrāddha ceremonies.

He is a Ćit-pāvan Brāhman (see note 1, p. 271), and generally opposed to all superstitious practices, yet he thinks it right to maintain his influence by conforming, as far as practicable, to old customs. Starting from Patnā, he had

---

[1] I mean Mr. G. H. Deshmukh, who was then judge at Nāsik and has been quoted before. The Government, in recognition of his services, has conferred on him the personal title of Rāo Bahādur.

to go through the ceremony of shaving (Kshaura) at a river called Punaḥ-punaḥ, about ten miles distant on the road. On reaching Gayā he was surrounded on all sides by thousands of persons offering Piṇḍas, some of whom were persons of high rank—Rājās and Mahārājas, on their way to the great imperial assemblage at Delhi. Many went through the entire round of ritual observances, necessitating the performance of at least a hundred Śrāddhas at different shrines. Mr. Deshmukh had to tell the Gaywāl priests that he was expected in a few days at Delhi, and had little time to spare for Gayā. He was therefore allowed to dispense with all but three ceremonies. These were—1. the Phalgu-Śrāddha, performed on the banks of the river; 2. the Vishṇu-pada-Śrāddha, at the temple containing Vishṇu's footprint; and 3. Vaṭa-Śrāddha, performed under a Banian tree. Two whole days were occupied in going through the necessary ritual of these Śrāddhas, which was most elaborate and tedious, and the fees were of course proportionately large. The Mahārāja of Kashmīr, who visited Gayā in the same year and stayed rather longer than Mr. Deshmukh, is said to have expended at least 15,000 rupees on the Gaywāl priests before their demands were satisfied.

I must confess that I myself came away from the Vishṇu-pada temple profoundly impressed by the solemnity and earnestness of manner displayed by some of the worshippers, their unfaltering faith in the efficacy of the acts in which they were engaged, and their intense anxiety to carry out every tittle and iota of the ceremonial in obedience to the directions of their priestly guides.

It was, however, a melancholy spectacle; for it seemed to make clear that, while the acquirement of European knowledge has acted like a solvent on the faith of the Hindūs, a long period must elapse before the influence of Christianity can prevail to uproot the time-honoured and inveterate superstitions of ages.

CHAPTER XII.

Worship of Animals, Trees, and Inanimate Objects.

SIR JOHN LUBBOCK in his work on the 'Origin of Civilization' has some interesting remarks on the subject of animal-worship, and shows that zoolatry has always prevailed among uncivilized and half-civilized races in every part of the globe. Mr. E. B. Tylor in the second volume of his 'Primitive Culture,' and Mr. Fergusson in his 'Tree and Serpent Worship,' go ably into the same subject.

It is found, for example, that serpents either have been or still are objects of worship in Egypt[1], Persia, Kashmīr, India, China, Tibet, Ceylon, Babylonia, Phœnicia, Greece, Italy, Lithuania, and among the Kalmucks and other uncultured tribes. I notice, too, that in the 'St. James's Gazette' for June 1, 1891, there is a curious account of a 'holy trout,' which is to be seen in a tank near Westport in Ireland, and is held sacred by the peasantry.

My remarks in the present chapter must of course be limited to India, but a difficult question meets us at the very threshold:—Can any satisfactory account be given of the origin of zoolatry in that country?

I need scarcely point out that, because animal-worship is common among numerous races in other parts of the world, it does not follow that it may not have originated

---

[1] The Egyptians, who were the first educators of the world, adored, as every one knows, the bull Apis, the bird Ibis, the hawk, the crocodile, and many other animals. The mummified cat is a familiar object in the British Museum.

independently in India. The human mind, like the body, goes through similar phases everywhere, develops similar proclivities, and is liable to similar diseases. It is certain that every form of Fetishism and Totemism, of stone-worship, tree-worship, and animal-worship, as well as every variety of polytheistic and pantheistic superstition, have sprung up spontaneously and flourished vigorously on Indian soil.

The motives, too, which have prompted men to worship animals in India, are probably similar to those which have actuated them elsewhere. It is thought by some that an animal may receive adoration for any one of three reasons. 1. Because, like an elephant or lion, it happens to possess superhuman strength and courage; 2. because it is believed to be an incarnation of the deity; 3. because it is regarded as a totem or representative of a tribe or family, the word totem being derived from an American Indian word *dodaim*, which signifies the patron or typical animal of a tribe. For it is remarkable that in America every member of a tribe or clan may be called by the name of some animal, as, for example, a bear, or a tortoise; pictures of these animals standing for the whole clan, very much as animals are used typically in the armorial bearings of some English families in England, and just as in South Africa we hear of men of the fish, men of the crocodile, etc. (Tylor's 'Primitive Culture,' ii. 235.)

One writer is inclined to lay great stress on Totemism as a motive for zoolatry. He thinks that an individual or family called after a bear would be inclined to worship the bear. I cannot believe that such a motive had much weight in India. It is true that the word *siṇh* (for Sanskṛit siṇha) is often appended to the names of men (as in Amara-siṇha, Raṇ-jit-siṇh); and in other parts of India the expressions 'man-lion,' 'man-tiger,' 'man-bull,' etc. denote a man remarkable for courage or strength; but as a matter of fact the names of the animals most worshipped in India—with the exception, perhaps, of Nāga—are not generally applied to human beings. It seems to me more probable that Indian animal-worship is to be accounted for by the working of one or other of the motives, gratitude, fear, or awe, operating separately, in separate cases.

For instance, a Hindū worships a cow because he is profoundly sensible of the services it renders him; he worships a serpent because he dreads its power of destroying him by the slightest puncture; and he worships a monkey because he stands in awe of the marvellous instinct it displays. In short, his zoolatry is simply the expression of an exaggerated or intensified feeling of admiration for the three qualities, utility, brute strength, and instinct, manifesting themselves in animal nature. It must not be forgotten, too, that with a Hindū all organic life is sacred. Even plant-life is to be respected, and must not wantonly be destroyed.

Without doubt this feeling is strengthened by the intense hold which the doctrine of metempsychosis has on the Hindū mind. It is difficult, as we have already seen, for any believer in Hindūism to draw a line of demarcation between gods, men, and animals. If men depend on animals, so also do the gods; if men are associated with animals, so also are the gods. Brahmā is carried on a goose (haṉsa); Vishṇu on an eagle (Garuḍa), which is also half a man; Śiva on a bull (Nandi).

Other deities are associated with other animals[1]. Nor must we forget that Vishṇu's first three incarnations are zoomorphic. He infuses his essence into the fish, the tortoise, and the boar (see pp. 107–109), with the object of delivering the world, or aiding it in certain special exigencies. This seems absurd to our ideas, but not to a Hindū who

[1] The association of great heroes and saints with animals is not confined to India, for we find three of the Evangelists (St. Mark, St. Luke, and St. John) associated with a lion, ox, and eagle, respectively.

firmly believes that the supreme soul of the universe, like the soul of man, may pass into any kind of animal form.

It is said of Dr. Duff—to whose labours in the cause of education India is so deeply indebted—that he was once examining an Indian school, and wishing to ridicule this idea of animal incarnations, said to the boys: 'Can any boy tell me whether it is likely that God's spirit would associate itself with a snail?' No one answered for some time; at last an intelligent lad said: 'I think He might condescend to do so, if any useful purpose were to be served thereby for the good of His creatures.' 'Then,' said Dr. Duff, 'you think as a fool.' But did the boy really think so very foolishly? and had he altogether the worst of the encounter in his little brush with the Scotch giant?

Again, it is owing to a belief in this same doctrine of metempsychosis that a Hindū has no difficulty in believing that a beast, bird, or reptile may at any moment develop human faculties and functions. According to popular belief there are eighty-four lakhs of different species of animals through which a man is liable to pass. Even a noxious insect, therefore, may enclose the soul of some person who was once a sage, a saint, or an orator. It is on this account that the excellent stories about talking animals and their sayings and doings, everywhere current in India, are to the generality of unthinking Hindūs not mere fables, but true narratives. A beast or bird may on special occasions speak with a human voice, engage in long arguments, acquire profound learning, and be troubled with a sense of right and wrong, without violating any law of organized life, or outraging any of the usual ideas of probability.

It is on this account, too, that no true religiously minded Hindū delights in killing animals, and certainly not for sport. India teems with animal life, and animals of every description appear to live on terms of the greatest confidence with human beings. Everywhere they dispute possession of the earth with man. Birds build their nests and lay their eggs in the fields, untroubled by fears or misgivings, before the very eyes of every passer-by, and within the reach of every village school-boy. Animals of all kinds rove over the soil as if they were the landlords. It is true that every thrifty farmer drives them from his crops; yet he would scarcely dare to question their claim to a portion of the food he eats and the house he occupies; while everywhere in the towns they are admitted, so to speak, to the privileges of fellow-citizens. Bulls walk about independently in the streets, and jostle you on the pavements; monkeys domesticate themselves jauntily on the roof of your house; parrots peer inquisitively from the eaves of your bedroom into the mysteries of your toilet; crows make themselves at home on your window-sill, and carry off impudently any portable article of jewelry that takes their fancy on your dressing-table; sparrows hop about impertinently, and take the bread off your table-cloth; a solitary mongoose emerges every morning from a hole in your verandah, and expects a share in your breakfast; swarms of insects claim a portion of your midday meal, and levy a tax on the choicest delicacies at your dinner table; bats career triumphantly about your head as you light yourself to your bed-room; and at certain seasons snakes domicile themselves unpleasantly in the folds of your cast-off garments.

It should be added, however, that although in the eyes of orthodox Hindūs every animal is more or less sacred, ill-treatment of such useful animals as draught-oxen is by no means uncommon in India.

I next proceed to note some of the more interesting examples of actual animal-worship, turning first to three classes of animals, the adoration of which probably results from the operation of the three motives I have already suggested.

In the forefront must be placed the worship of the cow and the bull. The utility of the cow as a source of nourishment to a people who never kill animals for food, and of the ox and bull to agriculturalists who have no cart-horses for draught, is manifest. The cow is of all animals the most sacred. Every part of its body is inhabited by some deity or other. Every hair on its body is inviolable. All its excreta are hallowed. Not a particle ought to be thrown away as impure. On the contrary, the water it ejects ought to be preserved as the best of all holy waters—a sin-destroying liquid which sanctifies everything it touches, while nothing purifies like cow-dung. Any spot which a cow has condescended to honour with the sacred deposit of her excrement is for ever afterwards consecrated ground, and the filthiest place plastered with it is at once cleansed and freed from pollution, while the ashes produced by burning this hallowed substance are of such a holy nature, that they not only make clean all material things, however previously unclean, but have only to be sprinkled over a sinner to convert him into a saint.

In an underground passage of the Agra fort there is an image of a man named Mukunda. The Brāhman who was my guide when I visited this place gravely informed me that it represented a celebrated saint who felt himself compelled to commit suicide by jumping into the neighbouring river as a penalty for having accidentally swallowed the hair of a cow by drinking milk without straining it. But even this was not deemed sufficient punishment, for he was condemned to become a Muhammadan in his next birth, though the sentence was mitigated by his being born again as the Emperor Akbar. We cannot wonder, therefore, that the heaven of Kṛishṇa is called Go-loka, 'cow-world' (p. 118).

It is worthy of note that the Hindūs believe in the existence of a typical divine cow called Surabhi or Kāma-dhenu, 'the cow of plenty,' yielding all desired objects, representations of which are to be seen in temples, or are kept in houses for purposes of domestic worship. This typical animal was produced from the ocean when it was churned by the gods and demons (see p. 108). Yet I nowhere saw any temple dedicated exclusively to Surabhi or to any other cow. It is rather the living animal which is a perpetual object of adoration. As to the bull, he is dedicated to Śiva, and constantly associated with the god as typical of generative power. Images of him are to be found near all Liṅga shrines. The letting loose of a bull (vṛishotsarga, bṛishotsarga)—stamped with Śiva's trident—in cities like Benares (p. 436) and Gayā (p. 309) is fraught with the highest merit. This setting free of a bull to roam about at will often takes place at Śrāddhas.

Passing on to the second class of animals, or those worshipped out of motives of fear, we must, of course, place the serpent at the head of the list. Much has been written on ophiolatry, and on the vexed question of its origin. The subject seems inexhaustible. Some writers maintain that snake-worship was the earliest form of religion prevalent among men in all parts of the globe, its general diffusion being partially accounted for by the fact that serpents are indigenous almost everywhere, and not, like monkeys and elephants, in certain localities only. All writers, however, are agreed that the chief factor in the universality of this phase of superstition is the dread inspired by a mysterious creeping creature, silent and stealthy in its movements, apparently quite unprovided with the most ordinary means of offence and defence, yet found to have at its command the most deadly of all known destructive weapons, and able to cause almost instantaneous death by merely pricking the skin of its adversary.

In India, as is well known, the habit of walking barefoot exposes the half-clad natives to constant peril from this source, so that, according to some authorities, at least 25,000 perish annually from snake-bites (many deaths being unregistered). Nevertheless, the feeling of antipathy that leads a man to recoil from contact with a snake of any kind does not seem to depend entirely on its power of doing harm.

A large majority of these animals are quite innocuous. Yet to many persons their sinuous movements, their habit of shunning observation, their concealment of themselves in holes, the cold fixity of their gaze, and the constant protrusion of their forked tongues, are in themselves typical of subtlety and malevolence; while to others these operations are not merely types of evil qualities, but evidences of actual demoniacal possession.

On the other hand, it is certain that to some Indian minds the beautiful markings, spiral movements, and generally striking aspect of many species of harmless snakes, are suggestive of reverential ideas. They are typical of divine beauty and beneficence, while the coiling of their bodies in rings and circles, and their annual rejuvenescence by the renewal of their skins, symbolize immortality and the never-ending cycles of eternal time. When they are accidentally killed they even sometimes receive funeral honours like human beings.

Hence serpents are either worshipped or propitiated in India under the most opposite characters even to the present day. Nor does a Hindū appear to see any inconsistency in regarding snakes as embodiments of the contradictory ideas of destruction and regeneration, malevolence and benevolence, demonism and divinity, death and immortality.

No authority, however, for any such diversified conceptions of serpent-nature is to be found in the more ancient sacred writings of India; nor is there any proof that the early Āryan immigrants were in any sense serpent-worshippers. On the contrary, their only feeling towards the serpent was one of dread and dislike. Hence in the Ṛig-veda (see VI. 20. 2) the demon of cloud and darkness, called Vṛitra, is either identified or associated with the serpent Ahi (Ὄφις); and the god Soma is described as delivering over all evil speakers and slanderers into the power of this serpent (see VII. 104. 9, and compare Vājasaneyi-saṃhitā VI. 12). We know, too, that even to this day the sight of a snake in the early morning is to a Brāhman so bad an omen, that after seeing it he will desist for the moment from the prosecution of any work in which he may be engaged[1]. Yet so elastic was the creed and practice of Brāhmanism, that, finding serpent-worship, like other aboriginal cults, established on Indian soil, it had no difficulty in adopting it, and ended by incorporating every superstitious idea connected with ophiolatry into the complex fabric of Hindūism.

In fact the gradual intertwining of serpent-worship with Śaivism, Vaishṇavism, and even Buddhism and Jainism, but more especially with Śaivism (see pp. 80, 105, and 113), is one of the most interesting features of this complex subject. Śiva has five heads, and a great majority of serpent images are five-headed also. Then I have often seen images of serpents coiled round the Liṅga, and five-headed snakes forming a canopy over it. A similar canopy is also found over idols of Kṛishṇa and Buddha; Vishṇu, too, is represented as sleeping on the thousand-headed serpent Śesha, the symbol of Infinity, which also forms a canopy over him (p. 323).

On the other hand, Garuḍa, the mythical bird of Vishṇu, half eagle, half man, destroys serpents in their character of representatives of evil. Kṛishṇa does the same; and the Mahā-bhārata—that greatest of all repositories of Hindū belief—opens with a long account of Janamejaya's sacrifice for the annihilation of the serpent or Nāga race (I. 1547–2197). Buddhism and Jainism, no doubt, became connected with serpent-worship not from any affinity with it, but because, like Hindūism, they adapted themselves to pre-existing cults.

And here it must be observed that the worship of serpents in India is closely connected with that of the Nāgas; or rather, is generally mixed up and confounded with that

[1] Yet a snake (as oviparous) is, like a Brāhman, called Dvi-ja, 'twice-born.' Birds for the same reason are 'twice-born.'

worship. Indeed the word Nāga frequently denotes an ordinary serpent, though it properly signifies a being half human, half serpentine in form[1], not necessarily evil, but often beautiful, wise, and good, and, although armed with a deadly venom, possessing also the elixir of life and immortality, and able to bestow it upon others (Mahā-bh. I. 1500–1505, 5018–5035).

The race of Nāgas is fabled to have sprung from Kadrū, one of the wives of the old patriarch Kaśyapa (her sister Vinatā being also a wife of Kaśyapa, and mother of Garuḍa). Kadrū gave birth to 1000 Nāgas, who became the progenitors of the serpent-race. Some of their females married human heroes (as Ulūpī married Arjuna, after carrying him off to the bottom of the Ganges, p. 233), and to this day there are tribes called Nāgas[2], and ancient families who claim to be of Nāga descent. The whole race of mythical Nāgas is sometimes represented as dwelling at the bottom of the ocean, or in the depths of rivers and lakes, but also as inhabiting the regions under the earth (see p. 233, and my 'Buddhism,' p. 220), and more especially Pātāla, or that portion of it called Nāga-loka, of which the capital is Bhogavatī.

The following curious story is told in the Mahā-bhārata (I. 5006):—

The Pāṇḍu princes in their boyish sports excelled the sons of Dhṛita-rāshṭra. This excited much ill-feeling; and Duryodhana, spiteful even when a boy, tried to destroy Bhīma

---

[1] According to Dr. K. M. Banerjea, the theory of a race of Nāgas, half serpents, half men, confirms the Biblical account of the serpent, which was originally perhaps of a species corresponding to the Nāgas, till the sentence was pronounced by which it became a creeping reptile.

I noticed, when at Rome, that Michael Angelo's fresco of Adam and Eve in the roof of the Sistine chapel, represents the serpent as shaped like an Indian Nāga; that is—the lower part of the body is coiled round the stem of the tree in serpent fashion, while the upper part in human form offers the fruit to Eve.

[2] For example, the Nāgas of Maṇipur, but they are not found to be snake-worshippers.

by mixing poison in his food, and then throwing him into the water when stupefied by its effects. Bhīma, however, was not drowned, but descended to the abode of the Nāgas, who freed him from the poison (I. 5052), and gave him an elixir to drink which endued him with the strength of ten thousand Nāgas, and made him a kind of Hercules.

The kings of the Nāgas are Śesha, Vāsuki, and Takshaka. Of these, the most conspicuous is the thousand-headed Śesha, also called An-anta, 'the Infinite,' sometimes represented as forming the couch and canopy of Vishṇu, while sleeping during the intervals of creation; sometimes as bearing the world on his thousand heads; sometimes as supporting Pātāla; and sometimes as having become man in the form of Bala-rāma, Rāmānuja, etc. (pp. 112, 119). According to popular belief all earthquakes are caused by his shaking one of his thousand heads.

A particular day called Nāga-pañćamī, about the end of July (Śrāvaṇa), is held sacred to the Nāgas, and in the districts of India where serpent-worship is especially rife, numbers flock to Nāga-shrines on that day. I should state, however, that temples dedicated to serpents are by no means common in Northern India. The only one I visited was that sacred to Vāsuki at Dārā-gañj, near Allahābād. This is a noted shrine, and pilgrims resort to it in large numbers on the Nāga-pañćamī festival. I found that the priest of this temple was not a Brāhman, but a man of low caste[1]. On my expressing a wish for some memorial of the place, he tore off a rude drawing of a many-headed serpent which was fastened to the door of the shrine, and presented it to me.

Other shrines in the neighbourhood of Nāgpur and certain districts of the central provinces (such as Chanda-puṛ, Bhāndhak, etc.) are much frequented at certain seasons. In

---

[1] This is, I believe, the case in all serpent-temples, and it is one evidence that Brāhmanism had originally no connexion with ophiolatry.

Southern India the whole of Kanara may be regarded as steeped in serpent-worship.

Mr. Walhouse informs us that one of the highest mountains of the South Kanara Ghāṭs, named Su-brahmaṇya, has a very celebrated serpent-temple. There great numbers of the 'coiling folk' reside in holes and crevices made for them. To propitiate these creatures, persons who have made vows roll and wriggle round the temple serpent-fashion, and some will even roll their bodies up to it from the foot of the hill, a mile distant. They also take home with them portions of earth from the sacred serpent-holes. This earth is believed to cleanse from leprosy (compare 2 Kings v. 17), if rubbed on the parts affected; it will moreover cure barrenness in women, if a little be daily put in the mouth. Serpentine body-wriggling is also practised further south, where small snake-temples (*Nāga-kovil* in Tamil) are common. Near one of these, not far from Madurā on the bank of the Vaiga river, there are men who for a few rupees will perform any number of wrigglings and rollings round the shrine, as proxies for persons who have vowed them[1].

Indeed it seems to be a fixed article of belief throughout Southern India, that all who have wilfully or accidentally killed a snake, especially a cobra, will certainly be punished either in this life or the next in one of three ways:—either by childlessness, or by leprosy, or by ophthalmia. It behoves all persons, therefore, who are afflicted with such diseases, or feel that they may have to undergo the inevitable penalty hereafter, to visit serpent-shrines and conciliate the serpent-gods by the most abject homage. In connexion with these ideas, I may mention that on the banks of the river Tāmraparṇī, near a bridge connecting Tinnevelly with Palamcottah, I noticed two or three Pīpal trees, under which were deposited hundreds of stone images of Kṛishṇa, and of the Liṅga of Śiva, each image having a five-headed Nāga so carved

[1] See 'Indian Antiquary,' for February 1878.

as to form a canopy over it. It is the custom in the South of India for any woman who is childless, and believes her barrenness to be caused by having killed a cobra in a former life, to perform the ceremony called Nāga-pratishṭhā; that is to say, she sets up a stone Nāga under a tree, taking care to have it duly consecrated by the repetition of texts and prayers. On the occasion of my visit to the Tāmra-parṇī, several women were assembled in the neighbourhood of the largest Pīpal tree. Some performed reverential circumambulation round the images, and some sprinkled them with water from vessels which they held in their hands.

In the same way childless women are in the habit of going to holes in the earth where snakes are supposed to dwell, and depositing offerings of milk with invocations and prayers.

I may note here another curious superstition connected with this subject. The heads of all Nāgas and of all serpents—especially cobras—are believed to contain precious stones and gems of magical properties. These, if extracted and carried about on the person, are capable of working as astounding miracles for their owners, as the wonderful lamp did for Aladdin. I met with no one who could show me a specimen of these so-called miraculous snake-stones, but they are described as dark and shining, and shaped like a horse-bean. A similar superstition exists in some parts of England in regard to supposed stones in the heads of toads.

As an example of other superstitious ideas about snakes, it is related that a certain village in Northern India was not long ago suddenly deserted by all its inhabitants. No persuasions would induce the people to return, and on inquiry it was found that the panic among the villagers was caused by an unexpected visitation of snakes, who had established themselves comfortably in the precincts of the village, and that these harmless immigrants were believed to be a colony of malevolent demons.

Again, it is said that a man once bought a piece of ground

and sat down to contemplate his purchase under a tree in the centre of his newly-acquired property. Suddenly he heard the hissing of a snake coiled in the branches above his head. Panic-struck, he ran off and escaped unharmed, but never dared to show his face on the ground again, being firmly convinced that the serpent was the indignant spirit of the former proprietor, whom he had imprudently neglected to propitiate before taking possession.

So much for the complex and difficult subject of serpent-worship in India.

Probably the best representative of the third class of animals whose worship originally arose from a deep reverence for instinct is the monkey. And here a difficult question presents itself as to the precise meaning of the term 'instinct.' Is it possible to define its exact nature and to give any reason for its claim to adoration? Without pretending to mathematical accuracy in attempting to solve insoluble problems, we may perhaps describe instinct, in a general way, as the mysterious exercise of certain powers and faculties of mind and body in obedience to the laws of organized life without conscious will. The working of these powers in the lower animals may well excite amazement and admiration, if not worship. What can be more wonderful than the sight of a feeble timid mother-bird suddenly transformed by instinct into a very tigress, and ready to fight hopelessly in defence of her young against an opponent immeasurably her superior?

To a Hindū such a sight would be an intense confirmation of his belief that the divine soul may occupy animals as well as men. And if instinct in the lower animals fills him with so deep an awe, he is the more inclined to attach sacredness to a higher order of animals in whom instinct almost impinges upon the domain of reason.

With regard to the actual worship of monkeys little need be added to what has already been stated in relation to Hanumān (see p. 220). In Hindū mythology apes and monkeys are as intimately connected with the worship of Vishṇu, as the bull is with that of Śiva; though the reverence for these animals probably preceded the full development of both Vaishṇavism and Śaivism (see note, p. 222). Indeed the idea of a close interconnexion between gods, demons, men, and animals dates from the earliest times; and the hold which such ideas have gained on the Hindū mind is often illustrated in a remarkable manner by present customs.

In Ward's 'Hindoos' an account is given of what to Europeans would appear an incredible occurrence:—A certain Bengal Rājā spent 100,000 rupees in marrying a male and female monkey, with all the paraphernalia, pageant, and expense usual at the weddings of high-caste human beings. The male monkey was borne along in a costly vehicle, had a crown fastened on his head, and a whole array of servants to wait on him. The festivities lasted for twelve days. Probably, after all, this remarkable proceeding was merely a mode of offering homage to Hanumān, whose worship, as already explained at p. 220, is prevalent everywhere.

I may note here as a curious circumstance that there is at Benares a well-known temple, commonly called the 'monkey-temple,' which is not really dedicated to Hanumān, but to Durgā. I witnessed the sacrifice of a goat in honour of the goddess outside the door of the shrine, while several intelligent monkeys, with true simian and mock-human curiosity, leaped from the neighbouring trees, took up a position on the vantage-ground of the roof, and seemed to be quite as interested in the ceremony as I was. These animals are daily fed by pious persons who frequent the temple. To feed one is a highly meritorious act; to injure one would be the most heinous of crimes.

I can only advert briefly to other animals usually held sacred in India. A large number are, as we have seen (p. 104, note 3), associated with gods, as their vehicles, servants, or companions, and worshipped accordingly.

Vishṇu's attendant, the divine Garuḍa (see p. 104), is represented by a species of eagle or similar bird, common in some parts of India, and held in great honour.

In some country districts, villagers are in the habit of invoking Garuḍa's protection against snakes every night before going to sleep. Again, in the North Koṅkan, I heard of a tribe called Wāralī, who worship Vāgho-bā, the 'tiger-lord' (Sanskṛit *Vyāghra*, 'a tiger'), from similar motives.

Then the goose (haṉsa) is, as we have seen, sacred to Brahmā, the elephant to Indra, the tiger to Durgā, the buffalo to Yama, the rat to Gaṇeśa, the ram to Agni, the peacock to Skanda, the parrot to Kāma-deva (god of love).

With regard to the sacredness of the elephant, it is notable that the earth is not only supported on Śesha (p. 323), but also on the vast heads and backs of eight male and eight female elephants, who all have names and distinct personalities. They are called the elephants of the eight quarters. When any one of these shakes its body the whole earth quakes (see Rāmāyaṇa I. 41). Sometimes they are described as roaming about in the neighbourhood of their stations.

The fish, the tortoise, and the boar are worshipped as incarnations of Vishṇu (pp. 107–109). Fish are often fed as a religious duty. At Mathurā (Muttra) I noticed a number of sacred tortoises and turtles. They swarm in the river and are daily fed by the pilgrims. The crocodile or alligator (makara) is sometimes held sacred to Kāma-deva. Children were at one time thrown into the Ganges as a sacrifice to these animals. The wag-tail (Khañjana) is regarded as a form of Vishṇu, the mark on its throat having some resemblance to a Śāla-grāma stone. The cat is sacred to the goddess Shashṭhī (p. 229), who is supposed to use it as her vehicle. The dog is connected with Śiva (p. 266, note) in his character of a Kirāta or mountaineer (p. 64), or rather perhaps with Rudra, who also presides over horses. Hence in the Śatarudriya hymn of the Yajur-veda (p. 76) we have

'Reverence to dogs and to the lords of dogs,' 'Reverence to horses and to the lords of horses.' Hence, too, the name Kṛita-jña, 'the grateful one,' is applied equally to Śiva and to dogs. In Western India dogs are sometimes fed as a sacred duty once a month. In the Bali-haraṇa (or Kāka-bali) ceremony (see p. 289), offerings of food are placed on the ground for Yama's two dogs, crows, etc. (see pp. 289, 422). Again, crows are fed at the end of the Śrāddha ceremonies (p. 311). On the other hand, dogs are sometimes described as unclean animals, and crows as birds of ill-omen. So also Śva-paća, 'dog-cooker,' and Tīrtha-kāka, 'crow at a place of pilgrimage,' Kūpa-maṇḍūka, 'frog in a well,' or Kūpa-kaććhapa, 'tortoise in a well,' are terms of reproach (Pāṇini II. 1. 42). There is a natural enmity between cat and mouse, dog and jackal, serpent and mongoose, crow and owl.

As to horses, in some parts of India at the Daśa-harā (Daśarā) festival, they are decorated with garlands. The mythical horse, Uććaiḥ-śravas, 'high-eared' (p. 108), supposed to be the prototype of all horses, is assigned to the god Indra. The Aśva-medha, 'horse-sacrifice,' was a very ancient ceremony (hymns 162 and 163 in Ṛig-veda I. being used at it). It was the chief animal sacrifice, and a hundred horse-sacrifices entitled the sacrificer to displace Indra from heaven. Indra, therefore, always tried to capture the horse which was allowed to roam about before immolation (see Rāmāyaṇa I. 13, and Mahā-bhārata XIV, Āśvamedhika-parvan)[1].

---

[1] A horse was selected by a prince who aimed at supremacy and was let loose to roam at large for a year. Those who disputed his claim tried to capture the roving horse and to hold it against the original owner and all comers. If no one succeeded the horse was brought back and sacrificed with long ceremonies, and the prince who held it was acknowledged as paramount sovereign. Yudhishṭhira in the Mahā-bhārata let loose a horse in this way, which wandered through many countries, having Arjuna for its champion. Among the places to which it came in its rovings was Maṇipur, whose king is described as virtuous, and who gave his daughter, Ćitrāṅgadā, to Arjuna in marriage.

Worship of Trees and Plants.

We learn from the numerous examples adduced by Sir John Lubbock, Mr. Tylor, and Mr. Fergusson, that the adoration of trees, shrubs and plants, in virtue of the supernatural qualities or divine essence supposed to be inherent in them, is almost as universally diffused over the globe as the worship of animals, and that both forms of religion are of the greatest antiquity. Every one is familiar with such instances as the prophetic oak of Dodona, the myrtle of Venus, the poplar sacred to Hercules, the oaks of the British Druids, and the sacred groves of Germany mentioned by Tacitus [1]; but every one does not know that there existed quite recently a particular oak-copse in the island of Skye which the inhabitants held inviolably sacred, and that here and there in remote parts of Europe simple-minded peasants are to be found who still pay homage to certain trees, still hang offerings on their branches, and still believe in willows that bleed, and in trees that speak when about to be cut down.

Tree-worship, we are told, was once common in Greece, France, Poland, Assyria, and many other countries. It has continually prevailed among uncultivated tribes in Africa, America, and Polynesia. In Persia travellers occasionally come across trees hung with offerings of rags and garments, and throughout the greater part of Asia a belief in a kind of divinity inherent in certain trees has always been a recognized element of the popular creed.

In India, as already observed, all life is sacred. It might even be affirmed that the Hindūs were the first believers in the law of continuity; for in their creed the life of gods is connected with that of demons, the life of demons with

---

[1] Pliny asserts that the earliest form of temple or church was a tree, and some think that the word kirk is cognate with quercus.

that of men, the life of men with that of animals, the life of animals with that of plants, the life of plants with a supposed life in rocks and stones, and the divine soul is thought to permeate all. In obedience to this law there is no break of any kind anywhere, and plant-worship follows, as a necessary consequence, on animal-worship. In fact, according to the Hindū theory of metempsychosis all trees and plants are conscious beings, having as distinct personalities and souls of their own as gods, demons, men, and animals (see Manu I. 49). But it must be borne in mind that although trees may in their turn become the receptacle of the spirits of gods, men, and animals[1], they are peculiarly liable to be occupied by demons. That is to say, these beings may not only occupy a tree as its spirit or soul; they may often resort to it as guests, or take up their abode in it as tenants, when it is already furnished with a soul of its own. The idea seems to be that demons require protection from the weather like human beings, and occasionally betake themselves to trees as convenient and agreeable places of shelter.

This explains the close connexion between tree-worship, serpent-worship[2], demon-worship, and Śiva-worship. Demons are believed to be fond of occupying both serpents and trees, and Śiva is lord of demons, of serpents, and of plants (see p. 77).

In relation to this subject, it may be noted that in India a tree is sometimes planted and then confided to the guardianship of a demon, who from that moment considers himself responsible for the safe-keeping of the tree, and if any one is rash enough to cut it down or even steal its fruit, punishes him by afflicting him with sickness[3].

---

[1] The great Buddha is said to have occupied trees forty-three times in the course of his transmigrations (see my 'Buddhism,' p. 112).

[2] The connexion of serpent-worship with tree-worship may have originally arisen from the fact that many snakes like to establish themselves in the roots of trees, especially in those of the sandal-wood tree.

[3] This is mentioned by Colonel Sleeman.

In Bīrbhūm the entire population does homage once a year to a cluster of three trees in the jungle, which are supposed to be the abodes of as many demons[1]. In the Madurā district there is a solitary Mimosa tree, growing near a tank. This tree always has numerous pieces of rag and cloth tied to its branches. The explanation given by the peasantry is that a traveller was once found dead near the tank and that his spirit has become a malignant demon which resides in the tree and requires to be propitiated by offerings[2].

Of course, however, adoration paid to the demons in such trees must not be confounded with the worship of plants and trees which are themselves deities, or are in themselves permeated by the essence of certain deities.

For instance, I need scarcely repeat that in the Vedic period the Soma plant was personified, and made an object of adoration (see pp. 12, 13, 368). It was not merely the abode of divinity, but itself a god.

Then just as the divine cow Surabhi (granting all desires) and the typical horse Uććaiḥ-śravas arose out of the ocean, when churned for the production of certain valuable objects, so arose also a divine tree called Pārijāta (see p. 108), which afterwards became the property of the god Indra, and was transferred to his heaven. This tree was called Kalpa-druma, as granting all desires to those who did homage to its divinity. So in the Śakuntalā the trees of the sacred grove are described as yielding beautiful robes and costly ornaments for the adornment of the heroine (see my translation, p. 99).

Moreover, just as a portion of the godhead or essence of Vishṇu descended in the fish, the tortoise, and the boar, so certain plants are embodiments of portions of the essence of particular deities.

---

[1] See Hunter's 'Annals of Rural Bengal,' p. 131.

[2] Mr. Walhouse states that he saw this tree. So also the tombs of Musalmān saints are often encircled by upright poles, to which are fastened streamers of many-coloured rags.

For example, the Tulasī, or holy Basil (popularly Tulsī, botanically *Ocymum Sanctum*), is not merely sacred to Vishṇu or to his wife Lakshmī; it is pervaded by the essence of these deities, and itself worshipped as a deity and prayed to accordingly. Many regard the Tulasī as a metamorphosis of Sītā, wife of Vishṇu's incarnation Rāma-ćandra; others identify this plant with Rukmiṇī, wife of Kṛishṇa [1], while others hold it to be an embodiment of all the deities together. It is certain that in whatever light regarded, the Tulasī is the object of more adoration than any other plant at present worshipped in India, and the following prayer is often addressed to it:—'I adore that Tulasī in whose roots are all the sacred places of pilgrimage, in whose centre are all the deities, and in whose upper branches are all the Vedas [2].'

Possibly its sanitary properties may have been the original cause of the homage it receives. Its leaves are believed to heal the sick, and to be a remedy against the poison of serpents [3].

But the great estimation in which the Tulasī is held is best indicated by the fact that it is to be found in almost every respectable Hindū household throughout India. It is a small shrub, not too big to be cultivated in a good-sized flower-pot, and often placed in rooms. Generally, however, it is planted in the court-yard of a well-to-do man's house, with a space round it for reverential circumambulation. In real fact the Tulasī is par excellence a domestic divinity, or rather, perhaps, a woman's divinity. The generality of Indian women are, unhappily, still shut out from the chief avenues leading to enlightenment. The great majority are unable to read and

---

[1] In Kālidāsa's celebrated drama Vikramorvaśī, the nymph Urvaśī is metamorphosed into a creeping plant, just as Daphne was into a laurel and the sisters of Phaethon into poplars.

[2] Yan-mūle sarva-tīrthāni yan-madhye sarva-devatāḥ | yad-agre sarva-vedaś-ća Tulasīṃ tāṃ namāmy aham.

[3] Sir H. Yule (who sojourned some time in Sicily) informed me that the Basil is venerated in Sicily for its sanitary properties. The inhabitants keep it in the windows of their houses.

write their own mother-tongue; yet, like the women in other countries, they are far more religious than the men, and have great influence. Their ignorance and narrow-mindedness make their religion take the form of unmitigated superstition. The ancient law-giver Manu affirms that women were created to be mothers and men to be fathers, and that religious rites ought to be performed by husbands with their wives (IX. 96). But in the present day women perform their religious services apart from their husbands, and as a rule, their one daily religious rite consists in walking round the Tulasī plant—considered as a form of either Vishṇu's wife Lakshmī or of Rāma's faithful wife Sītā, or of Kṛishṇa's wife Rukmiṇī—in saying prayers to it, or in placing offerings of flowers and rice before it.

In a central space in most of the villages I visited in India, I noticed a small raised platform of rough masonry on which grew a Pīpal tree and a Tulasī shrub, and on particular occasions I observed poor women, who were probably not rich enough to possess the Tulasī plant in their own houses, performing circumambulation round the village shrub. In one village, especially, I watched a woman who was in the act of walking 108 times round the sacred plant with her right shoulder always turned towards it[1]. Her simple object, no doubt, was to propitiate the goddess with a view to securing long life for her husband and gaining a large family of sons for herself.

I should note that as animals are made to go through the ceremonial of marriage (see p. 327), so also are plants. The ceremony of marrying the Tulasī shrub to the idol of the youthful Kṛishṇa takes place annually in every Hindū family in the month Kārttika. In Western India an idol of the young Kṛishṇa is often brought in procession from the house of one of the Vallabhāćārya Mahārājas (see p. 136), to

[1] Hence this reverential circumambulation is called pradakshiṇā. It must follow the course of the sun, or all its efficacy is destroyed.

some residence where the Tulasī is kept. The idol is placed in a gorgeous palanquin and followed by a long train of attendants. Then the marriage festivities are celebrated at the cost of, perhaps, several thousand rupees.

Similarly in other parts of India the Tulasī is married to the black Śāla-grāma pebble (see p. 69), which even more than the idol represents the god Kṛishṇa, for the god is present in the stone, even without consecration.

Sleeman describes a marriage of this kind. There was a procession of eight elephants, 200 camels, and 400 horses. The pebble-bridegroom was placed on the leading elephant sumptuously decorated, and about 100,000 persons were present at the nuptials. It is usual to maintain the supposed matrimonial union between the Tulasī and Kṛishṇa by keeping a Tulasī leaf always resting on the Śāla-grāma stone.

The marriage of other trees—as of a mango with a Nimba (or Nīm) or of a mango with a jasmine (compare my translation of Śakuntalā, p. 17)—is frequently celebrated with similar rejoicings. In my journey from Mirzapore to Vindhyāćal I passed a Nīm tree (p. 339) and a Pīpal growing together by the road-side. This was the result of a marriage celebrated many years before.

The next most noteworthy example of sacred plant-life in India is certainly the Pippala or Aśvattha tree (popularly Pīpal, botanically the *Ficus Religiosa*, or holy fig-tree). This also is held to be a most holy tree. It has a divine personality of its own. It is occupied by the essence of the god Brahmā [1], and is sometimes invested with the sacred thread, as if it were a Brāhman, all the ceremonies of investiture (Upanayana) being performed over it. The mysterious

[1] Others say that the Pīpal is pervaded by the three gods Brahmā, Vishṇu, and Śiva, but especially by the latter in his Kṛishṇa manifestation. In the Bhagavad-gītā Kṛishṇa says :—'I am Aśvattha among the trees.' It is believed that spirits delight to sit in the branches of this tree and listen to the rustling of the leaves.

rustling of its tremulous leaves, which resemble those of the poplar, is no doubt one cause of the superstitious awe with which this tree is regarded. Its roots also display a kind of miraculous power of undermining thick walls, and houses built of the strongest masonry, causing in this way much serious damage to property. Yet no native of India would venture to cut down or in any way injure or interfere with the growth of this tree. It is remarkable, too, that no native would venture to tell an untruth or deviate from the strictest rectitude of conduct while standing under a Pīpal tree. The following amusing circumstance illustrative of this point came to my knowledge when I was in India :—

A certain magistrate, well known for his energy and good nature, knowing that all Hindūs regard it as a work of immense religious merit to plant these trees, hit upon the clever idea of trying to conciliate the good-will of the inhabitants of his district by planting some Pīpal trees in the market-place of a large town where a number of traders were in the habit of transacting their business. This he accordingly proceeded to do, fully expecting to entitle himself to their gratitude, but imagine his surprise when a deputation of these traders made its appearance one day and entreated him to desist, urging with the most naïve candour that their business could not be carried on without a certain amount of deception, and that the neighbourhood of the Pīpal trees would paralyze all their negotiations[1].

The third most sacred tree in India is the Bilva or Vilva (popularly called Bel, botanically *Ægle Marmelos*, or wood-apple). Its leaf is of a triple form—with three leaflets—and probably on that account consecrated to Śiva with his triple

[1] In the same way, although the telling of untruths for the good of one's caste or village is justifiable under certain circumstances—as, for example, the saving of life—no native would venture to tell a falsehood with a piece of gold in his mouth. (Compare Manu VIII. 103, 104.) In all countries a loose code of morality prevails in regard to shielding caste-fellows and companions by untruthful statements.

functions. Offerings of these leaves are constantly placed on the Liṅga and on the Bull (see last line of p. 90).

Of other holy trees and plants, the Vaṭa or Banyan (popularly Var for Vaḍ, botanically *Ficus Indica*) is sacred to Kāla or Time. This and the Pīpal tree already described are supposed to enjoy a kind of immortality. When a man plants either of these trees he repeats a prayer to the following effect:—'May I abide in heaven as many years as this tree continues growing on the earth.' The method by which the Banyan tree propagates itself is too well known to require description. A tree of this kind called the Kabīr-Var, on the banks of the Narbadā near Broach, continued multiplying itself every year by sending down roots from its branches till it became a forest capable of sheltering an army of 7000 men. This tree, though gradually decaying[1], is still at particular seasons a great resort of pilgrims.

Again, in the underground passage of the Allahābād fort there is the stump of a tree called the Akshaya-vaṭa, or 'undecaying Banyan,' which once overhung the river and is said to be the same as that mentioned by the Chinese traveller Hiouen Thsang. Whether this be the real tree or not, it is still an attractive rendezvous for pilgrims, and was formerly a favourite place for committing suicide. Hundreds have at different times thrown themselves from that overhanging stem into the river. When I visited the place I could detect no life in what appeared to me a mere decaying stump. I was gravely informed by the priest who accompanied me that a further underground passage conducts from the tree to Lākshā-gṛiha (Lāchā-gir), the 'lac-house,' twenty miles distant on the Ganges, and again another thence to Benares.

---

[1] At any rate it had lost its forest character when I visited Broach in 1876. It was not the pilgrimage season, and only one solitary devotee then occupied a hut under one of the branches. The tree is believed to have grown from a twig which the sage Kabīr used as a tooth-brush and then threw away as impure. The largest Banyan trees seen by me were in the South of India.

With reference to the long life of the Pīpal tree, I may mention that when I visited Bodh-Gayā (six miles from the city of Gayā), in 1876, I saw growing there on a terrace behind the celebrated tower-like Buddhist monument said to be more than 2,000 years old, a very old Pīpal which was alleged to be the identical Bo-tree (Bodhi-druma) under which Gautama Buddha attained supreme knowledge in the fifth century B.C. No doubt a succession of trees was secured by planting new shoots inside the old decaying stem (see my 'Buddhism,' pp. 392, 393). An off-shoot from the tree was conveyed in the time of Aśoka (nearly three hundred years B.C.) to Anurādha-pura in Ceylon, and its descendant is said to be still growing there.

Of the other trees, the Aśoka (botanically *Jonesia Asoka*) is sacred to Śiva, the Arka or sun-plant to the Sun (Sūrya), while the Śamī or Acacia is a goddess on her own account and is supposed to contain fire[1].

The Dūrvā grass (popularly Panic grass, botanically *Panicum Dactylon*) is sacred to Gaṇeśa.

But of all the grasses the Kuśa or Darbha (*Poa Cynosuroides*) is the holiest. It is used at all religious ceremonies and strewn on the ground before all sacrificial rites; it sanctifies the soil, forms the most sacred of all seats, cleanses everything it touches, purifies the impure, and when wound around the fingers makes them fit to engage in the most sacred acts.

The lotus (padma), which is a species of water-lily, is constantly alluded to in Indian poetry[2]. It is not directly worshipped, but is perhaps more sacred, as a symbol, than any other flower. The Creator—Brahmā himself—was born

---

[1] The following prayer is addressed to the Śamī tree:—Śamī śamayate pāpaṃ Śamī śatru-vināśinī, 'the Śamī removes guilt, the Śamī is the destroyer of enemies.'

[2] It is curious that the rose is scarcely ever mentioned in Indian literature, though it is the favourite flower of Persia. In point of fact the rose is not indigenous in India, though found in the Himālaya mountains.

in the lotus which sprang from the navel of Vishṇu, and the goddess Lakshmī arose out of the ocean holding a lotus in her hand. She is connected with the lotus in other legends, and appeared at the creation floating over the water on the expanded petals of a lotus-flower. In short, the lotus is typical of perfection (see my 'Buddhism,' p. 522).

The Āmra or Mango, the Nimba or Nīm, the Bakula (*Mimusops Elengi*), and the Āmalakī (*Emblic Myrobalan*) are also sacred trees. Some Pandits assert that the Āmra is an incarnation of the god of love.

Of all fruits the cocoa-nut (nārikela) is perhaps the most sacred. It is called the fruit of the goddess of prosperity (Śrī-phala). The custard apple is the fruit of Sītā (Sītā-phala).

Worship of Material and Natural Objects.

The worship of inanimate natural objects opens out a wide field of inquiry. I can only direct attention to some of the most interesting and important phases of the subject.

We must bear in mind that objects which are inanimate to us are animate to the Hindūs. According to their belief every material or natural object is pervaded by a spirit. In fact the same doctrine of metempsychosis, which has continually forced itself upon our notice throughout our investigations, meets us again here. The spirit of a man in whom the dark quality (tamas, see p. 36) dominates is liable to pass into inert (jaḍa) motionless matter (see Manu XII. 9, 42), and to occupy a rock, a stone, a post, or any similar material form. Even the divine Spirit may infuse itself into images and objects of stone, metal, and wood, into idols such as those of Kṛishṇa, Rāma and Durgā, into symbols like the Liṅga and Yoni, or into pebbles like the Śāla-grāma (sometimes written Śāli-grāma) and Bāṇa-liṅga (see p. 69). And it does this not merely in its character of a universal Spirit pervading all matter. It is present in a special manner in all such material forms.

But it is to be observed that material objects which are thus, as it were, animated and endowed with personal souls, do not necessarily, when worshipped, become mere fetishes. Fetishism may be described as the expression of the spiritual instinct of a child and of a savage. A doll, or a ball, or any plaything is made a kind of fetish when it is endowed with personality and addressed as if it were alive. A savage makes a fetish of a lucifer match when, believing it to be occupied by a spirit, he stands in awe of it or tries to control it for his own benefit. In the same way he may make fetishes of his tools or weapons —of his axe, his knife, or his bow—or of any particular idol.

But a fetish, as Sir John Lubbock has pointed out, is not necessarily an object of worship. It is only worshipped if it answers prayers or confers benefits. If it appears to neglect the interests of its possessor, it is itself neglected, and if misfortunes occur it is abused or ill-treated. In short, it is essential to the idea of a fetish that, consisting in the first instance of some peculiar form of material object with a distinct individuality and special character of its own, it should be occupied by a spirit devoted to the interests of the person possessing it, and pledged, like the genius of Aladdin's lamp, to execute his behests. Hence, any stone idol which, in common with a number of other idols, represents a deity invariably held in honour, is not a fetish in the proper sense of the term.

It is difficult, however, to draw any hard and fast line between Animism and Fetishism, or to say where one ends and the other begins. It is certain that much true Fetishism and much of a kind of half-fetishism co-exist with higher religious ideas in most of the religions of the world.

I believe that in India some images (such as those of Khaṇḍo-bā) are exposed to actual ill-treatment, when any calamity occurs which is attributed to the neglect of the god, but I have never verified this by personal observation.

It must be admitted that what may be called Animistic and Fetish ideas run through the whole of Hindūism. For instance, in Atharva-veda (XVIII. 4. 5) the sacrificial ladles, the oblation, the sacrificial grass (IV. 35. 3–6; XIX. 32. 9), and even the remains of the sacrifice are described as animated and as possessing divine powers. We know, too, that on particular holy days, the merchant worships his books, the writer his inkstand, the husbandman his plough, the weaver his loom, the carpenter his axe, chisel, and tools, and the fisherman his net. Every object that benefits its possessor and helps to provide him with a livelihood becomes for the time-being his fetish. Nevertheless, I doubt whether the religion of the Āryan Hindūs has ever shown any great tendency to lapse into the worst forms of fetish-worship, such as those which undoubtedly prevailed among the aboriginal inhabitants, and are common everywhere among uncultivated races. Placed in the midst of striking physical phenomena and feeling themselves surrounded by mighty material forces, the Āryans on their arrival in India were simple nature-worshippers, and those natural objects and natural forces which had motion appeared to them more especially instinct with divinity. Hence the Sun, the Moon, Fire, Wind, and the Waters were the chief deities in Vedic times (pp. 9; 16).

Worship of the Sun.

Without doubt the great luminary to which the world owes light, heat, and vegetation, has always been one of the earliest objects of the world's adoration. In the Ṛig-veda (X. 88. 11) the Sun is said to be a son of Aditi, and has two chief names—Sūrya (Ἥλιος) and Savitṛi (p. 16)—both significant of his generative power. Probably his more ancient title was Prajā-pati, 'lord of creatures.' He is represented as a golden deity borne along in a chariot drawn by seven ruddy horses or mares, and his charioteer is the Dawn. By his wife Saṃjñā he had twin children, the Aśvins (p. 9), who are called heavenly physicians. The Sun himself is also described as a healer of diseases. In the Epic poems he is 'the eye of the world' and 'the soul of all.'

Passing on to medieval times, it is clear that in the days of Śaṅkara there were distinct sects of Sauras or Sun-worshippers (see p. 59); that is, a large number of persons adored the Sun as their exclusive divinity. They were divided, as we learn from the Śaṅkara-vijaya (chap. 13), into six sub-sects as follow:—1. Worshippers of the rising Sun as identified with Brahmā. 2. Worshippers of the meridian Sun as identified with Śiva. 3. Worshippers of the setting Sun as identified with Vishṇu. 4. Worshippers of the Sun in all three of the above phases as identified with the Tri-mūrti (p. 45). 5. Worshippers of the Sun regarded as a material being in the form of a man with a golden beard and golden hair[1]. Zealous members of this sect refused to eat anything in the morning till they had seen the Sun rise. 6. Worshippers of an image of the Sun formed in the mind. These spent all their time in meditating on the Sun. They were in the habit of branding circular representations of his disk on their foreheads, arms, and breasts.

Coming now to modern times, we find that, although the sect of Sun-worshippers has apparently died out and although the Sun-god has few temples like those of Śiva or Vishṇu, he still continues to be the object of universal adoration. Every Hindū—be he Śaiva or Vaishṇava, or to whatever sect he may belong—does homage to the rising Sun every morning by repeating the Gāyatrī (Ṛig-veda III. 62. 10), a prayer addressed to the Sun's vivifying essence (see pp. 19, 403; 406). Then at the midday service he ought to repeat the Sūrya-sūkta or Saura-sūkta (Ṛig-veda I. 50, partly translated at p. 16).

It certainly surprised me that I saw so few temples or

---

[1] It is remarkable that the Hindūs talk of the god in the Sun (called by them Sūrya-Nārāyaṇa) rather than of the man in the Moon. The spots in the Sun are supposed to give the idea of a man's face, while those in the Moon are compared to the markings on a rabbit.

shrines dedicated to the Sun in any part of India. His most celebrated temple was at Koṇārak (for Koṇārka, 'corner-sun') in Orissa. It is said that a sum equal to twelve years' revenues of Orissa was spent on this temple. Yet it is now deserted and in ruins. I visited a well-known sacred temple of the Sun at Gayā near to a tank consecrated to the same luminary. No one appeared to be worshipping in the shrine, but rude images of the disk of the Sun made of red cotton were affixed by women to the walls above the door-way.

The hymn to the Sun called Sūryā-sūkta (Ṛig-veda X. 85) is still in common use at marriage-ceremonies (p. 363 note).

Worship of the Moon.

Passing from the Sun to the Moon, we find that the latter seems never to have had any exclusive adorers in India. Yet, like the Sun, the Moon is often regarded as one of the nine planets, and is treated as a male deity. In the Purāṇas he is said to be borne along in a chariot with three wheels drawn by ten horses. Poets are never tired of alluding to the Moon's beauty, its brilliancy being far greater in India than in Europe; but the only worship it receives in the present day is in conjunction with the Sun and the other planets.

The sphere of the Moon is sometimes regarded as the abode of the spirits of deceased ancestors (Pitṛis); and its orb is usually held to consist of sixteen digits (Kalās), which are composed of nectar (amṛita) supplied to it from the Sun for the support of the gods. In Ṛig-veda X. 85. 5 there is an allusion to the gods drinking up the nectar and so causing the Moon to wane.

The name Soma, which first belonged to the plant only, came to be applied to the Moon in post-vedic mythology, traces of this application being also observable in Ṛig-veda X. 85, in Atharva-veda XI. 6, 7, and in several passages of the Śatapatha-Brāhmaṇa. In the later mythology (see

Vishṇu-purāṇa I. 22) Brahmā is said to have appointed Soma or the Moon to be the 'monarch of planets, of plants, of sacrifices, and penances,' and one of the names of the Moon is Oshadhi-pati or Oshadhīśa, 'lord of plants and herbs,' which he is supposed to nourish with his light. Again, at the churning of the ocean, as described in the Purāṇas, after all sorts of medicinal plants and healing herbs had been thrown into the waters, three of the precious things produced were the Moon (Soma), nectar (amṛita), and spirituous liquor (surā), though in other legends this nectar is said to be preserved in the body of the Moon, or even to constitute its substance. In Manu V. 96 Soma is called one of the eight Loka-pālas or guardians of the world.

Worship of the Planets.

The Sun and Moon, Mercury (Budha), Venus (Śukra), Mars (Maṅgala or Aṅgāraka), Jupiter (Vṛihaspati), Saturn (Śani), Rāhu and Ketu [1]—the former being fabled as a planet with a head and no body, the latter as a planet with a body and no head—together form the group of what is called the Nava-graha, nine planets, the first seven giving names to the days of the week [2]. In the Purāṇas they are all represented as deities borne in cars. Thus the car of Mars is of gold drawn by eight red horses, that of Jupiter is drawn by eight pale horses, that of Saturn is a slow-going car drawn by piebald horses, those of Rāhu and Ketu are drawn by eight dark horses. Rāhu is thought to have a spite against the Sun and Moon, and occasionally displays his enmity by swallowing them for a time and so causing eclipses, while Ketu gives birth to an awful progeny of comets and fiery meteors.

---

[1] These are sometimes identified with the Moon's ascending and descending nodes.

[2] The planets, however, are variously mentioned as five, seven, and nine in number.

The whole array of nine luminaries constitutes in the eyes of every Hindū a most formidable group of deities, whose power over every living person's career from the first moment of his coming into the world, and over the whole course of mundane events, no one for an instant thinks of doubting.

The influences of Saturn, Rāhu and Ketu are supposed to be sinister, and these planets are therefore most propitiated. If they are in the ascendant when a man is born they are sure to shorten his life or cause him trouble of some kind. Their anger, therefore, must be deprecated, and counteracting influences must be sought for by astrologers in drawing up horoscopes. They cause diseases, such as influenza, fevers, etc.

On the other hand, Jupiter, Venus, Mercury, Mars, and the Sun exert favourable influences only, and the first three are thought to be special sources of knowledge and wisdom. The favour of all must be conciliated before marriages and other auspicious events can be successfully accomplished.

I saw a celebrated temple dedicated to the nine planets at Benares, and another sacred to Saturn and to the bodiless Rāhu. Numbers of people as they passed these temples cast flowers and offerings before the images, but did not stop to worship.

The Nakshatras, or twenty-seven constellations through which the Moon passes[1], and which separate his path into twenty-seven divisions—as the signs of the Zodiac do that of the Sun into twelve—are, like the planets, regarded in the present day as deities who exert a vast influence on the destiny of men, not only at the moment of their entrance into the world, but during their whole passage through it. These formidable constellations are consulted at births, marriages, and on all occasions of family rejoicing, distress, or

---

[1] In the Ṛig-veda the word Nakshatra has the general sense of a constellation. In the Yajur and Atharva-veda the Nakshatras are distinctly connected with the path of the Moon, and in the latter (XIX. 8. 1) their number is given as twenty-eight.

calamity. No one undertakes a journey or any important matter except on days which the aspect of the Nakshatras renders lucky and auspicious. If any constellation is unfavourable, its anger must by all means be appeased by a ceremony called Śānti, 'propitiation.'

Worship of Fire.

The worship of Fire, like that of the Sun, was, as we have already seen, one of the earliest cults of India (see p. 9), and Fire is still a general object of homage [1]. Further allusions to this homage will be made subsequently. I will only here draw attention to the remarkable idea prevalent in India that fire is produced from water. In the Veda fire is called Apām-napāt, 'son of the waters,' and this name is also once applied to the Sun (I. 22. 6) [2]. Doubtless the idea arose from the apparent production of lightning from rain-clouds.

Worship of Water and Rivers.

Passing on to the worship of Water, especially running water, it is to be observed that river-water is throughout India held to be instinct with divinity [3]. It is not merely holy, it is pervaded by the divine essence. We must, however, be careful to distinguish between the mere sacredness of either fire or water and their worship as personal deities.

In Ṛig-veda X. 30, X. 9, VII. 47, and other passages of the Veda, the Waters are personified, deified, and honoured as goddesses, and called the Mothers of the earth. In

---

[1] As the medium of bearing the sacrifice to heaven it is always sacred, even when not worshipped as a personal god. The adoration of fire in Assyria, Phœnicia, Persia, etc., is well known. No doubt the difficulty of generating fire led to its adoration among uncivilized tribes.

[2] Some see a connexion between Apām-napāt and Neptunus.

[3] The worship of water is by no means confined to India, as the number of holy wells in our own country proves.

X. 17. 10 their purifying power, and in VI. 50. 7 their healing power, is celebrated. They cleanse their worshippers from sin and untruthfulness (I. 23. 22); and, as noted above, they give birth to Fire (X. 2. 7, X. 91. 6).

Of course some rivers are more sacred than others, and as the Ganges, which issues from Vishṇu's foot and falls on Śiva's head (p. 80), is the most majestic, so it is the holiest of all rivers. No sin is too heinous to be removed, no character too black to be washed clean by its waters. Hence the countless temples with flights of steps lining its banks; hence the array of priests, called 'Sons of the Ganges,' sitting on the edge of its streams, ready to aid the ablutions of conscience-stricken bathers, and stamp them as white-washed when they emerge from its waters. Hence also the constant traffic carried on in transporting Ganges water in small bottles to all parts of the country. The river Sarasvatī—called 'the purifier' in Ṛig-veda I. 3. 10—was to the earlier Hindūs what the Ganges was to the later; she was instinct with divinity, and her influence permeated the writers of the Vedic hymns. Sometimes she is identified with the Vedic goddess Vāć, 'speech,' and invoked as the patroness of science.

The river Indus (Sindhu) is also celebrated very early in the Ṛig-veda (see X. 75. 4).

But the confluence of the Ganges with the Jumnā (Yamunā) and Sarasvatī (supposed to flow underground) at Allahābād (Prayāga) is perhaps one of the most hallowed spots in all India. These three sacred streams form a sort of Tri-mūrti, or triad of rivers, often personified as goddesses, and called 'Mothers.' Then other celebrated rivers—such as the Godāvarī (also called Godā and Vṛiddha-gaṅgā, 'the ancient Gaṅges'), Narbadā (properly Narma-dā, 'bliss-giver,' also called Revā), Taptī (properly Tapatī, also called Tāpī), Sābarmatī (possibly for Śubhramatī), Gaṇḍakī, Kistna (properly Kṛishṇā), Veṇā, Sarayū, Tuṅga-bhadrā (called 'the Ganges of the South'), and Kāverī—became rivals of this original sacred triad.

The Narbadā has its special admirers, who exalt it even above the Ganges. It is said to have sprung from the perspiration of the god Rudra (p. 75). 'One day's ablution,' they say, 'in the Ganges frees from sin, but the mere sight of the Narbadā purifies from guilt.' The sanctity of the Ganges will, it is predicted, cease in 1895. The Narbadā will then supersede it and become the most sacred river of India. Moreover, all water thirty miles from the Narbadā's bank northward and eighteen miles southward is sanctified by it. Furthermore, either bank may be used for burning the dead, whereas only the northern bank of the Ganges is effectual for that purpose.

At Mahābaleśvar I visited the source of the Kṛishṇā (Kistna) which flows into a sacred tank after issuing from a Go-mukha (representation of a cow's mouth). Both are under the cover of a temple, and while I was there a pilgrim who had walked all the way from Benares, entered the building and taking off his dust-soiled garments began repeating his Mantras before performing his ablutions.

Chapters called Māhātmyas, assigning special sacredness to particular rivers and waters, have been at various times introduced into the Purāṇas.

At Kumbha-koṇam is a sacred pool which cleanses from guilt all those who are able to crowd into it at a particular moment once in twelve years. On the other hand, a river called Karma-nāśā, 'destroyer of good works,' which falls into the Ganges not far from Benares, is an unholy and accursed stream, and if a man touches its water he loses all his store of religious merit accumulated for years.

And here we may note that the whole length of the banks of all the chief rivers of India, from their source to the sea, is regarded as holy ground. To follow their course on foot is considered a highly meritorious act. A pilgrim, for example, sets out from the source of the Ganges, at Gaṅgotrī in the Himālayas, and walks by the left bank of the river to its mouth at Gaṅgā-sāgara; then, turning round, he proceeds by the right side back to Gaṅgotrī, whence he departed. This is called Pradakshiṇā, or Parikrama of the river, and takes six years to accomplish. In the same way a pilgrim starts from the source of the Narbadā, at Amara-kaṇṭaka,—a peak of the Vindhya chain in Goṇḍwāna,—and walks to the mouth, near Broach, and back. This pilgrimage takes nearly three years. The rivers Godāvarī and Kṛishṇā require only two years for the same process. As these rivers often pass through wild country, the pilgrims who perform such tasks are exposed to many hardships. Of course, the merit accumulated is in proportion to the length and difficulty of the pilgrimage (yātrā) and the ground traversed.

The sea is also held sacred, and on special occasions propitiated. When any one is compelled to take a voyage, it is not uncommon for his nearest relatives to throw milk into the sea as an offering to the waves.

Worship of Mountains, Rocks, and Stones.

With regard to the worship of immovable objects, many mountains and hills are holy ground. Of course the Himālaya range takes the lead. It is personified and extolled as a god. (Compare the first verses of Kālidāsa's Kumāra-sambhava.) There are temples (especially of Śiva) among its eternal snows, and pilgrims often perish in their efforts to reach the loftiest heights. Among other hills regarded as specially sacred are Ćitra-kūṭa (commonly called Chateerkoṭ) in the Banda district, the Pulney hills, Pārasnāth, Mount Abū, and Girnār in Kāthiāwār[1]. In short, nearly every hill in India is consecrated by temples and shrines.

There are some sand-hills in the Sātpura range dedicated

---

[1] Ćitra-kūṭa was the first residence of Rāma-ćandra after his banishment. Abū (corrupted from Sanskṛit *arbuda*), Pārasnāth, and Girnār are hills more particularly celebrated for their Jaina temples.

to Mahādeva, supposed, as Mahākāla, to preside over destruction. From a rock on these hills many youths have precipitated themselves, because their mothers, when childless, dedicated their first-born sons to the god. This mode of suicide is called Bhṛigu-pāta, 'throwing one's self from a precipice.' It was once equally common at the rock of Girnār, and has only recently been prohibited.

Particular rocks all over India are treated as divine. They are not only pervaded by the divine soul of the Universe which permeates all nature, God is specially present in them, just as he is in the Śāla-grāma pebble found in the Gaṇḍakī river, and in the Bāṇa-liṅga found in the Narbadā (see pp. 69, 412). A great deal of fraud is practised in selling these stones. If they come from other rivers they enjoy no special presence of the deity.

A simple Bilva-leaf offered on a true Bāṇa-liṅga brought from the Narbadā is an act of enormous merit (puṇya), but if offered on a spurious pebble is inefficacious.

I might continue the enumeration of sacred objects almost indefinitely, but enough has been said to make it clear that there is not an object in heaven or earth which a Hindū is not prepared to worship—sun, moon, and stars; rocks, stocks, and stones; trees, shrubs, and grass; sea, pools, and rivers; his own implements of trade; the animals he finds most useful, the noxious reptiles he fears; men remarkable for any extraordinary qualities—for great valour, sanctity, virtue, or even vice; good and evil demons, ghosts and goblins; the spirits of departed ancestors; an infinite number of semi-human and semi-divine existences; inhabitants of the seven upper and the seven lower worlds—each and all come in for a share of divine honour or a tribute of more or less adoration.

CHAPTER XIII.

The Hindū Religion in Ancient Family-life.

It has been well said that common life is the proper field for the exercise of Christianity; or, in other words, that true religion is not to be separated from every-day actions.

Turning to India we find a similar doctrine taught, although of course a different meaning is attached to the word 'religion.'

Without doubt it must be admitted that the actual life of a large number of Hindūs is not so complete a falling away from the moral standard set up in their sacred books (see pp. 532, 533), as some have represented. At the same time it must be confessed that the religion of a modern Hindū mainly consists in domestic rites, ceremonies and usages, all of which are superintended or carried out by the Brāhmans, although no central ecclesiastical government exists which has any power to impose or enforce any particular observances.

In fairness, too, it must be admitted that a genuine Hindū does not lead two lives. His religion, such as it is, may be described as bound up in the bundle of his every-day existence. The religion of a Hindū is his constant companion. Nor does he think it necessary, as a Christian does, to satisfy the claims of a corporate as well as of a personal and domestic religion. Any idea of congregational religious duties has no place in his mind. A Hindū never enters a place of worship with the object of offering up common prayer in company with his fellow-men. He has no conception of performing the kind of religious act which a Christian performs when he 'goes to church.' Occasionally, it is true, and on stated days, he visits idol shrines. But he does not go there with any idea of praying with others. He goes to the temple to perform what is called Darśana; that is, to look at the idol, the sight of which, when duly dressed and decorated by the priest, is supposed to confer merit. After viewing the image he may endeavour to propitiate the favour or avert the anger of the god it represents, by prostrations of the body, repetitions of its name, or presentation of offerings. But this is not an essential duty. His real religion is an affair of family usage, domestic ritual, and private observance. Not that his domestic worship is free from priestly interference. Sacerdotalism, uncontrolled by any central authority, exerts a strong power over personal and family religion in India, and all the stronger from the absence of congregational religion.

Nevertheless it is immemorial usage rather than ecclesiastical law which governs every operation in Indian home life. Each man finds himself cribbed and confined in all his movements, bound and fettered in all he does by minute traditional regulations. He sleeps and wakes, dresses and undresses, sits down and stands up, goes out and comes in, eats and drinks, speaks and is silent, acts and refrains from acting, according to ancient rule. And by the same rule the intervention of the priestly caste begins with his first unconscious existence as a living organism. From that moment to death, and even long after death, every Hindū is held to be the lawful property of the priests, who exact fees for innumerable offices performed on his behalf.

It is on this account that nearly every village has first its religious teacher (Guru), who teaches the Vedic Gāyatrī or the initiatory prayer (p. 61) to those whose caste or sect requires them to repeat it, and secondly its ceremonial priest, who serves as a domestic chaplain (Purohita) to all the families of the village. Not a single religious rite can be performed without this latter functionary, and though other priests may be asked to be present and assist at some of the ceremonies (such as marriage and initiation), the regular village priest must always take the lead and have his appointed duties and customary fees. In fact in no country of the world are domestic religion and sacerdotalism so curiously associated together and carried to such extremes as in India. There a complicated religious code has always been as necessary to the priest as an intricate civil code to the lawyer. It has supplied him with his meat, drink, and whole means of livelihood.

We must, however, be careful not to speak of Brāhmanism and Sacerdotalism in India as if these expressions were convertible terms. Every Brāhman is not a priest, though every priest is a Brāhman. The Brāhmans are simply an order of men divided into clergy and laity, and in ancient times a layman did many religious acts now performed by priests only.

To begin, then, with ancient times.

Twelve purificatory rites, called Saṇskāras, were prescribed in the ancient collections of domestic rules (Gṛihya-sūtras) and in the code of Manu, for the purification of the three higher castes—Brāhmans, Kshatriyas, and Vaiśyas—from the taint transmitted through the womb of the mother. They were, 1. Impregnation (Garbhādhāna or Garbha-lambhana); 2. Male-production (Puṃsavana); 3. Hair-parting (Sīmantonnayana); 4. Birth-ceremony (Jāta-karman); 5. Name-giving (Nāma-karaṇa); 6. Carrying out (Nishkramaṇa); 7. Food-giving (Anna-prāśana); 8 and 9. Tonsure or shaving and cutting off the hair (Ćaula or Kshaura and Keśānta)[1]; 10. Initiation (Upanayana); 11. Return from the house of the preceptor (Samāvartana); 12. Marriage (Vivāha). See Manu II. 27, etc.

Some account of these twelve ceremonies—supposed to purify from original or rather natal sin — ought to precede a description of the householder's daily observances; for no

[1] Manu places Ćaula 8th and Keśānta 10th, with Upanayana between, but the first two may be taken together as kindred ceremonies.

one whose body (tainted by its abode in the womb) has not been purified by these rites is held qualified to perform the ordinary religious duties of domestic life.

Turning then to one of the most important of the Saṇskāras—marriage—we find that it stands last. It will be necessary, however, to begin by supposing the recent union of a young couple in wedlock, so that every one of the Saṇskāras—beginning with that which is believed to be essential to the purification of the human embryo from its earliest origin in the womb—may be successively described. It must also be taken for granted that the newly-married pair in ancient times were of good family, that they were bent on acting up to the precepts of their religion, and that they brought with them to their own home a portion of the sacred fire which witnessed their union (see p. 363) and which, when once kindled on their own family hearth, had to be maintained ever afterwards for use in all domestic ceremonies and sacrifices, including the last sacrifice of all, the final burning of their own bodies at death.

The first Saṇskāra, which as a matter of course followed immediately on every matrimonial union, was called the 'Impregnation-rite' (Garbhādhāna). In ancient times no bridegroom approached the bride till the fourth night after the completion of the marriage ceremony[1]. Hence the consummation-rite was sometimes called Ćaturthī-karma. During the previous day the young married woman was made to look towards the sun, or in some way exposed to its rays. In the evening she was required to bathe. Her husband also per-

[1] This interval is prescribed by Gobhila. The present interval of two, three, or four years in the case of child-marriages is quite unsupported by the authority of ancient lawgivers. Dhanvantari (in the Suśruta) declares that the Garbhādhāna should not take place till a girl is sixteen. Dr. Bühler has shown (from the Vivāha-mantras) that in olden times girls were married long after they had reached the age of puberty, and infant-marriages were unknown; moreover, that the human husband is the 4th husband, the three gods, Soma, Viśva-vasu, and Agni, being the first three at the period of a girl's becoming marriageable.

formed his ablutions and went through other prescribed forms. Before approaching his wife he was careful to secure the solemn imprimatur of religion on an act which might lead to the introduction of another human being into the world. He therefore repeated two Mantras or texts of Ṛig-veda X. 184, the first of which may be thus translated :—'Let (all-pervading) Vishṇu prepare her womb; let the Creator shape its forms; let Prajāpati be the Impregnator; let the Creator give the embryo.'

The Impregnation-rite was followed after an interval of three months by that called 'Male-production' (Puṃsavana). This is not unusual even in the present day. We Europeans can scarcely understand the craving of Asiatic parents for the birth of a male child. The very word for a son (put-tra) is fancifully said to mean one who delivers a parent from a hell called Put. Whether any intelligent Hindū married man in modern times seriously looks forward to punishment in a place of torment hereafter as the penalty for not having sons or for having only daughters may be doubtful. We have seen, however, that the well-being of the parent's soul after death is believed to depend on the proper performance of the Śrāddha ceremonies by a son, and that the partition of the family inheritance is by law made dependent on that performance. Hence the craving for sons.

In short, a son is to every pious Hindū the first and last of all necessary things. Through a son he pays his own father the debt he owes him for his own life, and secures similar payment for the gift of life bestowed by himself.

What says the Aitareya-Brāhmaṇa of the Ṛig-veda (VII. 3. 13)? 'When a father sees the face of a living son he pays a debt in him, and gains immortality. The pleasure which a father has in his son exceeds all other enjoyments. His wife is a friend, his daughter an object of compassion, his son shines as his light in the highest world.' What says Manu? 'A man is perfect when he consists of three—himself, his wife, and his son' (VII. 3). What says Yājñavalkya? 'Immortality in future worlds and heavenly bliss are obtained by means of sons, grandsons, and great-grandsons.'

A story is told in some Brāhmaṇa of a certain pious man of ascetical temperament who determined to shirk the religious duty of taking a wife. Quietly skipping over the second prescribed period of life, during which he ought to have become a householder (gṛihastha), he entered at once upon the third period—that is to say, he became an ascetic, abjured all female society, and retired to the woods. Wandering about one day, absorbed in meditation, he was startled by an extraordinary spectacle. He saw before him a deep and apparently bottomless pit. Around its edge some unhappy men were hanging suspended by ropes of grass, at which here and there a rat was nibbling. On asking their history, he discovered to his horror that they were his own ancestors compelled to hang in this unpleasant manner, and doomed eventually to fall into the abyss, unless he went back into the world, did his duty like a man, married a suitable wife, and had a son, who would be able to release them from their critical predicament.

It is not, therefore, difficult to understand the object of the 'Male-production' ceremony (Puṃsavana). It was performed in the third month of gestation and before the period of quickening. According to Āśvalāyana the wife was to keep a solemn fast. She was then fed by her husband with two beans and a grain of barley[1] mixed with a handful of curds, and made to pray three times for the production of male-offspring.

A further supplementary rite for the prevention of miscarriage was customary in some localities. It was performed by sprinkling the juice of a stalk of fresh Dūrbā grass in the wife's right nostril, with the repetition of certain Mantras. This ceremony was called Anavalopana (or Anavalobhana).

---

[1] Symbolical of the Liṅga.

The next purificatory rite was called 'Hair-parting' (Sīmantonnayana).

First an oblation was made in fire, with repetition of the Vedic texts from Atharva-veda VII. 17. 1, Ṛig-veda III. 59. 1, V. 25. 2, II. 32. 4–5. Then the woman performed her ablutions in pure water; fragrant oil was poured on her head. and a line or parting (sīmanta) was drawn three times through her hair from the forehead upwards with three stalks of Kuśa grass bound together—the three sacred words called Vyāhṛitis (Bhūr, Bhuvar, Svar) and the hallowed syllable *Om* being uttered during each operation (pp. 402, 403). Certain medicinal substances supposed to have a purifying efficacy were also given, and a particular regimen prescribed for the remaining period of gestation. Musical performances also took place during the ceremony, the promotion of cheerfulness in the mind of the mother being thought essential to the proper development of the unborn child.

This rite was only performed at a woman's first pregnancy, and though, like the preceding, it purified the whole person of the wife, it also had reference to the well-being of the unborn child. The idea was that the body of the mother should be consecrated and protected from evil influences at the most critical period of gestation, the proper time for the ceremony being the fourth month, though it might be deferred until the sixth or eighth.

Immediately after the birth of the infant and before the severing of the umbilical cord the father performed the next Saṉskāra, called the 'Birth-ceremony' (Jāta-karman). Honey and clarified butter were mixed together and stirred—if possible, with a golden rod or spoon—to symbolize good-fortune. Then a small portion of the mixture was introduced into the mouth of the new-born infant and certain texts were repeated (Ṛig-veda II. 21. 6, III. 36. 10, Kaus.-Up. II. 11), with the following prayer: 'O long-lived one, mayst thou live a hundred years in this world, protected by the gods!' Both the ears of the infant were then touched with the golden rod, and another prayer repeated: 'May Savitṛi, may Sarasvatī, may the Aśvins grant thee wisdom.' Lastly, the shoulders were rubbed and these words uttered: 'Become firm as a rock, sharp as an axe, pure as gold; thou art the Veda called a son, live thou a hundred years. May Indra bestow on thee his best treasures.'

The next Saṇskāra, called 'Name-giving' (Nāma-karaṇa), took place on the tenth day after the birth of the child.

The Hindūs regard the giving of a name as a solemn religious act fraught with important consequences in its bearing on the future prospects of the child. The sound and meaning of the name must be auspicious. Āśvalāyana laid down the rule that a boy's name should either consist of two or of four syllables, not of an odd number, and have a soft consonant for its first letter and a semi-vowel in the middle (for example, Bhadra, Deva, Bhava, Nāga-deva, Bhadra-datta, Deva-datta, Yajña-datta). Lawgivers prescribed that the word Śarman, 'prosperity,' should form part of a Brāhman's name; Varman, 'armour,' of a Kshatriya's; Gupta, 'protected,' of a Vaiśya's; and Dāsa, 'slave,' of a Śūdra's (compare Manu II. 32). The names of women were required to be agreeable, soft, clear, captivating, auspicious, and ending in long vowels.

The next ceremony, called 'Carrying out' (Nishkramaṇa), was of less importance. In the fourth month after birth the child was carried out into the open air to look at the rising sun, while the following prayers were said: 'That eye-like luminary, the cause of blessings to the gods (or placed in the sky by the gods), rises in the east; may we behold it for a hundred years.' 'May we hear, may we speak, may we be free from poverty for a hundred years and more' (Ṛig-veda VII. 66. 16; Vāj.-Saṃhita XXXVI. 24).

The sixth Saṇskāra, called 'Food-giving' (Anna-prāśana), performed in the sixth month after birth, was of more importance. The child was carried in the arms of its father and placed in the midst of a party of friends, including the family priest, who offered prayers for its welfare and presented it with gifts. A little solid food (generally rice) was then for the first time put into its mouth, and various qualities were supposed to be imparted, according to the nature of the food given, whether rice, butter, honey, milk, or the flesh of partridges or goats (see Āśvalāyana Gṛihya-s. I. 17). At the same time a verse from the White Yajur-veda (II. 83) was recited.

After this sixth ceremony there was a pause, and the child was allowed to develop in peace for two or three years.

The next important Saṉskāras were those of 'Tonsure,' 'Shaving,' and 'Cutting off the hair' (Ćaula, Ćūḍā-karma, Keśānta, Kshaura). These were kindred operations, and may be explained together [1]. When performed for the first time they were held to have a purificatory effect on the whole character. In the case of a Brāhman the ceremony of tonsure was performed in the third year, but was often delayed, and sometimes did not take place till the seventh or eighth year. According to Āśvalāyana the child was to be placed on the lap of its mother to the west of the sacred fire. The father was to take up his station to the south of the mother, holding in his hand twenty-one stalks of Kuśa grass. He was to sprinkle the head of the child three times with a mixture of warm water, butter and curds. He was to insert three stalks of Kuśa grass seven times into the child's hair on the right side, saying: 'O divine grass, protect him!' Then he was to cut off a portion of the hair and give it to the mother, with recitation of various texts, leaving one lock (*śikhā* or *ćūḍā*) on the top of the head, or occasionally three or five locks, according to the custom of the family. The operation of shaving was some-

---

[1] Manu makes Keśānta, 'cutting off the hair,' a later Saṉskāra than Ćaula or Kshaura, 'shaving;' see note, p. 353. In the Roman Catholic Church the ceremony of tonsure is the first ceremony for devoting a young man to the service of God. In England this is done by cutting off a single lock; actual shaving is dispensed with.

times regarded as a different ceremony from that of cutting. It had to be continued after the age of puberty at regular intervals throughout life.

Another ceremony followed, called 'Ear-boring' (Karṇa-vedha). This was treated by some as a distinct religious rite, and had to take place after tonsure at three or five years of age. Pāraskara made it a Saṇskāra, but not so Āśvalāyana or Gobhila. The boy was fed with honey or something sweet, and made to sit down with his face towards the east. Then two perforations were made in his right ear, and a particular Mantra from the last hymn of the Sāma-veda was recited. Its first words may be thus translated: 'Let us hear what is good with the ears, let us see what is good with the eyes.' A similar operation was performed on the left ear, except that three perforations were made and a different Mantra from the Ṛig-veda (VI. 75. 3) recited. The text may be thus translated: 'This bowstring drawn tight upon the bow and leading to success in battle, repeatedly approaches *the ear*[1], as if embracing its friend, and wishing to say something agreeable, just as a woman makes a murmuring sound (in her husband's ear).'

The next Saṇskāra was 'Initiation' (Upanayana). Brāhmans underwent this at eight years of age, Kshatriyas at eleven, Vaiśyas at twelve, though it might be delayed to 16, 21, and 24 respectively. This and marriage were perhaps the most important of all the Saṇskāras. The nature of initiation could scarcely be inferred from its name, Upanayana, which simply means 'leading or bringing a boy to his Guru or spiritual preceptor.' But in real fact, until the boy was so brought, he could not be invested with the sacred thread, and until he was so invested he could not be reckoned among the 'twice-born,' and until he was spiritually regenerated by the act of investiture he could not be permitted to use a single

---

[1] The only apparent reason for reciting this Mantra at the Karṇa-vedha Saṇskāra is that the word *Karṇa* occurs in it.

prayer, or repeat the Veda, or engage in any single religious service or sacrificial rite. Nor was any ceremonial observance effectual unless the thread was worn. Indeed even in the present day a Brāhman before initiation has no right to any other name than Vipra. It is only when he has been invested with the sacred thread that he has a right to the title Dvi-ja, 'twice-born.' Nor ought the name Brāhman to be applied to him until the assumption of the thread has qualified him to learn the Veda (Brahmă) by heart.

If we inquire a little closely into the nature of the sacred symbol supposed to be capable of effecting so vast a transformation in a human being's condition, we find that now, as formerly, it consists of three slender cotton threads—white in colour to typify purity, and tied together in one spot by a sacred knot of peculiar construction (called *brahma-granthi*), each of the three threads also consisting of three finer threads tightly twisted into one. The construction of this cord is no doubt simple, but it must be borne in mind that the thread when formed is of no use unless blessed by Brāhmans and consecrated by the recitation of Vedic texts. The texts usually repeated during the process of arranging the threads are the Gāyatrī and certain other texts from the Black Yajur-veda. At the same time holy water is repeatedly sprinkled on the cord by means of Kuśa grass. So soon as the Hindū boy had been made regenerate by the solemn putting on of this mystic symbol his religious education and spiritual life really began. And now for the first time he was taught to repeat that remarkable Vedic prayer for illumination called Sāvitrī, or Gāyatrī (from Ṛig-veda III. 62. 10), thus translatable: 'Let us meditate on that excellent glory of the divine Vivifier, may he illumine our understandings,'—that most ancient of all Āryan prayers, which was first uttered more than three thousand years ago, and which still rises day by day towards heaven, incessantly ejaculated by millions of our Indian fellow-subjects. Then, again, every initiated boy was admitted to the privilege of reading and reciting other portions of the Veda. He was taught to pronounce the sacred syllable Om, the names of the seven worlds (Bhūr, Bhuvar, Svar, etc.), and other Vedic texts. He was furthermore required to learn by heart certain moral precepts taken from Manu or other Sanskṛit law-books, enjoining abstinence from injury to others, unselfishness, truth, honesty, chastity, and self-control (see Chap. XXI). The whole process of teaching him these various formularies was by some regarded as a separate Saṉskāra called Vedārambha-saṉskāra, or sometimes Vaidika upadeśa or Gāyatrī upadeśa. When he had been thus initiated he was for the first time permitted to perform other religious acts, such as the worship of gods, saints, spirits and ancestors, but these were generally deferred until, as a married man, he had a house of his own and was able to undertake a householder's duties.

According to Manu a Brāhman's life was properly to be divided into the four states or stages (called Āśramas) of 'unmarried religious student' (brahma-ćārī), 'married householder' (gṛihastha), 'anchorite' (vānaprastha), 'religious mendicant' (bhikshu) or 'abandoner of all worldly concerns' (sannyāsī). Hence on investiture with the sacred thread (p. 360) he had to leave his father and reside with a religious preceptor for several years as an unmarried student, till he had acquired a knowledge of the Veda, unless he took the vow of perpetual [naishṭhika] celibacy or of a life-long brahma-ćārī. On leaving his preceptor he performed the Saṉskāra called 'Return' (Samāvartana). This was formerly a solemn religious observance in which prayers were recited, ablutions performed, and gifts given to his spiritual teacher. After its celebration the youthful Brāhman returned to his father's house, and not till then was he supposed to take a wife and commence life as a householder. This proves that early marriages were not the rule in ancient times (compare p. 379). In real fact the next Saṉskāra, or Marriage (Vivāha), was not performed till a man and woman were able to live in a house of their own. According to Manu (IX. 90. 91), Gautama, Bodhāyana, and others, the postponement of marriage till three years after puberty is not sinful. The whole detail of the ancient marriage rite is given in the domestic rules (Gṛihya-sūtras) of Āśvalāyana, Gobhila, Pāraskara, and others. A wife was to be selected after proper inquiry as to family and condition. Before the marriage ceremony an oblation of clarified butter was to be offered in fire, with repetition of a Vedic text (Ṛig-veda V. 3. 2). The following are some particulars of the wedding ceremonial taken from Āśvalāyana (I. 7).

West of the sacred fire was placed a stone (for grinding corn and condiments such as is used by women in all households), and north-east a water-jar. The bridegroom offered an oblation, standing towards the west, and taking hold of the bride's hands, while she sat down and looked towards the east. If he wished only for sons he clasped her thumbs, and if for daughters the fingers alone. Then, whilst he led her towards the right three times round the fire and round the water-jar, he said in a low tone: 'I am male, thou art female; come; let us marry, let us possess offspring; united in affection, illustrious, well-disposed towards each other, let us live for a hundred years.' Every time he led her round he made her ascend the mill-stone, and said: 'Ascend thou this stone, be thou firm as a rock.' Then the bride's brother, after spreading melted butter on the joined palms of her hands, scattered parched grains of rice on them twice. Then, after pouring the oblation of butter on the fire, Vedic texts were recited (especially from Ṛig-veda X. 85[1]). Then the

[1] This is the Sūryā-sūkta, or well-known Marriage-hymn of the Ṛig-veda, translated by Prof. A. Weber in Ind. Studien, v. 177, etc., and discussed in full by Dr. Haas. In that hymn we have a description of the marriage of Sūryā daughter of the Sun to Soma (here probably personified as the Moon), whereas in Ṛig-veda IV. 43. 6 the two Aśvins are said to be Sūryā's husbands (compare p. 271). The Atharva-veda has also many marriage-hymns and texts (see I. 14, and many in Book XIV).

bridegroom unloosed the two braided tresses of hair, one on each side of the top of the bride's head, repeating the Vedic text: 'I loose thee from the fetters of Varuṇa with which the very auspicious Savitṛi has bound thee' (Ṛig-veda X. 85. 24). Then he caused her to step seven steps towards the north-east quarter, saying to her: 'Take thou one step for the acquirement of force; take thou two steps for strength; take thou three steps for the increase of wealth; take thou four steps for well-being; take thou five steps for offspring; take thou six steps for the seasons; take thou seven steps as a friend; be faithfully devoted to me; may we obtain many sons; may they attain to a good old age.' Then bringing both their heads into close juxtaposition, some one sprinkled them with water from the jar.

The fire used in the ceremonial was kindled by the friction of two pieces of sacred wood called Araṇī (Ṛig-veda VII. 1. 1), and this same fire which witnessed the union of the young couple was brought by them to their own home. There a room on the ground-floor was consecrated as a sanctuary for its reception and perpetual maintenance. Great reverence was shown to the fire so kindled. It was never blown upon with the mouth. Nothing impure was ever thrown into it, nor was it ever used for warming the feet (Manu IV. 53).

For what was the pious Brāhman's idea of fire? Two texts of the Ṛig-veda assert that the Supreme Being developed the whole order of existing entities (*ṛitaṃ-ća satyaṃ-ća*) through the operation of heat. Another verse of the Ṛig-veda says: 'All gods are comprehended in fire' (V. 3. 1); 'He surrounds them all as the circumference of a wheel does the spokes' (V. 13. 6). In fact, fire was to a Hindū a visible embodiment not only of heat but of all the other forces of nature. It had three forms, as fire on earth, as lightning—associated with rain and water—in the air, as the sun in the heavens. And yet these three forms were often regarded as comprehended in the one form of earthly fire (see p. 16). Hence fire was not merely a symbol of the Supreme Being's presence among men. It was an emblem of His creative, fostering, and disintegrating energies, a type of His three eternal attributes, Life, Thought, and Joy.

The Sun, too, as fire in the Heaven, had a triune aspect. It was called the 'three-stepped' (tri-vikrama). It differed in its attributes and qualities as the morning, the mid-day, and the evening sun (see p. 342). It was adored every day in the oft-repeated Gāyatrī prayer, which was in three measures, though all three measures were connected in sense. And yet there were not three Suns worshipped, but only three forms of one Sun.

The Sun, however, was inaccessible and not always visible. Fire could always be maintained, or, if extinguished, could be rekindled whenever religious rites were performed. As a general rule the householder was content with kindling the sacred fire in a single hearth or circular clay receptacle. This was called the Gṛihyāgni, 'household fire,' and was sufficient for all domestic ceremonies (smārta-karman). Those however who were more pious, or who wished to engage in Vedic sacrificial rites (śrauta-karman) which were of a more complicated character, took care to construct a more elaborate Homa-śālā, or room for fire-sacrifices, on the ground-floor. In that sanctuary fire was kindled in three differently-shaped receptacles, the fire in each having a different name (*Āhavanīya*, *Gārhapatya*, and *Dakshiṇa*). When the sacred fire was thus lighted it was regarded as a symbol of God present in the house,—as the 'brilliant guest' who lived in the midst of the family (Ṛig-veda X. 91. 2), the divine mediator who bore the savour of daily offerings towards heaven, the golden link of union between men on earth and the celestial denizens of air and sky.

Every morning and evening the head of the family, with his wife and children, went together into the room dedicated to worship [1]. There they seated themselves around the sacred hearth, saying: 'We approach thee, O fire, daily both morning and evening, with reverential adoration in our thoughts.' Then they fed the sacred fire [2] with pieces of consecrated wood (samidh), generally taken from the Palāśa tree, and with offerings of rice and butter, eating portions of this offering themselves. The oblation thus cast into the flame was supposed to ascend to the Sun. 'From the Sun,' says Manu, 'it falls again in rain, from rain comes food, and from food animals subsist' (III. 76). Then while they fed the fire they chanted hymns; they sang the glories of their divine guest, calling him Father, King, Protector, Illuminator of truth. They spoke of his subtle essence, of his universal presence in all nature, in water, in plants, in the bodies of men and animals. They prayed for forgiveness, saying:—

> Deliver, mighty lord, thy worshippers,
> Purge us from taint of sin, and when we die,
> Deal mercifully with us on the pyre,
> Burning our bodies with their load of guilt,
> But bearing our eternal part on high
> To luminous abodes and realms of bliss,
> For ever there to dwell with righteous men.

They prayed also for prosperity in their worldly affairs, and, if they were soldiers, for warlike sons and success in battle, saying: 'Be ever present with us, O God of fire, for our good [3].'

And here observe that as every religious idea was exaggerated by Brāhmanism, so it was not enough for a pious Hindū to be born twice during his earthly career. Even when regenerated by the sacred thread, he was held to be

---

[1] In Manu IX. 96 we read that religious rites are ordained in the Veda to be performed by the husband together with the wife.

[2] This was called the Homa Sacrifice. In the intervals of feeding the flame the fire was allowed to smoulder.

[3] Mr. M. M. Kunte has given a good account of ancient family fire-worship in his Shaḍ-darśana-ćintanikā, and many of my statements in this chapter are based on his authority. For the Vedic texts used in the worship of Fire and here paraphrased, see Muir's Texts, v. 197–220, 303–305, and my Indian Wisdom, p. 18.

again regenerated by his performance of the Homa or daily sacrifice to fire. Manu says: 'The first birth is from the natural mother, the second from the sacred thread, the third from due performance of the sacrifice' (II. 169).

Of course, it was most important to keep the smouldering embers of the sacred element perpetually burning. If through any accident the flame was extinguished, the whole household fell into confusion. Everything went wrong until an expiatory ceremony (prāyaśćitta)—sometimes consisting of a solemn fast observed by both husband and wife—had been performed, and the fire was rekindled.

And this daily service was not all. Every fourteenth day was to every pious and orthodox Hindū a high and holy day. It was set apart for special religious observances. Every new-moon day (darśa) and every full-moon day (paurṇamāsa) the head of the family—whatever his rank or occupation—laid them both aside. Clad in humble attire and accompanied by his wife, he went into the woods. There he collected fuel (samidh) and sacred sacrificial grass, placed them on his head, carried them home, and made preparation for the solemn fortnightly ceremonial. First he consecrated the fuel, constructed seats and a kind of broom out of the grass, spread deer-skins, and arranged the sacrificial instruments, made of a particular kind of wood (*khadira* or *śamī*), on the domestic altar. Then, with the assistance of his wife, he prepared the sacrificial cake. Having consecrated a certain quantity of rice—called *nirvāpa*—and pounded it in a mortar with a proper pestle, he kneaded the flour with his own hands into a ball. This was laid on eight fragments of brick (*kapāla*), taken up in a particular order, and placed in a circle on the fire. The ball of flour was then shaped into a rounded sacrificial cake (*puro-ḍāśa*) resembling the back of a tortoise, and, when baked, taken off the fire. Clarified butter was next poured by means of wooden ladles five times into the fire—such oblations being called the *pañća-prayāga*—and other oblations of butter—called Ājya—were made to various gods. The consecrated cake was then cut up, and the pieces (*avadāna*) were sprinkled with butter and thrown into the flames in the name of various deities, including the god of fire himself. Other portions were also reverently eaten by the assembled family, hymns were chanted, the sins of the past fortnight confessed, repentance expressed, and forgiveness asked. The whole ceremonial was not always performed by husband and wife alone. If they were rich they sent for regularly ordained priests—generally four in number—who kindled fire from two pieces of sacred wood (araṇī) by friction, and carried out the detail of the ritual with great elaboration and with all the sacrificial implements—including a sacred sword for keeping off demons—and, of course, with greater merit to the householder.

Then every four months another ceremony, called the Ćāturmāsya sacrifice, was performed at the beginning of the three seasons. Probably this was solemnized, like a harvest-thanksgiving, in gratitude for the fruits of the earth, gathered in at the end of the three seasons of summer, autumn, and winter. It was conducted with as much solemnity as the fortnightly rite, and in much the same manner. Another special sacrificial ceremony on a grander scale, with the addition of animal sacrifice (Manu IV. 26, VI. 10), was usually performed half-yearly at the summer and winter solstice (*uttarāyaṇa, dakshiṇāyana*).

Finally, every householder instituted once a year a Soma-sacrifice (Jyotishṭoma), when the first hymns, called Pavamāna, from Maṇḍala IX. of the Ṛig-veda (beginning Svādishṭhayā Madishṭhayā) were recited. This was a ceremony requiring at least sixteen different priests, who were well paid for its effective celebration. The simplest annual Soma-sacrifice, called *Agnishṭoma*, lasted for five days. Others were protracted for weeks and months, and there were even sacrificial sessions (*sattra*) which lasted for years. And in these public rites—

usually called *Śrauta-karman*, to distinguish them from *Smārta-karman*, or domestic rites—two entirely new elements were introduced; first the flesh of slaughtered animals, and secondly the juice of the Soma plant mentioned before (pp. 12; 13; 22; 332). At one time all kinds of animals were sacrificed, as, for example, horses (see p. 329), but in the end a goat was usually selected. Parts of the flesh were burned as offerings to the gods, and parts were eaten by the priests.

But the great central act of the whole ceremony was the presentation of the exhilarating Soma-juice to the gods, some of it being poured out for the deities and some being drunk by the performers and institutors of the sacrifice. This was done on the fifth day at the morning, midday, and evening libations (*savana*). In fact the animal sacrifice, though it preceded the Soma-libation, was really subordinate to it. The idea seems to have been that the sacrificer killed the animal instead of sacrificing himself; and as the body of the animal when sacrificed in the fire was borne upwards to the gods, so did the sacrificer—represented by the animal—ascend to the skies. It was only after he had been thus admitted to the society of the gods in heaven that he became fit to quaff the divine beverage, and to become one with the heavenly king Soma himself.

Indeed this purifying and invigorating juice, supposed to confer physical strength and to make the heart of men and gods glad, came to be regarded as the water of life—the nectar which purified body and soul and conferred immortality. It was then itself personified and deified. The god Soma was the Bacchus of India, and the fermented juice of the Soma plant was in ancient times to the Indian community very much what the juice of the grape was to the Greeks and Romans (compare p. 12). Happily for Indian households, the drinking of stimulating liquor has never been permitted except at special religious ceremonials.

CHAPTER XIV.

The Hindū Religion in Modern Family-life.

TURN we now to the daily life of the modern householder. And what I shall have to say will refer mainly to the castes corresponding to Brāhmans, Kshatriyas, and Vaiśyas[1] who alone have a right to the title 'twice-born,' and to go through the Sanskāras supposed to purify the child from the taint contracted in the womb. It will be seen that Hindūism is still an affair of minute ceremonial and elaborate purificatory rites, yet without any central ecclesiastical authority having power to enforce or regulate their application.

Of the twelve Sanskāras only a few remain in force. Passing over the first four, which have now fallen into desuetude, we come to the Name-giving ceremony (Nāma-karaṇa), performed about the tenth or twelfth day after birth.

It is worth while to take note here of a superstitious idea which prevails very generally throughout India, that on the sixth day after birth the Creator writes the child's future destiny on its forehead. Yet I know of no special ceremony instituted to mark this particular day, or to propitiate the deity on so momentous an occasion.

With regard to the present custom of Name-giving, the ceremony is performed in some parts of India on the day when the child is first fed with a little rice. Then to secure good fortune a boy is usually called after some favourite god (ishṭa-devatā)[2]; for example, Kṛishṇa, Gopāla,

---

[1] These are Manu's three chief castes. The Brāhmaṇs claim to be the only pure one left. See pp. 53, 452 of this volume.

[2] But not so usually in former days. Witness such names as Pāṇini, Patañjali, Śaunaka, Āśvalāyana, etc.

(Gopāl), Rāma, Rāma-ćandra, Nārāyaṇa, Śiva, Śaṅkara[1], Gaṇeśa ; or the name may indicate that he is to be the god's servant, as, for instance, Rāma-dāsa (Rām-dās), Kṛishṇa-dāsa, Nārāyaṇa-dāsa (Nārāyan-dās), Lakshmī-dāsa. Often the honorific affix Jī (probably thought to be auspicious as derived from either the root jīv, 'to live,' or ji, 'to conquer') is added to the name, as in Rāma-jī (Rām-jī), Śiva-jī, Deva-jī. Ćandra, the moon—corrupted into Ćandar and Ćand—is believed to bring good luck when used in a name (Motī-ćand, etc.).

Again, in the present day as in ancient times, the names of girls, like those of boys, are often taken from those of goddesses, such as Lakshmī, Durgā, Sītā, Rādhā ; or from celebrated women, such as Sāvitrī, Yaśodā, Subhadrā, Sumaṅgalā ; or from rivers, such as Gaṅgā, Yamunā, Bhāgīrathī, Godāvarī, Narmadā, Kṛishṇā ; or from jewels, such as Mānak (for Sanskṛit Māṇikya), a ruby ; Motī (Sanskṛit Muktā), a pearl ; Rattan (Sanskṛit ratna), a precious stone ; Maṇi, a gem ; or from flowers, such as Padma, a lily ; Phulli, a blossom ; or from words like Sundarī, beautiful ; Prema, love, etc.

It is often considered unlucky, and not unlikely to bring down a judgment on a child, if the name it receives is indicative of any good quality it may happen to possess at birth. Therefore it is not uncommon for a fair child to be called 'Black' (Kṛishṇa). Moreover, a parent will sometimes give an infant an ugly or inauspicious name from a superstitious fear that the child's beauty may excite the envious glances or 'evil eye' of malicious persons ; for it is remarkable that when a family has suffered early bereavements by death these are attributed to evil influences exerted through the instrumentality of the human eye (see p. 253).

As a general rule, the name given on the tenth day is only that by which the child is commonly known and addressed

---

[1] Narmadā-śaṅkar is the name of a celebrated living Gujarātī poet.

in conversation. But the infant often receives a second or private name, which is considered to be its real name, and is whispered inaudibly by its parent or the family preceptor (guru), and not revealed to others. The idea is that a man's name is in some mysterious manner connected with his personality, and the object of concealing it is to protect him from the power of sorcerers, who are unable to injure him by their enchantments unless they know and can pronounce his real name[1].

I ought to mention, too, that besides the common name and the secret name, another is generally added which may be called the astrological name, because it contains a letter from the name of the constellation (nakshatra) under which the child was born. It is well known that nothing of importance is done by a true Hindū without consulting the stars. Therefore soon after the Name-giving ceremony has been performed the family Astrologer (Jyotisha, corrupted into Jyoshī or Joshī) is sent for and commissioned to draw up a horoscope of the exact time of the child's nativity, the constellation under which it was born, with a prophecy of the duration of its life, and the circumstances, good or evil, of its probable career. This is called the birth-record (Janma-patra). It is always written in Sanskṛit, and, if the parents are rich, sometimes on a roll sixty yards long, takes three or four months to prepare, and costs a large sum of money. The name given in the horoscope is the Nakshatra name, and not the one given at the Name-giving ceremony. For example, if the child's common name is Yādava Ćandra Ghosh, this name is not mentioned in the horoscope, but a different name is given, such, for example, as Raghu-nātha,

---

[1] It is well known that no wife in India likes to utter her husband's name. According to Sir J. Lubbock a Sumatran scrupulously abstains from pronouncing his own name, and a similar superstition prevails among the Negroes, Abyssinians, and Australians.

or Hari-hara[1]. I subjoin a translation of part of a genuine Janma-patra or horoscope[2]:—

Adoration to the Sun. May the Sun and all other planets and stars and constellations prolong the life of him for whom this horoscope is prepared. Let that series of characters which is written by the Disposer of all things on the forehead of the child, and which is another name for Astrology, be seen clearly by eyes purified by the same science. May good fortune smile on the instant which came to pass after 1784 years, 7 months, 26 days, 22 daṇḍas, and 27 palas of the era styled the Sakābda had passed away, or after 1269 years, 7 months, 26 days, 22 daṇḍas, and 27 palas of the era styled the Sana had passed away.

First, the measure of the day of birth is 26 daṇḍas, 35 palas, 0 vipala, and of the night is 33 daṇḍas, 25 palas, 0 vipala; of half the day, 13 daṇḍas, 17 palas, 30 vipalas, and of half the night 16 daṇḍas, 42 palas, 30 vipalas; of a fourth part of the day, 6 daṇḍas, 38 palas, 45 vipalas; and of a fourth part of the night 8 daṇḍas, 12 palas, 15 vipalas; of an eighth part of the day, 3 daṇḍas, 19 palas, 22 vipalas; and of an eighth part of the night 4 daṇḍas, 10 palas, 37 vipalas.

The moment of his birth being next after the 27th pala, after the 22nd daṇḍa of the day, the child was born in that eighth part of the day which was presided over by the planet Śukra (Venus), and in that daṇḍa of the day which was presided over by Rāhu, and consequently the aspect of Rāhu was then not such that it could have had its position in the same degree with the constellation of the child's birth or with any of the coordinate constellations (compare p. 345).

At the instant following the 27th pala, after 22 daṇḍas of the 27th day of the solar month of Āgrahāyaṇa, being a Thursday and the 5th day of the fortnight succeeding the full moon, in that lagna or period during which the constellation Aries was visible in the sky, and which was ruled over by Mars, in that half of the lagna which was guarded by the Moon, and in that 3rd part of the lagna which was governed by Jupiter, etc., the second son of * * * * * was born under the star Aśleshā, and when the moon had revolved to the constellation Cancer.

The child, who will live a long life and be capable of attaining to great prosperity, belongs to the Devāri-gaṇa or demon class, and to the Vipra-varṇa or Brāhman caste, and his astrological name is Harihara Devaśarmā. To him doth this horoscope of happy results belong.

As the deity presiding over his birth-lagna is propitious, the child will

---

[1] The Rev. Nehemiah Goreh (a converted Brāhman) told me that each Nakshatra or constellation has four divisions, and that he was born under the third, in which the letter *r* occurs. Hence his Nakshatra name was Raghu-nātha. It might just as well have been Rāma or any name in which the letter *R* occurs.

[2] The late Mr. Woodrow, Inspector of Schools, is my authority here.

turn out to be a person of a good disposition and a favourite of fortune, he shall beget many sons, and have ample dwelling-places, enjoy pleasures, and possess gems of various descriptions.

Now are to be described the planetary periods according to the birth-star of the child. He was born under the star of Aśleshā, and hence 2 years 4 months and 18 days of the lunar period were passed, and 1 year 4 months and 12 days of the same remained, at the date of the child's birth. The result of this shall be the gain of clothes by the boy. The age of the boy will be 1 year 4 months 12 days at the expiration of the period of the Moon; 9 years 4 months 12 days at the expiration of the period of Mars, which is 8 years; 26 years 4 months 12 days at the expiration of the period of Mercury, which is 17 years; 36 years 4 months 12 days at the expiration of the period of Saturn, which is 10 years; 55 years 4 months 12 days at the expiration of the period of Jupiter, which is 19 years; 67 years 4 months 12 days at the expiration of the period of the Earth's shadow, which is 12 years; 88 years 4 months 12 days at the expiration of the period of Venus, which is 21 years.

With regard to the right of tonsure or shaving described at p. 359, it is to be observed that in modern times rich people are shaved every day, ordinary people once a week, poor people once a fortnight. No one, as a general rule, shaves himself, or even cuts his own nails. Both these necessary acts are performed by a caste of barbers (nāpita), and ought not to be carried on in a room, for the simple reason that fragments of hair and nail-parings are supposed to cause pollution. The operation is usually conducted under a shed or tree, or in an open verandah or street. Numbers of barbers may be seen plying their occupation every morning outside the houses of a native town.

In former days, as we have seen, a Brāhman had to part with all his hair except a tuft at the top of his head, this top-knot (śikhā) and the sacred thread being the two chief badges of Brāhmanhood. Only when he became a Sannyāsī (see p. 362) was he allowed to dispense with these two badges.

In the present day few persons, except Brāhmans of the strictest orthodoxy, allow themselves to be reduced to a single tuft on the top of their heads; but every respectable Hindū who has reached puberty gets rid of the hair on his face[1] (except his mustaches), unless he is an ascetic[2], or has taken some other religious vow, or belongs to the very lowest castes. It should also be noted that special religious shavings are performed at sacred places of pilgrimage on the banks of rivers, and are held to be very efficacious in purifying soul and body from pollution. Persons who have committed great crimes or are troubled by uneasy consciences, travel hundreds of miles to Prayāga (Allahābād), Mathurā (Muttra), or other holy places for the sole purpose of submitting themselves to the tonsorial skill of the professional barbers who frequent such localities. There they may be released from every sin by first being relieved of every hair and then plunging into the sacred stream. Forthwith they emerge new creatures, with all the accumulated guilt of a long life effaced.

Women, on the other hand, are most careful to preserve their hair intact. They pride themselves on its length and weight. For a woman to have to part with her hair is one of the greatest of degradations, and the most terrible of all trials. It is the mark of widowhood. Yet in some sacred places, especially at the confluence of rivers, the cutting off and offering of a few locks of hair (Veṇī-dānam) by a virtuous wife is considered a highly meritorious act.

A Brāhman gentleman of high rank in India once described to me how he had taken his wife for the performance of this ceremonial to Prayāga, which, as the point of meeting of the Ganges and Jumnā, is regarded as one of the holiest places of pilgrimage in India. She was escorted to the banks of the river by a troop of priests—there called Prayāgwāl—carrying cocoa-nuts, areca-nuts, flowers, kuṅkuma, etc. At the confluence she was made to sit down and offer worship (pūjā) to the

---

[1] This, in most parts of India, is one point of distinction between Hindūs and Muḥammadans, whose former hatred of each other made them adopt opposite practices out of mere antagonism.

[2] Some Sannyāsīs allow all their hair to grow, some shave it all off, including the Śikhā. These latter are the most orthodox.

Ganges. Then one of the priests recited certain texts and prayers from the Veda, and holding a pair of golden scissors in his hand cut off about two inches of her long hair. The locks thus severed were deposited as a precious offering in a costly metal vessel, but not without the addition of five rupees to make the gift more acceptable. Then the husband, in ratification of the ceremony, poured water into the hand of the priest, who thereupon took the money for himself and cast the locks of hair into the river. The shorn woman regarded this presentation of her precious locks to the river-goddess as a great privilege, for it can only be performed by a devoted wife who is living virtuously with her husband, and only in his presence.

I may observe here that if a really orthodox Hindū woman ever loses her hair or becomes partially bald from sickness or any other cause she never resorts to the artifice of using false hair. She would consider herself eternally defiled and condemned to prolonged suffering in a future state of existence by such an act.

It may be mentioned in connection with the religious duty of shaving that daily teeth-cleaning is also regarded as a religious act partaking of the nature of a ceremonial observance. It is performed, like shaving, in the open air. Any one who passes through a native village in the early morning may see a large proportion of its population engaged in the serious duty of cleansing their teeth. The instrument used is a twig or small stick. After its application to the teeth the twig serves the purpose of cleaning the tongue—another important duty. It is never used a second time, but always thrown away. No words can express the abhorrence with which a strict Hindū regards the European practice of using a tooth-brush a second time. Saliva is of all things the most utterly polluting.

Ear-boring is also a religious ceremony. Girls have their ears bored about the same age as boys (see p. 360), but often have three perforations made in each ear, besides one in the left nostril. Nose-rings are universal among women in all parts of India. Even boys in some places have one nostril bored, but this is an exceptional circumstance.

The ceremony of betrothal (vāg-dāna) generally succeeds tonsure and ear-boring, but is not reckoned among the Saṉskāras. In India a parent's first thought for its child is not for its health—not for its wealth—not for its physical, moral or mental well-being—but for its betrothal and marriage. To look out for a child's future wife, to lay by money for the cost of the nuptial festivities, to fee and conciliate the priests who promote the match—these are far more important duties than to make arrangements for a boy's proper education. When a boy attains the age of five his father deputes a professional match-maker (Ghaṭaka) to negotiate a promise of marriage with the daughter of a man of at least equal caste. It must be admitted that caste-equality in India is regarded as a more important requisite than riches. Money is quite a secondary consideration. Nor is character so important. In some parts of Northern India the match-maker for some castes is the family barber; but for the higher castes he is more generally a Brāhman, who goes about from one house to another till he discovers a baby-girl of suitable rank. Forthwith he reports to one of the parents that the young lady has all her members complete—the full number of eyes, teeth, fingers and toes—and to the other that the young gentleman is equally perfect in every particular. Next, he brings the two parents together. Genealogies are investigated, and pedigrees certified. Then the boy and girl are solemnly betrothed. This is called in Sanskṛit *vāg-dāna*, and in Hindūstānī *nisbat*.

The important Saṉskāra of initiation (upanayana) into the Brāhmanical religion by investiture with the sacred thread is restricted to the castes corresponding to Brāhmans, Kshatriyas, and Vaiśyas (p. 360). Once invested with this hallowed symbol of second birth, the twice-born man never parts with it. In this respect he has an advantage over his Christian brother. For the latter is admitted into the Church by a single ceremony performed in his infancy, and brought to his recollection by one other ceremony only; whereas the Indian twice-born man has a sacred symbol always in contact with his person, which must always be worn and its position changed during the performance of his daily religious services, constantly reminding him of his regenerate condition, and with its three white threads, united by a sacred knot, perpetually setting before him a typical representation of what may be called the triads of the Hindū religion. For example, it is probable that the triple form of the sacred thread symbolizes that the Supreme Being is Existence, Thought, and Joy (p. 34); that He has been manifested in three forms as Creator, Preserver, and Disintegrator of all material things; that He pervades the three worlds, Earth, Air, and Heaven; that He has revealed His will in three principal books called the Ṛig, Yajur, and Sāma Vedas, with other similar dogmas of the Hindū system in which the sacred number three constantly recurs. I have heard a Brāhman described as the greatest of all ritualists. This is true in regard to the multiplicity of rites which he ought to perform. But his ritualism in the present day is confined to private worship and domestic ceremonies, and his ritualistic vestments are restricted to the sacred coil of cotton thread, the name of which (yajñopavīta) denotes that it is put on (upavīta) during the performance of devotional rites (yajña). And just as a Roman Catholic priest changes his ecclesiastical vestments according to variations in his own ceremonial, so the Brāhman alters the position of his thread. For example, when he worships the gods he puts it over his left shoulder and under his right, being then called Upavītī; when he worships his departed ancestors he suspends it over his right shoulder and under his left, being then called Prāćīnāvītī; and when he worships the saints he hangs it round his neck like a long necklace, being then called Nivītī. It would be premature to pursue the subject of domestic worship until we have given some account of

Marriage Ceremonies.

We have seen (p. 362) that in ancient times the young Brāhman, after his initiation, left his father's house and resided for several years as an unmarried student with a religious preceptor. At present a boy's initiation is followed immediately afterwards by a mere formal performance of the rite called 'Return' (Samāvartana, p. 362), and generally, after a day or two's interval, by the ceremony of marriage. That is, he is made, while still a boy at the age of about nine or ten and before he is really marriageable, to go through the second matrimonial act with a girl of about seven, his previous betrothal having constituted the first, and cohabitation at the age of fifteen or sixteen with his child-wife at the age of twelve (but see note, p. 387) constituting the third. In fact, a Hindū marriage is a kind of drama in three acts. But the second is the religious and legal ceremony, and is a most tedious process, involving large fees to the priests and festivities prolonged for many days, at a cost, in the case of rich people, of perhaps 100,000 rupees. Often the savings of a whole lifetime are so spent. This is one of the greatest evils of Indian society. Every well-to-do parent is compelled to squander large sums on mere idlers and pleasure-seekers, instead of giving the money as a grant in aid to the newly-married pair on first starting in life. He knows, in fact, that if he were to allow the wedding to be conducted with an eye to economy he would sink irretrievably in the estimation of his friends and caste-fellows. He would never be able to hold up his head again in his own social circle. Nor must it be supposed that he spends his money unwillingly. On the contrary, the more lavishly he spends the more pride and satisfaction he afterwards feels in looking back on what he regards as the most meritorious act of his life [1].

As to the two persons chiefly concerned in a wedding, their wishes are never consulted about any of the arrangements. Yet it is thought highly important to consult the stars. A wedding ought never to take place except in a fortunate month and during fortunate days. The most favourable time is believed to be in spring—that is in the three or four months from February to April and May. The months generally chosen are Māgha, Phālguna, and Vaiśākha [2]. It is out of the power of any European, to whom the inner apartments of Indian households are forbidden ground, to give a complete description of the entire marriage ceremonial. The more ancient form has already been described at p. 363. The modern ceremonies—which last for many days—are marked by many similar acts, and especially by the following essential features: the night procession of the bridegroom to the house of the bride, tying the vestments of bride and bridegroom together with a piece of consecrated cloth under which their hands are joined, winding a cord round their necks, marking their faces with paint, making them walk three times round the sacred fire, each time in seven steps [3], with repetition of prayers and Vedic texts. Noisy music during some part of the ceremony is held to be essential. In fact no one in India would believe in the validity of a marriage ceremony conducted without loud and often uproarious festivities. For it is a common idea, which no contact with European habits of thought has yet eradicated, that the efficacy of religious services is greatly enhanced by noise.

Every sort of deafening musical instrument is brought into

---

[1] In one way the expense of marriages acts beneficially; for although it is lawful for a Hindū to have more than one wife, scarcely any one can afford to do so.

[2] In some parts of India Ćaitra is avoided.

[3] This part of the ceremony is called the Sapta-padī, and generally comes last (see p. 364).

requisition. Players on trumpets, horns, pipes, and drums are eagerly sought for, and every performer seems intent on overpowering the sounds produced by his fellow performers, as if his musical reputation depended on his being heard above the general din.

In the higher circles of Indian society the wedding entertainments, often repeated for several days, are on a magnificent scale, and when Europeans are invited every kind of expensive luxury is provided for them.

Soon after my arrival at Bombay in 1875 I was invited to be present at the wedding of Sir Maṅgaldās Nathoobhāī's two sons. The festivities and religious ceremonies lasted for eight days, and were on a scale of unusual magnificence. Such a wedding is rarely witnessed even in India. The residence of Sir Maṅgaldās was called Girgaum House—a magnificent mansion in the middle of a large garden. When we arrived at eight o'clock in the evening of the first day of the ceremonies, both house and garden were brilliantly illuminated—all the trees festooned with Chinese lanterns, all the lines of the architecture sparkling with light, and every bed and fountain in the garden encircled with thousands of coloured lamps. A splendid drawing-room blazing with light was thronged with native gentlemen and Rājās, most of whom sat round in a double row, intently gazing at the movements and listening to the songs of two jewel-bedecked Nāch girls. These girls wore bright-coloured silk trousers and were decorously enveloped in voluminous folds of drapery. They did not really dance, but merely sang in a monotonous minor key with continuous trills and turns of the voice, while they waved their arms gracefully to and fro, occasionally lifting one hand to the ear, and frequently advancing a few steps up the room and then retiring again, closely followed from behind by two or three musicians who played accompaniments on instruments called Sāraṅgī and Tabla (tom-toms). The loves, quarrels, and reconciliations of Kṛishṇa and his wives, especially his wife Rādhā, formed the subject of their songs, which were kept up incessantly for hours, no native spectators appearing to find them tedious. I was told that a fee of 1000 rupees is sometimes paid to a first-rate Nāch girl for one night's performance.

The European guests congregated in the balcony. From that vantage ground we looked down on a sea of turbaned heads and coloured dresses, brilliantly lighted up and set off by a glorious background of cocoa-nut palms, tropical plants, and trees in full foliage. It was like a fairy scene on enchanted ground, and our host, with his high hat and spotless white dress, might have been taken for the magician by whose art the marvellous spectacle had been conjured up before us.

A more human exhibition of his power followed, when, after garlanding us himself with jasmine wreaths, he beckoned to his servants, who feasted us with iced champagne, and presented every European visitor with bouquets of roses sprinkled with rose-water. Then we were all formally introduced to the two bridegrooms, whose ages were about twenty and eighteen —for our host was too enlightened a man to allow his sons to marry when mere children — the brides, respectively aged fourteen and twelve, being carefully kept out of sight.

On the fourth evening, when we were again invited, there was a still greater assemblage of people. On our arrival a vast multitude were preparing to accompany the night-procession to the houses of the brides. Again the whole garden was illuminated. Again it was crowded with visitors, or rather on this occasion literally alive and resonant with an excited throng of about 5000 people, who surged like a roaring ocean, while four bands of music struck up different tunes in different parts of the grounds, and the same Nāch girls entertained the guests in the drawing-room.

Then the procession gradually formed to conduct the bridegrooms to the houses of the brides. The two bridegrooms in superb dresses of gold tissue, with high jewelled hats—each of which was said to be worth two or three thousand pounds—and necklaces of emeralds and diamonds, were placed on richly caparisoned horses covered with white flowers. Crimson umbrellas were held over their heads, and silver fans waved near them. About 3000 native gentlemen and 1000 ladies—Hindū and Pārsī—in brilliant coloured dresses, closely packed and all talking and singing together, formed themselves into a procession, while the bands led the way. The men went first, then came the mounted bridegrooms, then two ladies carrying lanterns, and then the whole crowd of ladies followed.

We European guests wound up the procession in carriages. At length we alighted and threaded our way through a lane made for us into a large tent, where we found all the ladies, gorgeously arrayed, and squatting, in what to us appeared rather unladylike positions, on the ground around the youngest of the bridegrooms, who was also squatting in their midst. The crushing, jostling, and heat were intense, and the talking, joking, and excitement quite bewildering. Meanwhile one of the brides was brought in and made to sit down on the ground in front of the bridegroom. She was carried in the arms of her uncle, her head and face closely veiled, and covered with a deep red and yellow silk shawl of great value.

Leaving this curious scene before it was concluded, we were taken through the crush of people to the top of a gallery, whence we viewed another stage of the marriage ceremony. This took place under another canopy equally crammed with people. The crowd here was in a fever of excitement waiting for the appearance of the elder bridegroom, who ought to have been received by his mother-in-law. This however was impossible, as she was a widow. Another lady, therefore, came forward on his entrance and made a red mark on his forehead. Next a number of Brāhmans, after placing the bridegroom on a stool, proceeded to worship the god Gaṇeśa—the god who, as we have seen (p. 216), defends every undertaking from the lets and hindrances caused by evil demons. Sacred texts were also repeated, or rather muttered in an inaudible tone. Then preparations were made for receiving the bride, who was brought in by her maternal uncle and placed on a stool opposite the bridegroom. Her face was of course completely veiled, and her body kept bent, in token, I presume, of maidenly modesty and feminine humility.

At the same time two officiating priests squatted down on one side of the pair, and the acting mother and father-in-law on the other side.

The principal religious ceremony now began. First of all, one of the Brāhmans took a piece of consecrated cloth and fastened one end of it to the bridegroom's dress and the other to that of the bride. Next the hands of the bridegroom and bride were joined together and crossed under this cloth, and two ladies made marks with red paint on their faces and threw garlands of flowers round their shoulders. After this, one of the priests took a sacred cord and wound it round the necks of bride and bridegroom, joining them thus together while muttering prayers and Vedic texts (see p. 363, note). Then the bridegroom's hands were placed in milk. Sundry sprinklings of red powder, rice grains, cocoa-nut milk, and water followed. The remainder of the ceremony was very complicated and tedious, and we were not allowed to witness it all.

The bridegroom and bride were, I believe, taken to another room, where more red marks were applied and money presented by the bridegroom. Then they were brought back to the tent, where earthen pots were placed at the four corners and a consecrated fire lighted. Afterwards the bride and bridegroom walked four times round the tent hand in hand. Then the bridegroom put his arm round the bride's neck, and threw barley, betel-nuts, and oil-seeds into the consecrated fire, the Brāhmans at the same time throwing in ghee, while the pair walked three times round the sacred flames, each time in seven steps as in the ancient ceremony (see p. 364).

It is easy from all this to see that some portions of the ceremonial are little changed since the time of Āśvalāyana (see p. 363), whose collection of rules (sūtras) was probably composed about 2500 years ago.

About midnight, when the whole day's ritual was brought to a close, the bride and bridegroom played together at a kind of game like that known among schoolboys as odd and even, money being used instead of marbles. More ceremonies followed on the succeeding days, till on the eighth day the bride and bridegroom went together to the temple of Lakshmī (Mahā-lakshmī), near Bombay, and worshipped the goddess of Prosperity there. This was the grand finale. The two brides then followed their husbands, and took up their abode in the house of their father-in-law. The sums spent on the festivities must have been enormous.

This remarkable marriage of two young men of high rank at the respective ages of 18 and 20 was quite an exceptional occurrence. The legal ceremony is generally performed eight or ten years earlier. It must not, however, be supposed that, when a boy is thus married in childhood, he therefore begins life early as a householder on his own account. His first lessons in reading and writing probably commenced at the time of his betrothal. When he has been made at the age of 9 or 10, or a little later, to undergo the ceremony of marriage, he is old enough to understand that he must commence learning in earnest. His boyish education is therefore carried on till he and his wife have attained puberty (generally at the age of 15 or 16 in the case of the boy and 11 or 12 in the case of the girl). Then comes the third and concluding matrimonial act, when he lives with his wife as her actual husband (see note, p. 387).

Even then his education is by no means ended. He is still a mere schoolboy or collegian residing at home with his parents, and continuing to do so long after he has children of his own. I have not unfrequently examined the senior classes at Indian High Schools and Colleges in which most of the boys have been fathers.

And here it should be mentioned that in Brāhman families of the present day a boy's parents may choose for him either a religious or secular career. Brāhmans, we know, are not necessarily priests, but simply a class of men divided, like ourselves, into two great divisions of clergy (sometimes designated by the general term Bhikshukas) and laity (Gṛihasthas[1]). The clergy may be family priests (purohita) who perform the Saṇskāra ceremonies, but are often very ignorant, or they may be spiritual teachers (Gurus) who teach the mantras and prayers, or they may be men trained in sacred learning. These become either Vaidik priests and are sent to special schools where they are trained in Vedic lore and ritual by Vaidik and Yājñika priests, or they may be sent to native schools of another sort, where they learn either grammar (vyākaraṇa) or philosophy, and become Śāstrīs or Pandits. Those who are taught grammar also read the poems (kāvyas). Those who are trained in philosophy usually confine themselves to the Vedānta and Nyāya systems. These and the Vaidik Brāhmans[2] generally become bigoted members of the clerical order.

As to the laity, or Gṛihasthas, they either go to native institutions for secular education, or to some of the numerous schools, high schools, and colleges established by us. Here they learn English, study Shakspeare, Milton, Tennyson, etc. instead of their own literatures, and aspire to become themselves writers of English, and even of English poetry.

---

[1] The term Gṛihastha ought properly to be restricted to 'a married man and householder,' but is now applied generally to those Brāhmans who do not live by priestly work, but by some worldly business, such as that of a clerk, etc.

[2] With regard to the Vaidik Brāhmans, it should be noted that they have really little to do with Vedic sacrificial rites (yajña, śrauta-karman), which are now out of fashion. Their chief work is connected with smārta-karma or domestic ritual.

In regard to women, the general feeling is that they are the necessary machines for producing children (Manu IX. 96); and without children there could be no due performance of the funeral rites essential to the peace of a man's soul after death. This is secured by early marriages. If the law required the consent of boys and girls before the marriage ceremony, they might decline to give it. Hence girls are betrothed at three or four years of age, and go through the ceremony of marriage at seven to boys of whom they know nothing, and if these boy-husbands die they remain virgin-widows all their lives. They may be taken to their boy-husbands' homes at the age of 10 and may even become mothers before 11 [1]. Be it observed, however, that the wives of India, unless they belong to the upper classes, have complete freedom and are allowed to go anywhere. It is noteworthy, too, that wives do not adopt their husband's name, as European wives do. It is only theoretically that they merge their individuality in his. Note, too, that they are generally loved, and that cruel treatment by brutal husbands is unknown. Nay, Indian wives often possess greater influence than the wives of Europe, and one old grandmother will sometimes rule a whole household with a rod of iron. It is true that, theoretically, they are ignored as separate units in society. It is true that they abstain from pronouncing their husband's name, calling him simply 'lord,' or 'master,' or 'the chosen' (vara); and they themselves are never directly alluded to by their husbands in conversation. It is true that for a male friend to mention their names or even enquire after their health would be a breach of etiquette. It is true, too, that their life is spent in petty household duties, in superintending the family cuisine,

[1] When the previous edition of this work was published the earliest age for cohabitation was 10, but the raising of the age to 12 became law on March 19, 1891. It remains to be seen whether this law will become almost a dead letter like the Act of 1856 for legalizing the marriage of widows (but see p. 500).

in a wearisome round of trivial acts. It is even true that in religion they are theoretically placed on the same level as Śūdras. They are allowed no formal initiation into the Hindū faith, no investiture with the sacred thread, no spiritual second birth. Marriage is to them the end and aim of life, and the only medium of regeneration. No other purificatory rite is permitted to them. They never read, repeat, nor listen to the Veda. Yet, for all that, the women of India are the main-stay of Hindūism. They are its principal stronghold and fortress. Without their support both Brāhmanism and Hindūism would rapidly collapse.

Of course those women of the upper classes who are cooped up behind Pardahs in secluded apartments vegetate in profound ignorance of the world around them, while the duty of training and forming the character of their children is, I fear, neglected by all.

Still the women of India are generally satisfied with their position and desire no change.

Moreover it must be noted that the seclusion and ignorance of women, which was once mainly due to the fear of the Muhammadan conquerors, do not exist to the same degree in provinces unaffected by the influence of those conquerors.

Nor are child-widows, though generally condemned to perpetual mourning and to a life of domestic drudgery, treated with equal harshness in all parts of India.

And before concluding I may direct attention to some of the rules laid down by the ancient Hindū sage Vātsyāyana (author of the Kāma-sūtra [1]) in regard to Indian domestic life.

In the first place he recommends parents to allow their children complete freedom and indulgence till they are five years of age. Then from five to sixteen they are to learn some of the fourteen sciences and the sixty-four arts. Among

[1] An ancient but impure work quite as old as the first century of our era. A book called 'Early Ideas,' by Anaryan, gives a summary of Vātsyāyana's rules, which I have found useful here.

the sciences are comprised the Vedas, Purāṇas, law, medicine, astronomy, arithmetic, grammar, etc. Among the arts are singing, instrumental music, dancing, painting, composing poems, chemistry, mineralogy, architecture, gymnastics, etc.

After education a man is to become a householder. He is to win a suitable wife for himself by his own efforts, and not to allow others to choose for him. The sage then expatiates on the most approved methods of making love, and declares that no fair maiden can ever be won without a good deal of talking. The house in which the husband and wife are to live should be in the neighbourhood of good men.

The wife is to keep her husband's secrets, never to reveal the amount of his wealth, to excel other women in attention to her husband, in cookery, in ruling her servants wisely, in hospitality, in thrift, in adapting expenditure to income, and in superintending every minute circumstance of her family's daily life. Finally, she is to co-operate with her husband in pursuing the three great objects of life—religious merit, wealth, and enjoyment (kāma); and to neglect the third is as sinful as to neglect the other two.

This kind of perfect woman is called a Padminī, or lotus-like woman. Three other kinds are specified: the Ćitriṇī, or woman of varied accomplishments; the Śaṅkhinī, or conch-like woman; and the Hastinī, or elephant-like woman.

In ancient and medieval times women were not unfrequently Sanskṛit scholars.

Here is a nearly literal version of the definition of a wife given in Mahā-bhārata I. 3028, etc.:—

> A wife is half the man, his truest friend;
> A loving wife is a perpetual spring
> Of virtue, pleasure, wealth; a faithful wife
> Is his best aid in seeking heavenly bliss;
> A sweetly-speaking wife is a companion
> In solitude, a father in advice,
> A mother in all seasons of distress,
> A rest in passing through life's wilderness.

CHAPTER XV.

Religious Life of the Orthodox Hindū Householder.

LET me next direct attention to the daily religious duties of the orthodox married man who has attained to the position of possessing a separate house of his own.

I pass over the home-life of the anglicized Brāhman of advanced ideas, who has been educated under the auspices of the British Government, but has not on that account been able to avert the calamity of marriage with an uneducated and bigoted wife of his own rank, or rid himself of all the troublesome fetters of custom and caste. Such a life combines social conditions which are incompatible. The result is unpleasing. A combination is produced which is not unlike the unwholesome product of a forced chemical union between elements which naturally repel each other. What I desire rather to describe in this chapter is the religious life of the husband and wife who strive to perform their daily duties according to the orthodox Brāhmanical usage of more modern times.

And here it may be well to introduce the subject of the householder's life by glancing at the arrangements of the material house which forms his abode.

Of course the houses of the poor in villages or in the native quarters of even large cities need no description. They are mere mud erections with bamboo roofs and thatch. Those of the grade next above the poorest are little better.

They may be occasionally built of brick and may be one story high, but have seldom more than two or three rooms. Those of the richer classes, on the other hand, are always constructed of brick or some durable material, and, like the houses of Pompeii, usually have an interior court or quadrangle. A door from the street, and sometimes a handsome archway, opens into this quadrangle, which is surrounded on all sides by high walls. Over the archway or entrance is a large room, which serves as a meeting-place for the men of the family and their male visitors. A similar large and airy apartment occupies the whole front of the house in every story.

It is a melancholy fact that, as a general rule, all the well-lighted rooms with windows and verandahs looking into the street are appropriated by the male members of the household. On each floor a gallery running round the entire court-yard leads to small chambers scarcely worthy of the name of rooms, where the female members of the family are to be found by those who have the right of entrée. When there is no court-yard the women occupy the upper floor, to reach which there is usually in one corner a steep wooden staircase. The women's apartments either look into the quadrangle below—where the family cows or goats are often the chief objects of interest—or on a dead wall, never on a street. There is little or no furniture anywhere in the house, but in one room is a strong box containing the family jewelry. The ground floor has a kitchen, which is usually also the dining-room. There are also the store-rooms for grain and fuel, and even stalls for cattle. In one of the lower apartments, or in an adjacent enclosure, there is usually a well or reservoir for water. Here there are numerous shelves with a store of well-burnished brass water-vessels in constant readiness.

Another room on the ground floor is dedicated to daily worship.

Here there is a small wooden temple (Mandira) or some sacred receptacle for the household gods—the Indian Lares and Penates—which in orthodox Brāhman families—more especially among the Marāṭha people—are generally five consecrated symbols representing the five principal Hindū gods; to wit, the two stones (Śāla-grāma and Bāṇa-liṅga), described at p. 69; a metallic stone representing the female energy in nature (Śakti); a crystal representing the Sun (Sūrya); and a red stone representing Gaṇeśa (Gaṇa-pati), the remover of obstacles (p. 211). Here domestic worship is commonly performed every day by each member of every respectable Hindū family. Here, too, or in an adjacent court, there is generally a sacred Tulasī plant (see p. 333), to which the women of the family offer adoration.

Finally, in this part of the house the few remaining orthodox (Smārta) Brāhmans in different parts of India sometimes maintain a sacred fire. For it must be noted here that, although the ancient fire-worship and sacrificial ritual have almost disappeared, yet at Benares and other strongholds of Brāhmanism a certain number of Brāhmans of the old school still offer daily oblations in a sacred fire which they maintain in their own houses, while they conform also to the more recent practices enjoined in the Purāṇas. Even the old Vedic Soma-sacrifices are sometimes performed by such men on great public occasions.

For example, a Soma-sacrifice was instituted not long ago at Poona, and at Wāi near Mahābaleśvar. Again, eight or nine years ago a rich man, named Ḍhuṇḍhirāj Vināyak Sudās, had three Agnishṭomas, one Vājapeya, and one Aptoryāma sacrifice (all of them parts of the Jyotishṭoma Soma-sacrifice) performed at Alībāg in the Koṅkan. He employed a vast number of Pandits, Yājñikas, Śrotriyas, and Agnihotrīs, and spent at least 20,000 rupees. In the course of the ceremonies forty-two goats were killed. They were cooked on the fire called Śāmitrāgni, and partly eaten by the priests, partly offered in the sacrificial fire. At the end of each ceremony a supplementary sacrifice (called Avabhṛita) was instituted with the sole object of atoning for mistakes, defects, or omissions in carrying out the detail of the preceding ritual. The supposed aim of all these elaborate and expensive ceremonies was to secure the sacrificers' admission into heaven (svarga) after death.

But such Vedic sacrifices are everywhere either obsolete or obsolescent, and animals are now seldom killed in India, except as offerings to the bloody goddess Kālī—a goddess unknown in Vedic times—who is supposed, as we have already seen (p. 190), to delight in drinking blood, and, if not satiated with the blood of animals, will take that of men; this kind of sacrifice (bali) being quite distinct from the old Vedic Yajña, Homa, and Soma sacrificial rites.

But although the daily ritual acts of a modern Brāhman are founded on the teaching of the later sacred works, called Purāṇas and Tantras, yet it is remarkable that the repetition of Vedic texts (mantras) is still retained and is still essential to the due performance of every modern religious service.

And let no one suppose that a pious Brāhman's daily services in the present day are less irksome or tedious than they were in olden times. If he was then fettered, he is now enchained. A modern Brāhman of the orthodox school will sometimes devote four or five hours a day to a laborious routine of religious forms. Every faculty and function of his nature is bound by an iron chain of traditional observance. For example, his daily duties now comprise—1. Religious bathing; 2. Worship of the Supreme Being by meditation and repetition of prayers etc. at the three Sandhyās, or morning, midday, and evening services (p. 401); 3. Brahma-yajña, or worship of the Supreme Being by a formal repetition of the first words of every sacred book (regarded also as an act of homage to all those saints and sages to whom the Veda was revealed); 4. Tarpaṇa, or the threefold daily oblation of water to the secondary gods, to the sages, and to the Pitṛis; 5. Homa, or sacrifice to fire by fuel, rice, clarified butter, etc. (described at p. 366); 6. Deva-pūjā, or the daily worship of the gods in the domestic sanctuary or in temples; but, as before stated (p. 352), Hindūism enjoins no assembling together for congregational worship.

There is, moreover, the Vaiśvadeva[1] service before the mid-day meal, with offerings of food (called bali-haraṇa) to all beings (bhūta), including animals. There is the daily homage to men by the offering of food, etc. to guests and beggars. There is the solitary visit to the neighbouring temple, not necessarily for prayer or praise, but simply for bowing before the idol or for merely looking at it (darśana) after its decoration by the idol-priest. There is the observance of solemn fasts twice a month, and on other special days. There is the reading of passages from some of the Purāṇas[2], held to be a highly meritorious act. There is the performance, if circumstances permit, of a pilgrimage to some holy shrine. Finally, there is the last great Saṇskāra performed at death, called the last sacrifice (antyeshṭi), when the body ought to be burnt by the same sacred fire which was originally kindled by husband and wife on the domestic hearth. This is an outline of an orthodox Brāhman householder's life in modern times.

I now proceed to fill in the details of some parts of the picture more fully.

In the first place, then, the orthodox Brāhman must rise from his bed before sunrise. And be it observed that his wife must be up and stirring long before him. She may have to light a

---

[1] Parāśara does not include the Vaiśvadeva in his account of the daily duties. According to him there are only 'shaṭ karmāṇi,' six acts which are nitya or āhnika acts, to be performed every day. These are—1. Snāna, 2. Sandhyā-japa, 3. Svādhyāya, 4. Pitṛi-tarpaṇa, 5. Homa, 6. Devatā-pūjana. A Brāhman's six duties as enjoined by Manu (X. 75) are different. They are—1. repeating the Veda, 2. teaching it, 3. sacrificing, 4. conducting sacrifices for others, 5. giving, 6. receiving gifts.

[2] Especially the Durgā-māhātmya of the Mārkaṇḍeya-purāṇa.

lamp, give the children a few sweetmeats, sweep out the rooms, sprinkle them with water, and occasionally smear the floor with a mixture of moist earth and the supposed purifying excreta of a cow. If she lives in a village and is poor—and a high-caste family may often be poor—she will probably stick cakes of this last substance on the outer walls of the house to dry for fuel. Then perhaps her next act may be to spin a little cotton, or to examine the state of the family garments.

And here a few particulars about the dress of the household may be suitably introduced.

The poorer classes in India are never oppressed by a superfluity of clothing. A shred of cloth round the loins satisfies a poor working man's ideas of propriety. Great ascetics and pretenders to extraordinary sanctity were once in the habit of going about perfectly nude, until British law interposed to prevent the continuance of the nuisance. Even respectable Hindūs are satisfied with two garments made of white cotton cloth, one called the Dhoti, or waist-cloth, tucked round the waist and reaching to the feet; the other, called the Uttarīya, a shawl-like upper garment without seam from top to bottom, which is thrown gracefully round the shoulders like a Roman toga. Often, however, an under-jacket, or close coat, cut into form and called an Aṅgaraksha or Aṅgarakhā (body-protector), is worn under this upper garment. Sometimes also a piece of cloth is carried over the arm to be used as a scarf in cold weather.

It has been said by some writer of homely truths in England that a good wife ought never to have 'a soul above buttons.' Happily for a Hindū wife's peace of mind her husband's two garments are gloriously independent of all fastenings. Nor need she trouble herself to learn needle-work. Yet in some parts of India she considers it a high honour to be permitted to wash any article of clothing which has covered the sacred person of her lord and master.

In regard to head-coverings, the greater number of people,

including the poorer Brāhmans, in Bengal, the Dekhan, and Southern India never wear anything, though in cold weather they like to muffle up their heads and faces in their upper garments. In other places the better classes wear turbans (Sanskṛit Ushṇīsha[1]), which in Western and Northern India are often made of a piece of fine cloth from twenty to fifty yards long, folded according to the caste, and called Pheṇṭā[2].

As to shoes, at least three-fourths of the inhabitants of India never use them at all, and even the rich—except those who are thoroughly Europeanized—dispense with stockings. Those who wear leather shoes like to get rid of them whenever they can, not from any idea of the inconvenience of leather, but from its supposed impurity. It is common for the most dignified and refined gentlemen to come into one's presence with naked feet, leaving their shoes outside the room.

A woman's dress, like a man's, also consists of two pieces, namely, a kind of bodice, and a long garment called a sārī (śāṭī)—sometimes ten or even fifteen yards long—which is first tucked round the waist with many folds in front, and then brought gracefully over the shoulder, and frequently over the head. A third garment is now occasionally worn underneath, and some adopt the Muhammadan fashion of wearing a kind of drawers. Happily for economical husbands, no such thing as fashion in women's dress exists in the East. Indeed it may be safely affirmed that there has been little change in the character of woman's apparel for 3000 years.

But what the householder gains by his wife's moderation in dress he loses by her taste for expensive jewelry and ornaments. No woman would dare to hold up her head among her female companions unless well provided with a sufficient assortment of ornaments of eight principal kinds—nose-rings, ear-rings, necklaces, bracelets (commonly called

[1] In Bombay the Baniyahs wear high hats slanting backwards, and the Pārsīs do the same.

[2] When made up into a head-dress it is called Pagṛī.

bangles), armlets, finger-rings, anklets and toe-rings, and some of these, notably the nose-rings, often contain costly gems.

As to children's attire, the children of the rich are for the most part innocent of all clothing till about the third year, while those of the poor run about as they came into the world up to six or seven years of age, without a single encumbrance, except possibly a waistband and a few wrist-ornaments.

To return to the duties of the householder's wife (gṛihiṇī). One of her earliest acts, if she is poor, will be to bruise the rice, cleanse it from husk, or grind some kind of grain. Then, whether rich or poor, she must above all things attend to her kitchen; and make it a model of absolute cleanliness—nay more, a sacred inviolable spot which nothing impure must ever enter (see p. 128).

With regard to the actual culinary operations, the whole comfort of the family depends of course on the wife's superintendence and skill. In this respect very few mothers of families in India ever fall short of the highest standard.

Omens.

Then one of a wife's duties should be to keep all bad omens out of her husband's way, or manage to make him look at something lucky in the early morning. I may here point out that a knowledge of omens (nimitta-jñāna) is included among the sixty-four arts enumerated by Vātsyāyana, and is not the least important of them. Different lists of inauspicious objects are given which, if looked upon in the early morning, might cause disaster. Thus some believe that if a householder's first act should be to cast his eyes on a crow on his left hand, a kite on his right, a snake, cat, jackal, or hare, an empty vessel, smoky fire, a bundle of sticks, a widow, a man with one eye, or even with a big nose, confusion might be introduced into the houschold for the rest of the day. Nay, grievous calamities might befall the family; and if the goodman of the house had any intention of undertaking a journey, he must, after any such sights, by all means desist from the project. On the other hand, should the householder's first glance rest on a cow, horse, elephant, parrot, a lizard on an east wall, a clear fire, a virgin, or two Brāhmans, all will go right. Again, if he should happen to sneeze once, it would be a sure forerunner of good luck for the day; but if twice, it would portend some serious mishap. Finally, if he should unfortunately yawn, it might lead to no less a catastrophe than the entrance of an evil demon into his body.

The Adbhuta-Brāhmaṇa (forming the sixth chapter of the Shaḍviṇśa-Brāhmaṇa) treats of portents and omens[1]. It is to be noted, too, that both the Ṛig-veda and Atharva-veda contain texts which prove that in Vedic times birds of ill-omen were greatly dreaded and their evil influences deprecated[2].

Let us imagine then all risks arising from inauspicious sights well avoided, and the householder started on his tedious round of daily religious duties. And here be it observed that one change has passed over every Indian household. Manu, we know, asserts that, according to a Vedic ordinance, the husband and wife ought to perform religious rites together (IX. 96), but the wife has now no religious life in common with her husband.

I once asked a well-educated Brāhman why he acquiesced in a different rule of religion for himself and his wife. 'Oh,' he replied, 'we are now in the Kali-yuga, or age of universal degeneracy. Our lawgivers have promulgated quite a new code for these times; oxen cannot be killed for sacrifices, and women in all religious matters are practically degraded to the position of Śūdras. They are not allowed to repeat the Veda, or to go through the morning and evening Sandhyā services. They never accompany their husbands to

---

[1] This has been published with translation and notes, together with another text on the same subject, by Professor A. Weber of Berlin.

[2] See Ṛig-veda II. 42, 43, X. 165; Atharva-veda VI. 29, VII. 64.

any places of worship, and if they wish to visit the temples they must go alone. They cannot be regenerated by investiture with the sacred thread. Their only sacrament is marriage.' Such was his explanation of an Indian wife's inferior religious status. Had he attributed her degradation and seclusion to Muhammadan influences he would probably have been more correct.

Alone then, and unassisted by his wife, must the Brāhman commence his diurnal course of ceremonial observances. His first important act after rising is to clean his teeth. A Brāhman ought to do this according to strict rule, on pain of forfeiting the whole merit of the day's religious acts. He ought properly to use a twig of the sacred fig-tree (Vaṭa), but other kinds of wood are also allowed[1]. Compare p. 376.

Teeth-cleaning, however, is only preliminary to the next important religious act of the day—bathing (snāna). This should be performed in some sacred stream, but in default of a river, the householder may use a pool or tank, or even, in case of dire necessity, a bath in his own house. Before entering the water the bather ought to say: 'I am about to perform morning ablution in this sacred stream (the Ganges or any other, as the case may be) in the presence of the gods and Brāhmans with a view to the removal of guilt resulting from act, speech, thought—from what has been touched and untouched, known and unknown, eaten and not eaten, drunk and not drunk.' During the process of bathing, a hymn to the personified Ganges, consisting of eight verses (called Gaṅgāshṭaka), is often recited. Its opening words may be thus translated :—

Daughter of Vishṇu, thou didst issue forth
From Vishṇu's foot, by him thou art beloved.
Therefore remove from us the stain of sin—
From birth to death protecting us thy servants.

---

[1] The most common wood employed in some parts of India is that of a thorny tree called Bāval (commonly Babul). Sometimes the Nimba (Nīm) is used.

After bathing comes the ceremony of Bhasma-dhāraṇa, or application of ashes. This is done by rubbing ashes taken from the sacred domestic hearth on the head and other parts of the body, with the repetition of a prayer to Śiva (from the Taittirīya Āraṇyaka X. 43):—'I offer homage to Śiva (Sadyojāta). May he preserve me in every birth. Homage to the source of all birth.'

At this time, also, every pious Hindū marks his forehead with the sacred mark (called puṇḍra or tilaka) of his own peculiar faith or religious views. When a man is a Śiva-worshipper, he does this with ashes, in which case it is merely a part of the Bhasma-dhāraṇa rite just described [1]. Sometimes a curved perpendicular mark, sometimes a circular one, sometimes three horizontal lines (tri-puṇḍra) are made with white earth or pigment [2]. Of these markings the upright (ūrdhva, p. 67) denotes the impress of the god Vishṇu's feet [3], and the three horizontal the three functions of Śiva (p. 80).

I once said to a Brāhman who seemed proud of his curved perpendicular mark: 'What's the difference between you and your friend there with his three horizontal marks?' 'Oh,' he replied, 'we are as different in opinions as the horizon from the zenith. He does his religion horizontally, I do mine perpendicularly. But we are very good friends notwithstanding.'

The next act is Śikhā-bandhana, or the tying up of the locks on the crown of the head (p. 374), lest any hair, thought to convey impurity, should fall on the ground or in the water.

---

[1] I am told that on Ash-Wednesday in the Roman Catholic Church members of the congregation go up to the altar and are marked with the sign of the cross. This, I believe, is sometimes done with the ashes of palms such as are used on Palm-Sunday. I am told, too, that the priest as he marks each person says: 'Dust thou art, and unto dust thou shalt return.'

[2] The worshippers of Vishṇu generally use Gopī-ćandana, a kind of white earth brought from Dvārikā.

[3] It usually consists of two upright lines joined by a curve at the bottom. The Rāmānuja Vaishṇavas, as we have seen, dispute over the form of this mark (see p. 126).

All preliminary acts and purifications being now completed, the pious Hindū proceeds to the regular Morning Service, called Prātaḥ-Sandhyā, performed at the junction[1] of night and day. Every one chooses, if possible, the side of a sacred river or tank for this purpose, and every one conducts the entire service by himself. Often in the early mornings or late in the evenings I have watched numerous worshippers seated at the water's edge and going through the Sandhyā ceremonial with mechanical precision—each one separately, and each perhaps with slight variations, omissions, or additions according to the usage of his own locality or his own school of the Veda. Indeed we are so accustomed to give all our attention to the Veda for purely literary or philological objects that we are apt to forget that directly or indirectly, for good or for evil, these ancient books—the oldest in the world, except, perhaps, portions of the Christian Bible—have for three thousand years moulded the faith, inspired the prayers, animated the aspirations, influenced the conduct, shaped the lives of a large proportion of the great Āryan race to which we ourselves belong. And to this very day the remarkable spectacle may be seen of millions of Indo-Āryans, comprising countless tribes of various origin, scattered over a vast area from the Panjāb to Cape Comorin, from Bombay to Assam, living distinct from each other in separate castes and communities, yet all united by the common bond of this Veda, which they still use as their daily prayer-book. The detail of these ceremonies, practised as they still are by millions who acknowledge our rule, are fraught with the deepest interest to every Englishman.

The first act of the Morning Sandhyā Service[2], and, as stated

---

[1] Some derive Sandhyā from *San-dhā*, 'to join together' (see my Sanskṛit-English Dictionary); others, with more reason, from *San-dhyai*, 'to meditate in prayer.' Compare the Gāyatrī prayer, p. 403.

[2] I follow a manual called Brahma-karma-pustaka, printed at Alībāg in the Koṅkan, and given to me, as the best authority for the ceremonies

before, the usual preliminary to all Hindū religious rites, is sipping water (āćamana); two or three mouthfuls being swallowed for internal ablution. The water is taken up in the hollowed palm of the right hand or poured from a spoon into the palm, and is supposed to cleanse body and soul in its downward course. This is done two or three times at the commencement of the Morning Sandhyā [1]. During the process of sipping, the twenty-four principal names of the god Vishṇu are invoked, thus: 'Glory to Keśava, to Nārāyaṇa, to Mādhava, to Govinda, to Vishṇu,' etc.

The second act is called the Prāṇāyāma, 'exercise or regulation of the breath.' This includes three distinct acts:—

1. Rećaka: pressing in the right nostril with the thumb and expelling the breath through the left, and then pressing in the left nostril and expelling the breath through the right. 2. Pūraka: pressing in the right nostril with the fore-finger and drawing in the breath through the left, and then pressing in the left nostril and drawing in the breath through the right. 3. Kumbhaka: pressing in both nostrils with the finger and thumb, and holding in the breath for as long as possible.

These preliminary acts, which ought to be concluded before the rising of the sun, are thought to be useful in fixing the mind, concentrating the thoughts, and bringing the worshipper into a proper attitude of attention. He is now in a position to begin the recitation of his prayers. But first comes the utterance of the monosyllable Om (called Praṇava), the sound being prolated to the length of three vowels.

This most sacred of all Hindū utterances, made up of the

---

of the Ṛig-vedi-Brāhmans of the Marāṭha country, by Mr. Deshmukh. It must be borne in mind that variations occur in different places; and that the number of Brāhmans who go through *all* these Sandhyā ceremonies is constantly decreasing. At Kshetras on the banks of sacred rivers, a few continue to practise the whole, and all good Brāhmans go through them in an abbreviated form.

[1] One manual says *dvir āćamya*, but Manu (II. 60) enjoins *three* sippings. It is a mistake to translate *āćamana* by 'rinsing the mouth.'

three letters A, U, M, and symbolical of the triple manifestation of the Supreme Being in the Tri-mūrti or Triad of gods, Brahmā, Vishṇu, and Śiva, is constantly repeated (pp. 44, 45, with note). It is as sacred as the name Jehovah with the Jews, but not too sacred for utterance.

Manu describes it as a monosyllable, imperishable and eternal as the Supreme Being himself. After Om comes the utterance of the names of the three worlds, Earth (Bhūr), Atmosphere (Bhuvaḥ), Heaven (Svar), to which are often added the four higher heavens, Mahaḥ, Janaḥ, Tapaḥ, and Satya.

The utterance of these seven names—called the seven Vyāhṛitis—preceded in each case by the syllable Om, is an act of homage to all the beings inhabiting the seven worlds (p. 102, 1). It is supposed to induce purity of thought and to prepare the worshipper for offering up his first prayer.

Turning towards the Eastern sky he repeats the Gāyatrī or Sāvitrī (from Ṛig-veda III. 62. 10): 'Let us meditate on that excellent glory of the divine Vivifying Sun, may he enlighten our understandings' (see p. 19).

This prayer is, as we have seen, the most sacred of all Vedic utterances, and like the Lord's Prayer among Christians, or like the Fātiḥah or opening chapter of the Kurān among Muhammadans, must always among Hindūs take precedence of all other forms of supplication.

The next division of the ceremonial is called Mārjana, 'sprinkling.' It is a kind of self-baptism performed by the worshipper himself by sprinkling water on the head while the first three verses of Ṛig-veda X. 9 are recited. These may be thus paraphrased:—

> O Waters, give us health, bestow on us
> Vigour and strength, so shall I see enjoyment.
> Rain down your dewy treasures o'er our path.
> Like loving mothers, pour on us your blessing,
> Make us partakers of your sacred essence.
> We come to you for cleansing from all guilt,
> Cause us to be productive, make us prosper

This is followed by another remarkable prayer from the Taittirīya Āraṇyaka (X. 25):—

> May Sun and Anger[1], may the lords of anger
> Preserve me from my sins of pride and passion.
> Whate'er the nightly sins of thought, word, deed,
> Wrought by my mind, my speech, my hands, my feet,
> Wrought through my appetite and sensual organs,
> May the departing Night remove them all!
> In thy immortal light, O radiant Sun,
> I offer up myself and this my guilt.

Then follows a second performance of Mārjana, or 'sprinkling,' and a repetition of all the nine verses of the Ṛig-veda hymn of which the first three verses had been previously recited.

The next act is the repetition of a well-known hymn of the Ṛig-veda (X. 190) called Agha-marshaṇa, 'sin-annihilating,' supposed to have an all-powerful effect in removing sin. This hymn contains a curious summary of the supposed process of creation, which may be thus paraphrased:—

> From glowing heat sprang all existing things,
> Yea, all the order of this universe (Ṛita).
> Thence also Night and heaving Ocean sprang;
> And next to heaving Ocean rose the Year,
> Dividing day from night. All mortal men
> Who close the eyelid are his subjects, he
> The great Disposer made in due succession
> Sun, moon, and sky, earth, middle air, and heaven.

Manu (XI. 259) affirms that this short hymn thrice repeated releases from the most heinous sins.

All the ceremonial up to this point is supposed to precede the actual appearance of the Sun above the horizon. The worshipper now prepares to render homage to the rising luminary by what is called Arghya or Arghya-dāna. At other times this is the general name for a respectful offering of water in a boat-shaped vessel, called Argha, to a Brāhman or guest of any kind. In the Sandhyā it is an act of homage

---

[1] Anger personified = Manyu (Sāy. = Krodhābhimānī devaḥ); the god or gods who help a man to restrain his anger.

to the Sun, by offering water, or throwing it into the air, sometimes from a hollow vessel, but oftener from the two open hands hollowed and joined together[1]. The offerer, standing in the water, throws a handful of it upwards towards the Sun three times, each time reciting the Gāyatrī prayer. The more he scatters the water in throwing it the better.

The next division of the service is called Kara-nyāsa, or 'imposition of fingers.' Its peculiar ritual is taught in the more modern religious works called Tantras.

Some orthodox Brāhmans omit every kind of Tāntrik ceremonial as not sanctioned by the Veda, but with the majority of Hindūs it is all important. To understand the Kara-nyāsa we must bear in mind that the five fingers and the palm of the hand are consecrated to various forms of Vishṇu, and that different gods are supposed to reside in different parts of the body, the Supreme Being occupying the top of the head[2]. Hence the act of placing the fingers or hand reverentially on the several organs is supposed to gratify and do honour to the deities whose essences pervade these organs, and to be completely efficacious in removing sin.

The tip of the thumb is held to be occupied by Govinda, the forefinger by Mahīdhara, the middle finger by Hṛishīkeśa, the next finger (called the nameless finger) by Tri-vikrama, the little finger by Vishṇu, the palm of the hand by Mādhava—all being different forms of the same god Vishṇu.

The worshipper then commences the Nyāsa ceremonial by saying: 'Homage to the two thumbs, to the two forefingers, to the two middle fingers, to the two nameless fingers

---

[1] The sacred thread (yajñopavīta), always worn as a type of regeneration, and necessary to the validity of every religious act (p. 361), is often at the same time put round the two thumbs.

[2] The right ear is a peculiarly sacred spot with Tāntrikas. Fire, water, sun, and moon all reside in the right ear. Some think it is for this reason that the sacred thread, which is supposed to be polluted by the functions of nature, is hung, when they are performed, over the right ear.

(i. e. the ring-fingers), to the two little fingers, to the two palms and the two backs of the hands.'

Then follows another division of the Nyāsa ceremonial called Indriya-sparśa, or the act of touching different parts of the body, such as the breast, eyes, ears, navel, throat, and head, with the fingers. (Compare Manu II. 60.)

Next comes the regular Gāyatrī-japa, or repeated muttering of the Gāyatrī-prayer to the Sun (see p. 19).

Before beginning this repetition, those who follow the Tāntrik system go through the process of making various mystical figures called Mudrās, twenty-four in number, by twisting, interlacing, or intertwining the fingers and hands together. Each of these figures, according to its name, bears some fanciful resemblance to animals or objects of various kinds, as, for example, to a fish, tortoise, boar, lion (these being forms in which the god Vishṇu became incarnate), or to a cart, noose, knot, garland ; the efficacy attributed to these peculiar intertwinings and twistings of the hands and fingers being enormous.

The correct number of repetitions is 108, and to insure accuracy of enumeration a rosary of 108 beads made of Tulasī wood is generally used, the hand being carefully concealed in a red bag (called Go-mukhī) or under a cloth.

The next division of the service is called Upasthāna (or Mitropasthāna), because the worshipper abandons his sitting posture, stands erect with his face towards the rising Sun, and invokes that luminary under the name of Mitra. The prayer he now repeats is Ṛig-veda III. 59, of which the first verse is to the following effect :—

> Mitra, raising his voice, calls men to activity.
> Mitra sustains the earth and the sky.
> Mitra with unwinking eye beholds all creatures.
> Offer to Mitra the oblation of butter.

The use of this hymn in the morning service of every Hindū is an interesting fact in its connection with the identification of the Indian Mitra with the Zoroastrian god Mithra, mentioned by Herodotus, and with the same Mithra of the Avesta. At the end the worshipper invokes the personified Dawns in the words of Ṛig-veda IV. 51. 11: 'Hail brilliant Dawns, daughters of Heaven, I invoke you, bearing (or having) the oblation as a sign (of my devotion). May we be honoured among men, may heaven and the divine earth effect that (for us).'

The last act but one is a recitation of the family pedigree (gotroććāra); for with every high-caste man the recitation of his own genealogy forms an important part of the daily Sandhyā. For example:—

'I belong to a particular Gotra (or tribe of Brāhmans); I have three ancestors—Āṅgirasa, Śainya, and Gārgya; I am a student of the Āśvalāyana Sūtra, and follow the Śākala-śākhā of the Ṛig-veda.' See also p. 425.

The ceremonial concludes with an acknowledgement that the one Supreme Being is the real object of adoration throughout the whole service: 'Glory to the world of Brahmā, to the world of Rudra, to the world of Vishṇu. May the One Supreme Lord of the Universe be pleased with this my morning service.'

The last act, like the first, is an internal purification of the body by āćamana, or sipping of water.

In the midday Sandhyā (madhyāhna-sandhyā, now seldom performed), a different text of the Taittirīya Āraṇyaka (X. 23) is substituted for that used before (pp. 400, 404), and at the Arghya-dāna (p. 404) two different Ṛig-veda texts are substituted (viz. I. 35. 2 and the Haṇsavatī Ṛić IV. 40. 5), and at the Upasthāna the Sūrya-sūkta (I. 50, see p. 16).

The evening Sandhyā service (Sāyam-sandhyā) is like the morning, except that at the Arghya-dāna the offering is made to Varuṇa and at the Upasthāna ten verses of Ṛig-veda I. 25 are recited—freely rendered thus:—

1. As often as, O Varuṇa, we infringe thy law, like other men, every

day, 2. So often deliver us not over to death, nor to the blows of the angry, nor to the wrath of the enraged. 3. As a charioteer his tethered steed, so do we set free thy thoughts by our hymns, O Varuṇa, to turn towards us graciously. 4. My wishes fly forth towards thee, as birds to their nest, that I may receive thy blessing (vasyas may mean 'excellent wealth'). 5. When shall we induce the far-seeing ruler (or leader) Varuṇa, glorious in his sovereignty, to be propitious to us? 6. Partake together (O Mitra and Varuṇa) of the very same oblation, being both of you propitious to us; depart not from those who present offerings and remain true to their vows. 7. He (Varuṇa) who knows the path of the birds flying through the air, he abiding in the ocean knows also the ships. 8. He the maintainer of law (and order) knows the twelve months with their offspring; he knows also the month which is born afterwards (i.e. the thirteenth or additional month of the Hindū year). 9. He knows the path of the wind, the far-reaching, lofty, mighty (wind), and those (Maruts) who are enthroned above it. 10. Varuṇa, the maintainer of law (and order), sits in his palace to exercise universal sovereignty, doing good acts, the almighty one.

We must now advert to the supplementary ceremonial observances which are necessary to the completion of the morning Sandhyā.

The first act is Brahma-yajña, or worship of the Supreme Being as represented in the sacred Veda or canon of inspired knowledge. And here mark that the Sandhyā service is itself regarded as a part of Brahma-yajña. Every portion of it is held to be for the sake of pleasing the Supreme Being (Brahmă), but the use of the term Brahma-yajña is more usually restricted to the Brahma-yajña par excellence; that is, to the special worship of Brahmă as identified with the Veda.

How then is this special Brahma-yajña to be performed? We must remember that in Hindūism every religious idea, including that of revelation, is exaggerated.

Instead of sixty-six Books to which our own Sacred Scriptures extend, the Hindū so-called revelation consists of a far larger number of works, all of which are accepted as either directly revealed or inspired. Even works on pronunciation, etymology, and grammar are included in the list as part and parcel of the sacred canon.

How, then, is this mass of sacred inspiration to be dealt

with by those religious Brāhmans who wish to fulfil the duty of repeating portions of it daily?

It cannot be affirmed of any Hindū, however pious, that he reads his own Bible, as a Christian does his, much less studies it. The Veda is not meant to be either read or studied. We have seen how portions of the first three Vedas are repeated at the daily Sandhyā prayers. Portions also of the Mahā-bhārata (e.g. the Bhagavad-gītā) and of the Purāṇas (e.g. the Bhāgavata and Mārkaṇḍeya) are occasionally recited. But the duty of paying homage to Brahmă by repeating the words of divine revelation is held to be sufficiently fulfilled by the daily exercise of repeating the first few words of all the principal books, except the first hymn of the Ṛig-veda, which is recited throughout. Then comes the first verse of the second hymn. These Vedic texts may be recited according to any one or more of the five different Pāṭhas, or modes of recitation, called Saṃhitā, Pada, Krama, Jaṭā, and Ghana—wonderful devices for securing the accuracy of the Vedic text. Then come the first words of the Aitareya Brāhmaṇa (Agnir vai devānām avamo) and of each of the five books of the Aitareya Āraṇyaka. Then the first words of the Yajur-veda; of the Sāma-veda; of the Atharva-veda; of the Nirukta; of the Ćhandas (Prosody); of the Nighaṇṭu; of the Jyotisha; of the Śikshā; of Pāṇini's grammar. Then certain passages from the Atharva-veda; then the first words of Yājñavalkya's law-book, of the Mahā-bhārata, and of the philosophical Sūtras, etc.

The Brahma-yajña service is followed by the Tarpaṇa ceremony, which is properly a triple act, consisting in offerings of water for refreshment (tarpaṇa) to the gods, inspired sages, and fathers. It is accordingly divided into three parts.

In the first part, called Deva-tarpaṇa, 'refreshing of the gods,' the sacred thread is worn over the left shoulder and under the right arm, the worshipper being then called Upavītī.

Water is taken up in the right hand and poured out over the straightened fingers.

In the second part of the Tarpaṇa service, called Ṛishi-tarpaṇa, 'refreshing of the inspired sages,' the sacred thread is worn round the neck like a necklace, the worshipper being then called Nivītī.

The water is then offered so as to flow over the side of the palm between the root of the thumb and fore-finger, the finger being bent inwards[1].

The worshipper now changes the position of his sacred thread, and placing it over his right shoulder and under his left arm (being then called Prāćīnāvītī) makes offerings of water to the Āćāryas, or inspired religious teachers. This is called Āćārya-tarpaṇa, and is regarded as supplementary to the Ṛishi-tarpaṇa and not as a distinct division of the service.

The third division of the Tarpaṇa ceremony is called Pitṛi-tarpaṇa, 'refreshing of deceased fathers or departed ancestors.'

The thread is worn over the right shoulder as in Āćārya-tarpaṇa, but the water is poured out over the side of the palm opposite to the root of the thumb. The words uttered are, 'Let the fathers be refreshed; let this water containing tila (sesamum seeds) be intended for all who inhabit the seven worlds as far as the abode of Brahmā (the seventh world), though they exceed many millions of families. Let the water consecrated by my sacred thread be accepted by those members of our family who have died without any sons.'

This concludes the series of Sandhyā, Brahma-yajña, and Tarpaṇa services.

Pañćāyatana Ceremony.

At the conclusion of the Tarpaṇa ceremony the worshipper ought to re-enter his house and perform the Homa, or offering

[1] The part of the hand between the thumb and fore-finger is called pitrya, and is sacred to the Pitṛis. (Compare Manu II. 51.)

of oblations to the gods through fire, described in a previous chapter (p. 366).

In Manu's time the worship of the gods (deva or devatā) through the Homa was regarded as one of the five Mahā-yajñas, or chief devotional acts, the other four being (1) homage to the Supreme Spirit and to that Spirit present in the Veda, performed by the Brahma-yajña service; (2) homage to the Pitṛis, or deceased progenitors, performed by the Tarpaṇa and Śrāddha ceremonies; (3) homage to all beings (bhūta), including animals, performed by offerings of food called bali; (4) homage to men, performed by hospitality to guests and almsgiving to beggars. Of these five acts the worship of the gods—deva-yajña or deva-pūjā—was formerly the simplest. It was generally sufficiently performed by putting oblations of rice or clarified butter in fire. In the present day, as already stated, no one, except the most orthodox Brāhmans, thinks it necessary to maintain a sacred fire, and the old fire ritual is gradually dying out.

Other forms of worshipping the gods are, however, substituted. In nearly every modern house there is a room containing a sanctuary, called Mandira. Here the religious service called Deva-pūjā is generally performed by pious householders, or by some member of the family deputed to represent the others every morning.

It is, we know, an essential part of the theory of Brāhmanism (p. 50) that all gods like Brahmā, Vishṇu, and Śiva, who are manifestations of the invisible and formless Brahmă, should be worshipped through visible forms. In the Deva-pūjā, therefore, homage is paid to these deities through images, or more commonly, in Central and Southern India and the Marāṭha country, through the worship of five stones or symbols which are believed to be permeated by the essences of the five chief deities.

The room dedicated to their worship need not be on the ground-floor, like the Homa-śālā. The five stones (as pointed out, pp. 69, 392) are—1. the black stone[1], representing Vishṇu; 2. the white stone[2], representing Śiva's essence; 3. the red stone, representing Gaṇeśa (Gaṇa-pati); 4. the small piece of metallic ore, representing the wife of Śiva; 5. the piece of crystal, representing the Sun. The first two stones—Śāla-grāma and Bāṇa-liṅga—are regarded as far more sacred than manufactured idols, for such idols must be consecrated, whereas these stones are occupied by Vishṇu and Śiva without any consecration whatever.

All five symbols are placed on a round open metal dish, called Pañćāyatana, and are arranged in five different methods, according to the preference given to any one of the five deities at the time of worship. These five methods are:—

1. Vishṇu in the middle; Śiva N. E. (i. e. towards the north-east quarter); Gaṇeśa S. E.; Sūrya S.W.; Devī N.W. 2. Śiva in the middle; Vishṇu N.W.; Sūrya S.E.; Gaṇeśa S.W; Devī N.W. 3. Sūrya in the middle; Śiva N.E.; Gaṇeśa S.E.; Vishṇu S.W.; Devī N.W. 4. Devī in the middle; Vishṇu N.E; Śiva S.E.; Gaṇeśa S.W.; Sūrya N.W. 5. Gaṇeśa in the middle; Vishṇu N.E.; Śiva S.E.; Sūrya S.W.; Devī N.W.

Then, again, on one side of the Pañćāyatana is a small bell, and on the other side a conch-shell[3], and near at hand is a water-vessel called Kalaśa or Abhisheka-pātra, with a small hole in the bottom of it, through which the water used for sprinkling the stones passes. These three objects are also held sacred and receive their share of worship.

I should state that near the metal receptacle containing the five sacred stones is placed another metal plate on which are

---

[1] Near the black Śāla-grāma stone there is often placed a kind of fossil with circular markings, also sacred to Vishṇu and symbolising his ćakra. The Muhammadans also worship a kind of black stone fixed in the Ka'ba. This stone-worship is doubtless a remnant of fetishism which has prevailed in all countries.

[2] It is curious that Vishṇu should be represented as of a black colour and Śiva as white, when the former is held to be connected with the Sattva-guṇa and the latter with the Tamo-guṇa (see p. 45).

[3] The conch-shell is specially sacred to Vishṇu (see p. 103).

arranged the Tulasī leaves for Vishṇu and the Bilva leaves for Śiva, besides offerings of flowers, perfumes, etc.

The worship of the five deities thus represented is performed by sixteen acts of homage (upaćāra), one for each of the sixteen verses of the Purusha-sūkta, or ninetieth hymn of the tenth Maṇḍala of the Ṛig-veda, and the ceremony is sometimes called Pañćāyatana-pūjā, from the receptacle (āyatana) in which the five symbols are placed.

Before commencing the service the worshipper goes through the usual sippings of water (āćamana) and suppressions of the breath before described (p. 402). Then after repeating certain preliminary prayers he invokes the god Gaṇeśa, employing a well-known text from the Ṛig-veda (II. 23): 'Om. We invoke thee who art lord of the hosts of hosts (Gaṇapatiṃ gaṇānām), the sage of sages, of most exalted fame, the most excellent king of Vedic mantras, O Lord of prayer[1], hear us with favour, and enter our dwelling to aid us (against the demons of obstruction).'

This invocation is followed by Nyāsa, or the reverential touching of various parts of the body, in connection with the recitation of a few words at the beginning and middle of each of the last six verses of the Purusha-sūkta (X. 90) of the Ṛig-veda.

The next act is adoration of the water-vessel (kalaśa), thus:—

'In the mouth of the water-vessel abideth Vishṇu, in its neck is Rudra, in its lower part is Brahmā, while the whole company of the Mothers (mātṛis) are congregated in its middle part. O Ganges, Yamunā, Godāvarī, Sarasvatī, Narmadā, Sindhu, and Kāverī, be present in this water.'

Next succeeds the worship of the conch-shell, thus:—

---

[1] Brahman is here used for the hymns, or rather mantras, of the Veda which in later times were used as spells to counteract the malice of demons. Gaṇeśa in his power over the troops of demons is thus identified with the Vedic Brahmaṇas-pati, or lord of prayer.

'O conch-shell (Pāñćajanya, see p. 103), thou wast produced in the sea, and art held by Vishṇu in his hand; thou art worshipped by all the gods. Receive my homage.'

Then follows adoration of the bell, thus:—

'O bell, make a sound for the approach of the gods, and for the departure of the demons. Homage to the goddess Ghaṇṭā (bell). I offer perfumes, grains of rice, and flowers, in token of rendering all due homage to the bell.'

Then after intertwining his fingers so as to make the mystical figure called Ghaṇṭā-mudrā, the worshipper must ring the bell. Next, after fixing his thoughts, he says a prayer to Vishṇu, Śiva, the son of Śiva (Gaṇa-pati), the Supreme Being (Nārāyaṇa) in the centre of the Sun's orb, and the goddess Devī. The worshipper now commences the sixteen acts of homage or offerings (upaćāra), each accompanied with the uttering of one of the sixteen verses of the Purusha hymn of the Ṛig-veda (X. 90), a literal translation of which I here subjoin (see also pp. 17, 33):—

1. Purusha has thousands of heads (thousands of arms, A.V.), thousands of eyes, and thousands of feet. On every side enveloping the earth, he transcended this mere space of ten fingers[1]. 2. Purusha himself is this whole (universe), whatever has been, and whatever shall be. He is also the lord of immortality, since through food he expands. 3. Such is his greatness; and Purusha is superior to this. All existing things are a quarter of him, and that which is immortal in the sky is three quarters of him. 4. With three quarters Purusha mounted upwards. A quarter of him again was produced here below. He then became diffused everywhere among things animate and inanimate. 5. From him Virāj was born, and from Virāj, Purusha. As soon as born he extended beyond the earth, both behind and before. 6. When the gods offered up Purusha as a sacrifice, the spring was its clarified butter, summer its fuel, and autumn the (accompanying) oblation. 7. This victim, Purusha born in the beginning, they consecrated on the sacrificial grass; with him as their offering, the gods, Sādhyas, and Ṛishis sacrificed. 8. From that universal oblation were produced curds and clarified butter. He (Purusha) formed the animals which are subject to the power of the air (vāyavya),

[1] The world is called Daśāṅgula, a mere span of ten fingers compared with God's infinite essence. I have chiefly followed Dr. John Muir's translation, but not throughout (see Texts, p. 368). A.V. is for Atharva-veda.

both wild and tame. 9. From that universal sacrifice sprang the hymns called Ṛić[1] and Sāman, the metres, and the Yajush. 10. From it were produced horses, and all animals with two rows of teeth, cows, goats, and sheep. 11. When they divided Purusha, into how many parts did they distribute him? What was his mouth? What were his arms? What were called his thighs and feet? 12. The Brāhman was his mouth; the Rājanya became his arms; the Vaiśya was his thighs; the Śūdra sprang from his feet. 13. The moon was produced from his soul; the sun from his eye; Indra and Agni from his mouth; the Vāyu from his breath. 14. From his navel came the atmosphere; from his head arose the sky; from his feet came the earth; from his ear the four quarters; so they formed the worlds. 15. When the gods, in performing their sacrifice, bound Purusha as a victim, there were seven pieces of wood laid for him round the fire, and thrice seven pieces of fuel employed. 16. With sacrifice the gods worshipped the Sacrifice. These were the primeval rites. These great beings attained to the heaven where the gods, the ancient Sādhyas, reside.

The sixteen acts of homage or offerings are—

1. Invocation (āvāhana); 2. a seat for sitting down (āsana) formed of Tulasī leaves; 3. foot water (pādya); 4. respectful oblation (arghya) of rice, etc.; 5. water for sipping (āćamanīya); 6. ablution or lustration (snāna) with milk and clarified butter, honey and sugar; 7. clothing (vastra) formed of Tulasī leaves; 8. upper clothing or ornaments (upavastra) formed of more Tulasī leaves; 9. perfumes and sandal (gandha, ćandana); 10. flowers (pushpa); 11. incense (dhūpa); 12. illumination (dīpa); 13. oblation of food (naivedya); 14. reverential circumambulation (pradakshiṇā); 15. flowers with recitation of texts (mantra-pushpa); 16. final act of adoration (namaskāra).

With each act of homage one of the sixteen verses of the Purusha hymn above translated is recited. The final act of adoration is as follows:—

Veneration to the infinite and eternal Male (Purusha), who has thousands of names, thousands of forms, thousands of feet, thousands of eyes, thousands of heads, thousands of thighs, thousands of arms, and who lives for ten millions of ages.

O great god, pardon my want of knowledge of the right way of worshipping thee. Sin, misery, and poverty are removed; happiness and purity are obtained by thy presence. O great god, I commit thousands of faults every day and night; forgive me, as I am thy servant. There is no other protection but from thee; thou only art my refuge; guard me, therefore, and defend me by thy mercy; pardon my mistakes and defects

---

[1] According to Sāyaṇa's introduction to the Ṛig-veda, this mention of the Ṛić first proves the priority of the Ṛig-veda.

in syllables, words, and measure; O mighty lord, be propitiated. I offer flowers with prayers. Let the five gods, of whom great Vishṇu is the first, be pleased with the worship I have made. Let all this be offered to the Supreme Being. I offer thee with my mouth, O Vishṇu, the sacred salutation Vashaṭ. Be pleased, O Śipivishṭa[1], with my oblation; let my songs of praise exalt thee; protect us ever with thy blessings (Ṛig-veda VII. 99. 7, 100. 7).

Then sipping water the worshipper says :—

'I take into my body the holy water which comes from the feet of Vishṇu, preventing untimely death and destroying all diseases.'

This concludes the Pañćāyatana ceremony as performed by Brāhmans in the Marāṭha country. Doubtless here and there local variations may occur.

In some districts where Śiva is worshipped a form of service called Śiva-pūjā is substituted for the Pañćāyatana-pūjā, and two hymns called the Rudra hymns, from the Yajur-veda (Vājasaneyi-Saṃhitā XVI; XVIII), are recited. These two hymns are still used by strict Brāhmans, and familiarly called Namak and Ćamak, because Namas te is constantly repeated in one and Ća me in the other.

Vaiśvadeva Ceremony.

An orthodox Brāhman's craving for religious ceremonial is not by any means satiated by the tedious round of forms he has gone through in the early morning. A pause of an hour or two brings him to the time when preparations for another solemn rite have to be made. This is the ceremony which ought to precede the midday meal.

It should be stated that an Indian household is satisfied with two principal daily meals—one about midday, another in the evening—but no pious householder of high caste will sit down to the former without first performing what is

[1] This epithet of Vishṇu is only applicable to him as a form of the Sun displaying his rays in all directions.

called the Vaiśvadeva ceremony, or offering to all the gods (viśve devāḥ)[1]. Nor is this held to be completed without the addition of another rite, called Bali-haraṇa, which is practically nothing more than the concluding act of the Vaiśvadeva[2].

The gods worshipped in the Vaiśvadeva are Vedic, and the ceremony is therefore from its antiquity far more interesting than the Pañćāyatana-pūjā, or any other modern form of the Deva-pūjā. It is described in its most ancient form in Manu III. 84–93. The idea involved in the entire service seems to be, that before a man begins eating he ought to consecrate and purify his food by making offerings of small portions of cooked rice and other food to all the deities through whose favour he is himself fed, and more especially to Fire, who is the bearer of the offering to heaven. In point of fact the whole ceremony resolves itself into a form of homage offered to the gods who give the food, and to the god of fire without whose aid this food could not be prepared for eating. There is also a notion that, in preparing the food by cooking, animals may have been accidentally destroyed, for which expiation should be made.

It should be observed that the Vaiśvadeva is not, like the Sandhyā, incumbent on every individual separately. It may be performed vicariously, like the Deva-pūjā, through one member of the family (generally a junior member) acting for the others. In performing it a small portable fire-receptacle, called a Kuṇḍa, is brought into the room where

---

[1] In reality only certain classes of deities are intended. It is curious that the number of the gods is sometimes asserted in the Ṛig-veda to be 33, while elsewhere (X. 6. 3) the number 3306 is given, and elsewhere (III. 9. 9) 3339. They are now popularly said to amount to 330 millions, but any limitation as to number is opposed to the Brāhmanical theory of infinite evolution. Moreover it must be borne in mind that no god in the Hindū Pantheon is eternal, except the one Brăhmă—the one self-existent Spirit—out of which all the gods are evolved and into which they will all be re-absorbed.

[2] Some manuals speak of the two in the dual, as Vaiśvadeva-balikarmaṇī. They are described by Colebrooke in his 'Religious Ceremonies of the Hindūs,' but in a confused and imperfect manner.

the eatables are collected. Consecrated fire—fed with consecrated fuel—is placed in it, sacred grass is spread around, and offerings of rice, etc. are cast into the flames for all the deities, with repetition of Vedic texts.

The Bali-haraṇa which follows requires for its proper performance an elaborate arrangement of portions of food in a circle [1], each portion being allotted to a particular deity, or class of superhuman beings, with the utterance of prescribed formularies.

The detail of both Vaiśvadeva and Bali-haraṇa as given in the most trustworthy manuals is as follows:—

The worshipper begins by the usual sippings of water (aćamana) and breath exercises (p. 402), and by declaring his intention (saṅkalpa) of performing the ceremony, thus:—

'I will to-day perform the morning and evening [2] Vaiśvadeva with the cooked food (siddhānna) cast into the fire, for the purification of that food and for my own purification, and to make expiation for the five destructive domestic implements [3] (Pañća-sūnā), and to obtain the reward prescribed by the Śruti, Smṛiti, and Purāṇas.'

Then after bringing in a small movable fire-receptacle, the service commences with an invocation (āvāhana) of the god of fire from the Ṛig-veda (V. 4. 5; I. 72. 6), which may be thus translated:—

'O all-wise god Agni, come to this our sacrifice as a loved domestic friend and household guest. Destroy all our enemies, and procure for us, O Agni, the food (and other possessions) of those who bear us enmity.'

'Come, Agni, hither and sit down here as our priest, and be to us a

---

[1] A diagram of the circle is given in most of the Directories, with the order in which the portions of food are to be arranged.

[2] The evening Vaiśvadeva is never, so far as I was able to ascertain, performed in the present day.

[3] The five places, or domestic implements, through the use of which animals may be accidentally destroyed in the process of preparing food, are—1. the fire-place; 2. the slab for grinding grain and condiments; 3. the pots and pans; 4. the pestle and mortar; and 5. the water-pot. See Manu III. 68.

trustworthy guide. May all-pervading heaven and earth defend thee! Bear our oblations to the gods for their complete satisfaction.'

After these invocations a covered dish of uncooked rice is brought in and the cover removed. Then sacred fire is placed in the receptacle, with these words: Om Bhūr bhuvaḥ svaḥ, 'I deposit the fire called Rukmaka[1] (bright as gold).' Consecrated fuel is next put on and the fire fanned, while the following well-known and remarkable text from Ṛig-veda IV. 58. 3 is recited: 'Four are his horns, three are his feet, two are his heads, seven are his hands. He the triply-bound bull roars. The mighty deity enters mortals[2].'

Next comes a text from the Śvetāśvatara Upanishad II. 16: 'This god (of fire) pervades all the quarters of the sky; he was the first-born of all things; he is within the womb; he was born and is to be born; he dwells in all men, and has his countenance in all directions.'

The collecting together and spreading of the consecrated fuel and sacred Kuśa grass employed in the ceremony are then made; and water is sprinkled round in a circle.

Next, the rice about to be eaten is consecrated by the sprinkling of water and placed on the fire. It is then taken off and deposited between the worshipper and the fire.

---

[1] Fire is of various kinds and has various names, and it is requisite to name the particular fire intended to be prepared.

[2] Prof. H. H. Wilson gives a note in his translation, showing that Sāyaṇa identifies Agni here with either Sacrifice or the Sun. The four horns are the Veda or the Cardinal points, the three feet are the three daily Sandhyās, or morning, noon, and evening; the heads are either two particular ceremonies, or day and night; the seven hands are the seven metres or seven solar rays. The bull is sacrifice, or the Sun as the pourer down of benefits; the triple bond is Mantra, Kalpa, and Brāhmaṇa, and the roaring sound is the recitation of the Veda. Patañjali in the Mahā-bhāshya (I. 1. 1) explains the four horns to mean the four kinds of words—nouns, verbs, prepositions and particles; the three feet the three tenses—past, present and future; the two heads the eternal and temporary (produced) words; the seven hands the seven case affixes; the triple bond is composed of the chest, the throat, and the head. The mighty deity is speech. (Compare St. John's Gospel, i. 1.)

The next act is called Upasthāna. A prayer from the Ṛig-veda (V. 4. 9) is addressed to the god of fire under his name Jāta-vedas[1], thus:—

'Carry us, O omniscient god (Jāta-vedas), through all our troubles and difficulties, as if thou wert conveying us over a river by means of a boat. O Fire, thou art glorified by us with as great honour as (was once offered thee) by Atri, be thou willing (be thou awake or active) to become the protector of our persons.'

After this prayer offerings are made with the usual reverential ejaculations, thus: 'Homage to Fire (Agni). I offer fragrant sandal for unguent (vilepana), I offer flowers for worship. I offer uncooked grains of rice (akshatāḥ) for every kind of offering[2].'

Next, the worshipper, after purifying his person and washing his hands, makes offerings to all the gods, throwing portions of cooked rice—each portion about equal to a mouthful—into the fire, with the following words:—

'Om. Homage to the Sun (Sūryāya-svāhā). This is offered for the Sun, and not for my own use; homage to Prajāpati, to Agni, to Soma Vanaspati, to Agni and Soma together, to Indra and Agni together, to Heaven and Earth, to Dhanvantari, to Indra alone, to all the gods (Viśvebhyo devebhyaḥ), to Brahmā, to Bhūr and Agni, to Bhuvar and Vāyu, to Svar and Sūrya[3],' etc.

The next act is the taking up of ashes (vibhūti-grahaṇa) from the fire in a deep-bowled spoon called Darvi, and the application of a small quantity with the finger to different parts of the body, with the following prayer to Rudra (Śiva): 'O Rudra, inflict not harm on our sons and grandsons, on

---

[1] Jāta-vedas probably means 'having knowledge of all that is born or created.' The 10th and 11th verses of this hymn are also recited after the 9th.

[2] That is as a substitute for all other oblations. Practically neither sandal, perfumes, nor flowers are offered on ordinary occasions, but only cooked rice is put into the fire in place of other offerings.

[3] The manuals give a diagram of the circle, and the names of all the gods to whom portions of food are offered on the ground in the concluding Bali-haraṇa ceremony. The cooked food appears to be offered in fire to these same gods in the same order.

our living men, on our cows and horses; destroy not our brave men in thy anger; we invoke thee continually, bringing thee oblations.' (Ṛig-veda I. 114. 8.)

Then, with the prayer:—'May I enjoy the triple life (tryāyusham) of Jamadagni[1], of Kaśyapa, of Agastya, of the gods; may I altogether live for a hundred years'—ashes are applied to the forehead, the neck, the navel, the right shoulder, the left shoulder, and the head respectively.

Another prayer to the god of fire concludes the Vaiśvadeva portion of the service, thus:—

'O bearer of the oblations, give me happiness, faith, understanding, fame, wisdom, learning, intellect, wealth, strength, long life, dignity, and health. I salute him whose name, when remembered and mentioned, makes incomplete religious services complete[2]. Let the deity who partakes of the sacrifice and has the form of Agni-nārāyaṇa be pleased with this ceremony. Let it be regarded as offered to the true essence of the Supreme Being (Brahmă).'

The Bali-haraṇa Service.

But the Vaiśvadeva ceremony is not complete without the Bali-haraṇa, or offering of food to all gods and all creatures, including all kinds of animals and spirits. This act is identical with Manu's Bhūta-yajña, or homage to all creatures (Manu III. 70. 81–IV. 21). The offering to all animals is sometimes called Kāka-bali, because crows are practically the chief devourers of the offerings. In fact, the Vaiśvadeva and Bali-haraṇa are complementary of each other, and are generally regarded as one ceremony.

The worshipper begins by placing small mouthfuls of cooked rice in a circle on the ground between himself and the fire-receptacle, allotting separate portions to all the gods to whom offerings have already been made in the fire, as well as to other beings outside the circle, in regular order, saying:—

---

[1] Compare White Yajur-veda (Vājasaneyi-S.) III. 62.

[2] According to the manual I have followed, a Śruti enjoins that if any part of the ceremony has been carelessly omitted, it is held to be completed by remembering and repeating the name of Vishṇu.

'Homage (1) to Sūrya, (2) to Prajāpati, (3) to Agni, (4) to Prajāpati, (5) to Soma with Vanaspati, (6) to Agni and Soma, (7) to Indra with Agni, (8) to Heaven and Earth, (9) to Dhanvantari [1], (10) to Indra, (11) to all the gods, (12) to Brahmā, (13) to the waters, (14) to the plants and trees, (15) to the house, (16) to the household deities, (17) to the gods of the foundation of the house.'

Then portions are placed on the ground just outside the circle for other gods and beings in the order of the quarters of the compass, beginning with the East, saying:—

'Homage (18) to Indra, (19) to Indra's attendants, (20) to Yama, (21) to Yama's attendants, (22) to Varuṇa, (23) to Varuṇa's attendants, (24) to Soma, (25) to Soma's attendants, (26) to Brahmā, (27) to Brahmā's attendants, (28) to all the Gods, (29) to all the Bhūtas or Spirits, (30) to all the Spirits who move about by day, (31) to all the Spirits who move about by night, (32) to all Rākshasas and evil spirits, (33) to the Pitṛis—the worshipper hanging his sacred thread over the right shoulder (see p. 410) and becoming Prāćīnāvītī, (34) to the dog Śyāma, (35) to the dog Śabala, (36) to Sanaka [2] and the other Ṛishis (the worshipper hanging his thread round his neck like a necklace and becoming Nivītī, see p. 410).' With regard to 34 and 35, see p. 289.

While making offerings of food to the spirits and animals he says:—

'I who am myself desirous of being fed, offer oblations of food to those spirits that move about day and night and delight in doing mischief. Let the lord of food grant me also to be nourished by the food I am about to eat.'

While offering portions of food outside the door of the house he says:—

'Let the crows that come from all the four quarters of the sky (presided over by Indra, Varuṇa, Vāyu, Yama, and Nirṛiti) take the portions of rice placed by me on the ground. I present a portion to the two dogs, called Śyāma and Śabala (see p. 289), belonging to the family of Vaivasvata, that they may protect me always in my path (through this world and the next). I place portions on the ground for dogs, for low-born persons (ćāṇḍālas) and outcasts, for all animals and for crows (Śva-ćāṇḍāla-patita-vāyasebhyaḥ [3]).'

---

[1] Dhanvantari is not the physician of the gods produced at the churning of the ocean, but an ancient deity.

[2] Sanaka was one of the four sons of Brahmā.

[3] The Rev. Nehemiah Goreh (a converted Brāhman) informed me that he used to repeat these words every day when he performed the Vaiśvadeva and Bali-haraṇa for his family.

The householder then waits at the door for a short interval, watching for some guest (atithi) who may be passing, or for some beggar to whom he may give a portion of food as alms [1].

He then washes his hands and feet, sips water, and re-enters the house, saying:—

'Let earth, atmosphere, and sky be favourable to us and make us free from fear of danger. Let all the quarters of the sky, the waters, and the lightnings protect us from all harm! Peace, peace, peace! homage to Vishṇu, homage to Vishṇu, homage to Vishṇu.'

The Ceremony of Dining.

After the due performance of the Vaiśvadeva and Bali-haraṇa ceremonies the cooked food is considered fit to be consumed, and it might be thought that after so long a religious service the members of the householder's family would have nothing further to do but to eat their dinner without further ceremony. But not so. The process of dining is itself regarded as a religious rite, and must be conducted according to prescribed forms.

Most of the manuals in my possession give directions for what is called Bhojana-vidhi, 'the ceremony of dining.' In practice, what generally happens in the families of orthodox Brāhmans and other high-caste natives [2] is nearly as follows:—

The males of the family sit down in a row on the ground with their legs folded under them in the usual manner. They are waited on by the wives, daughters [3], and widows of the family; for no woman in any Indian household will venture to eat till the men have finished. Boiled rice and other kinds of grain or pulse cooked with condiments and

---

[1] The object of waiting at the door is that the worshipper may feel he has done his best to discharge the duty of performing the Manushya-yajña or Atithi-pūjana, 'homage to men or guests,' enjoined by Manu (in Book III. 70).

[2] Of course great variations occur even among Brāhman families, especially in large cities where anti-brāhmanic influences are at work.

[3] Daughters, however, are often privileged to eat with their fathers.

sometimes various kinds of sweetmeats are served up on plates made of leaves[1] (often of the palāśa tree or the plantain) and placed before each person; but no one begins eating till certain religious forms have been gone through. In the first place, there is the usual āćamana or sipping of water for internal purification (p. 402). Each person pours water with a spoon into the palm of the hand, then some one leads the others, and all sip together. Next, water is sprinkled in a circle round each plate, and some one of the company repeats a grace or prayer before eating. The most common prayer is from two passages in the Taittirīya Brāhmaṇa[2], as follows:—

'Let rivers continue to flow, let clouds rain, let plants produce good fruit (for the support of the world), may I be the lord of lands (grāma Com.) that produce food, rice, and curds.'

'They extol food (saying): that which is food is certainly a great divine power, since it leads a man (him) to supreme prosperity.'

The first clause of this curious prayer seems to be a benediction spoken for the benefit of the world at large; the second is for the good of the speaker; the third is a glorification of the food which the speaker is about to eat. Sometimes the following text from the Ṛig-veda (X. 121. 10) precedes the prayer:—

'O Lord of all creatures, no one else but thou keepest all these living beings encircled by thy care; with whatever desires we sacrifice to thee, let the fruit of that be to us; may we become possessors of wealth[3].'

---

[1] In large towns plates of metal are generally used.

[2] Taittirīya Brāhmaṇa II. 7. 16. 4, and I. 7. 10. 6. The following is the Sanskṛit text: Yantu nadayo varshantu parjanyāḥ supippalā oshadhayo bhavantu, annavatām odanavatām āmikshavatām eshāṃ rājā bhūyāsam.

Odanam udbruvate, parameshṭhī vā eshaḥ, yad odanaḥ paramām evainaṃ śriyaṃ gamayati.

[3] Prajāpate na tvad etāny anyo viśvā jātāni pari tā babhūva, yat-kāmās te juhumas tan no astu, vayam syāma patayo rayīṇām. In Kullūka's Commentary to Manu (II. 54) a much simpler form of grace before meat is given. The eater is told that he is always to honour his food and never despise it, and to pray that he may always obtain it (nityam asmākam etad astu).

After the recitation of this grace the actual business of eating may begin, but each person first places either four or five small mouthfuls (grāsa) of food on the ground on the right side of his leaf-plate. These are called simply āhuti, 'offerings[1],' or sometimes Ćitrāhuti, 'offerings to Ćitra,' or to Ćitra-gupta, whose power in the intermediate state after death is especially dreaded (see p. 292). While placing the mouthfuls he ought to say: 'Homage to Ćitra[2], to Ćitra-gupta[3], to Yama, to Yama-dharma, to Bhur bhuvaḥ svar.'

After the dinner is over these mouthfuls are left to be eaten by cats (if there are any in the house), or together with the leaf-plates and whatever is left upon them, they are thrown to the cows, or simply thrown out of the house to be eaten by dogs or animals of any kind. The evening family meal is a less formal ceremony.

With reference to the form of salutation used at the end of the morning Sandhyā service (see p. 407), I may mention that I was told by the Brāhman, Mr. Nehemiah Goreh, that before he became a Christian his daily form of words addressed to his father (Guru) were :—

Bhārgava - ćyāvanāpnavānaurva - jāmadagnyeti - pañća-pravarānvita - jāmadagnyavatsa-gotrotpanno 'ham Ṛig-vedāntargata-śākala-śākhādhyāyī Raghunātha-śarmā 'ham bho Guro tvām abhivādayāmi. 'O Father, I Raghunātha-śarmā, a student of the Śākala branch of the Ṛig-veda, born in the family of the children of Jamadagni, possessing five lines of progenitors—Bhārgava, Ćyāvana, Āpnavāna, Aurva, and Jāmadagnya—salute thee.'

It might be thought that every complete account of Hindū domestic rites would require to end with a description of funeral and Śrāddha ceremonies, but for these see p. 274.

---

[1] In the same way, whenever a Roman family sat down to meals, a portion of the food was presented to the Lares, regarded as departed spirits.

[2] Ćitrāya namaḥ, etc., or svāhā, may be substituted for namaḥ.

[3] Ćitra-gupta is the recorder who records the sins and merits of mankind in Yama's world.

CHAPTER XVI.

Hindū Fasts, Festivals, and Holy Days.

ALTHOUGH Hindūism has no ecclesiastical organization under any central authority it has a longer list of festivals (utsava), and seasons of rejoicing, qualified by fasts (upavāsa, vrata), vigils (jāgaraṇa), and seasons of mortification, than any other religion. Most of these take place on certain lunar days (tithi), each lunation of rather more than twenty-seven solar days being divided into thirty lunar days, fifteen of which during the moon's increase constitute the light half of the month, and the other fifteen the dark half. Some festivals are regulated by the supposed motions of the sun. To describe all the fasts and festivals would require a volume. I can only indicate some of the most common.

And first, with regard to the custom of fasting, it may be worth while to point out that no Christian man—be he Roman Catholic or Anglican—not even the most austere stickler for the most strict observance of every appointed period of humiliation and abstinence, can for a moment hope to compete with any religious native of India—Hindū or Muhammadan—who may have entered on a course of fasting, abstinence, and bodily maceration.

In point of fact, the constant action of a tropical climate, and the peculiar social habits of the sons of the soil in Eastern countries continued for centuries, have induced a condition of body which enables them to practise the most severe and protracted abstinence with impunity, and even with benefit; while European Christians, who, with a view of increasing their influence, endeavour to set an example of self-mortification, find themselves quite outdone and left hopelessly in the rear by a thousand devotees in every sacred city of India[1].

It must of course be borne in mind that fasting is practised by Indian devotees, not as a penitential exercise, but as a means of accumulating religious merit. Moreover, severe self-mortification is always connected with the fancied attainment of extraordinary sanctity or superhuman powers. Amongst other objects aimed at is the acquirement of a kind of preter-natural or ethereal lightness of body. By long fasting a man is believed to achieve what is called Laghimā, 'lightness'; that is to say, his frame becomes so buoyant and sublimated by abstinence, that the force of gravitation loses its power of binding him to the earth, and he is able to sit or float in the air. It may seem the very height of credulity to give credence to an emaciated Hindū claiming to triumph in this way over the laws of matter; yet cool-headed and sceptical Englishmen of unimpeachable sincerity have been invited to witness the achievements of these so-called Yogīs, and have come away convinced of their genuineness and ready to testify to the absence of all fraud.

Nevertheless, it must be noted that the rules of fasting, as practised by natives of India in the present day, are by no means so stringent as they were in ancient times. Several severe forms of abstinence are specified by Manu. For example, the fast called 'very painful' (ati-kṛiććhra) consisted in eating only a single mouthful every day for nine days, and then abstaining from all food for the three following days (Manu XI. 213).

Another notable fast was that called 'the lunar vow' (ćān-

---

[1] The truth is that any breach of the Creator's physical laws and laws of adaptation is sure to be followed by a Nemesis, and those devoted Englishmen who practise protracted abstinence from food in an exhausting Indian atmosphere cannot expect to be exempt from the operation of these laws. We have recently had examples of useful careers arrested through neglecting to study the account of the second or 'pinnacle temptation' of Christ (St. Matthew iv. 6).

drāyaṇa-vrata). It consisted in diminishing the consumption of food every day by one mouthful for the waning half of the lunar month, beginning with fifteen mouthfuls at the full moon until the quantity was reduced to nil at the new moon, and then increasing it in like manner during the fortnight of the moon's increase (Manu VI. 20, XI. 216).

In the present day every religious Hindū fasts twice in every lunar month—that is on the eleventh day (ekādaśī) in each fortnight. These fasts are usually kept in honour of Vishṇu, but are not very strictly observed, as fruit and milk are allowed. The Śaivas usually fast on the thirteenth or fourteenth day of the dark half of every month, on the day and night called Śiva-rātri, 'Śiva's night,' in anticipation of the great fast on the night of Śiva, kept once a year (p. 430). The evening before is called Pradosha. Some, again, fast in honour of Gaṇeśa on the fourth lunar day (ćaturthī) once a month, in anticipation of the chief Gaṇeśa fast once a year (p. 431).

An Indian friend of mine told me that, when a little boy, he accidentally crushed a sparrow; whereupon his mother made him keep an eleventh-day fast, the merit (puṇya) of which was credited to the spirit of the dead sparrow.

Other chief festivals and fasts beginning with Māgha—corresponding to our January–February—are as follow:—

Makara-saṅkrānti (popularly Sankrānt), in celebration of the commencement of the sun's northern course (uttarāyaṇa) in the heavens. To mark this, a kind of New Year's festival is observed towards the end of Pausha or beginning of Māgha (about January 12). The sun has then reached the most southern point of the ecliptic. It is a period of rejoicing everywhere, especially as marking the termination of the inauspicious month Pausha (December–January); but it is not really the beginning of a new year, which varies in different parts of India. In Bengal it may be called the 'Festival of good cheer.' Practically, at least, it is kept by free indulgence in the eating of cakes, sweetmeats, and other good things. At one of the most sacred places in India, Prayāga (Allahābād), where the Jumnā and Ganges meet, a celebrated religious fair (Melā) takes place during this season.

The same festival in the South of India is commonly called Pongal (or Pungal). It marks the commencement of the Tamil year, and is the day for congratulatory visits. People purchase new cooking-pots and boil fresh rice in milk. Then they salute each other with the question—'Has the milk boiled?' to which the answer is given that 'the boiling (pongal) is over.' In reality the South Indian festival seems to be dedicated to the glorification of agriculture. Cattle are decorated with garlands, their horns coloured, and mango leaves hung round their necks. Then they are led about in procession, exempted from all labour, and virtually, if not actually, worshipped.

Vasanta-pañćamī, on the 5th of the light half of Māgha (January-February). This is a spring festival. In Bengal Sarasvatī (also, like Lakshmī, called Śrī), goddess of arts and learning, is worshipped at this season. The day is a holiday in all public and mercantile offices. Reading and writing are honoured by being suspended, but people worship an image of the goddess, or ink-stands, pens, paper, and other writing implements taken to represent the image. Sometimes an officiating priest is called in who reads the prescribed formulæ, and presents rice, fruits, sweetmeats, flowers, etc., while the lay-worshippers stand before the images or symbols with flowers in their hands, beseeching the goddess to grant them the blessings of learning, wealth, and fame.

Moreover, on this day, according to Mr. S. C. Bose, every Pandit in Bengal who keeps a school sets up an image of Sarasvatī and invites his patrons and friends to call upon him and do honour to the goddess. This they do by making offerings of rupees, which really form an important part of the Pandit's annual income. It is a significant fact that females are not allowed to take part in the worship of this goddess, though she be of their own sex.

Mahā-Śiva-rātri, or 'great Śiva-night,' is held on the 14th of the dark half of Māgha (about the middle or end of February). A fast is observed during the day, and a vigil kept at night, when the Liṅga is worshipped (see p. 90). At this season many pilgrims flock to the places dedicated to Śiva.

Holī or Hutāśanī festival—identified with the Dolā-yātrā, or rocking of the image of Kṛishṇa[1]—is celebrated, especially in the upper provinces, as a kind of Hindū Saturnalia or Carnival, and is therefore very popular. It begins about ten days before the full moon of Phālguna (February–March), but is usually only observed for the last three or four days, ending with the full moon. Boys dance about in the streets, and inhabitants of houses sprinkle the passers-by with red or yellow powder, use squirts and play practical jokes. It is marked by rough sports, loud music, merriment, mid-night orgies, obscene songs, excesses and abominations. Towards the close of the festival, about the night of full moon, a bonfire is lighted and games—representing the frolics of the young Kṛishṇa—take place around the expiring embers.

Rāma-navamī—the birthday of Rāma-ćandra—is observed on the 9th of the light half of the month Ćaitra (March–April), and is kept by some as a strict fast. The temples of Rāma are illuminated, and his image adorned with costly ornaments. The Rāmāyaṇa is read in the temples, and dances (Nautches) are kept up during the night.

Nāga-pañćamī is held on the 5th day of the light half of Śrāvaṇa, in honour of the Nāgas.

Two days later comes the Śītalā-saptamī, in honour of the Small-pox goddess (p. 228), when only cold food is eaten.

Kṛishṇa-janmāshṭamī, the birthday of Kṛishṇa—kept on

---

[1] The meaning of Holī is doubtful. It may be merely an imitation of the sounds and cries made by the revellers. By some the festival is said to be in commemoration of the killing of the demon Madhu by Kṛishṇa.

the 8th of the dark half of the month Bhādra or (in Bombay and the South) of Śrāvaṇa (July–August)—is one of the greatest of all Hindū holidays (see p. 113).

The variation in time in this and other festivals is caused by the circumstance that the months of the Northern and Southern Brāhmans differ in the dark fortnight.

Gaṇeśa-ćaturthī—the birthday of Gaṇeśa—is observed on the 4th of the light half of the month Bhādra (August–September). Clay figures of the deity are made, and after being worshipped for a few days, thrown into the water.

Sixteen consecutive lunar days are devoted to the performance of Śrāddhas in the dark half of Bhādra, which is therefore called the Pitṛi-paksha (see p. 308).

Durgā-pūjā, or Nava-rātra, 'nine nights,' beginning on the 1st and ending on the 10th day of the light half of Āśvina (September–October), are celebrated in many places as a great holiday, especially in Bengal, and connected with the autumnal equinox. Nominally they commemorate the victory of Durgā, wife of Śiva, over a buffalo-headed demon (Mahishāsur). The form under which she is adored is that of an image with ten arms and a weapon in each hand, her right leg resting on a lion and her left on the buffalo demon. This image is worshipped for nine days—following on the sixteen Śrāddhas of the Pitṛi-paksha—and then cast into the water.

The tenth day is called Vijaya-daśamī, or Daśa-harā.

Kālī-pūjā is a kindred festival in Bengal, lasting only for one night, and that the darkest night of the dark fortnight of the month Kārttika. The image worshipped is that of Kālī, the dark and terrible form of Śiva's wife described at p. 189. The well-known temple at Kālī Ghāṭ near Calcutta and other shrines of the goddess are during this night drenched with the blood of goats, sheep and buffaloes, sacrificed in honour of the sanguinary goddess.

Rāma-līlā, 'Rama-play,' is celebrated in some parts of India on the day when the Bengālīs commit their images of Durgā to the waters. It is a dramatic representation of the abduction of Sītā by Rāvaṇa, concluding with the death of Rāvaṇa.

Dīvālī (properly Dīpālī or Dīpāvalī), 'the feast of lamps,' is observed twenty days after the Nava-rātra on the last two days of the dark half of Āśvina, and on the new moon and four following days of Kārttika, in honour of Vishṇu's wife Lakshmī or of Śiva's wife Bhavānī (Pārvatī). It is marked by beautiful illuminations, in the preparation of which Indians far excel Europeans.

In some parts of India the Sarasvatī-pūjā (described p. 429) is kept at this season, on the 8th of the light half of Āśvina.

The Dīvālī should be seen at Benares. There its magnificence is heightened by the situation of the city on the bank of the river and the unique grouping and somewhat bizarre outline of the buildings. At the approach of night small earthen lamps, fed with oil, are prepared in millions, and placed close together so as to mark out the architectural form of mansion, palace, temple, minaret, and dome in lines of fire. All the boats on the river are lighted up, and the city, under the serene sky of an Indian autumn, is a blaze of calm effulgence. Viewed from the water it presents a dazzling spectacle—a scene of fairy-like splendour, which cannot be matched in any other city of the world. Indeed similar spectacles in the great European capitals appear absolutely paltry by comparison. Perhaps the illuminations which took place on the occasion of the Prince of Wales' visit to India in 1876 reached the climax of perfection, and will never be equalled for beauty and magnificence.

Kārttika-pūrṇimā is a festival kept on the full moon of the month Kārttika (October–November), in honour of Śiva's victory over the demon called Tripurāsura.

It must be noted that the months are lunar and that the calendar varies in different parts of India. Every month, such as Śrāvaṇa, Vaiśākha, and the intercalary or thirteenth month [1]

[1] There is an allusion to this thirteenth month in Ṛig-veda I. 25. 8, and in Atharva-veda V. 6. 4, XIII. 3. 8.

(Adhika-māsa), has its Māhātmya or special excellence. When the intercalary month comes round every third year, preachers make the most of their opportunity, and recite its Māhātmya, hoping thereby to stimulate the generosity of the people. Then, again, if a conjunction of the moon (or in some places a full moon) fall on a Monday, this is an astronomical coincidence that must be turned to the best account. It is a conjuncture peculiarly favourable to charitable acts. The same may be said of eclipses. A single rupee given at such seasons is worth a thousand rupees at other times.

Moreover, every day of the week has its sacred character. Monday is especially sacred to Śiva (Mahā-deva). Pious persons often fast on this day and worship the Liṅga in the evening. Saturday is Hanumān's day, and offerings are especially made to him on that day. Then the eighth day in every lunar fortnight is sacred to Durgā. This is a day when no study is allowed, and therefore called An-adhyāya. Indeed holy days or non-reading days may be multiplied indefinitely. Thus a pupil will stop reading and go home if it happens to thunder, if any person or animal chances to pass between himself and his teacher, if a guest arrives, and often during the greater part of the rainy season.

No less than four eras are commonly current among the Hindūs in India:—1. Saṃvat (of King Vikramāditya), reckoned from 57 B.C.; 2. Śaka (of King Śālivāhana), reckoned from 78 A.D.; 3. San, current in Bengal, reckoned from 593 A.D.; 4. The era of Paraśu-rāma, current in Malabar, reckoned from 1176 B.C. In almanacks it is usual to state how many years of the present age of the world or Kali-yuga (p. 398) have elapsed; thus at present 4984 out of 432,000 years have gone by. The three previous ages are the Kṛita or Satya, Tretā, or Dvāpara. Almanacks which follow the Śaka era begin the year with the light half of the month Ćaitra, but the Saṃvat year usually commences with Kārttika.

CHAPTER XVII.

Temples and Sacred Places of Pilgrimage.

It is well known that the principal seat and great centre of the cultus of Śiva is Benares (Vārāṇasī)[1]—a city whose world-wide celebrity has earned for it the title of Kāśī, 'the resplendent.' In the Kāśī-khaṇḍa of the Skanda-purāṇa it is recorded how the god himself chose that city for his special abode, and how after having undergone severe austerities in the neighbourhood he made it sacred to himself and to his sons Gaṇeśa and Skanda (p. 211).

Elsewhere Benares is described as a special creation of the Creator, who formed it of pure unpolluted earth, separated it from the rest of the world, and caused it to rest on one of the points of Śiva's trident.

No doubt Benares was one of the first cities to acquire a reputation for sanctity, and is still regarded as the most sacred spot in all India. It is the Hindū's Jerusalem and Mecca. Here, temples, shrines, and idols are multiplied beyond all calculation. Here every inch of ground, every clod of earth is hallowed, and the very air is holy.

No wonder, then, that every pious Hindū is ambitious of accomplishing at least one pilgrimage to what he regards as a portion of heaven let down upon earth, and if he can happily manage to die within the magic circle of what is called the Pañćakośī—that is to say, within a circuit of ten miles round the centre of the holy city—nay, if the most desperate

[1] The popular name is more properly written Banāras. The name Vārāṇasī, of which it is a corruption, is said to be derived from two small rivers outside the city, the Varaṇā or Varṇā and the Asī.

criminal from any part of the world—be he of any religious denomination, Christian, Buddhist, or Muhammadan—die there, no amount of the most heinous guilt, not even the deadly sin of eating beef, can prevent his immediate transportation to the heaven of Śiva. Yet Benares is by no means exclusively dedicated to Śiva; nor are its inhabitants exclusively devoted to the worship of any one favourite deity (ishṭa-devatā). Nor is it the seat of any ecclesiastical organization or of any council or central sacerdotal government, which indeed exist nowhere in India. Still Benares is the citadel of Brāhmanism—the stronghold of Hindūism. It is the focus from which all the lines of the most complicated religious system in the world diverge, and to which they converge. Here priestcraft reigns supreme in all its plenitude and power. Nay it is not too much to say that here a population of about 200,000 persons and a countless number of pilgrims deliver themselves up to be deluded, defrauded, and kept in religious slavery by 25,000 arrogant Brāhmans.

Picturesquely situated on the Ganges and stretching for three or four miles along this most sacred of all rivers, with magnificent Ghāṭs or flights of steps conducting pilgrims by thousands into the very midst of its hallowed waters, Benares is the home of every form of Hindū religious earnestness and enthusiasm, combined with every conceivable variety of hideous superstition and fanaticism.

No description indeed can give the slightest idea of the reality of the sight presented to the eye by this unique city. The traveller bent on investigating its inner mysteries, and eager to solve for himself the riddle of the grosser forms of its superstition and fanaticism, finds that his only hope of traversing its tortuous streets, or penetrating the living tide which daily ebbs and flows in its leading thoroughfares, is by trusting to his personal powers as a pedestrian. Pushing his way through the seething throng he beholds everywhere, as he advances, the most striking contrasts and curious incongruities—princely mansions and mean tenements, handsome edifices and fantastic freaks of architecture, crowded shrines and empty sanctuaries, bright new temples and dilapidated fanes, freshly gilded domes and mildewed pinnacles, graceful minarets and unsightly cupolas, open streets and impassable lanes. dirty squares and well-kept quadrangles—everywhere and from every point of view a strange intermingling of the beautiful and the grotesque, the tasteful and the bizarre, the simple and the extravagant.

The living objects which meet his eye as he proceeds are not less interesting, odd, and incongruous. Now he is jostled by sacred bulls which wander everywhere free and uncontrolled; now a number of impudent monkeys bound over his head or spring from roof to roof; now a dozen sacred pigeons fly fearlessly almost into his face, or a flight of parrots circle noisily around his head. In one part of the city he is hemmed in before some sacred pool or noted temple by a motley throng of pilgrims, some pressing forward to perform their ablutions, some carrying Ganges water for use at the idol-shrines, some vociferating the name of their favourite gods. In another quarter he is surrounded by groups of half-naked mendicants and dirty devotees, many of whom parade their bodily austerities in a manner highly repulsive to European eyes. Here he struggles with difficulty through streets of coppersmiths and workers in brass. There his path is obstructed by the stalls of vendors of coarse sweetmeats, sellers of flower-garlands, or money-changers sitting behind heaps of cowries and piles of gold and silver coins. Everywhere temples, shrines, mosques, images and symbols, holy wells, pools, and sacred trees present themselves in bewildering confusion.

The number of principal temples is at least two thousand. Smaller shrines are, of course, innumerable. Of Muhammadan mosques the total is said to amount to three hundred. The tale of idols is computed at about half a million. The chief temple called the 'golden temple,' dedicated to Śiva or

Mahā-deva (see p. 78), is disappointing to any one who has seen the south Indian temples; for although Śiva is specially worshipped and propitiated at Benares he has nowhere so many earnest votaries as in the South, and the Benares temple in respect of size, external appearance and importance is to the great temples of Tanjore, Madurā and Tinnevelly, what a small village church is to St. Paul's Cathedral.

The fact is that the waves of Muhammadan invasion which swept over the North-west and Central provinces of India, and seemed at one time likely to obliterate Brāhmanism altogether, were either arrested in their onward course or else spent themselves before reaching the South. This is remarkably illustrated at Benares, where the most conspicuous building is the great mosque of Aurangzīb with its lofty minarets on the Ganges. Even the old original Śaiva temple of Viśveśvara does not exist. It was pulled down by the ruthless Aurangzīb and a mosque built on its foundations [1]. Another temple, however, speedily arose close at hand and rivalled the old one in picturesque beauty, if not in size. It stands at a distance of two or three hundred yards from its predecessor.

Between them is the Jñāna-vāpī, or holy well of knowledge —a spot greatly frequented and held in high veneration by pilgrims from all parts of the country—a legend being universally current that, when Aurangzīb destroyed the Hindū temple, its idol took refuge of its own accord at the bottom of this holy well. Thither therefore a constant throng of worshippers continually resort, bringing with them offerings of flowers, rice, and other grain, which they throw into the water thirty or forty feet below the ground. A Brāhman is perpetually employed in drawing up the putrid liquid, the smell or rather stench of which, from incessant admixture of decaying flowers and vegetable matter, makes the neighbourhood

---

[1] According to Mr. Sherring—whose book on Benares is well worthy of perusal—there was a still earlier temple on a site not far distant.

almost unbearable. This he pours with a ladle into the hands of expectant crowds, who either drink it with avidity or sprinkle it reverentially over their persons.

Another sacred well, called Maṇi-karṇikā, situated on one of the chief Ghāṭs on the Ganges, owes its origin, in popular belief, to the fortunate circumstance that one of Śiva's ear-rings happened to fall on the spot.

This well is near the surface and quite exposed to view. It forms a small quadrangular pool not more than three feet deep. Four flights of steps on the four sides lead to the water, the disgusting foulness of which vastly enhances—in the estimation of countless pilgrims—its efficacy for the removal of sin. The most abandoned criminals journey from distant parts of India to the margin of this sacred pool. There they pay large fees to secure the services of the Brāhman officials, and descending with them into the water are made to mutter certain texts and mystic formulæ, the meaning of which they are wholly unable to understand. Then while in the act of repeating the words put into their mouths they eagerly immerse their entire persons beneath the offensive liquid. The longed-for dip over, a miraculous transformation is the result; for the foul water has cleansed the still fouler soul. Few orthodox Hindūs venture to doubt that the most depraved sinner in existence may thus be converted into an immaculate saint, worthy of being translated at once to the highest heaven of the god of Benares.

But to return to the temple of Viśveśvara. I found, when I visited it, a constant stream of worshippers passing in and out. In fact, Śiva in his character of lord of the universe (see p. 78) is the supreme deity of Benares. Not that the pilgrims are prohibited from worshipping at the shrines of other gods, but that Śiva is here paramount and claims the first homage. Yet this supreme god has no image; he is represented by a plain conical stone—to wit, the Liṅga or symbol of male generative power. The method of performing worship in this great central and typical temple of Hindūism appeared to me very remarkable in its contrast with all Christian ideas as to the true nature of worship. All that each worshipper did was to bring Ganges water in a small metal vessel and pour the water over the stone Liṅga, at the same time ringing one of the bells hanging from the roof to attract the god's attention towards himself, bowing low in obeisance, and muttering a few texts with repetition of the god's name. In this way the god's symbol was kept deluged with water (see p. 68), while the crowds who passed in and out lingered for a time close to the shrine, talking to each other in loud tones. Nor did any idea of irreverence seem to be attached to noisy vociferation in the interior of the sanctuary itself. Nor was any objection made to an unbeliever like myself approaching and looking inside; whereas in the South of India I was strictly excluded from all the avenues to the inner Liṅga-sanctuaries (see p. 447). In the courts adjacent to the Liṅga were other shrines dedicated to various deities, and in a kind of cloister or gallery which encircled the temple were thousands of stone Liṅgas crowded together carelessly and apparently only intended as votive-offerings. I noticed the coil of a serpent carved round one or two of the most conspicuous symbols of male generative energy, and the combination appeared to me very significant.

The goddess Anna-pūrṇā has a temple close at hand. She is thought to be charged by the god Śiva with the duty of keeping the inhabitants of Benares supplied with abundance of food. I found the quadrangle which surrounds this shrine crowded with bulls, cows, priests, and mendicants, who are daily fed by the offerings of the rich. The effluvium emitted by the filth and dirt was insufferable. It was here that I met with an Ūrdhva-bāhu ascetic (described at p. 88).

Among Southern Śaiva temples the finest is at Tanjore.

It is contained within a vast quadrangle, the floor of which is paved with bricks and kept scrupulously clean. Two lofty

Gopuras or gateways surmounted by high pyramidal towers[1] lead into this square, and a sort of double cloister or arcade surrounds it. Then in the second or hinder part of two sides of the arcade are arranged a hundred and eight black stone Liṅgas of different sizes, one for each of the hundred and eight principal names of Śiva, and behind these again are sixty-four frescoes painted on the wall—many of them highly grotesque—representing various exploits of the god or his attendants[2]. A catalogue of sixty-three saints or distinguished personages whose devotion to Śiva gave them the power of performing miracles and supernatural feats is sometimes enumerated (see p. 85)[3]. On the left of the quadrangle as you enter is a pleasant grove of palms and other trees. In the centre is the principal temple, containing the Garbha-gṛiham or inner-most sanctuary of the sacred Liṅga, a kind of holy of holies to which I was not allowed access. This is an imposing structure, made still more so by the fine Maṇḍapa or open hall erected in front of it as a shrine for the stone image of Śiva's bull (nandi), which is a magnificent specimen of Indian sculpture of great size. Near the principal temple are four subordinate ones, two behind and two on one side. Those behind are dedicated to the two sons of Śiva, one to Gaṇeśa and the other to Su-brahmaṇya (p. 211). In front of Gaṇeśa is the image of his vehicle, the rat, looking into the shrine, as the bull does into the shrine of Śiva. The rat is an emblem of sagacity, as the bull is of generative power (see pp. 319, 328).

---

[1] These structures are of oblong form, and sometimes of immense height. They are only pyramidal in the sense of being broader at the base than at the summit. It is remarkable that Vaishṇava carvings are found on these Tanjore Gopuras, showing that the temple may have once belonged to the Vaishṇavas. Everywhere the two systems seem intermingled.

[2] In one of these a Liṅga is represented with a face inside it. Another has a serpent for a canopy. In another Gaṇḍodara, an attendant of Śiva, is swallowing mountains of rice and drinking up a river.

[3] The catalogue is given by Mr. Foulkes in his Śaiva Catechism.

The image of Su-brahmaṇya or Skanda is seated on a peacock and has six faces. As to Su-brahmaṇya, see p. 214.

One of the side temples near the entrance of the quadrangle contains an image of Śiva, lifting up his left leg while dancing the Tāṇḍava dance and trampling on the demon Apa-smāra. He holds the Ḍamaru in one hand, using it for a musical instrument or rattle, as a dancer would castanets. This temple has some curious pictures on the walls. One is of Bhṛiṅgi, an attendant of Śiva, who became so feeble and attenuated through self-mortification[1] that the god furnished him with a third leg for support; another represents an attendant with the lower part of his body terminating in a snake; a third depicts one of Śiva's servants with the feet of a tiger. In a fourth the sage Mārkaṇḍeya is about to be carried off by the king of death (Yama), when he grasps Śiva's Liṅga and saves himself. A fifth represents the story of Kāla-hasta, a pious forester who habitually did homage to Śiva with offerings of flowers. One day having forgotten his usual oblation he without any hesitation tore out one of his own eyes from its socket, and having offered it as a substitute was proceeding to take out the other, when Śiva prevented him.

The second side temple is an oblong chamber containing an image of Pārvatī at the further end, with lights always burning in front. Near the entrance is a representation of Pārvatī's darpaṇa or mirror. On one of the walls is portrayed a large Liṅga, canopied by the serpent Śesha.

To describe all the principal Śaiva temples of India would require volumes. One thousand and eight are said to exist, one for each of the one thousand and eight names of the god. One hundred and eight are regarded as important. Kālī's temples are equally numerous; see the Kālī-pūjā at p. 431 and the description of the Vindyāćal temple at p. 575.

---

[1] He was a model ascetic, and fasted so continuously that he became not only emaciated, but an actual living skeleton. He is so represented in the sculptures of the caves of Elephanta near Bombay.

Of the others which I visited, the temples at Madurā, Rāmeśvara, Trichinopoly, Kāñjīvaram, Tinnevelly, and the shrine of Kapāleśvara at Nāsik (one of the oldest), appeared to me most worthy of note.

At the Madurā temple Śiva is worshipped as Sundareśvara, a name given to him as the husband of Mīnākshī (corrupted into Mīnāćī), the deified daughter of a Pāṇḍya king[1].

A very extensive and imposing series of shrines, passages, and galleries, including a thousand-pillared open hall of great beauty, constitutes the temple. These are enclosed by a high wall, inside of which and encircling the interior building is an open road or way for the benefit of pious persons who use it for reverential circumambulation (pradakshiṇā) round the sacred shrine. Two lofty Gopuras form the entrance to the temple, each leading by long corridors to the two principal shrines. That on the left leads to the shrine of Mīnākshī (commonly called Mīnāćī); that on the right terminates with the Liṅga shrine. It is noteworthy that near the latter are images of the five Pāṇḍava princes who are generally connected with the worship of Kṛishṇa[2]. Various interesting carvings and sculptured figures are in the neighbouring corridors. It is evident that Mīnākshī is the real popular deity of the district, and that in the estimation of the inhabitants of Madurā her consort Śiva is quite secondary.

I happened accidentally to witness a festival held in her honour called Tailotsava, 'the oil festival.' A coarse image of the goddess, profusely decorated with jewels and having a high head-dress of hair, was carried in the centre of a long proces-

---

[1] The temple is commonly called the Mīnākshī-sundareśvara pagoda, the wife's name being placed first, as it generally is in other cases also (see p. 184). The legend is that Mīnākshī was born with three breasts, but one disappeared on meeting with her future husband Śiva. She was then converted into a local goddess of great celebrity.

[2] This is an evidence of the tolerant spirit which marks Hindūism. Where Śaivism got the better of Vaishṇavism in the South, the Vaishṇava ornaments were respected and allowed to remain in Śaiva temples.

sion on a canopied throne borne by eight Brāhmans to a platform in the magnificent hall or Maṇḍapa of the Tirumell Nāyak opposite the temple. There the ceremony of undressing the idol, removing its ornaments, anointing its head with oil, bathing, redecorating and redressing it was gone through amid shouting, singing, beating of tom-toms, waving of lights and cowries, ringing of bells, and deafening discord from forty or fifty so-called musical instruments, each played by a man who did his best to overpower the sound of all the others combined. At the head of the procession was borne an image of Gaṇeśa. Then followed three elephants, a long line of priests, musicians, attendants bearing cowries and umbrellas, with a troop of dancing girls bringing up the rear.

No sight I witnessed in India made me more sick at heart than this. It furnished a sad example of the utterly debasing character of the idolatry which, notwithstanding the counteracting influences of education and Christianity, still enslaves the masses of the population, deadening their intellects, corrupting their imaginations, warping their affections, perverting their consciences, disfiguring the fair soil of a beautiful country with hideous images, and encouraging practices unsanctioned even by their own most ancient sacred works.

Probably the Rāmeśvara temple ranks next to those of Tanjore and Madurā in magnificence, and to those of Benares in sanctity. It is situated in a small town at the further side of the island of Rāmeśvara—an island about eight miles long by four broad—which, with the coral reef stretching for twenty-one miles from its furthest extremity and appearing like a broken bridge above the sea[1], nearly connects India with Manaar and Ceylon. The narrow channel separating the island from the mainland is called Pāmbam (or Pāmben). The journey to it caused me great discomfort and fatigue.

---

[1] The natives still believe this to be the remains of the bridge formed by Hanumān and Rāma's army of monkeys, when he invaded Ceylon for the recovery of his wife Sītā (see Indian Wisdom, p. 358).

Starting from Rāmnād a vast sandy waste has to be traversed before this sacred island can be reached. Yet thousands of pilgrims walk first to Benares and thence to Rāmeśvara. And perhaps such a double pilgrimage (yātrā) is the most meritorious act a Hindū can perform. It is true that enormous merit (puṇya) may be accumulated by simply visiting Rāmeśvara, but this is as nothing compared to what may be obtained by going first to Benares.

In my own case I had visited both Benares and Rāmeśvara, though not on foot, and I was rewarded at the latter place by being met on my arrival by a number of Pandits, who brought a band of musicians and conducted me in state, amid a deafening din, through the streets of the town. The musicians, though they preceded me, all walked backwards.

In fact, if a man wish for the perfection of bliss hereafter, he has only one course open to him. He must first journey to Benares, there go through at least a hundred ceremonies at a hundred shrines in the sacred circle surrounding the centre of the city, pay large fees to the Brāhmans at innumerable temples, and especially pour plenty of Ganges water over the symbol of Śiva at the Viśveśvara shrine. Then he must fill a jar with more holy water from the Ganges, and toil with it on foot through dust and sand for about twelve hundred miles to Rāmeśvara. There the sacred water is to be poured over the symbol of Śiva with the certainty of securing complete beatitude hereafter, provided sufficient fees are paid to the Brāhmans, and the process is wound up by a bath in the sea at Dhanush-koṭi, a little further on.

Shortly before my arrival at the temple a father and son had just completed their self-imposed task, and after months of hard walking succeeded in transporting their precious burden of Ganges water to the other side of the channel. The longed-for goal was nearly reached and the temple of Rāmeśvara already in sight, when the father died suddenly on the road, leaving his son, a mere child, utterly destitute.

The boy, however, had one treasure left—his jar of Ganges water. This, if only it could be poured upon the sacred symbol, would prove a complete panacea for all his earthly troubles. Eagerly therefore he grasped his burden once more and hurried on to the shrine. Imagine the child's outburst of grief when the door was closed against him. He had no fee for the presiding priest.

The temple of Rāmeśvara itself I found to be a vast oblong structure containing an immense collection of Liṅga shrines, open halls and tanks surrounded by long beautiful galleries and corridors, one entrance to which is from the small town of Rāmeśvara and the other from the sea-shore. The principal sanctuary or Garbha is well secluded and carefully protected from all unhallowed eyes in the centre of the structure. It contains the celebrated Liṅga set up by Rāma after his return from Ceylon (Laṅkā).

The legend is that, anxious to expiate the impurity contracted by the slaughter of Rāvaṇa in the battle which ended in the demon's death (p. 111), Rāma despatched Hanumān to bring a Liṅga from Benares that he might erect a shrine over it and so propitiate Śiva. But the monkey-god was so long in executing the commission that Sītā prepared a Liṅga of sand with her own hands, and Rāma having then and there performed the ceremony of setting it up (pratishṭhā) and consecrating it, proceeded to worship it. He then bathed in the sea from the neighbouring promontory at a spot which was afterwards called Thanush-koḍi (Dhanush-koṭi), because marked by the corner of his bow. Hence a visit to this spot is essential to a completely meritorious performance of the Rāmeśvara pilgrimage.

The Śaiva temple at Trichinopoly is dedicated to Śiva in his character of Jambukeśvara, lord of the Jambu tree[1]. It is one of the most important and interesting shrines in

[1] The connexion of Śiva worship with tree and serpent worship seemed to me traceable everywhere in Southern India (compare p. 331).

India. No one could fail to be impressed with its beautiful colonnades, cloisters, and thousand-pillared Maṇḍapa, though when I visited it in 1877 it was in a somewhat decaying condition. In the central court of the temple is a metal column (stambha) supporting a flag (dhvaja)[1], and near it is the Jambu tree over which Śiva is supposed to preside.

The chief object of worship is a stone Liṅga, always kept under water and thence called the Ap-liṅga. The Pandits informed me that four other celebrated Liṅga-shrines in India represent the remaining four elements—fire, air, earth, and ether[2], all of which are believed to be manifestations of Śiva (compare p. 85).

At Kāñjīvaram (the ancient Kāñćī), one of the most sacred places in India[3], not far distant from Madras, there are two principal temples at opposite ends of the town, one dedicated to Vishṇu (as Varada-rāja), the other to Śiva. Both were visited by me, and both I found to be striking examples of South Indian architecture, containing a very considerable collection of imposing buildings within their exterior walls. According to a local legend the goddess Pārvatī once performed penance under a mango-tree (āmra) on the spot where the Śaiva temple now stands. There her husband Śiva appeared to her, and there he is worshipped as Ekāmra-nātha, 'the peerless lord of the mango[4].'

The Tinnevelly Śaiva temple is also highly interesting and instructive. Śiva is here again worshipped in connexion with a sacred tree, the Vaṭa or Banian tree, whence his name Vaṭeśvara, 'lord of the Vaṭa-tree[5];' but here, as at Madurā, his

---

[1] A similar column is in other South Indian shrines.

[2] They are called the Tejo-liṅga, Vāyu-liṅga, Pṛithivī-liṅga, and Ākāśa-liṅga respectively.

[3] It is enumerated among the seven most sacred places.

[4] So he was described to me by a Pandit in the temple. Otherwise his name might literally be 'lord of the one mango.'

[5] Here is another instance of Śiva's association with trees (compare p. 331). The Pandits who took me round the temple described the god as

wife Pārvatī, who has a shrine on the left side of the temple, under the name of Kāntimatī, 'the lovely one,' is the most popular object of adoration[1]. The Liṅga of Śiva, in a kind of holy of holies in this temple, is very sacred. The approach to it is by a long corridor; but the sanctuary itself is not visible at the end of the vista. It is protected by three other approaches or vestibules, each increasing in sanctity (called the Ghaṇṭā-maṇḍapa, the Mahā-maṇḍapa, and the Arddha-maṇḍapa), into none of which was I permitted to enter.

The Liṅga is, of course, never moved from its place in the penetralia of the temple, but an image of Śiva, called the Utsava-mūrti, is carried about in procession on certain festival days, especially when the annual ceremony of marrying the god and the goddess is performed every October. The god of love (Kāma-deva) and his wife (Rati) have also images in this temple, and a festival is held in their honour every spring. Two magnificent open halls—one with a thousand columns, the other with a hundred and eight—a tank, garden, and grove of palms are all within the enclosure of the temple.

I will not advert to the ruins of the marvellous Kailāsa temple cut out of the solid rock at Ellorā, which I visited in 1877 (pp. 70, 118, 291), further than to say that it is one of the wonders of India and indeed of the world. As to the celebrated Vishṇu-temple of Jagan-nāth at Purī in Orissa, its sanctity is such that 100,000 pilgrims annually eat the sacred food (*prasāda*) distributed in its courts to priest, prince and peasant alike; for no distinctions of caste are recognized in the presence of Kṛishṇa (Vishṇu) 'the lord of the world.' (The car-festival is described in my 'Modern India,' p. 68.)

The temple of Vishṇu at Gayā has been described at p. 309, and temples of Kṛishṇa at p. 144, and again at p. 152.

Śālīvaṭīśvara (or in Tamil, Nel vellī-nātha). I was informed that, at a sacred shrine south of the Vindhya, Śiva is worshipped as Drākshārāme-śvara, 'lord of the vineyard.'

[1] Live parrots and cockatoos are hung before her shrine as offerings.

We pass on to the Śrī-raṅgam temple at Trichinopoly which contains in one of its courts a shrine of Rāmānuja, the great Vaishṇava teacher (p. 119), who is supposed to have lived here for a considerable time before his death. Śrī-raṅgam is, indeed, rather a sacred city than a temple. Hundreds of Brāhmans dwell within its precincts, thousands of pilgrims throng its streets, and on great anniversaries myriads of worshippers crowd its corridors, and press towards its sanctuary. No sight is to be seen in any part of India that can at all compare with the unique effect produced by its series of seven quadrangular enclosures formed by seven squares of massive walls, one within the other—every square pierced by four lofty gateways, and each gateway surmounted by pyramidal towers rivalling in altitude the adjacent rock of Trichinopoly.

The construction of this marvellous congeries of sacred buildings must have cost millions of rupees, and since its first construction fabulous sums have been spent on its maintenance and enlargement. It is said that kings and princes have emptied their coffers and given up their revenues for the completion and extension of its many-storied towers; rich men of every rank have parted with their treasures for the adding of column after column to its thousand-pillared courts; misers have yielded up their hoards for the decoration of its jewelled images; capitalists have bequeathed vast benefactions for the support of its priests; architects and artists have exhausted all their resources for the production of a perfect shrine, the worthy receptacle of an idol of transcendent glory.

The idea is that each investing square of walls shall form courts of increasing sanctity which shall conduct the worshipper by regular gradations to a central holy of holies of unique shape and proportions. In fact, the entire fabric of shrines, edifices, towers, and enclosures is supposed to be a terrestrial counterpart of Vishṇu's heaven (Vaikuṇṭha), to which his votaries are destined to be transported.

The idol itself is recumbent, and its legendary history is curious. When Rāma dismissed his ally Vibhīshaṇa—the brother of the conquered demon Rāvaṇa who had carried off Sītā to Ceylon—he gave him, out of gratitude for his services, a golden idol of Vishṇu, with instructions not to lay it down till he had reached home. Vibhīshaṇa accordingly set out on his return to Ceylon, taking the precious image with him. Passing near Śrī-raṅgam, and wishing to bathe in the sacred tank, he gave the image to one of his followers, charging him to hold it upright, and on no account to let it pass out of his hands. But Vibhīshaṇa was so long over his ablutions, that the holder of the image, finding its weight insupportable, deposited it on the ground, intending to take it up again before Vibhīshaṇa's return. The dismay of all parties concerned was great when they discovered that the idol obstinately declined to be removed from its comfortable position. It had, therefore, to be left in a recumbent attitude, and a shrine was built over it, shaped like the sacred monosyllable Om, supposed to be a combination of the three letters A, U, M, mystically significant of the Supreme Being's three principal manifestations, Brahmā, Vishṇu, and Śiva (pp. 44; 402; 403). On the summit of the shrine were placed four pinnacles to denote the four Vedas, and around it were constructed seven walls built in squares, one within the other, and forming seven quadrangular courts, figuring the seven divisions or degrees of bliss in Vishṇu's heaven.

Of course the original idol of Vishṇu is supposed to be still immovable; but another image has been consecrated (called the utsava-vigraha), which is carried about in processions on certain anniversaries—such, for example, as the car-festival, when the enormous car, attached to every Vaishṇava temple in Southern India, is dragged through the streets of the town by thousands of men.

The dress, decorations, and jewelry belonging to this portable idol were all exhibited to me. I saw the idol-crown covered with diamonds, pearls, and rubies—worth at least eighty thousand rupees—with a breastplate, ornaments for the feet, and necklace, worth a similar sum.

In the centre of the inner wall of the temple, near the interior shrine on the north side, is a narrow door called heaven's gate. I happened to visit Śrī-raṅgam at the time of the annual festival celebrated on the 27th of December. This is the one day in the year on which the gate is opened, and on the occasion of my visit the opening took place at four o'clock in the morning. First the idol—bedecked and bejewelled to the full—was borne through the narrow portal, followed by eighteen images of Vaishṇava saints and devotees; then came innumerable priests chanting Vedic hymns and repeating the thousand names of Vishṇu; then dancing girls and bands of musicians—the invariable attendants upon idol-shrines in the South of India. Finally, a vast throng—probably fifty thousand persons—crowded for hours through the contracted passage, amid deafening shouts and vociferations, beating of drums, and discordant sounds of all kinds of music.

Not a single human being passed through that strait and narrow portal without presenting offerings to the idol, and gifts to the priests. Many, doubtless, joined the surging throng from a vague sense of duty, or because their fathers and grandfathers had joined it from time immemorial; but the motive which actuated the majority was a firm conviction that the passage of the earthly heaven's gate, kept by the priests, and unlocked at their bidding, would be a sure passport to Vishṇu's heaven after death.

I may mention in conclusion that most of the South Indian temples are sufficiently well endowed to maintain a band of musicians. That of Tanjore has fifty. The number and variety of their musical instruments struck me as extraordinary, though the resulting sounds at the time of morning and evening service, when a noisy orchestra is thought to contribute largely to the merit of religious worship, are productive, at least to European ears, of excruciating discord.

All the temples also maintain troops of dancing girls. The Tanjore temple possesses fifteen, ten of whom danced before me in the court of the temple with far livelier movements than are customary among the Nāch girls of Western and Northern India. There can be no doubt that dancing in the East was once exclusively connected with religious devotion, especially with homage paid to Śiva in his character of lord of dancing (see p. 85). Further, it is well-known that in ancient times women were dedicated to the service of the temples, like the Vestal virgins of Europe. They were held to be married to the god, and had no other duty but to dance before his shrine. Hence they were called the god's slaves (deva-dāsī), and were generally patterns of piety and propriety. In the present day they are still called by the same name, but are rather slaves to the licentious passions of the profligate Brāhmans of the temples to which they belong.

What surprised me most was the number and weight of their ornaments, especially in the case of those attached to the temples in Southern India. Some wore nose-rings and finger-rings glittering with rubies and pearls. Their ears were pierced all round and filled with costly ear-rings. Their limbs were encumbered with bangles, anklets, armlets, toe-rings, necklaces, chain-ornaments, head-ornaments, and the like. One of the Tanjore girls informed me that she had been recently robbed of jewels to the value of Rs. 25,000. No doubt they drive a profitable trade under the sanction of religion, and some courtezans have been known to amass enormous fortunes. Nor do they think it inconsistent with their method of making money to spend it in works of piety. Here and there Indian bridges and other useful public works owe their existence to the liberality of the frail sisterhood.

CHAPTER XVIII.

Caste, especially in relation to Occupations.

THE Portuguese, who were the first to trade with India, used the word 'casta,' 'race,' to denote the infinite number of classes into which Indian society is divided. This word was changed by us into 'caste'—a word unrecognized by the natives, but now universally adopted by all writers on Hindūism. Caste in India is closely bound up with religion.

Indeed it might fairly be asserted that Hindūism, allowing as it does the most perfect freedom in regard to religious opinions, is rather a religion of caste-rules and caste-usages, of forms and ceremonies, than of doctrines and dogmas.

The four original castes of Manu's time have been already described (p. 53). His word for caste was varṇa, 'colour,' which implied some ethnological distinction of complexion as separating the dominant from the inferior classes. The modern word is jāti (jāt), 'birth,' indicating that in whatever station or profession a man is born to that he is indissolubly bound. Of these four castes not one remains in its purity, not even that of the Brāhmans, who are divided and subdivided into countless sub-castes. Nevertheless the Brāhmans are still the purest caste of the four, though the Rājputs claim to be pure Kshatriyas, and the Baniyahs or traders call themselves pure Vaiśyas, and in some parts of India there are so-called pure Śūdras. All these four castes consider themselves superior to the countless mixed castes, each one of which is generally confined to its own employment, and these again look down upon the outcastes or sweepers who in the South are called Pariahs. It has recently been asserted that certain sections of the Pariah class are so down-trodden as to be kept in practical slavery. As a rule, however, the lower castes are not oppressed by the higher or even held in contempt by them. It is remarkable, too, that the lower the caste the more tenacious are its members of their own caste-rules and the more pride do they take in observing them, and the more strict are they in enforcing them.

Doubtless railroads by necessitating personal contact and facilitating communication have relaxed the rigour of caste in some few particulars. Yet its power is still exerted with almost irresistible force in imposing certain social restrictions which may be classed under four heads as follow:—

1. Restrictions as to the kind of food allowed to be eaten and as to its preparation by cooks who must not be of a caste inferior to that of the eaters.

2. Restrictions as to commensality,—that is, as to persons of different castes eating together[1], outcastes being excluded from all commensality, except among themselves.

3. Restrictions as to marriage, including the enforcement of child-marriages, the prohibition of widow-remarriage, and the prevention of intermarriage between persons of different castes.

4. Restriction of particular occupations to particular castes.

It is to the last of these four heads that the present chapter will mainly be confined.

It is remarkable that notwithstanding India's vast potentiality of wealth, all her ancient superiority in arts, sciences, and

---

[1] Fruits and dry food may be eaten by all castes together. The moment food is cooked caste comes in with strict prohibitions. Nothing cooked in water can be eaten by people of different castes together, nor can water be accepted by high caste from low caste persons.

industries, carried back through countless generations for at least 3500 years, it is impossible to deny that she has never advanced beyond a certain point, and that she is at present both scientifically and commercially left far behind by European nations. Let us go back to the beginning. Let us try to trace the causes which first promoted and then impeded the development of her trades and industries.

It is generally supposed that the first Āryan settlers on Indian soil were all tillers of the land. Parties of immigrants from Central Asia gained possession of fertile tracts in Northern India and formed themselves into separate agricultural communities. Soon the richness of the soil on the plains of the Indus and the Ganges enabled them to support a considerable surplus population. New wants arose with the gradual growth of the community. Soldiers were needed to fight their battles, watchmen to protect their crops, priests to perform their religious duties, weavers to weave their garments, artisans to supply them with common articles of every-day use, servants to do menial work. Hence arose a complete system of division of labour. To every man his place, work, rank, and remuneration were assigned. Hence, too, every member of the body so constituted acquired great skill in his own particular craft, and took a pride in continually improving it. This skill and these feelings of pride he transmitted to his children, by whom again they were developed and intensified. In this manner a strong *esprit de corps* was generated, and associations of persons engaged in the same occupations were ultimately formed, each of which fenced itself round with rules and regulations necessary for the protection of its own rights and privileges.

It is easy to see, therefore, that caste and occupation were formerly convertible terms. The number of these trade-castes is at present quite incalculable. There seems to be no limit to their formation. New ones are continually forming. Old ones are continually passing away. Even to enumerate their names would be impossible. In all probability they have all grown out of the primitive constitution of village communities.

And here I may observe that no circumstance in the history of India is more worthy of investigation than the antiquity and permanence of her village and municipal institutions. The importance of the study lies in the light thereby thrown on the parcelling out of rural society into autonomous divisions, like those of our own English parishes, wherever Āryan races have occupied the soil in Asia or in Europe. The Indian village or township, meaning thereby not merely a collection of houses forming a village or town, but a division of territory, perhaps three or four square miles or more in extent, with its careful distribution of fixed occupations for the common good, with its intertwining and inter-dependence of individual, family, and communal interests, with its perfect provision for political independence and autonomy, is the original type—the first germ of all the divisions of rural and civic society in medieval and modern Europe. It has existed almost unaltered since the description of its organization in Manu's code, two or three centuries before the Christian era. It has survived all the religious, political, and physical convulsions from which India has suffered from time immemorial. Invader after invader has ravaged the country with fire and sword; internal wars have carried devastation into every corner of the land; tyrannical oppressors have desolated its homesteads; famine has decimated its peasantry; pestilence has depopulated entire districts; floods and earthquakes have changed the face of nature; folly, superstition, and delusion have made havoc of all religion and morality—but the simple, self-contained Indian township has preserved its constitution intact, its customs, precedents, and peculiar institutions unchanged and unchangeable amid all other changes.

Let us endeavour to draw a picture of one of these Indian communities. And in the first place let us bear in mind that it consists mainly of tillers of the soil. At least three-fourths of the whole body are common field-labourers. Each man tills a small plot of ground of his own, which may vary in extent according to his position and capabilities. In some parts of India the cultivators form a separate caste, but as a rule almost any low-caste man may become a tiller of the ground. The implements are of the rudest kind. An Indian plough is exactly what it was two or three thousand years ago, not unlike a thin anchor, one claw of which pierces the ground while the other is held by the ploughman. It may be carried on a man's back, and scarcely does more than scratch the soil.

How, then, does this body of agriculturists provide for the management of its own affairs and the maintenance of order and organization? Each community forms itself into a little republic; bound, however, to the central Government by the regular payment of an assessment or tax on the produce. The first step is to elect their Headman or President, who is paid by a fixed proportion of the land, and is a kind of mayor or civic magistrate. He is the chairman of the village or town council—called a panchāyat—a kind of local board, which often holds its sittings under a large tree. He decides disputes, apportions the labour and the amount of produce each labourer is to receive as remuneration, and is responsible for the annual proportion due to the Government. It will astonish an English workman to learn that the amount of grain required for the support of an adult man in Bengal is only valued at three shillings a month, and for a woman at eighteen pence. A large family may be supported for fourteen shillings a month.

The next important personage in the community is the accountant or notary, a kind of local attorney, who transacts the village business and keeps an account of the land, the produce, the rents, and assessment. In some respects a far more important functionary than either headman or notary is the priest (purohita), the spiritual head of the society, who performs all religious ceremonies for its members, whether at births, marriages, or deaths, and is supported by fixed allotments of grain, or special offerings on solemn occasions. As a Brāhman he may be of higher caste than either the headman or notary (who are not generally Brāhmans), and his spiritual power is unbounded. His anger is as terrible as that of the gods. His blessing makes rich, his curse withers. Nay, more, he is himself actually worshipped as a god. No marvel, no prodigy in nature is believed to be beyond the limits of his power to accomplish. If the priest were to threaten to bring down the sun from the sky or arrest it in its daily course in the heavens, no villager would for a moment doubt his ability to do so. And indeed the priests of India, in their character of Brāhmans, claim to have worked a few notable miracles at different times and on various occasions. One of their number once swallowed the ocean in three sips, another manufactured fire, another created animals, and another turned the moon into a cinder. The priest confers incalculable benefits on the community of which he is a member by merely receiving their presents. A cow given to him secures heaven of a certainty to the lucky donor. The consequences of injuring him are terrific. The man who does him the smallest harm must make up his mind to be whirled about after death, for at least a century, in a hell of total darkness. This will suffice to account for the respect paid to the Brāhman-priest by the peasants, who sometimes drink the water in which his feet have been washed, by way of getting rid of their sins with the least possible difficulty. It by no means follows, however, that every Brāhman is a priest.

Sometimes the priest combines the functions of village astrologer—a very necessary official, since a chief part of the religion of all Indian peasants consists in a fear of the evil influence of stars and planets (p. 372). The astrologer determines the lucky days for sowing and reaping, tells fortunes, prepares horoscopes, and knows how to counteract bad omens—to avert the evil consequences of an envious look, of a sudden sneeze, of the yell of a jackal or chirping of a lizard. If the astrologer also practises magic it becomes necessary to conciliate him; for he has power over demons and evil spirits. He can cause diseases as well as cure them, and can destroy life by the repetition of magical texts. He is, I fear, the only physician. The true art of healing and of sanitation is unknown.

Then nearly every Indian village possesses a schoolmaster, and his functions also are sometimes united in those of the priest. In passing through a large village in Bengal, I came upon a group of at least fifty naked children squatting under a tree near a homestead, some engaged in scratching the letters of the alphabet on leaves, and some learning to write on the dust of the ground. This was the national school, presided over by a nearly naked pedagogue who, on my approach, made his pupils show off their knowledge of arithmetic before me, by shouting out their multiplication table with deafening screams. It may be noted as remarkable, that no religious teacher in the native schools of India receives money for teaching. Divine knowledge is too sacred a thing to be sold. It is, therefore, nominally imparted gratis, though the teacher has no objection to receive presents from the parents on festive occasions. Some of the national punishments are certainly curious from our point of view. For instance, a boy is condemned to stand for half-an-hour on one foot. Another is made to sit on the floor with one leg turned up behind his neck. Another is made to hang for a few minutes with his head downwards from the branch of a neighbouring tree. Another is made to bend down and grasp his own toes and remain in that position for a fixed period of time. Another is made to measure so many cubits on the ground by marking it with the tip of his nose.

Another is made to pull his own ears, and dilate them to a given point on pain of worse chastisement. Two boys, when both have done wrong, are made to knock their heads several times against each other.

Amongst the most important functionaries of the community I ought to mention the barber, who with the roughest implements does his appointed work admirably. An Indian barber can, if he likes, shave without soap. Shaving is, as we have seen, a religious duty with all Hindūs, but no one ever thinks of shaving himself. He sends for the barber, as he would for the priest or the doctor. Nor are this functionary's duties restricted to shaving. He cuts the nails, cleans the ears, kneads the body, cracks the joints, and often does the work of a homely surgeon. The natives of India are particularly fond of having their joints cracked. A rich man's barber performs all these operations for him every day, and is content with two shillings a month wages.

Next we have the village carpenter. If you enter a village at early dawn you will probably find him engaged in making handles for ploughs. You will see him saw as much by the help of his feet as his hands; for a Hindū's toes are never cramped or made useless by tight shoes, but early begin to assist his fingers. The ground is our carpenter's only bench, while the tools he uses are of the rudest kind, perhaps nothing beyond a coarse saw, hammer, plane, chisel, and wedge.

Next look at the village blacksmith, he has only a hammer, file, pair of tongs, and bellows. His forge is hollowed out of the ground or constructed of a few broken bricks, and his only anvil is a stone. Sitting on his hams he fashions old hoop-iron into bill-hooks, nails, and ferrules for ploughs.

Then there is the cowman, who furnishes the milk, curds, and a kind of butter, but not cheese; for cheese is an article of manufacture quite unknown to the Hindūs. No such trade as that of a cheesemonger is to be found throughout India.

Again, in some parts of India, behind the low huts of the irregular village street is sure to be seen the weaver's loom. For India, as Sir George Birdwood has well shown, is probably the first of all countries that perfected weaving. The weaver's art is alluded to in the Ṛig-veda, 1500 years before Christ, and as the original source of any textile fabric is often indicated by its name, so we find that calico takes its name from *Calicut*, on the western coast of India; chintz from the Sanskṛit *ćitra*, 'variegated;' shawl from *śālā*, 'a hall;' just as damask is from Damascus, dimity from Damietta, muslin from Mosul, nankeen from Nankin, drugget from Drogheda. The cotton thread used in India is spun by women of all castes. They spin it on a thin rod of iron with a ball of clay at the end, but the coarser thread is spun by means of a wheel similar to that of an English spinster.

Another useful functionary is the village shoemaker. If you wish him to make you a pair of shoes you must pay him in advance, that he may first purchase a prepared hide from the tanner, or prepare one himself, for he has no stock of leather. Then with a rough last, a knife and an awl, he will turn you out a very respectable pair of shoes, if you only give him plenty of time.

Then on the outskirts of the village is sure to be established another indispensable and much respected functionary, the hereditary potter. There he sits on a slightly elevated piece of ground outside the door of his hut with his apparatus ready for use—the ideal of a man who has achieved perfect mastery over the mechanism of his fingers, and is conscious of the power of the human hand, as the instrument of bringing beautiful shapes within the reach of the humblest cottager. The apparatus with which he effects this object is a simple circular horizontal well-balanced fly-wheel, generally two or three feet in diameter, which can be made to rotate for two or three minutes by a slight impulse. This he loads with clay, and then with a few easy sweeps and turns of his hands he moulds his material into beautiful curves and symmetrical shapes, and leaves the products of his skill to bake by themselves in the sun. In fact, the sun is the Indian workman's head assistant—nay, rather, his ever-present benefactor, from whom he gets coals, candles, clothing, and almost every necessary of life, free of all cost[1]. This relieves him from a deadweight of care, and enables him to give to his work—which in India is always regarded as a religious function—that placidity of mind, that pride and pleasure in it for its own sake, which are essential to all artistic excellence and perfection. And no man takes a greater pride and pleasure in his work, no man displays a greater air of dignity, self-respect, and contentment than the village potter (kumbhakāra, corrupted into kumbhār). No man furnishes a better illustration of that excellent doggerel of ours,

> If I were a cobbler, it would be my pride
> The best of all cobblers to be;
> If I were a tinker, no tinker beside
> Should mend a tin-kettle like me.

It never enters into his head to work for merely mercenary motives or with any idea of making money. He simply works because it is his appointed duty—the sacred duty for which God created him—to supply the villagers with as many pots, pans, bowls, and jars as they need, and to make them in the best and most workmanlike manner possible. Nor does his ambition ever soar above simple earthenware. Such a man never dreams of aspiring to the manufacture of valuable china dishes or vessels and plates of porcelain. He has no idea of rising above the art received from his fathers. One reason for this may be that in India there is no demand for chinaware. No orthodox Hindū likes to eat off anything but plates of leaves freshly prepared for every meal and never used again. Even earthenware dishes ought to be thrown

---

[1] All this, too, has been shown by Sir George Birdwood, K.C.I.E., to whose able works on Indian art my descriptions are greatly indebted.

away immediately after use. The great demand for earthenware vessels in India arises from the impurity supposed to be contracted by using any such articles a second time. It is noteworthy that during an eclipse the very poorest people fling them away.

I could go on to speak of the dyer, the washerman, the druggist, the oilman, the water-carrier, the watchman, and last but not the least useful functionary—the sweeper.

As to the towns, they are often of immense size and have teeming populations. Calcutta and Bombay are larger cities than any in the British Empire except, of course, London. They have a larger population than Liverpool and Manchester, and every conceivable kind of trade is represented in their streets. Even in the days of Rāma, several centuries B.C., the procession that went out to meet him from the capital of Oudh included metal-workers, copper-smiths, ivory-workers, crystal-cutters, glass-makers, inlayers, umbrella-makers, perfumers, hair-dressers, fishmongers, musical instrument-makers, painters, distillers, seedsmen, gardeners, partridge dealers, basket-makers, brick-makers, plasterers, architects, clothiers, exorcists, with the headmen of guilds bringing up the rear. In an ancient work (already alluded to) by a sage named Vātsyāyana sixty-four arts are enumerated. Among them are the following:—singing; dancing; playing on musical instruments; playing on musical glasses filled with water; tattooing; colouring the teeth, hair, and nails; dyeing and painting; writing and drawing; scenic representations, stage-playing; fixing stained glass into floors; magic or sorcery; culinary art; making lemonades, sherbets, and acidulated drinks; practice with sword, single-stick, quarter-staff, and bow and arrow; carpentry; architecture; knowledge about gold and silver coins, jewels and gems; chemistry and mineralogy; gardening; knowledge of treating the diseases of trees and plants, of nourishing them and determining their ages; cock-fighting, quail-fighting, and ram-fighting; teaching parrots and Maina birds to speak; knowledge of languages and vernacular dialects; obtaining possession of the property of others by means of incantations; skill in youthful sports and gymnastics; knowledge of the art of war, arms, armies, etc.; knowledge of the rules of society and how to pay respects and compliments to others; art of knowing the character of a man from his features.

It is curious to compare this ancient list with a modern one published by the Indian Census Office, in which, among other remarkable varieties of modern trades, the following are enumerated:—professional makers of speeches, professional ear-cleaners, vendors of drugs to promote digestion, professional givers of evidence, and professional devil-extractors.

Now, in India, all who practise the same trade are congregated in one quarter of the town. Some artisans are scarcely numerous enough to form a street of their own; but you might find whole streets of ironmongers, copper-smiths, braziers, weavers and confectioners, and these streets of shops are called bazaars. Let us wander for a few minutes through one of these native bazaars. We see nowhere any closed shops resembling those of Europe. On both sides of us are open recesses with dark interiors, wholly destitute of glass windows, but protected towards the street by projecting wooden eaves, often covered with cocoa-nut leaves or bamboos, and sometimes supported by well-carved wooden pillars. In these recesses, or under the open projections, are exposed for sale all kinds of commodities, their scantily clothed owners squatting in an apathetic manner on the ground, and apparently by no means eager to serve their customers. Here, in one quarter, we find vendors of coarse confectionery—strange concoctions of ghee, sugar, almonds, pistachio nuts, and saffron, or sellers of vegetables prepared with turmeric and flavoured with assafetida. There, in another street, are the workers in metal or wood. Everywhere we see open workshops filled with artisans patiently and persistently plying their occupation after the fashion of their fathers. Even artificers of a higher grade carry on their work almost in the open street before your eyes, not at all disturbed by the jostling throng of passengers around them, and not at all objecting to their operations being watched or the secrets of their craft studied. The patience, perseverance, and power of physical endurance displayed by an Indian workman are well worthy of imitation by us in Europe. He seems to be profoundly conscious of the truth that nothing of any kind can be well done, and no success of any kind achieved in this workday world of ours, without the application of the most common-place patient drudgery.

It is curious that in some trades even strict holidays are made a source of revenue to the general body. One shop in each market is then allowed to be kept open. The right to open this shop is put up to auction and given to the highest bidder, the amount being devoted to the general purposes of the caste.

In a few trades children help the men. The aid of their lithe and supple fingers is of great importance in all delicate manipulations. It must, however, be admitted that the Hindū is a slow worker; he will take a whole day about a thing which an active European would finish off in a couple of hours. Yet for all that, if we watch a party of Hindū workmen for a sufficient length of time we shall see the crudest raw material transformed before our eyes into excellent articles of every-day use; not very rapidly—not by any striking processes of inventive art—but by simple dexterity of manipulation, by skilful movements of hands and feet, aided by a few rough implements according to the most primitive methods.

Often these humble artisans have no workshops of their own. They bring their implements and their whole stock-in-trade to the houses of those who need their services, and when the work required of them is finished, pack up their tools and seek another employer. Nor does it ever enter into the heads of even the better class of workmen to think of availing themselves of any modern scientific improvements. If the most wonderful labour-saving machine were offered for their use, they would still prefer the machinery of their fingers, and the old traditionary practices received from their fathers.

And, perhaps, the great secret of the beauty of Indian art lies in the suppleness and flexibility of Indian fingers, and the consequent delicacy of Indian manipulation. The hand of the commonest menial servant in an Indian household is often as delicately formed as that of the most refined aristocratic beauty at a European court. Yes, we must go to India for the best illustration of the truth that the human hand is the most wonderful of all machines. In Europe, manufacture is no longer, as it ought to be according to its etymology, hand-work. But in India the hand is still the chief implement employed; and a fervent hope may be expressed that no European machinery may soon take its place. No greater calamity could befall Indian art than that it should abandon its own traditions and principles for meretricious ideas derived from European sources. If any one doubts this, let him visit the Indian Museum at South Kensington and examine the specimens there collected. No one could fail to admire the exquisite carvings, the delicate silver filigree work, the artistic feeling displayed in the fashioning of ornaments; the gorgeous richness of the Kincob work, with its gold, silver, and silken threads, woven into the texture of the fabric; the tasteful designs and matchless colouring of Cashmere and Delhi scarfs and shawls; the marvellous skill and taste displayed in the sandal wood-carving and inlaid wood-work; the sumptuous gold and silver plate-work and highly-tempered steel weapons of Kutch; the admirable embroidery and needlework of Amritsar and Delhi; the exquisitely fine muslin produced at Dacca.

In this last kind of manufacture the Hindū artisan is

absolutely unrivalled. With a loom of the simplest construction, formed of a few rough sticks and reeds, he produces something which no European machinery can equal; for the mysteries of his craft have been transmitted from father to son for thousands of years. The names given to different kinds of these muslins, such as 'woven air,' 'web of the wind,' 'evening dew,' 'running water,' indicate the extreme fineness and subtlety of their texture. A whole dress of the finest quality may easily be passed through a small finger ring, and a piece thirty feet in length may be packed in a case not much bigger than an egg shell—yet such a piece may take a workman at least four months to fabricate, and be worth forty pounds.

It is recorded that a cow-keeper was once prosecuted by a weaver because one of his cows had eaten up three dresses of this muslin accidentally left on the grass. The cow-keeper pleaded before the Judge that the muslin was too fine to be distinguished by a hungry cow, and his plea was accepted.

Again, a story is told of a young lady who appeared at the court of a Muhammadan Emperor in much too transparent garments to be thought respectable. When accused of exhibiting rather too much of the surface of her body in a questionable manner, she indignantly repudiated the charge, on the ground that she had carefully enveloped her entire person in seven folds of Dacca muslin.

It would be easy to dilate on other examples of the higher artistic genius of India. We are astonished at the Indian workman's mastery over his materials. Even in the more common work great regard is paid to beauty of form and right proportion, and great taste in the arrangement and distribution of the ornament.

As to jewelry, Sir Sourindro Mohun Tagore has written two thick volumes on the virtues and supernatural properties of Indian gems. The Purāṇas regard diamonds as differing in gender and as divided into castes. Kṛishṇa or Vishṇu has two marvellous jewels (see p. 104) about which long histories have been written. And doubtless jewelry is of all Indian arts the most ancient; for what would Indian women, from the lowest to the highest, be without their jewels? In most large Indian houses belonging to rich natives a jeweller will be found in some ante-room manufacturing jewelry for the family, or repairing that in daily use (p. 396). Here is a description of a typical Indian bride of high rank in ancient times:—

'She has no other clothing but one light garment, ten yards in length, of a rosy red colour, embroidered with gold, wound round her body in graceful folds; she has jewelled butterflies in her raven hair; her ears are bored in six places, and loaded with resplendent gems; a magnificent nose-ring of emeralds and pearls sparkles in one nostril; bright golden bracelets encircle her wrists, and shining armlets her arms: a golden zone binds her slender waist; she has jewelled rings on her fingers, and golden rings on her toes, and golden anklets, with musical bells attached, are fastened round her ankles, which make a tinkling sound as she walks.'

Those who were in India during the Prince of Wales' visit, and saw the jewelled dresses of the Indian chiefs, will not easily forget the sight. I was myself present in Sir Richard Temple's house, when the Mahārāja of Patiāla happened to make a morning call. His coat was of blue satin, beautifully embroidered with rows of pearls; he had costly ear-rings, and a necklace of diamonds worth £60,000 was suspended carelessly about his neck. Strings of immense uncut jewels ornamented his white turban. Even the humblest woman would lose her self-respect if she appeared before her family without a nose-ring and bangles. Children are often left without a shred of clothing, till they are six years of age, but are rarely without wrist-bands, or jewelled ornaments of some kind.

When the sister of the late Bishop of Calcutta once visited some native ladies in a Zenāna, she made some remark about the simplicity of their attire. 'Look,' she said, 'at the number and weight of my garments.' 'Yes,' they replied, 'but look at the number and weight of our jewelry.' The use of jewels, especially diamonds, as amulets, is very common. Certain gems are believed to possess magical properties. A celebrated amulet once existed in ancient India, supposed to be all-potent in protecting from evil. It consisted of nine gems—pearl, ruby, sapphire, topaz, diamond, emerald, lapis lazuli, coral, and Gomeda. (We may compare the Hebrew High Priest's breastplate containing twelve gems.) Even the commonest Indian jewelry presents examples of every variety of beautiful design. The forms have come down by unbroken tradition from the earliest times.

The fact is, that in India, artisans are not obliged to be ever pandering to the mania for novelty, ever racking their brains to invent some new fashion. They plod on in the old beaten paths; they are able to devote their energies to the beautifying, improving, and perfecting of what already exists. Perhaps the most beautiful ornaments are the work of artificers, who have continued in the service of a particular line of Rājās for centuries. These men dare not work for other employers. The secret of their skill is preserved religiously in their own families, and held to be the property of their masters.

Sometimes the work of such men is made subservient to the spiritual interests of their masters in rather a remarkable manner. For example, it is recorded of a certain king of Travancore, that feeling the blood he had spilt in his many wars lie heavily on his conscience, he sought counsel of his priests, who told him that if he wished to be cleansed from his guilt his only course was to pass through the body of a cow—that being the most sacred of all animals. This seemed rather a difficult task to perform, but it was eventually accomplished by help of the court jeweller and goldsmith, who manufactured a jewelled cow of the purest gold of immense value. Into the interior of this golden image the king solemnly crept, and there lay for many days in a state of abject contrition, till at length the process of purification being completed, he was permitted to emerge with all his blood-guiltiness removed, all his sins atoned for, and all his cheerfulness of mind restored.

Then as to sculpture and painting, would it be possible to see anywhere more admirable specimens of modelling than the clay figures made at Kṛishnagar? Such exquisite modelling, and the beauty of Indian miniature paintings on wood, talc, and ivory, prove that had the arts of sculpture and painting been cultivated by the Hindūs, they might have attained great perfection. As it is, not a single fine large painting, nor beautiful statue is to be seen throughout India. Even the images of gods are only remarkable for their utter hideousness; nor do we see anywhere good specimens of household furniture, for in India the houses of the richest natives are, to European eyes, almost furnitureless. Even in princely palaces we may pass through beautifully decorated rooms, we may see elaborate carved wood in niches and verandahs; yet the rooms appear to us bare and empty. Not a chair or table is to be seen except in apartments set apart for Europeans; and the owner of the mansion will probably be found seated on a rug with a pillow behind his back.

And here let me say, that if the excellence of the articles which the Indian artificer produces, with no other appliances than his hands, and the rudest tools, and the admirable traditions of form, design, and colour preserved in his productions, excite our surprise, we are no less astonished at the low cost of his workmanship. I visited a turner's shop in Benares, where a man was making a set of twenty toy boxes, some lacquered, some coloured, all neatly constructed and furnished with lids, and fitting one inside the other so that the smallest box in the interior of all was not bigger than the head of a knitting-needle. The price of the whole nest of twenty boxes was not more than fourpence or sixpence, although twenty-three different manipulations were needed to complete each box.

Again, I went into a brass-worker's shop in the braziers' quarter at Benares, where men were engaged in manufacturing drinking cups, salvers, vases, and other vessels. These workmen were seen chiselling out the most intricate and beautiful patterns with no other implements than a hammer and a nail. A purchaser of any such articles requests to have them weighed before buying them, and only pays a shilling or two beyond the actual value of the brass.

Frequently, indeed, it strikes a European as strange, that if he desires to purchase any of the beautiful articles he sees before him in native workshops, scarcely a single thing is to be had; they have all been made to order. There is little stock kept, and whatever a customer wants must be made specially to order, and not without an advance in money. There is little capital to be found in India; and this perhaps will account for the undoubted fact, that Indian industries are left behind in the race of competition by those of Europe.

During the American war, vast quantities of Indian cotton—to the annual value of twenty-two million pounds sterling—found its way to England, to be returned in the form of printed calico to India. The Manchester cotton cloth was far inferior to that spun and woven, and decorated with ornamental patterns, by men's hands in India, but it was much cheaper, because even the most active hand workers, working with imperfect implements and tools, according to antiquated methods for the lowest possible wages, cannot compete with machine-made goods, or make head against the combination of European science, capital, and enterprise. It is on this account that cotton mills have recently been established at Bombay, and in some other parts of India. No less than fifty-three spinning and weaving mills had been erected ten years ago, while others were in process of erection. Is it likely, then, that Indian trades and industries will be injuriously affected by the introduction of English ideas, English machinery, and English education? Time will show. But Caste is a strong conservative force, and as long as its strength continues, and the present intimate connexion between religion and caste is maintained, so long may Indian artisans be expected to work on in their old grooves, Indian agriculturalists to plod on in their old ruts, and primitive customs to hold their own against all modern inventions.

And be it borne in mind that an Indian caste is more than a mere union for trading and industrial objects. It is certainly much more than a mere social division into classes of men. It is part of a man's religious creed.

Its prohibitions extend, as we have seen (p. 453), to food, commensality and intermarriage as well as to occupations.

And, in truth, the idea of a man's birth in a particular circle, and of his being unalterably prohibited by the laws of his religion from eating, marrying, or engaging in any occupation except within the boundaries of that circle is essential to the idea of caste. This applies even to certain criminal castes in India, whose fixed business, inherited from their fathers and grandfathers, is that of plundering or even murdering others.

Even in England caste feeling operates strongly, although Christianity proclaims all men equal before God. In India any individual who might try to break down the barriers of caste, would find it impossible to withstand the opposition of the Brāhmans and his own caste-fellows.

Of course there are some exceptions to caste-rules. In some instances castes have changed their occupations without changing their names, just as the members of our great city Companies are no longer goldsmiths, drapers, merchant tailors, or fishmongers. The higher castes, too, are allowed considerable liberty of employment. A Brāhman may devote himself to almost any pursuit not absolutely degrading. He may be a cook, or even a soldier. Occasionally, too, men of the lower castes may rise to higher professions, though not to higher castes; but these exceptions only prove the rule. A Hindū is taught by his religious books to believe that God created orders of men, with fixed employments, as He created varieties of animals and plants (see p. 53).

In Europe, the laws of society are supposed to be of inferior obligation to the laws of the nation and the laws of religion. An educated Englishman, for instance, is ready to submit to the unwritten laws of his own social circle, but never allows any rule of caste to supersede the higher laws of the nation and of Christianity. In India, on the contrary, the laws of caste, and the laws of religion, are part and parcel of one Divine law, of which the Brāhman is the interpreter, and the laws of caste are stronger and more effectual than any of the laws imposed by Government.

Perhaps the nearest parallel to the action of Indian caste to be found in Europe is in such a social confederation as the late Land-League of Ireland, the members of which were bound together by an iron bond, were allowed no individual liberty of action, were forced to submit their lives to the will of the League, and made to subordinate the laws of the state to the laws and mandates of their own leaders.

India has furnished examples of Boycotters, and Boycottees, for many centuries. If a man offend against the rules of caste, a meeting of his caste-fellows is instantly called, and the offence being proved, he is thereupon condemned to a form of persecution of which Boycotting is a bad imitation.

When I was in Gujarāt, in 1875, a man named Lallu-bhāī, a cloth merchant of Ahmedābād, was proved to have committed a heinous caste crime. He had married a widow of his own caste, and to marry a widow is, in the eyes of a Hindū, a most awful offence. A woman once married, belongs to one husband, for time and eternity. Forthwith, he was sentenced to complete excommunication. No one, either of his own or any other caste, was to be allowed to associate with him; no one was to eat with him; no one was to have any trade-dealings with him; no one was to marry any of his children; no temple was to receive him as a worshipper; and, if he died, no one was to carry his body to the burning ground. On the morning after the sentence was passed, he went into the bazaar as usual, but not a person would buy from him or sell to him; he could get no home to live in; and none of his debtors would pay him. It was impossible to sue them, as no one would give evidence. He was a ruined man, and had to leave the country, and obtain Government employment in a distant city.

This may seem an extreme case, but it would be easy to multiply similar instances of the tyranny and terrorism of caste-leagues in our Indian Empire. Yet, it cannot be doubted, that as a matter of fact, the caste system of India really resulted from a natural and beneficial process of division of labour. Nor can there be a greater mistake than to conclude that the lower castes are in a condition of unhappiness.

In the present day, moreover, caste is certainly becoming relaxed, and re-admission, after violating any of its rules (especially that against a sea-voyage to Europe), can generally be accomplished by a money-indemnity, and by the religious ceremony of swallowing the Pañćagavya (or five products of a cow, viz. milk, curds, butter, and the two excreta).

The truth is, that of all masters, caste is the worst when allowed to become a despot. It is then a league of the worst kind; and we have not far to look, even in our own favoured country, if we wish to see the tyranny and terrorism such a league may establish. Its action tends to arrest progress, to paralyse energy, to crush manly independence, to stifle healthy public opinion, to make nationality, patriotism, and true liberty almost impossible. At the same time caste-leagues have their good as well as their bad side, and at a particular stage of a nation's life may do good service. In India, caste has been useful in promoting self-sacrifice, in securing subordination of the individual to an organized body, in restraining from vice, in preventing pauperism. And certainly the antagonism of these caste associations and trade leagues has helped us to govern the country by making political combinations impracticable[1]. Our wisest policy will be to convert caste from a master into a servant; to defeat its evil action, not indeed by forcible suppression but by the gradual application of corrective influences; to counteract its false teaching by imparting true ideas of liberty—true principles of political economy, social science, and morality; to supplant its tyrannical enactments by considerate legislation, based on the ancient laws and customs of the country; to make its hard support and iron grasp needless by helping the masses to ameliorate their own social condition, and stimulating them to improve their own national arts, trades, and industries in their own way. By doing this will England best fulfil her mission; best discharge her sacred trust; best advance the cause of true religion and justice; best promote the well-being and conciliate the affections of the countless millions of her Eastern Empire.

---

[1] The great diversity of languages and dialects, numbering at least 200—not to mention religious and sectarian differences which accompany caste—is doubtless another great element of safety. It may be well, however, to point out that education, scepticism in regard to religious dogma, and the increasing employment of English as a common medium of communication among an increasing number of intelligent natives in every separate district and province of India, are contributing in no small degree towards making national union possible, and towards weakening the walls of partition.

CHAPTER XIX.

Modern Hindū Theism[1]. *Rāmmohun Roy.*

It is a mistake to suppose that the first introduction of Theism into India was due to the founders of the Brāhma-Samāj (in Bengal written Brāhmo-Somāj), or modern Theistic Churches of Bengal. Some of the oldest hymns of the Ṛig-veda are monotheistic, and all the most pronounced forms of Indian pantheism rest on the fundamental doctrine of God's unity. 'There is one Being without a second,' 'Nothing really exists but the one eternal omnipresent Spirit,' was the dogma enunciated by ancient Hindū thinkers. It was a dogma accepted by the philosophical Brāhman with all its consequences and corollaries. He firmly believed himself and the Universe to be parts of the one eternal Essence, and wrapped himself up accordingly in a kind of serene indifference to all the illusions of external phenomena. Again even the ordinary Hindū who practises the most corrupt forms of polytheism is never found to deny the doctrine of God's unity. On the contrary, he will always maintain that God is essentially one, though he holds that the one God exhibits Himself variously, and that He is to be worshipped

---

[1] The two following chapters, which are principally the result of my own researches in India, have had the advantage of being revised and corrected by the venerable Debendra Nāth Tagore himself, so that their accuracy can be depended upon. Miss Collet's Brāhma Year-book, once published at the end of every year, gave a lucid and impartial account of the progress of the Indian theistical movement, and to her labours we are all indebted.

through an endless diversity of manifestations, incarnations, and material forms.

It is to be observed, too, that as often as pantheistic and polytheistic ideas have been pushed to preposterous extremes in India, a reaction has always taken place towards simple monotheism. The Vaishṇava Reformers of the 12th, 13th, 15th, and 16th centuries inculcated a doctrine which was an approximation towards the Christian idea of God's Unity and Personality, as set forth in the first article of the Church of England. Rāmānuja, Madhva, Vallabha, and Ćaitanya, all, as we have seen, taught the existence of one supreme personal God of infinite power, wisdom, and goodness, the Maker and Preserver of all things—a God whom they called Vishṇu, and whom they believed to be distinct from the human soul and the material world.

But none of these great Reformers succeeded in counteracting the corrupt tendencies inherent in the Vaishṇava system. That system contains within itself the seeds of constant morbid growth and unhealthy development. It cannot get rid of its dogma of repeated incarnations, or, to speak more correctly, repeated descents (avatāra). Vishṇu, it is believed, has ever been accustomed to descend in the shape of great warriors, great teachers, and even animals, to deliver the world in seasons of special exigence and peril. Of course such a theory opens the door to every kind of extravagant superstition. Notwithstanding, therefore, the partial reformation accomplished by Rāmānuja, Madhva, Vallabha, and Ćaitanya, the tide of degrading idolatrous practices set in more strongly than ever.

Then followed the monotheistic reaction led by Kabīr in the 16th century and improved upon afterwards by Nānak, the founder of the Sikh religion (p. 161). These movements were in a great measure due to Muhammadan influences. Both Kabīr and Nānak did their best to purify the Augean stable of corrupt Hindū doctrine, but met with only partial success. They taught devotion to one personal God, whether called Vishṇu or Kṛishṇa, or designated by any of his established epithets or synonyms. They even endeavoured to unite Hindūs and Muhammadans on the common ground of belief in the Unity of the Godhead. But in this they were wholly unsuccessful, and the tenth Sikh Guru, Govind, made religious fusion impossible by converting Sikhs and Muslims into bitter mutual opponents.

It became, indeed, a question whether the followers of Kabīr and Nānak were not destined to become exterminated under the persecutions to which they were exposed in the reign of Aurangzīb. Under that Emperor India suffered everywhere from an outburst of Muhammadan fanaticism. Nor was the stability of Islām shaken or its hold over the people of India weakened, when the political power of the Muhammadans declined. On the contrary, the number of Muslims increased, and their bigotry and intolerance gathered strength in opposition to the advance of British domination, and the diffusion of European knowledge.

The Hindūs, on the other hand, were not too proud to profit by contact with European ideas. Everywhere at the great centres of British authority a mighty stir of thought began to be set in motion, and able men, educated by us, made no secret of their dissatisfaction with the national religion, and their desire for a purer faith than that received from their fathers. At the moment when thoughtful Hindūs were thus asking for light and leading, the right leader appeared. The Hindū reformation inaugurated by Rāmmohun Roy was the first reformation due to Christian influences, and to the diffusion of European ideas through English education. He was the first great modern theistical reformer of what may be called British India.

Unhappily no biographies of India's eminent men have ever been written. Neither Hindūs nor Muhammadans have ever shown any appreciation of the value of such writings.

A good life of Rāmmohun Roy, composed in Sanskṛit or Bengālī, and translated into Hindūstānī and other principal vernaculars, together with a collection of his writings, were for a long time greatly needed[1]; but these wants have been recently to a great extent supplied by Nāgendra-nāth Chatterjea and Rāj Narāin Bose. The former has published a life of the Rājā and the latter a new edition of his Bengālī writings. What little is known of his early history is soon told. According to Nāgendra-nāth he was born in May, 1774, at a village called Rādhānagar, in the district of Murshidābād. His father, Rām Kānt Roy, was a Brāhman of high caste, and his grandfather had held offices under the Mogul Emperor. At an early age Rāmmohun Roy was sent to study Persian and Arabic literature, including the Kurān itself, at the great seat of Muhammadan learning, Patnā. It was thought that his proficiency in Muhammadan lore might lead to his advancement at the Mogul court. Not that he neglected Sanskṛit or his Brāhmanical studies. His father was a worshipper of Vishṇu. Every morning the son was accustomed to read a chapter of the Vaishṇava bible—the Bhāgavata Purāṇa. Naturally thoughtful and intelligent, he soon began to think for himself, and to see through the absurd tissue of fable by which its authority is supported. Wholly unable to acquiesce in its extravagant mythology, he betook himself to the simple Vedic system, and the Vedānta as expressed in the Upanishads attracted his special attention.

At the age of sixteen he composed a spirited tract against idolatry. This for a mere boy was a sufficiently remarkable achievement, and not likely to pass unnoticed. As a matter of course it roused the anger not only of his own immediate

---

[1] The Rev. K. S. Macdonald gave a short and interesting summary of his life in a paper read at Darjeeling (June, 1879), and Miss Mary Carpenter published an interesting account of his 'Last Days' in 1866. Mr. Macdonald's anecdotes were chiefly taken from a speech delivered by Rāj Narāin Bose at one of the annual meetings for commemorating the memory of the Rājā.

family, but of all his relatives and superiors. In consequence of the enmity thus excited against him, it was thought advisable that he should leave his father's home for a time. He resided first at Benares, the stronghold of Brāhmanism, and afterwards in Tibet, where he gave himself with much zeal to the study of Buddhism, and had many controversies with Buddhist priests. Probably Rāmmohun Roy was the first earnest-minded investigator of the science of comparative religion that the world has produced. From his earliest years he displayed an eagerness to become an unbiased student of all the religions of the globe. His sole aim in such studies was to seek out religious truth for himself with perfect fairness and impartiality. Hence he spared himself no trouble in endeavouring to master the several languages of the world's sacred books, each of which claimed to be the sole depositaries of such truth. As he studied the Hindū Veda in Sanskṛit, so he is believed to have given his attention to the Buddhist Tripiṭaka in the original Pāli. He is known, too, to have mastered Arabic that he might read the Kurān, and later in life he learnt Hebrew that he might form a just estimate of the authority of the Old Testament, and even began Greek that he might gain a complete knowledge of the New Testament.

On his return home about the year 1796, he appears to have been reinstated in the favour of his family and relations. This led him to apply himself with more zeal than ever to the study of Sanskṛit literature and an examination of the doctrines of his ancestral religion. He had too logical a mind to be deceived by Brāhmanical sophistries. Yet he was accustomed to assert that he had found nothing in the works of any other country, Asiatic or European, equal to the scholastic philosophy of the Hindūs. It was at about this period that he gave himself seriously to the study of English. At the same time he began to shake off the prejudices he had imbibed against social intercourse with his country's rulers, and to derive benefit from mixing in European society. After his father's death in 1803[1], Rāmmohun Roy became bolder in his controversies with the Brāhmans. Soon he began to publish various pamphlets and treatises against the errors of Hindūism. This he did at considerable risk to his own worldly prospects. His father had left his property to be divided among his three sons; but it was not long before, by their death, Rāmmohun Roy became possessed of considerable patrimony, which would have been forfeited had he formally abjured his family religion, and legally lost caste. With an increase of wealth came an increased desire for extension of usefulness. Notwithstanding an inheritance sufficiently ample for his own personal wants, Rāmmohun Roy found himself cramped in the carrying out of the vast objects he had in view. This led him to seek Government employment, and we find him acting for ten years as Dīwān or managing officer to the judges and collectors of Rangpūr, Bhāgalpūr and Rāmgarh, especially to a Mr. Digby. Hence he was often called Dīwān-jī,—a title by which he continued to be known until he received that of Rājā from the ex-Emperor of Delhi, on the occasion of his embassy to England. One object he had in undertaking revenue work was to gain a practical knowledge of the working of the British administration. Some have spitefully accused him of augmenting his own legitimate earnings by doubtful and underhand transactions. It is far more likely that his prosperous career was due to his righteous dealings, which made him popular among the landed proprietors, and to the skill he displayed in the settlement of Zamīndārī accounts, which made his services indispensable to his masters.

Notwithstanding his assiduous attention to business, he

[1] Some give 1804 as the date of his death. His mother, who was at first very bitter against him, lived to acknowledge that he was right, though she could not give up her old faith, 'which was a comfort to her.'

found ample time for study and for the prosecution of his schemes of reform. Every year his attitude of antagonism to the idolatry of his fellow-countrymen became more and more marked and decided. The ground he took, according to his own statement, was not that of opposition to the national faith, but to a perversion of it. He endeavoured to show that the idolatry of the Hindūs was contrary to the practice of their ancestors, and to the doctrine of the ancient books and authorities which they profess to revere and obey. Very soon after his father's death he had written a book in Persian: 'Against the idolatry of all religions.' This was followed at intervals by various treatises, and especially translations of some of the Upanishads. In the preface to the Muṇḍaka Upanishad of the Atharva-veda, he says:

'An attentive perusal of this, as well as of the remaining books of the Vedānta, will, I trust, convince every unprejudiced mind that they, with great consistency, inculcate the unity of God; instructing men, at the same time, in the pure mode of adoring him in spirit. It will also appear evident, that the Vedas, although they tolerate idolatry as the last provision for those who are totally incapable of raising their minds to the contemplation of the invisible God of Nature, yet repeatedly urge the relinquishment of the rites of idol-worship, and the adoption of a purer system of religion, on the express grounds that the observance of idolatrous rites can never be productive of eternal beatitude. These are left to be practised by such persons only as, notwithstanding the constant teaching of spiritual guides, cannot be brought to see perspicuously the Majesty of God through the works of Nature.

'The public will, I hope, be assured that nothing but the natural inclination of the ignorant towards the worship of objects resembling their own nature, and to the external form of rites palpable to their grosser senses, joined to the self-interested motives of their pretended guides, has rendered the generality of the Hindū community (in defiance of their sacred books) devoted to idol-worship :—the source of prejudice and superstition, and the total destruction of moral principle, as countenancing criminal intercourse, suicide, female murder, and human sacrifice.'

Perhaps the most important point to which he awakened attention was the absence of all Vedic sanction for the self-immolation of widows (Suttee = Sanskṛit Satī). It was principally his vehement denunciation of this practice, and the agitation against it set on foot by him, which ultimately led to the abolition of Satī by statute throughout British India in 1829.

Long before that period, however, the effect of his publications and addresses was to make his position one of increasing isolation, until, in 1814, finding himself surrounded by religious opponents, and ostracised by his own social circle, he retired to Calcutta. His property by that time had so far increased that he could reckon on an income of £1000 per annum, and he was able to purchase a residence there.

It was only to be expected that among the inhabitants of the metropolis would be many thoughtful persons capable of sympathizing with his lofty aspirations. Accordingly he attracted a number of adherents from Hindūs and Jains of rank, wealth, and influence. They gathered round him in a small but united band, and agreed to co-operate with him for the purification of their religion.

It may well be imagined that opinions like those which Rāmmohun Roy laboured to propagate could not have been adopted by any body of Hindūs without, so to speak, loosening the anchorage by which they held on to the foundations of their ancient faith. Yet in seeking their co-operation, he never swerved from his original position. He continued to declare that his only object was to bring back his countrymen to what he believed to be the true monotheistic doctrine underlying the Vedic hymns and brought out more clearly in the Upanishad portion of the Veda.

The first step taken was to establish a private society for spiritual improvement. The association was called Ātmīya-Sabhā, spiritual society, and was first formed about the year 1816. It consisted chiefly of Rāmmohun Roy's own personal friends, among whom was Dvārakā-nāth (Dwārkanāth) Tāgore. It met in Rāmmohun Roy's house at Manictolah, for discussion at periodical intervals; but the hostility of the Brāhmans and Pandits who were sometimes present, and who were offended and alarmed at the crushing demolition of their arguments by the reforming party, proved too strong for its continued existence. One by one its members dropped off, till by degrees the society ceased to exist. The great leader of the movement, however, was not to be so easily suppressed. On the contrary, he braced himself up with greater energy than ever, to continue the conflict single-handed. His zeal and industry in writing books, pamphlets, and addresses, only increased in vehemence.

It is clear that even at that time his study of the sayings of Christ in the New Testament had brought him to a qualified acceptance of Christianity; for in 1820 he published in Bengālī and English a book called 'The Precepts of Jesus, the Guide to Peace and Happiness.' In the preface he wrote:—

> 'This simple code of religion and morality is so admirably calculated to elevate men's ideas to high and liberal notions of one God, . . . and is so well fitted to regulate the conduct of the human race in the discharge of their various duties to God, to themselves, and to society, that I cannot but hope the best effects from its promulgation in its present form.'

In a letter prefixed to one of his later works (an edition of the Kena Upanishad) he makes the following admission:—

> 'The consequence of my long and uninterrupted researches into religious truth has been that I have found the doctrines of Christ more conducive to moral principles, and better adapted for the use of rational beings, than any other which have come to my knowledge.'

It is said that on being one day shown a picture of Christ, he remarked that the painter had represented Him falsely, for he had given Him a European countenance, forgetting that Jesus Christ was an Oriental, and that, in keeping with the Eastern origin of Christianity, the Christian scriptures glow throughout with rich Oriental colouring.

Some indeed, have not hesitated to affirm that Rāmmohun Roy, though he never abjured caste, was in reality a true Christian. But that he ever had the slightest leaning towards Trinitarian Christianity is altogether unlikely.

In his 'Final Appeal[1]' he says:—

'After I have long relinquished every idea of a plurality of Gods, or of the persons of the Godhead, taught under different systems of modern Hindooism, I cannot conscientiously and consistently embrace one of a similar nature, though greatly refined by the religious reformations of modern times. Since whatever arguments can be adduced against a plurality of Gods strike with equal force against the doctrine of a plurality of persons of the Godhead; and on the other hand, whatever excuse may be pleaded in favour of a plurality of persons of the Deity, can be offered with equal propriety in defence of polytheism.'

In fact his sympathies with the Unitarian sect were always strongly marked, and it is certain that, whenever his mind could free itself from the influence of Vedāntic proclivities, it gravitated towards a form of Unitarian Christianity.

But in truth the dominant feeling in Rāmmohun Roy's mind was a craving for a kind of eclectic catholicity. Throughout life he shrank from connecting himself with any particular school of thought. He seems to have felt a satisfaction in being claimed as a Vedāntist by Hindūs, as a Theist by Unitarians, as a Christian by Christians, and as a Muslim by Muhammadans. His idea of inspiration was that it was not confined to any age or any nation, but a gift co-extensive with the human race. He believed it to be a kind of divine illumination, or intuitive perception of truth, granted in a greater or less degree to every good man in every country. Whatever was good in the Vedas, in the Christian Scriptures, in the Kurān, in the Zand Avasta, or in any book of any nation anywhere, was to be accepted and assimilated as coming from the 'God of truth,' and to be regarded as a revelation. The only test of the validity of any doctrine was its conformity to the natural and healthy working of man's reason, and the intuitions and cravings of the human heart. 'My view of Christianity,' he says in a letter to a friend, 'is, that in representing all mankind as the

[1] He published three 'Appeals to the Christian public' against the unfair construction which Dr. Marsham and others had put on his 'Precepts of Jesus.'

children of one eternal Father, it enjoins them to love one another, without making any distinction of country, caste. colour, or creed.' It was easy for a man of so catholic and liberal a spirit to become all things to all men. Hence, it is not surprising that he cultivated friendship with Christian Missionaries of all denominations. He assisted them in their translation of the Scriptures, and occasionally joined in their worship. It is well known that he aided Dr. Duff in the establishment of his educational institution in Calcutta, recommending that its daily work should be commenced with the Lord's Prayer, and declaring that he had studied the Brāhman's Veda, the Muslim's Kurān, and the Buddhist's Tripiṭaka, without finding anywhere any other prayer so brief, comprehensive, and suitable to man's wants.

In 1828 occurred an event which may be regarded as an important turning-point in the history of the Theistic movement. Mr. W. Adam, a Protestant Missionary, had entered into friendly communications with Rāmmohun Roy, and had been led through his influence to adopt a decidedly Unitarian form of Christianity. This led to his being called 'the second fallen Adam' by his opponents. But not content with changing his own creed, he sought to disseminate the opinions he had adopted by holding meetings and giving lectures in a room attached to the Bengal Hurkaru Newspaper Office. For some time Rāmmohun Roy, with a few of his friends, was accustomed to be present, till at last the thought struck them that, instead of being dependent upon a foreigner for religious edification, they might establish a meeting-house of their own. Dvārakā-nāth (Dwārkanāth) Tāgore, Prosonno Kumār Tāgore, and others, came forward with pecuniary aid. Temporary rooms in the Chitpore Road were hired by Rāmmohun Roy, and prayer-meetings held there every Saturday evening. The service was divided into four parts—recitation of Vedic texts; reading from the Upanishads; delivery of a sermon; and singing hymns.

It was thus that the germ of the first Theistic church was planted at Calcutta in 1828. The commencement of its existence as a living growing organization did not take place till two years later. The beginning of 1830, now more than sixty years ago, inaugurated a new era in the history of Indian religious thought. It ushered in the dawn of the greatest change that has ever passed over the Hindū mind. A new phase of the Hindū religion then took definite shape—a phase which differed essentially from every other that had preceded it. For no other reformation has resulted in the same way from the influence of European education and Christian ideas.

The increase of contributions had enabled Rāmmohun Roy to purchase a large house in the Chitpore Road, and endow it with a maintenance fund. Trustees were appointed, and the first Hindū Theistic Church, or, as it was sometimes called by English-speaking natives, the Hindū Unitarian Church [1], was then opened in Calcutta on the 11th Māgha, 1751, equivalent to January 23, 1830. The name given to it by Rāmmohun Roy indicated its Unitarian character, and yet connected it with the national faith. It was called Brāhma-Sabhā, or Brahmīya-Samāj, that is to say, 'the society of believers in God,' the word Brāhma being an adjective formed from Brahman (nom. case Brăhmă), the name of the one self-existent God of orthodox Hindūism.

The trust-deed of the building laid down that it was to be used as a place of meeting for the worship of the One Eternal, Unsearchable, and Immutable Being, the Author and Preserver of the Universe, to the promotion of piety, morality, and charity, and the strengthening of the bonds of union between men of all religious classes and creeds [2].

---

[1] So the Press at which Rāmmohun Roy's publications were printed was called the Unitarian Press.

[2] It is said that in accordance with this principle, Eurasian boys used to sing the Psalms of David in English, and Hindū musicians religious songs in Bengālī.

Moreover, that no image, print, picture, portrait, or likeness, should be admitted within the building, that no sacrifice should be offered there, and that nothing recognized as an object of worship by other men should be spoken of contemptuously there. Yet Rāmmohun Roy still held fast to his original position. He was careful to make the members of the new society understand that he had no idea of founding a new sect or new system, or even a new church in the ordinary sense of the word. He simply claimed to have established a pure monotheistic worship for the first time in a building where men of all castes, all classes, and all creeds, Hindūs, Muhammadans, and Christians, were invited to worship together, the only unity of faith demanded being belief in the Unity of God. This first introduction of congregational worship and united prayer—before unknown among the Hindūs (pp. 351, 352)—was not the least of the benefits effected by Rāmmohun Roy. Yet he never quite abandoned the idea of an order of men ordained by God to be special teachers of divine truth. It is said that the meeting-house of the Samāj had a private room open only to Brāhmans, where special readings of the Veda were conducted by them.

And, in truth, Rāmmohun Roy's attitude towards his national religion continued that of a friendly reformer, even to the end of his life—a reformer who aimed at retaining all that was good and true in Brāhmanism, while sweeping away all that was corrupt and false. The weak point in his plan is manifest. The form of theology he propounded was too vague, undogmatic, and comprehensive. He was, in fact, by natural character too intensely patriotic not to be swayed, even to the last, by an ardent love of old national ideas. He had denounced caste as a demoralizing institution[1]; he had

---

[1] Thus, in the introduction to his translation of the Īśopanishad, he says: 'The chief part of the theory and practice of Hindooism, I am sorry to say, is made to consist in the adoption of a peculiar mode of diet, the least aberration from which is punished by exclusion from both family and

adopted a nearly true theory of the unity and personality of God; he had abandoned the doctrines of transmigration and final absorption of the soul; he had professed his belief in a day of judgment; he had accepted the Christian miracles, and had even declared Jesus Christ to be the 'Founder of truth and true religion,' and had admitted that the Son of God was empowered by God to forgive sins; but he never entirely delivered himself from his old prepossessions, and the alleged purity of his monotheism was ever liable to be adulterated with pantheistic ideas. In the eyes of the law he always remained a Brāhman. He never abandoned the Brāhmanical thread, and had too lively a sense of the value of money to risk the forfeiture of his property, and the consequent diminution of his usefulness and influence, by formally giving up his caste. In fact, though far in advance of his age as a thinker, he laid no claim to perfection, or to perfect disinterestedness of motive as a man.

Unfortunately for the interests of India, Rāmmohun Roy's career was cut short prematurely. In 1830 the ex-Emperor of Delhi, having long felt himself ill-treated by the Indian Government, deputed Rāmmohun Roy to lay a representation of his grievances before the Court of Great Britain, at the same time conferring on him the title of Rājā. The Rājā's great wish had always been to visit England and interchange ideas with the Western thinkers. He also wished to oppose in person a threatened appeal against the law for the abolition of Suttee (Satī), the passing of which had been just effected through his exertions, and which only required the royal assent. He was aware, too, that the granting of a new charter to the East India Company was about to be discussed in Parliament, and he felt the importance of

friends. Murder, theft, or perjury, though brought home to the party by a judicial sentence, so far from inducing loss of caste, is visited with no peculiar mark of infamy.'

watching the proceedings on behalf of the natives of India, and for the furtherance of their interests.

No better time for carrying these objects into execution seemed possible than the period which followed the opening of his new Church. He therefore sailed for Liverpool in November, 1830, and arrived there on the 8th of April, 1831, being the first native of rank and influence who had ventured to break through the inveterate prejudices of centuries by crossing 'the black water.' In England his enlightened views, courteous manners, and dignified bearing attracted much attention. During his residence in London he took great interest in the exciting political conflicts then raging, and the passing of the Reform Bill caused him unmixed satisfaction. He was presented to the King, and was present at the coronation. The evidence he gave on Indian affairs before a Committee of the House of Commons was of course highly valuable, and ought to be reprinted. In one of his replies to the questions addressed to him we find him asserting that the only course of policy likely to insure the attachment of the intelligent part of the native community to English rule was 'the making them eligible to gradual promotion, according to their respective abilities and merits, to situations of trust and respectability in the State.' Unhappily Rāmmohun Roy had not sufficient physical strength to contend with the severity of a European climate. After visiting Paris and other parts of France in 1833, he began to show symptoms of declining health. He had been invited to visit Bristol, and to take up his residence at the house of Miss Castle—a ward of Dr. Carpenter—in the vicinity of that city. He arrived there early in September, 1833, and shortly afterwards was taken ill with fever. Every attention was lavished on him, and the best medical skill called in; but all in vain. His death took place at Bristol on September 27th, 1833. He died a Hindū in respect of external observances; his Brāhman servant performed the usual rites required by his master's caste, and his Brāhmanical thread was found coiled round his person when his spirit passed away. In all his Anti-Brāhmanism he continued a Brāhman to the end.

Even after his death it was thought advisable to keep up the fiction of a due maintenance of caste. His body was not interred in a Christian burial-ground, but in the shrubbery at Stapleton Grove, and without a religious service of any kind. It was not till about ten years afterwards that Dwārkanāth Tāgore, on the occasion of his visiting England in 1843, had the coffin removed to Arno's Vale Cemetery, and a suitable monument erected over the remains of one of the greatest men that India has ever produced. Yet his grave is rarely now visited, even by Indians, and few care to make themselves acquainted with the particulars of his last days. For India is not alive to the magnitude of the debt she owes to her greatest modern Reformer. Nor have his merits yet received adequate recognition at the hands of European writers. Nor indeed has it been possible within the compass of the present summary to give even a brief description of all the services rendered by Rāmmohun Roy to his country as a social as well as religious Reformer, of his labours for the elevation of women and for the education of the people generally, of his invaluable suggestions made from time to time for the carrying out of Lord William Bentinck's political reforms, and of his efforts for the improvement of the Bengālī language, and the formation of a native literature. Assuredly the memory of such a man is a precious possession to be cherished not by India alone, but by the whole human race.

CHAPTER XX.

Modern Hindū Theism. Rāmmohun Roy's successors.

It was not to be expected that the void caused by the death of so great a patriot as Rāmmohun Roy could be filled up immediately. The church he had founded in Calcutta languished for a time, notwithstanding that his friend Dwārkanāth Tāgore and his learned coadjutor Rāmachandra Vidyābāgīsh made efforts to maintain its vitality, the latter acting very regularly as minister of the Samāj. At length, after the interval of a few years, a not unworthy successor to Rāmmohun Roy was found in Dwārkanāth's son, Deben-dra-nāth Tāgore.

This remarkable man, who was born in 1818, and is now, if alive, seventy-three years of age, received a good English education at the old Hindū College[1], and was the first to give real organization to Rāmmohun Roy's Theistic Church. But he imitated his great predecessor in doing as little violence as possible to the creed and practice of his forefathers. He aimed at being a purifier rather than a destroyer. He had the advantage and disadvantage of a rich and liberal father. The luxury in which he passed his youth was for some time a drawback rather than an aid. It was not till he was twenty years of age that he began to be conscious of spiritual aspirations. Utterly dissatisfied with the religious condition of his own people, and with the ideas of God presented by Brāhmanical teaching, he

[1] Under the teaching of a man to whom Bengal is perhaps as much indebted as to David Hare.

set himself to discover a purer system. It was highly creditable to his earnestness and sincerity that he took time for consideration before joining Rāmmohun Roy's Brāhma-Sabhā, or, as it came to be called, Brāhma-Samāj (Brāhmo-Somāj).

In 1839, he established a society of his own, called the 'Truth-investigating' or 'Truth-teaching Society' (Tattva-bodhinī Sabhā), the object of which, according to its founder, was to sustain and carry on the labours of Rājā Rāmmohun Roy, and to assist in restoring the monotheistic system of divine worship in the original Hindū scriptures.

This Society lasted for twenty years, and was not finally merged in the Brāhma-Samāj till 1859. It met every week for discussion at Debendra-nāth's house, and had also monthly meetings for worship and prayer, and the exposition of the Upanishad portion of the Veda. It had its organ in a monthly periodical, called the Tattva-bodhinī patrikā. This journal was started in August, 1843, and was well edited by Akhay Kumār Datta, an earnest member of the theistic party. Its first aim seems to have been the dissemination of Vedāntic doctrine, though its editor had no belief in the infallibility of the Veda, and was himself in favour of the widest catholicity[1]. He afterwards converted Debendra-nāth to his own views.

It was not till 1841 that Debendra-nāth, without giving up occasional meetings at his own house, formally joined the church founded by Rāmmohun Roy. He soon saw that if Indian Theists were to maintain their ground in India, they needed organization, and that if the Samāj was to exist as a permanent church, it wanted a properly appointed president, a regularly ordained minister, a settled form of worship, and a fixed standard of faith and practice. He himself undertook the task of preparing what is sometimes called the Brāhma covenant, consisting of seven solemn declarations,

---

[1] The Tattva-bodhinī patrikā is, I believe, still in existence and is now known as the organ of the Ādi Brāhma-Samāj.

or vows to be taken by all candidates for admission into the Theistic Society.

By the most important of these declarations every member of the Society bound himself to abstain from idolatry; to worship no created object, but to worship through the love of God, and through doing the works dear to God (Para-brahmaṇi prītyā tat-priya-kārya-sādhanena), the One God, the Creator, Preserver, Dissolver (sṛishṭi-sthiti-pralaya-kartṛi), the Causer of emancipation (mukti-kāraṇa), the Partless (nir-avayava), the One only without a second (ekamātrādvitīya); to lead holy lives, and to seek forgiveness through abandonment of sin. At the same time a few short formulæ for worshipping God (Brahmopāsanā), consisting of prayers, invocations, hymns, and meditations, were promulgated for use in the daily services. This took place at the end of 1843.

Pandit Rām Chandra Vidyā-bāg-īsh was appointed minister of the newly-organized church, and not long afterwards Debendra-nāth, with twenty friends, solemnly took the oaths of the new Theistic covenant in his presence. The year 1844 may be given as the date of the real commencement of the first organized Theistic Church of India, hence afterwards called the Ādi Brāhma-Samāj, though at that time and until the first secession it was simply denominated the Calcutta Brāhma-Samāj.

Three years later, in 1847, the number of covenanted Brāhmans had increased to seven hundred and sixty-seven.

But, as usual, with the accession of new members, the growing church began to be agitated by contending opinions. It was affirmed that the Vedas had never been thoroughly examined with a view of arriving at a just estimate of their value as an authoritative guide to truth. Four young Brāhmans were therefore sent to Benares. Each was commissioned to copy out and study one of the four Vedas. The result of a careful examination of the sacred books was, that some members of the Samāj maintained their authority, and even their infallibility, while others rejected them as abounding in error. A serious conflict of opinion continued for some time. In the end it was decided by the majority, that neither Vedas nor Upanishads were to be accepted as an infallible guide. Only such precepts and ideas in them were to be admitted as harmonized with pure Theistic truth, such truth resting on the two chief foundations of external nature and internal intuition. Moreover, the religion of Indian Theists was held to be one of equilibrium—that is, a system balanced by intuition, reason, authority, personal experience, observation, and faith.

This took place about the year 1850, by which time other Samājes had begun to be established in the provinces, such as those at Midnapur, Kṛishnagar, and Dacca. Rāj Narāin Bose was minister of the Midnapur Samāj for many years.

A new Theistic Directory was then put forth by Debendranāth, called Brāhma-Dharma, or 'the Theistic Religion.' It contained a statement in Sanskṛit of the four fundamental principles of Indian Theism, together with the seven declarations revised, and approved extracts from the Veda, Upanishads, and later Hindū scriptures, as, for example, from the Īśopanishad, Śatapatha-Brāhmaṇa, and Manu. Selections from these works were thought to commend themselves to national predilections. Otherwise they were not regarded as possessing any special inspiration, or inherent superiority over other good books. It is to be noted that the *neuter* word Brăhmă is used for God—a word which seems inconsistent with the idea of personality and Fatherhood.

And any one who examines the whole compendium with impartiality must come to the conclusion that, although the quotations it gives are pervaded throughout by a strong aroma of Vedāntic and Pantheistic ideas, it marks an advance in the Theistic movement. It presents us for the first time with a definite exposition of Indian Theistic doctrine, which may be held by those who reject Vedāntism. Its four fundamental principles (called Brāhma-dharma-vīja) translated from the Sanskṛit are:—

I.—In the beginning before this Universe was, the One Supreme Being was (Brahma vā ekam idam-agra āsīt); nothing else whatever was (nānyat kiñćanāsīt); He has created all this universe (tad idam sarvam asṛijat).

II.—He is eternal (tadeva nityam), intelligent (jñānam), infinite (anantam), blissful (śivam), self-dependent (sva-tantram), formless (nir-avayavam), one only without a second (ekam evādvitīyam), all-pervading (sarva-vyāpī), all-governing (sarva-niyantṛi), all-sheltering (sarvāśraya), all-knowing (sarva-vid), all-powerful (sarva-śaktimat), unmovable (dhruvam), perfect (pūrṇam), and without a parallel (apratimam).

III.—By Worship of Him alone can happiness be secured in this world and the next (Ekasya tasyaivopāsanayā pāratrikam aihikaṃ ća śubham bhavati).

IV.—Love towards Him (Tasmin prītis), and performing the works He loves (priya-kārya-sādhanaṃ ća), constitute His worship (tad-upāsanam eva). Note that, although the word 'He' is used, Brāhmă is neuter.

Any one who subscribed to these four principles was admitted a member of the Calcutta Brāhma-Samāj. The seven more stringent declarations were only required of those who desired a more formal initiation into the system.

The substance of this improved Theistic teaching may be thus summarized:—

Intuition and the book of Nature form the original basis of the Brāhman's creed, but divine truth is to be thankfully accepted from any portion of the ancient Hindū scriptures as from any other good books in which it may be contained. According to the truth thus received, man is led to regard God as his Heavenly Father, endowed with a distinct personality, and with moral attributes befitting His nature. God has never become incarnate, but He takes providential care of His creatures. Prayer to Him is efficacious. Repentance is the only way to atonement, forgiveness, and salvation. The religious condition of man is progressive. Good works, charity, attainment of knowledge, contemplation, and devotion, are the only religious rites. Penances and pilgrimages are useless. The only sacrifice is the sacrifice of self, the only place of pilgrimage is the company of the good, the only true Temple is the pure heart. There is no distinction of castes.

The Hindū doctrine of transmigration of souls was given up. Yet great latitude in regard to the maintenance of old national customs was still allowed, and a friendly demeanour towards the national religion encouraged.

In fact, the Mission of the Calcutta Brāhma-Samāj, according to its president and most able literary representative Rāj Narāin Bose[1], was to fulfil or at least to purify the old religion, not to destroy it.

Such a compromise appeared wholly unsatisfactory to the more thoughtful members of the Samāj, especially to those who were beginning to be influenced by the opinions of a clever eloquent young man, Keshab Chandar Sen, who joined it in 1858. They felt that a more complete Reform was needed before the Samāj could deliver itself from all complicity with degrading social customs.

The youthful Keshab addressed himself to the task of radical reform with the ardour of a young man full of spirit and energy, who had his knightly spurs to win.

It must be borne in mind that we in Europe are wholly unable to realize the difficulties which beset the career of a radical religious reformer in India. There, religious and social life are so intimately interwoven—there, the ordinary creed of the people, their debasing idolatry and demoralizing superstitions, are so intertwined with the texture of their daily life, with their domestic manners and institutions, and even with the common law of the land, that to strike at the root of the national faith is to subvert the very foundations of the whole social fabric. Let a man enter on the path of progress, let him abandon the ideas inherited from his parents, let him set

---

[1] Rāj Narāin Bose has rendered good service to the Ādi Brāhma-Samāj by his able writings, just as Mr. P. C. Mozoomdār (see p. 521) has done to the later development of Theism about to be described—the Brāhma-Samāj of India.

his face against the time-honoured usages of his country, let him stand up boldly as the champion of truth, the eradicator of error, the regenerator of a degenerate age, the purifier of a corrupt condition of society, and what are the consequences? He has to fight his way through a host of antagonisms and obstructions, sufficient to appal, if not to overpower, a man of ordinary courage and determination. The inveterate prejudices of centuries, deeply-seated antipathies, national pride, popular passion, a thousand vested interests of tradition, ignorance, bigotry, superstition, indolence, priestcraft. conspire to crush his efforts and impede his advance. Every inch of the ground is disputed by a host of bitter antagonists. Humiliation, insult, threat, invective, vituperation are heaped upon his head. Father, mother, wife, children, relatives and friends hold him fast in their embraces or unite their efforts to drag him backwards. No one stirs a finger to help him onwards. At length, by the force of his own resolute character, by patience and conciliation, by firmness and gentleness, by persuasion and earnestness, by carrying people with him against their will, by making his work theirs as well as his own, he gains a few adherents; for nowhere do qualities such as these command so much admiration as in India. Then his progress becomes easier. But if his attitude towards ancient creeds and social abuses continues that of an uncompromising enemy, he will still have to do battle at the head of a little band of followers against countless adversaries. and will only triumph over opposition in one quarter, to find it renewed with increased acrimony and vehemence in other directions.

This may be taken as a description of the early career of the third great Theistic Reformer of British India, Keshab Chandar Sen, who was born in 1838 and died in 1884.

A few particulars of Mr. Sen's life ought to be given here. He was a grandson of a well-known member of the Vaidya caste, Rām Comul Sen, who was a man of great worth, talent and literary culture[1], but a bigoted Hindū of the Vaishṇava school. The young Keshab was brought up in an atmosphere of Hindū superstition and idolatry. As might have been expected, the Vishṇu-worship in which he was trained predisposed him to emotional religion and to a belief in one supreme personal God. Subsequently he received a thorough English education at the Presidency College, Calcutta. There, of course, the foundations of his family faith crumbled to pieces. It could not bear collision with scientific truth as imparted by European teachers. Nor was any new faith built up immediately on the ruins of the old. His attitude towards all religion became one of absolute indifference. Happily, in a character like that of Keshab, the void caused by the over-development of one part of his nature was not long left unfilled. With a greater advance in intellectual culture came a greater consciousness of spiritual aspirations, and a greater sense of dependence upon the Almighty Ruler of the Universe. He began to crave for a knowledge of the true God. One day, when he was twenty years of age, some sermons by Rāj Narāin Bose fell into his hands, and he found to his astonishment that a pure Theistic Church had been already founded in Calcutta. Without a moment's hesitation he decided to enroll himself a member of the Calcutta Brāhma-Samāj. This happened towards the end of 1858, when he was in his twentieth year.

The English culture and freedom of thought, not unmixed with Christian ideas, which Keshab imported into the Calcutta (Ādi) Samāj, could not fail to leaven its whole constitution. Not that Debendra-nāth had been uninfluenced by similar culture in his reorganization of the Brāhma-Samāj. The fear however was that Keshab's enthusiasm might lead him to put himself forward prematurely. Happily his extreme youth-

[1] He was held in great esteem by Prof. H. H. Wilson, and was the author of a useful English and Bengālī dictionary, to which my own lexicography is under some obligations.

fulness and inexperience compelled him to veil his own individuality. He longed from the first to bring all the impetuosity of his fervid nature to bear on the accomplishment of vast changes. He was ambitious of penetrating to the very springs of social life and altering their whole course. But he was sensible enough to perceive that he could not enter upon such a Herculean task without feeling his way and testing his powers. He, therefore, commenced his mission as a fellow-worker with Debendra-nāth, and in due subordination to him as his recognized leader. Their fellowship and co-operation lasted for about five years. Nothing, however, could keep the enthusiastic Keshab long in the background. It was not sufficient for him that idolatry had been eliminated from Hindū usages. They remained Hindū usages still. He soon began to urge a complete abolition of all caste-restrictions. The first change he advocated was that all who conducted the services in the Mandir should abandon the sacred thread (upavīta, p. 378) which distinguished the Brāhmans and higher castes from the lower. But Debendra-nāth, though he consented to give up this sacred badge in his own case, declined to force a similar renunciation upon others. Unhappily this was the commencement of a difference of opinion between the progressive and conservative Reformers, which afterwards led to a more complete rupture.

Next to the abandonment of the thread came the alteration of the Śrāddha, or worship of deceased ancestors—a rite involving ideas incompatible with the Brāhma doctrine of a future state. This was followed by a remodelling of the ritual at the ceremonies of birth (jāta-karma, p. 353), name-giving (nāma-karaṇa, p. 353), and cremation of the dead (antyeshṭi, p. 354). Then a solemn and impressive form of initiation into the Brāhma faith was substituted for the Upanayana, or initiatory rite of Brāhmanism (p. 377). Of course, efforts were made for the education and elevation of women. They were encouraged to join the Brāhma-Samāj, which many eventually did under the name of Brāhmikās, worshipping at first either behind screens, or in a separate room.

A still more important matter was the reform of marriage customs. Vast difficulties beset any reform in this direction. Marriage is the most ancient, sacred, and inviolable of all Hindū institutions, and its due performance the most complicated of all religious acts. It involves intricate questions of caste, creed, property, family usage, consanguinity, and age. To remodel the institution of marriage is to reorganize the whole constitution of Indian society, and to create, so to speak, an entirely new social atmosphere. The first change advocated by the Reformers had reference to the abolition of child-marriages. Nothing has tended to the physical and moral deterioration of the people so much as child-marriage. It has not only resulted in excessive population, rapidly multiplying till reduced to so low a standard of moral and physical stamina that every failure of crops adds demoralization to starvation. It is an ever-present source of weakness and impoverishment, destructive of all national vigour, and fatal to the development of national thrift and economy. The progressive Reformers felt that until this evil was removed there could be no hope of India's regeneration.

Of course, no man was to be allowed more than one wife. The idea that child-widowhood was the result of crimes committed in former births was scouted, and widows were to be released from enforced celibacy. Rāj Narāin Bose was the first to introduce the remarriage of widows into his family—a reform for which the inhabitants of the village in which he was born threatened to stone him to death (compare p. 473). As to the marriage ceremony itself, all semblance of idolatrous worship, all foolish ritual, all noisy music, needless display and unnecessary expense, caused by spreading the festivities over many days, were to be eliminated. Debendranāth himself was induced to set the example of celebrating a nuptial ceremony in his own family according to this simple

Brāhmic form. His second daughter was engaged to be married to Babu H. N. Mukerjea. The rite was performed on the 26th of July, 1861, quietly, solemnly, simply, and without protracted festivities, in the presence of nearly two hundred co-religionists. This was the first Brāhmic marriage.

A still more momentous reform was attempted by Keshab Chandar Sen when he performed a marriage ceremony between two persons of different castes in August, 1864. An innovation so revolutionary gave great dissatisfaction to Debendra-nāth. In fact, Mr. Sen, notwithstanding the real good he had effected by his influence, example, and personal efforts, found himself hampered by his connexion with the too conservative Calcutta Ādi-Samāj. He was like a man working in chains. He felt himself powerless to penetrate beneath the outer crust of the social fabric. The old caste-customs, the old superstitious rites, were still practised by a large number of Theists, while others who professed sympathy with the advanced Reformer, and adopted his opinions in public, secretly reverted to their old ways. It was not to be expected that a man of Mr. Sen's temperament would long acquiesce in merely superficial changes and patchy incomplete reformations. He was willing to accept half measures as an instalment. But nothing short of a thorough reconstruction of the whole religious and social fabric could afford him permanent satisfaction. He was bent on laying the axe to the very root of the tree. He felt his own mission to be very different from that of Debendra-nāth. He was to destroy rather than to renovate the old Vedic system with all its train of ceremonial rites and observances.

Of course, he no sooner gave up all idea of compromise than instantly he found himself plunged in a slough of obstruction. Difficulties and opposition met him at every turn. At length, in February, 1865, the inevitable crisis arrived. Keshab Chandar Sen with a large number of the younger members of the Samāj formed themselves into a separate body of advanced or progressive reformers, and seceded from the old Society, leaving behind them all its accumulated property. It was not, however, till November, 1866, that they were able to organize themselves into a new Theistic Church called the Brāhma-Samāj of India (Bhāratavarshīya Brāhma-Samāj[1]), a church which gloried in having broken entirely with Brāhmanism, and severed every link which connected it with the national religion.

At a meeting held on November 11th, 1866, the day of the incorporation of the new society, Mr. Sen announced that the aim of the new Church would be to unite all Brāhmas into one body, to reduce their labours to a well-organized system of co-operation, and to establish a central metropolitan Brāhma-Samāj of all India, to which all other Samājes throughout the country might be affiliated, or with which they might establish friendly relations. This idea was not a new one. An effort had been made in 1864 to establish a General Representative Assembly or Council of all the existing Brāhma Samājes. A meeting was then convened, and twenty-eight out of the existing fifty Samājes sent representatives, but little further was done. Nor did Mr. Sen ever succeed in making his own Samāj a centre of union and authority, though for a long time his talents as an orator secured him a position as chief leader of the Brāhma community.

The first stone of the new Mandir or place of worship of the Brāhma-Samāj of India was laid on the 23rd of January, 1868, but the building was not opened until August (Bhādra), 1869. As might have been expected, the new Samāj exhibited from its first foundation a decided reflection of its founder's individuality. He had imbibed Vaishṇava ideas with his earliest impressions. Yet the peculiar vein of

---

[1] This new Church has been sometimes called the progressive Brāhma-Samāj.

Hindū theology which permeated his mind only operated beneficially. The introduction of faith (bhakti), emotional religion, and devotional fervour into the Brāhma system was a real advantage. It infused warmth and light into a cold inanimate Theology, and brought the latest development of Indian Theism into closer harmony with Christian ideas.

It remains to describe more fully the nature of that development. No sooner was Brāhmanism finally discarded than it became necessary to formulate more definite articles of faith. Briefly the new creed might have been described as 'the Fatherhood of God and the Brotherhood of Man.' Its most essential points are as follow:—

God is the first cause of the Universe. By His will He created all objects out of nothing and continually upholds them. He is spirit, not matter. He is perfect, infinite, all-powerful, all-merciful, all-holy. He is our Father, Preserver, Master, King, and Saviour.

The soul is immortal. Death is only the dissolution of the body. There is no new birth on earth after death; the future life is a continuation and development of the present life. The men that now live are the embryos of the men that are to be.

The true scriptures are two,—the volume of nature, and the natural intuitions implanted in the mind. The wisdom, power, and mercy of the Creator are written on the Universe. All ideas about immortality and morality are primary convictions rooted in the constitution of man.

God Himself never becomes man by putting on a human body. His divinity dwells in every man, and is displayed more vividly in some; as in Moses, Jesus Christ, Muhammad, Nānak, Ćaitanya, and other great Teachers, who appeared at special times, and conferred vast benefits on the world. They are entitled to universal gratitude and love.

The Brāhma religion is distinct from all other systems of religion; yet it is the essence of all. It is not hostile to other creeds. What is true in them it accepts. It is based on the constitution of man, and is, therefore, eternal and universal. It is not confined to age or country.

All mankind are of one brotherhood. The Brāhma religion recognizes no distinction between high and low caste. It is the aim of this religion to bind all mankind into one family.

Duties are of four kinds: (1) Duties *towards God*—such as belief in Him, love, worship, and service; (2) Duties *towards self*—such as preservation of bodily health, acquisition of knowledge, sanctification of soul; (3) Duties *towards others*—such as veracity, justice, gratitude, the promotion of the welfare of all mankind; (4) Duties *towards animals* and inferior creatures—such as kind treatment.

Every sinner must suffer the consequences of his own sins sooner or later, in this world or the next. Man must labour after holiness by the worship of God, by subjugation of the passions, by repentance, by the study of nature and of good books, by good company and by solitary contemplation. These will lead through the action of God's grace to salvation.

Salvation is deliverance of the soul from the root of corruption and moral disease, and its perpetual growth in purity. Such growth continues through all eternity, and the soul becomes more and more godly and happy in Him who is the fountain of infinite holiness and joy. The companionship of God is the Indian Theists' heaven.

With regard to the worship of God, it was declared to be 'a wholly spiritual act.'

The form of divine service was as follows:—First a hymn; then an invocation of God by the minister, followed by another hymn; then adoration of God, chanted by the whole congregation together, and continued by the minister alone; then silent communion for some minutes. Then the following united prayer[1], chanted by the whole congregation standing:—

'Lead us, O God! from untruth to truth, from darkness to light, from death to immortality. O! thou Father of truth, reveal thyself before us. Thou art merciful, do thou protect us always in thy unbounded goodness. Peace! Peace! Peace!

Then a prayer for the well-being of the whole world by the minister alone standing, succeeded by another hymn, and by a recitation of texts from Hindū and other scriptures. Finally, a sermon, followed by a prayer, a benediction, and a hymn (see pp. 527, 528).

Services of this kind still take place—generally on Sundays, and often on a week-day in addition. There are also grand anniversary festivals to celebrate the foundation of the Brāhma Church. The chief festival, called Māghotsab (Māghotsava), on the 23rd of January (11th of Māgha), is kept by all the Samājes in commemoration of the founding of monotheistic worship by Rāmmohun Roy. Another, called Bhādrotsab

---

[1] This was taken from the form used by the Ādi Brāhma-Samāj.

(Bhādrotsava), is held by the Brāhma-Samāj of India in celebration of the opening of the Mandir in August, 1869. Solemn initiation services for the admission of new members are also performed. They correspond in an interesting manner to our Confirmation services.

Clearly it would be easy to prove that the advanced Indian Reformers, trained and educated by us, and imbued unconsciously with Western theological ideas, have borrowed largely from our Christian system in formulating their own creed. The points of agreement are too obvious to need indicating. One noteworthy point of contact with Christianity is the active missionary spirit displayed by progressive Brāhmas, which indeed was originated by the members of the Ādi-Samāj. Such a spirit is, of course, essential to the growth and vitality of all new systems. Keshab Chandar Sen has made several Missionary tours in India, and in 1870 he came to England, giving out that his mission was to excite the interest of Englishmen in the religious, social, and political progress of his fellow-countrymen. Here he visited fourteen of the chief towns of England and Scotland, and conducted religious services in the pulpits of Baptist, Congregational, and Unitarian chapels. He preached to large congregations in East London, and addressed seventy meetings in different places in behalf of such objects as Temperance, Peace, Reformatories, Ragged Schools, and general education. He had interviews with Her Majesty and several eminent Statesmen.

And what were the impressions he formed of Christian religious life and doctrine in England? It may do us no harm to listen once more to the Hindū Theist's utterances before he left our shores:—

'One institution,' he said, 'in England I have looked upon with peculiar feelings of delight—the happy English home, in which the utmost warmth and cordiality of affection, and sympathy, are mingled with the highest moral and religious restraint and discipline. The spirit of prayer and worship seems mixed up with daily household duties, and the influence of the spirit of Christ is manifest in domestic concerns.' 'Yet,' he added, 'it grieves me to find that the once crucified Jesus is crucified hundreds of times every day in the midst of Christendom. The Christian world has not imbibed Christ's spirit.'

At Birmingham he said :—

'Since my arrival in England I have found myself incessantly surrounded by various religious denominations, professing to be Christians. Methinks I have come into a vast market. Every sect is like a small shop where a peculiar kind of Christianity is offered for sale. As I go from door to door, from shop to shop—each sect steps forward and offers for my acceptance its own interpretations of the Bible, and its own peculiar Christian beliefs. I cannot but feel perplexed and even amused amidst countless and quarrelling sects. It appears to me, and has always appeared to me, that no Christian nation on earth represents fully and thoroughly Christ's idea of the kingdom of God. I do believe, and I must candidly say, that no Christian sect puts forth the genuine and full Christ as He was and as He is, but, in some cases, a mutilated, disfigured Christ, and, what is more shameful, in many cases, a counterfeit Christ. Now, I wish to say that I have not come to England as one who has yet to find Christ. When the Roman Catholic, the Protestant, the Unitarian, the Trinitarian, the Broad Church, the Low Church, the High Church, all come round me, and offer me their respective Christs, I desire to say to one and all : "Think you that I have no Christ within me? Though an Indian, I can still humbly say, thank God that I have my Christ."'

This remarkable statement has become invested with far deeper significance and interest since the publication of Mr. Sen's striking lecture, on the subject 'India asks, Who is Christ?' It might have been expected that his English visit would have brought his Theism into closer affinity with Christian dogma. But such was not really the case. I may state, however, as an interesting fact, that two of his Hindū travelling companions were afterwards baptized.

On his return to India Mr. Sen applied himself zealously to the work of social reform, and at once started what was called 'The Indian Reform Association' for female improvement, for the promotion of education among men and women, for the suppression of intemperance, and generally for the social and moral reformation of the people of India. This society, open to all classes and creeds, was founded November 2nd,

1870, and a female Normal and Adult School was opened in 1871.

The most important Reform of all—that relating to marriage—to which Mr. Sen's efforts had already been directed, had not made much progress. The example so well set by the marriage of Debendra-nāth Tāgore's daughter in 1861 had created hopes of a better state of things, but little real advance had been achieved. It is true that similar marriages had followed, but the legality of such marriages was disputed, though a form of ritual had been adopted which was thought to be sufficiently conformable to Hindū usage to insure their validity. It was not encouraging that between 1864 and 1867 only seven or eight Ādi Samāj Brāhma marriages and four or five Progressive Brāhma intermarriages between persons of different castes had been solemnized. Nor had much success attended the attempt to prevent early marriages. Mr. Sen and his followers now threw themselves more vigorously than ever into the marriage-reform movement. The best medical opinions were sought, and the proper marriageable age fixed. But the most important step was to memorialize the Government for a new Marriage Act, to relieve Brāhmas from their disability to contract legal marriages according to their own forms. Much agitation ensued. The native mind became greatly excited, and Indian society was stirred to its depths by a conflict of opinion on a matter which affected the very framework of its whole structure and composition.

At length a Bill was drawn up by Sir Henry Maine—the legal Member of Council—and improved upon by his successor Sir Fitzjames Stephen. This pleased no one. It was violently opposed not only by the orthodox Brāhmans, but by the more conservative Theists. The struggle was protracted with much bitterness on the part of the natives for four years. Finally, after many ineffectual attempts at obtaining a general agreement of opinion, a third Bill was elaborated, and under the able management of Sir Fitzjames Stephen the Native Marriage Act became law on the 22nd of March, 1872. It commences thus :—

'Whereas it is expedient to provide a form of marriage for persons who do not profess the Christian, Jewish, Hindū, Muhammadan, Pārsī, Buddhist, Sikh or Jaina religion, and to legalize certain marriages the validity of which is doubtful; it is hereby enacted,' etc.

The Act, in fact, introduced for the first time the institution of civil marriage into Hindū society. It sanctioned matrimonial union without any necessary religious ceremonial. It legalized marriages between different castes. It fixed the minimum age for a bridegroom at 18 and of a bride at 14, but required the written consent of parents or guardians when either party was under 21. It prevented marriage within certain degrees of consanguinity. It prohibited bigamy, and permitted the remarriage of widows, which had been before legalized generally by the Act of 1856.

After the passing of the Act of 1872 fifty-eight marriages took place in the eight and a half years ending August, 1879, against fifty-one in the ten and a half years preceding its ratification. The average of widow marriages has not as yet been greatly increased by the passing of the Act. The same may be said of intermarriages between persons of different castes, though these are said to have become more numerous during the Prince of Wales's visit. All the marriages which took place before the Act might have been registered retrospectively, and in this manner legalized, but only twenty-one were so registered. Singularly enough, too, even to this day, some Hindū Theists continue to prefer being married according to Brāhmic rites, without availing themselves of the Act. There appears to be a dislike to the Registrar, as if he were required to take the place of the minister of religion, whereas he simply witnesses the contract between the bride and bridegroom, and listens to the words by which they bind themselves to matrimonial union. Some Theists also object to the categorical repudiation of the Hindū religion which must precede the performance of the civil marriage, considering that because they are Brāhmas they are not, therefore, un-Hindūized.

Yet, it cannot be doubted that Mr. Sen and his followers deserve the gratitude of their fellow-countrymen for their labours in agitating for and obtaining the ratification of so useful an Act. At any rate the events of the year 1872 must always constitute an epoch in the history of the reforming movement.

For some time afterwards the Ādi Brāhma-Samāj led by Debendra-nāth, and the Brāhma-Samāj of India under Keshab Chandar Sen, achieved good work in their respective spheres, and in not unfriendly co-operation with each other. The two leaders, though very different in character, were both men of unusual ability, and both penetrated by a sincere desire for the regeneration of India. Each Samāj, too, had its able Secretary and Writer; the Ādi-Samāj in Rāj Narāin Bose, and the more Progressive Samāj in Mr. Sen's cousin Pratāp Chandar Mozoomdār[1]. Moreover, the Conservative Samāj had its literary organ in the Tattva-bodhinī patrikā, and the Progressive in a daily newspaper called 'The Indian Mirror.'

No better proof of the activity of the two societies could be given than the success of their missionary operations. By the end of 1877 the number of Brāhma Samājes scattered throughout India, including Assam, had increased to a hundred and seven, some following the Conservative pattern, and some the Progressive. In 1875 fresh attempts were made to establish a general representative Council of all the Samājes, and one or two meetings were held, but no definite scheme has yet been matured.

Meanwhile, lamentable dissensions, leading to a serious

---

[1] This gentleman was in England for three or four months in the year 1883. He kindly called to see me at Oxford and much impressed me by his conversation. I have given an account of my conversation with him at p. 522. He has lately published a very interesting summary of the doctrines of his Samāj.

schism, have taken place in the Progressive Brāhma-Samāj. Without doubt the career of this Samāj continued for several years to be one of real progress. It did sterling work in propagating its own reforming principles. It sent forth earnest missionaries to all parts of India. It put forth an ably written Sunday edition of its daily newspaper the 'Indian Mirror [1].' It encouraged fervour of faith and devotion (bhakti) to such an extent that it was accused of making religion an affair of mere emotion and excitement. One direction in which the devotional side of the movement developed itself was in the rapturous singing of hymns in chorus (saṃkīrtana), sometimes performed in procession through the streets. Another form of development was the establishment of Brāhmotsavas, or periodical religious festivals as seasons of special prayer, faith, and rejoicing. Besides all this, many members of the Society were remarkable for austerity of life, and the Samāj had a niche for those who gave themselves up to severe self-discipline and asceticism (Vairāgya).

The rock on which it split was its too unquestioning submission to the commanding ability of its leader. Keshab Chandar Sen had fought his way through difficulties, hardships and perils, with indomitable energy, but was not prepared for an unsuspected danger—the danger of success—the danger that too much praise would be lavished on the work he had accomplished. For many years his daily path had certainly not led him through clover; nor had his nightly rest been taken on a bed of roses. Nowhere is eminent ability worshipped with more fervour than in India. So conspicuous were Mr. Sen's talents that he soon became the object of a kind of adoration. He was even accused of accepting divine

---

[1] Besides the 'Indian Mirror' the *Sulabh Samāchār* ('Cheap News') and *Dharma-tattva*, 'Religious Truth,' have long been exponents of Mr. Sen's teaching. Mr. Mozoomdār's 'Theistic Annual,' and his 'Theistic Quarterly Review' which has lately taken its place, are more recent advocates on the same side.

honours. This, of course, he denied, and his followers have always indignantly repelled the charge, but his old Vaishṇava training was not without its influence on his own estimate of his own mission and office. He certainly supposed himself to be in some special manner a partaker of divine gifts. It is noticeable that in his address, delivered January, 1879, though he answered the question, 'Am I an inspired prophet?' in the negative, he laid claim to a kind of direct inspiration. He declared that he had had visions[1] of John the Baptist, Jesus Christ, and St. Paul, who all favoured him with personal communications, that the Lord said he was to have perennial inspiration from heaven, that all his actions were regulated by divine command (ādeśa), and that men should remember that to protest against the cause which he upheld was to protest against the dispensations of God Almighty.

Then, again, Keshab Chandar Sen was not merely an autocrat among his own people in matters of faith and doctrine. He was the sole administrator of the affairs of the Society, and ruled it with the rod of an irresponsible dictator. People began to complain that the Progressive Brāhma-Samāj was without a constitutional government. It had no freedom of discussion in the management of its own affairs. Keshab Chandar Sen was not only its Bishop, Priest, and Deacon all in one; he was a kind of Pope[2], from whose decision there was no appeal.

---

[1] A great part of the matter in this chapter was written by me soon after my second travels in India, about the year 1879. Not long afterwards a Brāhma Missionary Conference held on Dec. 22, 1880, commissioned the brother of Mr. Sen to write me a letter calling in question some of my statements. In that letter the members of the Conference objected to the expression 'visions,' and declared that on the occasion here alluded to Mr. Sen only meant to use metaphorical expressions. Further, they assert that Mr. Sen was not regarded by them as a Pope, but only as an inspired apostle commissioned by God.

[2] Rāj Narāin Bose considered that Mr. Sen was justly amenable to this charge, as he (Mr. Sen) brought the same charge against Debendra-nāth at the time of the schism.

While all these elements of discontent were at work, a most unexpected revelation took place, the effect of which was to precipitate the disruption of the Samāj. It turned out, in fact, that Keshab Chandar Sen, with all his almost superhuman eloquence, ability, and genius, was nothing after all but a plain human being, with very human infirmities. It appears that as early as August, 1877, it began to be anxiously whispered that the great social Reformer was likely to sacrifice his own cherished principles at the altar of ambition. He, who had denounced early marriages as the curse of India, was said to be inclined to accept an offer of marriage for his own daughter not yet fourteen, from the young Mahārāja of Kuch Behār not yet sixteen years of age. The rumour proved to be too true, and the 'Indian Mirror' of February 6, 1878, formally announced that the marriage had been arranged. Protests from every conceivable quarter poured in upon the great social Reformer, but they were not only unheeded, they were absolutely ignored. The marriage ceremony[1] took place on March 6, 1878, and not without idolatrous rites on the bride's side, though these were not performed in the presence of Mr. Sen himself[2]. In point of fact, the performance of certain ceremonies—such as the Homa, or fire-oblation—was necessary to secure the validity of the marriage in a Native State protected by our Government, but not subject to the operation of the Marriage Act. Immediately after the wedding the young Mahārāja set out

[1] The Missionary Conference of Dec. 22, 1880, commissioned Mr. Sen to inform me that this ceremony was only a betrothal and that the parties did not live together as man and wife till a final ceremony had been performed in the Brāhma Mandir on Oct. 20, 1880. But the ceremony of March 6 was surely the legal ceremony.

[2] The 'Indian Mirror' of March 17, 1878, informed its readers that 'though the Rājā's Purohits, who were orthodox Brahmins, were allowed to officiate at the ceremony, the Homa was not performed *during* the marriage; but after the bride and her party left the place. The principles of Brāhma marriage were barely preserved.'

for England, and the bridegroom and bride did not live together as man and wife till a final ceremony had been performed on Oct. 20, 1880.

Subsequently the Dharma-tattva and the 'Indian Mirror' published an elaborate justification of Mr. Sen's conduct. The defence set up was that Mr. Sen had no choice in the matter. He had acted, it was said—as was said of Muhammad of old—under divine command (ādeśa), and in obedience to God's will. Moreover, it was contended that the marriage of his daughter with a Mahārāja had dealt a blow at caste-marriages, while the propagation of Theistic opinions in Kuch Behār and other Native States was likely to be materially promoted. Another line of defence taken was that Keshab Chandar Sen's mission had always been that of a religious and not secular Reformer.

As might have been expected, the Protestors, who objected to Mr. Sen's proceedings in regard to the marriage, met together, soon after he left for Kuch Behār, to decide on their line of action. An unsuccessful attempt was then made to depose Mr. Sen from his office as Minister, and an unseemly struggle took place for the possession of the Mandir. In the end it was determined to establish a new church on a constitutional and catholic basis. All the provincial Samājes were consulted, and with the approval of the majority, a meeting was held in the Town Hall, Calcutta, May 15, 1878, Mr. Ānanda Mohan Bose being in the chair, when the following resolution was passed :—

'That this meeting deeply deplores the want of a constitutional organization in the Brāhma-Samāj, and does hereby establish a Samāj to be called "The Sādhāraṇa [or general] Brāhma-Samāj," with a view to remove the serious and manifold evils resulting from this state of things, and to secure the representation of the views and the harmonious co-operation of the general Brāhma community, in all that affects the progress and well-being of the Theistic cause and Theistic work in India.'

At first the Prayer Meetings of this new Brāhma-Samāj, of

which Mr. Ānanda Bose was the first President [1], were held in temporary rooms, but the foundation stone of a new Prayer Hall (211, Cornwallis Street) was laid on January 23, 1879, and the building finished and consecrated on January 22, 1881. Moreover, the Brāhma Public Opinion [2] newspaper, and the Tattva-kaumudī, 'Moonlight of Truth,' a fortnightly paper, were started as religious and literary organs of the protesting party.

It is not possible for me to speak with certainty as to the success of this fourth development of the Brāhma Theistic movement although I visited its Mandir. Its name, *Sādhāraṇa*, implied that it aimed at more catholicity, and a more democratic government, but its organization, though promising well under Mr. Ā. M. Bose and Pandit Śivanāth Śāstrī (a man of eloquence and ability), did not appear to be complete in relation to the rest of India. There appeared, at that time, to be no one man among its members who had the religious genius of either Keshab Chandar Sen, or of Debendra-nāth Tāgore, or the literary culture which characterized the best productions of Mr. P. C. Mozoomdār and Rāj Narāin Bose. Yet there seemed to be a large number of practical men—men of good sound sense, religious earnestness, and sufficient ability, who were likely to accomplish a great deal of useful work together, and to make their society one of the leading Samājes of India.

After the unhappy breach of harmony, caused by Mr. Sen's conduct in regard to the marriage of his daughter, he appears to have made extraordinary efforts to restore his own prestige by the elaboration of novel ideas. The year 1879 was signalized by the institution of an order of professed

[1] He was succeeded by Bābū Shib Chandar Deb, the Secretary being Bābū Dvārkā Nāth Gāṅguli. Whether these still continue I know not.

[2] This has now become a purely secular paper and has changed its name to 'Bengal Public Opinion,' while the 'Indian Messenger,' well edited by Śivanāth Śāstrī, M. A., was started on September 9, 1883, and has taken its place as the religious organ.

teachers of religion, called Adhyāpakas. Four teachers were ordained by Mr. Sen on September 7, 1879, among whom was Mr. Mozoomdār. A curious practice was also introduced of holding supposed conversations and passing days and nights as imaginary pilgrims with the great prophets, apostles, and saints of the world—as, for example, with Moses, Socrates, Ćaitanya, the Ṛishis, Muhammad, Buddha—who were supposed to be present and to take part in the dialogues and to inspire the pilgrims with the fire of their own nature.

Furthermore, a remarkable 'Proclamation' was issued in the 'Sunday Mirror' of December 14, 1879, purporting to come from 'India's Mother.' It is here abridged:—

'To all my soldiers in India my affectionate greeting. Believe that this Proclamation goeth forth from Heaven in the name and with the love of your Mother. Carry out its behests like loyal soldiers. The British Government is my Government. The Brāhma-Samāj is my Church. My daughter Queen Victoria have I ordained. Come direct to me, without a mediator, as your Mother. The influence of the earthly Mother at home, of the Queen Mother at the head of the Government, will raise the head of my Indian children to their Supreme Mother. I will give them peace and salvation. Soldiers, fight bravely and establish my dominion.'

This idea of God's Motherhood as a correlative to God's Fatherhood is, as I have already pointed out, an essential characteristic of Hindūism (see Chapter VII. pp. 180-208).

Mr. Sen's lecture delivered on the 24th of January, 1880, called 'God-vision,' was full of rhapsody mixed up with many fine thoughts; but that delivered in the Town Hall, Calcutta, on the 9th of April, 1879, before at least a thousand persons, on the subject, 'India asks, Who is Christ?' was pronounced by those who heard it to be a masterpiece of oratory[1]. He not only entranced his hearers by an extraordinary effort of eloquence; he surprised them by calling upon India to accept Christ. According to Mr. Sen,

[1] The Rev. Luke Rivington was my authority. He was present with the Bishop of Calcutta and a few other Europeans. Indeed the subject chosen was due to a previous conversation with Mr. Rivington at a dinner-party given by Mr. Sen to him and a large number of thoughtful natives.

Christianity is the true national religion of his fellow-countrymen. India is destined to become Christian, and cannot escape her destiny. 'You, my countrymen,' he says, 'cannot help accepting Christ in the spirit of your national scriptures.' In another part of the lecture we find him using these remarkable words:—

> 'Gentlemen, you cannot deny that your hearts have been touched, conquered, and subjugated by a superior power. That power, need I tell you? is Christ. It is Christ who rules British India, and not the British Government. England has sent out a tremendous moral force in the life and character of that mighty prophet to conquer and hold this vast empire. None but Jesus, none but Jesus, none but Jesus, ever deserved this bright, this precious diadem, India, and Jesus shall have it.'

It is evident, however, that Mr. Sen intends Christ to be accepted by his fellow-countrymen as the greatest of all Asiatic saints and not in the character ascribed to Him by the Church of England. 'Christ comes to us,' he says, 'as an Asiatic in race, as a Hindū in faith, as a kinsman and as a brother. . . . Christ is a true Yogī, and will surely help us to realize our national ideal of a Yogī. . . . In accepting Him, therefore, you accept the fulfilment of your national scriptures and prophets.' This is all very striking, but seems rather like presenting Christianity to the Hindūs in the light of an advanced phase of Hindūism.

A still more recent annual sermon delivered by Mr. Sen at Calcutta, in January, 1881, announced the advent of a New Dispensation, which any one perusing the discourse will be surprised to find, is a kind of amalgamation of Hindūism, Muhammadanism, and Christianity. Thenceforth the Brāhma-Samāj of India was to be called the 'New Dispensation Church.' The present Bishop of Exeter (the Right Rev. Dr. Bickersteth) was present on the occasion and recorded his impression of the address in a letter written from Bishop's Palace, Calcutta:—

> 'This afternoon Keshab Chandar Sen gave his annual address to the Brāhma-Samāj in the Town Hall. The huge hall was crammed—I should

say 3500 men and some six ladies; almost all were Hindūs, thoughtful, earnest-looking men. He spoke for one hour and forty minutes—a torrent of eloquence. He denies the Godhead of Christ, though, with this grave and grievous lack, nothing in parts could be more impassioned than his language of devotion to Christ. He thinks himself the prophet of a "New Dispensation," as he calls it, which is to affirm the Unity of the Godhead, and the unity of all earnest creeds—Hindū, Moslem, and Christian—who worship God. Of course it is a great advance upon the multiform idolatry of this land; and again and again I said to myself, "Quoniam talis es, utinam noster esses."'

This New Dispensation was proclaimed on January 26, 1881. Then, on January 1, 1883, Mr. Sen, as chief apostle of the Church of this Dispensation, put forth another manifesto. I here give the greater portion as it appeared in the Indian newspapers of about that date (see 'Times of India' for Jan. 12, 1883):—

'Keshab Chandar Sen, a servant of God, called to be an apostle of the Church of the New Dispensation, which is in the holy city of Calcutta, the metropolis of Āryāvarta,

'To all the great nations in the world, and to the chief religious sects in the East and the West,

'To the followers of Moses, of Jesus, of Buddha, of Confucius, of Zoroaster, of Mahomet, of Nānak, and the various branches of the Hindū Church,

'Grace be to you, and peace everlasting.

'Whereas sectarian discord and strife, schisms and enmities prevail in our Father's family, causing much bitterness and unhappiness, impurity and unrighteousness, and even war, carnage, and bloodshed,

'Whereas this setting of brother against brother and sister against sister in the name of religion has proved a fruitful source of evils, and is itself a sin against God and man:

'It has pleased the Holy God to send unto the world a message of peace and love, of harmony and reconciliation.

'This New Dispensation hath He in boundless mercy vouchsafed to us in the East, and we have been commanded to bear witness unto it among the nations of the earth.

'Thus saith the Lord—Sectarianism is an abomination unto Me, and unbrotherliness I will not tolerate.

'I desire love and unity, and My children shall be of one heart, even as I am one.

'At sundry times have I spoken through My prophets, and through My many and various dispensations; there is unity in them.

'Hear ye men, there is one music but many instruments, one body but many limbs, one spirit but diverse gifts, one blood yet many nations, one church yet many churches.

'Blessed are the peace-makers, who reconcile differences and establish peace, good-will, and brotherhood in the name of the Father.

'These words hath the Lord our God spoken unto us, and His new Gospel He hath revealed unto us—a gospel of exceeding joy.

'And these blessed tidings the Loving Father hath charged me and my brother apostles to declare unto all the nations of the world, that being of one blood they may also be of one faith and rejoice in one Lord.

'Gather ye the wisdom of the East and the West, and accept and assimilate the examples of the saints of all ages.

'Above all, love one another and merge all differences in universal brotherhood.

'Let Asia, Europe, Africa, and America, with diverse instruments, praise the New Dispensation, and sing the Fatherhood of God and the Brotherhood of Man.'

Soon after this proclamation the health of the apostle of the 'New Dispensation,' which had been for a long time subject to severe disturbances, began to decline very rapidly, and, a year afterwards, on the 8th of January, 1884, he died. On the evening of that day his body was burnt at the Nīm Tollah burning-Ghāṭ on the Ganges, and, being at Calcutta, I went to the cremation.

The Ghāṭ had no flight of steps down to the river, but was simply a long brick building, with three enclosing walls, open upwards to the sky, and on one side towards the river. All cremations took place on its stone floor. Nothing was to be seen inside this utterly bare and dreary structure, except bodies in the process of burning, surrounded here and there by attendants and relations.

The sun was setting as I entered the building, and a lurid afterglow—like that observed all over Europe during the winter of 1883, 1884—lingered in the sky, suffusing the river, the shipping, and the whole surroundings of the Ghāṭ with a weird unearthly light. Just inside the entrance were two pyres nearly burnt out, but with embers still smouldering. At the farther end a crowd of perhaps three hundred people were collected [1]. These constituted the principal members and

[1] The small number present surprised me. I looked in vain for the Mahārāja of Kuch Behār.

friends of the Brāhma community of which Keshab was head.

In their midst was an enormous pyre of sandal-wood which quite concealed the dead body of their leader. I was allowed to stand on a raised parapet, and from that vantage-ground witnessed the first application of the lighted torch by some near relative. Then other relatives and friends brought contributions of sandal-wood and combustible substances, while others cast flowers, garlands, and fragrant powder on the burning pyre, amid the solemn chanting of hymns in Gregorian tones.

'The mercy of God alone availeth' (Brahma-kṛipā hi kevalam), was the burden of the cry of grief uttered by the mourners.

Meanwhile, the lurid twilight gave place to gathering gloom. The mourners ranged in a circle round the pyre swayed to and fro as the flames darted forth from the blazing wood. Their faces, now lighted up by a fitful glare, now enveloped in clouds of smoke, had a ghastly unearthly look. It was, in truth, an extraordinary scene, the like of which I had never seen before, and shall probably never witness again. Every detail will remain indelibly imprinted upon my memory.

A greater contrast to a Christian funeral could scarcely be imagined [1], and the contrast was the more remarkable, as this

---

[1] It was equally, however, a contrast to the form of cremation now in vogue among orthodox Hindūs, as may be proved by referring to pp. 295–303 of this volume, as well as by perusing the following account of the cremation of the Hon. Kristo-dās Pāl, which appeared in the 'Times of India Overland Summary' for July 29, 1884:—'The remains of Kristo-dās Pāl were cremated at Nīm Tollah burning-Ghāṭ in accordance with the orthodox Hindū custom. A few moments before he expired, his son poured a few drops of Ganges water into his mouth and anointed his forehead with mud from the river; placing a few leaves of tulsī on the forehead. The mourners then chanted the names of Hindū gods and goddesses whilst anointing the corpse. The family priest also chanted prayers. After the deceased had breathed his last, his eyelids and lips were closed by his son, who was chief mourner. The remains were then

was the Keshab who in the impassioned address already noticed, had called on India to accept Christ. I believe that a further religious ceremony (corresponding to the Śrāddha) was performed at the private residence of the deceased man a few days later, but to this I was not invited. Such ceremonies make it abundantly clear how wide a chasm separates the followers of Keshab, the enthusiastic admirer of Christ, from the community of Christians at Calcutta.

But it is equally clear that Keshab was one of India's greatest social and religious reformers, and, notwithstanding his errors of judgment, a worthy successor of Rāmmohun Roy. Before I left Calcutta a meeting was held to organize some suitable plan for perpetuating his memory, and a large sum had been collected in subscriptions. But I doubt whether the time has yet arrived for an adequate appreciation of his character, and it is to be feared that jealousies and disputes among some of his former followers may impair the good effect of what he has done for the cause of progress.

---

put into a cot and brought down into the court-yard. The chief mourner applied nine bits of gold to the mouth, nostrils, eyes, and head of the deceased, and anointed the body with otto of spikenard and otto of sandal-wood. The corpse was then dressed in clean clothes, after which garlands of flowers were placed on it. A small plant—the sacred tulsī—with its root and flowers was placed on the head during this period. Large crowds flocked in to see the last of the well-known patriot. At three o'clock the cortège proceeded to the Ghāṭ. The corpse was borne by the friends and relatives of the deceased. On the way it was deposited opposite the temple near the Ghāṭ, where prayers were offered. It was then taken to the side of the river, where the son anointed it with Ganges water. The funeral pyre was composed partly of sandal-wood. A clean piece of cloth was then put on the pyre, and the body was uncovered up to the waist. After this the son was summoned to the side of the remains, when ghee was placed on his hand, with which he anointed the head of the corpse. Ganges water was again sprinkled on the body, after which the priest gave the son two rings composed apparently of tulsī leaves, which he placed round the forefinger of the deceased. The priest then chanted some invocations in a low tone, which the son repeated. The body was then placed on the funeral pyre and cremated. During the cremation rice, dāl, and pice were distributed to the poor. The deceased wished that the cremation should not be attended with any pomp.'

It might indeed have been thought that the return of Mr. Pratāp Chandar Mozoomdār very soon after the death of Keshab Chandar Sen would have made his election as Mr. Sen's successor, and as leader of the New Dispensation Church, certain. He had been travelling round the world, but hurried back on hearing of Mr. Sen's illness. No one could deny that he was the one man intellectually qualified to succeed the great Reformer, and he himself was bent on becoming a religious guide, if not a ruler. Nothing short of this was likely to satisfy his aspirations. But he seemed to lack the tact needed for keeping the great Keshab's Samāj together, and he failed at first to bring about any settlement of the unseemly disputes which had arisen in regard to the ownership of the place of worship.

On inquiry in August, 1884, I was told that he conducted religious services in his own house, and that he had started a Bengālī paper (called the Ālok) as an organ for disseminating his own views and the doctrines of the 'New Dispensation,' of which he still believed himself to be the exponent. He maintained that the public utterances of the late minister showed that it was never his desire to appropriate for the use of his own family and most intimate friends any of the property of the Samāj, such as the prayer hall (Mandir) which was erected by public subscription.

In opposition to this view, the near relatives and adherents of the late Keshab Chandar Sen called themselves the true members of the Apostolic Darbār, and claimed the Mandir as their own, declining to recognize Mr. Mozoomdār as their leader. They were for some time like a flock without a shepherd, and appeared likely to lapse—as their leader also seemed latterly inclined to do—into many superstitious practices, or even into a form of Theism nearly approaching Vaishṇavism.

I have at present (1891) no information as to Mr. Mozoomdār's exact position; but his great energy and ability, combined with his oratorical powers, must have secured for him a large number of adherents, and perhaps have led to his organizing a Samāj of a purer character than that of his predecessor Mr. Sen. It may be interesting, therefore, if I here put on record a conversation I had with him, nearly in the following words :—

What is your name for God?

Brăhmă is our chief name, though this (being neuter) is rather our philosophical one. Our house of God is called Brahma-mandira. But our common name for God is Hari (also one of the common names of Vishṇu), which means 'the Taker away of sin and evil.' We also use the names Parameśvara, 'Supreme Lord,' and Paramātmā, 'Supreme Spirit,' and Parama-pitā, 'Supreme Father,' and even Parama-mātā, 'Supreme Mother.' Perhaps one reason for these last names may be that we cannot get rid of the idea of Purusha and Prakṛiti, which is ingrained in the Hindū mind (see p. 223 of this volume).

Do you hold that God created the world out of nothing, or that He developed it out of His own essence?

We consider this inquiry too recondite and too much beyond the reach of our intellects. We do not attempt to go into it. But we hold that God did not create the world all at once, but by gradual evolution. Everything in creation proceeds progressively by fixed law, and not per saltum.

Your late leader, Keshab Chandar Sen, called on India to accept Christ; what did he mean by this?

We do accept Christ in our own way. We regard Him as our supreme Exemplar, our ideal Man. He was the Spirit of God incarnate—the ideal of the life of God in man. We do not believe this of any one else. Moses was a good man, and David a devoted man full of faith and trust in God. But these were only partially good. Paul conforms most nearly to the Christ-like pattern—Christ is the concentration and combination of all.

Do you claim anything similar for your late leader, Keshab Chandar Sen?

No. True, he was a good and holy man and had the Spirit of God; he was inspired, but not perpetually; the Spirit was not always present in him, and certainly he was not inspired in the sense Christ is thought to have been by Christians. He was only inspired when he placed himself in a devotional frame of mind and gave himself to earnest prayer. Then great spiritual impulses were imparted to him, in response to such prayers. And similar responses are given to other men also. Inspiration was not confined to Mr. Keshab Chandar Sen. He had his allotted place and work as our chief leader, and we yielded him allegiance. He was not a guide to any except to those brought into association with him—not to all the world. There is a common inspiration given to each member of our church in his own special sphere of work.

What are your views on the subject of Christ's death?

We accept Christ's death as an atonement spiritually. But there is no mere mechanical and material application of Christ's merits. If we are to profit by Christ's death we must go through the same processes. Christ's death was the victory of pain and suffering over pleasure and carnality. It was also a self-sacrifice. It was God living and dying for the good of the world. It effected a reconciliation between sinful man and God. In this sense we recognise the atonement. Any one who adopts the same principle of self-sacrifice helps to effect reconciliation between man and God. Christ has taught us to die.

Do you believe in the resurrection of Christ?

Not in His bodily, but in His spiritual resurrection.

What are your ideas about Heaven?

Our heaven is called Svarga. It is an eternal condition, and not necessarily connected with any particular locality.

We do not believe in the transmigration of souls (metempsychosis).

Do you believe in a Hell?

Yes, our Hell is called Naraka, but it is a temporary condition, like the Purgatory of the Roman Catholics. It is not necessarily connected with a locality.

What do you hold in regard to a personal Spirit of evil?

We do not believe in a personal Devil, nor in the Bhūtas and Pretas of the Hindūs (see p. 241 of this volume). Evil is negative, and sin is a positive act proceeding from weakness or disease of the will.

Do you keep up any of the Hindū domestic ceremonies, or have you ceremonies of your own?

We have some domestic ceremonies, of course, which we call Anushṭhāna. They are performed without idolatry, and according to forms of our own and with our own prayers. Thus we have Birth, Marriage, and Funeral ceremonies. We have also Baptism and a rite called Homa (using fire as a symbol). Moreover, we have a ceremony corresponding to the Christian Communion, performed with rice and milk, which are supposed to have the same symbolical significance as bread and wine,—that is, they typify union and assimilation as food is assimilated. But we do not consider our ceremonies (anushṭhāna) binding on all. Any member of our church may retain the Hindū domestic ceremonies, going through them as a matter of routine. Still, we do not consider any one a strict Brāhma unless he adopts the Brāhma (sometimes called Brāhmic) ceremonies, and these strict Brāhmas we call Anushṭhānikas.

With regard to the question of Brāhma ceremonies, it should be carefully noted that, after all, the Brāhma-Samāj Theist who has not given up Hindū domestic rites and caste-customs can scarcely be said to have severed himself from Hindūism. The mere holding of Theistic opinions has nothing in it opposed to Hindūism, nor even to Brāhmanism. I once asked a Brāhman if he had any short creed which he could write down for me. He immediately wrote in Sanskṛit a few words which may be thus translated: 'I bow down before the One God, who is the only existing Being, who is eternal, who is all joy, and the giver of all joy; who is all knowledge; who is unchangeable and present as a witness in all consciences.'

Indeed the foregoing pages of this volume will have been written in vain if they have not made it evident that Vaishṇavism and Śaivism—especially the former—are in reality forms of Theism (pp. 54, 73, 96, 475). The Vaishṇavas are Theists who worship one personal God under the name of Vishṇu. They maintain that the idolatry connected with that worship is not a necessary part of its essence. Adoration of images (mūrti-pūjā) is allowed as a help to weak-minded people, but the mental and spiritual form of devotion (mānasī pūjā) is repeatedly declared to be the highest (see p. 123), and that to which all lower forms lead up. If, therefore, a Vaishṇava abstains from idolatry in his daily worship, and confines himself to spiritual adoration, it may be contended that he is as good a Theist as any member of a Brāhma-Samāj, bearing in mind that some of these latter also worship God under one of the names of Vishṇu (Hari). Every such Vaishṇava may be a sympathizer with the members of modern Theistic societies so far as mere monotheistic doctrines are concerned. There remains, however, the doctrine of metempsychosis.

The crucial test of pure Theism among the Hindūs lies in the rejection of that doctrine and of the old domestic ceremonies and caste-customs. If a man adheres to caste, and to the old superstitious and idolatrous methods of performing family rites, and to the Hindū doctrine of metempsychosis, he cannot be said to have joined the ranks of true Theistic Reformers.

And in real fact no one ought to be allowed to register his name as a member of any Brāhma-Samāj unless he has the courage of his opinions, and is prepared to become an Anushṭhānika; that is to say, unless he engages to shake off all the fetters of caste, and perform all domestic rites and ceremonies at births, initiation, marriages, deaths, etc., according to Brāhma (Brāhmic) rules and forms; and of these Anushṭhānikas I believe there are little more than eight hundred all told. So much, then, for the actual advance of pure Theism in India.

Nevertheless it is matter of congratulation that many thousands are now to be found who, though they do not adopt pure Theistic forms, or renounce caste-customs, nevertheless sympathize with the members of the Brāhma-Samāj to the extent of renouncing idolatry.

And it is much to be hoped that the bitterness of feeling produced by constant disputes and schisms may in the end pass away, and that the various bodies of Theists which the operation of our educational system is rapidly calling into existence, may ere long forget their petty differences, and agree upon some course of combined and systematic action for the promotion of social reform. Surely the present little band of Reformers, however courageous, is not strong enough to bear weakening by internal divisions. A compact and serried front is urgently needed in the presence of countless foes, who neglect no opportunity of marshalling their forces, and uniting in active co-operation for the destruction of the scattered ranks of their opponents.

Ten years ago the Census showed that there were 178 Theistic Churches established in different localities throughout India. The present Census will no doubt prove them to be now more numerous; but it must be borne in mind that many of them have few registered Anushṭhānika members, though they have numerous sympathizers.

The Madras Samāj, founded in 1871, and developed out of a previous Veda-Samāj, was well led by Srīdhāralu Naidu (under the Ādi Brāhma-Samāj), but at his death languished. It revived in 1879, but soon split into two parties, some siding with Keshab Chandar Sen and some with the Sādhāraṇa

Church. When I was last in India the latter party was the strongest, and had formed a new Samāj. At Bombay, the Prārthanā-Samāj, or 'Prayer Society,' was the first Theistic Church of Western India. It was founded in 1867, and owed much of its continued vitality to the support of an enlightened native, Dr. Ātmārām Pāndurang.

Some of the Samājes follow on the lines first laid down by Keshab Chandar Sen, and are liberal and progressive. Many are more conservative, and conform to the pattern of the Ādi Brāhma-Samāj at Calcutta[1]. Some, again, take an independent line, and call their creed 'Theosophy.'

Such Theosophical societies define 'Theosophy' to mean 'divine wisdom or science,' 'spiritual philosophy.' They hold that all religions have elements of truth which spring from the one Fountain of Truth, and that Theosophy is the synthesis of all religions. Hence pure Brāhmanism, pure Buddhism, pure Islām, pure Christianity may be equivalent to Theosophy. It may be true that Theosophy is spreading, but in India it seems to be little more than another name for the Vedānta philosophy.

Let me now describe the meetings which I myself attended (1) of Keshab's Progressive Samāj or New Dispensation Church at Calcutta; (2) of the Ādi Brāhma-Samāj at Calcutta; (3) of the Prārthanā-Samāj at Bombay.

The meeting of the Progressive Brāhma-Samāj at which I was present, took place on the Sunday previous to Keshab Chandar Sen's death, when he was lying dangerously ill. The religious service was conducted by some relative who acted as his deputy. His Secretary, Mr. Pratāp Chandar Mozoomdār, who, as already mentioned, had been on a tour round the world,

[1] According to Rāj Narāin Bose, the Ādi Brāhma-Samāj, though *generally* conservative, contains *individual* members who have taken part in very progressive reforms, such as discarding the thread, the remarriage of widows, emancipation of females, etc. The Ādi-Samāj in fact is conservative in religious reform, basing it on Vedas and Vedānta, but leaves social reform to the judgment and taste of individual members.

had not at that time returned. The building used for these services is situated in a handsome street in the native quarter of Calcutta, and has a spire and an exterior elevation copied from our Christian churches; while its interior arrangements, though Oriental in points of detail, give it an appearance not unlike that of a plain unadorned dissenting chapel. This is the building which since the death of Keshab Chandar Sen has caused a dispute as to its ownership, terminating in a serious disruption (see p. 520). On driving up to the entrance I noticed two temporary screens stretching from the road to a side-door. This was to enable the female Brāhmas (usually called Brāhmikās) to enter without being seen.

No doubt it is a most unusual circumstance in India for the women of a family to meet in the same place of worship and to join in the same devotions with their male relatives; but, I confess, I did not expect to find the female members of the congregation of the great social Reformer immured in a gallery with a wooden screen in front of it.

On entering the Church I found the interior nearly full of men, almost every one of whom wore the shawl which constitutes the favourite winter costume of a Bengālī Bābū drawn closely around him.

They began by repeating a litany in a standing attitude, and I observed that the responses of the congregation were uttered with much apparent devotion. The preacher, who was also wrapped in a shawl, sat in the middle of a slightly raised platform surrounded by a railing. When the litany was concluded he repeated a prayer in Bengālī. Then came a hymn sung to an organ accompaniment, apparently played with one finger in single notes and in a minor key, a kind of drum-beating time. After the hymn the preacher sat down and in that attitude gave us an exhortation or sermon in a very unimpassioned manner, interweaving many quotations from the sacred scriptures of India and other nations, the congregation listening with great attention.

The simple character of the service and the absence of all idolatry was very refreshing after a recent visit I had made to the temple of the goddess Kālī.

The services at the Ādi Brāhma-Samāj were conducted by a son of Debendra-nāth. The sermon was preached from a raised platform or altar (Vedi); and three singers, seated in front of a kind of organ, chanted the hymns in loud tones, and with much warmth of manner and energetic gesticulation.

At Bombay the Manual used by the Prārthanā-Samāj contained selections from the Veda, Upanishads, Christian Bible, Kurān, and Zand-Avastā. Hymns were sung with much fervour in a thoroughly Hindū fashion to an accompaniment played on the Vīṇā or Indian lute, and prayers were said, consisting chiefly of invocations of the Supreme Being, with praise and adoration of His attributes, but without confession of guilt, while the congregation remained seated, though their hands were joined in reverence. After the prayer an able sermon was preached by Professor Bhāṇḍārkar (Professor of Sanskṛit at Deccan College, Poona) who took for his text a passage from the Kaṭhopanishad (VI. 15), thus translatable:—'Man cannot obtain immortality till all the knots in his heart caused by ignorance and unbelief are cut (yadā sarve prabhidyante hṛidayasya granthayaḥ).' He then illustrated his text by quotations from other books. For example—a passage from Tukārām—the most popular Marāṭha poet: 'There is no happiness other than peace. Therefore preserve peace, and you will cross over to yonder shore.'

What chiefly struck me at the Bombay meeting was the apparent absence of sympathy or *rapport* between the official performers of the services and the general congregation. The hymns were energetically sung by the appointed singers, the prayers earnestly repeated, and the address solemnly delivered by the minister, but the congregation neither stood nor knelt, and seemed to take no really cordial part in the proceedings. It is true that a sitting posture at prayer is customary, and by no means intended to imply irreverence; yet I came away persuaded that the Prārthanā-Samāj of Bombay, in spite of honest strivings after a pure soul-stirring Theism, is still chilled and numbed by the lingering influence of Vedāntic Pantheism, which it is unable wholly to shake off. And this, I believe, is true of many of the Churches of Western India which number many learned and philosophical men among their members—men who have little sympathy with the Vaishṇava tendencies of the Bengālī Brāhmas.

Before concluding this sketch of modern Hindū Theism, I should note that occasional Reformers still arise who make efforts to found a purely Indian Theism on the doctrines supposed to be contained in the hymns of the Veda. A movement for the diffusion of this kind of Vedic Theism was not long ago inaugurated by a remarkable Gujarātī Brāhman, named Dayānanda Sarasvatī, who called his new church the Ārya-Samāj. I made his acquaintance at Bombay in 1876, and was much struck by his fine countenance and figure. There I heard him preach an eloquent discourse on the religious development of the Āryan race. He began by repeating a hymn to Varuṇa (see p. 15) preceded by the syllable Om (p. 10), prolating the vowel in deep sonorous tones. Just before I reached India in the autumn of 1883 he died suddenly (some say by poison) at Ajmere during the Dīvālī festival. In the spring of 1884 I visited Ajmere, and saw the place of his cremation. I found that, although after his death vast numbers declared their sympathy with him, their admiration of his character and their willingness to subscribe large sums to perpetuate his memory and his teaching, yet that, while alive, he had many bitter enemies among the Brāhmans; for he was a strong opponent of idolatry as well as of all forms of Polytheism. The peculiarity of his teaching was that he contended that the four collections of Vedic hymns (Mantras), as distinct from the Brāhmaṇas and Upanishads (pp. 8, 21, 26), are the only true non-human (a-paurusheya) revelation, and that the hymns to Agni, Indra, and Sūrya are to One God under different names. In his printed creed he declared that he was not an independent thinker (nāhaṃ svatantraḥ), but a follower of the Veda; that the four Saṃhitā texts of the Vedas—including the Īśā Upanishad—are to be received as a primary authority in all matters relating to human conduct; that the other Upanishads, the Brāhmaṇas, beginning with the Śatapatha; the six Aṅgas or limbs of the Veda, beginning with Śikshā; the four Upa-vedas; the six Darśanas or Schools of Philosophy, and the 1130 schools or branches[1] (śākhās) of Vedic teaching are to be accepted as secondary authority in expounding the meaning of the Vedic texts, and that adoration, prayer, and devotion are to be offered to One God only, abstracted from all idea of shape and form, and without any second, as set forth in the Vedas.

In one of my interviews with him, I asked him for his definition of religion, he replied in Sanskṛit:—'Religion (Dharmaḥ) is a true and just view (nyāyaḥ), and the abandonment of all prejudice and partiality (pakshapāta-rāhityam)—that is to say, it is an impartial inquiry into the truth by means of the senses and the two other instruments of knowledge (pramāṇa), reason, and revelation.'

Dayānanda's teaching, however, included the doctrine of metempsychosis (punar-janma), which it would be difficult to found on Vedic authority. Of course, both this and all his more peculiar doctrines are repudiated by the various Brāhma Samājes, and even by the Ādi Samāj of Calcutta. Nor would Dayānanda himself have admitted an identity of teaching with the Brāhma Theistic movement. Nevertheless he has done undoubted good by his uncompromising opposition

[1] Of these there are one thousand for the Sāma-veda, one hundred for the Yajur-veda, twenty-one for the Ṛig-veda, and nine for the Atharva-veda. See Patañjali's Mahābhāshya I. 1. 1.

to idolatry and to the later developments of Hindūism, including the whole circle of Purānic mythology. He was also a Social Reformer and often preached against child-marriages. He left a will (svīkāra-patra), written in Hindī, and by that constituted what he called a Paropakāriṇī Sabhā—that is to say, a Society, or more properly a Committee, consisting of twenty-three members who are bound to assist each other (the Mahārāṇā of Udaypur being President). The duty of this Committee is (1) to publish and disseminate the Veda and Vedāṅgas; (2) to send missionaries to different countries and by their means persuade every one to accept truth and abandon error; (3) to educate poor people in India (Āryāvarta) in the principles of the Ārya-Samāj, as founded by himself. He also left money to be spent in promoting these objects.

And let us not be slow to acknowledge the good results likely to flow from all this agitation in Indian religious thought—all this upheaval of old ideas, all this activity and movement in Indian religious life. Still less let us regard with distrust the efforts of these modern Theistic Reformers, as if they were unfavourable to the progress of Christian truth. We may be quite sure that men like Debendra-nāth Tāgore, and the other leaders of the chief Brāhma-Samāj or Theistic churches, are doing good work in a Christian self-sacrificing spirit, though they may fall into many errors. And we shall do well not to be too censorious and critical in our animadversions on their opinions and practices.

Rather let us hold out the right hand of fellowship to these noble-minded Patriots; for, indeed, they need every encouragement in their almost hopeless struggle with their country's worst enemies, Ignorance, Prejudice, and Superstition, in whose train may generally be found Pride, Untruthfulness, Selfishness, and Immorality. Intense darkness still broods over the land; let Christianity thankfully welcome and wisely make use of every gleam and glimmer of true light, from whatever quarter it may shine.

CHAPTER XXI.

Examples of the Moral Precepts of Brāhmanism and Hindūism.

In treating of Indian morality it is usual to affirm that there is no connexion between a Hindū's creed and his moral conduct. This is scarcely correct, because an essential part of his creed is the doctrine of metempsychosis, which teaches that a man may, on dying, return to earth in higher or lower forms of existence according to the merit or demerit of his acts—after passing through intermediate periods of bliss or torment in temporary heavens or temporary hells (see pp. 232, 291–293). A belief in such a doctrine is of course likely to have a powerful effect in impelling a man to good actions and deterring him from evil. Every man is likely to control his appetites, if, through indulging them to excess, he may be born as an unclean animal in his next birth; and every man is careful not to steal, if theft may lead to his being born as a rat; and to abstain from murder, if the killing of his neighbour may lead to his own degradation in his next life to the condition of some noxious brute or reptile. Constantly in the sacred books of the Hindūs morality is summed up in three precepts, 'good thoughts,' 'good words,' 'good deeds,' and these are enjoined upon every man; but no motive is put before him, except the dread of the evil consequences which bad thoughts, bad words and bad deeds will certainly entail, not only in this life but in many subsequent states of existence. See pp. 52, 53.

For no Hindū is a believer in the possibility of obtaining any supernatural external aid which may help him to lead a moral life. He is no believer in any divine spring or source of power, outside himself, which may act like a purifying, energizing force upon his character, and make his obedience to the laws of morality not only a duty, but a delight.

With regard to the mere letter of the Hindū moral code it is admitted that the noble precepts scattered throughout the sacred literature of Brāhmanism and Hindūism often rise to the level of Christian teaching, and present a picture which, although it is here and there disfigured by dark spots and blemishes, cannot but produce a favourable impression on every candid critic (p. 52).

The present chapter will be devoted to the exhibiting of a few samples of the best of these precepts which I have selected from different works, beginning with the 'Laws of Manu.' As the originals are in verse, the translations are also metrical, and as nearly literal as possible[1].

Precepts from Manu. General Precepts.

With pain the mother to her child gives birth,
With pain the father rears him; as he grows
He heaps up cares and troubles for his parents;
Incurring thus a debt he ne'er can pay,
Though he should strive through centuries of time (II. 227).

Think constantly, O son, how thou mayest please
Thy father, mother, teacher—these obey.
By deep devotion seek thy debt to pay.
This is thy highest duty and religion (II. 228).

Even though wronged, treat not with disrespect
Thy father, mother, teacher, elder brother (II. 226).

---

[1] These translations are my own, and will be found scattered in some of my other works, especially 'Indian Wisdom,' now out of print.

From poison thou mayest take the food of life,
The purest gold from lumps of impure earth,
Examples of good conduct from a foe,
Sweet speech and gentleness from e'en a child,
Something from all; from men of low degree
Lessons of wisdom, if thou humble be (II. 238, 239).

Wound not another, though by him provoked,
Do no one injury by thought or deed,
Utter no word to pain thy fellow-creatures (II. 161).

Say what is true, speak not agreeable falsehood (IV. 138).

Treat no one with disdain[1], with patience bear
Reviling language; with an angry man
Be never angry; blessings give for curses (VI. 47, 48).

E'en as a driver checks his restive steeds,
Do thou, if thou art wise, restrain thy passions,
Which, running wild, will hurry thee away (II. 88).

When asked, give something, though a very trifle,
Ungrudgingly and with a cheerful heart,
According to thy substance; only see
That he to whom thou givest worthy be (IV. 227, 228).

Pride not thyself on thy religious works,
Give to the poor, but talk not of thy gifts,
By pride religious merit melts away,
The merit of thy alms by ostentation (IV. 236, 237).

None sees us, say the sinful in their hearts;
Yes, the gods see them, and the omniscient Spirit
Within their breasts. Thou thinkest, O good friend,

---

[1] In IV. 135 the householder is especially warned against treating with contempt a Brāhman well versed in the Veda, a Kshatriya, and a serpent, because (says Kullūka) the first has the power of destroying him by his unseen power of magical texts and spells, the other two by their seen power (*drishṭa-śaktyā*). Cf. the passages relative to the power of the Brāhmans at pp. 201, 202.

'I am alone,' but there resides within thee
A Being who inspects thy every act,
Knows all thy goodness and thy wickedness (VIII. 85, 91).

The soul is its own witness; yea, the soul
Itself is its own refuge; grieve thou not,
O man, thy soul, the great internal Witness (VIII. 84).

The Firmament, the Earth, the Sea, the Moon,
The Sun, the Fire, the Wind, the Night, and both
The sacred Twilights[1], and the Judge of souls[2],
The god of Justice, and the Heart itself—
All constantly survey the acts of men (VIII. 86).

When thou hast sinned, think not to hide thy guilt
Under a cloak of penance and austerity (IV. 198).

No study of the Veda nor oblation,
No gift of alms, nor round of strict observance
Can lead the inwardly depraved to heaven (II. 97).

If with the great Divinity, who dwells
Within thy breast, thou hast no controversy,
Go not to Ganges' water to be cleansed,
Nor make a pilgrimage to Kuru's fields (VIII. 92).

Iniquity once practised, like a seed,
Fails not to yield its fruit to him who wrought it,
If not to him, yet to his sons and grandsons (IV. 173).

Contentment is the root of happiness,
And discontent the root of misery.
Wouldst thou be happy, be thou moderate (IV. 12).

Honour thy food, receive it thankfully,
Eat it contentedly and joyfully,
Ne'er hold it in contempt; avoid excess,
For gluttony is hateful, injures health,

---

[1] See the account of the Sandhyās, p. 401. [2] Yama, see p. 289.

May lead to death, and surely bars the road
To holy merit and celestial bliss (II. 54, 57).

Shrink thou from worldly honour as from poison,
Seek rather scorn; the scorn'd may sleep in peace,
In peace awake; the scorner perishes (II. 162, 163).

Daily perform thy own appointed work
Unweariedly; and to obtain a friend—
A sure companion to the future world—
Collect a store of virtue like the ants
Who garner up their treasures into heaps;
For neither father, mother, wife, nor son,
Nor kinsman, will remain beside thee then,
When thou art passing to that other home—
Thy virtue will thy only comrade be (IV. 238, 239).

Single is every living creature born,
Single he passes to another world,
Single he eats the fruit of evil deeds,
Single, the fruit of good; and when he leaves
His body like a log or heap of clay
Upon the ground, his kinsmen walk away;
Virtue alone stays by him at the tomb,
And bears him through the dreary trackless gloom.
(IV. 240–242)[1].

Thou canst not gather what thou dost not sow;
As thou dost plant the tree so will it grow (IX. 40).

Depend not on another, rather lean
Upon thyself; trust to thine own exertions.
Subjection to another's will gives pain;
True happiness consists in self-reliance (IV. 160).

---

[1] Dr. Muir has pointed out that the expression *tamas tarati dustaram*, 'he crosses the gloom difficult to be passed,' may be taken from Atharva-veda IX. 5. 1, *tīrtvā tamāṃsi bahudhā mahānti.*

Strive to complete the task thou hast commenced;
Wearied, renew thy efforts once again;
Again fatigued, once more the work begin,
So shalt thou earn success and fortune win (IX. 300).

Be courteous to thy guest who visits thee;
Offer a seat, bed, water, food enough,
According to thy substance, hospitably;
Naught taking for thyself till he be served;
Homage to guests brings wealth, fame, life, and heaven.
(III. 106, IV. 29).

Though thou mayst suffer for thy righteous acts,
Ne'er give thy mind to aught but honest gain (IV. 171).

So act in thy brief passage through this world
That thy apparel, speech, and inner store
Of knowledge be adapted to thy age,
Thy occupation, means, and parentage (IV. 18).

According to a man's sincerity
In penitent confession of his crime,
And detestation of the evil deed,
Shall he be pardoned and his soul released
From taint of guilt, like serpent from its skin (XI. 227, 228).

If he do wrong, 'tis not enough to say
I will not sin again; release from guilt
Depends on true contrition, which consists
In actual abstinence from sinful deeds (XI. 230).

Revolving in his mind the certainty
Of retribution in a future state,
Let him be pure in thought, in word, in deed[1] (XI. 231).

By free confession, penitence, and penance,
By daily repetition of the Veda[2],

---

[1] Here is another example of Manu's triple division of 'thought, word, and deed.' The same triple division is frequent in Buddhistic writings.

[2] *Khyāpanena, anutāpena, tapasā, adhyayena ća.*

By the five holy acts[1], by giving alms,
By patience, and by bearing injuries,
The greatest sinner may obtain release (XI. 227, 245).

The man who keeps his senses in control,
His speech, heart, actions pure and ever guarded,
Gains all the fruit of holy study; he
Needs neither penance nor austerity (II. 160).

Contentment, patience under injury,
Self-subjugation, honesty, restraint
Of all the sensual organs, purity,
Devotion, knowledge of the Deity[2],
Veracity, and abstinence from anger,
These form the tenfold summary of duty (VI. 92).

Long not for death, nor hanker after life;
Calmly expect thy own appointed time,
E'en as a servant reckons on his hire (IV. 45).

This mansion of the soul, composed of earth,
Subject to sorrow and decrepitude,
Inhabited by sicknesses and pains,
Bound by the bonds of ignorance and darkness,
Let a wise man with cheerfulness abandon (VI. 77).

Quitting this body, he resembles merely
A bird that leaves a tree. Thus is he freed
From the fell monster of an evil world[3] (VI. 78).

Whate'er the act a man commits, whate'er
His state of mind, of that the recompense
Must he receive in corresponding body (XII. 81).

Action of every kind, whether of mind
Or speech or body, must bear fruit, entailing

---

[1] That is, the five Mahā-yajñas; see p. 411.

[2] *Vidyā*, 'knowledge of the supreme Spirit.'—Kullūka.

[3] *Kṛiććhrād grāhāt=saṃsāra-kashṭād grāhād iva.*

Fresh births through multifarious conditions,
In highest, mean, and lowest transmigrations (XII. 3).

This universal Soul is all the gods,
Is all the worlds, and is the only source
Of all the actions of embodied spirits (XII. 119).

He is their ruler, brighter than pure gold,
Subtler than atoms, imperceptible,
Except by minds abstracted, all-pervading,
Investing all with rudiments of matter,
Causing all beings to revolve like wheels
In regular and constant revolution
Through birth and growth, decay and dissolution.
(XII. 122, 124).

Duties of Women and Wives.

In childhood must a father guard his daughter;
In youth the husband shields his wife; in age
A mother is protected by her sons—
Ne'er should a woman lean upon herself (V. 148, IX. 3).

A faithful wife who wishes to attain
The heaven of her lord, must serve him here
As if he were a god, and ne'er do aught
To pain him, whatsoever be his state,
And even though devoid of every virtue (V. 154, 156).

Be it her duty to preserve with care
Her husband's substance; let her too be trusted
With its expenditure, with management
Of household property and furniture,
Of cooking and purveying daily food.
Let her be ever cheerful, skilled in all
Domestic work, and not too free in spending (V. 150).

Then only is a man a perfect man
When he is three—himself, his wife, his son—

For thus have learned men the law declared,
'A husband is one person with his wife' (IX. 45).

Fidelity till death, this is the sum
Of mutual duties for a married pair (IX. 101).

And if the wife survives, let her remain
Constant and true, nor sully her fair fame
E'en by the utterance of another's name (V. 157).

Duties of Kings.

The Lord of all in pity to our needs
Created kings, to rule and guard us here;
Without a king this world would rock with fear (VII. 3).

A king, e'en though a child, must not be treated
As if he were a mortal; rather he
Is a divinity in human shape (VII. 8).

Dread of the rod alone restrains the bad,
Controls the good, and makes a nation happy (VII. 15).

The king must therefore punish fearlessly;
Else would the strong oppress the weak, the bad
Would wrong the good, and pierce them as with iron[1];
The crow would eat the consecrated rice,
The dog the burnt oblation; ownership
And rights of property would be subverted;
All ranks and classes would become confused,
All barriers and bridges broken down,
And all the world turned wrong side uppermost.
(VII. 20, 21, 24).

But let the monarch, ere he wield his rod,
Consider place and time, the written law
Of justice, and the measure of his strength (VII. 16).

---

[1] The literal translation of the text here is 'the stronger would roast the weaker like fish on a spit' (*śūle matsyān ivāpakshyan durbalān balavattarāḥ*).

When Goodness, wounded by Iniquity,
Comes to a court of justice, and the judge
Extracts not tenderly the pointed dart,
That very shaft shall pierce him to the heart (VIII. 12).

Let him with full deliberation weigh
The evidence, the place, the mode, the time,
The facts, the truth, and his own frame of mind,
Firmly adhering to the rules of law (VIII. 45).

The court must not be entered by a witness,
Unless he speaks the truth without reserve;
For equally does he commit a crime,
Who tells not all the facts, or tells them falsely (VIII. 13).

A witness who gives evidence with truth
Shall be absolved from every sin, and gain
Exalted glory here and bliss above (VIII. 81, 83).

Headlong in utter darkness shall the wretch
Fall into hell, who in a court of justice
Answers a single question falsely; he
Shall be tormented through a hundred births (VIII. 82, 94).

And all the merit of his virtuous acts
Shall be transferred to dogs. Therefore be true,
Speak the whole truth without equivocation (VIII. 90, 101).

Let no considerate witness take an oath
Lightly, or in a trifling matter; he
Who does so shall incur eternal ruin (VIII. 111).

He who by firmness gains the mastery
Over his words, his mind, and his whole body,
Is justly called a triple-governor[1] (XII. 10).

---

[1] His title in Sanskṛit is Tri-daṇḍin. It is noticeable that the Indian ascetic, who is described by Arrian (VII. 2) as exciting the wonder of Alexander the Great by his *καρτερία*, is named Δάνδαμις, probably from the same root as *daṇḍa* (*dam*, 'to subdue,' in Intens.). By others he is called Mandanis (root *maṇḍ?*).

Exerting thus a threefold self-command
Towards himself and every living creature,
Subduing lust and wrath, he may aspire
To that perfection which the good desire (XII. 11).

Examples of Precepts from the Epic Poems.

To carry out an enterprise in words
Is easy; to accomplish it by acts
Is the sole test of man's capacity.

Rāmāyaṇa (ed. Gorresio) IV. lxvii. 10.

Where'er we walk, Death marches at our side;
Where'er we sit, Death seats himself beside us;
However far we journey, Death continues
Our fellow-pilgrim and goes with us home.
Men take delight in each returning dawn,
And with admiring gaze, behold the glow
Of sunset. Every season, as it comes,
Fills them with gladness, yet they never reck
That each recurring season, every day
Fragment by fragment bears their life away.
As drifting logs of wood may haply meet
On Ocean's waters, surging to and fro,
And having met, drift once again apart;
So fleeting is a man's association
With wife and children, relatives and wealth,
So surely must a time of parting come.

Rāmāyaṇa (ed. Bombay) II. cv. 24–27.

Whate'er the work a man performs,
The most effective aid to its completion—
The most prolific source of true success—
Is energy without despondency.

Rāmāyaṇa (ed. Bombay) V. xii. 11.

Time is awake while mortals are asleep,

None can elude its grasp or curb its course,
It passes unrestrained o'er all alike.
Mahā-bhārata I. 243.

Thou thinkest: I am single and alone—
Perceiving not the great eternal Sage
Who dwells within thy breast. Whatever wrong
Is done by thee, he sees and notes it all.
Mahā-bhārata I. 3015.

Heaven, Earth, and Sea, Sun, Moon, and Wind, and Fire,
Day, Night, the Twilights, and the Judge of Souls,
The god of Justice and the Heart itself,
All see and note the conduct of a man.
Mahā-bhārata I. 3017.

A wife is half the man, his truest friend.
Source of his virtue, pleasure, wealth—the root
Whence springs the line of his posterity.
Mahā-bhārata I. 3028.

An evil-minded man is quick to see
His neighbour's faults, though small as mustard-seed;
But when he turns his eyes towards his own,
Though large as Bilva[1] fruit, he none descries.
Mahā-bhārata I. 3069.

If Truth and thousands of Horse-sacrifices
Were weighed together, Truth would weigh the most[2].
Mahā-bhārata I. 3095.

Death follows life by an unerring law;
Why grieve for that which is inevitable?
Mahā-bhārata I. 6144.

---

[1] This is the Aegle Marmelos (*Bel*) or Bengal Quince, bearing a large fruit. It is esteemed sacred to Mahā-deva. Compare St. Matthew vii. 3, 4.

[2] Hitopadeśa IV. 135.

Conquer a man who never gives by gifts;
Subdue untruthful men by truthfulness;
Vanquish an angry man by gentleness;
And overcome the evil man by goodness[1].

Mahā-bhārata III. 13253.

Triple restraint of thought and word and deed,
Strict vow of silence, coil of matted hair,
Close shaven head, garments of skin or bark,
Keeping of fasts, ablutions, maintenance
Of sacrificial fires, a hermit's life,
Emaciation—these are all in vain,
Unless the inward soul be free from stain.

Mahā-bhārata III. 13445.

To injure none by thought or word or deed,
To give to others, and be kind to all—
This is the constant duty of the good.
High-minded men delight in doing good,
Without a thought of their own interest;
When they confer a benefit on others,
They reckon not on favours in return[2].

Mahā-bhārata III. 16782, 16796.

Two persons will hereafter be exalted
Above the heavens—the man with boundless power
Who yet forbears to use it indiscreetly,
And he who is not rich and yet can give[3].

Mahā-bhārata V. 1028.

Sufficient wealth, unbroken health, a friend,
A wife of gentle speech, a docile son,

---

[1] See Rom. xii. 21. Compare the Pāli Rājovāda Jātaka (Fausböll's Ten Jātakas, p. 5), *Akkodhena jine kodham, Asādhum sādhunā jine, Jine kadariyam dānena, Saććena alika-vādinam.* See also Dhammapada 223.

[2] Compare St. Luke vi. 35.

[3] Compare St. Mark xii. 41-44.

And learning that subserves some useful end—
These are a living man's six greatest blessings.
Mahā-bhārata v. 1057.

Good words, good deeds, and beautiful expressions
A wise man ever culls from every quarter,
E'en as a gleaner gathers ears of corn.
Mahā-bhārata v. 1126.

To curb the tongue and moderate the speech,
Is held to be the hardest of all tasks [1].
The words of him who talks too volubly
Have neither substance nor variety.
Mahā-bhārata v. 1170.

Darts, barbëd arrows, iron-headed spears,
However deep they penetrate the flesh,
May be extracted; but a cutting speech,
That pierces, like a javelin, to the heart,
None can remove; it lies and rankles there.
Mahā-bhārata v. 1173.

Bear railing words with patience, never meet
An angry man with anger, nor return
Reviling for reviling, smite not him
Who smites thee; let thy speech and acts be gentle.
Mahā-bhārata v. 1270, 9972.

If thou art wise, seek ease and happiness
In deeds of virtue and of usefulness;
And ever act in such a way by day
That in the night thy sleep may tranquil be;
And so comport thyself when thou art young,
That when thou art grown old, thine age may pass
In calm serenity. So ply thy task

---

[1] St. James iii. 8.

Throughout thy life, that when thy days are ended,
Thou may'st enjoy eternal bliss hereafter.
Mahā-bhārata v. 1248.

Reflect that health is transient, death impends,
Ne'er in thy day of youthful strength do aught
To grieve thy conscience, lest when weakness comes,
And thou art on a bed of sickness laid,
Fear and remorse augment thy sufferings.
Mahā-bhārata v. 1474.

Do naught to others which if done to thee
Would cause thee pain; this is the sum of duty.
Mahā-bhārata v. 1517.

A king must first subdue himself, and then
Vanquish his enemies. How can a prince
Who cannot rule himself, enthral his foes?
To curb the senses, is to conquer self.
Mahā-bhārata XII. 2599.

Who in this world is able to distinguish
The virtuous from the wicked, both alike
The fruitful earth supports, on both alike
The sun pours down his beams, on both alike
Refreshing breezes blow, and both alike
The waters purify? Not so hereafter—
Then shall the good be severed from the bad;
Then in a region bright with golden lustre—
Centre of light and immortality—
The righteous after death shall dwell in bliss[1].
Then a terrific hell awaits the wicked—
Profound abyss of utter misery—
Into the depths of which bad men shall fall
Headlong, and mourn their doom for countless years.
Mahā-bhārata XII. 2798.

[1] Compare St. Matthew xiii. 43, xxv. 46.

Enjoy thou the prosperity of others,
Although thyself unprosperous; noble men
Take pleasure in their neighbour's happiness.
Mahā-bhārata XII. 3880.

Even to foes who visit us as guests
Due hospitality should be displayed;
The tree screens with its leaves, the man who fells it[1].
Mahā-bhārata XII. 5528.

What need has he who subjugates himself
To live secluded in a hermit's cell?
Where'er resides the self-subduing sage,
That place to him is like a hermitage.
Mahā-bhārata XII. 5961.

Let none reject the meanest suppliant
Or send him empty-handed from his door.
A gift bestowed on outcasts or on dogs
Is never thrown away or unrequited.
Mahā-bhārata XIII. 3212.

Time passes, and the man who older grows
Finds hair and teeth and eyes grow ever older.
One thing alone within him ne'er grows old—
The thirst for riches and the love of gold.
Mahā-bhārata XIII. 3676, 368a.

This is the sum of all true righteousness—
Treat others, as thou would'st thyself be treated.
Do nothing to thy neighbour, which hereafter
Thou would'st not have thy neighbour do to thee.
In causing pleasure, or in giving pain,
In doing good, or injury to others,

---

[1] This verse occurs in Hitopadeśa I. 60. Cf. Rom. xii. 20. Professor H. H. Wilson was induced to commence the study of Sanskṛit by reading somewhere that this sentiment was to be met with in Sanskṛit literature.

In granting, or refusing a request,
A man obtains a proper rule of action
By looking on his neighbour as himself[1].

Mahā-bhārata XIII. 5571.

Before infirmities creep o'er thy flesh;
Before decay impairs thy strength and mars
The beauty of thy limbs; before the Ender,
Whose charioteer is sickness, hastes towards thee,
Breaks up thy fragile frame and ends thy life[2],
Lay up the only treasure; do good deeds;
Practise sobriety and self-control;
Amass that wealth which thieves cannot abstract,
Nor tyrants seize, which follows thee at death,
Which never wastes away, nor is corrupted[3].

Mahā-bhārata XIII. 12084.

Heaven's gate is very narrow and minute[4],
It cannot be perceived by foolish men,
Blinded by vain illusions of the world.
E'en the clear-sighted who discern the way,
And seek to enter, find the portal barred
And hard to be unlocked. Its massive bolts
Are pride and passion, avarice and lust.

Mahā-bhārata XIV. 2784.

Just heaven is not so pleased with costly gifts,
Offered in hope of future recompense,
As with the merest trifle set apart
From honest gains, and sanctified by faith[5].

Mahā-bhārata XIV. 2788.

---

[1] Compare St. Matthew xxii. 39, St. Luke vi. 31.
[2] Compare Eccles. xii. 1.
[3] Compare St. Matthew vi. 19, Prov. xxiii. 4, 5.
[4] Compare St. Matthew vii. 14.
[5] Compare St. Matthew vi. 1–4, St. Mark xii. 43, 44.

Examples of Precepts from Bhartṛi-hari.

Blinded by self-conceit and knowing nothing,
Like elephant infatuate with passion,
I thought within myself, I all things knew;
But when by slow degrees I somewhat learnt,
By aid of wise preceptors, my conceit,
Like some disease, passed off; and now I live
In the plain sense of what a fool I am (II. 8).

The attribute most noble of the hand
Is readiness in giving; of the head,
Bending before a teacher; of the mouth,
Veracious speaking; of a victor's arms,
Undaunted valour; of the inner heart,
Pureness the most unsullied; of the ears,
Delight in hearing and receiving truth—
These are adornments of high-minded men
Better than all the majesty of Empire (II. 55).

Now for a little while a child, and now
An amorous youth; then for a season turned
Into the wealthy householder; then stripped
Of all his riches, with decrepit limbs
And wrinkled frame, man creeps towards the end
Of life's erratic course; and, like an actor,
Passes behind Death's curtain out of view[1] (III. 51).

Examples from the Kirātārjunīya of Bhāravi.

Those who wish well towards their friends disdain
To please them by fair words which are not true (I. 2).

Better to have a great man for one's foe
Than court association with the low (I. 8).

---

[1] The parallel in Shakespeare need scarcely be suggested.

In matters difficult and dark, concealed
By doubt and disagreement of opinion,
The Veda, handed down by holy men,
Explained with clearness, and well put in practice,
Like a bright lamp throws light upon the way,
Guiding the prudent lest they go astray (II. 33).

Would'st thou be eminent, all passion shun,
Drive wrath away by wisdom; e'en the sun
Ascends not to display his fullest light
Till he has chased away the mists of night (II. 36).

The noble-minded dedicate themselves
To the promotion of the happiness
Of others—e'en of those who injure them.
True happiness consists in making happy (VII. 13, 28).

Let not a little fault in him who does
An act of kindness, minish aught its value (VII. 15).

Youth's glories are as transient as the shadow
Of an autumnal cloud; and sensual joys,
Though pleasant at the moment, end in pain (XI. 12).

Riches and pleasure are the root of evil;
Hold them not dear, encourage not their growth;
They are aggressors hard to be subdued,
Destroyers of all knowledge and of truth (XI. 20).

The enemies which rise within the body,
Hard to be overcome—thy evil passions—
Should manfully be fought; who conquers these
Is equal to the conqueror of worlds (XI. 32).

The friendship of the bad is like the shade
Of some precipitous bank with crumbling sides,
Which falling buries him who sits beneath (XI. 55).

The natural hostility of beasts
Is laid aside when flying from pursuers;

So also when calamities impend
The enmity of rivals has an end (XII. 46).

Examples of Precepts from the Śiśupāla-badha of Māgha.

He who by virtue of his rank, his actions,
And qualities, effects no useful purpose,
Is like a chance-invented word; his birth
Is useless, for he merely bears a name (47).

A man of feeble character resembles
A reed that bends with every gust of wind (50).

Two only sources of success are known—
Wisdom and effort; make them both thine own
If thou would'st rise and haply gain a throne (76).

Science is like a couch to sapient men;
Reclining there, they never feel fatigue (77).

A monarch's weapon is his intellect;
His minister and servants are his limbs;
Close secresy of counsel is his armour;
Spies are his eyes; ambassadors, his mouth (82).

That energy which veils itself in mildness
Is most effective of its object; so
The lamp that burns most brightly owes its force
To oil drawn upwards by a hidden wick (85).

Wise men rest not on destiny alone,
Nor yet on manly effort, but on both (86).

Weak persons gain their object when allied
With strong associates; the rivulet
Reaches the ocean by the river's aid (100).

A good man's intellect is piercing, yet
Inflicts no wound; his actions are deliberate,
Yet bold; his heart is warm, but never burns;
His speech is eloquent, yet ever true (109).

Examples of Precepts from the Pañća-tantra.

Praise not the goodness of the grateful man
Who acts with kindness to his benefactors.
He who does good to those who do him wrong
Alone deserves the epithet of good (I. 277).

Hear thou a summary of righteousness,
And ponder well the maxim: Never do
To other persons what would pain thyself (III. 104).

The little-minded ask: Belongs this man
To our own family? The noble-hearted
Regard the human race as all akin (V. 38).

Examples of Precepts from the Hitopadeśa or book of 'friendly advice.'

A man of truest wisdom will resign
His wealth, and e'en his life, for good of others;
Better abandon life in a good cause,
When death in any case is sure to happen (I. 45).

He has all wealth who has a mind contented.
To one whose foot is covered with a shoe
The earth appears all carpeted with leather (I. 152).

Strive not too anxiously for a subsistence,
Thy Maker will provide thee sustenance;
No sooner is a human being born
Than milk for his support streams from the breast.
(I. 190).

He by whose hand the swans were painted white,
And parrots green, and peacocks many-hued,
Will make provision for thy maintenance[1] (I. 191).

---

[1] Compare St. Matthew vi. 26.

How can true happiness proceed from wealth,
Which in its acquisition causes pain;
In loss, affliction; in abundance, folly (I. 192)?

Whoever, quitting certainties, pursues
Uncertain things, may lose his certainties (I. 227).

By drops of water falling one by one,
Little by little, may a jar be filled;
Such is the law of all accumulations
Of money, knowledge, and religious merit (II. 10).

That man is sapient who knows how to suit
His words to each occasion, his kind acts
To each man's worth, his anger to his power (II. 48).

If glass be used to decorate a crown,
While gems are taken to bedeck a foot,
'Tis not that any fault lies in the gem,
But in the want of knowledge of the setter [1] (II. 72).

A man may on affliction's touchstone learn
The worth of his own kindred, wife, and servants;
Also of his own mind and character (II. 79).

A feverish display of over-zeal
At the first outset, is an obstacle
To all success; water, however cold,
Will penetrate the ground by slow degrees (III. 48).

E'en as a traveller, meeting with the shade
Of some o'erhanging tree, awhile reposes,
Then leaves its shelter to pursue his way,
So men meet friends, then part with them for ever.
(IV. 73).

---

[1] 'Is such a thing as an emerald made worse than it was, if it is not praised?' Marcus Aurelius. Farrar's 'Seekers after God,' p. 306.

Thou art thyself a stream whose sacred ford
Is self-restraint, whose water is veracity,
Whose bank is virtue, and whose waves are love;
Here practise thy ablutions; by mere water
The inner man can ne'er be purified (IV. 90).

It must not, of course, be inferred from a perusal of the above selection of examples that all the moral precepts of the Hindūs are all equally unexceptionable. It would be easy to give specimens of a very different character, and I here subjoin a prose translation of two verses of a less favourable type from the code of Manu.

'In certain cases a man stating a case falsely from a pious motive, even though he knows the truth, is not excluded from heaven; such a statement they call divine speech.

'Whenever the death of a Brāhman, Kshatriya, Vaiśya or Śūdra may result from speaking the truth, then an untruth may be told; for falsehood in this case is preferable to truth (VIII. 103, 104. Compare p. 336, note 1, of this volume).'

I could easily multiply examples of a far more objectionable character. Nay, I do not hesitate to declare my conviction that the gems of truth, which I have carefully and with much trouble unearthed from the sacred literature of the Hindūs and exhibited in the foregoing pages, are generally so buried under a superincumbent mass of erroneous teaching or so set in a false framework of fable and fiction, as to be practically of little or no value as rules of life, or as guides to the performance of a man's duty towards God, his neighbour, and himself.

CHAPTER XXII.

SUPPLEMENTARY[1].

The Worship of Brahmā at Pushkara, with some Account of the Śara-śayyā or 'Arrowy-bed' form of self-mortification (tapasyā).

WE have seen that Brāhmanism has no Creator in our sense. The personal god Brahmā (masculine) who is called 'the Creator,' is himself evolved out of the one impersonal self-existent Being, Brahmă (neuter). The personal Brahmā then becomes the Evolver of the Universe, while Vishṇu is associated with him as its Maintainer, and Śiva as its Dissolver. These three gods constitute the well-known Hindū Triad (Tri-mūrti, pp. 44, 45). How then has the worship of the first fallen into comparative desuetude?

According to the Abbé Dubois in his interesting work on the religions of India (English translation, p. 430) a legend is current that the god Brahmā indulged an incestuous passion for Sarasvatī, who, being really his daughter, afterwards became his wife. He states that the god's supposed violation of the most sacred laws of nature is the true cause of his being without any temples and ceremonies in India. Elsewhere he relates another legend that the absence of temples dedicated to Brahmā arose from a curse pronounced upon him by a holy man, whom he had treated with irreverence. To say, however, that Brahmā is wholly without temples is, as I shall show, inaccurate. Rodriguez in his exhaustive

[1] Supplementary notes collected during my Indian travels in 1884.

'Hindū Pantheon' (published at Madras in 1841) affirms that Brahmā is never adopted by any Hindū as his guardian deity, and, like Dubois, repeats the legend of Brahmā's unnatural passion for his daughter; assigning the neglect of the god's worship to this cause. Furthermore he adds a legend from the Skanda-purāṇa, in which it is declared that Brahmā once had five heads, but that one was cut off by the god Śiva inflamed with anger because Brahmā boasted that he was the greater god of the two. Others again explain the neglect of Brahmā's worship by asserting that his only office is to create, and that having once created men and endowed them with life he has no further benefit to confer upon them, while men, on the other hand, have nothing to gain by propitiating him. Probably the origin of these fanciful notions is to be traced to some of the Purāṇas, or possibly to the Upapurāṇas and Tantras; but it seems scarcely worth while to ransack these immense repositories of myths in the hope of discovering the source of a few grotesque legends; and the less so as I hold that the true reason for the rarity of Brahmā's temples is to be sought for in the fact that, according to orthodox Brāhmanism, the functions of Brahmā, Vishṇu and Śiva are interchangeable, and that both Vishṇu and Śiva may be identified with Brahmā, or be worshipped as Brahmā. This has been already pointed out (p. 45), and the remarkable verse in Kālidāsa's Kumāra-sambhava which expresses the doctrine, may be repeated here :—

> In those three Persons the one God was shown—
> Each first in place, each last—not one alone;
> Of Śiva, Vishṇu, Brahmā, each may be
> First, second, third among the blessed Three[1].

Others declare that Brahmā's inferiority is indicated by the legend which makes him spring from Vishṇu's navel (see p. 66).

---

[1] Translated by Griffith. The Sanskṛit words are as follow :—
'Ekaiva mūrtir bibhide tridhā sā sāmānyam eshām prathamāvaratvam
Vishṇor Haras tasya Hariḥ kadāćid Vedhās tayos tāvapi Dhātur ādyau.'

It is certainly incorrect to compare (as some have done) the Hindū doctrine of a Triad with the Christian dogma of a Unity in Trinity and a Trinity in Unity. For it must be borne in mind that Brahmā, Vishṇu and Śiva are all three held to be subordinate deities, and that all three have celestial bodies (antecedent to their earthly incarnations), and that all three are believed to be corporeal manifestations of the one sole self-existent, bodiless, impersonal Essence of the Universe, and destined to be reabsorbed into that Essence. Their coequality and interaction as personal manifestations of the one Self-existent God is nobly symbolized in the caves of Elephanta at Bombay, where may be seen sculptured out of the rock, three majestic heads springing out of one body. Such representations, however, are rare in other parts of India, and the intelligent traveller who judges of the Hindū religion by what meets the eye finds that he may generally regard the apparent medley of Indian divinities as forms of the two chief gods Vishṇu and Śiva with their wives. He would see little or no evidence of any worship paid to the male god Brahmā.

Indeed, so far as I was able to ascertain I could only hear of two temples dedicated directly and primarily to Brahmā, amid the vast number which may be observed dedicated to forms of Vishṇu, Śiva, or to their wives or offspring. And this is the more remarkable as certain localities are held to be consecrated through a sacrifice supposed to have been performed by Brahmā in the neighbourhood[1]. Moreover among the various idols and symbols scattered throughout India, those of Vishṇu and Śiva are by far the most abundant and often imply that these gods are worshipped as Brahmā, or are identified with him in his character of Evolver of the Universe[2], whereas the image of Brahmā with his four faces

[1] The remarkable myth of Brahmā offering himself up as a victim in the form of Purusha rests on a hymn of the Ṛig-veda (X. 90).

[2] Images of Vishṇu with Brahmā in the act of being evolved out of his navel are common enough, and, as I have stated further on, the Liṅga with four faces carved round it is by no means uncommon.

looking in all directions[1], though carved and sold by image-vendors, and even found in houses or in the precincts of Śaiva and Vaishṇava temples, do not imply that he combines in his own person all the functions of the Triad.

Of course the substitution of a kind of ditheism for tritheistic ideas is quite in harmony with the dualism which I have already described as an essential element in Hindū philosophy.

It is exactly what every student of the Sāṅkhya and Vedānta aphorisms would be led to expect (p. 38). But the general falling off in the direct worship of Brahmā is nevertheless a point of great interest in the development of Indian religious thought, and I therefore determined, when last travelling in India, to make a detour with the object of accomplishing a journey to Pushkara (Pokhar), where the most celebrated of the two temples of Brahmā now stands.

Pushkara, I should state at the outset, is one of the most sacred Tīrthas in all India. It is said that Brahmā having once performed a particular sacrifice (yajña) there, the waters of the small lake near the present town were thereby so sanctified that they ever afterwards became a potent specific for the removal of every kind of guilt. The greatest sinner has only to bathe in them to be at once purified and rendered fit for admission to Brahmā's heaven (Brahma-loka)[2].

In the Tīrtha-yātrā-parva of the Mahā-bhārata (Vana-parva, sec. 82) the precedence over all other places of pilgrimage is given to Pushkara:—'Any one who sojourns there,' so it affirms, 'becomes equal to the God of gods (deva-devasya). It was there that the gods, Daityas and Brahmarshis, having performed self-mortifying austerities (tapas taptvā) accumulated

---

[1] And, as some say, symbolizing the four Vedas. In Kumāra-sambhava (II. 3) Brahmā is called Vāg-īśa, 'The lord of speech or of word;' but his epithet is Sarvato-mukha, 'looking in all directions.'

[2] I need not repeat here that Brahmā, Vishṇu and Śiva each has his own special heaven (see pp. 54, 291). The Kṛishṇa form of Vishṇu also has a heaven of his own.

vast merit and attained to the rank of deities. Men of self-control are cleansed from their sins by ever thinking of Pushkara. The great Brahmā (pitāmahaḥ), who has the lotus for his seat (Kamalāsanaḥ), dwelt with great delight at this Tīrtha.' No wonder, then, that the little lake is lined with bathing Ghāṭs, and according to Sir W. W. Hunter's 'Imperial Gazetteer,' surrounded with houses belonging to most of the Rājput princes. It is stated that no living thing is allowed to be put to death within the precincts of the town, though how this rule can be enforced seems difficult to understand, considering that, at the great fair held there in October and November, at least 100,000 pilgrims throng the neighbourhood.

It was with the assistance of Mr. L. Saunders, whose guest I was when he was collector at Ajmere in Rājputāna, that I made an expedition from Ajmere to Pushkara (popularly called Pokhar), on February 22, 1884. The distance was only about seven miles from Mr. Saunders' house, and he arranged that I should be accompanied by an intelligent, well-educated Brāhman Pandit who knew the country thoroughly, and would be able to point out every object which was likely to interest me.

The road, like most of the roads made by Anglo-Indian engineers, seemed to me admirably constructed, and as pleasant to travel on as the best macadamized road in England. Soon after leaving the town of Ajmere it passes through a deep cutting in the hills, and then emerges on rather a wild country. I noticed here and there in the adjoining fields traps for catching tigers, leopards, and other less formidable beasts of prey, while occasional rude paintings, images, and shrines by the road-side warned us to be on our guard against prowling demons, especially those most spiteful of all evil spirits—the spirits of recently deceased human beings who, through some failure in the due performance of their funeral rites, were believed to rove about and haunt the neighbourhood. It was hinted to me that some of these malignant and unrestful spirits were in the habit of making themselves troublesome to any travellers or passers by who might neglect to propitiate them by offerings.

When we had accomplished about half of our journey and were approaching Pushkara we came upon a very interesting anthropological curiosity. This was a Vairāgī or Vaishṇava ascetic, whose appearance would certainly have shocked any one fresh from London Society and inclined to be a stickler for the proprieties of life. His demeanour seemed to be that of a human being, who, though just alive himself, seemed to be supremely indifferent to the existence of everything else in creation, including demons and beasts of prey. He had, however, erected for his own protection close to the road a rough covering consisting of a mat supported on four poles, open to all the winds of heaven. Like other ascetics of his type still to be seen in India, he was not altogether an inviting object to be looked upon by any one at all fastidious in regard to the realities of human anatomy, for he was absolutely nude with the exception of the smallest conceivable patch of cloth, three or four inches square. Nor was he a very promising object of investigation to any one, who, like myself, was bent on extracting information from every possible source; for he was under a vow of silence (mauna-vrata) which was supposed to be inviolable for at least six years. Yet, for all that, he made a kind of mumbling sound through his closed lips, and tried to make himself intelligible to us by signs, when, descending from our vehicle, we approached his hermitage to examine his condition and surroundings more closely.

An inscription written in rude characters indicated his name—Khākī Jñāna-dās. Round his neck was a rosary (japa-mālā) consisting of eighteen large rough Tulasī beads (see p. 67). He was seated in the usual way on the ground, but close to him on his right hand was his only bed—an iron framework resting on four short legs, and unprovided with mattress or coverlet, but studded instead with rows of iron spikes, somewhat blunted at the points, while at the pillow-end there was a spiky head-rest. This remarkable couch was called by my Brāhman companion the devotee's Kaṇṭaka-śayyā, 'bed of thorns,' though I noticed that it had an inscription in Sanskṛit letters designating it as 'a bed of arrows' (Bāṇa-śayyā). This convinced me that it was intended to represent Bhīshma's Śara-śayyā or 'arrowy bed' described in the Mahā-bhārata (Bhīshma-parva and Anuśāsana-parva 7732), and, on my mentioning this to my companion, the Vairāgī gave a grunt of assent and approval, evidently pleased with my acquaintance with the story of Bhīshma.

I should observe that, resting on the spiky bed, was a wooden stand on which were deposited (1) the black stone (Śāla-grāma) of Vishṇu, (2) the white stone (Bāṇa-liṅga) of Śiva, and (3) the red stone of Gaṇeśa (see pp. 69, 70, 412). I noticed no symbol of the divine mother (generally identified with Śiva's consort) nor of the Sun, which, together with the three just named, usually represent a Pentarchy of divinities worshipped at the Pañćāyatana ceremony (see pp. 410–416).

It was a great satisfaction to me that I had at length met with a genuine example of the spiky-bed form of self-mortification (tapas); for during my numerous travels in different parts of India I had hitherto sought for one in vain, and had begun to doubt the truth of the story told in a paper read before the Asiatic Society of Bengal in 1792 (see the fifth volume of the Asiatic Researches), relative to a Brāhman ascetic at Benares, who is depicted as actually lying naked day and night on one of these spiky couches which he is described as having used for thirty-five years. That man's name was Parama Svatantrī Prakāśānanda. He had travelled much as a devotee through many countries, and part of his process of self-mortification, during winter, consisted in placing himself beneath a perforated pot full of water which fell drop by drop on his head, and, during summer, in reclining between four blazing fires with the rays of the burning sun beating down upon him from above. Questioned as to his reason for punishing himself by such severe forms of self-torture (tapasyā), he repudiated the idea of resorting to what we call 'penance' as an atonement for the commission of sin or of any special crime. The simple reason he gave was that since a celebrated Ṛishi or holy man named Agni-varṇa had undergone the spiky-bed form of austerity in the Satya-yuga or first age of the world, and since the demon Rāvaṇa had done the same for ten thousand years in the Tretā or second age of the world, and since Bhīshma had done the same in the Dvāpara or third age, it had been assigned to him as a peculiar privilege to go through similar austerities in the present age of the world. Of course, as we have already shown (see pp. 72, 87), the efficacy of bodily mortification is an essential element in the Hindū creed, and the ostensible motive of all self-torture is either to accumulate merit, or to acquire supernatural power, or to achieve complete absorption of individual personality in the one eternal Essence of the Universe.

The story of Bhīshma's arrowy couch is one of those extravagant figments, occurring here and there in Indian sacred literature, which has hitherto been passed over or little noticed by European writers on Hindūism. Nor indeed is it easy to disentangle this remarkable episode of the Mahā-bhārata from the tedious succession of legendary stories with which it is interwoven; although it constitutes an important link in the continuity of the leading narrative. It will be sufficient to note here that the Bhīshma-parva of that immense Epic poem relates how the two armies of the Pāṇḍavas and Kauravas met on Kuru-kshetra—a vast plain north-west of Delhi; the Kauravas (or Kurus) being commanded by Bhīshma. Long tedious descriptions of the battles which ensued are closed with an account of the terrific duel between Bhīshma and Arjuna—the bravest of the Pāṇḍavas. In the end Arjuna transfixed Bhīshma with innumerable arrows, so that there was not a space of two fingers' breadth left unpierced on the surface of his body. Then Bhīshma fell from his chariot, but the countless arrows which had penetrated his frame prevented it from touching the ground, so that instead of lying prostrate it remained suspended, and, as it were, reclining on an arrowy couch (śara-talpe śayāna). In that condition the old warrior continued alive and conscious. The story goes on to relate that he had been endowed with the supernatural power of fixing the time of his own death, and that, although pierced through and through and grievously wounded, he resolved not to die, but to remain alive till the sun had entered its northern course in the heavens. All the warriors on both sides thereupon ceased fighting that they might view this wonderful sight. As he lay on his arrowy bed his head hanging down, he begged for a pillow; whereupon the chiefs brought all kinds of soft supports, which Bhīshma rejected. Arjuna then made a pillow for his head with three sharp arrows, which Bhīshma approved. Soon after this he asked for water, and Arjuna thereupon struck the ground with an arrow, causing a pure spring to burst forth. This so refreshed Bhīshma that he remained alive on the field of battle for fifty-eight days and nights, pouring forth words of wisdom for the benefit of the listening warriors, and enunciating many excellent moral precepts and sage counsels on social and political subjects[1]. When the time came for him to die, the arrows suddenly and of their own accord left his body, his skull divided, and his spirit, bright as a meteor, ascended through the top of his head (see p. 291) to the skies.

Doubtless the voluntary bodily suffering undergone by Bhīshma for so long a period, pierced and agonized by sharp arrows, was the supposed efficient cause of the divine knowledge of which he became possessed and which he was able to impart to others in his long series of discourses.

---

[1] These precepts are all collected in the Śānti and Anuśāsana Parvas of the Mahā-bhārata, two of the longest books in that vast thesaurus of Hindū legendary tradition. Compare p. 546 of this volume.

A picture of the old warrior sage, lying in a moribund condition on his arrowy bed, is given in the Bombay edition of the Mahā-bhārata [1], and always interested me, whenever I had occasion to refer to its pages. Here then I had at last accidentally come across a living specimen of a 'holy man' intent on practising a similar method of obtaining divine knowledge and union with the Deity; and that, too, under our own matter-of-fact work-a-day rule, and notwithstanding the expected collapse of superstition under the pressure of steam, electricity, and generally advancing civilization and education.

Of course my interest in the example before me led me to scrutinize his condition and habits rather critically, and in the absence of all power of cross-questioning this utterly apathetic ascetic under a vow of silence, I confess that I soon began to feel somewhat sceptical as to his sincerity, or at least as to the fact of his torturing himself by too close a contact with his spiky bed. To test therefore the reality of his self-imposed bodily suffering, as well as his freedom from all worldly desires and consequent right to the title of Vairāgī, I offered him half a rupee if he would rise from the ground and lie on the spikes for a few minutes; but he declined either to gratify my curiosity or to satisfy my doubts, pointing to his pebble-gods, and making signs to intimate that they were asleep on the spiky bed and could not be disturbed without impiety.

Perhaps it was unfair to place an uncharitable construction on his excuses, without first paying him a nocturnal visit. Possibly his vow debarred him from taking a recumbent posture except at night, and he might not improbably have been found at a later hour, reposing on his bed of thorns under the protection of his then wakeful and vigilant gods. Or possibly my silvery offering was not liberal enough to

---

[1] I saw one also in the Comte de Gubernatis' Indian Museum at Florence.

be tempting, yet I noticed that he evinced no particular contempt for money doles tendered in the form of metal of the baser kind. He had a Tulasī shrub in front of him, and even during our short sojourn near his hermitage two or three passers by approached him, bowed their heads reverently before the divinity supposed to be embodied in the 'holy man,' and offered him one or two pice which he accepted without demur, while giving in return one or two leaves of the sacred plant to be preserved by the recipients as preservatives against evil. We, too, were honoured by the gift of a few leaves presented to us quite gratuitously, but evidently only intended as a parting memento, or as a token that the prolongation of our visit would be unwelcome.

On our reaching the outskirts of the town of Pushkara, my companion pointed out on the right of the road a celebrated Varāha-mandira—that is—a temple of Vishṇu in his Boar-incarnation. It was a striking structure, built on an elevation, and approached by a long flight of steps. I ascended, and was allowed to inspect the image of the god represented here in his boar-form and in the act of destroying the demon Hiraṇyāksha (see p. 109). Willingly would I have lingered and taken note of all the surroundings had not my presence attracted a number of temple-attendants who began to crowd round us and clamour for fees in an excited manner.

It was with difficulty that we escaped to our carriage and proceeded on our way to the town. Before entering the main street, I noticed a temple dedicated to Śiva (Mahā-deva), which, like the other temples, was raised above the level of the road. On ascending the steps leading to the shrine, I found the usual image of a bull (Nandi) looking into it and the usual liṅga of Śiva in the sanctuary, but with four human faces carved round it. This was to show that Śiva was worshipped there as identified with Brahmā. I saw a similar four-faced liṅga in a shrine between Jaipur and Ambar.

With reference to this point, I may observe that in the

Sauptika Parva (770) of the Mahā-bhārata there is a curious account of the subordinate part which Brahmā instigated Śiva to take in the creation of the world, and of the delay caused by the preparatory course of austerity which Śiva thought it necessary to perform immersed in water. In the Śiva-purāṇa, on the other hand, the god Śiva is described as the direct author of creation, and the liṅga is asserted to be the source of the whole visible universe.

But to return to Pushkara, no sooner did we enter the town and reach the margin of the sacred waters than a crowd of Brāhman Harpies surrounded us, intent on exacting money-fees. It was useless maintaining that the shore of the lake was open to the public ; the mob was not to be reasoned with, and the demeanour of a few individuals close to us became so threatening that I unwisely tendered two or three rupees as a peace-offering. My proffered coins were instantly snatched by those nearest to us, and snatched at again by others who considered that they had a right to a share in my gifts. Then a free fight ensued—no mere good-natured scramble between a few idlers, but the fierce struggle of a mass of half-frantic human beings, each grappling the other in savage embrace, and all vociferating together, while they surged hither and thither in remarkable contrast to the peaceful surface of the lake. Happily under cover of the confusion caused by this battle-royal, we effected a retreat, congratulating ourselves that our garments had not been torn off our backs in the melée.

Of course the chief object of my journey was the all but unique temple of the god Brahmā. The first impression made on me by this structure was one of surprise at its massiveness. It is erected on an elevated piece of ground at the further end of the town in full view of the picturesque temple of Sāvitrī which crowns the sugar-loaf peak of a hill in the Ārāvalī range close at hand. No doubt Sāvitrī, or Gāyatrī (pp. 19; 403; 406) is there personified and worshipped in connexion with the god Brahmā as his wife. The temple of

Brahmā itself is approached by successive flights of solid stone steps, and has rather the appearance of a small fortress with loop-holed bastions. The present structure is said to be of no great antiquity, and is believed to be not much older than the present century. I ascended the steps along with my Brāhman companion, and passing through the portal entered a spacious court-yard surrounded by cloisters. This cloistered quadrangle constitutes the precincts of the temple. Looking back I noticed above the entrance gate a covered place for the temple-musicians, and just below an image of a goose-like bird (Sanskṛit, haṉsa) carved in the stone-work—this animal being the vehicle or symbol of the god Brahmā (see pp. 104, 3; 328).

In the centre of the quadrangle was the actual shrine of Brahmā—an isolated temple of some architectural pretensions, with columns supporting a roof on which was a low central dome and the usual pyramidal tapering tower rising above the sanctuary, where Brahmā's image is enshrined. In front of the entrance was the inevitable bell. I was allowed to look through the well-carved wooden gates at the image which was clearly visible in its sanctuary at the end of the vista of open columns. I observed that it had four black faces, each one of which was supposed to be directed towards one of the four quarters of the compass. In point of fact, however, three of the faces were made to look at the observer, each face having two great staring glass eyes. Covering the four-faced head was a broad red turban, and over that were hanging five umbrella-shaped ornaments. I noticed that the image was dressed in red clothes with flaps of coloured cloth hanging round the waist. On one side of the god's image was that of his wife worshipped here as Gāyatrī or Sāvitrī (p. 19)[1], and behind both was the image of Kāma-dhenu—the sacred cow

[1] The Gāyatrī or most sacred verse of the Veda is personified and sometimes identified with Sarasvatī and called the Mother of the four Vedas. She is also regarded as the daughter of Prajāpati (Brahmā).

granting all desires. On the marble floor in front of the shrine was the carved representation of a tortoise,—significant, no doubt, of Brahmā's connexion with Vishṇu (p. 108), out of whose navel he is fabled to have sprung, seated on a lotus.

In the court-yard surrounding the inner temple and in front of it on one side was a small shrine dedicated to the liṅga of Śiva, which here—as in the instances already mentioned—really represents Brahmā. It consists of a dwarf stone column with four faces carved round it, while underneath is the usual female symbol (yoni). Near it is a shrine of Vishṇu—doubtless here identified with Brahmā. Again, there is a shrine close at hand dedicated to the Ardha-nārī form of Śiva, and another to Dattātreya, regarded as an incarnation of Brahmā, Vishṇu and Śiva united in one person (see p. 267). Elsewhere in the precincts, I noticed images of Indra and Kuvera, both riding on elephants, and of course, here, supposed to be subservient to the god of the temple. I ought to mention, that reclining lazily on the ground in the cloisters of the quadrangle were two devotees, of the Parama-haṇsa class. One of these was a sleek stalwart youth, who looked as if he lived well and was daily fed on the fat of the land. Both devotees were supposed to be wholly devoted to the contemplation of Brahmă (here manifested as Brahmā), and to do nothing else whatever. I could not help addressing them and suggesting that the god Brahmā would be more honoured by their doing some useful work for the good of his creatures.

Several sacred trees were growing in the court-yard of the temple—for instance, a Pīpal tree (see p. 335), two Banian trees (Vaṭa), a Nīm, an Aśoka, an Āmalakī, and the sacred Tulasī (Tulsī) shrub. In one spot I noticed a Śamī tree married to a Banian (see p. 335).

With regard to the other temple of Brahmā, which is said to be the only other temple existing in India, and to which I believe I was the first to draw attention in a note to the first edition of my Manual of Hindūism (p. 90), it is to be found near Īdar (or Edar), but I was unable to make an expedition to this place.

Mr. G. P. Taylor, a missionary, having observed my note, made inquiries of a friend living in the Īdar state, which is situated about sixty miles N. E. of Ahmedābād, and not very far S. of Mount Abū, and ascertained the following particulars :—

This second temple dedicated to Brahmā is not in the town of Īdar itself, but about fifteen miles distant, on a plain called Brahma-kheḍ (Brahma-kshetra). It is constructed of white sandstone and bricks covered with cement. It is seven feet long, thirty broad, and thirty-six high, and is traditionally believed to have been built by Brahmā's reputed son, Bhṛigu —probably the identical personage who gave his name to Broach (Bhṛigu-kaććha). Though not so celebrated as the Pushkara temple, it is nevertheless held in high esteem and much resorted to by pilgrims and others at certain seasons of the year.

An Account of the late Mahārāṇī of Nuddea's Cremation and the subsequent Funeral and Śrāddha Ceremonies as performed by her Son, Kshitīśa Chandra Rāya, Mahārāja of Nuddea.

The young Mahārāja of Nuddea paid me a visit whilst I was Lord Ripon's guest at Government House, Calcutta, in the early part of the year 1884, attended by his English tutor ; and knowing that I was interested in the religious ceremonies of the Hindūs, gave me an account of the cremation of his mother, written by himself. I here give it nearly in his own words :—

'On the evening of Dec. 26, 1883, my mother died at Kṛishṇa-nagar (Krishnagar), in the Nuddea district (Bengal). Some Brāhmans were at once called in to remove the dead body to Nuddea, that they might burn it near the Ganges. Having wrapped the body up in the bedding on which she died, we fastened it with strings, and put a small piece of iron in the wrappings. The dead body was then laid on a charpoy, and covered with a curtain. This was carried by Brāhmans only. Soon after midnight we started for Nuddea, arriving there early on the morning of the 27th. Having collected wood, ghee, earthen vessels, etc., we summoned our priests, and the Pandit Braja-nāth Vidyā-ratna, the chief expounder of Smṛiti —who all lived at Nuddea. Then the man who makes arrangements for cremation, called 'Gaṅgā-putra' (p. 347), enclosed a space near the Ganges with a long sheet, there being an opening only on the river side. As a boat was passing at the time we ordered it to the other side. Removing the curtain we took the body off the charpoy, and laid it on the bank, covered only with a simple white cloth. The feet up to the ankle were immersed in the water, the rest of the body was on the dry land. The priest then repeated some texts (Mantras), corrected from time to time by the chief Pandit. The deceased meanwhile was supposed to be assisted by this ceremony in crossing the river Baitaraṇī (Vaitaraṇī), the river supposed by all good Hindūs to lie between this world and the next (see p. 297 of this volume).

'I then plunged into the Ganges, and on coming out boiled a mixture of rice, sesamum, plantain, and ghee, which I took near the dead body of my mother. Then dividing the mixture into two parts, and repeating some Mantras, I threw it into the river. This ceremony is called the giving of Piṇḍa (Piṇḍa-dāna, see pp. 285, 293)—that is to say, presenting the dead with an oblation of food. Then I bathed again, and rubbed some ghee, etc. on my deceased mother's head, and threw some water over the body. I then re-covered the face. Next, we removed the body to a pile of wood about two feet high, called a Chelu, within the enclosure. Then laying the body on this pile, I uncovered the face, and with a torch in my right hand burned the hair, but my back was turned, and I was not allowed to see the face. The whole pile was then set on fire, and soon after I threw seven pieces of sandal-wood into the flames, repeating a Mantra. Some two hours afterwards I took a sharp-pointed bamboo, and piercing the backbone which is never totally consumed, placed it in the water. This concluded the actual ceremony of cremation.

'Then after a substitute had dipped ten times in the river for me, and, instead of my dipping, had touched me ten times, I prepared my breakfast with my own hands, and after taking it returned to my home at Kṛishṇa-nagar on the evening of December 27. For the twelve days during which the mourning lasts the use of all luxurious food—such as fish or flesh,—of good clothes, of beds, of chairs, of shoes, and of an umbrella, is forbidden to the nearest surviving relative; but in my case, I being an adopted son, the prohibition only took effect for five days, during which period I slept—wrapped up in a blanket on the floor, and ate no rich food, nor used luxurious oils when bathing.

'On the morning of the 28th, or second day, the priest and the chief Pandit came from Nuddea, and we went to a neighbouring tank, and boiled some simple food, such as ghee, sesamum, rice, and plantain; dividing it into eight portions, we threw each portion into the river, repeating a Mantra.

'Thus altogether ten portions had been given as food for the deceased during ten days (see p. 293 of this volume). I then shaved my hair off, the other relatives shaving their moustache only. Next I cooked my simple food of rice and ghee (Havishya). On the third day, or December the 29th, the first thing I did was to bathe in the tank, using no towel, soap, or luxurious oils. I then put on my simple clothing, consisting of a white sheet known as Kacha, which was the only clothing I was allowed to wear during the five days prescribed for the period of mourning, called the *Aśauća*. I then went to a room and dedicated fruit, money, a bed, rice, shoes, and umbrellas to Vishṇu, in the presence of the Priest, the Guru, and other Brāhmans. These offerings were then distributed amongst the Brāhmans who were present. This is called the Tri-rātra or 'Three-night ceremony,' after which the spirit of the deceased, having been judged (see p. 292 of this volume), is sent to its own place. A short time after the performance of this rite I again went to the tank, and cooked and dedicated a Piṇḍa, or funeral cake, to Vishṇu. I also dedicated to him a bull-calf marked on one side with the Tri-śūla or Trident, and on the other with the Ćakra or Circle, and four young heifers, which were all let loose, and allowed to roam where they pleased. These ceremonies over I breakfasted.

'On the fourth day I was not called upon to do anything. On the fifth day I fixed a wooden pole, with the image of a bull in a small shrine on its summit, in the ground a few yards from the house. After walking round it seven times I went to the tank and bathed, being now allowed to use soap, towels, and fragrant oils. I then breakfasted for the first time after my mother's death on fish and the flesh of kid; and from this day was again allowed to use fine clothes, chairs, shoes, beds, and umbrellas, first presenting some Brāhman with one of each.

'On January 5, or the tenth day, I dedicated to Vishṇu a large number of shoes, umbrellas, beds, brass and silver cooking utensils, copper, silver, and gold coin, lampstands of silver and brass, carpets, shawls, and clothes. After the dedication the things were distributed amongst the Pandits, Brāhmans, and relatives present. In the evening we entertained them all at a feast, to the number of about one thousand; and during the night some thirteen thousand poor were fed with rice and sweetmeats, and each man, woman, and child received four annas (=*6d.*). On January 7, or the twelfth day, the Śrāddha ceremonies were concluded by another feast given to some five hundred relatives and Brāhmans.'

An Account of the daily Deva-pūjā performed by the Mahārāja of Dhol-pur.

When (in 1884) I was the guest of General Dennehy at the Residency, Dhol-pur, the youthful Mahārāja (named Rāṇā Nihāl Siṇh)—whose education the General was then ably superintending—very obligingly performed his usual diurnal Deva-pūjā, or 'worship of the gods,' in my presence.

The ceremony took place in one of the courts of his palace, under a Maṇḍapa or open hall leading to a shrine of Vishṇu, worshipped as Narasiṇha. A square piece of ground was marked out and consecrated on the floor, and in the centre of the ground so prepared was a small rectangular silver platform or low stand on legs, and in the centre of this again a little round platter with a silver cup containing several Bāṇa-liṅgas, Śāla-grāmas, etc. (see pp. 69, 392, 412). On the right of this was a little white conch-shell resting on a small silver stand, on the left a silver bell, and at the opposite corner a cocoa-nut. All around on the ground were arranged sacrificial implements, sacred vessels, cups, lotās, and flowers. On one side of the prepared ground and close to the silver stand sat the Mahārāja, with his legs folded under him in the usual manner, having the sacred vessels and implements in front of him within easy reach of his hands. Behind him sat his domestic priest (Purohit) ready to give him directions for the due performance of the ceremonial, and on one side of the prepared ground sat a row of four Brāhmans who took part in the muttering of prayers, the repetition of texts and chanting. Not far off, on an elevated step, was the altar (vedi) for the Homa or sacrifice to fire. This altar was made of clay well plastered with cow-dung, but only rising a few inches from the ground. It was of an oblong form, with a Svastika (p. 91, note 1) or auspicious mark in the centre. It was also consecrated by water scattered on its surface with Kuśa grass.

On it was kindled the sacred fire which was fed with Samidh or fuel, composed of pieces of wood of six different kinds (Palāśa, Śamī, Khadira, Aśvattha, Uḍumbara, etc.), and was made to blaze up by ghee poured on the wood with sacrificial ladles (Śruva, darvi).

At the commencement of the Deva-pūjā a piece of silk was bound round the Mahārāja's arm, with repetition of benedictory formulas, to protect him from the evil influence of demons always on the watch to counteract the good effect of religious ceremonies. This is called Rakshā-bandhana.

Much of the detail of the ceremonial resembled that of the Pañćāyatana-pūjā, described at p. 410 of this volume. The Mahārāja, under the direction of his Purohit, performed the usual acts of worship by the offering of flowers (pushpa), by placing garlands of yellow flowers round the sacred vessels, by the burning of incense (dhūpa), by the waving of lights (dīpa), by oblations of rice-grains etc. (naivedya), by offering a cloth (vastra) placed on the central stand, by the pouring of water with a little spoon into his own hand, or into a boat-shaped vessel, by repeatedly sprinkling the Bāṇa-liṅgas etc. with water taken out of the larger sacred water-vessel (Kalaśa), by again pouring water into the Kalaśa, and by putting yellow flowers into it, and by again pouring out water with these flowers.

It seemed to me that the most important part of the ceremonial consisted in the constant sprinkling and pouring out of water and scattering of rice-grains. Some of the latter the Rāṇā threw behind his head, while during the entire ceremony the Purohit and Brāhmans recited texts, muttered prayers, and chanted verses. There was also a hymn to Śiva (Śiva-stotra), with repetition of some of his 1008 names (see pp. 81, 106), preceded by adoration of the nine planets (p. 344) represented by nine areca nuts placed in rice and arranged in order on the ground. The repetitions were concluded by the exclamation, 'Om phaṭ,' and by clapping of hands.

How far the young Rāṇā himself believed in the efficacy of

these ceremonies, I cannot undertake to say, but he went through them with an evident desire to fulfil every minute requirement of the ritual in a careful and reverential manner.

An Account of the Temple of Kālī at Vindhyāćal.

When I was at Mirzapur in the spring of 1884, I visited the neighbouring temple of Kālī (about five miles distant), worshipped under the name of Vindhyāćala-vāsinī (popularly Vindhyāćal), 'dweller on the Vindhya mountains.' This was the form of the goddess to which the Ṭhags were supposed to offer up their victims, and here was the particular shrine to which they made pilgrimages from all parts of the country. It is still one of the most popular temples in India, and on the day of my visit at least a thousand worshippers were collected in the precincts. There is a small central temple with a low roof, on which several flags were kept flying. As it was the time of *darśana*—i. e. homage paid to the idol by viewing it when dressed and decorated—the surging, struggling crowd passed in through a narrow door on one side, and out at an equally narrow exit on the other, amidst a deafening din of yelling, shouting, and tolling of bells. I was informed that between the hours of 12 and 3 in the day, and of 12 and 5 at night, the goddess is put to sleep on a silver bed, and the shrine is then closed.

The temple has a space round it for pradakshiṇā (p. 68, 2) or reverential circumambulation, and round this again is an open area, on three sides of which are rows of shrines to various deities behind finely carved screens. I noticed an image of Sarasvatī in a particularly beautiful shrine, behind an exquisitely carved lace-like stone screen. Near this was the place for sacrificing goats. The priests seemed to take especial pleasure in chopping off the heads of as many goats as possible while I was examining the shrines, perhaps to make atonement for the pollution caused by my presence. The animals were then flayed, and dogs came and licked up the blood.

Close to the exit of the temple the Homa sacrifice to fire was being performed by a number of Brāhmans seated in a semi-circle round it. I observed two or three women at one end of the semi-circle. All were engaged in putting ghee into the fire with wooden ladles and then scattering grain, camphor, and sawdust of sandal-wood on the flames, the Brāhmans chanting texts (see p. 367).

What struck me as most curious in the conduct of the crowd was that some of the worshippers before leaving the temple left an impress of their hands—dipped in some dark colouring matter—on the exterior wall, close to the entrance. I was told that this was intended as the record of a vow, binding the worshipper, if he obtained some particular boon which he had prayed for, to sacrifice a goat to the goddess. When the boon was obtained, and the vow fulfilled, the mark on the wall was to be effaced.

Account of the Customs and Religious Tenets of the Santāls.

One of my objects in travelling through India in 1883–1884, was to gain a better knowledge of the Jains and of the points of difference which distinguish Jainism from Buddhism. I therefore determined to visit Pārasnāth, which is perhaps the most sacred of all the hills dedicated to Jaina saints. At any rate numerous Jaina temples crown the table-land on the summit, and are daily visited by hundreds of Jaina pilgrims from all parts of India.

Yet this pilgrim-frequented mountain, rising, as it does, about 4,500 feet above the sea, is surrounded by tiger-haunted jungles, and is by no means easy of access. My ascent of it is briefly described in my work on Buddhism (p. 509) and I propose referring to it more particularly in another work.

As my way led me through a tract of country inhabited by

the Santāls, I availed myself of the opportunity to make myself acquainted with some of the customs of that aboriginal race—a race generally classified under what is usually called the Kolarian group of aborigines.

I had received an invitation to stay with Mr. Stevenson, an energetic missionary of the Free Church of Scotland, who had laboured for many years among the Santāls and at that time had fixed his residence at Pāchambā [1] about three miles from Girīdi—a station of the narrow guage railway leading from Madhupur—and about 200 miles north-west of Calcutta.

The whole of the plain extending for thirty miles between Girīdi and the Pārasnāth range, forms part of the District officially known as the Santāl Parganas. According to the Imperial Gazetteer this district, which is under the Lieutenant Governorship of Bengal, has an area of 5,488 square miles and a population (at the last census) of 1,259,287 souls inhabiting 9,872 villages.

Colonel Dalton considers, that there were in 1872 about 200,000 Santāls, and the same authority states, that they form about one-third of the total number of the aboriginal races of Bengal [2].

On the 28th of January, 1884, I started with Mr. Stevenson from Pāchambā with the view of gaining some knowledge of these people and with the special object of observing the relation between their usages and those of Hindūism.

We drove through a pleasant undulating country, passing

[1] Mr. Stevenson died of cholera at Pāchambā three years ago, to the great grief of those among whom he laboured and of all who knew him; but his influence still lives in Santālia. In 1887 he published a little pamphlet containing a brief history of the Scotch Mission to the Santāls, and of Santāl customs, and this I have consulted. Most of the information, however, embodied in this part of my book was gathered from his own lips. Much has been written on the same subject by Colonel Dalton, Sir W. W. Hunter, and others. According to Mr. Stevenson the name Santāl should properly be spelt *Saontāl.*

[2] The whole number of Santāls amounted in Mr. Stevenson's time to about a million, and of these about 8,000 were Christians.

many villages and rice-fields, till we came to what appeared to be a good typical example of a Santāl village-community. The village—called, I believe, Chamarkho—lay about a quarter of a mile from the road, and to reach it, we had to leave our carriage and follow a well-beaten path across a paddy-field bordered here and there by palm-trees. We found the primitive inhabitants quite as unprepared for our visit, as we had hoped to find them. No head-man made his appearance for some time after our arrival, and few human beings, except children, were at first visible. I noticed that the huts and homesteads which constituted the village were not grouped together in an irregular cluster, as is usual in the rural districts of India, but were arranged in one long straight line, protected on both sides by a high thick fence, made of boughs of trees wattled together and strengthened by thick sticks, while here and there the monotony of the line of fencing was broken by the stems of living palms and tamarind trees, and castor-oil plants. The fence ran parallel on one side with the homesteads, but so as to leave an intervening space, which formed a kind of long straight street. Each homestead, too, was surrounded by a similar protection, enclosing a kind of separate compound. Of course the usual troop of village dogs and yelping curs surrounded us, and had to be kept off by the free use of our sticks. Their barking, however, had the effect of rousing some of the villagers, who approached us and greeted Mr. Stevenson with exclamations of pleasure, appearing to recognize him as an old friend and benefactor, and talking familiarly with him in their own peculiar speech. Parenthetically I may remark that the Santāl language offers to scholars an interesting example of the Kolarian family, and those philologists who have investigated it have shewn that it contains some remarkable curiosities of complex grammatical structure and idiom. All the difficulties and intricacies of the dialect had been mastered by my companion, Mr. Stevenson, and another excellent missionary (Mr. Campbell), who had heard of our expedition and joined us. Both missionaries spoke to the natives with as much case and fluency as if Santālī was as familiar to them as their own mother-tongue. I noticed that the Santāl men were branded or tattooed on three places on the left arm under the elbow. Such marks are supposed to act as charms against evil influences. The women have the arms and chest tattooed in the same way and for the same purpose. They chattered as unconstrainedly as the men, and seemed to enjoy quite as much freedom and liberty of action. It was not long before the head-man, called Manjhī, appeared —a venerable old gentleman who welcomed us to the village in the name of all the inhabitants.

We found the main-street not particularly clean, but entering one of the compounds at the invitation of its smiling owners, we observed a marked contrast to the state of the street in the well-swept floors and great tidiness and good order of all the interior arrangements of the homestead. On the left of us was a buffalo-shed, and near it a shed for cooking and another for other domestic purposes. On our right was the dwelling-place of the family, consisting of a large shed with a thatched roof and walls made of mud-cement and floors smeared with mud. The one door-way was so low, that we had to stoop on entering. Creeping inside we noticed that the dimly-lighted apartment had a vacant space in the middle with a solitary piece of furniture in the shape of a small charpoy, barely big enough for the father and mother to lie upon, while the children slept on the floor. All around the wall were about fourteen huge bee-hive shaped receptacles for stored grain bound round and round with straw bands. We noticed also a weaving-loom, some gourds for holding water, some native-made umbrellas and a collection of bows and arrows.

As to wardrobe, nothing of the kind was visible. Nor was it needed, since the only dress of the men is a strip of cloth, while a single Sārī satisfies the women, though this one article of dress may consist of a strip of calico, five or six yards long. The women, however, have very heavy brass ornaments on their neck, arms, ancles and toes, besides curious brass finger-rings; the whole collection of ornaments often weighing sixteen pounds. We observed that the girls and women were generally tolerably clean and always bright and cheerful; but the men were dirty, rough and unkempt, with long locks of dark hair hanging down over their shoulders. As to the children, they ran about innocent of all clothing, and to all appearances utterly untended and uncared for, in the full enjoyment of unmitigated dirt. Each child, too, held in its hand a stick of sugar-cane, the continued sucking of which was not conducive to its facial cleanliness.

And I may mention here that throughout India there exists a superstition according to which it is unlucky to wash children until they reach a certain age, or until they have been taken to some far distant temple, to the deity of which they have been dedicated at their birth.

I was informed that Santāl parents exercise little or no control over their offspring, and for no other reason than a rooted dislike to trouble of any kind. Girls are not generally married till fourteen or even fifteen or sixteen years of age, betrothal taking place three or four days previously. It is important to choose a lucky day for both betrothal and wedding. This is done by observing omens, and strange to say, the sight of a dead body is considered auspicious. Santāl wives, however, must always be purchased, and the price of a bride ranges from five to sixteen rupees. With regard to intermarriage there are no distinctions of caste among the Santāls, but there are differences of tribe; each tribe forming a kind of separate caste. A curious custom prevails of not permitting a youth to take a wife of the same tribe as himself.

Emerging from the homestead, which served as a fair sample of Santāl family-life, we proceeded to the centre of the village, where in an open space was a small shed roofed over with circular tiles and supported by four posts and a central pole. Its clay floor, smeared with cow-dung, was raised about two feet from the ground, and on one side of the central pole were ranged what resembled three thick nine-pins, roughly moulded out of clay and made somewhat thicker in the centre. The whole Santāl community firmly believe that these are tenanted by the spirits of the last three head-men (Manjhī) of the village. and the simple shed-like shrine which contains them is therefore called the Manjhī-thān or abode of the Manjhīs. To these clay representatives of their dead chiefs daily offerings are made, and it struck me that Africa itself could not afford a better illustration of genuine fetish-worship. 'They cleared the jungle for us, they watched over the cultivation of our fields, and it is now our turn to support them by our offerings.' Such was the explanation given by the villagers themselves.

Further on we came upon the village-weaver. His loom was of the simplest construction. A hole dug in the ground served as a receptacle for his legs and a quantity of branches formed a roof over his head. Half hidden in that well-like cavity he sat patiently at work to supply the wants of his fellow-villagers. We were told, that a hard-working man could weave five yards a day of a kind of rough unbleached cloth.

Before leaving the street we were invited to witness a Santāl dance. Three young men stood in a row holding drums (tom-toms), two of which were beaten with the hand and one with sticks. Then a row of eight girls filed out of their dwellings looking bright and modest. These clasped hands together, each girl bending her fingers upwards through the fingers of the next girl and turning the other palm towards us. In this way they made a quiet movement backwards and forwards, advancing and retiring with joined hands to the sound of the drums or occasionally moving sideways and singing a low quaint melody. The effect was simple and the combination of dance and song was on the whole pleasing and attractive. It seems that dancing, singing and feasting together make up a considerable portion of the every-day life of every Santāl community.

Passing out of the street we noticed that the village was surrounded with well-cultivated paddy fields. Here and there flocks and herds were grazing and nowhere could we detect any signs of poverty. Yet Santāl men are decidedly lazy, and in the winter do very little work beyond using their bows and arrows in hunting for game. When the rain comes they may be seen exerting themselves a little to turn up the soil. But even then the women have to make up for the laziness of the men. They not only cook for the family, but are expected to work in the fields, reap the harvest and carry the grain on their heads for storing at home.

Just outside the village was the sacred grove, which always consists of Ṡāl-trees—tall stately trees, not unlike poplars. Under a cluster of three of these trees planted close together (compare p. 332) we noticed rude erections consisting of four poles with three crossing at the top to keep the structures together. It is in these that the six great Bongās or Demon-Spirits named Jāhererā, Monreko, Turuiko, Marāng Buru, Gosāeera and Pergana Bongā are believed to reside. Of these six Marāng Buru is thought to have most power over human beings. Indeed, although the Santāls believe in the existence of one Supreme God, they consider that He need not be worshipped since He has no dealings with His creatures except through the great demon-spirit Marāng Buru, who alone requires any real adoration and propitiation. He is a supreme Being it is true, but He resides too far away in the inaccessible orb of the Sun; He is even identified with the Sun, and the Sun is therefore saluted every morning (compare pp. 62, 406), and a festival held in his honour at intervals of three, five, seven or ten years.

Yet it is certain that Heliolatry is not a real element in the religion of the Santāls. Such religion as they possess consists rather in Demonolatry—that is, in the worship of demon-spirits (Bongās) combined with ancestor-worship. In this respect the aboriginal tribes closely resemble the great majority of the unlettered and ignorant Hindūs of the mixed Āryan race who live around them.

Yet it should be noted that the worship of a man's own deceased ancestors is thought to be a duty which is not so obligatory on a Santāl as the homage due to the departed spirits of the head-men of his own village; for his belief is that the interests of the community ought to take precedence of those of the family.

As to the worship of demons and spirits, it is not, of course, limited to Marāng Buru or to any of the six enumerated above; for demon-spirits are innumerable. They haunt the air, pervade the waters, ride on the winds, and are to be found everywhere, being particularly fond of residing in trees and sometimes dwelling in animals and even in men. They influence for good or evil all the affairs and events of life; and if they are not well supplied with food and offerings, they become very spiteful and vindictive, causing diseases, producing storms and blighting crops [1].

These demon-spirits, however, are not represented by images (compare pp. 243; 249). We have already seen that rude nine-pins like lumps of clay are set up in roughly constructed shrines, as representatives of the spirits of the head-men. In contradistinction to these clay fetishes, lumps of quartz, smeared with red paint, are deposited under trees to represent the demon-spirits (Bongās) dwelling in the sacred groves. Several feasts are held in honour of the demon-spirits, but the chief festival of the year is that called Soharai at the begin-

---

[1] They will apparently take possession of hysterical persons, who, when so possessed, jump and run about, writhe and contort their limbs, or speak in the name of some demon, perhaps, to some terrified villager, or calling out and saying:—'I am come to eat your wife, if you do not wish her to be killed (by some disease) you must give a goat to propitiate the demon.'

ning of January. Mr. Stevenson describes it as a kind of harvest festival, which lasts for four or five days in each village; but as the period of its celebration varies in different places, every community invites the other to its own feast, and in this way the feasting may be prolonged for a month. There is much drinking of strong liquor, distilled from Mahwa flowers, the method of distilling which is supposed to have been revealed by the chief demon, Marāng Buru.

In fact, a Santāl has no idea of any form of worship except that of propitiating an irascible being by offerings of food and sacrifices of fowls and other animals, of which the worshippers partake themselves. His religion is one of much eating and drinking and carousing. He has no conception of sin in the Christian sense; nor would he dream of asking pardon for any error, except that of omitting to make a sufficient number of oblations. No act of immorality, according to his ideas, can possibly offend a Bongā. If a villager sins against a fellow-villager, a money compensation to the person sinned against expiates all the guilt.

Then each family has its own special Bongā belonging to the household which must be propitiated every day, and is on special occasions very exacting. If, after receiving his due mead of offerings and invocations, he does nothing for the fulfilment of the wishes of the family, he is abused in decidedly strong and vituperative language[1].

Then Bongās often dwell in ferocious animals, such as tigers and leopards, and when a Bongā occupies human beings or otherwise harmless animals, it may make them fierce and dangerous.

When we were passing through the Santāl district, we were gravely warned to beware of an elephant which had been

---

[1] For instance:—'I gave you a goat and you ought to be ashamed of yourself, you are a brute (or some equivalent expression) for not having cured my son.'

selected by a Bongā for its habitation, and had killed several people who had before found it tractable and good-tempered.

In regard to death-ceremonies, I was informed that the occasion of a death among the Santāls is always made an excuse for a feast. Then after the corpse is cremated, five small bones or pieces of bone are searched for among the ashes. If portions of the skull or collar-bone can be found they are preferred to any other fragments[1]. These are carefully placed in an earthen lotā, and are either preserved in the house of the nearest relative or are buried under a tree until an opportunity occurs of making a pilgrimage to the river Dāmodar[2], which is the sacred river of the Santāls. In due course of time the nearest relative carries these pieces of bone to the sacred stream, taking with him some bread for offerings. Next he erects three rude altars on the bank, and entering the water, first immerses his own body and then scatters the bony fragments on the stream, allowing the current to bear them away.

Finally he makes three offerings of bread on the altars—one to Marāng Buru, calling on that spirit to introduce his relative to the world of spirits; another to the spirits of his ancestors, inviting them to receive the recently deceased man; and a third to the spirit of the dead man himself, at the same time expressing a hope that every possible steps have been taken for the furtherance of his welfare in the other world.

These strange superstitions, as well as those previously described, point to a close connexion with Hindūism, and testify to the fact of a constant interaction and interfusion of religious ideas between Āryan and Non-Āryan races (see pp. 274–312).

It is this interaction between Brāhmanical pantheism and the pre-existing cults and superstitions, not only of aboriginal

---

[1] Compare the funeral ceremony witnessed by me at Bombay, described in my work 'Modern India and the Indians' (Trübner and Co.), p. 97.

[2] Dāmodara is a name of Kṛishṇa and also of a river in Bengal.

races, but of Drāviḍians and Buddhists, that has led to the production of the composite and complex religious system which, from the absence of any one founder or supreme Head, and from the want of a general name applied to it by the Hindūs themselves, we have been obliged to designate by the double title—'Brāhmanism and Hindūism'—a system which, as I have explained in the Preface to this volume, is really no system, but rather a vast mosaic, inlaid with every variety of idea which the human mind, unaided by any true supernatural inspiration, is able to conceive and elaborate for itself.

And the reader who looks back on the foregoing pages will, I think, bear me out when I assert that I have had no light task in endeavouring to bring some kind of order out of a chaotic confusion of creeds, traditions and usages, overlaid with some of the worst superstitions which have ever degraded the human race at any time or in any country.

We may speak of this complicated system as peculiar to India and the Indians, but in real fact the pantheistic ideas on which it rests and its cardinal doctrines of Self-evolution, self-evolved righteousness, and self-created new-births, belong quite as much to other nations, and are the spontaneous product of every human thinker's inborn faculties and instincts, when they work naturally.

Our conviction is that Hindūism will ultimately crumble to pieces when brought more fully into contact with the truths of Christianity. But it may be predicted that, as long as human nature and the human mind remain what they are, so long will this subjectively evolved creed, though its doctrines and its gods may be called by other names, continue to prevail in various parts of the world, and its more philosophic phases continue to commend themselves to those who deny that there is any other source of authority in religion than a man's own innate personal intuitions, and any other external revelation than the book of Nature.

INDEX.

OBSERVE—In the following Index the numbers indicate the pages. When more than one page is given the numbers are separated by semicolons. A unit separated from a preceding number by a comma indicates the number of a foot-note.

Abbé Dubois, 555.
Abhisheka, 68.
Abhisheka-pātra (vessel), 412.
Abstinence (total), 195.
Ābū (Mount), 349.
Āćamana, 144; 401; 407.
Āćamanīya, 415.
Āćārya (worship of), 101; 116; 117.
Aćārya-tarpaṇa, 410.
A-ćit, 120.
Activity, 36.
Acts (five Śākta), 192–196.
Adam (Mr. W.), 485.
Adbhuta-brāhmaṇa, 398.
Adhika-māsa, 433.
Adhishṭhāna-deha, 28; 293, 1.
Adhyāpaka, 515.
Ādibrāhma-Samāj, 493; 526.
Ādi-Granth, 161; 169.
Aditi, 15; 182; 223.
Āditya, 75.
Ādityas, 10.
A-dvaita, 122; 139; 142.
Advaita-drohiṇaḥ, 86.
Afghānistān, 4.
Āgama, 185; (Sacred Books of the Śaivas), 89.
Āgama-prakāśa, 94; 189, 1.
Agastya, 421.
Age (Dvāpara), 111; (Kali), 114; 163; (Satya), 109; (Tretā), 110.
Ages (four), 433.
Agha-marshaṇa, 404.
Aghora-panthī, 87; 94.
Aghorī, 87; 94.
Agnāyī, 14; 182.
Agni, 5; 9; 10; 15.
Agnihotṛi-Brāhmans, 50.
Agni-Nārāyaṇa, 50.
Agnishṭoma, 368.
Agra, 175; (Fort), 272.
Aham-kāra, 31; 32.
Ahi, 320.
Ahmedābād, 149.
Ahobala, 129.
Āhuti (offerings), 425.
Air, 20; 30.
Airāvata, 109.
Aitareya-brāhmaṇa, 21; 24; 102.
Ajagava, 81.
Ajmere, 529; 559.
Ajñāna, 35.
Ājya, 367.
Akālī, 175.
Ākāśa (ether), 30.
Akbar (Emperor), 318.
Akhay Kumār Datta, 492.
Akshatāḥ, 420.
Akshaya-vaṭa (tree), 337.
Alchemy (Śākta idea of), 206.
Alībāg, 392.
Allahābād (camp-meeting at), 136.
All Souls' day, 275, 3.
Alopī (shrine of), 226.
Āmalakī, 339; 568.
Amar-dās, 164.
Amaru-Śataka, 56, 2.
Ambā (mother), 222.
Ammans (mothers), 228.
Amṛita, 108.
Amṛita-sar (tank), 165; (temple at), 175; (town), 166.
Amṛita-vapuḥ, 106, 1.
Amṛitsar. *See* Amṛita-sar.
Amulet, 204; 468.
An-adhyāya, 433.
Anala, 82.
Ānanda, 34.
Ānanda-giri, 59.
Ānanda-tīrtha, 130.
An-anta, 323.
Ananteśvar, 130.
Anaryan, 388, 1.
Anavalopana, 356.
Ancestor-worship, 72; 274.
Andhaka, 81.
Aṅga, 164.
Aṅgada, 164.
Aṅgarakha, 395.
Anger (personified), 404, 1.
Āṅgirasa, 407.
Aṅgushṭha-mātra, 291.
Animal-life (sacredness of), 118; 316.
Animal-marriages, 327.
Animal-sacrifice, 13; 369; 393.
Animal-worship, 72; 313.
Animals (sacred), 327; 328.
Animishaḥ, 106, 1.
Animism, 339; 340.
Aṅkana (branding), 132.
Anna-prāśana, 353; 358.
Anna-pūrṇā, 87, 2; 439.
Aṇśa, 142.
Aṇśa-rūpiṇī, 187.
Antar-vedi, 282.
Antaryāmin, 123.
Anthropomorphism, 7.
Antyeshṭi, 22; 394; 532.
Anumāna, 39.
An-upalabdhi, 39, 1.
Anurādha-pura, 338.
Anuśāsana-parvan, 78; 105.
Anushṭhānika, 524.
Anustaraṇī, 282, 1.
Āpaḥ (water), 30.
Apām-napāt, 346.
Apa-smāra, 441.
Ap-liṅga, 446.
Apsaras, 237; 238.
Araṇi, 9; 364; 368.
Arddha-maṇḍapa, 447.
Ardha-nārī, 85.
Ardha-nārīśa, 225.

Arghya, 404; 415.
Arghya-dāna, 404.
Arishṭa, 193.
Aristotle, 105, 1.
Arjun, 164; 165; (tomb of), 174; 175.
Arjuna, 63; 271; 272.
Arka (tree), 338.
Arrack, 193.
Arrows (five, of Love), 200.
Arrowy bed, 560; 561.
Artha, 388.
Arthāpatti, 39, 1.
Ārti, 94.
Arts (Indian), 462; 468.
Aruṇa, 104, 3.
Ārya, 4.
Ārya-dharma, 20; 53; 55.
Aryaman, 5.
Āryans, 223; 244; (early religion of), 11.
Ārya-Samāj, 529.
Āryāvarta, 517; 531.
Āsana, 415.
Āśāpūrā, 227.
Aśauća, 288; 571.
Ascetics (Aghora-panthī), 87; (Ākāśa-mukhin), 87; (Kāpālika), 88; Liṅgavat), 88; (Śaiva), 86-88; (Ūrdhva-bāhu), 87; (at Benares), 87, 2; (at Bombay), 91; (at Gayā), 87, 2; (Daṇḍin), 87.
Asclepias Acida, 12.
Ashes (application of), 400; (act of taking up), 420.
Asiatic (Journal), 432; 511, 1.
Aśoka (tree), 338.
Āśrama, 154.
Āśramas (four), 362.
Association (Reform), 506.
Asthi-sañćaya, 284; 300; 302.
Asthi-vilaya-tīrtham (at Nāsik), 301.
Astrologer (family), 372; (village), 457.
Āsura, 235; 236; 237.
Āśvalāyana, 281; 356; 358.
Aśva-medha, 8; 24; 329.
Aśvattha (tree), 83; 335.
Aśvāvatāra, 114.
Aśvins, 9; 271; 341.
Atala, 102, 1.
Atharva-veda, 8; 9; 15; 21; 182, 2; 238.
Ati-kṛićchra (fast), 427.
Atithi-pūjana, 423, 1.
Ātivāhika, 28.
Ātman (or Ātmā), 20; 26; 27; 31, 2; 33; 34; 37; 85; 95, 2; xxi.
Ātmārām Pāndurang (Dr.), 526.
Ātmīya-Sabhā (society), 482.
Atmosphere, 5.
AUM, 44.
Aurangzīb (Emperor), 166; 168; 477; (mosque of), 437.
Aurdhva-dehikam, 293, 1.
Aushadham, 106.
Avadāna, 368.
Āvāhana (invocation), 19; 415; 418.
Avatāra, 47; 62; 63; 97.
Avayava, 39.
A-vyakta, 30.
Axe (Rāma with), 110.
Āyatana, 413.
Ayenār, 209; 218-220; 245.
Ayenār-appan, 218.
Ayodhyā (Oudh), 110.

Bābar (Emperor), 161.
Babylonia, 313.
Bacchus (Indian), 12.
Baḍavā-mukhaḥ, 106.
Badrināth, 55, 1.
Bagalā (or Vagalā), 118.
Bahādur Shāh, 168.
Baitaraṇī. See Vaitaraṇī.
Bālā-ji, 267.
Bālak-dās, 179.
Bāla-Kṛishṇa, 136.
Bala-rāma, 112; 113; 195; 270; 323.
Bali (sacrifice), 25; 393.
Bali (tyrant-demon), 104, 2; 110; 233.
Bali-gāyatrī, 201.
Bali-haraṇa (ceremony), 329; 394; 418; 421.
Balinī, 188.
Balkh, 4.
Bām-i-dunyā, 3.
Bāṇa, 104, 2.
Bāṇa-liṅga, 69; 392; 412; 561.
Banāras, 434, 1.
Banerjea (Dr. K. M.), 121; 123; 322, 1.
Banyan, 337.
Baptism (self), 403.
Barber (village), 459; (professional), 374.
Barth (A.), 19; 211, 1.
Basaba, 88; (purāṇa), 88.
Basil (holy), 333.
Bathing (religious), 393; 399.
Bāval or Babul (tree), 399, 1.
Bazaars (Indian), 463.
Beaconsfield, Lord (late), 88, 2.
Beatification, 41; 118; 234.
Bećarājī, 227.
Bell (adoration of), 414.
Benares, 50; 272; 434; (Śrāddha at), 308.
Bentinck (Lord W.), 490.
Berāī, 227.
Berkeley, 33, 1; 132.
Betrothal (ceremony of), 377.
Bhādrotsab, 504.
Bhagat, 87, 1; (Sikh saints), 162; 169.
Bhagavad-gītā, 63, 2; 116; 235.
Bhāgavata-purāṇa, 45; 116; 141.
Bhairava, 82; 85.
Bhairavī, 188.
Bhakta, 87, 1.
Bhakta-mālā, 147.
Bhakti, 97.
Bhakti-mārga, 63.
Bhakti-sūtras, 63, 2; 97.
Bhāṇḍāra (of a Bhūta), 248.
Bhāṇḍārkar (Prof.), 121, 1; 528.
Bharata, 47.
Bhāratavarshīya Brāhma-Samāj, 502.
Bhāskarāćārya (astronomer), 146; 202.
Bhasma-dhāraṇa, 399.
Bhāṭ, 169.
Bhava, 85.
Bhavānī, 79.
Bhikshu, 53; 55; 362.
Bhikshukas, 386
Bhīma, 271; 272; 322.
Bhīshma, 561-564.
Bhog, 170.
Bhogavatī, 322.
Bhojana-vidhi, 423.
Bhṛigu, 45; 46; 52, 1; 264.
Bhṛigu-pāta (suicide), 349.
Bhṛiṅgi, 441.
Bhroach, 337; 569.
Bhūmyā, 243.
Bhūr, 9; 102, 1; 403.
Bhūta, 82; 241.
Bhūta-bhāvana, 83.
Bhūta-pūjā, 71.
Bhūta-sthān, 249.
Bhūta-śuddhi, 197.
Bhūta-yajña, 421.
Bhuvaḥ, 9.
Bhuvaneśvara (temple of), 68, 3; 93.
Bhuvaneśvarī, 188.
Bhuvar, 102, 1; 234; 403.

Bible (Hindu), 8; (of nomistic Brāhmanism), 52; (Śaiva), 73; (Śākta), 184; (Sikh), 158; 161; 165; (Vaishṇava), 116; (of tenth Guru), 167.
Bickersteth (Bishop), 516.
Bīja, 197–202.
Bīl (leaves), 90.
Bilva (Vilva-tree), 336.
Bīrbhūm, 332.
Bird (Garuḍa), 104; 327.
Birds (of ill-omen), 329; 398.
Birdwood (Sir George), 460.
Birth-record, 372.
Blacksmith (village), 459.
Blessedness (stages of), 10.
Bliss (pure), 34; (method of obtaining), 444; (three conditions of), 118.
Boar, 109.
Bodh-gayā. *See* Buddha-Gayā.
Body (causal), 35; (gross), 28; 35; (subtle), 28; 35.
Bombay (burning-ground), 284; 302.
Bone-gathering ceremony, 284; 300; 302.
Bose (Ānanda Mohan), 513; (Rāj Narāin), 478; 494; 496; 500; 511, 2; 514; 526, 1; (S. C.), 295; 306; 307; 429.
Bo-tree (Bodhi-druma), 338.
Bow (miraculous), 109; (Vishṇu's), 104.
Brahmā, 2; 3; 21; 25; 34; 35; 43; 409.
Brahma, 2; 3; 102, 1.
Brahmā, 31, 2; 36; 44; 48; 65; 66, 1; 95; (worship of), 555–569.
Brahmaćārī, 55; 84; 151; 362.
Brahmādi-stamba, 44, 1.
Brahma-dvish, 237.
Brahma-karma-pustaka, 401.
Brahma-loka, 54; 291.
Brahman (the God), 21; 26.
Brāhman. *See* Brāhmans.
Brāhma-dharma, 494.
Brāhmaṇas, 21; 52; (story in), 356; (doctrine of), 140.
Brāhmanhood (two badges of), 374.
Brāhmanism, 2; 3; 19–55; 97; (four phases of), 21; (fundamental doctrine of), 20; 21; (mythological), 41–51; (nomistic), 51–53; (pantheism of), 224; (philosophical), 25–41; (ritualistic), 21–24; (theory of), 180.
Brāhmans, 2; 53; (acts and duties of), 393; 394; (A-yengār), 129; (god of), 84; (Mantra-śāstrīs), 199; (race), 353; (two classes of), 386; (Vaidik), 386; (Vedic), 50; (wife of), 394.
Brahmaṇyaḥ, 106, 1.
Brahma-randhram, 291.
Brāhma-Sabhā, 486.
Brāhma-Samāj, 491–529; (of India), 502–526; (schism in), 510; (festivals), 504.
Brahma-sambandha, 136.
Brahma-vid, 84.
Brahma-yajña, 393; 408.
Brahmīya-Samāj, 486.
Brahmopāsanā, 493.
Brāhmotsava (festival), 510.
Branding (ceremony of), 129; (Madhva), 132; 133.
Brands (Śaiva), 67; (Ten-galai), 127; (Vaishṇava), 67; 118.
Breath (exercise), 402.
Bṛihad-āraṇyaka Upanishad, 26; 29; 182.
Bṛihas-pati, 215.
Bṛishotsarga. *See* Vṛishotsarga.
Broach. *See* Bhroach.
Buddha, 42; 58; 64; 114; 338.
Buddha-Gayā, 272; 338.
Buddhi, 27; 31; 32; 215, 2.
Buddhism, 3; 41; 58; 97; 114.
Buddhists, 3.
Buffalo (Yama's), 104, 3.
Bull (Śiva's), 104, 3.
Burial-ground, 94.
Burnell, Dr. (late), 13, 1; 52, 1; 56, 1; 62, 1; 247.
Burning-ground, 279; 284; 302.
Butter (clarified), 6.

C'aitanya (life of), 138; 139; 140; 142; 476; 515.
C'aitanya-ćaritāmṛita, 144.
C'akra, 103.
C'akravartī (Nīlāmbar), 138.
Caldwell (Bishop), 251.
Camp-meeting, 261.
C'ampāraṇya (forest), 134.
C'āmuṇḍā, 188, 1; 228.
C'āṇḍālas, 422.
C'andana (sandal), 144; 308; 415.
C'andra, 108.
C'āndrāyaṇa-vrata (fast), 427.
C'araṇāmṛita, 137.
Car-festival (Jagan-nāth), 447.
Carpenter (Miss Mary), 478, 1.
Carpenter (village), 459.
Cashmere, 1; 4.
Caste (institution of), 17; 18; 53; 128, 1; (in relation to trades and industries), 452–474; 487, 1; (abolition of, among Sikhs), 167; (definition of), 471; (kingly and military), 98; 110; (subordination of), 139; (temporary suppression of), 192, 1; (tyranny of), 298; 472; (equality of), 377; (abolition of), 499.
Cat (sacred), 328.
Cat-hold theory, 125.
C'āturmāsya (sacrifice), 368.
C'aturthī-karma, 354.
C'aula, 353; 359.
Cause (material), 119.
Caves (Buddhistic), 271.
Census, 452; 525.
Ceremonies (at Liṅga Shrine), 89–91; (domestic), 52; (funeral and Śrāddha), 288; (over a corpse), 297; (Śaiva), 89–94; (name-giving), 370; (Śākta), 192–196; (Śrāddha), 284; (Tambila), 248.
Ceylon, 245; 313.
Chamār, 179.
Chanda-pur, 323.
C'handas, 7.
C'hāndogya Upanishad, 26; 34.
Chapāī, 148.
Charms, 197–202; 254.
C'haṭhī (goddess), 229.
Chatīsgarh, 179.
Chatterjea (Nagendra-nāth), 478.
Child-marriages, 385; 387; 500.
Child-widows, 388.
Children's attire, 397.
China, 313.
C'hinna-mastakā, 188.
Christianity, 3, and Vaishṇavism (compared), 119.
Churel (demon), 229.
Circles (holy), 196.
Circumambulation, 68, 2; 145; 334; 348; 415.
C'it, 34; 120.

C'it-pāvan (tribe of Brāhmans), 271, 1; 311.
C'itra-gupta, 292; 425.
C'itrāhuti, 425.
C'itra-kūṭa, 147; 349.
C'itriṇī (woman), 389.
C'itta-vṛitti-nirodha, 48.
Class (Smārta), 95; (Śaivas), 95; (Vaishṇava), 95.
Classes (four distinct), 53; (three principal Hindū), 95.
Cleanliness, 88.
Club (Musala), 112; (Vishṇu's), 103; 104.
Coiling-folk, 324.
Colebrooke, 417, 2.
Collet (Miss S. G.), 475, 1.
Colombo, 247.
Commerce (Indian and European compared), 454.
Conch-shell, 92; 103; 104; 109; 412; 413.
Conjīvaram = Kāñjīvaram.
Continuity (law of), 330.
Converts (Christian), 1.
Cooking (of food), 128; 423.
Council (village), 456.
Courtezans (Indian), 451.
Cow (of plenty), 108; (sacredness of), 172; (worship of), 317; 318.
Cowell (Prof.), 119; 122; 123; 133.
Cowherdesses, 136.
Cowman (village), 459.
Cows (sacrificed), 195.
Creation (description of), 13.
Creator, 45.
Creed (Āryan), 53; (Brāhman), 523; (Hindū), 37; (of modern Theism), 503.
Cremation, 281; 299; 518; 519, 1; 569–572.
Crocodiles (sacred), 328.
Crosses (sacred), 90.
Crows (sacred), 329.
C'uḍel (demon), 229.

Dādū, 178; 268.
Dādū-panthī, 178.
Daityas, 233; 238.
Daiva, 235.
Daivika (Śrāddha), 305.
Ḍākiṇī, 189.
Daksha (sage), 82.
Dakshiṇā (gift), 308.
Dakshiṇa-mārgī, 185.
Ḍamaru, 81.
Damdamā, 168.
Dānavas, 233; 238.
Dancing (religious), 141; 451; (demoniacal), 246; 247; 248.
Daṇḍa, xxi note.
Daṇḍa-dhara, 290.
Daṇḍin (Śaiva ascetic), 87.
Dārā-gañj, 323.
Darbār Sāhib, 175.
Darbha Śrāddha, 306.
Darkness (indifference), 31.
Darśana, 61, 1; 152.
Dāruṇī rātriḥ, 204.
Darvi (spoon), 420.
Dāsa (slave), 358.
Daśa-harā (festival), 329.
Daśa-nāmī Daṇḍins, 87.
Daśāṅgula, 414, 1.
Daśa-ratha, 110.
Dāsya, 141.
Dasyus, 237.
Datta (Akhay Kumār), 492.
Dattātreya, 205; 267.
Dawn, 9; (goddess), 182.
Dawns (personified), 407.
Dayābhāga, 286, 1.
Dayānanda Sarasvatī, 529–531.
Dead (the condition of), 274.
Death, 274; (present Hindū creed regarding), 291.
Debendra-nāth Tāgore, 491; 498; 514; 531.
Dehū, 265.
Deification, 258; (Chinese), 262; (local), 263.
Deities (favourite presiding), 50; (tutelary), 209–229.
Demon-dancing, 246; 247.
Demon and devil (not convertible terms), 231.
Demon-festivals, 247.
Demon-host (lord of), 215; 218; (three classes), 241.
Demon-kings (seven), 236.
Demonophobia, 210.
Demons (character of), 234; (corporeal organization of), 235; (destroyed by Vishṇu), 104, 2; (numbers of), 234; (orders of), 213; (two great divisions of), 236.
Demon-shrines, 243.
Demon-worship, 71; 230–256.
Dennehy (General), 534.
Dervishes, 141, 1.
Deshmukh (Gopāl Hari), 94, 2; 189, 1; 200, 2; 208; 311; 401, 2.
Destroying-god, 9.
Dev (deva, god), 272, 1.
Deva-ćakra, 196.
Deva-dāsī, 451.
Devakī, 111; 112; 113.
Deva-pūja, 394; 411; 573.
Devas, 4.
Devatā-pūjana, 394, 1.
Deva-tarpaṇa, 409.
Devayānī, 194, 1; 214.
Devī, 185.
Devil and demon (not convertible terms), 231.
Devil-dancing, 246; 247; 248.
Devil-region, 245.
Devil-worship, 244; 251.
Devotee (at Bombay), 92.
Dhan, 117.
Dhanna, 169.
Dhanus, 109.
Dhanush-koṭi, 444; 445.
Dhanvantari, 108; 422.
Dharma, 290; 388.
Dharma-rāja, 290.
Dharma-śālā (clergy asylum), 153.
Dharma-śāstra, 51.
Dharma-tattva, 510, 1; 513.
Dhēr, 249; 250.
Dhol-pur (ceremony at), 573.
Dhoti, 395.
Dhṛita-rāshṭra, 322.
Dhūmāvatī, 188.
Ḍhunḍhi-rāja, 218, 1.
Ḍhunḍhirāj Vināyak Sudās, 392.
Dhūpa, 415.
Dhūrjaṭi, 83.
Diagrams (mystical), 203.
Dig-ambara, 83.
Digby (Mr.), 480.
Dīkshā, 61; 117; 191.
Dīnanāth, 155.
Dining (ceremony of), 423.
Dīpa, 415.
Directory (Theistic), 494.
Disintegration (act of), 74; 75.
Dissolver, 44.
Diti, 182.
Dīvālī (festival), 432; 529.
Dṅyāneśvara, 266.
Dṅyāno-bā, 266.
Doctrine (Vedānta), 53; (Hindū, various phases of), 71; 72; (four principles of theistic), 495.
Dog (sacred), 328.
Dog-demon, 243.
Dogs (watch), 289.
Dolā-yātrā (festival), 430.
Domestic rules (Ancient Hindū), 353.
Domestic worship (Hindū), 352.

Drākshā, 192.
Drākshārāmeśvara, 446, 5.
Draupadī, 271.
Draupadī-Amman, 271.
Drāvaṇa-bāṇa, 200.
Drāviḍians, 244.
Dravya, 40.
Dress (of Indian household), 395.
Dṛishadvatī (river), 51.
Dṛishṭi-dosha, 128.
Dṛiśyam, 119.
Dualism, 37.
Duality (in the divine unity), 29; (doctrine of), 130; 131; (first dawn of), 181; (enunciated), 182; 183.
Dubois, 202, 1.
Duff (Dr.), 316; 485.
Durgā, 72; 188, 1; 185; 197; 198.
Durgā-pūjā, 197; 198; 431.
Dūrvā (grass), 338.
Duryodhana, 322.
Duties (six daily), 158, 1.
Dvaita, 130.
Dvāpara (age), 111; 433.
Dvārakā-nāth Tāgore, 482; 485.
Dvārikā, 55, 1; 113; 400, 2.
Dvi-ja, 361.
Dwarf, 110.
Dyaus (heaven), 182.
Dyaus, Zeus (worship of), 223.
Dyaus-pitar, Jupiter (worship of), 223.
Dynasties (warrior), 43.
Dyu (or Dyaus), 8.
Dyupitar, 4.

Ear (sacredness of), 405, 2.
Ear-boring, 360; 376.
Early Ideas (by Anaryan), 388, 1.
Earth (Pṛithivī or Bhūmi), 30; 182.
Earth-spirit, 243.
Egypt, 313.
Ekam-eva-advitīyam, 34.
Ekāmranātha, 446.
Ekoddishṭam (Śrāddha), 305.
Elements (five subtle), 30.
Elephant (Indra's), 104, 3; (mythical), 108.
Elephanta (caves of), 74, 1; 82; 85, 1; 236, 1.
Elephant-worship, 328.
Ella-amman, 228.
Ellorā (caves of), 84, 2; (temple at), 71, 1.

Entity, 2; 29.
Entities (tri-unity of), 34.
Envelopes (three corporeal), 35.
Epicureans of India, 135.
Epithets (of Śiva and Vishṇu), 105; 106; 107; 239.
Eras (four Hindū), 433.
Ether (Ākāśa), 30.
Evil eye, 253; 254.
Evil (impersonations of), 238.
Evolution (doctrine of), 43.
Existence, 34.
Exorcisers (professional), 241; 246.

Fair (religious), 429.
Faith (doctrine of), 63, 1; 97.
Fakīrs, 87, 1.
Family-religion (Hindū), 352; 370.
Fasting (Hindū powers of), 426.
Fasts (special Hindū), 427.
Fātiḥah, 403.
Fergusson (Mr.), 313; 330.
Festival (Pūrṇimā), 151; 152.
Festivals (of the left-hand worshippers), 204; (time of), 431; (special), 428; (Brāhma-Samāj), 504.
Fetishism, 340; 341.
Fever-gāyatrī, 201.
Fig-tree (sacred), 9; 399.
Figures (twenty-four mystical), 406.
Fingers (consecration of), 405.
Fire, 10; 20; (god of), 420; (Tejas or Jyotis), 30.
Fire-god, 9; 15.
Fires (sacred), 281; 282.
Fire-worship, 2; 346; 364.
Fish, 107; (sacred), 328; (Varuṇa's), 104, 3.
Fish-gāyatrī, 201.
Flood, 107.
Food (secrecy in preparation of), 128.
Fortune-tellers, 202.
Foulkes (Mr.), 440, 3.
Free-will (doctrine of), 125.
Fruits (sacred), 339.
Funeral (and Śrāddha ceremonies compared), 285; (ceremonies), 278; (ceremonies in Vedic times), 279; (Hindū), 276; (of a child), 287.
Funeral-pile, 299.
Funerals (expense of), 278.
Furniss (Rev. J.), 232, 3.

Gadā, 103.
Gadaḍā, 150.
Gādi (chair), 135.
Gaṇa, 85.
Gaṇa-pati, 77; 211.
Gaṇapatim gaṇānām, 413.
Gāṇapatyas, 59.
Gaṇas, 79.
Gaṇḍakī (river), 69; 347.
Gandha, 66; 415.
Gandharvas, 237; 238.
Gāṇḍiva, 272.
Gaṇeśa, 48; 62; 79; 392; (temple), 440; (worship of), 211-217.
Gaṇeśa and Sūbrahmaṇya (contrasted), 215.
Gaṇeśa-ćaturthī (festival), 431.
Gaṅgā-putra, 347; 570.
Gaṅgāshṭaka, 399.
Ganges, 80; 295; 347.
Garbha (sanctuary), 445.
Garbhādhāna, 353; 354.
Garbha-gṛiham, 440.
Gārgya, 407.
Gārpagāri, 241.
Garuḍa (vehicle), 65; (bird), 104; 288; 321; 327.
Garuḍa-purāṇa, 288; 293; 298; 301.
Gati (refuge), 260.
Gauḍī, 193.
Gaurī, 80, 2.
Gautama, 42.
Gautamīya (Tantra), 207.
Gaya, 81; 309.
Gāyatrī, 19; 342; 403; (translation of), 19; 361; (upadeśa), 362.
Gāyatrī-japa, 406.
Gāyatrī Mantras, 200; 201.
Gayāwāls, 310.
Gems (magical), 468.
Genesis (viii. 21), 12, 1.
Ghana (recitation), 409.
Ghaṇṭā (bell), 144.
Ghaṇṭā-maṇḍapa, 447.
Ghaṇṭā-mudrā, 414.
Ghāsī-dās, 179.
Ghāṭ (at Benares), 435; (Nim Tollah), 518; 519, 1.
Ghaṭaka, 377.
Ghose (Pratāpa-ćandra), 197.
Girgaum House, 381.
Girls (dancing), 450; (Indian), 387.
Girnār (hill), 349.
Gīta-govinda, 114; 146.
Gobhila, 354, 1.
Godāvarī, 295.

Goddess-worship, 180–196.
Gods (ancient Vedic), 182; (animal attendants of), 104, 3; (Brāhman), 44; (five Hindū), 392; (number of), 417, 1; (offerings to all the), 420; (structure of the bodies of), 28; (worship of the), 411.
Gokula, 113.
Golden temple, 436.
Goloka, 118; 291.
Gomeda (gem), 468.
Go-mukha, 348.
Gomukhī (bag), 92; 406.
Goodness, 36.
Gopāl Hari Deshmukh, 94, 2; 189, 1; 200, 2; 208.
Gopatha-brāhmaṇa, 21.
Gopī-ćandana, 67; 400, 2.
Gopīs (cowherdesses), 113; 136.
Gorakhpur, 158.
Goreh (Rev. Nehemiah), 373, 1; 422, 2; 536.
Gosāins, 87; 135; 142.
Gosāinjī, 135.
Goshṭhī-Śrāddha, 305.
Gospel (St. John's), 419, 2.
Gotroććāra (ceremony), 407.
Gough (Prof.), 37, 1; 119; 122; 130; 131; 133.
Govardhana (mountain), 113.
Govind (bible of), 167; (character of), 168; (shrine of), 175; 176.
Govinda, 405.
Govind-Siṇh, 164; 166; 167.
Grace (before dinner), 424.
Grain (parched), 192; 193.
Grāma-devatā, 209.
Grant (Sir A.), 265.
Granth or Grantha (bible of Sikhs), 158; 165; (arrangement of), 170; (passages from), 171; (teaching of), 172; (worship of), 172; 177.
Graphic, 255, 1.
Grasses (sacred), 338.
Greece, 313.
Gṛihastha (householder), 138; 150; 362; 386.
Gṛihiṇī, 397.
Gṛihyāgni, 365.
Gṛihya-Sūtras, 281.
Groves (sacred), 332.
Guhyaḥ, 106, 1.
Gujarāt, 113; 225.
Guṇas, 30; 31; 36; 163.
Gupta (protected), 358.
Guru, 352; (derivation of), 161; (Vaishṇava), 142.
Guru-mukhī (alphabet), 164; 170.
Gurus, 61; (ten chief Sikh), 164.

Haas (Dr.), 363, 1.
Haḍakāī, 227.
Hair (cutting off the), 359; (the pride of women), 375.
Haṇsa, 104, 3.
Han Tan Hien, 262.
Hanumān, 48; 111; 326; 445; (temple of), 65, 2; (worship of), 220–222.
Hapta Hendu, 7.
Hara, 82.
Hare (David), 491, 1.
Har-Govind, 164.
Hari (name), 522; (temple), 175; 176; (bol), 297.
Hari-dās, 142.
Haridrā-Gaṇapati, 217.
Hari-Hara, 65.
Hari-jana, 269.
Hari-Kṛishṇa, 269.
Hariś-ćandra, 24.
Hari-vaṇśa (chap. clxxxi), 65.
Har-Kisan, 164.
Har-Rāi, 164.
Hastinī, 389.
Haug's Ṛig-veda, 102.
Haya-gardabhiḥ, 107.
Head-coverings, 395.
Headman (duties of), 456.
Heaven, 22; 23; 232; (Dyaus), 182; (Indra's), 13; 49; (Kṛishṇa's), 118; (Vaishṇava), 70; (Vishṇu's), 118; (Śaiva), 70; (five heavens), 102; 403.
Heaven's gate, 449.
Heber (Bishop), 149.
Hell (twenty-one), 127, 1; 232.
Heramba, 218.
Hercules (Indian), 112.
Hermaphrodite, 183.
Hero-worship, 71; 257–273.
Hetu, 39.
Hills (sacred), 349.
Himālaya, 4.
Hindū Religious Sects, 160, 1.
Hindū-ī, 170.
Hindūism, 2; 3; 54–72; (compared to banian-tree), 98; (Śākta form of), 180; 186; (Theism of), 224.
Hindūs (naturally religious), 100; (as they are), 296, 1.
Hingrāj, 227.
Hiouen Thsang, 337.
Hiraṇya-garbha, 14; 35; 44.
Hiraṇya-kaśipu (tyrant), 109.
Hiraṇyāksha (demon), 109.
Hiraṇya-Śrāddha, 306.
History (absence of), 38.
Holī (festival), 430.
Homa (ceremony), 299; 394; (sacrifice), 367; 576.
Homage (acts of), 415.
Homa-śālā, 365; 411.
Hongi, 273, 1.
Horoscope, 372; 373.
Horse (high-eared), 108.
Horse-sacrifice, 8; 24; 329.
Horses (clay), 219; 220.
House (arrangement of), 391.
Householder's wife, 397.
Hṛishīkeśa, 405.
Human life (three great objects of), 388.
Hunter's Annals of Rural Bengal, 332, 1.
Hutāśanī (festival), 430.
Hymn (creation), 404.
Hymns, 7; 8; (to the Vedic triad), 15; 16; (character of Vedic), 18.
Hymn-veda, 8.

Iḍā, 5.
Īdar (temple), 569.
Idol-crown, 449.
Idols, 123; (artificial), 70.
Ikshu, 193.
Illeććhida Nema (festival), 247.
Illusion, 27; 36; 37; 41.
Images (sanctity of), 69.
Implements (agricultural), 456; (five destructive), 418; (for shaving), 459.
Inca, 273, 1.
Incarnation (Hindū doctrine of), 62; 63.
Incarnations (Vishṇu's), 107–116; 115; 315.
Incense, 415.
India's Mother, 513.
Indian Antiquary, 265.
Indian Mirror, 509; 512; 513.
Indian Wisdom, 13; 112.
Indifference, 36.
Indische Studien, 363, 1.
Indra, 9; 10; 12; 16; 63; 271.
Indrāṇī, 14; 182; 188.
Indriya-sparśa (ceremony), 406.
Influenza, 227.

Initiation, 117; 360; 377.
Instruments (musical), 145; 381; 450.
Interchangeableness (of Indian religious beliefs), 159.
Īśa (or Īśāna), 85.
Īśa Upanishad, 26.
Ishṭaḥ, 106, 1.
Ishṭa-devatā, xiv; 370; 435.
Islām, 3.
Islands (seven circular), 232, 1.
Īśopanishad, 487, 1.
Īśvara, 35; 85; 89; 119.
Itihāsa, 41; (verses), 287.

Jaḍa, 132.
Jagad-ambā, 185.
Jagan-mātā, 185.
Jagannāth (temple of), 59, 1; 139; 447; (car of), 118.
Jagannāth-purī, 55, 1; 447.
Jag-jīvan-dās, 179.
Jahāngīr (Emperor), 166.
Jaimini, 198.
Jaleśvara, 201.
Jamadagni, 110; 421.
Jambukeśvara (Śiva), 445; (temple), 446.
Jambu-tree, 445.
Janaḥ (heaven), 102, 1; 403.
Janamejaya, 321.
Janam-sākhī, 162.
Janar (heaven), 403.
Jaṅgamas, 88.
Janitrī, 182.
Janma-patra, 372.
Janmāshṭamī, 113, 2.
Jap-jī, 170.
Japu, 170.
Jaṭā (recitation), 409.
Jāta-karman, 353; 357.
Jātavedas, 420.
Jāti (Jāt), caste, 471.
Jāti-mālā, 207, 1.
Jaya-deva (poet), 146.
Jetalpur, 149.
Jewel (miraculous), 108; (Vishṇu's), 104.
Jewelry (Indian), 396; 466.
Jīva (or Jīvātman), 26; 27; 28.
Jīvan-mukti, 206.
Jīvātman, 37; 40.
Jñān-mārga, 63.
Jñāna (knowledge), 27; 140.
Jñāna-prakāśa, 179.
Jñāna-vāpī, 437.
Jñāneśvara, 266.
Jñeyam, 49.
John (St., Gospel, i. 1), 419, 2.
Journal (Asiatic), 432; 511, 1.

Jupiter, 4.
Jvara, 201.
Jyotisha (Jyoshī, or Joshī), 372.
Jyotishṭoma, 22; 368.

Kabīr, 99, 1; 148; 169; 476; (life of), 158; (sayings and precepts of), 160; (twelve disciples of), 178.
Kabīr-panthīs, 160.
Kabīr-Var (tree), 337.
Kaća, 194, 1.
Kādambarī, 193.
Kadrū, 233; 322.
Kaḥ, 106, 1.
Kailāsa, 70; 78; 84; 103; 291; 447.
Kaira, 269.
Kāka-bali (ceremony), 329; 421.
Kālahasta, 441.
Kalāṅśa-rūpiṇī, 187.
Kāla-rātri, 204.
Kalā-rūpiṇī, 187.
Kalās (of Moon), 343.
Kalaśa (vessel), 412; 413; 513.
Kali (age), 52; 114.
Kālī (goddess), 25; 79; 187; 393; (description of), 189; (worship of), 185.
Kālī-ćaturdaśī, 204.
Kālidāsa, 45; 333, 1.
Kālī Ghāṭ (temple), 431.
Kālī-pūjā (festival), 431.
Kāliya (serpent), 113.
Kali-yuga (age), 60; 163; 398; 433.
Kālkā, 227.
Kalkatti, 250.
Kalki, 114.
Kalkin, 114.
Kalkuḍa, 250.
Kallurti, 250.
Kallyāta (festival), 247.
Kalmucks, 313.
Kalpa (age), 82.
Kalpa-druma, 332.
Kāma, 388.
Kāmāćī, 228.
Kāma-deva, 83; 114; 115; 200; 447.
Kāma-dhenu, 108; 318.
Kāmākhyā (Tantra), 207.
Kamalātmikā, 188.
Kamaṇḍalu, xxi, note.
Kāmya (Śrāddha), 305.
Kanara, 250.
Kāñći-puram (= Kāñjīvaram), 119.

Kāñjīvaram, 124; 446.
Kaṇsa, 104, 2; 111; 113.
Kaṇṭaka (a thorn), 191, 1.
Kaṇṭhī (rosary), 117; 135.
Kāntimatī (Pārvatī), 447.
Kapāla, 367.
Kāpālika, 59.
Kapardin, 77.
Kārakal, 250.
Kāraṇa-śarīra, 35; 36.
Kara-nyāsa, 405.
Karma (works), 140.
Karma-mārga, 63.
Karma-nāśā (river), 348.
Karman, 22.
Karmāṅga (Śrāddha), 305.
Karṇa, 273.
Kartā, 89.
Kārttika-pūrṇimā (festival), 432.
Kārttikeya, 48; 211; 213.
Kārya, 89.
Kashmīr, 312; 313.
Kāśī, 434.
Kaśyapa, 104, 3; 233; 322; 421.
Kāśyapa (sage), 123, 1.
Katak, 139.
Kāterī, 228.
Kaṭha Upanishad, 26.
Kaṭhopanishad, 121, 1; 528.
Katwa, 179.
Kaula (Upanishad), 185.
Kauleśī, 188.
Kaumodakī, 103.
Kaupīneśvara, 50.
Kaustubha, 104; 108.
Kavaćas (or Amulets), 204.
Kāverī (river), 119; 347.
Kāyastha (caste), 292, 1.
Kedārnāth, 56.
Kerala (Malabar), 55.
Keśānta, 353; 359.
Keshab Chandar Sen, 496; 497; 499; 505; 510; 512–523; 525; 526.
Ketu, 344.
Khadira, 367; 535.
Khālsā, 167.
Khaṇḍe-Rao, 266.
Khaṇḍo-bā, 266.
Khañjana, 328.
Kharjūrī, 192.
Khaṭvāṅga, 81.
Khelā, 163.
Khoḍiyār (shrine of), 225; 226.
Kim, 106, 1.
Kimidins, 237.
Kimpurushas, 238.
King (deification of), 259.

Kinnaras, 238.
Kirāta, 84.
Kīrtana, 264.
Kistna (river), 348.
Kitchen (Indian), 128.
Knowledge (salvation by), 63.
Koli, 193.
Kolla (festival), 249.
Koṇārak, 343.
Kookas. *See* Kūkas.
Krama (recitation), 84; 409.
Kravyād, 237.
Kṛishṇa, 47; 98; 111–114; 116; 259; (worship of), 144; 145; 447; (life of), 112; (miracles of), 113; (repetition of name of), 143; (sons of), 114.
Kṛishṇā (Kistna), 295; 348.
Kṛishṇa-dās, 144.
Kṛishṇa-deva, 134.
Kṛishṇa-janmāshṭamī, 430.
Kṛishṇa-nagar, 569.
Kristo-dās Pāl, 519, 1.
Kṛita (age), 433.
Kṛita-jña, 329.
Kṛittikās (six), 213.
Kshatriyas, 53; (god of the), 84.
Kshaura (shaving), 312; 353; 359.
Kubera, 238; 268.
Kuber-bhaktas, 269.
Kuch Behār (Mahārāja, marriage of), 512; 518, 1.
Kūkas (sect of Sikhs), 268.
Kulārṇava (Tantra), 207.
Kullūka, 184.
Kulumāndī-amman, 228.
Kumāra, 214.
Kumāra-sambhava, 45.
Kumbhaka, 402.
Kumbha-Konam, 348.
Kuṇḍa, 417.
Kuṅkuma, 91.
Kunte (Mr. M. M.), 366, 2.
Kuntī, 271.
Kūpa-kaććhapa, 329.
Kūpa-maṇḍuka, 329.
Kūrma, 108.
Kūrma-purāṇa, 74.
Kurukulyā, 188, 1.
Kuśa, 48, 1; (grass), 296; 338.
Kūsh (Hindū), 3.
Kuvera, 59; 79; 238.

Laghimā, 427.
Lahanā, 164.
Lake-temple, 165.
Lakshmaṇa, 47.
Lakshmī, 14; 103; 108; 182.
Lakshmī-Nārāyaṇa (temple of), 151; 184.
Lamps (feast of), 432; 529.
Lares (Indian), 392.
Lares, 425, 1.
Larvæ, 274, 1.
Laukikāgni, 287.
Lava, 48, 1.
Law-books and Law Schools, 51; 52; 286, 1.
Leader (religious), 101.
Leaves (Bilva), 68; 90; (as plates), 461.
Lecture (by Keshab), 515.
Left-hand worshippers, 185.
Lemures, 274, 1.
Līlā (sport), 43; 138.
Liṅga (body), 28; (phallus), 33; 68; 70; 83; 90; 447; (typical), 224; (number of), 78, 1; (worship of), 439; 440; 567; 568.
Liṅgāits, 88.
Liṅga-purāṇa, 65; 74.
Liṅga-śarīra, 35; 297.
Liquor (spirituous), 108; 112; 193; 194.
Liquors (twelve Śākta), 192.
Lithuania, 313.
Loango (king of), 273, 1.
Lokas (seven), 102, 1.
Lotus-flower, 103; 338.
Love (god of), 83.
Lubbock (Sir John), 273, 1; 313; 330; 340; 372, 1.
Luther (Martin), 138; 139; 162.
Lyall (Sir A.), 262.

Macdonald (Rev. K.), 478, 1.
Machinery, 470.
Madagascar (bishop of), 274, 3.
Mādhava, 405.
Madhu, 104, 2.
Mādhūka, 193.
Mādhurya, 141.
Madhva, 96; 130; 476.
Mādhvīka (plant), 193.
Madhyāhna-sandhyā, 407.
Madras (Missionary Record), 179.
Madurā (temple of), 58, 1; 65; 79, 1; 442; (town), 182, 2; 219; 228; 272.
Madya, 192.
Magar, 158.
Māghotsab, 504.
Mahaḥ (heaven), 102, 1; 403.
Mahābaleśvar, 216; 217; 348.
Mahā-bhārata, 41; 47; 63; 116; 232, 1; 241; 271–273; 292; 321; 389.
Mahābhāshya, 198; 419, 2; 519, 1.
Mahā-bhūta, 31, 2.
Mahā-ćakra, 196.
Mahā-deva, 78; 85.
Mahā-devī (manifestations of), 186.
Mahā-Gaṇapati, 217.
Mahā-kāla, 82.
Mahā-krodhaḥ, 107.
Mahā-lakshmī, 385.
Mahā-maṇḍapa, 447.
Mahā-mātṛis, 188.
Mahā-māyaḥ, 106.
Mahā-nirvāṇa (Tantra), 207.
Mahant, 87, 1.
Mahā-pralaya, 179.
Mahar (heaven), 403.
Mahārāja (title of), 135; (homage to), 136; 137.
Mahā-rātri, 204.
Mahā-Śiva-rātri (festival), 430.
Mahātala, 102, 1.
Mahā-tapāḥ, 83.
Mahātmā, xii, 1.
Māhātmya, 433.
Mahā-vidyā (ten), 187.
Mahāyajña (five), 411.
Mahā-yogī, 83.
Mahīdhara, 405.
Mahisha, 104, 3.
Mahishāsur (demon), 431.
Maine (Sir Henry), 507.
Maintenance, 74; 75.
Maireya, 193.
Maithuna, 192.
Ma-kāras (five), 192, 2.
Makara-saṅkrānti, 428.
Mallāri, 266.
Mallāsura, 266.
Malwa, 168.
Man (divine and human), 235.
Manas, 27; 31; 32; 40.
Mānasī-pūjā, 524.
Mānavas, 51.
Maṇḍapa, 440.
Mandara (mountain), 108.
Mandir (or Mandira), 151; 392; 411; 513.
Manes, 274, 1.
Mangalor (district), 247.
Maṅgal Siṇh Rāmgharia, 175.
Mango (tree), 446.
Maṇi-karṇikā, 308; 438.
Maṇi-pur, 322, 2; 329, 1.

Man-lion, 109.
Māṇsa, 192.
Mantra, 7; 8; (importance of), 61; (Śākta), 197; (eight-syllabled), 297; (number of Mantras), 199; (efficacy of), 199; (translations of), 200; 197–202.
Mantra-pushpa, 415.
Mantra-śāstrī (power of), 201; 202; (decline of power of), 208.
Mantra-vid, 84.
Manu, 30; 52, 1; 107; (Book I. 5), 30; (I. 49), 331; (II. 60), 406; (III. 68), 418, 3; (III. 70. 81), 421; (III. 84-93), 417; (III. 237), 285; (IV. 21), 421; (IV. 26), 368; (IV. 173), 287, 1; (IV. 88-90), 232; (V. 68), 287; (VI. 10), 368; (VI. 20), 428; (Seventh), 237; (VII. 41), 241; (IX. 96), 334; 387; (IX. 317. 319), 260; (X. 75), 394, 1; (XI. 84), 260; (XI. 216), 428; (XI. 243. 244), 235; (code of), 51; 52; (doctrine of), 53; (teaching of), 129.
Manushya-yajña, 423, 1.
Man-worship, 71; 273, 1.
Manyu, 404, 1.
Marakī, 227.
Mārgaḥ, 106.
Mārī-amman, 226; 228.
Mārjana (sprinkling), 403; 404.
Mārjāra-nyāya, 125.
Mark (sectarial), 66; (nāma), 66; (puṇḍra), 66; (tilaka), 66; (tri-puṇḍra), 66; (ūrdhva-puṇḍra), 67; (Śrī-vatsa), 103; 113; Svastika), 104, 1; (sacred), 400.
Mārkaṇḍeya, 441.
Markaṭa-nyāya, 125.
Markī, 227.
Markings (religious), 400.
Marks (Śaiva), 66; (Vaishṇava), 66; 118; (Ten-galai), 126; (Vada-galai), 126; (Madhva), 133.
Marriage-act, 508.
Marriage-ceremonies (ancient form of), 354; 363; (reform in), 500; 507; (expense of), 379; (modern), 379; (in Brāhma-Samāj), 501; (marriage of trees), 335.
Marriage-hymn, 363, 1.
Marriages (early), 362; 385.
Mars (Hindū), 212.
Marshman (Dr.), 484, 1.
Marudāyī, 228.
Māruta, 221.
Maruts, 9.
Mata (religious sect), 61, 1.
Mātā (mother), 106; (worship), 222.
Mātaṅgī, 188.
Mātarā, 182.
Match-maker (professional), 377.
Maṭha (monastery), 55; 129.
Mathurā, 113; 375.
Mātṛi (or Mother forms of Śiva's wife), 188; 188, 1.
Mātṛikā, 188.
Mātṛikā-bheda Tantra, 193.
Matṛis, or Mothers, 223.
Matsya, 107; 192.
Māyā, 35; 37; 44; 85; 120.
Māyā-ćid-yoga, 37, 1.
Meu-eaters, 237.
Metempsychosis, 18; 26; 27; 41; 53; 57; 60; 115; 173; 316; 331; 339.
Midnapur Samāj, 494.
Milton, 386.
Mīmāṇsā (Sūtra), 26.
Mīnāći (goddess), 58, 1; 228; 442.
Mīnākshī, 58, 1; 228; 442.
Mīnākshī-sundareśvara (pagoda), 442, 1.
Minos (Hindū), 290.
Mīrā-bāī, 268.
Miracles, 266.
Miśra (Jagannāth), 138.
Missionary Conference, 512, 1.
Mitāksharā (law-book), 52; 286, 1.
Mitchell (Dr. Murray), 265.
Mithra, 406.
Mitra, 5; 9; 10; 406.
Mitra (Dr. Rājendra-lāla), 282, 1.
Mitropasthāna, 406.
Modelling (art of), 469.
Model-wife, 389.
Moha-rātri, 204.
Mohinī, 65, 1.
Monasteries (founded by Śaṅkara), 55.
Monkeys (veneration of); 222; 326.
Monkey-temple, 327.
Monkey-theory, 125.
Monotheism, 11; 17.
Months (lunar), 432.
Moon, 108.
Moon-worship, 343.
Morning Sandhyā Service, 401.
Moses, 515; 517.
Mothers (number of), 225; (shrines of), 226; (special), 227; 228; (Tāntrikas), 229; 245.
Mother-worship, 188; 222–229.
Mountain-worship, 349.
Mourning (time of), 306, 3.
Mozoomdār (Mr. P. C.), 496, 1; 509; 510, 1; 514; 515; 521–523; 526.
Mṛićchakaṭikā (drama), 77, 1.
Mudrā, 204; 406; (double meaning of), 192, 2.
Muir (Dr. John), 182, 2; 237, 1; 414, 1.
Muir's Texts, 366.
Mukunda, 318.
Mūla (root), 107.
Muṇḍaka Upanishad, 26; 120.
Munich (church at), 229, 1.
Mura, 104, 2.
Muralīs, 266.
Mūrti-pūjā, 524.
Musala (club), 112.
Muslin (Indian), 465.
Mystical formulæ, 197.

Nābhājī, 147.
Nāch (girls), 381; 382; 451.
Nāches, 430.
Nadīya, 138.
Nāga (serpents), 233; 237; 321–326.
Nāga-kanyā, 233.
Nāga-pañćamī, 323; 40.
Nāga-pratishṭhā, 324.
Nāga-shrines, 323.
Nāgendra-nāth, 478.
Nāg-loka, 322.
Nāgpur, 323.
Nahusha, 241.
Naimittika (Śrāddha), 305.
Naivedya (food), 144; 415.
Nakshatra, 345; (name), 372; (constellation), 373, 1.
Nakula, 271; 272.
Nala, 235.
Nālāyira, 125.
Namak and Ćamak, 416.
Nāma-karaṇa, 132; 353; 358; 370.

Nāma-kīrtana, 141.
Nāma-saṅkīrtana, 105.
Namaskāra, 415.
Nāmdev, 169.
Name (importance of), 358; (for sorcery), 372; (name-giving), 358; 370; 371.
Names (special), 358; (of Vishṇu and Śiva), 105–107.
Nānak (life and teaching of), 161; 162; 163; 476.
Nanda (herdsman), 113.
Nandaka, 104.
Nandi (bull), 81; 440.
Nāpita (barber), 374; 459.
Nara-bali (human sacrifice), 190.
Narāin Bose, 478. *See* Bose.
Nara-siṇha, 109.
Nārāyaṇa, 62, 1; 102.
Narbadā (river), 69; 347; 348.
Nariād (temples of), 269.
Nārikela, 192.
Narmadā, 295.
Narmadā-śaṅkar, 371, 1.
Nāsik, 272; 301.
Naṭeśvara, 84.
Nāthubhāī (Sir Maṅgaldās), 381.
Nature-worship, 2; 4; 5; 72.
Navanīta-Gaṇapati, 218.
Nava-rātra (festival), 431.
Nayars (aborigines), 271, 2.
Nāyikā (forms of Śiva's wife), 188.
Necklace (thread), 35.
Nectar-gāyatrī, 201.
Netā (guide), 106, 1.
New Dispensation, 516; 517; 526.
Nicholson (General), 260.
Nigamana, 39; 185.
NikkalSen (worshippers), 260.
Nimbārka (miracle of), 146.
Nimitta-jñāna, 397.
Nīm Tollah (Ghāṭ), 518; 519, 1.
Nirguṇa, 31, 1; 36, 1; 121.
Nirṇaya-sindhu, 303; 305.
Nirvāṇa, 106.
Nirvāpa, 367.
Niśāćaraḥ, 106.
Nishkramaṇa, 353; 358.
Nitya (Śrāddha), 305.
Nityānanda, 139; 142.
Nivīti, 379; 410.
Noah, 107.
Non-duality (doctrine of), 86.
Non-entity, 29.
Notary (village), 456.
Nṛitya-priyaḥ, 84.
Nuddea (cremation at), 569.
Numismatic Chronicle, 104, 1.
Nyāsa (ceremony), 204; 405; 413.
Nyāya (Sūtra), 26.

Objects (worship of), 339; 349.
Oblations (to fire), 365; 366; 367.
Obstacles (lord of), 216.
Odyssey (Homer's), 274, 1.
Offerings, 6; (at dinner), 425.
Oil (festival), 442.
Om, 10; 44; 357; 402; 449.
Omens, 320; 397.
Ophiolatry, 319.
Origin of Civilization (Lubbock's), 273, 1; 313.
Orissa, 447.
Ornaments (eight kinds), 396.
Oudh (Ayodhyā), 110; (princes of), 113, 1.
Oxus (river), 3.

Pāchambā (village), 577.
Pada (recitation), 409.
Padārtha-tritayam, 119.
Padma, 103.
Padminī, 389.
Pādya, 415.
Pagrī, 396, 2.
Pāhul, 167.
Paishṭī, 193.
Pāla, 151.
Panasa, 192.
Pāñćajana (demon), 103, 2.
Pañćakośī (Benares), 218, 1; 435.
Pañćānana, 79.
Pañća-pātra, xxi, note.
Pañća-prayāga, 367.
Pañćasūnā, 418.
Pañćāyatana (ceremony), 410–416.
Panchāyat, 456.
Pāṇḍavas, 112; 271.
Paṇḍharpur, 50; 263; 264.
Paṇḍitaḥ, 84.
Paṇḍit (lady), 389.
Pāṇḍu, 271; (princes), 322.
Pāṇḍu-leṇe, 272.
Pāṇḍya (kingdom), 58, 1.
Pāṇini, 84; 184, 1; 329; 519, 1.
Panjāb, 7.
Pañjūrli, 250.
Pannagas, 238.
Pān-supārī, 137.
Pantheism, 2; 7; 11; 17.
Pāpa (demerit), 292.
Paradise (temporary), 118.
Parāli, 268.
Parama-haṇsa, 87.
Pāramārthika, 38.
Paramātman, 37; xii, 1.
Parameśvara, 35; 36; 44; 45; 50.
Parāśara (code of), 51; 52; 394, 1.
Paraśu-rāma, 110; 270.
Pārijāta, 108; 332.
Parikrama (of a river), 349.
Pariṇāma, 269.
Parrot (Kāma's), 104, 3.
Pārtha-sārathi, 107.
Pārvaṇa (Śrāddha), 305.
Pārvatī (goddess), 46; 47; 446; (will of), 65; (different names of), 79.
Pāśa (fetter), 81; 89.
Pāśin, 290.
Passion (or activity), 31.
Paśu (an animal), 89; 191.
Pāśupata, 59.
Paśupati (Śiva), 85; 89.
Pātāla, 102, 1; 233; 322; 323.
Patañjali, 198; 419, 2.
Pāṭhas (five Veda), 409.
Pati, 89.
Patiāla (Mahārāja), 467.
Patnā, 166; (temple at), 174.
Patrimony, 286.
Paurāṇika, 25.
Pavamāna (hymns), 368.
Pavana, 221.
Pavitram, 106.
Peacock (Skanda's), 104, 3.
Pebbles (sacred), 69; 349.
Penance (six courses of), 87.
Penates (Indian), 392.
People (social condition), 18.
Permagudy, 219.
Persia, 313.
Peterborough (Bishop), 275, 2.
Phalgu-Śrāddha, 312.
Phallus, 68, 1. *See* Liṅga.
Pheṇṭa, 396.
Philosophy (Vedānta), 33; 85; (Sāṅkhya), 30; 85.
Phœnicia, 313.
Pictures (on temple walls), 441.
Pīdārī, 228.
Pilgrimages, 311; 348; 349; 434; 444; 570.
Pināka, 81.
Piṇḍas, 293; 298–310.
Pīpā, 148; 169.

Pīpal or Pippala-tree, 83; 334; 335; 336.
Piśāćas, 82; 237; 241; 242.
Pitā, 106; 182; 244.
Pitarā, 182.
Pitṛi (departed ancestors), 10.
Pitṛi-loka, 28.
Pitṛi-paksha, 329; 431.
Pitṛi-tarpaṇa, 394, 1; 410.
Pitrya, 410, 1.
Planet-worship, 344.
Plant-marriages, 334.
Plants (sacred), 338.
Plant-worship, 72; 330; 332.
Plateau (Pamīr), 3.
Plates (of leaves), 424; 461.
Pliny, 330, 1.
Plough (Indian), 456.
Pluto (Hindū), 290.
Poems (heroic), 42.
Poison (deadly), 109.
Polyandry, 271.
Polygamy (forbidden), 500.
Polytheism, 7; 11; 17.
Pomlā (caste), 229.
Pongal (festival), 429.
Poona (temple at), 144.
Population (Hindū), 2.
Potter (village), 460; xxii.
Prabhus, 142.
Prāćīnāvītī, 378; 410.
Pradakshiṇā (worship by), 68, 2; 145; 348; 415.
Pradhāna, 30.
Pradyumna, 114; 116.
Prahlāda, 109.
Prajā-pati, 35; 237; 341; 355.
Prakṛiti, 30; 31; 32; 36; 85; 223.
Pramā, 27.
Pramāṇa (four), 39.
Pramāṇam, 106, 1.
Pramathas, 238.
Prāṇa, 35.
Prāṇaḥ, 106.
Praṇava, 402.
Prāṇāyāma, 402.
Prārthanā (prayer), 19.
Prārthanā-Samāj (manual of), 526; 528; 529.
Prasāda (sacred food), 69; 94; 145; 168; 447.
Prātaḥ-sandhyā, 401.
Pratāpa-ćandra Ghosha, 197.
Prathama-grantha, 179.
Prātibhāsika, 38.
Pratijñā, 39.
Pratishṭhā, 70.
Pratyaksha, 39.
Prayāga, 375.
Prayāgwāl (priests), 375.
Prāyaśćitta, 41; 367.
Prayer (eight-syllabled), 136.
Prayers (for the dead), 275.
Preta, 241; 242.
Preta-śarīra, 28.
Priests, 386; 457.
Primitive Culture (Tylor's), 274, 2; 313; 314.
Princes (Rājputāna), 113, 1; (Oudh), 113, 1; (Pāṇḍava), 271; 272.
Principles (triad of), 119.
Pṛithā, 271.
Pṛithivī, 8; 30; 182.
Priya-kṛit, 106, 1.
Proclamation (Keshab's), 515.
Profession (choice of), 386.
Progressive Samāj, 526.
Prosonno Kumār Tāgore, 485.
Prosperity (temple of), 385.
Pudkalā, 219.
Pūjāri (priest), 249.
Pulastya, 192.
Puliyār, 211; 217.
Pulney Hills, 214, 2; 349.
Puṃsavana, 353; 355.
Puṇḍalika (or Puṇḍarīka), 263.
Puṇḍra, 66; 67; 118; 400.
Punishment (future), 295; (of school-boys), 458.
Puṇya (merit), 292.
Pura, 81.
Pūraka, 402.
Purāṇas, 63; 99.
Pūraṇī, 219.
Purgatories (temporary), 232.
Purī, 142; 447.
Purity (or goodness), 31; (age of), 114.
Pūrṇa-prajña, 130.
Pūrṇā śakti, 187.
Pūrṇimā (festival), 151; 152.
Puro-ḍāśa, 367.
Purohita (priests), 352; 386; 457.
Purusha, 31; 33; 34; 35; (division of), 415.
Purusha-hymn (or sūkta), 17; 23; 33; 414.
Purusha-kāra, 125.
Pūrva-mīmāṃsā, 198.
Pūshan, 9.
Pushkara (Pokhar), 558.
Pushpa (flowers), 144; 415.
Pushṭi-mārga, 134.
Pushṭy-artha (Śrāddha), 305.
Put (hell), 287.
Pūtātmā, 106.
Put-tra, 287; 355.
Race (great Āryan), 3; (Anārya), 19; (Dasyu), 19; (Drāviḍian), 3; 19; (Kolarian), 3; (lunar), 112; (Nāga), 233; (Non-Āryan), 3; (Nishāda), 19; (pastoral), 3; (Serpent), 321.
Rādhā, 113.
Rādhā-Kṛishṇau, 184.
Rāg (or Rāgas), 170; (Āsā), 170; (Gaurī), 170; (Mājh), 170.
Rāhu, 344.
Rain-god, 9; 12; 16.
Rain-worship, 2.
Rāja-ćakra, 196.
Rājanya, 415.
Rajas, 31; 36.
Rājendralāla Mitra (Dr.), 93; 108, 2; 193; 194, 1; 195, 3; 282, 1.
Rajo-guṇa, 45.
Rājput (tribe), 233, 1.
Rājputāna, 113; 559; (princes of), 113, 1.
Rākshasas, 237; 244.
Ram (Agni's vehicle), 104, 3.
Rāma, 47; 62, 1; 98; 111; 220; 259; 445; 462.
Rāma-ćandra, 110; 220; 270.
Rāma-līlā, 431.
Rāmānand, 169; (disciples of), 148.
Rāmānanda-Svāmī, 149.
Rāma-navamī (festival), 430.
Rāmānuja (doctrine of), 119; 120; 121; 476.
Rāmāyaṇa, 41; 42; 47; 111; 116; 148; 220; 328; 329; (of Tulsī-dās), 116.
Rambhā, 108.
Rām-dās, 164; 165; 268.
Rāmeśvara (island), 443.
Rām Kānt Roy, 478.
Rāmmohun Roy, 475–490.
Rāmnād, 444.
Rām-singh, 268.
Raṇ-chor, 152.
Raujit Siṇh (tomb of), 174; 177.
Rasātala, 102, 1.
Raseśvara-darśana, 206, 1.
Rat (Gaṇeśa's), 104, 3.
Rati, 447.
Raurava (hell), 127, 1.
Rāvaṇa (tyrant-demon), 110; 220; 238; 445.
Rāvī, 162.
Ravi-dās, 148; 169.
Reasoning (logical), 39.

Rećaka, 402.
Redeemer (universal belief in), 114.
Reformation (Hindū), 477.
Reformers (Vaishṇava), 476; (advanced Indian), 505.
Reforms (religious), 496.
Regions (seven lower), 102, 1; 232; 233; (seven upper), 232; 233.
Reintegration, 74; 75.
Religio-Philosophical Journal, 256.
Religion (social equality in), 64; (Hindū daily), 351; (in modern family-life), 370.
Religious Truth, 510, 1.
Remarriage of widows, 472; 500; 508.
Reproach (terms of), 329.
Reproducer, 44.
Revatī, 112.
Revā (river), 347.
Ṛić (hymn), 415.
Rice, 6; (consecration of), 419.
Ṛiddhi, 215.
Right-hand worshippers, 185.
Ṛig-veda, 8; 12; 13; 14; 21; 281; (I. 25), 407; (I. 34. 11), 10; (I. 45. 2), 10; (I. 72. 6), 418; (I. 114. 8), 421; (I. 164. 20), 120; (I. 164. 46), 51; (II. 23. 1), 216; (III. 59), 406; (III. 62. 10), 403; (IV. 5. 5), 281, 1; (IV. 51. 11), 407; (IV. 58. 3), 419; (V. 4. 5). 418; (V. 4. 9), 420; (VI. 20. 2), 320; (VII. 89. 1), 280; (VII. 99. 7, 100. 7), 416; (VII. 104. 3), 281, 1; (VIII. 58. 2), 51; (IX. 73. 8), 281, 1; (X. 9), 403; (X. 10), 289; (X. 14. 9), 282; (X. 14. 7. 11), 283; (X. 17. 3), 299; (X. 18. 3), 283; (X. 18. 8), 280; (X. 71. 2), 182, 2; (X. 85). 363; (X. 85. 5), 343; (X. 86), 222, 1; (X. 88. 11), 341; (X. 90), 23; 414; (X. 121. 10), 424; (X. 129), 29.
Ripon (Lord), 569.
Ṛishis, 2; 7; (seven), 107.
Ṛishi-tarpaṇa, 410.
Ṛita, 404.
Rite (Agnishṭoma), 22; (Aptoryāma), 22; (Aśvamedha), 22; (Branding), 132; 133; (Funeral), 274; (Jyotishṭoma), 22; (Vājapeya), 22, 194; (Dedication), 117; (purificatory), 157; 353; (sacrificial), 22; 367; (Sikh, baptismal), 167; (Vaitaraṇī), 297; (Sautrāmaṇi), 194.
River-god, 182.
River-goddess, 182.
Rivers (sacred), 295; 347; (trinity of), 347.
Rivington (Rev. Luke), 515, 1.
Rocks (sacred), 349.
Roër, 183.
Rohiṇī, 113.
Rosary, 67; 135; 406; (Vaishṇava), 67; 117; (Śaiva), 67; 82; (of ascetic), 92.
Rudra, 9; 36; 75; 76; 77; 82; 85; (hymns), 416.
Rudrāksha (tree), 67; (berries), 82.
Rudras (eleven), 10.
Rudra-Śiva, 44; 75.
Rudra-yāmala (Tantra), 207.
Rukmaka (fire), 419.
Rukmiṇī, 114.
Rules (of life), 51; 281.

Śabala, 289; 422.
Sābarmatī, 347.
Śabda (or āptopadeśa), 39.
Sabhā-maṇḍapa (assembly hall), 153.
Sacerdotalism (Hindū), 352.
Sacrifice (meaning of), 12; 13, 1; (foreshadowing of), 17; (efficacy of), 22; 23; (Brāhmanical), 22; 23; (human), 24; 166; (animal), 24.
Sacrificial-rites, 367.
Sadā-Śiva, 83.
Sādhāraṇa (Brāhma-Samāj), 513; 514.
Sādhus (holy men), 87, 1; 150.
Sadyo-jāta, 400.
Saffron, 91.
Saguṇa, 31, 1; 36, 1; 121.
Sahadeva, 271; 272.
Sahajānanda, 148; 149; 268.
Sahishṇuḥ, 106, 1.
Saint-worship, 257–273.
Śainya, 407.
Saira, 193.
Śaiva (worshippers of Śiva), 59; 60; 73; 96.
Śaiva-darśana, 89.
Śaivism, 71; 73–94; (prevalency of), 244; (compared with Vaishṇavism), 64.
Śaka (era), 433.
Śākhā (of the Veda), 530, and note.
Sākhya, 141.
Śākinīs, 189.
Sākshī, 106, 1.
Sākshin (witness), 218, 1.
Sākshi-Vināyaka, 218, 1.
Śāktas, 59; 140.
Śakti, 33; 62; 187; 392.
Śakti-saṅgama (Tantra), 207.
Śāktism, 71; 180–196; (definition of), 180; (theory of), 181; (licentiousness of), 190; (initiation into), 191.
Śāl (tree), 582.
Śālagrāma, 46; 69; 296; 335; 392; 412; 561.
Śālivāhana, 433.
Sālivaṭīśvara, 446, 5.
Sālokya, 41; 71; 118.
Salutation (at Sandhyā), 536.
Samādh (tomb), 179.
Samādhi, 48; 261.
Samājes (various), 494; (compared), 509.
Sāman (hymn), 415.
Samānodakas, 286.
Samarpaṇa, 117; 137.
Samāvartana, 353; 362; 379.
Sāma-veda, 8; 21.
Śambhu, 83.
Saṃhitā (recitation), 409.
Saṃhitās (of the Veda), 8.
Śamī (tree), 338; 535.
Samidh (fuel), 367.
Sāmīpya, 41; 71; 118.
Saṃjñā, 341.
Sammohana, 200.
Sampradāya, 61; 62.
Saṃvat (era), 433.
Saṃvatsara-karaḥ, 106.
Sāmya, 30.
San (era), 433.
Sanaka, 422.
Sanat-kumāra (Tantra), 207.
Sandal, 144; 415, 1.
Sandaṇśa, 232.
Sandhyā (morning), 401; (mid-day), 407; (evening), 407.
Sandhyā-japa, 394, 1.
Śāṇḍilya, 63, 2; 97.
Sandīpana, 200.
Śaṅkalpa, 23; 27.
Śaṅkara, 55; 56; 83; (doctrine of), 120.
Śaṅkarāćārya, 53; 59.

Śaṅkara-Nārāyaṇa, 65.
Śaṅkara-vijaya, 59; 67, 2; 86; 217; 236; 342.
Śaṅkha (shell), 65; 92; 103; 109; 299.
Śaṅkhinī, 389.
Sāṅkhya (Sūtra), 26.
Saṅkīrtana, 141.
Sankrānt (festival), 428.
Sannyāsī, 53; 55; 87; 129; 261; 362; 375; xxi.
Sanskāras (twelve), 353.
Sanskṛit Texts (Muir's), 182, 2; 237, 1.
Sanskṛita (language), 4.
Santāls and Santālia, 576–585.
Santāna-Gaṇapati, 218.
Santa-Rām, 269.
Śānti, 141; 346.
Śānti-da, 106, 1.
Śānti-parvan (13140), 66.
Sapiṇḍana (Śrāddha), 305.
Sapiṇḍas, 286.
Sapta-padī, 364; 380, 3.
Sapta Sindhu, 7.
Śāradā-tilaka (Tantra), 207.
Śaraṇam, 106, 1.
Sāraṅgī, 381.
Śara-śayyā, 561.
Sarasvat, 182.
Sarasvatī (goddess), 14; 47; 182; 211; 536; (worship of), 429; (river), 51.
Sarayu, 347.
Sarcostema Viminalis, 12.
Sārī, 396.
Śārīraka-bhāshya, 121.
Śarman (prosperity), 358.
Śārṅga, 104.
Sārsā, 268.
Sārshṭi, 205.
Sārūpya, 41; 71; 118.
Śarva, 85.
Sarva-bhūta-hara, 82.
Sarva-darśana-saṅgraha, 119; 121, 1; 122; 124, 1; 131; 133.
Sarvaḥ, 106, 1.
Śāstā, 218.
Śāstrīs (Paṇḍits), 386.
Sat, 34.
Sātāni (school), 125, 1.
Satāpana, 200.
Śatapatha-brāhmaṇa, 21; 24; 29; 182.
Śatarudriya, 76; 79; 328.
Satī, 79; 261; 279, 1; 299; 481.
Satnāmī, 178; 179.
Śatru-ghna, 47.
Sattārā, 267; 268.
Sattra, 368.
Sattva, 31; 36.
Sattva-guṇa, 45; 412, 2.
Saturnalia (Hindū), 430.
Satya, 102, 1; (age), 109; 114; 433.
Satyaḥ, 106; 403.
Sauras, 59; 342.
Saura-sūkta, 342.
Śāvam āśaućam, 288.
Savana, 369.
Sāvitrī, 9; 75; 341; 361; 403.
Sāyam-sandhyā, 407.
Sāyaṇa, 78, 2; 419, 2.
Sāyaṇa-Mādhava, 56.
Sāyujya, 41; 71; 118.
Sāyujya-mukti, 196.
Scape-goat, 227.
Schädel-haus, 275, 1.
Schoolmaster (village), 458.
Schools (village), 458.
Scriptures (Hindū), 408.
Sea (of milk, &c.), 108.
Sect (Hindū), 60; (Bhaṭṭa), 86; (C'aitanya), 138–145; (Gāṇapatya), 217; (Jaṅgama), 86; (Mādhva), 129–134; (Nimbāditya), 146; (Nimbārka), 146; (Pāśupata), 86; 89; (Rām-ānuja), 119–129; (Rāmā-nanda), 147; (Raudra), 86; (Śaiva), 86–89; (Sikh), 161–178; (Smārta), 95; (Svami-Nārāyaṇa), 148–158; (of Kabīr), 158–161; (Vaishṇava), 116–161.
Sectarianism (Hindū), 60; (Śaiva), 86–89; (Vaish-ṇava), 116–160.
Sen (Keshab Chandar), 496; 497; 510; 512–523; 525; 526.
Sen (Rām Comul), 497.
Serpent, 80; 105; (Kāliya), 113; (demons), 233; (temple), 323; (worship), 313; 319–326.
Services (religious), 392.
Sesamum (seed), 296.
Śesha (serpent-god), 59; 63; 105; 112; 232, 1; 321; 323; 332, 1.
Setuḥ, 106, 1.
Seven (steps), 364; (seas), 108; (worlds), 403.
Shaḍviṇśa-brāhmaṇa, 398.
Shakespeare, 386.
Shamanism, 246.
Shānārs (religion of), 251.
Shaṇ-mata-sthāpaka, 59.
Shashṭhī (goddess), 229; 328.
Shaṭ karmāṇi, 394, 1.
Shaving (religious), 127; 359; 374; (of corpse), 297.
Sherring (Mr.), 437, 1.
Shoḍaśī, 188.
Shoemaker (village), 460.
Shoes, 396.
Shrines (celebrated), 139; 434–451; (demon), 249.
Siddha (perfect ones), 191.
Siddhi, 215.
Sights (inauspicious), 397; (auspicious), 398.
Sikandar Shāh Lodi, 158.
Sikh (sect), 161–178.
Śikhā, 374.
Śikhā-bandhana, 400.
Śikshā-patrī (translated), 155.
Sīmantonnayana, 353; 357.
Sindūra (vermilion), 221.
Singing (religious), 141; 264; 527; 528.
Śipivishṭa, 416.
Sipping water, 144; 401.
Śiraś-ćheda, 201.
Sirī Rāg, 170.
Śiśu-pāla, 143; 259, 1.
Sītā, 48, 1; 220; 445.
Śītalā Devī, 228.
Śītalā-saptamī (festival), 430.
Sītā-Rāmau, 184.
Śiva, 3; 45; 46; 47; 54; 56; 62; 65; 66; 67; 68; 69; (supremacy of), 74; (symbol of), 78; (names of), 78; 82; 106; (description of), 78; 79; (names of attendants of), 79, 1; (five faces of), 79, 3; (eyes of), 80; (weapons of), 81; (five chief characters of), 81–86; (representation of), 82; (feminine counterpart), 83; (eight material forms of), 85; (miracles), 85; (eight principal manifestations), 85; (female energy), 187; (contradictory qualities), 186; (incarnation), 266.
Śivā-jī, 265.
Śivanāth Śāstri (Paṇḍit), 514.
Śiva-purāṇa, 74; 78.
Śiva-rāt, 90.
Śiva-rātri, 204; 428.
Śiva-stotra, 535.
Śiva-sūtras, 84, 1.
Skanda, 48; 62; 79; 214.

Skanda-purāṇa, 74.
Skull (cracking), 299.
Sky, 5; 9; 20.
Sky-god, 15.
Sleeman (Col.), 331, 3; 335.
Small-pox (goddess of), 227.
Smārta Brahmans, 55; 95.
Smārta-karman, 365.
Śmaśāna, 203; 281.
Śmaśāna-vāsin, 82.
Smṛiti, 53.
Smṛiti-karman, 52.
Smṛiti-śāstra, 51.
Snake-chiefs, 233.
Snake-stones, 325.
Snake-superstitions, 324.
Snake-worship, 319.
Snāna (bathing), 394, 1; 399; 415.
Societies (Theistic), 485–520.
Socrates, 515.
So-daru, 170.
Sohilā, 170.
Soma (moon), 343.
Soma-god, 12.
Soma-juice, 25; 369.
Soma (plant), 6; 8; 12; 332.
Soma-sacrifice, 25; 368; 392.
Son (importance of), 355.
Sons (of the Ganges), 347.
So-purkhu, 170.
Sorcerer (story of a), 299.
Soul (restless state of), 277, 1.
Sound (eternity of), 198.
Spell-Veda, 8.
Spiky bed, 561.
Spirit (Supreme), 14; (bodily coverings of), 26; 27; (mode of worshipping), 49; 50; (disembodied), 291; 292; (embodied), 293.
Spirit-worship, 71; 230–256.
Śrāddha (ceremonies), 276; 303; (object of), 304; (twelve Śrāddhas), 305; (payment for), 307; (time and place of), 308; (special), 308; 310; 311; (expense of), 278; 312.
Śramaṇa, 58.
Śrauta-karman, 365; 368.
Śrī, 103.
Śrī-ćakra, 196; 203.
Srīdhāralu Naidu, 525.
Śṛiṅga-giri, 55.
Śrī-phala, 299.
Śrī-raṅgam, 119; (temple of), 70, 1; 447–451.
Sṛishṭi-sthiti-laya, 44.
Śruti, 7.
Śruti-karman, 52.
Stages (four, of Brâhman's life), 362.
Stambhana, 200.
Statue (Jain), 250.
Stephen (Sir Fitzjames), 507.
Sthāṇu, 83.
Sthūla-śarīra, 28; 35.
Sthūṇā (column), 280.
Stones, 272; (five), 349; 411; (five methods of arrangement of), 412.
Storm-god, 9.
Strī Parambattūr, 119.
Stuti (praise), 19.
Styx (Hindū), 297.
Subrahmaṇya, 48; 211–218; 323; (contrasted with Gaṇeśa), 215.
Sudarśana, 103; 133; xxi.
Śuddhy-artha (Śrāddha), 305.
Śūdra, 53; 415; (god of the), 84; 212.
Sugrīva (king), 221.
Suhṛid, 106, 1.
Sukh-nidhān, 160.
Śuklaḥ (name of Śiva), 107.
Śukra, 194, 1.
Sūkshma, 123.
Sūkshma-śarīra, 28.
Sulabh Samāchar, 510, 1.
Sun, 10; 20; 104; 365; (titles of), 341.
Śunahśepa, 24.
Sundareśvara, 442.
Sun-god, 9; 10; 16.
Sun-temples, 342.
Sun-worship, 2; 5; 341.
Sun-worshippers, 62; 342.
Superstition, 210; 230; 344; 370.
Surā (wine-goddess), 108; 193; 195.
Surabhi, 108; 318.
Sūr-dās (poet), 147; 169.
Sūrya, 9; 16; 75; 341; 392.
Sūrya-Nārāyaṇa, 342, 1.
Sūrya-sūkta, 342.
Sūryā-sūkta, 343; 363, note.
Sutala, 102, 1.
Sūtra (aphorism), 26.
Sūtrātman, 35.
Suttee (for Satī). *See* Satī.
Svadhā, 304.
Svādhyāya, 394, 1.
Svāmī. *See* Dayānanda.
Svāmi-Nārāyaṇa (sect), 148; 268; (manual), 155.
Śva-paća, 329.
Svar, 9; 102, 1; 403.
Svarga, 13; 49; 71; 118.
Svarṇa-Gaṇapati, 218.
Svastika (mark), 90, 2; 104, 1; 573.
Svayam-bhū, 30; 69.
Śveta, 80, 2.
Śvetāśvatara Upanishad, 419.
Swan (Brahmā's), 104, 3.
Sword (Vishṇu's), 104.
Swords (sacred), 175.
Śyāmā, 187; 289; 422.
Śyāmā-rahasya (Tantra), 207.
Symbols (of Śiva), 67; 239; (of Vishṇu), 127; 239; (sanctity of), 69.

Tabla (tom-toms), 381.
Tacitus, 330.
Tāgore (Debendra-nāth), 491; 498; 514; 531; (Dvārakā-nāth), 482; 485; 491; (Prosonno Kumār), 485.
Tailotsava (festival), 442.
Taittirīya Āraṇyaka, 400; 403.
Taittirīya-brāhmaṇa, 23; 195, 3.
Taittirīya-saṃhitā (VI. 4. 10. 1), 237.
Tāj at Agra, 175; 176.
Takshaka, 233; 323.
Talātala, 102, 1.
Tālī (toddy), 192.
Talismans, 197–202; 204; 254.
Talvandī, 162.
Tamas, 31; 36.
Tamatoa (king), 273, 1.
Tambila (ceremony), 248.
Tamo-guṇa, 45; 412, 2.
Tāmraparṇī (river), 324.
Tāṇḍava (dance), 85.
Tāṇḍya-brāhmaṇa, 21; 23.
Tanjore, 66, 2; 439.
Ṭāṅka, 193.
Tanmātra, 30; 31, 2.
Tantra (Mātṛikā-bheda), 193.
Tantras, 63; 85; 184; (extracts from), 189; (Vaishṇava), 207; (authorship and character of), 205; 206.
Tantra-sāra, 200, 1.
Tāntrikas, 25.
Tanus (eight), 85.
Tapaḥ or Tapar (heaven), 102, 1; 403.
Tāpana, 86.
Tapas, 72; 87.
Tapasvī, 83.
Tapta-kumbha, 232.
Tapta-loha, 232.
Taptī (river), 347.

Tārā, 187.
Tāraka-mantra, 297.
Tarpaṇa (ceremony), 394; 409.
Tattva, 106.
Tattva-bodhinī-patrikā, 509.
Tattva-bodhinī-sabhā, 492.
Tattva-muktāvali, 122.
Teachers (Vaishṇava), 86.
Teeth-cleaning (religious act), 376; 399.
Teg-Bahādur, 164; 166.
Tejas (fire), 30.
Temple (golden), 175; 176; 436; (of Vishṇu-pada), 309; (of Gaṇeśa), 217.
Temples (description of), 434–451.
Temple (Sir Richard), 467.
Ten-galai, 125–127.
Tennyson, 386.
Ṭhag. *See* Thug.
Thānā (temples of), 50.
Thanush-koḍi, 445.
Theism, 7; (introduced into India), 475; (forms of), 524; (modern Hindū), 492.
Theistic Annual, 510, 1.
Theistic Church (first Hindū), 486.
Theistic Churches (number of), 517.
Theistic Society, 493.
Theistic Quarterly Review, 510, 1.
Theists (Vaishṇava), 179.
Theosophy, 526; xii, 1.
Thomas (Mr. Edw.), 104, 1.
Thread (Brāhmanical), 84; 360; 361; 378; 409.
Threefold pains of life, 97.
Thug (ṭhag), 260; 575.
Tibet, 3; 313.
Tiger (Durgā's), 104, 3.
Tilaka, 66; 67; 118; 400.
Tinnevelly, 272; (Śaiva temple), 446.
Tīrtha (water), 145.
Tīrtha-kāka, 329.
Tirumell Nāyak, 443.
Todas (aborigines), 271, 2.
Tonsure, 359; (modern), 375.
Torment (regions of), 293.
Tortoise, 108; 328.
Totemism, 314.
Towns (Indian), 462.
Trade (Indian), 453.
Trade-castes, 454.
Tradition (Brāhmanical), 53.
Transfiguration, 206.
Transmigration, 24; 52; 235. *See* Metempsychosis.
Travancore (king of), 468.
Tree (celestial), 108.
Tree and Serpent Worship, 313.
Trees (sacred), 338; (Śiva's association with), 446.
Tree-worship, 72; 330; 332.
Tretā (age), 110; 433.
Triad (sacred), 5; 9; 44; 45; 49; 74; (of Principles), 119; (Vaishṇava), 142.
Tribe (Yādava), 112; (Rājput), 233, 1.
Trichinopoly, 70, 1; 119; (temples), 217; 445; 447; (Vaishṇava temple at), 447.
Tri-daṇḍin, 541, 1.
Trikoṇa, 45.
Tri-mūrti, 45; 74.
Trinity (Hindū, wrongly called), 44; (contrasted with Christian Trinity), 49.
Tri-pati, 267.
Tripura, 81.
Tripurā, 188.
Tripurāsura (demon), 432.
Tritheism, 11.
Tri-vikrama, 365; 405.
Trumpp (Prof.), 161; 164; 169; 170, 1.
Tryāyusham, 421.
Tukārām or Tukā-rāma, 264; 265; 528.
Tulasi or Tulsī (shrub), 46; 67; 296; (healing qualities of), 333; (worship of), 333.
Tulsi-dās (poet), 147; 148.
Tuṅga-bhadrā, 347.
Turbans, 396.
Turīya, 35.
Tutelary deities, 71.
Tylor (E. B.), 274, 2; 313; 314; 330.

Uććaiḥ-śravas, 108; 329.
Uććhishṭa-Gaṇapati, 218.
Udāharaṇa, 39.
Udāsa, 154.
Uḍḍīśa (Tantra), 207.
Uḍumbara, 535.
Uḍupī, 130.
Ugra, 76; 85.
Ujjhī Puliyār, 217.
Ulūpī, 233, 1; 322.
Umā, 79; 229.
Uṇṭāi, 227.
Upaćāra, 413.
Upādana, 119.
Upādāna-kārana, 120.
Upadeśa (knowledge), 191.
Upamāna, 39.
Upanaya, 39.
Upanayana (ceremony), 353; 360; 377.
Upanishad (Kaula), 185.
Upanishads, 26; (philosophy of), 37, 1.
Upāsanā (meditation), 19.
Upasthāna (service), 406; (prayer), 407; (act), 420.
Upavastra, 415.
Upavīta, 378.
Upavītī, 409.
Upāya (means), 125.
Ūrdhva-bāhu, 88; 439.
Ūrdhva-deha, 293, 1.
Ūrdhva-puṇḍra, 67; 118.
Urvaśī (nymph), 333, 1.
Ushas, 5; 9; 182.
Utsava-mūrti, 447.
Utsava-vigraha, 449.
Uttarīya, 395.

Vada-galai, 125–127.
Vagalā or Bagalā, 188.
Vāg-dāna, 377.
Vāghobā, 328.
Vāhana, 104, 3.
Vaidika Upadeśa, 362.
Vaidyaḥ, 106.
Vaikuṇṭha, 70; 102; 118; 124; 142; 291; (terrestrial counterpart of), 448.
Vairāgī, 87; 561.
Vairāgya, 48; 510.
Vaiśeshika (Sūtra), 26.
Vaishṇavas, 59; 60; 95–160.
Vaishṇavism, 71; (general characteristics), 95–106; (compared with Śaivism), 64; (with Christianity), 119.
Vaiśvadeva (ceremony), 394; 416.
Vaiśvadeva-balikarmaṇi, 417, 2.
Vaiśvānara, 35.
Vaiśya, 53; 415; (god of the), 84.
Vaitaraṇī, 290; 297; 570.
Vājasaneyi-saṃhitā, 76.
Vajra, 81.
Vallabha or Vallabhāćārya (life of), 134; 135; (teaching of), 476; (Mahārājas), 335.
Vallī-amman, 214.
Vālmīki, 196.
Vāma-mārgīs, 185.